Corporate Finance for Business

# Corporate Finance for Business

## John-Paul Marney

Teaching Fellow, School of Management and Languages,
Heriot-Watt University, Edinburgh

## Heather Tarbert

Professor of Financial Management at the University of the West of
Scotland

Formerly Professor of Finance and Head of Dundee Business School,
University of Abertay, Dundee

OXFORD
UNIVERSITY PRESS

# OXFORD
UNIVERSITY PRESS

Great Clarendon Street, Oxford OX2 6DP

Oxford University Press is a department of the University of Oxford.
It furthers the University's objective of excellence in research, scholarship,
and education by publishing worldwide in

Oxford  New York

Auckland  Cape Town  Dar es Salaam  Hong Kong  Karachi
Kuala Lumpur  Madrid  Melbourne  Mexico City  Nairobi
New Delhi  Shanghai  Taipei  Toronto

With offices in

Argentina  Austria  Brazil  Chile  Czech Republic  France  Greece
Guatemala  Hungary  Italy  Japan  Poland  Portugal  Singapore
South Korea  Switzerland  Thailand  Turkey  Ukraine  Vietnam

Oxford is a registered trade mark of Oxford University Press
in the UK and in certain other countries

Published in the United States
by Oxford University Press Inc., New York

British Library Cataloguing in Publication Data

Data available

Library of Congress Cataloguing in Publication Data

Data available

Typeset by TechType
Printed in Italy
on acid-free paper by
L.E.G.O. S.p.A. – Lavis TN

ISBN 978–0–19–956339–5

1 3 5 7 9 10 8 6 4 2

I dedicate this book to my wonderful mother, Mrs Agnes Heaver, and to my six fabulous sons.

*Heather*


For my part, this book is respectfully dedicated to the memory of my late father John Marney of Glasgow, 24 April 1938 to 27 June 2002. He came from a generation that did not go on to higher education, but left school at an early age to seek employment in the shipyards. Despite his lack of formal qualifications, he was an intelligent man with an enormous respect for scholarship and learning. I am sure he would have been thrilled to have his name associated with this educational endeavour. Rest in peace Dad.

Your son, *John-Paul*

# Preface

There are many very good introductory books in Corporate Finance, so the reader may well be asking the question, why another one? The reason that we have chosen to make our humble addition to a rather crowded market is that, within the constraints of the syllabus which must necessarily be offered, we genuinely feel that we have been able to take a fresh look at the subject. So how, then, does this fresh approach manifest itself?

Firstly, we give some consideration to small and medium scale enterprise. Of course, the emphasis in Corporate Finance for the foreseeable future must be on large corporations. However, we have tried where possible to change this emphasis slightly, particularly in our Practical implications text boxes, so that our text will have relevance for graduates who go on to start their own companies or who may eventually make their career in smaller enterprises.

Secondly, we are conscious that vast majority of Corporate Finance books are American, with a smaller proportion from Britain, and very few textbooks from other countries. However, Corporate Finance has become a global subject studied by students from across the world. Therefore we have modified this Anglophone tone by including numerous international examples, along with material from the UK and the US. While the canonical literature of Corporate Finance remains predominantly Anglophone, and more particularly American, we hope our international readers recognize a world which is more familiar to them, and that our English speaking readers will realize that the world of finance is increasingly a global and international one.

Thirdly, we have tried to move away from class-bound textbooks by referring to as many real life examples as possible. There are numerous quotes and case studies throughout, from very well known, to some less well known, but no less prestigious, financial sources. We now know why so many textbooks tend to keep things fairly abstract by referring almost entirely to imaginary situations and companies, as it took quite a lot of our time and a great deal of our resource to secure the very many copyright permissions required. However, we really think it has improved the quality of our offering, and gives our book a much more authoritative 'feel'.

Fourthly, another merit of the book which we would particularly like to emphasize is that, where relevant, we have given due consideration to issues which are perhaps sometimes neglected in the context of Corporate Finance, including Corporate Governance and Social Responsibility, the changing nature of Corporate Finance, and Corporate Finance in Emerging Countries.

Fifthly, learning objectives are clearly set out at the start of each chapter. We know this will be particularly useful for tutors.

Sixthly, we have had some very encouraging comments from our anonymous referees on the 'readability' of the book. At the risk of sounding unduly immodest, we hope that you, our readership, will agree that this is a distinct quality of our text and will particularly enjoy the start-of-chapter running case studies.

Finally, although there are many Corporate Finance books out there, there are not so many custom-designed for one semester 'stand-alone' courses, unlike, this, our own.

Having emphasized the particular merits of our book, there are two additional points we would like to make. The first point concerns the fact that your authors have come to the conclusion that it is very difficult to fit basic Portfolio and Investment Theory within a one semester 'stand-alone' course in Corporate Finance, while also achieving the desirable goal of covering a representative selection of the other basic topics . This is strongly evidenced in our book by the sheer size of Chapter 5, which covers both Investment and Portfolio Theory, and the closely associated topic of the Capital Asset Pricing Model. As you will readily observe, Chapter 5 is much bigger than any of our other chapters. After struggling with this problem for a number of years, the authors had a 'eureka' moment recently. Why not 'skip' portfolio theory and get straight on to the CAPM? After all, the point ultimately from a Corporate Finance point of view is to introduce the CAPM as a primary means of working out Required Return on Equity. One could do this a) by introducing a simple account of the benefits of portfolio diversification, followed by; b) the idea of the Market Portfolio as the ultimate in diversified portfolios, and finally; c) by introducing Beta as a measure of volatility of return over the Business Cycle relative to the diversified Market Index. If, as a tutor or student, you wish to take this approach, you could start Chapter 5 at section 5.5 and pick up with the CAPM at this point. Of course, we realize that many of our colleagues would not wish to skip Portfolio and Investment Theory, which is why it constitutes the first two thirds of the chapter. The choice is there however.

In writing this book, we have had to take a particular view on how the book should be written. It seemed to us, first and foremost, that it was important to engage the reader and to encourage Corporate Finance students to make the journey through what can potentially be perceived as a boring and difficult subject area. Therefore, particularly in the first few chapters, we took a deliberate decision to keep the tone relatively light-hearted by comparison with the normal academic text. We had a clear purpose in mind; namely to get the basic principles across as best we could without turning off our students to what we feel is now the most exciting and relevant field of applied economics. Therefore, we had a noble reason for giving ourselves dispensation to take a slight deviation from the normal textbook style. We enliven the learning process by engaging the reader in action learning activities and in contemporary cases, and in relating what can often be perceived as ancient history, by our Facebook-literate students, to modern practice.  Chapter by chapter, the themes of our book are as follows:

In Chapter 1, we start by considering the increasingly complex role of that the financial manager within the firm. Financial managers were at one time mainly cash managers. However, as we will discover, there is a great deal more to Corporate Financial Management in the twenty-first century. Subsequently, we go on to consider some particularly powerful theoretical frameworks underpinning Corporate Finance, including free market economics and perfect competition, behavioural finance and agency theory. This is followed by a discussion of three of the most central principle of the discipline; discounting and present value, the relation between risk and return; and the business cycle. We then go on to take a general look at what is typically assumed about business motivation, and a specific look at the profit motive versus the stakeholder view, and the tradeoff between the pursuit of profit and good Corporate Governance. Finally, we examine some current topics in finance, namely the reasons for the credit crunch and issues such as the emergence of microfinance in Bangladesh.

In Chapter 2 we examine one of the most critically important aspects of Corporate Finance and of finance generally. This is the time value of money. Money now is not the same as money in the future, and the way that we bring it all to a common measure is in the form of discounting. The discounting process is the reverse of the process of adding interest to a deposit. We also look at how to calculate a return when an investment has only one future value. On the basis of discounting, we have available two different techniques for investment appraisal, namely Net Present Value (NPV) and Internal Rate of Return (IRR). Internal rate of return is the technique which is used when there is more than one future cash flow and one cannot calculate using the simpler return formulation. We look in detail at how to calculate internal rate of return (IRR), and the potential drawbacks of IRR, before moving on to other methods of investment appraisal, viz accounting rate of return and payback, both of which are limited by the fact that they are not based on the time value of money concept. We then go on to look at some of the basics of discounted cash flow, and in particular the difference between incremental cash flow and profit-loss. We conclude with a meditation on intangible benefits and the reliability of assumptions.

In Chapter 3 we look at the big financial markets, particularly the stock markets and the bond markets; that is, the market for corporate equity, and the markets for corporate, governmental and institutional debt. We then go on to look at the key functions and features of these markets which are: to allow firms to obtain funds and grow; to facilitate the allocation of capital to its most productive uses; to provide a central point for those who wish to invest and those who wish to borrow; to provide a means for companies to raise funds; to provide a means for investors to choose investments according to their risk and return profiles; to enable holders of financial instruments to sell speedily and cheaply and to allow them to value their financial assets easily; to facilitate diversification of risk; and to facilitate improvements in corporate behaviour because of the high level of public awareness of the business and the considerable financial reporting and other disclosure requirements on the main financial markets. In addition, we look at the fundamentals of pricing bonds and pricing equity.

Chapter 4 is concerned with the important concept of the valuation of the firm, and the three fundamental approaches that can be used; cash flow based, earnings based and asset based. Cash flow approaches are based on inferring firm value from dividends or on inferring value from incremental cash flow. The earnings based approach uses either the stock market's valuation of the firm's earnings, namely the p-e ratio, or infers this by using a p-e ratio for a similar company. Finally we consider valuation based on net asset value. A major problem in this respect is the valuation of intangible assets, an increasingly important part of overall firm value.

Chapter 5 is by far the longest of our chapters. It basically falls into two parts. In the first two thirds of the chapter, we explain the basic nature of financial risk which can be broadly defined as variation in expected outcomes. The chapter then goes on to examine the various measures used to appraise risk-versus-return; specifically, expected return and standard deviation of return. We also look at correlation; the degree to which two assets returns vary in relation to each other. Having looked at the 'supply side' of risk return, we also look at how the investor might make choices among risk-return assets using utility theory and indifference curves. The chapter then sets out the fundamental concepts of portfolio theory, specifically, the Efficient Frontier and the Market Portfolio. With the aid of these concepts we are able to analyse choices by investors between different portfolios. The reader who is confident of their grasp of basic statistics and basic investment theory may wish to 'skip' this section in order to move on to the last third and a more germane topic for those purely interested in the cost of capital – the capital asset pricing model (CAPM). The last third of the chapter sets out the CAPM, which relates individual security return to the undiversifiable Beta risk of the individual security. Beta is calculated with reference to the covariance of a stock return to the *market portfolio*, an important concept in finance. Once we understand the CAPM, we can understand how the required return on equity is calculated. As we say, it may not be absolutely necessary for every student of corporate finance to delve deeply into the investment and portfolio theory set out in the first two thirds of the chapter to grasp the CAPM set out in the last third.

Chapter 6 opens with a discussion of derivative instruments, that is to say financial instruments which are derived from ordinary *underlying* instruments such as agricultural contracts, bonds or even stock indices. The chapter then goes on to give some institutional background to the foreign exchange market before discussing the major shift of world forex regime from fixed to floating exchange rates in the 1970s. The new floating exchange rate system was unexpectedly volatile giving rise to *exchange rate risk*, because of the fundamental unpredictability of exchange rates. We go on to explain that exchange rates are fundamentally determined by long-run supply and demand factors and that in theory we should be able to calculate the appropriate exchange rate using the *Fundamental Equilibrium Exchange Rate* or *FEER*. However, given the limitations of FEER as a practical approach, other approaches in common use are Purchasing Power Parity and Covered Interest Parity. We also examine some of the practical ways in which a firm could manage exchange rate risk.

In Chapter 7 we extend the applicability of the techniques of project appraisal by considering how internal rate of return and net present value can be applied in the case of capital rationing. Next we go on to discuss the practical considerations that must be taken into account when making decisions about investment projects, and in particular the various costs which should and should not be included. The concept of project risk, as opposed to financial investment risk is also introduced and some consideration is given to how this can be analysed. Finally, we look at real options, which is the value of various path-dependent courses of action that are open to us over the course of the project's life.

In Chapter 8 we go on to look at a core concept in finance, the Weighted Average Cost of Capital (WACC). This is the weighted average cost of the firm's use of debt and equity capital. In principle, the firm's discount rate should be the weighted average cost of capital. Following from this, we look at the effect of gearing, or leverage, which is defined as the proportion of debt to equity in the capital structure, and the issue of whether or not there is an optimal capital structure which minimizes the weighted average cost of capital. In this respect, both the theoretical contribution of Modigliani and Miller and the 'empirical' school are given equal prominence.

In Chapter 9 we examine dividend policy. Dividend policy concerns the firm's decision whether or not to issue a dividend, and also what proportion of earnings to pay as dividend and what proportion to retain for investment. Such decisions are very important, because if the firm does not retain enough for investment, then that will threaten future growth: while if the firm retains too much, it is not achieving best value for investors. Furthermore, it is rarely a good idea to radically alter the dividend without careful consideration, as a change in dividend sends a powerful signal to the market. This is due to the problems of imperfect and asymmetrical information: an investor does not know everything there is to know about the firm he is investing in, and a company insider will know more. We examine both the theoretical contributions in the area of dividend policy, chiefly by Modigliani and Miller, and also look at some more applied aspects of dividend policy.

Chapter 10 is concerned with the management of day to day cash flow, liquidity and working capital. As we shall discover, working capital is capital which is not used up in the course of production and, in principle should be returned at the end of a particular investment project. Because of the highly cyclical nature of business, even over the shorter time perspective of days, weeks and years, the level of working capital will tend to rise and fall depending in the behaviour of current assets relative to current liabilities. The factors that are particularly influential in the ebb and flow of net current assets are payables (-), receivables (+) and inventory (+). As a result of the effect of these on working capital it is necessary to carefully manage these areas with particular respect to their impact on the availability of cash. We also consider how cash itself might be managed in order to cope with variation in these items.

In Chapter 11 we examine mergers and acquisitions in detail. A merger is when two companies combine into a new entity. An acquisition, or takeover, is when one company buys all, or most, of the assets of another company. The goal of M&A is to create value, though it is a moot point as to whether or not this goal is actually achieved. We discuss the main reasons for M&A, including economies of scale and scope, vertical integration, rapid growth, reduction of competition, efficiency gains, tax advantages, risk reduction, expropriation and shutdown, hubris, empire building, synergy, critical mass, obtaining a listing, and avoiding government interference. We also look at the problem of agency and whether or not managers always undertake M&A for the right reasons. In addition, we look at types of M&A, M&A strategies (including defensive strategies) financing issues and methods of valuation.

Chapter 12 is essentially concerned with reviewing and revising the various mathematical techniques used throughout the book.

Our hope is that we can excite students and give them an interest in finding out more about corporate finance. We ourselves have a passion for the subjects that follow, and if we can communicate that passion to our readers, we will have fulfilled our purpose.

# Brief contents

# Detailed contents

# About the authors

## John-Paul Marney

Dr Marney has lectured full time in both Finance and Economics at the Universities of Paisley, Northumbria and East London and on a visiting basis at Strathclyde and Stirling. He has also been visiting research fellow at the Universities of Madeira and Buenos Aires. He is currently employed as a teaching fellow at Heriot-Watt University, Edinburgh.

## Heather Tarbert

Heather Tarbert is now Professor of Financial Management at the University of the West of Scotland. She was formerly Professor of Finance and Head of Dundee Business School, University of Abertay. She has published in many accountancy and finance-related subjects including commercial property economics and finance; financial markets; economics methodology; oil and gas economics and finance; remuneration for senior executives; alternative ways of organising businesses; accountancy education; and studies of careers within the accountancy profession. She passionately believes that the study of corporate finance is both inherently extremely interesting and of key importance to any student who will engage in any way with the wider corporate world.

# Acknowledgements

It behoves us to give thanks to various people who have helped us along the way. Our heartfelt thanks go to the patient, hard-working, and encouraging staff at Oxford University Press, including Emily Medina Davis, Kirsty Reade, Sarah Brett, and Philippa Hendry, and to the panel of anonymous reviewers, all of whom have done sterling work, for which we are truly and eternally grateful.

Thanks also to all of those many people and institutions who were very patient and helpful with our applications for copyright permission.

## Alan Ballantyne

Finally, thanks to *Alan Ballantyne*, a research assistant at Glasgow Caledonian, who has done some very useful service and shown maturity beyond his years in helping us get the manuscript finalised. Alan graduated from Strathclyde University with a 2:1 in Business Law and Finance in 2009. Since then he has been employed as a research assistant at Glasgow Caledonian University where he also tutors in Managerial Finance. Alan was invaluable in helping to source material and composing questions and activities which he thought would be interesting to students. Given his much closer proximity to the student experience, I strongly believe that his input was critical in making this book readable and engaging for our target audience.

The publishers would like to thank the following who granted us permission to reproduce copyrighted material:

The Financial Times
The Economist
Martin Wolf
Associated Content
Fortune
International Corporate Governance Network
World Exchanges

Megastock
Carl Gustav Linden
Burton Malkiel
The Guardian
New York Times
IMF
University of Hawaii
G Frederick Thompson
Evening Standard
Telegraph Media Group Limited

Tel Aviv University
London Stock Exchange plc

The publishers would be pleased to clear permission with any copyright holders that we have inadvertently failed or been unable to contact.

# List of case studies

## Case studies

## Mini case studies

# Guided tour of the textbook features

The text is enriched with a range of learning features to help you navigate the text material and reinforce your knowledge of Corporate Finance. This guided tour shows you how to get the most out of your textbook.

## Fictional case study

A fictional case study runs through the book, mapping the development of a company from start-up to takeover. A portion of the case study, at the beginning of each chapter, introduces the themes and issues that the chapter deals with, helping you to appreciate the relevance of the topics covered, and the context within which they may operate.

## Skills-based and knowledge-based objectives

at the beginning of each chapter focus your learning. These are intended as a revision aid.

## Practical implications for managers

Practical implications for managers boxes can be found throughout the text, at points where it is relevant for you to think about the topic or issue from the point of view of a manager, or to consider the business implications of the topic.

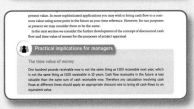

## Active learning activities

Throughout the text, active learning activities encourage you to stop, engage, and interact with the topic under discussion, helping you to learn more effectively.

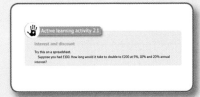

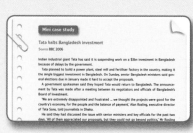

## Mini case studies

There are numerous mini case studies, which are presented throughout each chapter, highlighting the real-world relevance of the topics under discussion. These are often real newspaper articles, which bring the subject alive, always making reference to topical points of interest.

## Key concepts

Key terms are highlighted in the text, and definitions are provided in key concepts sections throughout the chapter, helping you to keep track of important and relevant terms and definitions.

## End-of-chapter case study

Longer case studies may be found at the end of each chapter. They allow you to further appreciate the real-world relevance of each topic.

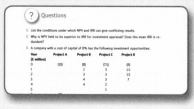

## Questions

A set of carefully devised questions is provided at the end of every chapter to help you assess your comprehension of core topics.

## Further reading

A further reading list is provided at the end of every chapter, to help you to take your learning further and to locate the key academic literature relevant to the chapter topic.

## Internet references

Web links at the end of each chapter guide you to relevant learning material on the web.

## Suggestions for presentations and suggestions for group work

provide ideas for seminars and self-study groups, helping you to engage further with the material, and to employ varied learning methods and skills.

# Guided tour of the Online Resource Centre

www.oxfordtextbooks.co.uk/orc/marney/

The Online Resource Centre that accompanies this book provides students and instructors with ready-to-use teaching and learning resources.

## For Students

### Learning objectives

The authors set out key learning objectives for you, with pointers as to how to meet the objective and page references to relevant parts of the book. Invaluable for revision purposes.

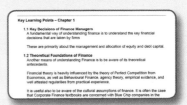

### Web links

Web links to relevant articles will help you take your leaning further. Each web link is accompanied by a brief summary of the article, and how it relates to the chapter topics.

### Multiple choice questions

A bank of self-marking multiple choice questions has been provided for each chapter of the text. It gives instant feedback on your answers to help strengthen your knowledge.

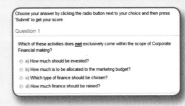

### Case studies

Additional case studies are provided online, adding even further to your appreciation of the real world of corporate finance.

MP3 (podcast) chapter introduction

The authors introduce each chapter of the book, setting out the main themes and issues that the chapter deals with. This can serve as an aide memoir; to prepare you before you begin your reading; or simply as another useful way to engage with the material.

MP3 (podcast) interviews relating to chapter contents

Interviews will help you appreciate the real-life relevance of the subject, adding depth to your knowledge and understanding.

## Registered Adopters of the Book

All the resources in the lecturer's section of the Online Resources Centre are password-protected and available only to lecturers who are adopting the book.

PowerPoint slides

A suite of customizable PowerPoint slides has been included for use in lectures. Arranged by chapter, the slides may also be used as handouts in class.

Suggestions for discursive/seminar questions

Discussion questions that are designed to draw out the themes and issues raised in each chapter have been provided for use in seminars and tutorials.

Solutions manual

A convenient solutions manual includes answers to all the questions in the book, as well as indicative answers to case study questions.

Test bank

A set of questions has been devised by the authors for each chapter. The test bank is customisable and fully automated for quick and convenient use in your assessment software: automatic grading allows you to access your students' progress via your university's Virtual Learning Environment, and instant feedback shows your students what they need to work on for revision purposes.

# 1 The Nature of Finance

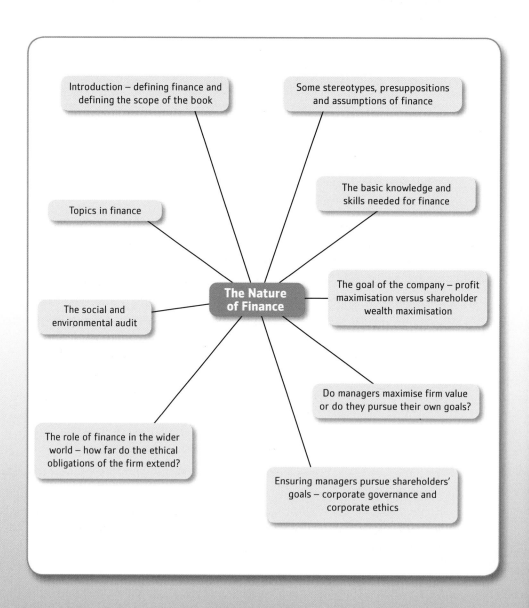

Introduction – defining finance and defining the scope of the book

Some stereotypes, presuppositions and assumptions of finance

The basic knowledge and skills needed for finance

Topics in finance

**The Nature of Finance**

The goal of the company – profit maximisation versus shareholder wealth maximisation

The social and environmental audit

Do managers maximise firm value or do they pursue their own goals?

The role of finance in the wider world – how far do the ethical obligations of the firm extend?

Ensuring managers pursue shareholders' goals – corporate governance and corporate ethics

## Knowledge learning objectives

When you have completed this chapter you will be able to:

✓ Understand the role and functions of a financial manager

✓ Understand the context of finance in terms of its theoretical and cultural background

✓ Understand the basic concept if not the precise detail of the time value of money and discounting

✓ Understand why firm value maximisation is preferred to profit maximisation as a goal

✓ Understand why the firm may have other subsidiary goals but that shareholder value maximisation has primacy

✓ Understand the reasons for the corporate governance framework

✓ Know who the main sources are for corporate governance codes

✓ Understand some of the main factors involved in the credit crunch

## Skills-based learning objectives development

✓ Business and financial environment consciousness: you should have developed an understanding of the nature of corporate finance.

✓ Numerical skills: you should have developed the ability to understand net present value.

✓ Analytical thinking and problem-solving skills: you should have developed the ability to know how to evaluate the main goals of a corporation.

✓ Problem-solving skills: you should have developed the ability to assess whether a corporation is meeting the main goal of shareholder value maximisation and any subsidiary goals.

✓ Critical-thinking skills: you should have developed the ability to understand the assumptions on which mainstream corporate finance is based and to know the limitations of these assumptions.

✓ Organisational skills: you should have developed your ability to organise your time and work efficiently and to gather data and information which you can translate into value-adding intelligence.

✓ Managerial soft skills: you should have developed the ability to know where judgement and interpersonal skills are needed within issues related to corporate governance.

✓ Presentation skills: you should have developed your ability to present your work clearly both verbally and in writing.

✓ Interpersonal skills: you should have developed your ability to present your work clearly both verbally and in writing and to interact with others effectively upon completion of the end of chapter questions.

## Online resource centre

Visit the Online Resource Centre that accompanies this book to listen to a podcast of the authors introducing the nature of corporate finance.

**www.oxfordtextbooks.co.uk/marney**

## Fictional case study

### And in the beginning ... OrganicX comes into being

Charlie and Kate are two very successful individuals who have left their employers to start up their own company which specialises in ethical investments. Charlie's career began in the time-honoured manner – as a mail boy, working his way up over 20 years to become the fixed income director in a small investment bank. Kate is very much a product of her education – an MBA and a professional accounting qualification in addition to 5 years' experience as a derivatives trader in a larger investment bank.

Together with some external investors they have started a new boutique investment company, OrganicX, and hope to list on the alternative investment market (AIM) within the next few months. They are currently working on the prospectus and, as usual, having some differences of opinion. Whilst both are committed to ethical investment principles, they cannot agree on the main, shareholder-orientated goal of their firm.

'Clearly, we need to maximise profits,' Charlie says. 'That's what shareholders want.'

Kate disagrees: 'That may have been the mantra in your old company, but that's what's wrong with mainstream companies – it's all about the short term and we are trying to do something different here. We need to look at the longer term and that's why shareholder **value maximisation** is the way to go.'

'Value? Value? What exactly do we mean by value?' asks Charlie. 'At least with profits you know where you are – revenues minus costs – simple!'

'You know the old joke, Charlie? 2 + 2 = whatever the accountants want it to be. There is nothing straightforward about profits.'

'That might be true,' replies Charlie, 'but "value"? It seems even more vague – so what exactly do you mean?'

Kate frowns, not having considered the matter in any great depth before. 'Well, obviously there *is* a profits dimension – we do need to make money – but value is a broader concept. It means that we maximise the wealth of our shareholders by good investment decisions designed to also ensure sustainability of our company and the companies we invest in – it's not about a quick hit, but rather about longer-term relationships.'

'But don't we need to make a profit at the same time?' asks Charlie.

'Yes, of course,' replies Kate. 'And at times, we will have to make some very difficult decisions. Hopefully we will attract the type of shareholders who understand our commitment to ethical investing, but they will still want a good return.'

# 1.1 Introduction

You are about to enter into the formal study of the academic discipline of corporate finance. Finance in general, and corporate finance in particular, is different from many other academic disciplines, in that it is intended to have fairly direct insights into the real business practices of finance departments and finance specialists within companies. In what follows, we try to maintain a balance between real-life practice and examples and the theory that is necessary to understand the conceptual framework which is shared by all financial professionals. However, given the introductory and pedagogic nature of this book, we may sometimes give slightly more weight to theory.

As you may imagine, given its multifaceted nature, corporate finance can be difficult to define exhaustively and comprehensively in just a few sentences. Traditionally the financial manager made sure that cash was available as and when needed, that there would be no unexpected cash shortages within the organisation, but that there were no underemployed cash surpluses either.

The role of the financial manager is much more complicated and much more difficult to categorise nowadays, particularly given the emergence of the finance role as something distinct from accountancy, and also because of the emergence of finance as an academic discipline, particularly since the 1950s. However, we might make a start by defining corporate finance as we intend to discuss it in this book. In the following section we look at the key decisions taken by financial managers.

## 1.1.1 Defining finance and defining the scope of the book

One way of looking at the role of finance in the organisation is in terms of the key decisions taken by financial managers. These are as follows:

1. How much should be invested?
2. Which projects should be chosen for investment purposes and which rejected?
3. How much finance should be raised?
4. Which type of finance? Should the firm rely on internal funds, intermediated bank loans, direct loans from the money markets in the form of bonds, etc. or equity finance in the form of external share ownership?
5. How should profits be used? Should they be re-invested in the business or returned to shareholders?
6. How is cash and **working capital** to be managed over the operating cycle in such a way as to be available when needed, but at the same time put to optimal use?

The list above is a basic textbook description of what a financial manager does. However, a number of other important modern roles for financial managers could be identified in addition to these core functions.

1. How is risk to be managed? One of the by-products of the development of finance as a profession and as an academic discipline is that there is much greater awareness of financial risk, particularly with the development of derivative instruments. The relationship between risk and return is certainly a core concept in what we will discuss in the course of the book. However, we will not be discussing **risk management** in detail, though we will offer some insights and brief comments. A thoroughgoing study of risk management can be made once the fundamental techniques offered here have been absorbed.

2. **Strategic value management**. An increasingly important role for the financial manager is to be found in strategic management. That is to say, the input of the financial manager is essential for strategic planning at various levels of the corporation, including at corporate level, at the strategic business unit (SBU) level and at the operational level.

Thus, decisions on takeovers and acquisitions would be considered strategic, decisions about the financial performance of individual units would be at business or competitive-strategy level, while decisions concerning how corporate-level decisions on, say, acceptable project returns or types of finance to be raised would be implemented at the operational level for each SBU.

Again, we do acknowledge in this book that decisions take place at different strategic levels. However, we do not take an integrated strategic financial management approach as we feel this would be better left until the fundamental and basic principles are thoroughly familiar.

In summary, the essential points we would hope to get across in this book are about the nature of investment, the nature and type of the various forms of capital available to the firm, the potential impact of financing decisions on the firm's performance, earnings distribution decisions, and the way in which the external economy and external markets such as the stock market and the foreign exchange market can affect the firm.

As we have hinted, this by no means defines and fully explains the complex modern role of financial manager, the precise nature of which is a 'work in progress' as we can see from the case study 'Book review: your finance officer's inner warrior'.

## Mini case study

### Your finance officer's inner warrior

Source Witzel 2006, Copyright *Financial Times*, 2006

Chief financial officers are under pressure. Their fellow directors and managers are demanding more and more information about business performance, risk factors and forecasts, while hawk-eyed regulators and angry shareholders scrutinise their every action.

At the same time – as Jeremy Hope writes in this book – most CFOs 'remain prisoners of dysfunctional systems and mental models that were developed for a role that is fast becoming obsolete'.

'Until the 1980s, the world of the CFO hadn't changed much for decades,' says Mr Hope, research director of the Beyond Budgeting Round Table, a think-tank. 'Success was seen in terms of balance sheets. The annual planning process dictated what was made and sold and informed people what they had to achieve by when.'

That is no longer the case. CFOs are now expected to be business generalists with full knowledge of what is happening across the business. By default, many have become custodians of organisational knowledge.

Most CFOs are not suited to this general management role, says Mr Hope. They tend to come from accounting backgrounds and have risen through the ranks within corporate finance departments. They have high levels of expertise in managing finance but are not equipped for the many other roles now heaped on them, especially forecasting and risk management.

He urges CFOs to take on other roles, too, becoming 'regulators of risk', 'champions of change' or 'architects of adaptive management'.

All of these require CFOs to become more proactive and to move away from their traditional roles as makers of plans and preparers of budgets.

1. Why might accountants not be 'suited to this general management role'? How can any deficiencies be overcome?

2. Should CFOs take on other roles? What dangers could arise from placing such a variety of extra responsibilities on one person?

As we can see from this extract, as well as the main explicit assumptions concerning the role of the financial manager discussed above, there are a number of implicit assumptions about what it is the financial managers do. Many of these implicit assumptions are valid and reasonable, though not all are. Just so we're explicitly clear on what kind of explicit assumptions tend to be made, at this point we should probably address some of the implicit assumptions and stereotypes of corporate finance . We consider this in the next section.

## Practical implications for managers

### Financial manager duties

The role of financial managers continues to evolve and grow over time. Managers must therefore keep up to date with market trends and research or they will run the risk of becoming antiquated, to the cost of their career, their company and the shareholders.

## Active learning activity 1.1

### What do financial managers need to know?

Reflect on the recent credit crisis and list five skills that a financial manager needs to cope during sudden downturns in business.

## Key concepts

- The increasingly sophisticated **role of financial manager** requires an increasing and demanding skill set and knowledge base
- **Working capital** represents the cash available to the business for operations
- **Risk management** involves achieving the minimum risk for a given level of return
- **Strategic value management** is the activity in which financial managers attempt to increase the value of the company through strategic decisions

## 1.2 Some stereotypes, presuppositions and assumptions of finance

Consider first the kinds of assumptions that the trained financial mind tends to make. Both the academic discipline and the profession of corporate finance were largely developed in North America and therefore they bear some characteristically North American cultural markers. These include:

1. The importance of markets in bringing about desirable outcomes. The US has this in common with other Anglophone countries which tend to be more enthusiastic about unrestricted market capitalism than, for example, Western European countries. The implicit assumption throughout standard corporate finance textbooks is that external markets for capital such as the bond market and the stock market work well and efficiently in finding correct prices for the supply of equity capital and debt capital.

2. This brings us to the next point – that much of the underlying theory of corporate finance is based on the theory of **perfect competition** and the **free market** – which comes in turn from economics. In this theory, competitive markets find the most efficient outcome because markets represent the actions of many atomistic individuals and firms trying to maximise their own gains. By maximising their own gains, for example, profit, they maximise efficiency in the market and welfare for society as a whole.

   This kind of theorising may at times strike the student as somewhat abstract and unrealistic. However, it is a well explored body of theory which merits at least initial consideration as a useful 'jumping off' point. It is up to us to provide alternative explanations as to why this type of theory does not hold if we feel it provides an unsustainable explanation.

3. Our alternatives to orthodox economic theory come from a number of sources. These are (1) the **behavioural school of finance** which is based more on psychology than economics; (2) **empirical observations by financial professionals** based on actual prac-

tice in finance; and (3) **asymmetric information** and **agency theory**, which explore the implications of a great deal of desirable information being unknown or incomplete when financial decisions are made.

## Active learning activity 1.2

### Assumptions, assumptions, everywhere we look

Reflect on the above assumptions and consider how realistic each assumption is in the context of a real-life large corporation.

It is important to be clear on where our key concepts come from and how ideas are organised in the discipline. Much of the implicit framework is strongly culturally influenced by Anglophone economic doctrine. However, this does not in any way invalidate its universal applicability, as can be ascertained from the extract below from a recent survey of senior female finance managers from Middle Eastern countries entitled Role models from banking and finance. [For further examples, see the full article by Patrikarakos and Asokan (2008).]

## Mini case study

### Role models from banking and finance
Source Patrikarakos and Asokan 2008, Copyright *Financial Times*, 2008

#### Hynd Bouhia, Morocco
It was only in March that Hynd Bouhia became director of Morocco's Casablanca Stock Exchange, and she is brimming with ideas. 'I want to position this stock exchange internationally,' she says. 'We need to provide more products and get more international companies to list here.'

Casablanca-born Ms Bouhia, 35, started her career at the World Bank in Washington, working on emerging economies. In 2004 she returned to Morocco as an economic adviser to the prime minister, then Driss Jettou. She says leading the country's successful bid for a $700m US development grant was one of her proudest achievements in that role.

Ms Bouhia, who has a degree in industrial engineering from École Centrale Paris and a PhD in operations research and economic development from Harvard, is optimistic about Morocco's economy. 'Many sectors such as agriculture and textiles are growing, so people are borrowing and lending more,' she says. 'The stock exchange, as the heart of that, has an important role.'

#### Maha al-Ghunaim, Kuwait
Maha al-Ghunaim, 48, is one of the most prominent businesswomen in the Gulf, with powerful family connections and a successful investment company. She set up Global Investment House in 1998 after spending 18 years at state-owned investment companies, and is managing director

and chairperson – a role she originally gave to a man, who could enter the dewanya or men-only part of a Kuwaiti house. GIH now has more than $9.5bn under management and operates in 16 countries.

Last month, GIH became the first Kuwaiti company to issue global depository receipts on the London Stock Exchange. 'Being on the LSE raises our profile and shows everyone who we are,' Ms Ghunaim says. Female entrepreneurs in the region must learn to network, she says: 'They are not used to social interaction with men as it's not considered acceptable. But they must learn to make links – and sometimes enemies.'

1.  What barriers to higher level positions might exist for females in the financial industry?

2.  What additional opportunities exist in developing countries?

Thus, corporate finance can be seent to be a multi-faceted and dynamic subject with global relevance. Therefore we have tried as far as possible to open up the subject's universality by finding examples from beyond the US and the UK. We hope we have not fallen short in this aim, though necessarily we have been somewhat limited for the following reasons.

First, much of the empirical evidence tends to be for the US or the UK. There are many more research studies done in the US than in any other country of the world; and as we have already observed, almost all the basic theory originated in the US. Second, as monolingual English speakers we can only access sources written in English. Third, as British citizens born in Scotland, we may have cultural baggage of which we are completely unconscious. Nevertheless, as far as possible, we have tried to keep the scope of this book as international as we are able within the limits imposed on us.

Another way in which we would have liked to keep the scope fairly wide is to address the needs of smaller businesses and non-profit organisations. Corporate finance as a subject is largely predicated on the implicit idea that we are dealing with a medium sized or large profit-making firm, or perhaps a small firm with very good growth prospects and the potential to become much larger. Thus, for example, it is implicitly assumed that the firm has full access to equity and bond markets, when in actual fact many smaller less well-known companies have limited or no access to these markets. The inescapable fact concerning corporate finance is that it is still mainly concerned with larger companies which are often multinational (MNCs).

## Practical implications for managers

### What happens when you assume?

Many business practices are based upon financial theory. However, the formulation of theory requires assumptions that may not always, or even often, hold true. Managers must take theory into account while also considering how their own circumstances differ from that of the theory's assumptions.

Having considered some of the assumptions that we and others tend to make about the subject, we turn now to the most central concepts in the discipline.

## Key concepts

- ☐ **Free market economics** assume no government intervention or regulations in financial markets

- ☐ **Perfect competition** describes a situation of ultimate competition between many buyers and sellers, which brings about a situation of maximum economic efficiency

- ☐ **Behavioural finance** attempts to attribute financial anomalies to psychological effects

- ☐ **Empirical observations in finance** are recorded results which shape corporate finance literature

- ☐ **Asymmetric information** occurs when one party to a transaction holds an information advantage over the other party

- ☐ **Agency theory** describes the conflicts of interest between the principal (such as the owner of a business) and the agent (such as the manager of that business)

## 1.3 The basic knowledge and skills needed for finance

Throughout the book, we draw your attention to the core skills and key knowledge we would have expected you to acquire as a result of reading it. We also provide a summary of key points at the end of each chapter. Nevertheless, if we were to put all these together as a list of key skills and knowledge, it would run to many pages. Which of these would we pick as the most essential?

A particularly essential skill in corporate finance is valuation. Many of the techniques of corporate finance require appreciation of the value of particular types of asset and whether the current price of the asset reflects its true value. Suppose that the current price of an ordinary share in Endymion Enterprises is £10. How do we know whether or not that is a fair price? Or, for example, suppose a new project is proposed which would involve building a new Arthurian Legend theme park called 'Idylls of the King' in Japan? Initial investment is ¥100 million and revenues are expected to be ¥3 million for the next 50 years. What is the value of the project? Is it a good investment or a bad investment?

The conventional approach to these kinds of problem is to add up all the net benefits in cash terms. Thus, for example, what dividend does Endymion pay and what will it pay in the future? Suppose it will pay £1 next year, then the same for the subsequent 19 years? Does this mean the share is actually worth the sum of £1 a year over 20 years? Well no, as £1 next year is not the same as £1 in 2 years and so on. The value of £1 receivable in 10 years is less than the value of £1 receivable in 2 years which is less valuable than £1 receivable now.

We have to use a technique called **discounting** based on the concept of the **time value of money** in order to allow for this. The discounting technique enables us to sum values occurring at different points of time to find a total value. This total value is known as **present value**. Thus a central idea in finance is that the value of any asset is equal to the present value of the cash flows involved. This is always a starting point in any valuation and can be fairly universally applied, for example in both share and project evaluation.

## Active learning activity 1.3

**Why take today what you could put off until tomorrow?**

Consider whether you would rather have £1 million pounds now or £2 million pounds in 10 years' time. What factors would influence your decision?

The technique of discounting brings us on to another fundamental concept in corporate finance. This is the **relationship between risk and return**. In the process of adding up future cash flows across different time periods, future cash flows are discounted or reduced in value. Those further away in time are discounted more than those nearer in time. The extent to which future cash flows should be discounted depends on the uncertainty or riskiness of the cash flows. The greater the uncertainty, the higher the risk and the higher the discount rate. Hence there is a positive relationship between risk and return.

For example, suppose an investor is offered two possible investment opportunities, both requiring an initial outlay of €1000. Investment 1 offers a guaranteed €1100 in 1 year. Thus the gain or return is €100 or 10% of the initial investment. Investment 2 is less certain. Either it will produce €1300 in 1 year or it will produce (with equal probability) €900 in 1 year. Thus the investor stands to gain €300 or to lose €100. The average expected return in this case is €200 (i.e. the average of €300 and –€100) or 20% of the initial investment. Even if risk averse, the investor might regard the extra return as adequate compensation for the extra risk. Now suppose that the return on Investment 2 is reduced and it now offers only the possibility of either €1200 or €900. There would be no takers, as this would be an average 10% return for an uncertain outcome when 10% is available *with certainty* from Investment 1. Thus, if a project or an investment has greater risk or uncertainty, it is required to offer higher returns to compensate investors for bearing the risk. This is why Investment 2 would have to offer a higher return than 10%.

The risk–return relationship is to be found in almost every aspect of corporate finance specifically and Finance generally. In fact it is such a universal principle that it almost seems unnecessary to stress it. Nevertheless it is worth stressing, as it is surprising how often professionals lose sight of the relationship in the pursuit of ever increasing profit. If you are making high returns, it is almost certainly because you are taking large risks.

Another fundamental financial and economic relationship which even very clever people can sometimes lose sight of and forget about is the **business cycle**. Consider overall economic activity as measured by the output of the whole economy for your country. Almost all economies tend to grow over time, so aggregate economic output tends to follow a rising trend. However, there can be substantial cyclical fluctuation around this trend, as can be seen in Figure 1.1.

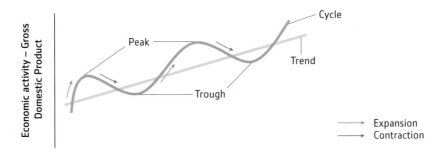

Figure 1.1 The business cycle

Figure 1.1 shows the four stages of the business cycle – expansion (growth), peak, recession (contraction) and trough. A fifth stage, recovery, is sometimes added. This is the stage at which the economy is just coming out of recession. The business cycle would not really be a major problem if it were as regular as the cycle indicated in Figure 1.1. The problem is that in real life the business cycle is much more likely to look like the graph presented in Figure 1.2.

Figure 1.2 shows a business cycle for the US. In this diagram, aggregate output is measured in terms of **Gross Domestic Product (GDP)**. Furthermore, the data are not presented in terms of absolute levels but in percentage rates of growth. Nevertheless, as we can see, there is a clear cycle in consumer expenditure, employment and GDP. In real life, as this diagram suggests, cycles are messy and irregular. If the business cycle was as regular as that suggested in the stylised picture in Figure 1.1, it would be easy to know when, for example, a recession was coming up and adapt accordingly. However, in real life, the important turning points in the cycle are difficult to predict.

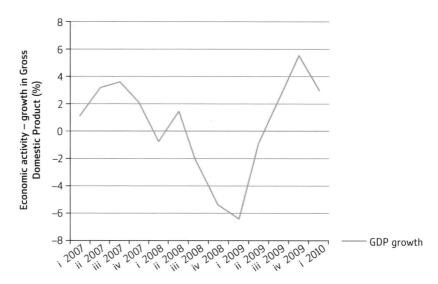

Figure 1.2  A more realistic business cycle

## Practical implications for managers

### Risky returns and global cycles

Managers must be aware that the 'no free lunch' principle generally holds true in markets. Higher returns come with higher risks, and periods of boom are followed by periods of bust. With proper foresight and planning managers can avoid the worst effects. If you assume that the good times will always continue, however, your company may be in trouble when they do not.

This is no mere exercise in pure economics. As you will find later when you tackle the Capital Asset Pricing Model (CAPM), the idea of the market cycle is intrinsic to financial theory. As businesses have found to their cost, the transition from one phase of the business cycle to another can have serious implications for corporate finance policies.

For example, during the long period of sustained growth which many countries experienced from around the mid-1990s to 2007, there was a high availability of credit and debt was cheap. Hence companies were encouraged to take on high levels of cheap debt. Companies with low proportions of debt to overall capital looked staid and overly conservative. However, all of this went into sharp reversal with the onset of the credit crunch in August 2007. Suddenly, it was very difficult for firms to **roll over** debt or to take out fresh loans. Consider the mini case study below, 'Desperately seeking a cash cure'.

## Desperately seeking a cash cure

Source *Economist* 2008a

... a new survey by the Federal Reserve Bank of Philadelphia has shown that many economists believe the United States went into recession in April and will not emerge from it until the middle of 2009.

Opinions differ as to how long and deep the global slowdown might be. But the combination of a battered banking system and shell-shocked consumers mired in debt suggests it could be particularly hard for many businesses, whatever the duration. So bosses are rushing to secure as much cash as they can now to see their companies through the downturn.

How times change. Not long ago companies with cash piles were assailed by corporate activists to return money to shareholders. Nowadays it is only a slight exaggeration to say that the more cash that investors see in a firm's coffers, the happier they are. A recent report from Citigroup's investment bank shows that since the credit crisis began the returns of firms with ample liquidity have outperformed those of their cash-strapped industry peers by almost 7%. Before the crunch, cash-rich firms were generally underperforming.

1. Why have companies with ample liquidity outperformed their peers during the credit crunch?

2. Are there any detrimental consequences to companies, 'rushing to secure as much cash as they can?'

The main point is that economies at both the world and international level are inherently cyclical and probably always will be. Furthermore the existence of the cycle affects more than just the decision to take on debt. The stages of the cycle can affect how businesses and markets behave with respect to their expectations of the future and their assessment of risk. For example, prior to the credit crunch, expectations of the future were over-optimistic.

Stock markets and companies themselves overestimated the ability of companies to pay future dividends to shareholders. Credit was too freely available and both the explicit and implicit cost of debt was too low. Finally, as the interest rate was lower than it should have been, so discount rates on the future were lower than they should have been. Thus a great number of corporate financial calculations were probably wrong because of excessive enthusiasm in the expansionary part of the cycle. Though it didn't appear so at the time, the world was living through an over-exaggerated boom that was followed almost inevitably by a 'bust', and this meant that the ability to make accurate financial decisions was badly hampered. Business cycle volatility and risk–return, the subject of this section, is an important constraint on the firm's financial decision making. In the next section, we examine the possible principal motivations in corporate decision making.

## Key concepts

- **Discounting** is the process of adjusting future cash flow so that it can be added to current cash flow
- The **time value of money** is the notion that cash flow receivable in the future is worth less than the same amount in the present
- **Present value** is the sum of present and future cash flows when future cash flows have been suitably adjusted using discounting
- The **relationship between risk and return** states that the higher the return, the higher the risk
- The **business cycle** is the inherent tendency for market economies to go through periods of boom and bust
- The **unpredictability of the business cycle** means that it is difficult to plan ahead for the downturn and the timing of the upturn is very difficult to predict
- **GDP** is the value of all the goods or services produced within a country in a year
- **Roll over** – most debt taken on by firms is for a given time period. At the end of the time period (known as **maturity**) the firm will often need to renew its loans. The firm may encounter problems in rolling over debt if the general level of credit has dried up, as was the case following the **credit crunch**.

## 1.4 The goal of the company – profit maximisation versus shareholder wealth maximisation

This is not a difficult question if the company is owned by a sole proprietor, or if ownership of the firm is dominated by a single family. However, one of the common features of modern commerce is the separation of ownership and control. Thus, the managers who run the company are a different set of people from the shareholders who own the company. However, given that managers are paid by shareholders it does not seem unreasonable to expect that the company is run in the interests of shareholders. A number of questions arise, however. First, how exactly is the shareholders' interest to be defined? Second, do managers always act in the interests of the firm's owners? Third, do shareholders and managers also have obligations to the wider community?

Businesses are by definition profit-making organisations. Therefore, it might be imagined that the interests of firms are best served by maximising profits. This is certainly the approach that is taken in economics, in which it is assumed that the firm does maximise profits.

However, outside the world of theory, profit maximisation can be problematic for two reasons. First, the amount of profit earned by a firm is determined according to accounting definitions which can take us quite far away from the simplicity of revenue minus cost. This is because accounting profit is defined as earnings after expenses, depreciation, interest, tax and amortisation. Although the concepts of depreciation and amortisation are extremely important for accounting purposes, they do not represent actual expenditure and can be misleading for the purposes of calculating shareholder welfare in terms of how much cash is available to shareholders now and in the future.

Furthermore, the amount to allow for items such as depreciation and amortisation requires a judgement call on the part of managers, and therefore this is to some extent subjective, which in turn makes accounting profit more uncertain as a measure of shareholder welfare. Indeed management are required to make judgements not only about the amounts to allow for amortisation and depreciation, but also sometimes on what to allow as revenue and cost.

For example, a potentially controversial issue which your authors have encountered in previous positions in the British University system is the allocation of overhead to university departments. The cost of university administration, management and marketing has to be allocated somehow. Should it be allocated in terms of staff head-count, student numbers or office floor space? There are quite a number of metrics that one could think of, and this doesn't help to dispel the idea that the allocation of overhead is somewhat arbitrary. What makes overhead allocation controversial is that a small change in overhead can have a big impact on a department's profitability.

However, it is not just the potential ambiguity of profit per se that makes it a problematic concept for measuring shareholder wealth maximisation. It is also the fact that the definitional ambiguity means that accounting profit can be manipulated by less scrupulous managers for their nefarious ends. Perhaps the best examples of this in recent years are the well-known corporate scandals involving Enron and Tyco, in which senior managers were accused of having misled their shareholders. Even though most managers are not criminally fraudulent, they may present accounts in such a way as to flatter their performance, given the amount of control they have over the definition of profit.

Quite apart from the problems involved in defining accounting profit, profit maximisation may not be an appropriate objective for management or even for shareholders. As Martin Wolf (2008) observes:

'Let us suppose, for example, that a business knows of an undetectable way of dumping poisonous waste, thereby saving itself vast sums of money. Do we believe that it 'ought' to do this? I certainly do not. Do we believe businesses ought to create cartels? No, again. Do we regard it as right for business leaders to manipulate their pay – by back-dating stock options, for example – in order to steal as much as possible from their shareholders? No, yet again. Yet all these people are doing is maximizing their personal profits, as individuals in the market economy supposedly should.'

Thus, the short-sighted and relentless pursuit of profit maximisation may lead to all kinds of undesirable and unforeseen consequences. For example, it is possible to 'flatter the bottom line' by drastically reducing costs. Suppose an ambitious manager decided to do this by scrapping expensive-to-use capital machinery, slashing the marketing budget, and encouraging more experienced but more expensive members of staff to leave the company. It is not impossible to imagine that these decisions, while boosting short-term profits, would harm the long-term prospects of the business. It might also be possible to make apparently substantial profits from excessive risk taking. As discussed above, this is the very characteristic of banking and financial companies that led to the credit crunch.

## Practical implications for managers

### Think of the future

Management can often be pressured by their superiors to reduce costs, and it may be tempting to do so without regard to future profits. This short-sighted view will only lead to more problems later.

Therefore, profit is not usually assumed to be an appropriate goal for managers to try to achieve on behalf of the owners of the firm. Rather, in corporate finance it is typically assumed that managers attempt to maximise shareholder wealth by **maximising the value of the firm**. The value of the firm in turn depends on the value of its investment projects and hence it is the value of these that should be maximised. To use the technical language, it is assumed that managers maximise the **net present value** of investment projects. This in turn will maximise the value of the firm.

The maximisation of net present value has a number of advantages over the maximisation of profit. First, it is defined *purely* in terms of cash flow; there are no 'notional' expenditures such as depreciation and therefore there is less ambiguity. Second, net present value takes account of current and *future* cash flows; therefore there is less risk of short-termism. Third, there is at least some account of **risk** in NPV calculations, which can be incorporated via the **discount rate**.

Having established the *reasons* for the assumed goal of managers in finance, there are two further questions that arise. First, what incentives do managers have to maximise shareholder wealth if this would conflict with their own goals? Second, is the pursuit of shareholder value maximisation appropriate from a societal point of view?

## Key concepts

- [ ] The **theoretical concept of profit maximisation** states that the point of a business is to make as much profit as possible
- [ ] **Separation of ownership and control** means that the managers who run the company are a different set of people from the shareholders who own the company
- [ ] **Present value maximisation** states that the point of a business should be to maximise firm value rather than profits
- [ ] The **discount rate** is a percentage rate applied to discount future cash flow
- [ ] **NPV** is a measure of the value of the future cash flows of a project in the present

## 1.5 Do managers maximise firm value or do they pursue their own goals?

Obviously, given the separation of ownership and control, the goals of owners and the goals of managers need not be the same thing at all. Indeed we could go further by observing that managers have an informational advantage, in that they know a great deal more about the inner workings of the firm than shareholders. Shareholders, being outsiders to the firm, have to rely on the limited information conveyed by managers. Clearly it would be physically burdensome and commercially unwise for managers to share absolutely every piece of information with shareholders.

However, this leaves managers in a position of knowing a great deal more than shareholders and other outsiders about the company and its prospects. To use the terminology, managers are in a position to be able to take advantage of an information asymmetry. What forms might the abuses of this advantage take, how can this be guarded against and how can managers be incentivised to pursue shareholders' and not their own interests?

### Active learning activity 1.4

#### Goals for companies

Look up a company's mission statement online and analyse how easy it would be to measure the goals of the company. Is there any contradiction between stated goals?

One possible problem that arises from asymmetric information is that managers may quite simply be dishonest. For example, one of the more alarming stories which emerged from the credit crunch was the fact that Bernard Madoff was running a multibillion dollar ponzi scheme.[1] However, apart from straightforward criminality, there is clearly a strong opportunity for managers to take unfair advantage of their position. This, for example, is why insider trading is illegal in most countries. It is held to be universally unfair that managers can successfully beat the stock market by dealing in their own company stock and using private information to which no one else has access.

While managers may not normally indulge in insider trading, it is not unknown for them to indulge in perks and benefits that, strictly speaking, they don't really need. For example, on 19 September 2005, Dennis Kozlowski, CEO of Tyco, was ordered by a New York state judge to repay $97 million of unauthorised bonuses and compensation.[2] Another notable case involving the misappropriation of funds concerned British and Canadian entrepreneur Conrad Black, who was convicted of fraud on 13 July 2007.[3]

However, managers need not be criminally fraudulent to be falling short of their proper mission to maximise value for shareholders. It is not unknown for senior managers to find ways of being generous to themselves in the matter of expenses, travel, corporate hospitality and so on while remaining well within the letter of the law.

It is not only in the matter of 'perks' that managers may deviate from the shareholders' interest; they may also deviate in terms of the goals they are interested in pursuing on behalf of the firm. Thus, for example, managers may indulge in excessive investment, unwise mergers and acquisitions, and overexpansion more in line with their own grandiose ambitions for empire building than with prudent investment on behalf of shareholders. A possible historical example from the UK is the virtual destruction of eminent company GEC Marconi through overinvestment and unwise takeovers. The concept of an ego-driven takeover where bidding managers pay too much and overestimate their ability to manage the acquired firm may be explained by **hubris** (which may be defined as excessive self-confidence). We discuss this case in more detail in a later chapter.

Overinvestment and unwise takeovers are only one way in which managers may imagine they are furthering the company's interests as well as their own. Another way in which this can happen is, for example, if senior managers, particularly those from a sales or marketing background, are overly focused on sales growth, market domination or brand recognition. Alternatively, those from the production side may be more concerned to produce a technically excellent product.

So how then can shareholders ensure that managers are actually pursuing the interests of the owners of the firm and not their own interests? One way is through corporate governance and corporate ethics.

## Key concepts

- **Private information** is an important concept in finance and it occurs when one party to a transaction has crucial private information which is not available to the other party
- **Information asymmetry** occurs when both parties to a transaction do not have equal access to information
- **Hubris** (excessive self-confidence) may drive overpayment for acquired firms rather than proper objective valuation criteria

## 1.6 Ensuring managers pursue shareholders' goals – corporate governance and corporate ethics

Roger Barker, Head of Corporate Governance at the UK's Institute of Directors, provides a neat summary of the comparatively new topic of corporate governance. It is based on the principle that everyone within a firm is accountable to someone else. Employees are accountable to their bosses, bosses to their shareholders, and shareholders – in the case of institutional investors – to their trustees and beneficiaries. Although company bosses certainly need autonomy and flexibility to manage their companies in an effective manner, they also need to be held directly accountable for their performance and remuneration.[4]

In what follows we use the basic Global Corporate Governance Principles framework suggested by the International Corporate Governance Network. We cannot possibly reproduce their 'best practice' code in detail, but we would recommend it to the interested reader. A similar detailed guide to international corporate governance has been provided by the international Organisation for Economic Co-operation and Development (OECD) and can be found at www.oecd.org.

1. **Corporate objective–shareholder returns**: this is basically the duty to ensure appropriate returns on investment and to ensure the long-term prosperity of the business.

2. **Disclosure and transparency**: corporations should disclose relevant and material information concerning the corporation on a timely basis. Ownership of company shares should also be transparent.

3. **Audit**: this should take place once a year and should show a fair and representative picture of the company's financial health. Auditors should be independent and have no conflicts of interest. Internal controls should ensure the financial probity of the firm.

4. **Shareholders' ownership, responsibilities, voting rights and remedies**: this concerns the rights of shareholders to be consulted on major decisions and to have all possible means to make their views known to management. Where possible, voting should be fair and in proportion to the number of ordinary shares held. Institutional shareholders are obliged to discharge their duties in accordance with the best interest of their clients.

5. **Corporate boards**: the duty of the board is to ensure that compensation and remuneration of executives is in line with the long-term interests of the company. In addition, the board is responsible for ensuring the integrity of the audit process, the transparency of board-level decision making, the avoidance of conflicts of interest and the assurance of independent opinion at board level in order to avoid the capture of the board by self-interested cliques with vested interests.

6. **Corporate remuneration policies**: this can often be the most controversial area of corporate governance. In the UK, for example, there is a perception that the executives of companies are 'fat cats' who are excessively rewarded or are rewarded for failure. In principle, the job of the company is to align **executive remuneration** with the interests of shareholders and this should be done by appointing a remuneration committee, which typically bases its estimate for fair pay and remuneration for senior executives on what is paid in comparable organisations. This approach has been criticised in the UK as providing a 'Buggins's turn' escalation of executive pay, in which pay is ratcheted up as remuneration committees use pay comparisons as a price list.[5]

7. **Corporate citizenship, stakeholder relations and the ethical conduct of business**: we deal with these issues in Section 1.7.

8. **Corporate governance implementation**: the board has a duty to ensure that current industry standards in terms of codes of practice have been enacted. Thus, for example, in the UK the relevant standards would be the Combined Code which can be found at http://www.frc.org.uk/corporate/ukcgcode.cfm.

Of course the codes of corporate governance remain a work in progress. For example, a recent news report suggests that shareholders in the UK still have a need for reform in the areas of pay, capital raising, communication and board composition.[6] Corporate governance in itself may not be enough if it is seen as a 'box-ticking' exercise. It is argued by many commentators that the firm should be imbued with a strong sense of ethics as well.

## Practical implications for managers

### Managers are only human

Managers should be aware of their own limitations. While hopefully you do not plan to deliberately overindulge in perks and bonuses, even the most well-meaning managers cannot be completely unbiased where their remuneration levels are concerned. That is why a robust system of checks and balances through good corporate governance and ethics is needed.

## Key concepts

- **Corporate governance** is the idea that a firm should be accountable to its owners/shareholders, to others directly involved with the firm and to wider society
- **Executive remuneration** deals with the payments of a firm's top management

## 1.7 The role of finance in the wider world – how far do the ethical obligations of the firm extend?

A powerful but potentially controversial idea from economics is that by pursuing their own interests, business people pursue society's interest at the same time. This is an old and very venerable idea put most memorably by Scottish economist Adam Smith in 1776.

> 'It is not from the benevolence of the butcher, the brewer, or the baker that we expect our dinner, but from their regard to their own interest.'[7]

What Smith meant by this was that if businesses such as the ones he mentions wish to gain and retain our custom, then they have to provide us with the things that we actually want to buy. Therefore by pursuing their own self-interest and attempting to make a profit, they also satisfy our needs by providing us with what we want, when and where we want it. This is an elegant and very neat idea which has attracted a great number of adherents over the years. This is not to say, however, that Smith was an uncritical admirer of business people and the business world. As he went on to observe in a later chapter:

> 'People of the same trade seldom meet together, even for merriment and diversion, but the conversation ends in a conspiracy against the public, or in some contrivance to raise prices.'[8]

Thus, the view of Smith and many other economists is that businesses serve both their owners' interests and those of wider society *provided* that they are *competing* with each other. Clearly if a firm exercises monopoly power through control of a vital resource or of a key distribution network or through dominant market spend, it may well not be maximising the potential benefit to society from its business efforts.

The most notable recent example of a leading thinker in the tradition of Smith is Nobel Prize winner Milton Friedman (1912–2006) who is associated with the classical view of the role and responsibilities of business in the wider community, which is that 'management's only social responsibility is to maximize profits' (Robbins *et al.* 2006, p. 161). Milton Friedman (1970, p. 6) asserted that 'there is one and only one social responsibility of business – to use its resources and engage in activities designed to increase its profits so long as it stays within the rules of the game, which is to say, engages in open and free competition without deception or fraud.'

Friedman (1962, 1970) argued that managers' main responsibility is to operate the organisation in the interest of the shareholders, by maximising the returns on the firm's investments. His view was that as the agents of shareholders, firms are ethically and contractually obliged to act in the shareholders' interests. Thus not only is the firm under no obligation to pursue wider social objectives, as many firm do nowadays, but also any social welfare activities on the part of the firm beyond this narrow remit would be an unethical and serious digression from the firm's true purpose, as activities of this kind would add to cost and reduce returns to shareholders. We might refer to this view as the **orthodox economist's view**.

The converse view to Friedman's is the **stakeholder view**. This is the view that the firm operates within a wider societal field which includes not only its investors, customers and employees, but also anyone who could be adversely affected by the company's operations. So, for example, it is fairly obvious that the firm owes a duty of care not to pollute excessively and also to be considerate in its use of potentially exhaustible resources, particularly those from fragile ecosystems. However, some would go further than that and argue that the firm has an obligation to allocate a significant proportion of its considerable resources to pro-bono projects to improve public welfare generally. Consider the next mini case study, 'Spotlighting companies that give back'.

## Active learning activity 1.5

### Ethics versus profits

Think about whether or not companies can afford to have ethical practices in an increasingly competitive and global economy. Go online and find an example of an ethical policy. What might be the costs of such a policy?

## Mini case study

### Spotlighting companies that give back

Source Clapper 2007 (from Associated Content)

#### Ben & Jerry's

This popular ice cream producer promotes a product mission that 'continued commitment to incorporating wholesome, natural ingredients and promoting business practices that respect the Earth and the Environment.' Ben & Jerry's openly states that capitalism does not create equal opportunities for everyone. The company seeks to provide balance there, promoting peace, minimising waste and maintaining safe food production standards.

#### Microsoft Corporation

Following CEO Bill Gates' lead, Microsoft employees individually donate generous amounts of money to non-profit organisations. Instead of direct involvement and CSR reporting, Microsoft focuses on providing software, training, business opportunities and technological advancements to areas of the world and communities that might not otherwise receive such opportunities.

#### Seventh Generation

The ultimate mission of Seventh Generation is to sell and promote the use of safe, non-toxic household products including biodegradable laundry products, chlorine-free diapers and baby wipes, and trash bags made mostly from recycled plastic product. Because of its products, Seventh Generation is a natural leader in Corporate Social Responsibility. Seventh Generation promotes consumer education, providing the public with information about toxins in most common household products. Seventh Generation products alone have saved 1,313,700 gallons of petroleum, among other non-renewable resources.

#### Starbucks Coffee Company

Starbucks Coffee Company takes Corporate Social Responsibility very seriously. Starbucks begins at the bean, ensuring fair pay and healthcare services for coffee bean growers. Starbucks also passes this immense profit on to its employees. Starbucks partners receive exemplary health benefits for working part-time, including dental, life insurance, AD&D [Accidental Death and

Dismemberment insurance], and more. Starbucks also offers its employees stock benefits and gives employees stock each quarter.

The company has also ensured environmental responsibility, making its drink sleeves out of 10% post-consumer product. The company's commitment to diversity and equality are ranked above profitability in its list of core values. Starbucks also stresses community involvement, encouraging partners to volunteer for community causes. Store donations to community events and fundraisers are frequent.

Lastly, Starbucks Coffee Company sells books with profits advocating literacy and sells Ethos Water. Five percent of profits from Ethos Water (bottled) goes to producing clean water for children in third world countries.

1. Which of the listed companies above seem to most embrace the stakeholder view?

2. What stakeholders are identified in the examples above?

Of course, businesses still have to earn a profit and make a good return for their shareholders. Stakeholder theory is comparatively new, so it would probably be wrong to talk of a hard and fast set of central principles. However, in terms of the basic framework, we might identify the following unifying concepts.

First, that companies should not be too focused on short-term profits. A focus on short-term profits can have dire consequences as we can see in the next mini case study where the Manville Corporation was reluctant to reveal information to employees that the company's product, asbestos, was damaging their health. The effect of too much focus on short-term profits is briefly illustrated in this case study entitled 'The only responsibility of managers is to maximise shareholder wealth'.

## Mini case study

### The only responsibility of managers is to maximise shareholder wealth
Source Zhu 2010 (from Bukisa)

However, a major flaw with the classical view is that its focus tends to be on short-term profit. A good example would be Manville Corporation in the United States: 50 years ago management decided to conceal information from employees that one of its products, asbestos, caused fatal lung disease. Chest X-ray results from employees were withheld from them. The rationale behind this was being able to save money and increase profits. Although this seemed to work for a short-term period, in the long run the company was forced into bankruptcy in 1982 in order to protect itself from the increasing lawsuits in relation to asbestos liabilities (Robbins et al. 2006).

1. Describe what the 'classical view' means in the context of this article.

2. How does this contrast with the stakeholder view?

3. What view do you most agree with?

Not only was Manville's behaviour unethical, but also it ultimately led to the demise of the company. It should be noted that Manville's behaviour is by no means condoned or encouraged in the orthodox economist's view of Milton Friedman, who was punctilious in pointing out that firms should not involve themselves in anything illegal or immoral. The argument is the more subtle one that by overly focusing on short-term profit firms may be led into the temptation of doing something illegal or immoral.

Other reasons for the increasing popularity of the stakeholder approach include:

1. **Globalisation and regulation**: as public opinion and governments now support businesses that pursue Corporate Social Responsibility (CSR) due to the increased awareness of globalisation and its effects, those who pursue CSR can also expect less government regulation.

2. **Responsibility**: large companies wield considerable power in modern societies. With power comes responsibility.

3. **Survival**: in order to ensure an organisation's survival, managers must be able to implement some social obligations and accept the costs that are attached (Robbins *et al.* 2006). Certainly in Western countries, there is an expectation on the part of the public that companies should both act responsibly and display a social concern.

4. **Preventive action to avoid adverse social impact**: some good examples of how this works in practice are given in an article in *Marketing Week*, 'Paved with good intentions', 15 March 2007).[9]

5. **Pre-emption of laws and regulation**: by participating proactively, the firm has an opportunity to shape public sector initiatives in a positive way rather than having to react to them.

6. **Global warming**: this may require firms to focus on more than the bottom line. A great deal has been written on global warming specifically and the environment generally – far more than we could possibly do justice to in a small section here. We reserve this as a topic for the next section.

Of course, between the more polar positions of the orthodox economist's view and the stakeholder view it is possible to take a position somewhere in the middle ground. Space does not permit expansion on this more nuanced approach, but the interested reader is particularly recommended to seek out the writing of distinguished contributors to the *Financial Times* such as Sam Brittan and Martin Wolf.[10]

Given that the stakeholder view has many proponents as to the value of recognising the wider social resopnsibilities of firms, the question then arises of how these responsibilities can be taken into account. This is the subject of the next section.

## Key concepts

- [ ] The **orthodox economist's view** of firms is that they are there to maximise present value or profit
- [ ] The **stakeholder view** is that firms should take full account of any societal impact

## Practical implications for managers

### A wider view

Businesses across the world are now increasingly subscribing to the stakeholder view, where not just the profitability of the company must be considered, but also the effect on the environment, suppliers, customers and so on. Managers must therefore take these stakeholders into account when making decisions.

## 1.8 The social and environmental audit

Given the various aspects of corporate responsibility outlined previously, it is necessary to consider how companies can formally respond to the expectations of the public so that they meet their corporate responsibilities without it seeming like a superficial publicity stunt.

One answer would be to incorporate a social and environmental audit into the normal financial audit. As we indicated in the previous section, a particular area in which companies will be expected to comply will be in meeting environmental standards. Indeed, although at present such reports are voluntary in many countries, particularly in the US, it would not be surprising if they eventually became compulsory in most countries. As Kate Galbraith (2007) observes in *The Economist*:

> 'In America, the world's great energy guzzler, 'sustainability reports' are voluntary. It is nice to learn how many tonnes of waste are recycled at UPS, and to read that Proctor & Gamble's Pampers are getting slimmer (so using less material). But what about the issues that companies don't want to report?'

It would be no surprise if one day California – which has already passed a cap on carbon emissions – decides to require, say, corporate water-usage reports,' says Janet Ranganathan of the World Resources Institute.

One big problem is that most sustainability reports are not audited by outsiders (verification is especially rare in America). This could change as investing in 'sustainable companies' grows. Environmentalists are putting pressure on America's Securities and Exchange Commission to require companies to disclose their carbon emissions, as well as to quantify (for the benefit of shareholders) the possible impact of climate change on companies' bottom lines.

Moreover, environmental issues are a global concern. For example, Daniel Esty (2007) observed a similar effect in China, as shown in the next mini case study, 'Is China turning green?'.

## Mini case study

### Is China turning green?

Source Esty 2007 (from Fortune Online Magazine)

For example, it set a target of cutting energy use per unit of GDP by 20 percent by 2010 – an ambitious goal for a country that gets 70 percent of its power from burning coal. It has adopted fuel-economy standards that will push average car mileage to nearly 40 miles a gallon over the next five years, much higher than in the U.S. And it has promised to reduce water pollution by 10 percent by 2020 and increase industrial solid-waste recycling by 60 percent.

Those aren't just empty promises. The State Environmental Protection Agency, which recently acknowledged that air- and water-quality levels are worsening, blocked 163 projects worth about $99 billion last year.

Start-up companies are being launched every day to develop pollution-control technologies, improve energy efficiency, and create alternate sources of power. The $220 million in clean-tech venture capital China received last year puts it ahead of Europe as a venue for new environmental companies.

1. How do China's 'green' initiatives compare with similar initiatives across the world?
2. Do these initiatives correspond with the classical view or the stakeholder view of how companies should do business?

Hence a future task for almost all future financial managers will be to include a social and environmental audit as well as financial figures in company reports, and for other reporting purposes. The problem is that there are a number of bodies offering advice, including the International Corporate Governance Network and the OECD, mentioned above, as well as, for example, the Global Reporting Initiative (GRI) based in the Netherlands and the Accounting for Sustainability Initiative founded by Britain's Prince Charles.

As far as we can see the latter two organisations offer actual reporting frameworks unlike the former two. We would recommend the GRI framework which is more general than Accounting for Sustainability which appears to be mainly focused on the physical environment. Space does not permit its reproduction here, but it can be found in the longer case study at the end of the chapter.

The suggested framework of Prince Charles is more focused on the physical environment. So far it has been taken up by Aviva, BT and HSBC, as well as the Cabinet and environment offices of the UK government.

As we have seen, there is plenty of guidance for CSR. However, it is unlikely that such audits will ever be legally enforced with the stringency of financial audits, and there will always to some extent be an element of voluntary practice in enforcing them, as the following mini case study, 'An onus on retailers to keep hands clean', suggests.

## Mini case study

### An onus on retailers to keep hands clean
Source Birchall 2007, Copyright *Financial Times*, 2007

It is unclear whether 10 years of effort have delivered oversight that is fundamentally better for workers.

'Millions of dollars have gone into codes of conduct and monitoring efforts, and the major output has been to create an army of fraudsters,' says Neil Kearney, head of ITGLWF, an international group of clothing worker unions. 'And the skill acquired has been how to pull the wool over the auditor's eyes.'

At the same time, suppliers complain of 'audit fatigue' from the need for factories to provide differing sets of data for a stream of different people. The inspectors come from retailers and brands, from independent assessors such as Verité, a non-profit auditing group, and from auditing initiatives run by groups including Social Accounting International and the US-based Fair Labor Association.

Some of the limits of monitoring were demonstrated last year in a report by Sussex University's institute of development studies for the ETI. The report found, broadly, that monitoring efforts had helped to eliminate child labour violations and improve factory safety but had far less impact on issues such as freedom of association and regular employment.

With little political support for regulation, two related views are emerging among companies and non-governmental organisations.

The first entails a fundamental shift in the way factories are run. Management and workers would be educated both about their legal rights and the standards buyers expect.

The approach has gained traction as more companies seek to draw supplies from a smaller number of factories. In a move that could reinforce such efforts, the US clothing retailer Gap has introduced an 'integrated vendor score card' that ranks suppliers in five tiers, combining overall factory conditions with factors such as speed and innovation. The scorecard, says Dan Henkle, who leads Gap's social responsibility efforts, demonstrates the 'close correlation' between factories with the best working conditions and those with the highest performance.

The argument touches on the second strand in current thinking: how purchasing and design decisions made by a retailer or brand at its home office can contribute to abuses such as unpaid

or excessive overtime. The ETI report found that downward pressure on prices and lead times from the companies themselves 'limited suppliers' ability to make improvements in labour practices'.

1. Have increased auditing regulations had any detrimental effects on the clothing industry?

2. Have clothing retailers encouraged suppliers to take a more stakeholder-centric or classical view of how their companies should operate? How?

In the next two sections, we close by looking at two current issues in finance, one rather sobering and the other giving quiet cause for optimism.

## Key concepts

☐ **Environmental audits** occur when a firm attempts to calculate the full social costs as well as the private cost of its activities and to determine its impact on the environment

☐ **Corporate social responsibility** describes the accountability firms have for the effects of the business on the environment and community

# 1.9 Topics in finance

## 1.9.1 The credit crunch

It was in August 2007 that a widespread perception began to emerge that there was something wrong with the banking sector. In an almost unprecedented development, liquidity in the interbank market began to dry up. The interbank market is the market where banks borrow short term from other banks and where they place any short-term surplus funds. The reason, it eventually transpired, was that banks were nervous of lending to each other, as many banks were exposed to bad debt from sub-prime mortgage lending in the US and it wasn't clear who exactly was exposed and by how much.

The reason this situation came about is that for a long time, particularly in the Anglophone countries, credit was too freely available at too low an interest rate. This led to excessive spending on consumer goods and services and also excessive spending on investment assets. In normal times, excessive spending on consumer goods would push prices up, causing interest rates to be raised to cope with the resulting general inflation.

However, inflation was kept low as the Anglophone countries were importing large amounts of goods from China. Because China has low labour costs and, arguably, a favourable exchange rate, it was able to keep prices down. Hence the excess spending spilled over into investment products, and there was **asset price inflation** instead. However, Central

Banks were more used to targeting consumer prices and did not intervene strongly when it became increasingly apparent that there was a **bubble** in asset prices.

The most striking aspect of this asset price bubble from the ordinary person's point of view was the rapid increase in house prices. House prices peaked in the US in 2005 and in the UK in 2007. The declining fortunes of the housing markets appear to be strongly correlated with the declining fortunes of the banking sector in most countries. This was not just because of the link between mortgage lending and house prices in local markets. It was also because banks throughout the world had become exposed to the 'burst bubble' in the US as they invested in US mortgage lending.

It might be asked how banks with no financial links to the US market could become exposed to mortgage lending in the US, traditionally a fairly localised financial activity, relying as it does on the knowledge of borrowers and knowledge of local housing market conditions. However, the link between local lender and local borrower had been severed by a process known as **securitisation**. Securitisation occurs when the underlying cash flows from a financial asset such as a loan book or a tranche of credit card customers are sold on to a third party. The problem was that investors from outside the US housing market overestimated the quality of their investment and default rates were much higher than they expected, triggering large bank losses.

## Practical implications for managers

### The credit crunch

The credit crunch has had a huge effect on markets worldwide and has led to an increased regulatory atmosphere in business. With many banks being bailed out with taxpayer money the public has grown increasingly angry with companies setting remuneration levels too high or acting irresponsibly. Managers should be aware of the potential public reaction to their actions. While setting high bonuses may be tempting, the public relations (PR) damage sustained may lead to it costing more than expected.

You might question why so many banks could make such costly mistakes. There were a number of factors at play here:

1. It is not unknown for banking investment at times to be driven by what are known as 'herd effects'. This is when one investment bank feels the need to get into a particular new type of 'hot' investment or risk being left trailing by their competitors. The very fact that other large institutions are already in a particular line of business may cause the institution to be less cautious about risk than normal.

2. Securitisation has worked very well in the past for things like credit cards. However, this might have been a securitisation too far. Certain types of lending may require a close relationship between lender and borrower in order to overcome risk stemming from asymmetric information.

3. It may have been more difficult for banks to assess the risk they were exposed to given that different grades of mortgage debt were wrapped or amalgamated and securitised as structured investment vehicles known as **collateralised debt options** (CDOs).

4. Firms thought they had offset the risk involved by using a type of financial insurance called a **credit default swap**. As it turned out this only offset *individual* risk, not *systemic* risk. Indeed, no insurance can offset systemic risk.

### 1.9.2  Microfinance

We close finally on some good news for finance, and that is the development of microfinance in less developed countries. This is the idea of making small loans at commercial rates to individuals who want to set up very small businesses. One of the most well-known practitioners of microfinance and microlending is the Grameen Bank of Bangladesh. As it says on its website:

> 'Grameen Bank branches are located in the rural areas, unlike the branches of conventional banks which try to locate themselves as close as possible to the business districts and urban centers. First principle of Grameen banking is that the clients should not go to the bank; it is the bank which should go to the people instead. Grameen Bank's 23,799 staff meet 7.80 million borrowers at their door-step in 84,096 villages spread out all over Bangladesh, every week, and deliver bank's service. Repayment of Grameen loans is also made very easy by splitting the loan amount in tiny weekly instalments. Doing business this way means a lot of work for the bank, but it is a lot more convenient for the borrowers.'

While loans tend to be made at commercial rates, loan conditions are less stringent than they would be with normal banks. The bank makes every effort not to foreclose and to help customers to work through any difficulties. So successful has Grameen been in furthering development objectives in Bangladesh that the bank and its founder, Professor Mohammed Yunus, were awarded the Nobel Peace Prize in 2006.

The interested reader is recommended to look at the bank's website (www.grameen-info. org ) to learn more about this heart-warming story. Another useful resource in the area of microfinance is provided by the Women's World Banking Network (www.swwb.org). For example, the interested reader is directed to the powerful story of Oyunchimeg Dendev, a seamstress and mother of five in Ulan Bator, Mongolia. In 1995 she left her factory job to start her own tailoring business in her home.

One word of caution: given the impressive rates of interest achievable in microfinance, it may well become of major interest to many banks not currently involved in this area. It would be a shame if the rather delicate ecostructure involved in providing this kind of finance were destroyed by a boom and bust cycle caused by a financial herd effect.

## Key concepts

☐ General inflation is when the prices of goods and services across the economy rise in general

☐ Asset price inflation is when the value of financial assets such as stocks or even housing rise beyond their true intrinsic worth

☐ Herd effects occur when investors place undue weight on the actions of others and don't place enough weight on their own independent judgement

☐ Securitisation is the practice of issuing securities such as bonds on the basis of cash flow from other financial assets, in effect selling on the cash flow

☐ Collateralised debt options are instruments for selling on debt such as mortgage debt from the original lender

☐ Credit default swaps are financial instruments that in effect insure against loss from other financial instruments held in collateralised debt options

## 1.10 Summary

We started this chapter by considering the various roles that the financial manager is expected to play, including investment and project manager, for example, and observed that the role of financial managers has become much more complex than in the days when they were simply expected to ensure money was available when needed and that the firm made the best use of surplus funds.

We then went on to elaborate on some of the theory underlying the academic discipline of finance, while at the same time pointing out that these theories are only ultimately useful if they help with actual practice. Particularly powerful influences on finance have been the concepts of free market economics and perfect competition, though this is changing with the advent of behavioural finance, more empirical observations and a greater appreciation of the agency theory. Subsequently we went on to examine the skills and knowledge needed in finance. We particularly emphasised:

1. Discounting and present value as a universal valuation technique.

2. The ever-present relationship between risk and return.

3. The risk engendered by the business cycle, in particular the risk of an unexpected downturn.

We then went on to look at the reason why value maximisation rather than profit maximisation is the assumed motive for firms and their employees in finance. Nevertheless, the assumed theoretical motive for firm behaviour is not necessarily always the case, as we discovered in the next section on how and why managers may pursue goals more suited to their own preferences rather than those that would be in the best interest of the firm. The topic of corporate governance is largely concerned with ensuring that managers act in the interests of owners and shareholders, and this was discussed in the subsequent section.

Nevertheless, corporate governance is about more than ensuring that managers maximise shareholder value. It is also about ensuring that firms and their employees act responsibly. This brought us on to the topic of corporate social responsibility and social auditing – codes of conduct to ensure corporate responsibility, for example with regard to the environment. Nevertheless, not everyone agrees that firms ought to take on a large social role, and thus we have a range of views of what firms ought to do – from the Friedmanite view that firms should concentrate solely on maximising value, to the stakeholder view that firms have extensive responsibilities towards society as a whole.

We closed by examining some current topics in finance, namely the reasons for the credit crunch and the difference being made in some of the emergent countries by microfinance.

## Case study

### GRI framework
Source www.globalreporting.org

### Part 1

#### 1.1 Reporting principles and guidance
The principles involved in the social audit are materiality, stakeholder inclusiveness, sustainability context and completeness, along with a brief set of tests for each principle. Application of these principles with the standard disclosures determines the topics and indicators to be reported. This is followed by principles of balance, comparability, accuracy, timeliness, reliability and clarity, along with tests that can be used to help achieve the appropriate quality of the reported information.

- **Strategy and profile**: disclosures that set the overall context for understanding organisational performance such as an organisation's strategy, profile and governance.
- **Management approach**: disclosures that cover how an organisation addresses a given set of topics in order to provide context for understanding performance in a specific area. These disclosures should provide a brief overview of the organisation's management approach in order to set the context for performance information. In other words, there should be a brief description of the line of responsibility and structures in place in order to manage particular issues.
- **Performance indicators**: indicators that elicit comparable information on the economic, environmental and social performance of the organisation.

*Materiality*
Definition: an organisation's significant economic, environmental and social impacts.

*Stakeholder inclusiveness*
Definition: the reporting organisation should identify its stakeholders and explain in the report how it has responded to their reasonable expectations and interests.

*Sustainability context*

Definition: the report should present the organisation's performance in the wider context of sustainability.

*Completeness*

Definition: coverage of the material topics and indicators and definition of the report boundary should be sufficient to reflect significant economic, environmental and social impacts and enable stakeholders to assess the reporting organisation's performance in the reporting period.

### 1.2 Reporting principles for defining quality

*Balance*

Definition: the report should reflect positive and negative aspects of the organisation's performance to enable a reasoned assessment of overall performance.

*Comparability*

Definition: issues and information should be selected, compiled and reported consistently. Reported information should be presented in a manner that enables stakeholders to analyse changes in the organisation's performance over time, and could support analysis relative to other organisations.

*Accuracy*

Definition: the reported information should be sufficiently accurate and detailed for stakeholders to assess the reporting organisation's performance.

*Timeliness*

Definition: reporting occurs on a regular schedule and information is available in time for stakeholders to make informed decisions.

*Clarity*

Definition: information should be made available in a manner that is understandable and accessible to stakeholders using the report.

*Reliability*

Definition: information and processes used in the preparation of a report should be gathered, recorded, compiled, analysed and disclosed in a way that could be subject to examination and that establishes the quality and materiality of the information.

## Part 2

### 2.1 Standard disclosures

This section specifies the base content that should appear in a sustainability report, subject to the guidance on determining content in Part 1 of the Guidelines. There are three different types of disclosures contained in this section:

- **Strategy and profile:** disclosures that set the overall context for understanding organisational performance such as an organisation's strategy, profile and governance.
- **Management approach:** disclosures that cover how an organisation addresses a given set of topics in order to provide context for understanding performance in a specific area. Again,

it should be stressed that these disclosures should provide a brief overview of the organisation's management approach in order to set the context for performance information (see above).

- **Performance indicators**: indicators that elicit comparable information on the economic, environmental and social performance of the organisation.

Choose an industry and see if you can find enough information to define in practical terms and apply each of the concepts identified.

## Questions

1. Outline five decisions that are taken by financial managers.

2. What is the theory of perfect competition and the market and how does this differ from behavioural theory?

3. In terms of the basic concept, what is meant by discounting, time value of money and present value?

4. What is information asymmetry and what kind of problem does it give rise to?

5. Why is there a need for corporate governance and what are some of the basic principles of corporate governance?

6. How might you characterise the two polar opposite viewpoints on social responsibility?

7. Give some examples of firms with social policies and discuss whether these can be measured in a meaningful manner.

8. What is the point of a social and environmental audit?

9. Outline and discuss some of the main factors leading to the credit crunch.

10. What is microfinance and how does it differ from ordinary finance?

## Online resource centre

Visit the Online Resource Centre that accompanies this book for the answers to these questions.

**www.oxfordtextbooks.co.uk/marney**

# Further reading

Carlton, J. (2006) Greenpeace grades PC makers; Dell, H-P step up recycling efforts; Apple is pressed to do more. *Wall Street Journal*, 21 September, sec. B5.

Forsythe, J. (2005) Leading with diversity. *New York Times*, 29 November.

Friedman, M. (1962) *Capitalism and Freedom*. University of Chicago Press, Chicago.

Friedman, M. (1970) The social responsibility of business is to increase profits. *New York Times Magazine*, 13 September, p. 6.

Hawken, P. (2005) *The Ecology of Commerce: A Declaration of Sustainability*, 1st edn. Harper Collins, New York, pp. 1–82.

Richardson, L.A. (1998) What is the constitutional status of affirmative action? Reading tea leaves. In: Affirmative Action: A Dialogue on Race, Gender, Equality and Law in America. ***Focus on Law Studies***, XIII(2). American Bar Association, Chicago.

US government award: see http://www.hispanicprwire.com/news.php? 1=insid=6031.

 # Internet references

In our discussion above, we recommended www.icgn.org and www.oecd.org as good sources for corporate governance codes.

Adam Smith, despite publishing his masterpiece The Wealth of Nations in 1776, still has a great deal of relevance today; not just for economists, but also for financiers, business generally and even politics. This may well be because he dealt mainly in actual observable entities rather than multiplying abstractions. See

http://www.internationaleconomics.net/bizfinance.html#finance

For various views on ethical business and the stakeholder approach a very useful resource is

www.associatedcontent.com.
For the 'common-sense' FT approach to business, see

www.ft.com, http://creativecapitalism.typepad.com
and

http://www.samuelbrittan.co.uk/.
Finally, if you are interested in microfinance, you could consult the Grameen Bank website

(http://www.grameen-info.org)
and Women's World Banking Network

(www.swwb.org).

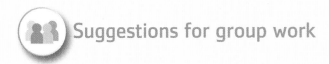 # Suggestions for group work

1. Students should discuss the key assumptions implicit in financial theory. How likely are they to hold true in practical situations?

2. Consider the cyclical nature of economies. Discuss possible reasons for this and how it should affect business practices.

 ## Suggestions for presentations

1. Choose an FTSE 100 company. Assume the role of a consultant for that company and create a presentation identifying the stakeholders and how their needs can be managed.

2. Create a presentation advocating value maximisation over profit maximisation. Explain the difference and justify the choice.

# 2 Investment Appraisal

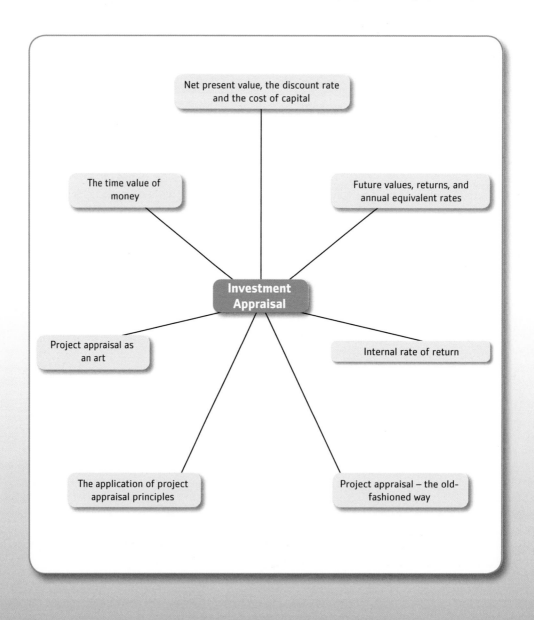

Net present value, the discount rate and the cost of capital

The time value of money

Future values, returns, and annual equivalent rates

**Investment Appraisal**

Project appraisal as an art

Internal rate of return

The application of project appraisal principles

Project appraisal – the old-fashioned way

## Knowledge-based learning objectives

When you have completed this chapter you will be able to:

✓ Calculate discount factors

✓ Explain discounted cash flow

✓ Explain a basic compound interest process and how it is used to calculate return

✓ Calculate net present value and internal rate of return

✓ Calculate payback and accounting rate of return

✓ Calculate future values

✓ Calculate annual equivalent returns

## Skills-based learning objectives development

✓ Business and financial environment consciousness: you should have developed an understanding of some fundamental techniques in basic finance.

✓ Numerical skills: you should have developed the ability to understand, manipulate and calculate standard measures of investment performance.

✓ Analytical thinking and problem-solving skills: you should have developed the ability to know why standard investment criteria are appropriate techniques for investment appraisal.

✓ Problem-solving skills: you should have developed the ability to assess the financing requirements of a company and evaluate possible solutions.

✓ Critical-thinking skills: you should have developed the ability to understand the assumptions on which appraisal techniques are based and to know the limitations of these techniques.

✓ Organisational skills: you should have developed your ability to organise your time and work efficiently and to gather data and information which you can translate into value-adding intelligence.

✓ Managerial soft skills: you should have developed the ability to know where judgement and interpersonal skill are needed with investment appraisal.

✓ Presentation skills: you should have developed your ability to present your work clearly both verbally and in writing.

✓ Interpersonal skills: your ability to present your work clearly both verbally and in writing and to interact effectively with others is further developed upon completion of the end of chapter questions.

## Online resource centre

Visit the Online Resource Centre that accompanies this book to listen to a podcast of the authors discussing the main principles of investment appeal.

**www.oxfordtextbooks.co.uk/marney**

### Decisions, decisions for OrganicX

Following the notable success of the Grameen Bank in Bangladesh and other microfinance initiatives in the emerging countries,
Charlie and Kate want to get involved to some extent in microfinance and local project development.

   One project they have been asked to consider is a mobile phone repair project. They have
discovered that there's no limit to how cell phones can be modified and how their life spans can
be extended. OrganicX would like to become involved in this kind of venture, initially in Delhi,
and then expand across India and Africa. Charlie and Kate are keen to apply the lessons learnt
from the Grameen Bank and other microfinance initiatives which reveal that these projects are
most successful when run on a strictly commercial basis. Any profits would be ploughed back
into further initiatives. They have been given the following figures. Premises of at least 10,000
ft$^2$ will be needed and the current cost of commercial property in Delhi is 100–150 rupees (Rs)
per ft$^2$ per month. They will need to employ 17 staff, at an annual cost of Rs1,500,000 each for
two managerial staff, Rs 250,000 each for five support staff and Rs 500,000 each for ten techni-
cal/educational staff. Other costs such as energy and consumables are estimated at Rs 500,000
per month. They estimate that they could attract 300 students for each self-contained weekly
training session in exactly how to expand the use of mobiles, and the limit to what they could
charge as a fee would be Rs 6,000. Their normal cost for raising capital is 15%. What they would
like to do is to get some project performance in terms of net present value and internal rate of
return. They would also like to make sure they have covered all the issues important in ensuring
that the project fulfils its private and social objectives. Kate is torn in two. She doesn't feel that
the figures really add up, especially once all the uncertainties with regard to training are taken
into account, but is keen to promote the ethos of OrganicX. Charlie, as usual, sees only the opportunity, and says 'Let's just go for it, Kate, how can we lose?'

## 2.1  The time value of money

   'Space, the final frontier ...'

For people of a certain age, including your authors, the phrase that introduces this chapter
has tremendous resonance. It was part of a little speech on space exploration which was always given by William Shatner at the start of every episode of the original series of *Star Trek*.
In the 1960s, when *Star Trek* was made, it was confidently expected that by the twenty-first
century humanity would have made serious inroads into the conquest of space and time
through advanced science. Alas, it wasn't to be. Surprisingly though, the less glamorous and
more workaday world of finance cracked the time problem years ago, by introducing the

concept of **discounting, time value of money (TVM), present value (PV)** and **net present value (NPV)**. It hardly needs emphasising that these are important concepts in financial management, and they have a wide variety of applications in a number of fields including, inter-alia, the comparison of investment alternatives and solving problems involving loans, mortgages, leases, savings and annuities. For our purposes at the moment, we will focus mainly on investment appraisal.

In order to gently lead into the idea of the time value of money, consider the following scenario. You have been asked for some help by Pauly. He wants your advice on a new Trattoria that he's thinking of setting up. Now it's important that you get this one right, as Pauly is an influential businessman. The basic details of the investment project are fairly simple. The Trattoria will cost £200,000 to set up, in terms of fixtures, fittings, etc. Thereafter, Pauly reckons that he should make £50,000 net income after deducting all expenses necessary to run the restaurant. After 5 years, the restaurant will need to be completely refurbished – the whole thing can be considered a 5-year investment. So your friend Pauly reckons that the project will put him £50,000 ahead. Is this right?

| | A | B |
|---|---|---|
| 1 | Year | Cash Flow |
| 2 | | |
| 3 | | |
| 4 | 0 (i.e. Now) | -200,000 |
| 5 | 1 (Next Year) | 50,000 |
| 6 | 2 (The year after) | 50,000 |
| 7 | 3 (etc.) | 50,000 |
| 8 | 4 | 50,000 |
| 9 | 5 | 50,000 |
| 10 | | |

Screenshot 2.1  Trattoria cash flow

'Erm, well, Pauly, not necessarily. You see the same monetary cash flow, if it occurs at different points in time, does not have the same value,' and warming to your theme, 'I mean, which would you rather have? £100 now or the promise of £100 in 1 year's time?' You quickly continue: 'Clearly a businessman like you would value £100 now more highly than £100 in a year's time.' He's still not looking absolutely convinced, so you reach for a copy of this book which you always happen to keep in your bag, and rifling through the well-thumbed pages you quickly find the relevant passage.

'£50,000 in 1 year's time is not the same as £50,000 in 2 years' time which is not the same thing as £50,000 in 3 years' time.'

His gaze begins to soften ever so slightly, and so you continue reading with him.

Cash flows received nearer the present are more valuable than cash flows received further in time. So before we add up the cash flows we have to adjust them so that they are on an equivalent standard. The way that we do this in finance is to use a technique called **discounting**. Once we've adjusted each cash flow by an appropriate **discount factor**, we can then safely add them up. For example, supposing you had a discount rate of 10%, the calculation would look like this:

| | A | B | C | D |
|---|---|---|---|---|
| 1 | T | CF | DF | DCF |
| 2 | Time | Cash Flow | Discount Factor | Discounted Cash Flow |
| 3 | 0 | -£200,000 | 1.0000 | -£200,000.00 |
| 4 | 1 | £50,000 | 0.9091 | £45,454.55 |
| 5 | 2 | £50,000 | 0.8264 | £41,322.31 |
| 6 | 3 | £50,000 | 0.7513 | £37,565.74 |
| 7 | 4 | £50,000 | 0.6830 | £34,150.67 |
| 8 | 5 | £50,000 | 0.6209 | £31,046.07 |
| 9 | | | | |
| 10 | | | NPV | -£10,460.66 |

Screenshot 2.2  Trattoria cash flow discounted @ 10%

What we have calculated is the sums of money receivable in each time period which are the equivalent to £50,000 receivable now. For year one, we find this equivalent by multiplying Year 1 cash flow by the factor 1/1.1. We explain why we do this later in the chapter; however, it does no harm at this point to reveal that 1/1.1 represents a reversal compound interest process for r, the discount rate of 10%, and n, the number of years until receipt of the cash flow. Having multiplied £50,000, receivable in 1 year, by 1/1.1, the discount factor, we find that £50,000 in 1 year is the equivalent of £45,450 now. We multiply the Year 2 cash flow by the factor 1/1.1, then again by the same factor, 1/1.1. That makes the £50,000 receivable in 2 years the equivalent of £41,320 now. And just to emphasise the point, we multiply the Year 3 cash flow by 1/1.1, 1/1.1 and then 1/1.1 again. Once we've done that for all the future cash flows, we can legitimately add up discounted cash flow, which gives us the net discounted cash flow for the Trattoria project at the equivalent of current monetary values. Sorry Pauly, the sums don't add up as DCF is negative. But Pauly still doesn't understand.

You explain as follows: 'You know the way you get interest on your money when you put it in the bank? Well, all I've done here is to apply the opposite process.' Look at this example in the book:

**Example of basic compound interest**: suppose you put £100 on deposit at an interest rate of 10%. If interest is applied annually, by the end of a year you will have £110. By the end of 2 years you will have £121.

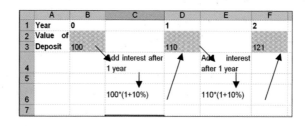

Screenshot 2.3  Basic compound interest @ 10% and annual compounding

Fairly obviously, the £110 is the result of the following process:

$$£110 = (1 + 0.1) \times £100 \ or \ £110 = (1 + 10\%) \times £100$$

Now if we were to write the same thing in symbols, it would say

$$FV_1 = (1 + r) \times PV$$

That is, the future value of your deposit in 1 year (FV1 or £110) is the result of the application of one plus some interest rate (1 + r or 1.1) to the amount you have now (PV or £100). We have called the £100 we have now 'PV,' as this stands for **present value**. So £100 at present value will have a **future value** of £110 in 1 year, *if* the appropriate interest rate is 10% and the compounding period is 1 year.

We can apply similar reasoning to the Year 2 calculation:

$$£121 = (1 + 0.1) \times (1 + 0.1) \times £100 = 1.1 \times £121 = 1.1^2 \times £100$$

Now if we were to write this equation in symbols, it would say

$$FV_2 = (1 + r)^2 \ PV$$

The interpretation of this equation is that £100 at present value will have a future value of £121 in 2 years, if the appropriate interest rate is 10% and the compounding period is 1 year.

So as promised at the start of this chapter, we have, in a sense, discovered a form of time-travel. We can take a present value and, through the simple application of the interest process, turn it into a future value. Table 3 at the back of the book contains future value multipliers.

At this point you notice that Pauly has visibly relaxed. Now is your chance to really get the point home. 'But that's not all, Pauly. What's even more impressive is that we can reverse the process.' You both return to the relevant page in the book to find out how it's done.

In most investment problems, one is faced with the reverse of the interest process. One does not want to translate present value forward into future value. **Rather one wants to translate future value** back to present value – so that all the cash flows are at a common standard of valuation and can be added up. All we do is reverse the logic.

$$If £110 = (1 + 0.1) \times £100 \ then \ £100 = £110/1.1 \ or \ £100 = £110 \times 1/(1.1)$$

Now if we were to write the same thing in symbols, it would say

$$If FV_1 = (1 + r) \times PV \ then \ PV = FV_1/(1 + r) \ or \ PV = FV_1 \times 1/(1 + r)$$

Exactly the same thing can be said for the future value in Year 2:

$$If £121 = (1 + 0.1)^2 \times £100 \ then \ £100 = £121/1.1^2 \ or \ £100 = £121 \times 1/(1.1)^2$$

Now if we were to write the same thing in symbols, it would say

$$If FV_2 = (1 + r)^2 \times PV \ then \ PV = FV_2/(1 + r)^2 \ or \ PV = FV_2 \times 1/(1 + r)^2$$

If we go back to Screenshot 2.2 and look at column 3, we can see that this is precisely what has been calculated. In Year 1 we have 1/1.1 or 0.9091 , in Year 2 we have $1/(1.1)^2$ or 0.8264, and in Year 3 we have $1/(1.1)^3$, or 0.7513; and so on. As we said above, these are the discount factors and each discount factor is multiplied by cash flow occurring in a given year to get discounted cash flow. Discounted cash flow is valued in the same time units and therefore is safe to add up. And when the cost of an investment is subtracted from the discounted value of cash received from the investment, this is known as **NPV**.

Pauly can now see the inexorable logic of what you have done and how important it is for assessing investment projects with future cash flow.

It is worth noting that discounted cash flow is not always necessarily the same thing as present value. In more sophisticated applications you may wish to bring cash flow to a common value using some point in the future as your time reference. However, for our purposes at present we may consider them to be the same.

In the next section we consider the further development of the concept of discounted cash flow and time value of money for the purposes of project appraisal.

## Practical implications for managers

### The time value of money

One hundred pounds receivable now is not the same thing as £100 receivable next year, which is not the same thing as £100 receivable in 10 years. Cash flow receivable in the future is less valuable than the same sum of cash receivable now. Therefore any calculation involving cash flows at different times should apply an appropriate discount rate to bring all cash flows to an equivalent value.

## Key concepts

- [ ] **Time value of money** – money receivable in the future has a lower value than the same sum receivable now
- [ ] **Basic compound interest process** – future value is the result of adding interest to a present value
- [ ] **Discounted cash flow** – in order to add up monetary values occurring at different periods of time it is necessary to discount them

## Active learning activity 2.1

### Interest and discount

Try this on a spreadsheet.

Suppose you had £100. How long would it take to double to £200 at 5%, 10% and 20% annual interest?

## 2.2 Net present value, the discount rate and the cost of capital

When you worked out that the sum of discounted cash flow for the Trattoria project was –£10,460.66, this was what is called the **NPV of the project**. The decision rule is as follows:

Accept if NPV ≥ 0.
Otherwise reject.

In other words, provided a project is generating a positive NPV then it is **adding to firm value and shareholder wealth**. If there is no limit to the amount of capital available for investment, all projects with positive NPV should be taken on. Even if the NPV = 0, the project should still be considered, as it is covering its **cost of capital**, a concept that will be examined in a later chapter. If there is a limit to the amount of capital that is available, then clearly the project with the biggest NPV should be taken on, then the next biggest and so on until there's no more investment capital left. By following these decision rules, the firm **maximises shareholder wealth**.

An important factor in this type of calculation is the discount rate used. The result of the NPV calculation will depend to a great extent on the **discount rate** that is assumed or calculated. For example, let's re-do the calculations for the Trattoria, this time using a discount rate of 5%.

| | A | B | C | D |
|---|---|---|---|---|
| 1 | T | CF | DF | DCF |
| 2 | Time | Cash Flow | Discount Factor | Discounted Cash Flow |
| 3 | 0 | -£200,000 | 1.0000 | -£200,000.00 |
| 4 | 1 | £50,000 | 0.9524 | £47,619.05 |
| 5 | 2 | £50,000 | 0.9070 | £45,351.47 |
| 6 | 3 | £50,000 | 0.8638 | £43,191.88 |
| 7 | 4 | £50,000 | 0.8227 | £41,135.12 |
| 8 | 5 | £50,000 | 0.7835 | £39,176.31 |
| 9 | | | | |
| 10 | | | NPV | £16,473.83 |

Screenshot 2.4   Trattoria cash flow discounted @ 5%

It is evident from the Screenshot that if the discount rate were 5%, instead of 10%, the project would give a positive NPV and therefore the project would now be acceptable under our NPV decision criteria. So, given the importance of the assumed discount rate, one is entitled to ask, where does the discount rate come from in the first place?

There are three reasons for applying a discount rate to future cash flow. First, **risk**. We have very little insight into the future. It used to be thought that with the application of very sophisticated statistical techniques, it would be possible in time to be able to predict important economic variables such as inflation and interest rates, years into the future. Most forecasters are much more humble now, and few would make confident predictions more than 6 months ahead and certainly no more than a year ahead. For example, in early 2008, the main topics being mulled over in financial circles were the Credit Crunch, the possibility of a recession and the ongoing problems at Northern Rock and Bear Sterns. None of these problems were seriously envisaged by most financial commentators in January 2007. Hence, it is always wise to discount future cash flow because of uncertainty. To use the old saying, 'Don't count your chickens before they've hatched.'

Another reason to discount future cash flow is to take account of the effects of inflation. In most countries and at most times there is positive and ongoing inflation. This means that the value of money is continually declining. For example, if the rate of inflation is 5%, this means that money is falling in value by 5% every year. If prices go up by 5%, then to be as well off as I am now and buy all the same things, I will need £105 in a year's time for every £100 I have now. More extreme examples can be calculated at the website http://www.measuringworth.com/ppoweruk/. For example, consider the year 1971. This was the year of decimalisation in the UK. To have the equivalent of £100 at 1971 prices, I would have to have had very nearly £1,000 in 2007.

The final factor in the equation is **time impatience**. As we discussed in the previous section, money receivable in the future is less valuable than an equivalent sum receivable now. And that's not just because of uncertainty, and it's not just because of the erosion of the purchasing power of money. It's also because few people like to wait for their money. Of course, you'll always get a few people who enjoy deferring gratification. But most of us are more impatient. One only has to look at the rates chargeable on store cards and credit cards to see that it is so. If we have the choice, we would rather have money and gratification now, than money and gratification later. This is part of the reason why we have an interest rate. If some people want to borrow money, then they have to offer other people a reason to lend and therefore defer gratification.

Thus, the discount rate is a number that reflects time impatience, inflation and risk. Time impatience is typically taken to be the same across most people, though it can vary considerably between different countries and cultures. Inflation is of course a national and global phenomenon. However, within a particular country, it is the specific riskiness of firms that will vary most, and hence the discount rate that is appropriate for risk will cause the most variation in firm discount rate. Even within a given firm, if a particular project is large and has a significantly different risk from the firm's normal business, a different discount rate will apply.

It is worth noting that the requirement that the discount rate compensate for the risk factors involved, in addition to time impatience and inflation, is from the point of view of those who supply the firm with capital. From the firm's point of view, the discount rate represents the cost of capital. For example, in the OrganicX case study, Charlie and Kate had to make 15% to cover their cost of capital. Thus **cost of capital** and discount rate are one and the same thing for those who run the firm. The cost of capital is the rate at which the firm's projects should be discounted. We will go on later in the book to discuss the appropriate discount rate and cost of capital for the firm under the heading **weighted average cost of capital**.

Finally we close this section by observing that there is potentially a great deal more to the art of assessing discounted cash flow from projects, including, for example, what does and does not count as cash flow, and how one would handle tax and inflation. However, we leave this for a later chapter. We turn next in the following section to another fundamental concept – how to calculate rates of return.

## Practical implications for managers

### Interest rates and discount rates

When the interest rate is used to discount a cash flow, it uses its alias, discount rate. As well as allowing us to calculate discount factors, the discount rate also alerts us to the fact that money has an opportunity cost, which is generally defined as the next best use of funds, but is often specifically defined as the interest foregone from tying cash up in projects. Projects should therefore earn at least this rate of return.

## Key concepts

- [ ] **Net present value** is the sum of discounted future value minus any investment outlay
- [ ] The **decision rule** for projects using NPV is that one should go ahead with all projects with an NPV greater than or equal to zero
- [ ] The **reasons for having a discount rate** are to compensate for risk, inflation and time impatience
- [ ] The **equivalence between the discount rate and the cost of capital** means that the cash flow should be discounted at the percentage cost of capital

## Mini case study

### BP raises oil price assumptions

Source *Financial Times* 2008a

Hidden amid grotty fourth-quarter figures from BP on Tuesday was the disclosure that it now believed oil prices would stay stronger for longer. BP will test projects' net present value on the basis of a Brent crude price of $60 per barrel for at least five years, up from $40. For chief executive Tony Hayward this marks a shift from his predecessor, Lord Browne, who expressed greater confidence that the oil price would revert rapidly to its mean.

That $60 figure is gaining currency across the industry. Suncor Energy used it in approving a huge C$21bn investment to upgrade its Canadian oil sands operation. Anything lower would

have threatened a modest 15 per cent hurdle for return on capital – only fractionally above the average return on exploration for conventional oils in the past three years, according to Wood Mackenzie.

The uplifts represent the industry catching up with reality. Natural conservatism – many executives will remember the 1970s price spikes and the 1980s crash – means planning assumptions have tended to lag spot prices by a significant margin. However, a survey of almost 250 oil companies by Citigroup in December found that the gap between the oil price used for planning compared with the market prices implied by futures had increased to more than $20 a barrel – the widest on record.

It is easy to understand the concerns of oil executives – after all, crude prices are volatile and the industry has a history of capital indiscipline. Still, raising price assumptions (in effect, lowering hurdle rates for investments) does look sensible. For one thing, the oil companies are struggling to replace their reserves in an environment of aggressive resource nationalism and rampant cost inflation.

And there is still a decent buffer between new planning assumptions and a Brent spot price of $90. Admittedly an easing of tensions could cut the estimated $15 to $30 geopolitical risk premium inherent in the oil price. But the chances of problems from Latin America to the Middle East evaporating any time soon look as remote as ever.

## BP's planning assumptions lag market prices

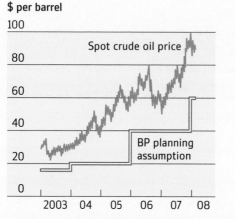

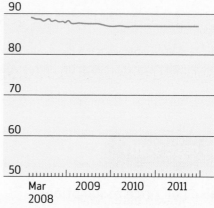

Figure a. Brent crude spot price

Figure b. Brent crude futures curve

*Sources*: Reuters; Thomson Datastream; company

1. Suggest reasons why BP would be particularly interested in capital appraisal techniques.

2. When this article was extracted (26 February 2008), the current price of crude oil had just spiked at $100 per barrel. Why does BP not use $100 as its projected price for NPV purposes?

3. Given BP's big problems in the US in 2010, what other factors do you think should be considered when evaluating oil investment?

## 2.3 Future values, returns, and annual equivalent rates

### 2.3.1 Calculating a return when there is only one future value

Sometimes, we don't actually start off with a *given* rate of return in order to calculate the discounted value of cash flow. Sometimes, when confronted by an investment cash flow, we want to know what the **return** is on the original investment. Easy? No! Take our compound interest example from Screenshot 2.3. If we invested £100 which then became £110 next year, we'd have made 10%. Now if we'd invested £100 and that became £121 at the end of 2 years, then that's 21% on the original investment. Interest rates are almost always quoted in annual terms, so that means we get 21% over 2 years or 10.5% per year.

But wait, that *can't* be right, because we know that at the bank they've been applying 10% interest once a year, so the rate of return should still be 10%. The problem is that if we just take a percentage change from initial investment to final value and divide it by the number of years, then it is a reasonable approximation, but it's not absolutely accurate. What we should have done is something like this. A rate of return, which is the same thing as a rate of interest, is a key determinant in how a sum of money grows. We already know this from Screenshot 2.3. The £110 next year was the application of an interest rate as follows:

$$£110 = (1 + 0.1) \times £100 \ or \ £110 = (1 + 10\%) \times £100$$

We applied an interest rate of 10% *once* in a year to get £110. In symbols we would say

$$FV_1 = (1 + \mathbf{r}) \times PV$$

Similarly, the £121 was the application of an interest rate of 10% *twice in 2 years,* as follows:

$$£121 = (1 + 0.1) \times (1 + 0.1) \times £100 = 1.1 \times £121 = 1.1^2 \times £100$$

In symbols we would say

$$FV_2 = (1 + \mathbf{r})^2 \, PV$$

Suppose now that we know the future value and present value cash flow, but we don't actually know what the underlying rate of interest is. We can solve for **r** as follows. Take the first process that generated the £110 (we know that it looks like this):

$$FV_1 = (1 + \mathbf{r}) \times PV$$

Divide both sides of this by the present value to get

$$\frac{FV_1}{PV} = (1 + \mathbf{r})$$

Now take away one from both sides:

$$\frac{FV_1}{PV} - 1 = \mathbf{r}$$

In words, over one period (in this case a year) the **rate of return** equals the ratio of future value to present value minus one. If we put the numbers in it reads as follows:

$$\left(\frac{£110}{£100}\right) - 1 = 1.1 - 1 = 0.1 = 10\%$$

The same thing would apply to the rate of return over 2 years, but this time we're going to have to deal with roots. Luckily it's a square root, which as we all know from school is the opposite operation from squaring, e.g. if $9 = 3^2$ then the square root of 9 is 3. In symbols, $\sqrt[2]{9} = 3$.

Or, since $16 = 4^2$, then the (positive) square root of 16 is 4. In symbols, $\sqrt[2]{16} = 4$. Having reminded ourselves of roots, we can tackle the calculation of return in the two period case:

$$FV_2 = (1 + \mathbf{r})^2 \times PV$$

If we divide both sides of this by the present value, then we get

$$\frac{FV_2}{PV} = (1 + r)^2$$

Take the square root of both sides:

$$\sqrt[2]{\left(\frac{FV_2}{PV}\right)} = 1 + \mathbf{r}$$

Finally, take one away from each side:

$$\sqrt[2]{\left(\frac{FV_2}{PV}\right)} - 1 = \mathbf{r}$$

Or in numbers:

$$\sqrt[2]{\left(\frac{121}{100}\right)} - 1 = \mathbf{r}$$

Now, we know that since $1.1^2 = 1.21$, then $\sqrt[2]{1.21} = 1.1$. So the solution is:

$$1.1 - 1 = 0.1 = \mathbf{10\%}$$

Magic, eh? Now more generally over n periods, the formula is:

$$\mathbf{r} = \sqrt[n]{\left(\frac{FV_2}{PV}\right)} - 1$$

Don't worry too much about the meaning of roots greater than 2; your calculator or spreadsheet will be able to work it out. The spreadsheet formula will be:

$$\mathbf{r} = \left(\frac{FV_n}{PV}\right)^{\left(\frac{1}{n}\right)} - 1$$

That is, the ratio of FV to PV is raised to the power 1/n. The power 1/n is just the same thing as the nth root, e.g. if the future value occurs in period 2, the ratio is raised to the power (1/2). If it occurs in period 10, then it is raised to the power (1/10).

In the next section we examine how to calculate overall return when future cash flow occurs within a time frame of less than a year.

## 2.3.2 Calculating the annual equivalent return/rate

You will notice that in all cases, no matter how far in the future your cash flow occurs, the return is always expressed as an annualised percentage. We have until now dealt in periods of a year or more, but it is a simple enough matter to adjust for future values occurring in years and fractions of years. Thus if our future value occurred in 2.5 years (2 years, 6 months):

$$r = \left(\frac{FV_{2.5}}{PV}\right)^{\left(\frac{1}{2.5}\right)} - 1$$

What would be slightly more difficult would be if we had to annualise the return on a future value which will occur *within a year.* Suppose our future value occurs in 1 month, which is one twelfth of a year. What we would have then is that n = 1/12 and $1/n = \frac{1}{\frac{1}{12}} = 12$. Thus the annual rate of return is:

$$r = \left(\frac{FV\frac{1}{12}}{PV}\right)^{(12)} - 1$$

This raises the question, what determines the monthly future value $FV_{(1/12)}$? Well, this will be determined by the application of the monthly interest rate to the present value. That is:

$$FV_{(1/12)} = \left(1 + r_{(1/12)}\right) \times PV$$

Substituting this *last* expression for future value in the *previous* expression for the interest rate gives:

$$r = \left(\frac{FV_{1/12}}{PV}\right)^{12} - 1 = \left(\frac{(1 + r_{1/12})PV}{PV}\right)^{12} - 1 = (1 + r_{1/12})^{12} - 1$$

So, for example, suppose you are receiving an interest rate of 1.5% per month on your bank deposit account. When this is compounded over a year, it is equivalent to $(1 + 0.015)^{12}$ − 1 or 19.56% **annual equivalent rate (AER)**, also known sometimes as the **effective interest rate**. The general expression for the AER for compounding periods of less than a year is:

$$r = AER = \left(1 + r_{\frac{1}{n}}\right)^{n}$$

where $1/n$ is the fraction of a year over which interest is compounded.

Suppose that you were now getting 0.05% per day on your bank account. That would compound as $(1 + 0.0005)^{365}$ − 1, which is an AER of 20.02%. Note the equivalence to the general formula for rate of return given above of the calculation of return for periods of a year or more. For example, if the compounding period is exactly a year, then the expression for AER is:

$$r = AER = (1 + r_{1/1})^{n} - 1 = 1 + r - 1$$

If we consider periods of more than a year, the compounding period will be less than 1, as a year is less than the period over which the return takes place. The index on the return (i.e. the 'n' part of $r_n$) will be greater than 1. For example, the AER for an investment over 2 years is:

$$r = AER = (1 + r_2)^{1/2} - 1$$

Generally,

$$r = AER = (1 + r_n)^{1/n} - 1$$

Recognising that $r_n = \dfrac{FV_n}{PV}$ we are back where we left off in Section 2.1 with an equation for determining the return on an investment with one future cash flow. In the next section, we look at a similar but subtly different problem – the impact of different compounding periods.

### 2.3.3 Compounding and the AER

In many financial situations you will be presented with a **nominal annual rate** and a **compounding period**. In our examples on simple compound interest, interest was added once a year on £100 at 10%. At the year's end, £100 became £110; that is, the 10% interest was added annually. If the 10% had been compounded twice a year instead of once, half of the interest would have been credited at 6 months, so you would have £105. The remaining interest would be credited at the year end, not just on the initial deposit, but on the initial deposit plus interim interest. That is, the 5% remaining interest would be added to £105 to give £110.25, slightly better than the £110 available from annual compounding. Other common compounding periods are monthly and daily. The effect of different compounding periods is demonstrated in the Screenshot below.

| | Compounding Period | Compounding Name | Value of £100 after 1 year | AER |
|---|---|---|---|---|
| 1 | Period | Name | | |
| 2 | 1 | Annual | £110.00 | 10.000% |
| 3 | 2 | Semi-Annual | £110.25 | 10.250% |
| 4 | 12 | Monthly | £110.47 | 10.471% |
| 5 | 365 | Daily | £110.52 | 10.516% |
| 6 | ∞ | Continuous | £110.52 | 10.517% |

Screenshot 2.5  The effect of different compounding periods

### 2.3.4 Calculating doubling time

One final point that is worth considering in the context of calculating a one period return is the calculation of the time needed for a particular event to take place.

Consider again the basic equation:

$$FV_n = (1 + r)^n \times PV$$

We can also solve this for n, the number of time periods if we have a specific objective in mind. We know that:

$FV_n/PV = (1 + r)^n$

Therefore if we take the log of either side of the equation:

$\log(FV_n/PV)= n \times \log(1 + r)$

This solves for n, the number of time periods:

$n = \log(FV_n/PV)/\log(1 + r)$

For example, in the learning activity 2.1, you were asked to work out the time it would take for £100 to double to £200 at 5, 10 and 20% annual interest. Note two things here. First, the ratio of interest $FV_n/PV = £200/£100 = 2$. Second, we have to specify a base for our logarithm. The normal base used in finance is the exponential, which means we take the natural log, ln. Thus the doubling time at 10% is:

$\ln(2)/\ln(1.1) = 7.27$

while at 20% it is

$\ln(2)/\ln(1.2) = 3.8$

Thus, you should have found on your spreadsheet that doubling your money would take just over 7 years at 10% per annum (p.a.) and just under 4 years at 20% p.a.

The main thrust of this section has been how to calculate return in the situation where there is only one future cash flow. However, a rather different technique is required if there is more than one future cash flow, as we find in the next section.

## Practical implications for managers

### Calculating returns and interest

You might be tempted to take return as simple percentage change. However, if we regard return as being the equivalent of the kind of simple interest that we'd get at the bank, then, as we have demonstrated, your answer wouldn't be strictly accurate. Though the proper formula for returns is slightly trickier than calculating a simple percentage, it is easily performed on a spreadsheet or calculator. You may also find that the effective interest rate is very different from the nominal or headline rate.

## Key concepts

- ☐ The proper way to calculate **return for a simple cash flow** is to reverse the interest process
- ☐ To calculate **return for periods of less than a year** divide the interest rate by the number of compounding periods while multiplying the exponent by the same number
- ☐ **Compounding and interest** – the more frequently interest is compounded within a given period, the greater the future value
- ☐ **Doubling time** is the time it takes a sum of money to double (in nominal terms)

## Active learning activity 2.2

### Interest and compounding

Credit card statements usually quote monthly rather than annual interest rates. It is tempting to simply multiply the monthly interest rate by 12 to get the annual equivalent. However, as credit card interest is applied every month, our new-found knowledge of the compound interest process should convince us that a more accurate way to calculate credit card interest over a year would be to take the monthly interest process as $(1 + r)^{12} - 1$, where 'r' is the monthly interest rate.

For example, if the monthly rate is 1%, the annual rate is not 12% but $(1 + 0.01)^{12} - 1 = 12.68\%$. The latter figure is the borrowing equivalent to the annual equivalent rate (AER). It is known as the annual percentage rate (APR). Calculate the APR for your own credit or store cards or look one up online. Why do you think the card companies quote interest in monthly terms?

## 2.4 Internal rate of return

### 2.4.1 Introduction

Suppose that you're very keen to try out your new-found formula on the kind of investment project we saw at the start of the chapter – viz Pauly's Trattoria:

$$r = \sqrt[n]{\frac{FV_n}{PV}} - 1$$

Now, we've hit a snag. While our return formula is fine for an investment that produces *one* future value, it's not so good at handling problems with *more than one* future value, as the maths gets hideously complicated. However, there is a solution. Simply find the rate of return that makes the value of the investment equal to the present value of the future cash flows or, to put it another way, **find the rate of return that makes NPV equal to zero**.

We can show that it works for our simple examples. Take the one period cash flow. We know that we can solve for 'r' by using the following equation:

$$FV_1 = (1 + r) \times PV$$

That is, we would find the rate of return that increases the **present value** of the initial investment by enough to **equal the future value**. This is the equivalent of:

$$FV_1/(1 + r) = PV$$

i.e. find the rate of interest that makes the future value of the future cash flow equal to the present value of the initial investment. This in turn is the equivalent of:

$$FV_1/(1 + r) - PV = 0$$

Find the rate of return (r) that makes the **NPV equal to zero**. You'll be relieved to hear that we can apply the same principle to much more complicated cash flows. And so, the golden rule is that for investments with more than one future cash flow, the appropriate way to calculate return is to use **internal rate of return**. This is the rate of return that makes the NPV equal to zero.

## 2.4.2 Finding the internal rate of return

The easiest way to work out internal rate of return is just to pop your cash flow into the appropriate Excel function. Take the following cash flow in the Screenshot below.

| B | C |
| --- | --- |
| Time | Cash Flow |
| 0 | -100 |
| 1 | 0 |
| 2 | 121 |

Screenshot 2.6   Simple cash flow – what's the IRR?

Reader – hang on, haven't we seen this one before? Why yes, of course. It's that old routine, £100 in now, £121 back in 2 years. We already know the rate of return for this one, don't we? But suppose that we didn't. We could use the Excel function '= IRR()' as we can see in the following Screenshot.

| | B | C |
| --- | --- | --- |
| | Time | Cash Flow |
| 1 | | |
| 2 | 0 | -100 |
| 3 | 1 | 0 |
| 4 | 2 | 121 |
| 5 | | |
| 6 | IRR | =IRR(C2:C4) |

Screenshot 2.7   IRR – Excel function

What we do in this case is just plug the appropriate cell references for the cash flow into the formula, and it'll give us 10% – the right answer, as we can see below in the following Screenshot.

| | B | C |
|---|---|---|
| | Time | Cash Flow |
| 1 | | |
| 2 | 0 | -100 |
| 3 | 1 | 0 |
| 4 | 2 | 121 |
| 5 | | |
| 6 IRR | | 10% |

Screenshot 2.8  IRR – Excel solution

But supposing we didn't know the Excel formula? Well, what we could also have done instead was to have taken some guesses. For example, let's try 5%, i.e. 0.05. This would give us a value of 9.75 for NPV, as in the Screenshot below.

| | A | B | C | D | E |
|---|---|---|---|---|---|
| | Discount Rate | Time | Cash Flow | Discount Factor | Discounted Cash Flow |
| 1 | | | | | |
| 2 | 5% | 0 | -100 | 1 | -100 |
| 3 | | 1 | 0 | | |
| 4 | | 2 | 121 | 0.907029 | 109.75057 |
| 5 | | | | | |
| 6 | | IRR | | 10% NPV | 9.7505669 |

Screenshot 2.9  IRR – try 5%, but 5% is too low!

So the discount rate we tried there was too low. We need to push it up a bit. How about 20%?

| | A | B | C | D | E |
|---|---|---|---|---|---|
| | Discount Rate | Time | Cash Flow | Discount Factor | Discounted Cash Flow |
| 1 | | | | | |
| 2 | 20% | 0 | -100 | 1 | -100 |
| 3 | | 1 | 0 | | |
| 4 | | 2 | 121 | 0.694444 | 84.027778 |
| 5 | | | | | |
| 6 | | IRR | | 10% NPV | 15.97222 |

Screenshot 2.10  IRR – try 20%, but 20% is too high!

Too high this time, I'm afraid! So we need to go lower. You could keep guessing, but let's short circuit this and suppose that by a process of iteration, we had reached the conclusion that the IRR was somewhere between one rate of return, 8%, which gave us an NPV of £3.74 and another rate of return, 12%, which gave us an NPV of –£3.54. So how do we go from here? Well, we could just keep messing about with the spreadsheet, getting closer and closer. But traditionally that's not the way we do it.

What we do is take a kind of average between the two. This approach is called linear interpolation, which despite the name is really just a fancy average. To explain how linear interpolation works, we're going to have to create some symbols. Let's call 3.75 $NPV^{positive}$, because it's the positive NPV. By the same token let's call 8% $r^{positive}$, because it represents a discount rate that gives us a positive NPV. By the same reasoning, $NPV^{negative} = -3.54$ and $r^{negative} = 12\%$. The linear interpolation formula is as follows:

$$IRR = r^{positive} + (NPV^{positive}/(NPV^{positive} - NPV^{negative})) \times (r^{negative} - r^{positive})$$

The minus sign in front of $NPV^{negative}$ is there to convert it from negative to positive. Alternatively we could have written:

$$IRR = r^{positive} + (NPV^{positive}/(NPV^{positive} + ABS(-NPV^{negative}))) \times (r^{negative} - r^{positive})$$

where $ABS(-NPV^{negative})$ means the absolute value of $NPV^{negative}$, in other words the value without the minus sign. Filling in the values:

$$IRR = 8\% + (3.74/(3.74 + 3.54)) \times (12\% - 8\%)$$

Therefore:

$$IRR = 8\% + (3.74/7.28) \times 4\% = 8\% + 0.5137 \times 4\% = 10.056\%$$

You will notice that we haven't got a value of exactly 10%. This is because **linear interpolation**, our fancy average, is an **approximation to the true value of the IRR.**

Now it never does any harm for us to reinforce our learning. Let's take a more complicated cash flow which is set out in the following Screenshot.

| | B | C |
|---|---|---|
| 1 | Time | Cash Flow |
| 2 | 0 | -4800 |
| 3 | 1 | 1000 |
| 4 | 2 | 1500 |
| 5 | 3 | 2000 |
| 6 | 4 | 3000 |
| 7 | | |

Screenshot 2.11   Another cash flow that needs an IRR

OK, let's try a ridiculously high discount rate, say 20%. The result is shown in Screenshot 2.12.

| | A | B | C | D | E |
|---|---|---|---|---|---|
| | Discount Rate | Time | Cash Flow | Discount Factor | Discounted Cash Flow |
| 1 | | | | | |
| 2 | 20% | 0 | -4800 | 1 | -4800.00 |
| 3 | | 1 | 1000 | 0.833333 | 833.33 |
| 4 | | 2 | 1500 | 0.694444 | 1041.67 |
| 5 | | 3 | 2000 | 0.578704 | 1157.41 |
| 6 | | 4 | 3000 | 0.482253 | 1446.76 |
| 7 | | | | | |
| 8 | | | | NPV | -320.83 |
| 9 | | | | | |

Screenshot 2.12   IRR – try 20%

As we might have guessed, NPV is negative at this high rate of discount. Now let's try 10%.

| | A | B | C | D | E |
|---|---|---|---|---|---|
| | Discount Rate | Time | Cash Flow | Discount Factor | Discounted Cash Flow |
| 1 | | | | | |
| 2 | 10% | 0 | -4800 | 1 | -4800.00 |
| 3 | | 1 | 1000 | 0.909091 | 909.09 |
| 4 | | 2 | 1500 | 0.826446 | 1239.67 |
| 5 | | 3 | 2000 | 0.751315 | 1502.63 |
| 6 | | 4 | 3000 | 0.683013 | 2049.04 |
| 7 | | | | | |
| 8 | | | | NPV | 900.43 |
| 9 | | | | | |

Screenshot 2.13   IRR – try 10%

Applying the formula, we get

$$10\% + (900.43/(900.43 + 320.83)) \times (20\% - 10\%) = 10\% + 0.737 \times 10\% = 17.37\%.$$

If we had done this calculation using the IRR function, we would have found that the correct value for the IRR is 17% exactly. The reason for the error is because linear interpolation is an approximation. This approximation will be less accurate the greater the difference between the two 'guesses' at the correct rate. Thus, when conducting linear interpolation, the trick is to make this difference, known as the **range**, as small as possible. For example, if we revisit the cash flow from the Trattoria example, we find that the IRR is 8%, as we can see from Figure 2.1.

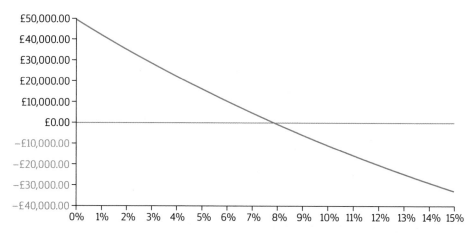

Figure 2.1   NPV versus discount rate

However, if we had used 5% and 15% for our guesses either side of the true IRR, we would have come up with 8.37%. We can see the difference in Figure 2.2.

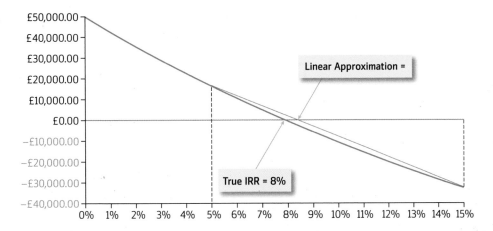

Figure 2.2  True IRR versus approximate IRR

The non-linear or curved nature of the underlying relationship between r and NPV is fairly subtle for this set of cash flow. Nevertheless, it is there as we have seen by drawing a straight line between the coordinates (5%, 16,473.83) and (15%, − 32,392.5). This is why our approximation is fairly accurate despite the rather large range of 10%. The relationship can be much more curved, and normally such a large range would give rise to a much bigger error.

Before we leave this section, we must mention the decision rule which is used with IRR. The decision rule is:

Accept if IRR ≥ k.
Otherwise reject.

The symbol k in finance is usually taken to mean the cost of capital. It *doesn't* mean the money cost of borrowed funds. What it means is the **percentage return** that those who provide loans or equity expect to get back. So the rule is that IRR or the percentage gain from the project should be greater than or equal to the percentage expected by those who are putting up the funds in the first place. However, in some senses, IRR isn't entirely straightforward sometimes, as we see in the next section.

### 2.4.3  NPV versus IRR – problems with the IRR

The IRR is based on very similar principles to the NPV. However, it can be argued that the IRR is less robust and less reliable than the NPV for the following reasons. First, the IRR does not cope well with what are called unconventional cash flows. Unconventional cash flow occurs when there is more than one 'change of sign' in the cash flow. Take, for example, the following:

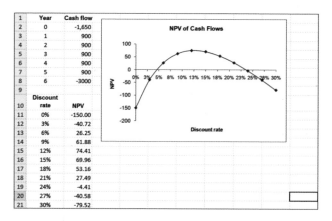

| | Year | Cash flow |
|---|---|---|
| 1 | | |
| 2 | 0 | -1,650 |
| 3 | 1 | 900 |
| 4 | 2 | 900 |
| 5 | 3 | 900 |
| 6 | 4 | 900 |
| 7 | 5 | 900 |
| 8 | 6 | -3000 |
| 9 | | |
| | Discount rate | NPV |
| 10 | 0% | -150.00 |
| 11 | 3% | -40.72 |
| 12 | 6% | 26.25 |
| 13 | 9% | 61.88 |
| 14 | 12% | 74.41 |
| 15 | 15% | 69.96 |
| 16 | 18% | 53.16 |
| 17 | 21% | 27.49 |
| 18 | 24% | -4.41 |
| 19 | 27% | -40.58 |
| 20 | 30% | -79.52 |

Screenshot 2.14  Unconventional cash flow

We can see that the sign of the cash flow changes from negative to positive, then positive to negative. Negative cash flows further on or towards the end of a project might represent disposal or clean-up costs. Nuclear power stations, for example, have very high decommissioning costs at the end of their life. Alternatively, in fashion-driven markets, further expenditure may be necessary later in the life of the project to 'refresh the brand' in order to continue the appeal for trend-driven consumers. This kind of cash flow representing more than one change of sign can cause considerable problems in calculating IRR. The reason is the underlying non-linearity or curvature of relationship between discount rate and NPV. The degree of non-linearity isn't a problem when there is only one change of sign. As we saw in the previous section, in some cases the relationship can be almost linear. However, when there is more than one change of sign, the underlying relationship becomes more highly non-linear and there is a possibility of two roots, or two solutions for r, the discount rate that makes NPV = 0, as we can see in Figure 2.3. At this point IRR stops making sense, and we should rely on NPV criteria instead.

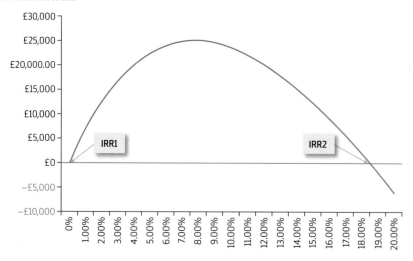

Figure 2.3  Two IRRs from unconventional cash flow

Another potential problem with IRR is that a very high IRR may disguise a relatively small project. For example, take the following cash flow in Screenshot 2.15.

| T | CF |
|---|---|
| Year | Cash Flow |
| 0 | -£1 |
| 1 | £5 |
| 2 | £5 |
| | |
| IRR | 485% |

Screenshot 2.15   Large IRR, low addition to shareholder wealth

We have deliberately chosen rather extreme and unlikely values to drive the point home. Although the sums involved are insignificant, the IRR is very high. If we didn't look too closely at the cash flows involved, we might think this was an outstanding project. If a project doubles in size, the NPV doubles in size. IRR, on the other hand, remains the same. This insensitivity to scale does not just affect IRR, but any capital budgeting criteria based on return. Thus you may get impressive looking IRRs for very small projects which would make little difference to the firm, while larger projects with significant NPVs may have less impressive IRRs. For example, suppose you ran a cafe in Nairobi which had a fairly spacious backroom. You decide to install a computer with internet connection. Given that there is low computer ownership and low access to the internet, you have a constant stream of customers. Furthermore, you anticipate that this situation is likely to continue for the foreseeable future.

Your annual cash flow from the computer is KES (Kenya Shillings) 137 per day or around KES 50,000 per year after costs such as electricity and maintenance. A personal computer will cost KES 62.4 and it will have to be replaced after 2 years because of the constant use it will receive. The IRR of the project is 38% while the NPV at 20% is KES 13,989. Now, demand is almost unlimited, so you reason that you could actually squeeze 20 PCs into your spacious backroom. As we can see from Screenshot 2.16, the NPV is multiplied by 20, but the IRR remains the same. Clearly, you and your business would be much better off with the 20 machines, but the IRR does not tell you this as it does not distinguish between small-scale projects and large-scale projects.

An additional potential problem with IRR is that it can conflict with NPV. Consider two projects A and B. The discounted cash flow (DCF) from A is more sensitive to the discount

| | A | B | C | D |
|---|---|---|---|---|
| | T | Costs and Revenue for 1 PC (KES) | Costs and Revenue for 20 PCs (KES) | |
| 1 | | | | |
| 2 | 0 | -62,400 | -1,248,000 | |
| 3 | 1 | 50,000 | 1,000,000 | |
| 4 | 2 | 50,000 | 1,000,000 | |
| 5 | | | | |
| 6 | IRR | 38% | 38% | |
| 7 | | | | |
| 8 | NPV | 13,989 | 279,778 | |

Screenshot 2.16   IRR and scale effects

rate and falls more sharply than the DCF from B as the discount rate is increased. This is illustrated in Figure 2.4.

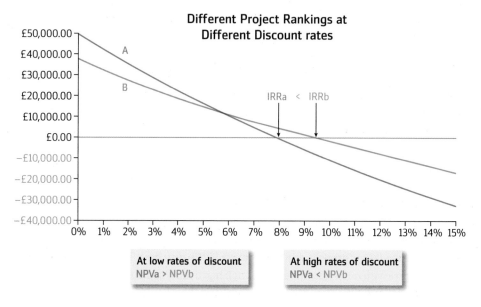

Figure 2.4  Contradictory rankings from the IRR and NPV

Hence, at low rates of discount NPVa > NPV b, and project A would be preferred to project B. However, IRRb > IRRa, which indicates that project B would be preferred to project A.

This kind of problem comes into particularly sharp focus when **capital is constrained or rationed**. When capital is limited, the absorption of capital by one project may leave insufficient funds for other projects, making some projects **mutually exclusive**. Therefore we will have to rank projects in order of their desirability. The limited capital available can then be allocated to the project that makes best use of limited capital, then the next best and so on, until all the capital is allocated. However, as we have seen this is potentially misleading when done in terms of IRR. Furthermore, ranking in terms of IRR does not tell us anything about the addition to shareholder wealth from each project. Thus, again, it is probably better to rank by NPV where capital is limited. NPV actually tells us about the addition to firm value and shareholder wealth for each project. Finally, NPVs can be added up to get a grand total for addition to shareholder wealth; IRR cannot be added up like this. Thus when capital is constrained, it probably makes more sense to rank projects by NPV. We give some actual figures in the Screenshot below which you can try for yourself.

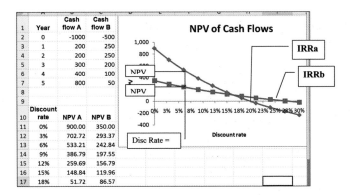

Screenshot 2.17   Contradictory rankings from the IRR and NPV

One final point of conflict between IRR and NPV is that they have different implicit assumptions concerning the rate at which cash flow received before the end of the project is reinvested. IRR assumes reinvestment at the IRR whereas NPV assumes reinvestment at the cost of capital. Given that the firm should have selected all projects that cover the cost of capital, the assumption of reinvestment at the IRR is unrealistic. This is the subject of the next section.

## 2.4.4 Reinvestment assumption of the IRR

Something that we haven't really discussed about the IRR is the implicit assumption about the rate at which any investment revenues can be reinvested. We can shed light on this subject by considering the following, which is the basic equation for deriving IRR:

$$NPV = -1_0 + FV_1 \times \frac{1}{(1+r)} + FV_2 \times \frac{1}{(1+r)^2} + FV_3 \times \frac{1}{(1+r)^3} \ldots \ldots + FV_n \times \frac{1}{(1+r)^n} = 0 \qquad (1)$$

If we multiply through by $(1+r)^n$ then we get the following:

$$NPV \times (1+r)^n = -1_0 \times (1+r)^n + FV_1 \times (1+r)^{n-1} + FV_2 \times (1+r)^{n-2}$$

$$+ FV_3 \times (1+r)^{n-3} \ldots \ldots + FV_n = 0 \qquad (2)$$

Now the sense of what we have just done is as follows. If Equation (1) is true then Equation (2) logically follows. In other words, by finding the discount rate that makes the NPV equal to zero, we are also necessarily invoking the underlying condition that $FV_1$, when it is realised from the investment, is reinvested at the rate, r, yielding $FV_1 \times (1+r)^{n-1}$ by the terminal period n. Also, for example, $FV_2$ when it is realised is reinvested at r yielding $FV_2 \times (1+r)^{n-2}$ by period n, and so on. We can also prove this point to ourselves on a spreadsheet by looking at the future value of cash flows when reinvested at the IRR. For example, in the Screenshot 2.18, 200 is received from project A in Year 1. When this is reinvested at the IRR, this will yield 411.55 by the end of the project. Similarly the 300 received in Year 3 will have a future value of 430.35 in Year 5 if reinvested. If all project cash flows are reinvested at the IRR in this way, they will sum to 2464.6048 – just enough to offset the Year 5 value of the initial £1,000 investment if it had been invested at the IRR. You might want to try this for both the A and B cash flows and confirm that it is true. The IRR as a technique assumes reinvestment of all intermediate cash flows at the IRR rate.

| | Year | Cash flow A | Interest Rate Multiple (at IRR) | Value at Year 5 when Reinvested | Year | Cash flow B | Interest Rate Multiple (at IRR) | Value at Year 5 when Reinvested |
|---|---|---|---|---|---|---|---|---|
| 1 | | | | | | | | |
| 2 | 0 | -1000 | 2.4646 | -2464.6048 | 0 | -500 | 3.35356 | -1676.78 |
| 3 | 1 | 200 | 2.05777 | 411.554954 | 1 | 250 | 2.63272 | 658.18 |
| 4 | 2 | 200 | 1.7181 | 343.619953 | 2 | 250 | 2.06682 | 516.706 |
| 5 | 3 | 300 | 1.43449 | 430.348381 | 3 | 200 | 1.62257 | 324.513 |
| 6 | 4 | 400 | 1.1977 | 479.081555 | 4 | 100 | 1.2738 | 127.38 |
| 7 | 5 | 800 | 1 | 800 | 5 | 50 | 1 | 50 |
| 8 | | | | | | | | |
| 9 | IRRa | 19.77% | Total | 0 | IRRb | 27.38% | Total | 0 |
| 10 | | | | | | | | |
| 11 | | | | | | | | |

Screenshot 2.18 Cash flows A and B reinvested at the IRR

Clearly, the firm will usually *not* have the opportunity to reinvest at the IRR, particularly if this is significantly different from k, the cost of capital.

## 2.4.5 Modified IRR

A method of calculating rate of return without making the reinvestment assumption of IRR is the technique known as the **modified internal rate of return (MIRR)**. The basis of this technique is to assume instead that project cash flows are reinvested at the **cost of capital, k.** The stages involved are as follows:

1. All cash received or **cash inflow** is multiplied by an interest rate multiple – based this time on the cost of capital (as opposed to the IRR). This represents the future value of the cash inflow reinvested at the cost of capital.

2. The value of the reinvested amounts is totalled to give a final figure for future value at the termination of the project.

3. The ratio of the **reinvested** cash inflow to the **initial (present value)** investment is calculated. In effect this is the ratio $\frac{FV_n}{PV}$.

4. The **simple return** is then in fact calculated as $\sqrt[n]{\frac{FV_n}{PV}}$.

5. The simple return is the return on the project or MIRR. If the MIRR is greater than (or equal to) the cost of capital, k, then the project goes ahead.

We go through the steps in the two examples A and B in Screenshot 2.19. You can see that the MIRR for A is 16.67% while that for B is 17.1%. As the cost of capital is 10%, both projects would be accepted.

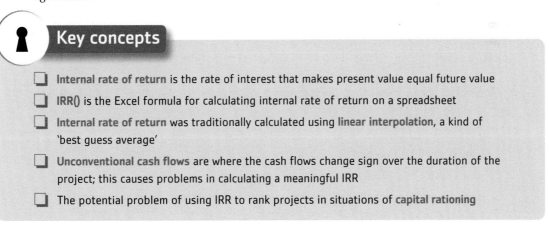

| | A | B | C | D | E | F | G | H | I |
|---|---|---|---|---|---|---|---|---|---|
| 20 | Year | Cash Flow A | 1a. Interest Rate Multiple (at k=10%) | Value at Year 5 when Reinvested | | Year | Cash Flow B | 1b. Interest Rate Multiple (at k=10%) | Value at Year 5 when Reinvested |
| 21 | T | | | | | T | | | |
| 22 | 0 | -1000 | | | | 0 | -500 | | |
| 23 | 1 | 200 | 1.4641 | 292.82 | | 1 | 250 | 1.4641 | 366.025 |
| 24 | 2 | 200 | 1.331 | 266.2 | | 2 | 250 | 1.331 | 332.75 |
| 25 | 3 | 300 | 1.21 | 363 | | 3 | 200 | 1.21 | 242 |
| 26 | 4 | 400 | 1.1 | 440 | | 4 | 100 | 1.1 | 110 |
| 27 | 5 | 800 | 1 | 800 | | 5 | 50 | 1 | 50 |
| 28 | | | | | | | | | |
| 29 | Cost of Capital k | 10% | 2a. Total Inflow Reinvested | 2162.02 | | Cost of Capital k | 10% | 2b. Total Inflow Reinvested | 1100.775 |
| 30 | | | 3a. Ratio of Sum(FVs)/PV | 2.16202 | | | | 3b. Ratio of Sum(FVs)/PV | 2.20155 |
| 31 | | | 4a. Rate of Return/MIRR | 16.67% | | | | 4b. Rate of Return/MIRR | 17.10% |

Screenshot 2.19   MIRR for cash flows A and B

### 2.4.6 Conclusion

Thus, to conclude, there are a number of problems with IRR which should be kept in mind when applying this technique. If in doubt, rely on NPV. However, both techniques are normally used together to provide a figure for both addition to shareholder wealth and percentage return.

## Key concepts

- Internal rate of return is the rate of interest that makes present value equal future value
- IRR() is the Excel formula for calculating internal rate of return on a spreadsheet
- Internal rate of return was traditionally calculated using linear interpolation, a kind of 'best guess average'
- Unconventional cash flows are where the cash flows change sign over the duration of the project; this causes problems in calculating a meaningful IRR
- The potential problem of using IRR to rank projects in situations of capital rationing

## Mini case study

### Buying sports stars

Source *Financial Times* 2008b

In an age of rapid player turnover and in-your-face merchandising, comedian Jerry Seinfeld memorably likened supporting a favourite sports team to little more than 'cheering for laundry'.

Having a bit of skin in the game can change all that. Private sports syndicates, in which investors can hold stakes representing as little as a leg of a greyhound, are one way of doing this. Now Randy Newsom, a minor league baseball player with big dreams, hopes to bring the concept to the masses. Mr Newsom's plan – yet to be cleared by baseball officials – would involve an initial public offering of himself, raising $50,000 to help him break into the big time. In return, investors would receive 4 per cent of post-tax earnings from any major league contract he might eventually sign.

Say you could buy a share today and Mr Newsom, a 25 year old pitcher, signed a three-year contract in 2009, paying $400,000 annually. He might double that in 2012 and, very optimistically, grow it to $3m per annum by 2015, holding it there for another few years. Discount the resulting cashflow at a private equity-like rate of 25 per cent, to reflect the risks involved, and in net present value terms you could roughly double your outlay.

Against that, one man's right arm is about as undiversified – and finite – as an investment gets. Investors might lose everything if Mr Newsom simply never impressed the talent scouts or injured himself. And while he hopes the venture might one day include other baseball hopefuls, liquidity would be virtually nil.

Regular investors, therefore, should give this a wide berth. Still, there would probably be no shortage of at least one class of buyer. One share in Mr Newsom's future would cost about the same as a cheap ticket for a major-league game – not a huge price to pay for those guys on the bleachers swilling beer and munching hot-dogs to feel part of the team.

The extract above reveals that sports investors in the US typically apply a 25% discount rate, which is fairly hefty. It implies that cash receivable in 3 years is only worth half of cash receivable now, while cash receivable in 6 years is only worth a quarter.

1. Why do you think they apply such a high rate?

2. Why is such a rate also 'typical of private equity'?

3. Is there a way in which the required return on sports investment could *be lowered*?

## 2.5 Project appraisal – the old-fashioned way

Many people in business also use two other techniques which are regarded somewhat sceptically in some academic circles. The techniques in question are payback and accounting rate of return.

### 2.5.1 Payback

Payback is astonishingly straightforward compared to almost everything else in finance; in fact we can explain it in one sentence. It's the length of time that it takes for the project cash flows to pay back the original investment. Let's see an example for projects A to D, which have the same initial investment but different cash flow profiles.

| | A | B | C | D | E |
|---|---|---|---|---|---|
| 1 | T | Project A | Project B | Project C | Project D |
| 2 | 0 | -2000 | -2000 | -2000 | -2000 |
| 3 | 1 | 500 | 400 | 200 | 100 |
| 4 | 2 | 500 | 400 | 300 | 500 |
| 5 | 3 | 500 | 400 | 1000 | 800 |
| 6 | 4 | 500 | 400 | 1000 | 300 |
| 7 | 5 | 500 | 400 | 0 | 1000 |
| 8 | | | | | |
| 9 | Payback in | 4 Years | 5 Years | 3.5 Years | 4.3 Years |
| 10 | | | | | |

Screenshot 2.20   Payback

The decision rule is:

Accept all projects with payback less than some predetermined maximum

Payback does have some fairly serious drawbacks. One serious flaw is that it doesn't take account of the time value of money. But that's easily remedied. All one would have to do is to discount the cash flow before calculating the payback period. In this case, clearly the payback period would be longer as discounted cash flow is always smaller than current cash flow. The following Screenshot shows payback periods for the same cash flows discounted at 5%.

| 9 | T | | Project A | Project B | Project C | Project D |
|---|---|---|---|---|---|---|
| 10 | | 0 | -2000 | -2000 | -2000 | -2000 |
| 11 | | 1 | 476.19 | 380.95 | 190.48 | 95.24 |
| 12 | | 2 | 453.51 | 362.81 | 272.11 | 453.51 |
| 13 | | 3 | 431.92 | 345.54 | 863.84 | 691.07 |
| 14 | | 4 | 411.35 | 329.08 | 822.70 | 246.81 |
| 15 | | 5 | 391.76 | 313.41 | 0.00 | 783.53 |
| 16 | | | | | | |
| 17 | Payback in | | 4.58 Years | DNP | 3.82 Years | 4.66 Years |
| 18 | | | | | | |

Screenshot 2.21   Discounted payback

As we can see, project B does not payback at all now. The other projects take longer to payback, but the ranking is still the same. The other potential problem with payback is that it is arbitrary and 'ad-hoc'. That is, how does one decide what constitutes an acceptable payback period? Is it 1 year, 2 years, 5 years? The answer is that we don't know, and the 'cut-off' is ultimately arbitrary and really not particularly scientific.

A further problem with payback is that it ignores cash flow occurring after the payback period, thus ignoring potential addition to shareholder wealth. In our example above the 'best' project is project C with the shortest (undiscounted) payback period of 3.5 years. However, if we add up the cash flows for each project when they are discounted at 5%, we find that project D is the best project with an NPV of 270.16.

|  | A | B | C | D | E |
|---|---|---|---|---|---|
| 11 | T | Project A | Project B | Project C | Project D |
| 12 | 0 | -2000.00 | -2000.00 | -2000.00 | -2000.00 |
| 13 | 1 | 476.19 | 380.95 | 190.48 | 95.24 |
| 14 | 2 | 453.51 | 362.81 | 272.11 | 453.51 |
| 15 | 3 | 431.92 | 345.54 | 863.84 | 691.07 |
| 16 | 4 | 411.35 | 329.08 | 822.70 | 246.81 |
| 17 | 5 | 391.76 | 313.41 | 0.00 | 783.53 |
| 18 |  |  |  |  |  |
| 19 | Payback in | 4.58 Years | DNP | 3.82 Years | 4.66 Years |
| 20 |  |  |  |  |  |
| 21 | NPV@5% | 164.74 | -268.21 | 149.13 | 270.16 |

Screenshot 2.22   NPV versus discounted payback

There may be some sense in the payback approach in its emphasis of recovering cash quickly. It is very hard to see what may happen in the future, and the further away the future is, the harder it gets to foresee what could potentially happen. Therefore, the longer that cash is tied up, the more uncertain we are going to be about whether our assumptions about returns, revenues and so on are actually accurate. However, it is not particularly recommended, given its arbitrary and ad-hoc nature. In the next section we turn to another traditional business practice that is regarded as somewhat unscientific by modern corporate finance practitioners, Accounting Rate of Return.

## 2.5.2 Accounting rate of return

Along with payback, accounting rate of return (ARR) is another of those popular techniques in business that attracts the scepticism of academics. This is because ARR has a number of well-documented weaknesses. Before examining these though, let's start by defining our terms. ARR is intended to measure the return on capital. In other words, given how much capital you've put in place, what kind of return on capital are you getting where return is expressed as a proportion of the capital put in place at the start of the investment process? Thus:

$$ARR = \frac{profit}{capital\ employed}$$

However, given that investment is a process that takes place over time, at which point in time do we measure both of these items, profit and capital employed? The easiest way is just to take the average value for profit over the life of the project and divide that by the initial investment, as we can see from the simple example in the following Screenshots.

| | A | B | C | D |
|---|---|---|---|---|
| 1 | Time | 1 | 2 | 3 |
| 2 | Profit after depreciation | 8000 | 9000 | 10000 |
| 3 | Initial Investment | 90000 | | |
| 4 | | | | |
| 5 | ARR | =AVERAGE(B2:D2)/B3 | | |

Screenshot 2.23  Accounting rate of return – Excel formula

| | A | B | C | D | E | F | G |
|---|---|---|---|---|---|---|---|
| 1 | Time | 1 | 2 | 3 | | | |
| 2 | | | | | | | |
| 3 | Profit after depreciation | 8000 | 9000 | 10000 | | | |
| 4 | Initial Investment | 90000 | | | | | |
| 5 | | | | | | | |
| 6 | ARR | 10.00% | | | | | |
| 7 | | | | | | | |

Screenshot 2.24  Accounting rate of return – calculation

So the ARR is 10%, right? Of course right! But hang on a second. Suppose we had calculated it as the average of all the annual ARRs. To do this we would have to have a value for capital in each year. We could, for example, have decided to 'write off' the investment over the life of the project. That is, by the end of the project, it is assumed that the capital will be worthless. In order to accommodate our depreciation scheme, capital is assumed to lose a third of its initial value every year. Thus, we can work out annual ARRs and average them as shown in Screenshot 2.25.

| | A | B | C | D |
|---|---|---|---|---|
| 1 | Time | 1 | 2 | 3 |
| 2 | | | | |
| 3 | Profit after depreciation | 8,000 | 9,000 | 10,000 |
| 4 | Value of Capital at Start of Year | 90,000 | 60,000 | 30,000 |
| 5 | | | | |
| 6 | ARR | 8.89% | 15.00% | 33.33% |
| 7 | | | | |
| 8 | Average ARR | 19.07% | | |
| 9 | | | | |

Screenshot 2.25  ARR – alternative method

The figure of 19.07% is very different from the figure of 10% which we got using the first method.

And these are not the only two ways in which we could have done the calculation. We could have taken the value of capital over the project life as the average of the start value of capital, £90,000 and the value at the end of Year 3, £0. This gives an average of £45,000. Average post-depreciation profit over the life of the project is £9,000. Hence, ARR in this case = 9,000/45,000, which is 1/5 or 20%. Again, we have a different figure.

As we can see, ARR can vary widely, depending on how you calculate it. Nevertheless, it is useful to know how it's calculated as it is widely used in industry, particularly in relation to both the performance of projects and the performance of managers. The decision rule is:

Accept all projects with ARR greater than some predetermined minimum cut-off.

Apart from the different ways average capital employed can be measured, there are a number of other problems with ARR. These are as follows:

1. The ARR does not take into account time value of money.

2. Accounting profit is not cash flow, and therefore ARR may not give an accurate picture of net addition to wealth for shareholders. For example, accounting profit is calculated as income minus depreciation. However, depreciation is a notional sum and does not represent actual cash flow.

3. Accounting profit is a definitional concept and can vary considerably depending on the accounting conventions used, e.g. how is capital to be depreciated?

4. Again there is the question of what constitutes an acceptable ARR cut-off rate. One is drawn to the conclusion that this is inherently ad-hoc.

## Practical implications for managers

### Payback and accounting rate of return

These techniques are still widely used in industry. However, you might want to take a 'belt and braces' view by using all four approaches, and having greater confidence if all four are 'pointing the same way'.

## Key concepts

- ☐ Payback – the time it takes to recover the initial investment from the project returns
- ☐ Accounting rate of return – the ratio of profit to capital employed

## Active learning activity 2.3

### Accounting rate of return

Pick three major blue chip companies. Find out what accounting rate of return they typically expect on new projects.

## 2.6 The application of project appraisal principles

The central thing in applying the time value of money principle to project appraisal is to count in only actual monetary cash flows, whether positive or negative. However, this information may not be easily found in the kind of data available. One of the main problems that you will face in applying time value of money principles to the assessment of project cash flow is that you will often have to extract your data from **profit and loss accounts**. A profit and loss account or income statement is a standard format for financial reporting in business and it consists of the calculation of income minus expenses. Though it might be tempting to take a profit and loss approach to project assessment, it can be highly misleading by comparison with the discounted cash flow approach for the following reasons:

1. Profit and loss accounting takes no cognisance of the time value of money. If I estimate that net profit for a project is £100,000 per year over 5 years, the profit and loss account treats the Year 5 net profit as exactly the same as the Year 1 net profit.

2. Cash flows are not recorded as and when they happen. Rather they are credited as and when transactions take place, orders are placed, goods are delivered and invoices are issued. However, all of the latter activity can take place without any money changing hands, particularly as a great deal of business activity relies on credit.

3. An accountant would allocate some of the firm's fixed and overhead cost if he/she wanted to calculate profit and loss. However, fixed and overhead cost is irrelevant for cash flow purposes unless the adoption of the project would imply *additional* overhead.

4. Accountants also include sunk or historical cost in the calculation of profit and loss. All that is relevant in project appraisal is **incremental cost** which is necessarily associated with the project.

5. If a profit and loss account is drawn up, any expenditure on capital equipment is depreciated over time. That is, a portion of the expenditure is allocated to each year of the project depending on the depreciation rule. However, any capital equipment will typically have to be bought and paid for in one big lump at the start of the project (unless of course it is leased), so again the profit and loss approach doesn't reflect actual cash expenditure.

In order to illustrate these principles, let's take the following example. Every night at the weekend, Hungry Joe comes out of his health and sports club very hungry, as surprisingly there are no fast food places within the vicinity of the club. He has the idea of setting up a hamburger van on a vacant piece of waste ground opposite the club. The van would also be handy for offices nearby so sales could also be made during the day. However, these sales would be on contract to local firms and would be paid by invoice 3 months in arrears. Sales would be as shown in the following Screenshot.

| | A | B | C | D | E | F | G |
|---|---|---|---|---|---|---|---|
| 1 | Sales | T | 2010 | 2011 | 2012 | 2013 | |
| 2 | Night | Sales (£) | 15000 | 16025 | 17050 | 18075 | |
| 3 | Day | Sales (£) | 19500 | 20833 | 22165 | 23498 | |
| 4 | | | | | | | |

Screenshot 2.26   Hungry Joe – projected sales

The van will cost £20,000. His accountant has advised him that this should be depreciated at 25% on a straight line basis with a zero residual value (which equals £20,000 divided by four). Hungry Joe has paid £10,000 to a market researcher to establish the likely sales figures. He estimates he will need a cash float of £30,000. He has also calculated annual staff costs and stock costs, that is **cost of goods sold**, as shown in Screenshot 2.27.

| | A | B | C | D | E | F | G | H |
|---|---|---|---|---|---|---|---|---|
| 1 | | | | 2010 | 2011 | 2012 | 2013 | |
| 2 | COSTS | | | | | | | |
| 3 | Staff | | | 6900 | 7372 | 7843 | 8315 | |
| 4 | Stock - Costs of Goods Sold | | | 10350 | 11057 | 11765 | 12472 | |
| 5 | | | | | | | | |

Screenshot 2.27   Hungry Joe – projected costs

Stock purchases from wholesalers are normally given 6 months credit.

Hungry Joe will undertake the initial expenditure in 2009. How would this project look on a profit and loss basis and what would the difference be on a discounted cash flow basis? Take first the profit and loss account, which is as shown in Screenshot 2.28.

| | A | B | C | D | E | F | G |
|---|---|---|---|---|---|---|---|
| 1 | ACCOUNTING APPROACH | | | | | | |
| 2 | | | 2010 | 2011 | 2012 | 2013 | |
| 3 | SALES (£) | | | | | | |
| 4 | Night | | 15000 | 16025 | 17050 | 18075 | |
| 5 | Day | | 19500 | 20833 | 22165 | 23498 | |
| 6 | | | | | | | |
| 7 | COSTS (£) | | | | | | |
| 8 | Staff | | 6900 | 7372 | 7843 | 8315 | |
| 9 | Stock - Costs of Goods Sold | | 10350 | 11057 | 11765 | 12472 | |
| 10 | Van | | 5000 | 5000 | 5000 | 5000 | |
| 11 | Research | | 2500 | 2500 | 2500 | 2500 | |
| 12 | | | | | | | |
| 13 | | | | | | | |
| 14 | Profit | | 9750 | 10929 | 12107 | 13286 | |

Screenshot 2.28   Hungry Joe – profit and loss approach

What's worth noting about the profit and loss account is as follows:

1. Accounting entries don't follow cash flow. For example, day sales and stock costs are included as and when they're invoiced. But we know that both of these are done on credit terms and are not paid right away, and therefore these entries do not reflect the true cash flow involved.

2. Research costs are included. Research cost is a **sunk cost**. A sunk cost is an expenditure that has already been incurred and will not recur in the future. The way in which the profit and loss account handles sunk cost does not reflect the economic principle that sunk costs are forever gone and should have no influence on current decisions on the allocation of resources such as investment capital.

3. Although the van has to be paid for 'up-front', before the project starts, the expenditure is recorded as occurring in four equal chunks over the course of the project. It is standard accounting practice to depreciate the capital expenditure in this way, but again it doesn't reflect actual cash flow.

The central principle involved is deciding whether or not a cash flow, whether negative or positive, represents **incremental cash flow** which is necessarily associated with the project. If the monetary benefit or cost would still exist without the project, we would not include it in project cash flow. OK, so let's illustrate the cash flow approach.

|  | A | B | C | D | E | F | G |
|---|---|---|---|---|---|---|---|
| 17 | NET PRESENT VALUE | | | | | | |
| 18 | | 2009 | 2010 | 2011 | 2012 | 2013 | 2014 |
| 19 | Cash Received (£) | | | | | | |
| 20 | Night Sales | | 15000 | 16025 | 17050 | 18075 | |
| 21 | Day Sales | | 14625 | 20499.8 | 21832 | 23164.8 | 5874.5 |
| 22 | Cash Float | | | | | | 30000 |
| 23 | | | | | | | |
| 24 | Cash Paid Out (£) | | | | | | |
| 25 | Staff | | 17550 | 18083 | 18616 | 19149 | |
| 26 | Stock - Costs of Goods Sold | | 5175 | 10703.5 | 11411 | 12118.5 | 6236 |
| 27 | Van | 20000 | | | | | |
| 28 | Cash Float | 30000 | | | | | |
| 29 | | | | | | | |
| 30 | Net Cash Flow | -50000.00 | 6900 | 7738.25 | 8855 | 9972.25 | 29638.5 |
| 31 | | | | | | | |
| 32 | Discount Factor@6.5% | 1 | 0.938967 | 0.88166 | 0.82785 | 0.77732 | 0.72988 |
| 33 | Discounted Cash Flow | -50000.00 | 6478.873 | 6822.5 | 7330.6 | 7751.66 | 21632.6 |
| 34 | | | | | | | |
| 35 | Sum DCF | 16.21 | | | | | |

Screenshot 2.29   Hungry Joe – cash flow approach

The main points to note here are as follows:

1. Cash flow occurs before and after the life of the project, namely in the years 2009 and 2014. The reason for this is that expenditure on the van and cash float must occur before the project starts, while the cash float is recoverable after the project finishes. Also, because of credit, some cost is payable and some revenue is receivable in 2014.

2. The cost of the van, i.e. the capital equipment involved, is not depreciated. It is recorded as and when it is paid for.

3. By contrast with the profit and loss account, the sunk cost of research is *not* included.

4. And again, by contrast with the profit and loss account, the cash float *is* included. The cash float is not used up in the course of the project and is returned at the end. However, as the float will involve negative cash flow at the beginning and positive cash flow at the end, then it should be included.

A more general point should be made here about the DCF approach. The following items are recorded as negative cash flow, for the simple reason that they tie up cash: (1) increase in cash float; (2) increase in stocks; (3) increase in debtors. We refer to the cash we need to make available for these items as **working capital**. Of course, there is a potential benefit to the firm's working capital in the sense that the firm itself will normally be able to buy on credit. Hence any increase in creditors is taken away from (1) to (3) above.

Finally note how stocks and sales to businesses are treated. These are sold on credit terms of respectively 6 months and 3 months. In the first year of the project, £10,350 worth of stock will be delivered to Hungry Joe's. However, only £5175 will be paid for as there is 6 months credit, i.e. any stock delivered after June 2010 will be paid for some time in 2011. The 2011 value in turn will be calculated as half the 2010 value of stock, which still has to be paid for, and half the 2011 value of stock delivery, which will have to be paid for within that particular year. As a result there will still be negative cash flow of £6236 in 2014, the year after the project has ended. This represents the remaining half of the stock purchased in 2013 which still has to be paid for.

Similarly, sales to businesses will not fully match cash flow in the first year. With 3 months' credit, only 75% of invoices to business will have been paid by the end of 2010. The remaining 25% will be paid in 2011 along with 75% of deliveries made in 2011. The good news is that there is a little drop of cash yet to come in 2014, representing the last 25% of credit sales invoiced in 2013.

In summary then, one can observe the following points of contrast between the discounted cash flow approach and the profit and loss accounting approach:

1. The DCF approach discounts cash flow in order to bring cash flow to the same common time measurement.

2. The DCF approach includes working capital items associated with the project. Changes in working capital won't necessarily be included in profit and loss unless they imply a change in the firm's assets and liabilities.

3. The DCF approach does not include sunk cost. Sunk costs are historical and not **incremental** and hence of no consequence to the value-adding possibilities of the project.

4. Neither does the DCF approach include overhead cost, unless there is additional overhead associated with the project. In the latter case, the overhead cost is incremental, but the firm's normal day to day overhead is not incremental.

5. The DCF approach tries as far as possible to include all incremental costs and revenues, benefits and negative effects that are associated with the project, even if they're not directly part of the project. For example, a new product might cannibalise an existing product, which is an external cost of the project. Or, the development of a garage forecourt (gas station) at a supermarket may attract more custom for the supermarket itself.

We've got as far as we can in the treatment of project appraisal in the context of this chapter. There is a great deal more to be said on the subject, and we will address this in Chapter 7 on Capital Budgeting. Before we do so, however we would point out that a great deal of project appraisal is also something of an art rather than a hard science. It is to these aspects of project appraisal that we turn, briefly, in the next section.

## Practical implications for managers

**The discounted cash flow approach to project appraisal**

As a manager, your mindset may be inherently 'profit and loss', with all that that entails. However, a different approach is needed when using the discounted cash flow approach. Specifically, you record expenditure and revenue as and when they occur and you don't include overhead or sunk cost as they have nothing to do with the project.

## Key concepts

- [ ] The discounted cash flow approach – which is concerned only with incremental cash flow
- [ ] The significant differences between the profit and loss approach and the discounted cash flow approach – and in particular actual and notional cash flows
- [ ] The concepts of sunk cost, overhead cost and depreciation and their treatment for DCF purposes
- [ ] The concepts of cash float, stock, debtors and creditors and how these are recorded in real time for project cash flow purposes

## 2.7 Project appraisal as an art

Despite the emphasis on calculation in the previous sections, there is also a substantial role for 'soft' skills such as managerial judgement and interpersonal ability. The intuitive elements can be listed as follows.

First, how reliable are your figures? Despite the fact that you have come up with very precise answers, these very precise calculations are based on a great deal of supposition and assumption. You may ask, why do we use this approach when it may be misleading? The answer is that investment is inherently bound up with trying to anticipate future events, and no one knows precisely what's going to happen in the future. Even the most sophisticated Government Treasury statistical models cannot supply meaningful predictions on the future of the economy beyond a time horizon of a year. And weather forecasts are only really accurate a day or two ahead. Beyond that, the doubts and uncertainties multiply geometrically.

So if governments and weather forecasters don't know the future, then what chance do businesses have? Well, we have to give it our best shot. Project appraisal is better than guessing as it is much more analytical and informed, bearing in mind of course that it is based on guesstimate. It is a worthwhile process to review one's assumptions as the future actually starts to unfold. For example, did the cash flows envisaged actually materialise? Have we kept to budgeted cost?

Second, many costs and benefits are intangible. For example, in the previous section we talked of a garage forecourt attracting additional customers to a supermarket. But how exactly do you quantify that? Or, to take another example, a case study in the *Journal of Business Logistics* in 1996 found the following benefits for reusable packaging:

> 'Other benefits reported by firms included better use of floor space on the assembly line, better housekeeping, and improved ergonomics for manually handled containers. Better housekeeping was the first benefit sought by respectful U.S. automakers, who saw returnable packages used on Japanese auto assembly lines in the early 1980s. The amount of trash in the assembly area is dramatically reduced, compared to expendable packages. Furthermore, packages in staging areas can be more neatly stacked.'
>
> (Rosenau *et al.* 1996)

So, how do you quantify all of that? This is a good question and one that is well outside the scope of this book as it is a specialist accounting topic in itself. But it will require judgement and skill, not all of it of a straightforward numerical kind. (The article referred to above is also recommended as a case study which discusses all of the techniques covered in this chapter.)

For those of you who work in the public and voluntary sector, project appraisal is known as cost-benefit analysis (CBA), which can get even more ethereal when applied to the costs and benefits of government policies. For example, how do you calculate the cost of the noise nuisance from building a new runway at Heathrow? CBA is often used to assess project work in less affluent countries, and again you might be confronted with problems such as how to put a value on clean drinking water? CBA is a very large subject which is well outside the scope of this book. However, it is even more the case that in CBA there is a great deal that depends on assumption and interpretation, so always question these as much as possible. One of your authors used to work for a firm of consultants who did a great deal of work for the public sector. The author in question learned to be somewhat sceptical whenever the phrase, 'a consultant's estimate suggests' cropped up in a document.

 ## Practical implications for managers

### Payback and accounting rate of return

Despite widespread use of sophisticated quantitative techniques in this area, there is still ample need for old-fashioned management skills such as shrewdness, judgement, prudence, intuition and people management.

## Key concepts

- [ ] **Reliability of assumptions** and why assumptions should always be examined
- [ ] **Intangible costs and benefits** and the difficulties of putting a value on them

## Mini case study

### The analytics of climate change

Source Anda 2007, Copyright *Financial Times*, 2007

John Kay implies that only a Marxist (Groucho or otherwise) could support climate policies that just benefit future generations ('Climate change: the (Groucho) Marxist approach', November 28). Yet the basis of his argument is a rather totalitarian belief in NPV (net present value) as the means to evaluate policy.

If a 5 per cent discount rate applied to base-case cost and damage estimates yields a negative NPV for policy, does that mean we reject it?

1. Why is the discount rate only 5% in this case?
2. The discount rate has a rather wider meaning in the context of carbon emissions policies. In what way do you think it would be different from a firm or project discount rate?
3. What do you think would be the problems involved in calculating NPV in the context of global warming and carbon emissions policies?

## 2.8 Summary

In this chapter we started by considering the concept of the time value of money, and in particular the notion that the further away in time a given sum is receivable, the less valuable it is. This gives rise to a problem when looking at investment cash flows as it means that sums receivable or payable at different points in time cannot simply be added up. However, we discovered that it is possible to add these values occurring at different points in time provided they are discounted. Discounting is essentially the reverse process of adding interest. Instead of adding interest to a present value to get a future value, we discount back from a future value to get a present value. Once that is done at a specified discount rate, which should reflect the cost of capital, we get a figure for the value of the investment net of cost which is called the net present value (NPV).

We went on to look at the specifics of calculating an annualised return both within and beyond a compounding period of a year. However, it was found that there was a problem with the simple return formula in that it only works if there is one future value. It does not work when there is more than one future value. In order to deal with more than one cash flow it is necessary to use the internal rate of return (IRR) in which one finds the rate of return that makes the NPV equal to zero. However, it was also discovered that the IRR is subject to a number of problems such as the potential confusion that can arise when cash flows are unconventional. Therefore it was argued that when in doubt one should use NPV alone.

The chapter than went on to look at two other techniques of investment appraisal. These were payback, which is the relatively simple calculation of how long the project takes to return its initial investment, and accounting rate of return (ARR), which measures the ratio of accounting profit to capital employed. Neither technique is recommended by corporate finance academics as these techniques do not take account of the time value of money and they are both based on somewhat arbitrary investment approval criteria.

Following this, we looked at some basic principles of discounted cash flow, with particular emphasis on the central idea that only incremental cash flow should be counted in any investment appraisal. A large part of the skill involved in investment appraisal is in knowing precisely what is and is not additional cost or monetary benefit directly associated with the project.

In the final section, we emphasised the importance of examining all assumptions used and in clearly identifying cost and benefits, though the more intangible costs and benefits can be very hard to quantify.

## Case study

### Comparing ARR and NPV

Source [The following question is reproduced by kind permission of the professional organisation the Chartered Institute of Management Accountants (CIMA).]

It is 2 January 20X1 and the management of G Ltd, a subsidiary of GER Group, has estimated the following results for the coming year ending 31 December 20X1:

|  | £'000 |
|---|---|
| Profit | 500 |
| Fixed assets | |
|   Original cost | 1,500 |
|   Accumulated depreciation at year end | 720 |
| Net current assets (average for year) | 375 |

GER group assesses new projects using discounted cash flow and a cost of capital of 15 per cent. But it assesses the performance of its subsidiaries and their managers using ROC [return on capital], based on the following:

1. Profit: depreciation of fixed assets is calculated on a straight-line basis on a presumed life of five years.

   Profit/loss on sale is included in the profit for the year.

2. Capital employed: fixed assets are valued at original cost less depreciation as at the end of the year.

Net current assets are valued at the average value for the year.

In addition to the normal transactions, the management of G Ltd is considering submitting the following proposals to GER:

1. At the start of the year it could sell for £35,000 a fixed asset which originally cost £300,000 and which has been depreciated by 4/5 of its expected life. If it is not sold the asset will generate a profit of £45,000 during the coming year.

2. At the start of the year it could buy for £180,000 plant that would achieve reductions of £57,000 per annum in production costs. The plant would have a life of five years after which it would have no resale value.

**Required**

Evaluate the two proposals from the point of view of:

1. G Ltd's CEO; and

2. GER group's chief accountant.

# ? Questions

1. My rich old auntie always sends me a £100 postal order on my birthday. To be honest, I need some cash up front. Do you think I could get £500 for the next 5 years' postal orders? If not, how could I work out a fair price for 5 years of postal orders?

2. What would it mean if I said that discounting was the reverse of the interest process?

3. I have £100 which my friend Larry would like to borrow for a sure-fire scheme. This will give me back £150 in 2 years. Tempting, as I will have made 50% over 2 years, or 25% p.a. Yes or no?

4. What is the difference between present value and *net* present value?

5. I invest £100 now and receive £110 in a year's time and £121 in 2 years.

   a) What is the NPV of this scheme at 10%?

   b) What is the NPV at 20%?

6. Describe in one sentence how to find the internal rate of return.

7. Find the internal rate of return for the data given in Q5. Hint – try 75% and 80%.

8. Describe some of the advantages and disadvantages of payback.

9.  Compare and contrast accounting rate of return with internal rate of return.

10. Why do companies sometimes use all four approaches to project appraisal?

11. The following cash flows have been estimated for four projects:

| Year | Project | | | |
|---|---|---|---|---|
| | **A** | **B** | **C** | **D** |
| 0 | −4,000 | −4,000 | −2,000 | −2,000 |
| 1 | 2,000 | 40 | 1,280 | 0 |
| 2 | 2,000 | 40 | 1,280 | 0 |
| 3 | 100 | 3,200 | 40 | 0 |
| 4 | 100 | 3,200 | 40 | 3,600 |

For each project, calculate:

a)  NPV at 15%

b)  Internal rate of return

c)  Payback

d)  Discounted payback at 10%

12. Calculate the ARR for each project. In order to do so, assume the following:

a)  The initial outflow in Year 0 represents the purchase of a fixed asset.

b)  The asset is depreciated on a straight line basis over the life of the project (no residual value).

c)  All cash flow in this example can be treated profit before depreciation.

# Online resource centre

Visit the Online Resource Centre that accompanies this book for the answers to these questions.
www.oxfordtextbooks.co.uk/marney

# Further reading

Much of the academic work on project appraisal consists of surveys of which techniques are used in practice by companies. A lot of the seminal work was done in the 1970s, including:

Gitman, L.J. and Forrester, J.R. Jr (1977) A survey of capital budgeting techniques used by major US firms. *Financial Management* 6(3):66–71.

Klammer, T. (1972) Empirical evidence of the adoption of sophisticated capital budgeting techniques. *Journal of Business* 45(3):387–397.

These can be accessed through Google Scholar.

More recent research for the UK has been done by Glen Arnold, a professor at Salford, and various co-authors. For example:

Arnold, G.C. and Hatzopoulos, P.D. (2000) The theory–practice gap in capital budgeting: evidence from the United Kingdom. *Journal of Business Finance and Accounting* 27(5&6):603–626.

See also:
Arya, A., Fellingham, J.C. and Glover, J.C. (1998) Capital budgeting; some exceptions to the net present value rule. *Issues in Accounting Education August:* 499–508.

 ## Internet references

http://www.measuringworth.com/ppoweruk/
This website can be used to calculate the change in the purchasing power of the pound.

http://www.hm-treasury.gov.uk/data_greenbook_index.htm
This is the web link for *The Green Book, the British government guide to project appraisal for public and voluntary sector projects. Chapters 2 and 5 may be of some interest for private sector practitioners.*

www.jstor.com
This useful website contains academic journal papers more than 5 years old.

http://scholar.google.co.uk/
More generally this is a good first port of call for journal articles.

 ## Suggestions for group work

1. Get together in groups to elaborate on the practical aspects of project appraisal, which were only briefly mentioned in the chapter.

2. How does this wider process relate to other business and management subjects that you have studied?

3. Compare notes with other groups in the form of presentations.

## Suggestions for presentations

1. Give a presentation on the main similarities and differences between private sector investment appraisal and public sector project appraisal.

2. Give a presentation on some recent high-profile business projects and how project appraisal was used in these. (Hint: try a quick search on www.ft.com.)

# 3

# Financial Markets

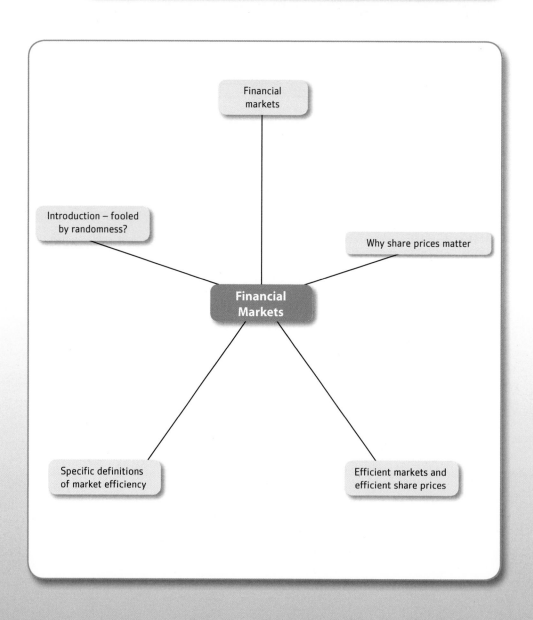

## Knowledge-based learning objectives

When you have completed this chapter you will be able to:

✓ Appreciate the functions of capital markets and the key features of mature financial markets

✓ Understand the roles of credit rating agencies, analysts and wider CSR issues on the stock or bond price

✓ Define and understand the three forms of the efficient markets hypothesis (EMH)

✓ Understand the basic pricing mechanisms of bonds and stocks

✓ Contrast the relative merits of behavioural finance as an alternative paradigm to efficient markets

## Skills-based learning objectives development

✓ Business and financial environment consciousness: you should have developed further understanding of the financial environment and the nature of business organisations within the global financial world.

✓ Numerical skills: you should have developed the ability to understand, manipulate and interpret numerical and statistical data in relation to stock and bond markets.

✓ Analytical thinking and problem-solving skills: you should have developed the ability to critically assess the main theories of how stock prices change.

✓ Problem-solving skills: you should have developed the ability to assess the financing requirements of a company and evaluate possible solutions.

✓ Organisational skills: you should have developed further your ability to organise your time and work efficiently and to gather data and information which you can translate into value-adding intelligence.

✓ Presentation skills: you should have developed further your ability to present your work clearly both verbally and in writing.

✓ Interpersonal skills: your ability to present your work clearly both verbally and in writing and to interact effectively with others is further developed upon completion of the end of chapter questions.

## Online resource centre

Visit the Online Resource Centre that accompanies this book to listen to a podcast of the authors discussing the functions of both mature and developing financial markets.

**www.oxfordtextbooks.co.uk/marney**

## OrganicX meets the Animal Spirits

The company has now successfully floated on the alternative investment market (AIM) at a cost of nearly £10 million. It has raised £150 million in new share capital and still has £50 million in debt. Charlie is still annoyed about the costs of the flotation. In addition to the direct costs, there was also the fact that the underwriters of the share capital made 4% on the spread – the difference between what the underwriters bought the stock for and what they then priced to sell to the actual investors. In addition, the stock seemed to be undervalued as it increased in value over 15% on the first day of trading. It seemed that the underwriters have not only fleeced OrganicX but also got the initial valuation wrong! Kate explained the reasons – the underwriters had entered into a firm commitment to buy the shares and sell them to investors and thus might have been left with unwanted shares. This is potentially risky and therefore costly. In addition, the underwriters had to give legal advice, arrange road shows for potential investors, and buy the shares prior to re-selling. However, it still seems to Charlie that the underwriters and investors made millions for doing virtually nothing whereas he had been working 16-hour days for the past 3 years.

Charlie is also very concerned because the stock price seems to fluctuate in a random manner and he cannot understand why this should be so. On one particular day, the share price of OrganicX falls by over 10% on the news that a rival company has been discovered to be supplying consumers with genetically modified produce – surely this should result in a share price increase for OrganicX? He calls a meeting with Kate so that she can explain why the share price moves in such a peculiar manner. How can the company be undervalued to begin with, then worth £150 million one day and only £135 million the next? Who or what decides what the share price should be?

## 3.1 Introduction – fooled by randomness?

The costs of raising equity, the way in which equity is priced and, of course, the tendency for share prices to fluctuate are considered as an important part of this chapter on financial markets. In the discussion on financial markets that follows, we address three key issues. These are, firstly, the nature of financial instruments, and the nature of the markets for these financial instruments. Although we will look at many fine distinctions between different types of financial markets, they are in essence markets for **debt**, allowing firms and institutions to borrow money, and for **equity**, allowing firms to sell partial shares in their enterprise in exchange for capital funds. As well as describing the various institutions that constitute the financial markets, we also consider, secondly, the question of the efficiency of markets, particularly the stock market. The question of efficiency is essentially a question of whether or not the stock market values corporate equity at its 'proper' worth. In order to shed some light on the nature of the problem of the 'correct' valuation of equity, we consider the problem of valuing equity by contrast with the rather more straightforward problem of valuing debt in the form of bonds. Thus, this second question of efficiency raises a third and final question of what the value of debt and, more particularly, equity ought to be. In essence, it is a question of valuation, and we introduce some elementary techniques of valuation of debt and equity in order to be absolutely clear what we seek in trying to establish what market efficiency actually is. But as Charlie and Kate found above, stock markets, in particular, can be rather unpredictable – so much so that we can consider it as essentially a random process – which some have likened to a guessing game.

Take, for example, the popular television programme *Deal or No Deal* which is syndicated by Dutch company Endemol in 65 countries. The game essentially involves contestants guessing which boxes, from a selection, have large sums of money and which have trivial sums of money. However, despite the fact that it is in essence a guessing game, the guests often behave as if there is causality involved, which can be uncovered by discovering the 'right strategy'. One might argue that they are 'fooled by randomness'. The book *Fooled by Randomness* by Nassim Taleb (Taleb 2007), an investment manager, more explicitly suggests that even very clever, well-paid people, whose job it is to analyse financial markets, can sometimes be fooled into attributing causality to what is essentially a random process. This certainly seems to be the case with both the audience and participants on *Deal or No Deal*, all of whom appear to believe that certain boxes are more likely than others to contain high or low quantities of money. Many people, including Taleb, believe that financial markets work in the same way. Despite the enormous amounts of resources that go into analysing and predicting the financial markets, they are essentially random and, by definition, unpredictable.

## Active learning activity 3.1

### Fooled by randomness?

Can you think of any other situation where people are fooled by randomness?

The great economist Keynes once said that financial markets 'were like a casino', and some people who have lost money recently may feel that way too. But, of course, many financial professionals such as fund managers, fundamental analysts and technical analysts would beg to differ. So who is right? As we journey through this chapter, we will try to answer that question and, along the way, discover the exciting world of financial markets where fortunes have been won and lost. And, rather surprisingly, we will find that efficient markets in which financial instruments are priced accurately should basically be unpredictable. What is more surprising about financial markets, however, is not so much their unpredictability as their **volatility**. Indeed, in 1987, stock markets fell 30% in one day and, even today, experts argue as to the causes of this market crash. More recently, markets have experienced severe volatility. In a common-sense way, volatility means that prices will oscillate, with large swings possible from one day to the next. More formally, we measure volatility in terms of standard deviation around the mean. The cause of this volatility – with occasionally very large shifts in financial markets – is still an open question.

However, before we get too carried away with 'Fooled by randomness' and other interesting stories, we need to describe what is actually traded on financial markets. This is the subject of the next section.

## 3.2 Financial markets

### 3.2.1 IOUs and bits of paper

Financial markets are essentially markets for borrowing and lending. The fact that borrowing and lending has taken place was traditionally recorded on a share or bond certificate. As well as allowing the transfer of funds from lender to borrower, these bits of paper also often record information such as how the lender is to be rewarded, and when – if ever – the principal sum advanced is to be repaid, particularly in the case of bonds. It might be argued that the financial markets are, in effect, markets for trading bits of paper which represent sophisticated IOUs. (Indeed, it is increasingly the case that no certificates change hands and that the whole transaction – including recording and registration – is done in cyberspace.) Of course, you and I don't normally participate in these markets as individuals, so it is worth pointing out that when we talk of financial markets, we typically mean **wholesale markets**. That is to say, markets where:

1. Firms deal with other firms
2. Very large quantities of money are at stake
3. Borrowing and lending are not intermediated

'Intermediated?' you may well be asking. Let us explain. When you yourself want to borrow money, you typically go to the bank, or you may let your credit card take the strain. These types of finance are what is known as **intermediated** finance. Banks, for example, do not offer you their own money for loan. They are acting as an intermediary for their depositors, who are the primary lenders. In the wholesale markets, by contrast, borrowers and lenders tend to deal much more directly with each other. There are two types of wholesale market, the **money markets** and the **capital markets**. The **money markets** are the markets for shorter-term finance, typically of a year or less. **Capital markets** are markets for longer-term finance, typically longer than a year.

It is the larger 'blue chip' companies, along with sovereign governments and international organisations, that we usually think of as having shares, bonds and other financial instruments which are widely held, traded and publicly quoted on stock, bond and other markets. Nevertheless, though smaller companies or less well-known companies often do not have access to the bond markets, they may well issue equity. They may publicly trade on a smaller exchange, such as the UK-based alternative investment market (AIM) for 'small cap' firms or raise equity capital from private investors, venture capitalists or private equity funds.

It should be pointed out, though, that smaller- to medium-sized companies may not deal directly with the wholesale markets. Indeed, particularly smaller firms may more typically use intermediated finance through business accounts at a bank, along with internally generated funds which are known as retained earnings or **internal equity**. If your own company relies on internal equity for a significant proportion of its finance, there are two things worth bearing in mind. First, this is not 'free' money, as there is an opportunity cost associated with retained earnings. Second, it is only actual cash available that can be used for funding. This is quite different from the figure in the profit and loss account of a company. Internal equity is an important concept which we will refer to later, particularly in the context of capital structuring decisions and those concerning working capital. In the next section we consider, first, the market for equity capital.

## Key concepts

- There are two types of **wholesale markets**: the **money markets** are the markets for shorter-term finance and the **capital markets** are for longer-term periods

### 3.2.2 Equity capital and the stock exchange

Stock markets, or **stock exchanges**, are centralised trading places where companies can raise equity share capital. Traditionally, the four biggest and most well known are the London Stock Exchange, the New York Stock Exchange (NYSE), the NASDAQ (which is also based in New York but is separate from the NYSE) and the Tokyo Stock Exchange. However, as always with finance, things are changing fast, as we can see from Table 3.1 which shows the world's top 10 stock exchanges, ranked by total value of share trade in 2008 and 2009.

Table 3.1 Largest exchanges by value of share trading in the electronic order book in 2009 and 2008

| Exchange | USD bn 2009 | USD bn 2008 | Percentage change in USD |
|---|---|---|---|
| 1 NYSE Euronext US | 17 521 | 27 651 | −36.6 |
| 2 NASDAQ OMX US | 13 608 | 23 845 | −42.9 |
| 3 Shanghai Stock Exchange | 5 056 | 2 584 | 95.7 |
| 4 Tokyo Stock Exchange Group | 3 704 | 5 243 | −29.4 |
| 5 Shenzhen Stock Exchange | 2 772 | 1 242 | 123.2 |
| 6 NYSE Euronext Europe | 1 935 | 3 837 | −49.6 |
| 7 London Stock Exchange | 1 772 | 3 844 | −53.9 |
| 8 Korea Exchange | 1 570 | 1 435 | 9.4 |
| 9 Deutsche Börse | 1 516 | 3 148 | −51.8 |
| 10 Hong Kong Exchanges | 1 416 | 1 562 | −9.3 |

*Source*: www.world-exchanges.com.

You can follow the fortunes of most stock markets by tracking a stock exchange index. A stock exchange index is a composite which measures the change in value of a selected group of stock traded on the market. So, for example, the fortunes of the London Stock Exchange are reflected in the performance of the FTSE 100 or the FTSE 250, the NYSE by the Dow-Jones or the S&P 500, and the Tokyo Stock Exchange by the Nikkei. Of course, in these days of globalisation and emerging markets, it's not just the big stock exchanges that are of interest to businesses and investors. Table 3.2 shows the fastest growing exchanges in 2008/2009.

Table 3.2  Top 10 performing broad market indexes in 2009, in local currency terms

|   | Exchange | Percentage change 2009/2008 |
|---|---|---|
| 1 | Colombo Stock Exchange | 125.2 |
| 2 | Shenzhen Stock Exchange | 117.1 |
| 3 | Buenos Aires Stock Exchange | 103.6 |
| 4 | Lima Stock Exchange | 101.0 |
| 5 | Istanbul Stock Exchange | 96.6 |
| 6 | Bombay Stock Exchange | 90.2 |
| 7 | National Stock Exchange India | 88.6 |
| 8 | Indonesia Stock Exchange | 87.0 |
| 9 | BM&FBOVESPA | 82.7 |
| 10 | Shanghai Stock Exchange | 80.0 |

*Source*: www.world-exchanges.com.

Many of these stock exchanges are probably new to you, though some may be familiar. You may well have heard of the Hong Kong market's stock index, the Hang-Seng, whose performance is often mentioned in the news. In a future career as a finance professional, you would become much more familiar with these slightly less well-known exchanges, as it is here where the highest growth and the greatest returns are experienced – along with the highest amounts of risk, it should be added! Always remember that risk and return are intimately related, or as economists are fond of saying, 'There is no such thing as a free lunch', as illustrated by the mini case study, 'Worse than a casino?'.

## Mini case study

### Worse than a casino?

Source Adapted from Wong 2006

Stock market development in China took off in the early 1990s, at roughly the same time as it did in other transitional economies. China's stock market has some interesting features. First, the government used it to raise funds for state-owned enterprises (SOEs). When the shares were initially offered, only one-third of the enterprises' equity capital sold to private shareholders and the remainder was held either by state asset management agencies or by SOEs themselves. Second, China's stock market was developed under a weak legal framework that offered shareholders little protection. Since one of the prerequisites of a well functioning capital market is held to be strong legal shareholder protection ..., it seems paradoxical that China's stock markets have developed so rapidly. Third, a typical listed firm in China has two types of shares. The first type includes shares issued to state-owned entities that are not allowed to be traded on China's two stock exchanges. Only these shares are backed by the assets of the company. The second type includes freely tradable shares issued to private individual investors.

In January 2001, Wu Jinglian, head of the Chinese State Council's Development Research Council, openly condemned China's stock market for being 'worse than a casino' – that is, like a casino without rules. Although such a stock market was not an investment venue for investors, it was a paradise for speculators.

The Chinese stock market is largely represented by two exchanges, the Shanghai and Shenzhen stock exchanges. The CSI 300 Index is representative of the top 300 companies from both of these exchanges. In 2006, the CSI 300 rose 116 percent and so far this year [2006] the index has soared by nearly 90 percent! Chinese investors have been jumping into the market en masse. Reports of over 300,000 new trading accounts opening every day are testament to the 'fear of missing out' mentality.

1. Why do you think such abnormally high returns have been made on the Chinese stock market?

The primary purpose of all stock exchanges is to raise equity capital for firms in return for securities issued in the form of **ordinary shares** or **preference shares**. The purpose of the issue of equity is to provide the firm with capital for investment purposes. Shareholders have a direct stake in the firm as their share certificate gives them fractional ownership in proportion to the amount of the firm's equity that they own. Ordinary shareholders are usually paid dividends out of any residual profit which is left after interest, tax and depreciation. Ordinary shareholders usually have voting rights, though this is not always the case.

**Preference shares** are less common than ordinary shares. Preference shareholders are paid a dividend which is a fixed percentage of the value of their share subscription and are paid before ordinary shareholders. If a preference dividend is not paid, it usually accrues until it can be paid. Preference shareholders do not usually have voting rights unless dividends fall into arrears. Preference shares are actually more like debt in their characteristics. They are also attractive to investors as, in the event of liquidation, they have precedence over ordinary shares and will be paid before ordinary shares. The seniority of preference shares over ordinary shares, along with the greater certainty of dividend, make preference shares less risky.

A new issue of shares such as, for example, an **initial public offering**, is when the stock market performs its primary function. Notwithstanding this, almost all of the activity that we think of as typical of stock markets, and which is reported widely in the press and on TV, is in second-hand shares, that is, shares that have been previously issued. Thus, most reported trading activity is concerned with the market's performance in its secondary role; that of trading previously issued shares. The secondary function provided by financial markets is important because it allows those who invest in shares or bonds to change their minds and switch their investment to some other asset should the need arise. The investor is not 'stuck' with a particular share. Unless there are very serious problems with the company, investors can almost always sell their share on, particularly in large publicly quoted companies. Thus, the secondary market function provides **liquidity**. Liquidity is the ability to sell at a fair price in a reasonable time period. The reassurance of being able to sell on an investment on a liquid secondary market makes investors more likely to invest in primary market investment vehicles such as new share issues.

The economic benefits of a well-run stock exchange can be considerable. Some of the benefits of a well-regulated exchange are that it:

- Allows firms to obtain funds and grow
- Facilitates the allocation of capital to its most productive uses
- Provides a central point for those who wish to invest and those who wish to borrow
- Provides a means for companies to raise funds
- Provides a means for investors to choose investments according to their risk and return profiles
- Allows shareholders to sell speedily and cheaply and allows them to value their financial assets easily and facilitates diversification of risk
- Facilitates improvements in corporate behaviour because of the high level of public awareness of the business and the considerable financial reporting and other disclosure requirements

Thus, with proper regulation, negligence, fraud and other abuses are minimised (but never eliminated altogether), and investors are presented with a 'fair game', i.e. the current share price reflects what is known about the firm and its future prospects, which encourages trade to take place, thus reducing transaction costs and increasing liquidity.

Consider the London and Nigerian Stock Markets in the learning activity below.

 **Active learning activity 3.2**

### Compare the London and Nigerian Stock Markets

The London Stock Market originated in the coffee houses of seventeenth century London. The next few hundred years saw the development of codified rule books and the building of a central exchange. In 1923, the exchange received its own coat of arms, with the motto Dictum Meum Pactum (*My Word Is My Bond*). The march of progress continued exorably, with female members admitted for the first time in 1973. In 1986, the London Stock Market deregulated following the so-called Big Bang. One of the main consequences of the deregulation is that trading is now done via computers and telephones, which is perhaps more efficient but does not seem as exciting as the open-outcry system. In 1991, the exchange became the London Stock Exchange (LSE). In 2001 the LSE celebrated its 200th anniversary by listing on its own exchange. In 2007, it merged with Borsa Italiana, creating the London Stock Exchange Group.

The Nigerian Stock Exchange was established in 1960 as the Lagos Stock Exchange. In December 1977 it became the Nigerian Stock Exchange, with branches established in some of the major commercial cities of the country. The Exchange started operations in 1961 with 19 securities listed for trading. In 2007, there were 262 securities listed on the Exchange, made up of 11 government stocks, 49 industrial loan (debenture/preference) stocks and 194 equity/ordinary shares of companies, all with a total market capitalisation of approximately N5.9 trillion ($46 billion).

Go to the official stock exchange websites:

- http://www.londonstockexchange.com
- http://www.nigerianstockexchange.com/index.jsp.

**1.** Compare how both these stock exchanges fulfil the specified functions of a stock market.

### 3.2.2.1 *Calculating share return*

Ordinary share capital holders expect two types of reward for investing in shares. They may expect the price of the shares to go up – capital appreciation – and they usually also expect periodic payments in the form of dividends. In symbols, the absolute gain over one period, for example over a year, is as follows:

$$d_t + P_t - P_{t-1}$$

where $d_t$ is the current dividend, $P_t$ is the current price and $P_{t-1}$ is the price in the previous period. That is, the gain from owning a share is the dividend plus any gain or loss on the price. Hence, **return** is normally any gain (or loss!) expressed as a percentage of the initial investment, the buying price, or the opening price. Therefore, the one period return for shares is as follows:

$$R_t = (d_t + P_t - P_{t-1})/P_{t-1}$$

Now we know how to calculate share return and having considered the markets for equity in some detail, we turn in the next section to the markets for debt.

## Key concepts

☐ **Stock exchanges** are centralised trading places where companies can raise equity share capital

☐ **Ordinary shares** are shares in the ownership of a company, allowing the owners to collect a share of profits after all other stakeholders have been paid

- **Preference shares** are shares in the ownership of a company which allow the holder the first claim on part of any dividend paid
- **Liquidity** is the ability to sell at a fair price in a reasonable time period
- An **initial public offering** is the first time a company offers its shares for sale to the public

### 3.2.3 Debt capital and the markets for debt

#### 3.2.3.1 *The advantages of debt for firms*

As observed above, when a firm issues shares, the buyers of these shares are not only making funds available to the firm for investment purposes, they also partly own the firm. This arrangement for financing the firm and its investments, whereby funding is attracted by offering ownership certificates, is known as **external equity**, as opposed to the **internal equity** provided by retained profits. The alternative to the issue of external equity on the capital market is the issue of **debt**. Firms issue debt in the form of, for example, corporate bonds, commercial paper, certificates of deposit, bills and notes.

Debt has a number of attractive features in comparison to share capital:

1. It reduces the amount of corporate tax payable by firms by reducing the amount of taxable profit. This is because taxable profit is calculated after interest has been deducted, by contrast with dividends which are an appropriation of profit – an after-tax sharing out of profit.

2. The cost of debt is generally cheaper than the cost of share capital and hence can lower the overall cost of capital for a firm. This is because, from the lender's point of view, debt is less risky than equity. Interest must be paid to the lender at the terms agreed, unless the firm wishes to risk insolvency, bankruptcy and foreclosure. By contrast, the share dividend is more uncertain. Indeed, technically, the firm is not obliged to pay a dividend at all. Also, debt is often secured through the use of **collateral** or **covenants**. Thus, lenders are prepared to take a lower return than those who provide the firm with equity capital because of the lower risk involved.

3. Debt does not give away ownership of the firm.

4. The costs of issuing debt are cheaper than the costs of issuing equity. A full listing on the LSE is a hideously expensive business. Put it this way: where do people get the money to pay high prices for property in the more salubrious parts of London? Well, they get it from their City bonuses. A significant part of what the City does is investment banking, and a significant part of what investment bankers do is manage share issues, advise on flotations, underwrite share issues and so on. And the money comes from firms issuing new equity on the stock market. Investment bankers employ highly skilled but highly expensive staff. Hence, the issuance costs of fully publicly listed equity can be prohibitive.

5. A fifth advantage, that we will explore more in Chapter 8 on Capital Structure, is that the addition of debt may, under certain circumstances, enhance the value of the company.

3.2.3.2  *The money markets*

The shorter-term markets for debt are known as the **money markets.** These are wholesale cash markets through which banks, firms and government bodies fund short-term deficits or invest short-term surpluses. (The process of balancing out short-term deficits and surpluses is known as liquidity management, or cash flow management.) The money markets are for financial instruments with maturities of less than 1 year, though actual maturities are often much shorter. For example, on the interbank market, it is not uncommon to find money being borrowed and lent overnight. Borrowing and lending in money markets is usually high volume, relatively low risk and, of course, short term, as previously described.

Major money market instruments include:

- Treasury bills – forms of central government debt
- Certificates of deposit (CDs) – securitised bank time deposits
- Bankers acceptances (BAs) – securitised commercial trade debt obligations
- Commercial paper (CP) – securitised debt issued by highly creditworthy corporations

As well as these markets for sophisticated forms of IOU paper, other important money markets are the interbank market and the local authority market. The London interbank market is the market for short-term borrowing or lending between banks. Those banks with temporary surpluses will lend to those with temporary shortfalls. The interbank market was the centre of dramatic events in August 2007, when liquidity on the interbank market dried up, accelerating the collapse of Northern Rock after the first run on a bank in the UK since the 1860s.[1]

The other reason why the London interbank market is better known than some of the other money markets is that the key rate in this market, LIBOR, is often used as a reference rate for borrowing and lending throughout the world. LIBOR stands for London interbank offered rate.

## Key concepts

- **Collateral** is the name given to assets which are required from the lender as guarantees to secure the loan
- **Covenants** are conditions placed on loans to ensure repayment
- The **money markets** are wholesale cash markets through which banks, firms and government bodies fund short-term deficits or invest short-term surpluses
- **Corporate debt** can be issued in a number of forms but usually involves interest payments and a commitment to repay the principal at a future specified date

### 3.2.3.3  The bond markets

A bond is a financial instrument that guarantees the holder a fixed sum of money at a pre-specified date in the future. The fixed sum is generally known as the face value or par value. This is the sum that has been lent in the first place and which will be repaid on maturity. Usually, the holder of the bond will also receive a series of interest payments which are fixed in monetary terms. These fixed money payments are known as coupons.

A typical bond cash flow is defined precisely by its **maturity, face value, coupon rate** and **payment frequency**. The **maturity** is the number of years that the bond runs from the time of issue to the time when the bond expires. The bond will expire or mature on repayment of the sum borrowed at the point of issue. The **face value** is the units in which the bond is nominally issued – normally £100 in the UK and $1,000 in the US. The **coupon rate** is the percentage of the face value that is paid as interest before the principal is repaid. Frequency of payment of coupon is, in real life, 6 months, but to keep things simple and avoid semi-annual compounding, it is often assumed to be paid annually in textbooks. Thus, suppose you had a 5-year bond with £1,000 face value and a coupon rate of 6%. The cash flows are shown in Screenshot 3.1.

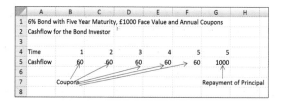

Screenshot 3.1  Cash flows for plain vanilla bond with 6% coupon and £1,000 face value

The type of bond structure described in the previous paragraph is an example of a plain vanilla bond. A **plain vanilla bond** has the following characteristics:

• Known maturity

• A series of regular coupons which are fixed in cash terms at issue. This is why bonds are often known as fixed income instruments

• A coupon rate which is a fixed percentage of face value

There are two main types of bonds: bonds issued by the government (whether central or local) and bonds issued by corporations. (A rare example of a personal issuer of bonds is shown in the mini case study, 'The thin white Duke'.) You can buy bonds directly from the issuer – for example, from the UK government. Once issued, the bonds are traded on a secondary bond market.

For reasons that will be explained in Section 3.3.2, bond yields move inversely to prices. This means that falling bond prices mean rising bond yields and vice versa. Changes in yield are the standard way of referring to bond markets. Thus, investors will not say 'bond prices fell' and would instead say 'bond yields rise'.

## Mini case study

### The thin white Duke

Source **BBC 1999**

As mentioned before, although bonds are really a form of sophisticated IOU, the market for these IOUs can only be accessed by large companies. However, one individual has had his own bond issue. International rock star David Bowie 'securitised' his future earnings in exchange for $55 million, to be paid back in 10 years' time. In fact, the enduring popularity of the 'thin white Duke' is so high that analysts at Moody's, a ratings agency, gave David Bowie's bond their highest accolade, a triple-A rating. In return, the artist had to pay less interest on his loan issue.

1. Would you consider investing in a bond issued by David Bowie?

Bonds come in a bewildering number of varieties. However, most of the important types can be illustrated with respect to UK government bonds, which are known as **gilts**. The UK government gilts market is the British market for all types of government bonds. The gilts market is the major borrowing source for the UK treasury and gilts account for over 60% of the total UK national debt. The UK gilts market is one of the largest in the world and it is regarded as one of the most liquid and well-organised markets in the world. UK gilts carry AAA ratings from credit rating agencies – this shows that they are regarded as very safe.

There are four types of gilt-edged securities:

1. **Conventional gilts**: this type of bond is the largest part of the UK gilt market. They have a semi-annual coupon and a bullet maturity. A bullet maturity means there is no repayment of principal until maturity. This form of bond is often known as a plain vanilla bond.

2. **Index-linked gilts**: the distinguishing feature of this type of bond is that the coupon rate is adjusted according to changes in the retail price index (RPI). The redemption value is also protected against inflation.

3. **Convertible bonds**: the distinguishing feature of this type of bond is that they allow the investor to convert the bond into longer-dated bonds on a pre-specified date. It should be noted that in the context of corporate bonds issued by firms, convertible usually refers to an option to convert the bond to an equity holding at some point.

4. **Irredeemable bonds** (also known as undated bonds): this type of bond is the smallest part of the UK gilts market. The distinguishing feature of these bonds is that they have no final maturity date. That is, there is no commitment by the UK government to redeem these bonds. However, should the British government choose, they can buy them back as they are callable at any time with 3 months' notice. Irredeemable bonds, also known as perpetuities, are something of a rarity and many governments do not issue them at all. However, it is unusual to find a finance textbook that does not mention UK government perpetuities, which usually take the form of consols. Consol stands for consolidat-

ed stock. The reason for the issue of this stock is lost in the mist of time. Some say it was to pay for the Napoleonic Wars, others that it was to pay for the Boer Wars. You may think that widespread interest in consols is to do with a keen interest by international finance academics in British history. Alas, it is not. It is because consols are a rare example of real-life perpetuities. Though not often found in reality, perpetuities, being an extreme kind of bond, have useful properties for financial calculation purposes, which we will explore later in the book.

## Key concepts

- The **maturity** is the number of years that the bond runs from the time of issue to the time when the bond expires
- The **face value** is the units in which the bond is nominally issued – normally £100 in the UK and $1,000 in the US
- The **coupon rate** is the percentage of the face value that is paid as interest before the principal is repaid
- **Frequency of payment** of coupon is in real life 6 months, but to keep things simple and avoid semi-annual compounding it is often assumed in textbooks to be paid annually
- A **gilt** is a bond issued by the UK government

### 3.2.3.4  *The role of credit rating agencies in bond markets*

If you ask for credit to buy a new car, a **credit rating agency** can provide a report assessing your creditworthiness. This report will influence how much you are able to borrow and at what rate. In much the same way, although using different criteria, companies and governments are also credit-rated in terms of their eligibility to issue bonds.

Well-known agencies, mainly based in the US – such as Moody's, and Standard & Poor's – grade corporate and institutional borrowers according to their ability to repay their debt. Bonds in other countries are also rated by these US rating agencies, or sometimes by local credit rating agencies. Rating scales vary; the most popular scale uses (in order of increasing risk) ratings of AAA, AA, A, BBB, BB, B, CCC, CC and C, with the additional rating D for debt already in arrears. Government bonds and bonds issued by government agencies are often considered to be in a zero-risk category above AAA; and categories like AA and A may sometimes be split into finer subdivisions like 'AA–' and 'AA+'. The analysis and ratings provided by rating agencies can be very influential in determining the interest rates that borrowers pay on their debt. There are two broad categories of ratings: investment grade and speculative grade (also known as junk bonds). Most investment and pension funds are not allowed to hold junk bonds as part of their portfolio.

Explore the credit rating of a country as described in the learning activity below.

**Active learning activity 3.3**

### How is your country rated?

**Source** Standard & Poor's

Standard & Poor's has been engaged in issuing credit ratings since 1916. Today, Standard & Poor's has credit ratings outstanding on approximately 150,000 securities in over 100 countries. The company rates and monitors developments pertaining to these securities and obligors from operations in more than 21 cities in 16 countries around the world. It rates more than 99.2% of publicly traded US debt obligations and preferred stock issues.

The UK has been rated as AAA/Stable/A–1+. Go to the website www.standardandpoors.com and click on 'Products and Services' and then on 'Sovereigns'. Click on 'Credit ratings list'. Choose a country and check out its credit rating. The definitions are available on the same page. Can you explain why your chosen country has the allocated rating?

Investment grade bonds are bonds with one of the higher credit ratings. They are less risky bonds with a low probability of default. For many borrowers, it is necessary to get an investment grade credit rating to ensure full uptake of their bond issue. This is because many investment funds and pension funds are constrained by law or by their own rules to buy only investment grade bonds.

Junk bonds are bonds with below investment grade ratings. They are usually corporate bonds with higher default risk than investment grade bonds. They are worth investing in for investors with a taste for risk and so investors need higher yields to induce them to take on the higher risk. The market for junk bonds or below investment grade bonds was developed by Michael Milken when he realised that bonds whose ratings had slipped below investment grade (termed **fallen angels**) had greater value than their bond rating suggested. He had the insight of pioneering the market for bonds that were never intended to be of investment grade due to the fact that they were intended to finance risky activities such as leveraged buy-outs.

This is, by no means, an exhaustive list of bonds and bond markets. Indeed, it is possible to find many books written on the subject of bonds alone. However, for the purposes of discussion in the rest of the book, we will consider bonds to be of the plain vanilla type described above. Bonds are known as **fixed income instruments** because the monetary value of the cash flows from the bond is fixed. As a variation on the plain vanilla bond, we will also make further reference to perpetuities later in the book.

In this rather long section, we have considered at some length the nature of debt markets, subsequent to our discussion of equity markets. In the next section we consider the impact that the markets have on society as a whole – particularly stock market prices.

**Key concepts**

☐ **Credit rating agencies** grade borrowers on their ability to repay their debt

☐ **Fallen angels** are bonds whose ratings have slipped below investment grade

☐ **Fixed income instruments** are bonds with fixed cash flows

## 3.3  Why share prices matter and why we don't normally hear much about bond prices

### 3.3.1  Share prices

'Stock prices have reached what looks like a permanently high plateau.'

(Fisher 1929)

Just after the bold statement above, Wall Street led the way in a frenetic wave of selling whereby stock prices fell. This led to the Great Depression of the 1920s and 1930s, the effect of which was felt worldwide.

The Great Depression, it goes without saying, was an historical event. So you may think that falling share prices are somewhat abstract and of no real concern to you. But share prices do matter as they indicate investor confidence. When share prices are generally trending downward – in what is called a 'bear market' – some of the consequences could be as follows:

- The company you work for has a lower market value. This makes it vulnerable to being taken over. You may very well lose your job.

- Your pension fund, which is invested in the stock market, is worth less. You may have to live a much more modest life in retirement.[2]

- Liquidity may dry up because of a general lack of investor confidence. This means it becomes difficult for both businesses and individuals to borrow. For example, in 2008 100% and 125% mortgages were withdrawn from the UK retail mortgage market. Private equity firms, for a few years the darlings of the markets, found it increasingly difficult to refinance their loans and some went out of business.

Consider the relevance of the stock markets to your own life by referring to the learning activity below.

**Active learning activity 3.4**

**I've never bought shares – why should I care if stock markets crash?**

Go online and read the article 'How falling stock markets affect you': http://news.bbc.co.uk/1/hi/business/2067010.stm.
   Discover at least three ways a market crash could affect you.

Share prices are also of concern to the firms that issued the shares in the first place. Again, this might be slightly puzzling. Once the firm has raised the capital it requires, what does it matter what price its share certificates are trading at? After all, the firm is under no obligation to pay equity capital back, while any dividend it pays is at its own discretion. However, share price is important to the firm for the following reasons:

1. A company's general success and financial health is often judged by the share price. The higher the price – or, more specifically, the higher the price per share relative to earnings per share – the more confidence the firm's management has that they are doing a good job. After all, the stock market normally provides a very good estimate of a firm's worth – particularly if the EMH, discussed below, is to be believed. A high stock market valuation is a big vote of confidence in the firm's management and workforce.

2. Senior management rewards are often directly linked to stock market performance in the form of stock options. The higher the firm's stock price, the more valuable these options.

3. Share price is important to the firm, even after capital has been issued, as it can affect the cost of any further finance, whether debt or equity capital. The more favourably the firm is perceived by the stock market, the easier it is to issue debt or additional equity on favourable terms.

4. There is the question of whether or not the firm is maximising shareholder wealth. As was discussed in Chapter 1, this is generally agreed to be the most appropriate goal for the firm. The stock market price is a reasonably reliable indicator as to whether or not this is being achieved.

5. Fifthly, and possibly more controversially, it may well be that the stock market price estimates not only shorter-term value maximisation but also longer-term corporate responsibility and the sustainability of the business. This is the subject of the next active learning activity.

## Active learning activity 3.5

### Does good corporate behaviour pay off in the stock market?

Over the past decade, a great deal of intellectual effort has been expended on whether 'ethical' investment delivers greater value for investors.

1. Go on the internet and track down some of the ways in which ethical investing is done, the companies involved and the indices or studies that assess the performance of these investments. You might try the *Financial Times* or *The Economist*. Or, for example, you could start by reading 'Finding the best measure of 'corporate citizenship'' by Phil Dvorak in the *Wall Street Journal*.

2. Why would shareholders value companies that behave ethically?

3. Look at the share price of a company you believe to have acted ethically or unethically in the past year. How has it performed? Do you think this is due to its behaviour or other factors?

## Key concept

☐ **Falling** or **rising share prices** have substantial effects on both the firms involved and the real economy

Now we've convinced ourselves of the importance of share prices, the following questions naturally follow:

1. What determines bond and share prices?

2. Is the share price efficient, in the sense that the share price is a true valuation of the firm and its business activities?

3. Is the stock market, as a whole, efficient in the sense that it typically reaches efficient valuations of share prices for stocks?

We follow these questions up in the next two sections.

### 3.3.2  Bond prices

In 2010, bond prices, particularly for Greek government bonds, are receiving a great deal of attention. This is an unusual situation, as bond prices usually receive less attention than share prices, particularly from the general public and TV news programmes. For technical reasons, which we will discuss below , bond prices and interest rates tend to go in opposite directions. So if bond prices are falling, this usually indicates that the bond markets anticipate higher future long-term interest rates, perhaps, for example, because of inflation, or perhaps because greater uncertainty now makes borrowing more risky. These possible causes of higher bond prices follow naturally from our discussion in Chapter 2 that the interest rate reflects risk, inflation and time impatience. However, **bond markets**, though an important feature of later chapters, will not be mentioned in the subsequent discussion in the next section on **efficient markets**. The question of market efficiency does not crop up very often in the market for debt. This is possibly because debt instruments such as bonds are much more clearly defined than equity instruments. The timing and amount of cash flow from a low risk, plain vanilla, highly rated sovereign government bond, for example, is exactly known when the bond is issued. As discussed in the previous section, a bond's cash flow is defined very precisely by its maturity, face value, coupon rate and payment frequency.

Now comes an important point – indeed, one of the main reasons that you have bought this book. We are going to initiate you into one of the three great secrets of finance. The first secret is that, to find the value of anything in finance, you take the discounted value of cash flow. Now, that may not seem like much of a secret to you, and neither does it seem like much of a secret to us, but along with our other two insights vouchsafed for later, we have to conclude that it must be a secret, otherwise why do intelligent well-paid professional financial people occasionally appear to act as if it was unknown, such as during the dotcom boom of the late 1990s when firms that were earning absolutely no revenue were valued at millions?

Applying our new-found secret, we can value a bond and its associated cash flow as long as we have a discount rate. It's just like valuing an investment project, with the sole difference that we take present value of the cash flow from the bond and *not* net present value. Suppose we have a plain vanilla bond which is issued with a maturity of 5 years and a face value of £1,000. At issue, the bond coupon rate of 6% is equal to the interest rate, which for bonds is called the yield to maturity. The bond price on a discounted cash flow (DCF) basis is £1,000, as shown in Screenshot 3.2.

| | A | B | C | D | E | F | G |
|---|---|---|---|---|---|---|---|
| 1 | 6% Bond with Five Year Maturity, £1000 Face Value and Annual Coupons | | | | | | |
| 2 | Cashflow for the Bond Investor | | | | | | |
| 3 | | | | | | | |
| 4 | Time | 1 | 2 | 3 | 4 | 5 | 5 |
| 5 | Cashflow | 60 | 60 | 60 | 60 | 60 | 1000 |
| 6 | Discount Factors @ 6% | 0.9434 | 0.89 | 0.83962 | 0.79209 | 0.74726 | 0.74726 |
| 7 | Discounted Cashflow | 56.6038 | 53.3998 | 50.3772 | 47.5256 | 44.8355 | 747.258 |
| 8 | | | | | | | |
| 9 | Price = Sum DCF | 1000 | | | | | |

Screenshot 3.2  At 6%, the bond is at par

When a bond's price is equal to its face value, it is said to be at **par**. For any bond at par, and not just this one, the bond price will equal face value.

Now, if the interest rate, and hence the discount rate, should happen to rise after the bond is issued, the future cash flow will be more heavily discounted and the bond will be worth less. Suppose, for example, the interest rate rose from 6% to 8%. The bond price will fall from £1,000 to £920.14. This is because the cash flow from the bond is more heavily discounted, as can be seen in Screenshot 3.3.

| | A | B | C | D | E | F | G |
|---|---|---|---|---|---|---|---|
| 1 | 6% Bond with Five Year Maturity, £1000 Face Value and Annual Coupons | | | | | | |
| 2 | Cashflow for the Bond Investor | | | | | | |
| 3 | | | | | | | |
| 4 | Time | 1 | 2 | 3 | 4 | 5 | 5 |
| 5 | Cashflow | 60 | 60 | 60 | 60 | 60 | 1000 |
| 6 | *Discount Factors @ 8%* | 0.92593 | 0.85734 | 0.79383 | 0.73503 | 0.68058 | 0.68058 |
| 7 | Discounted Cashflow | 55.5556 | 51.4403 | 47.6299 | 44.1018 | 40.835 | 680.583 |
| 8 | | | | | | | |
| 9 | Price = Sum DCF | 920.146 | | | | | |

Screenshot 3.3  At 8%, the bond is at a discount to face value

The bond is no longer at par but is now said to be at a discount to face value. As we already know, the technical reason why this is the case is, of course, because the cash flow from the bond is now more heavily discounted. However, we might also explain the discount as follows. The 6% bond with its £60 coupons can no longer compete with bonds now being issued at 8% and offering £80 coupons. Hence those investors now holding 6%/£60 bonds would have to offer an added inducement to potential buyers in the form of a discount in price sufficient to make the old 6% coupon bond equivalent to the newer 8%/£80 bond for investors seeking to buy. For technical reasons, which we won't go into at this point, the discount on face value is just sufficient to offset the disadvantage of the lower coupons of the 6% bond, making the overall return equal to 8%.

Of course, the opposite could happen after issue and the interest rate could fall after the 6% bond is issued. For example, if the interest rate fell from 6% to 4% after the 6% bond was issued, the bond price would rise from £1,000 to £1,089.04, as illustrated in Screenshot 3.3.

| | A | B | C | D | E | F | G |
|---|---|---|---|---|---|---|---|
| 1 | 6% Bond with Five Year Maturity, £1000 Face Value and Annual Coupons | | | | | | |
| 2 | Cashflow for the Bond Investor | | | | | | |
| 3 | | | | | | | |
| 4 | Time | 1 | 2 | 3 | 4 | 5 | 5 |
| 5 | Cashflow | 60 | 60 | 60 | 60 | 60 | 1000 |
| 6 | *Discount Factors @ 4%* | 0.96154 | 0.92456 | 0.889 | 0.8548 | 0.82193 | 0.82193 |
| 7 | Discounted Cashflow | 57.6923 | 55.4734 | 53.3398 | 51.2883 | 49.3156 | 821.927 |
| 8 | | | | | | | |
| 9 | Price = Sum DCF | 1089.04 | | | | | |

Screenshot 3.4 At 4%, the bond is at a premium to face value

The rise in price is, of course, because the bond's cash flows are now *less* heavily discounted. Or to put it more intuitively, those investors now holding 6% bonds are in possession of a fixed income instrument which offers bigger coupons than the 4% bonds now being issued. Thus, if they wish to sell, they can put the price up a bit and sell at a premium. Again, for technical reasons which we won't go into at this point, the premium on face value is just sufficient to offset the advantage of the higher coupons, making the overall return equal to 4%.

Notice that we have now also established the inverse relationship between bond yield and bond price. The yield, or yield to maturity, to give it its full name, is just the bond rate of return, or indeed the bond's rate of interest. When general interest rates go up, bond yields usually go up and bond prices fall. And, of course, falling interest rates usually mean falling yields and rising bond prices.

Note that there is a shortcut method for valuing bonds. This is to treat the coupon payments of the bond as an **annuity cash flow**. An annuity cash flow can be defined as a recurring cash flow, i.e. the same sum repeats at regular intervals over a fixed period of time. With such a recurring cash flow there is no need to multiply each identical cash flow (in this instance £60 recurring every year) by each different discount factor for each different year. All we have to do is to multiply the recurring cash flow (RCF) once by the appropriate annuity factor, and that will give us the discounted value of the RCF.

The annuity factor for an n period annuity with discount rate r can be defined as follows:

$$A^n_r = \frac{1 - \frac{1}{(1+r)^n}}{r}$$

Or:

$$A^n_r = \frac{1 - DF^n_r}{r}$$

That is the **annuity factor** for an n-period annuity is equal to one minus the appropriate **discount factor** for r and n divided by the **discount rate**, r. The value of a bond of course is only partial determined by the annuity value of the coupons. One must also add the discounted face value of the bond. That is the overall price of the five year bond at 6% yield to maturity is as follows:

$$Price = Sum(DCF) = Coupon * AF \begin{smallmatrix} n = 5 \\ r = 6\% \end{smallmatrix} + Face\ Value * DF \begin{smallmatrix} n = 5 \\ r = 6\% \end{smallmatrix}$$

Therefore, the calculation for our £60 coupon bond is as follows:

$$Price = Sum(DCF) = 60 * AF \begin{smallmatrix} n = 5 \\ r = 6\% \end{smallmatrix} + 1000 * DF \begin{smallmatrix} n = 5 \\ r = 6\% \end{smallmatrix}$$

The discount factor $DF \begin{smallmatrix} n = 5 \\ r = 6\% \end{smallmatrix}$ is 0.74726. Thus the annuity factor, $\dfrac{1 - DF_n}{r}$ is equal to

$\dfrac{1 - 0.74726}{0.06}$ or 4.2133... The value of the bond at 6% is

$$60 * 4.2133 .. + 1000 * 0.74726 = 1000$$

By a similar line of reasoning, the values of the bonds at 8% and 4% may be calculated as follows using the annuity factor

$$60 * 3.9927 + 1000 * 0.68058 = 920.14$$
$$60 * 4.4518 + 1000 * 0.82193 = 1089.04$$

See Chapter 12 for more details.

And that's just about it. You have two basic uncertainties with a bond. One is the possibility of an interest rate increase. In this case, the price will fall below the £1,000 the bond commanded at issue (known as the par price) and you will have made a capital loss. The other uncertainty is the possibility of default. While neither capital loss nor default can be predicted, they can be quantified in terms of statistical probability. In short, questions of efficient markets don't crop up as much in bond markets as the valuation of bonds is relatively straightforward and there are fewer unknowns than in the case of equity pricing, which is the subject of the next section.

## Key concepts

- [ ] DCF stands for **discounted cash flow**, a method used to value financial instruments
- [ ] If a bond is at **par** value, its price is equal to its face value
- [ ] **Bonds** are relatively easy to price. The price is a function of the maturity **face value, coupon rate** and **payment frequency**

## 3.4 Efficient markets and efficient share prices

Before we can explain what constitutes an efficient stock market, we need to explain what constitutes an efficient or 'fair' share price. In fact, the valuation of a share is deceptively simple. A firm's cash flows are not expected to end any time soon, and therefore they can be treated as perpetuity cash flows, as can the firm's dividends. Assuming that no change is expected in the dividends, then it is just a case of applying **fundamental law no. 1** of finance and taking the discounted value of constant dividend cash flow. Right? Well, there is a small problem. How do you value a cash flow to infinity? This looks like it could be a tricky problem, but it turns out to be very straightforward. The problem is as follows:

$$P_t = (1/(1+r) + 1/(1+r)^2 + 1/(1+r)^3 + \ldots\ldots\ldots 1/(1+r)^\infty) \times d$$

where P is the share price, d is the constant dividend and r is the discount rate.

That is, the share price valuation problem is that of valuing a perpetuity cash flow. (This is a recurring cash flow without a finite time limit.) It looks impossible, but it isn't. We can make progress here by trying a moderately large number, rather than an impossibly large number such as infinity. Suppose the discount rate was 10% and we assumed that the firm will pay a dividend every year for 50 years. The price of a share in the firm would depend on all 50 discounted cash flows as follows:

$$P_t = (1/(1+r) + 1/(1+r)^2 + 1/(1+r)^3 + \ldots\ldots\ldots 1/(1+r)^{50}) \times d$$

If you do all of the 50 calculations involved on a spreadsheet, you will find that the price can be expressed as follows:

$$P_t = 9.915 \times d$$

Now, suppose the firm will pay a dividend over the next 100 years. The price would now depend on 100 discounted cash flows. If you did the calculation, it would be as follows:

$$P_t = 9.999274 \times d$$

(Of course, you might just want to use the annuity factor for r = 10% and n = 50, n = 100, respectively – far simpler!)

In other words, the longer the period over which the firm pays a dividend, the closer the price gets to 10 times the dividend. There is a sound technical reason for this. The longer the time over which a regular repeated cash flow is discounted, the closer the sum of all discount factors, $(1/(1+r) + 1/(1+r)^2 + 1/(1+r)^3 + \ldots\ldots\ldots 1/(1+r)^n)$, gets to 1/r. For example, if the discount rate is 10%, 1/r = 1/0.1 = 10.

Just to prove the point, suppose we took a discount rate of 20% and found the sum of all the discount factors for a 100 period cash flow. We would find that $(1/(1+0.2) + 1/(1+0.2)^2 + 1/(1+0.2)^3 + \ldots\ldots\ldots 1/(1+0.2)^{100})$ is very, very close to 5, which is the same thing as 1/20% or 1/0.2. So, the value of a share is easy to work out in DCF terms. Just divide the constant dividend by the discount rate as follows:

$$P_t = d/r$$

This looks simple enough. In practice, it can be very difficult to apply this valuation to shares, because it is difficult to know what the correct assumptions about dividend and discount rate ought to be. Also, another element of uncertainty is introduced when there is expected to be growth in the dividend. We reserve discussion of the pricing formula with dividend growth for Chapter 4, and full details, including mathematical derivation, can be found in Chapter 12 together with a more appropriate context.

In the long run, dividends are determined as the residual that is left over from profit after all expenses have been deducted. But future profit depends on a myriad of factors such as future demand, future competitors and future technology, to name but three. Future risk, and hence the appropriate discount rate, will also depend on these kinds of factors which can only be seen through a glass darkly. And there's a final problem that what is known to market participants may well fall short of the full information required, which is known only within the firm. Given the obvious difficulty, no individual could possibly come up with precise values for the correct share price which will always turn out to be correct. What happens is that the market comes up with a kind of 'best guess' average value based on what is known now with certainty about the riskiness of the firm, future cash flows and dividends and potential for growth. This best guess average is not always correct and may be quite badly wrong at times. However, taken over all stocks in the long run, the market's best guess average should turn out to be less wrong than any alternative method of pricing shares.

An efficient market, then, is one in which the market's best guess average price for the typical stock turns out to be less wrong than any other conceivable way of forecasting future income and risk for firms. There is, of course, a more precise technical definition, which is as follows:

'A market is efficient with respect to information set θ *t* if it is impossible to make economic profits by trading on the basis of information set θ *t*.'

(Jensen 1978)

This basically means that, on average, no-one can make above average profits by trading a share based on information already known because all the information is already reflected in the current price. What is the average return in the market? Well, measured over a year, say, it's your dividend over the year, plus any capital gain or loss over the year. In other words, it's just a simple percentage return. Just in case you missed it, here it is again:

$$R_t = (d_t + P_t - P_{t-1})/P_{t-1}$$

Let's suppose **t-1** is 31 December 2014 and **t** is 31 December 2015. We will further suppose that the firm is Acme. (You know, the fictional mail order people who always send far-fetched items – such as outsized butterfly nets or home-assembly rocket kits – to cartoon characters by post in a matter of seconds.) Now, in order to have beaten our old friend **market return**, by investing in Acme, you would have to have bought at smarter prices than the rest of the market, given that there is, of course, no changing the dividend. Suppose that the dividend is £1 and that $P_{31/12/2014}$ is £10 and $P_{31/12/2015}$ is £11. The market return over the year is $(11 + 1 - 10)/10 = 20\%$. One way of beating this return would have been to have **bought at**

**a lower price** than £10. In order to do this, you would have to have held off from buying on 31/12/2014 in anticipation of a dip in price at some point before 31/12/2015.

Let's say you think that Acme's quarterly results – to be released on 31 March – will be unexpectedly poor and the price will fall to £9. If you bought at this price and sold at £11, you would make a return of £3/£9 which is 33%. Actually your **annualised** return would be slightly higher than this on an annualised basis as you would only have held the stock for 9 months. But let's not get too complicated for the moment.

But why would you be able to see this whereas the market wouldn't? In order to pull it off, you would have to have known something about Acme that the market didn't; some piece of information concealed from the market that justified your private belief that the price would go lower, perhaps because of bad results or unanticipated problems. Otherwise, everyone else in the market would have held off to wait for the lower buying price too. The very act of holding off by the market would have reduced demand to the point where the new price would have prevailed straight away, given how quickly financial markets respond to new information. In addition, notice that you would also have to have been clever enough to know that the price would eventually recover to the expected price of £11 by the end of 2015.

The other way of beating the market would have been to have **sold** Acme shares **at a higher price**. So, for example, you might alternatively have bought at the price of £10 on 31/12/2014, like the rest of the market. Over the course of the year, the share price ticks up, perhaps on a succession of good news stories about the firm, and reaches the dizzy heights of £12. You, however, know that £12 isn't sustainable, as you have a feeling that the quarterly results on 31 September will be disappointing.

But again, you would have to know something that the market didn't. Just to add to your frustration, some advocates of the idea of efficient markets would argue that the very act of trying to sell Acme would alert the rest of the market to your private information and the price would immediately jump from £12 to £11 before you had time to profit. Thus, your effort to **sell at a higher price** would also be nullified.

The speed of response of the market would also have frustrated your efforts in the previous example where you attempted to **buy at a lower price**, in the circumstances that you were already holding the stock. In this case, you would have sold the stock in order to buy back cheaper. However, an efficient market would have spotted this move, and the price would fall very rapidly. Thus, the act of trying to take advantage of information unknown to the market actually reveals the information to the market and frustrates any attempt to make returns greater than market returns. Returns greater than normal market returns are known as **abnormal returns**. In order to make abnormal returns, you will have to have private information and/or be able to beat the market with your speed of response. The EMH argues that you would only have useful private information if you had **insider information**, that is, information that is known only inside the company and is not available to the general public. This is why attempts to trade using insider information are illegal in most countries. You could, of course, try to get to market quicker on the release of information to the public, but given the mad scramble to be first off the starting blocks on these occasions, you're unlikely to win this race consistently.

In short, then, the EMH says that no one can beat the market in the sense of earning a consistently abnormal return, unless they have insider information. In a way, then, we're back to *Deal or no Deal*. If you're a contestant on the show, there's always a chance that you will walk away with the big prize (£250,000 in the UK), but it is highly unlikely. You're much more likely to walk away with the average payment, which is much less. Of course, in the event that you were a contestant on the programme, it is highly unlikely that someone from the TV company would be willing to tell you where the money was located, as that would be deeply unethical, so you can't benefit from insider information. What you're left with is a guessing game, where the money is distributed at random in various boxes. The random aspect of the money boxes applies also to stock prices, which brings us neatly to our next topic. This is the observation that patterns in price behaviour are essentially random and no one can actually beat the market on the basis of previous patterns in price. In the next section we consider more explicit definitions of market efficiency and what they imply.

## Key concepts

- [ ] **Abnormal returns** are returns greater than normal market returns
- [ ] **Insider information** is information that is known only inside the company and is not available to the general public
- [ ] An **efficient market** means that prices fairly reflect all information almost instantaneously

## 3.5 Specific definitions of market efficiency

### 3.5.1 Weak form market efficiency

Technical analysts believe in their powers to find patterns in share prices with which they can predict future price in order to make profitable trades. This is in contrast to academics, who tend to believe in the EMH, which says that they have no such power. Technical analysts, or 'chartists', believe that there is information content in past prices. That is, patterns in prices observed in the past will be repeated and therefore they can help to predict the future. On the basis of previously observed pattern, technical analysts constantly scan price data looking for repeats to emerge. They devise simple or complex rules designed to signal buy or sell. Technical traders attribute much significance to patterns, such as those shown in Figure 3.1.

These are what are called resistance and support lines. Technical analysts argue that these lines put a 'ceiling' or maximum on price and 'floor', or impose a minimum, on price – that is, until there is a 'breakout', when a new resistance and support line are established.

Another common technical trading pattern is the head and shoulders, which is shown in Figure 3.2. The head and shoulders pattern is argued by technical analysts as indicating when a market has 'peaked', or, in the case of the inverse head and shoulders, when it has 'bottomed out'.

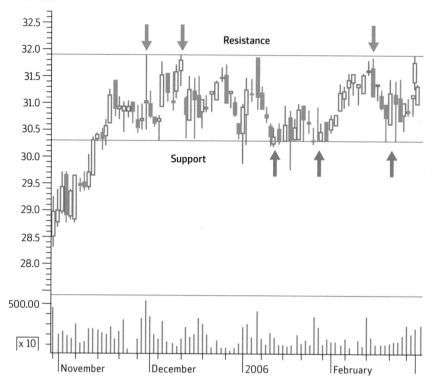

Figure 3.1 A typical technical analysis diagram showing what technical analysts believe is a current maximum and minimum for price fluctuation
*Source*: chart courtesy of MetaStock.

Figure 3.2 Technical analysis diagram showing a 'head and shoulders' pattern (market top) and an inverse 'head and shoulders' (market bottom)
*Source*: chart courtesy of MetaStock.

Sceptics argue that the patterns that technical analysts claim to see are just random fluctuations due to constant information update which leads to more or less continuous trading in popular stocks. Even supposing the patterns did contain valuable information, the information advantage would be lost almost instantaneously, as the rest of the market would notice, as well, and rush in to trade. Thus, technical analysis should not generate abnormal profit under the weak form version of the EMH.

For years, technical analysis was simply dismissed as irrational by financial economists. However, the more recent research has reached some surprising conclusions, which is that there may be some value in technical analysis. For example, Lo *et al.* (2000) published an article giving qualified support to the technique in the most prestigious journal in finance, the *Journal of Finance*. Your authors have also published research in this area (Fyfe *et al.* 1999, 2005; Marney *et al.* 2008). Our findings suggest that apparent abnormal profits from technical trading may well be possible. However, even this is only when one does not allow for risk. As we know, return and risk always go together, and what ultimately matters is **return relative to risk**. Our calculations suggest that, although superficially technical trading might earn abnormal profits, once you take the risks into account, the abnormal profits disappear.

In summary, then, weak form market efficiency means that there should be no discernible pattern in share price which allows prediction of future share price and the possibility of abnormal profit, or, more specifically, abnormal return relative to risk, and, on the whole, the empirical evidence tends to support this proposition. What about other information concerning the company itself – would that help 'beat the market'? We consider this in the next section. First, however, consider your own ability to predict the future, by referring to the learning activity below.

## Active learning activity 3.6

### Can the past predict the future?

Think about what happened to you last Friday. Does this help you to predict what will happen next Friday? How sure can you be? How credible is the proposition that you can exactly predict what will happen next Friday?

## Key concepts

☐ **Technical analysis**, also known as chartism, is the practice of searching for exploitable patterns in share data. It is useless if markets are weak form efficient

## 3.5.2 Semi-strong form market efficiency

Semi-strong form market efficiency is the idea that no publicly available information can be used to beat the market to make abnormal profit. This includes both past price information and any information on a firm such as accounts, marketing reports and news stories about management successes or problems within the firm. Analysis of the firm's worth, and therefore the correct value of shares using this approach, is known as **fundamental analysis**. Fundamental analysis is carried out by professional analysts who examine the performance and trading prospects of a particular firm or company sector and produce reports that rate a share as a buy, sell or hold. The reports produced by analysts may influence the decisions of professional or private investors as to whether to buy or sell shares in a particular company. Analysts come in two categories. There is the sell-side who put out research recommendations on behalf of the stockbrokers and investment banks they work for; their recommendations are often reproduced in the press. Then there's the much lower profile buy-side who work for an investment institution and play a role in stock selection. This particular group is more important for the investor relations department.

### 3.5.2.1 *Can fundamental analysis beat the market? Event study evidence*

The usual method of testing for semi-strong efficiency is to undertake studies of how prices react to events. Clearly, a fundamental analyst's buy/sell/hold recommendations are a matter of public knowledge. The question is: does this recommendation allow one to beat the market? From the available empirical evidence, the answer to this question would appear to be 'no'. First, any given analyst will not be alone. There will be other market participants using the same publicly available information, and in an efficient market this will be factored into the price almost instantaneously. Thus, the analyst will be unable to beat the market or to help his clients to beat the market by 'being ahead of the game'.

The alleged speed of reaction of the efficient marker, and hence the inability of the fundamental analyst to beat the market, is borne out by event studies. The term events refers to a piece of news that markets will normally regard as being fundamentally significant in its ability to change the correct valuation of the share in question.

Examples of events can be takeovers, earnings announcements, stock splits and political events. Researchers examine the reaction of prices to such events and determine whether or not the reaction is significant (this is measured by statistical significance). The general conclusion is that not only do stock prices quickly incorporate the news of events, but also the market appears to anticipate the information, and most of the price adjustment is complete before the event is revealed to the market. When news is released, the remaining price adjustment takes place rapidly and accurately.

Again, we have found that even fundamental analysis cannot beat the market. What about insider information? We consider this in the next section on strong form market efficiency.

## Practical implications for managers

### Creative accounting

The EMH implies that creative accounting techniques are useless. The market cannot be fooled by (legal) manipulation of accounting data if there are no cash flow consequences.

Furthermore, in an efficient market it does not matter when companies sell stocks. No one can predict what will happen in the future, and therefore, it is impossible to pick the 'best' time to issue securities. Companies can sell as many shares as they want without depressing the price. There is no price pressure effect. The company's share price will reflect the net present value of the company's future cash flows, so managers must only ensure that all investments are expected to exceed the company's cost of capital.

## Key concept

☐ **Fundamental analysis** is the practice of studying current information, such as company accounts, to try to discover exploitable information. If markets are semi-strong efficient, then fundamental analysis will not yield information that will allow an investor to beat the market.

### 3.5.3 Strong form market efficiency

In a previous section, we argued that in order to beat the market, one would have to have information that the market didn't have. That is to say, one would have to have **inside information**. The strong form of the EMH says that the market is so efficient that not even insider information can beat the market. Even the very act of trying to buy or sell on the basis of private information unknown to the market, in general, would alert the market. Though the market was not privy to the private information, it would know that something was motivating any transaction one undertook on the basis of private information and would adjust the price instantaneously, thereby cancelling any advantage.

This is clearly a rather extreme form of the EMH, and the evidence does not support it. The fact that it is possible to make excess returns from privately held information is further supported by the fact that insider trading is illegal in most countries, as it conveys an unfair advantage on the holder of the information. Take the experience of Martha Stewart. Martha Stewart is famous in the US and beyond for her TV shows on the domestic arts and home craft, particularly interior decor. It is hard to imagine such a homely wholesome national icon ending up in prison. But this is what happened when the US Securities and Exchange Commission (SEC) alleged that Martha Stewart had been warned by her friend Sam Waksal that his company ImClone's cancer drug had been rejected by the Food and Drug Administration. The SEC maintained that the warning came before the information was made public and allowed Stewart to sell her shares in ImClone before the price plummeted. She was subsequently imprisoned on charges relating to her alleged obstruction of the subsequent investigation of the insider trade from October 2004 to March 2005. She was also fined $195,000 by the SEC.

Stewart's case illustrates that allegations of insider trading can lead to very serious trouble. The rules on insider trading are in place because the market is probably not strong form efficient, giving insiders an unfair advantage.

## 3.6  Summary

We started this chapter by considering the stock market. The stock market may have a big impact on our lives and the general economy. Stock markets were argued to be inherently unpredictable in both levels and in volatility and the reasons for these features were examined.

The chapter then went on to consider the main debt and equity markets. The fundamental characteristics and functions of each type of market was considered in turn.

It was observed that the financial markets are, essentially, markets for corporate equity, or markets for corporate, governmental and institutional debt. The functions and key features of these markets are: to allow firms to obtain funds and grow, to facilitate the allocation of capital to its most productive uses, to provide a central point for those who wish to invest and those who wish to borrow, and to provide a means for companies to raise funds. In addition they provide a means for investors to choose investments according to their risk and return profiles, to enable holders of financial instruments to sell speedily and cheaply and to allow them to value their financial assets easily. Moreover, the financial markets facilitate diversification of risk, and facilitate improvements in corporate behaviour because of the high level of public awareness of the business and the considerable financial reporting and other disclosure requirements.

In the course of our discussion we outlined the following specific sub-topics: the advantages to firms of debt, the nature of bonds and the role of credit rating agencies. We then went on to discover the basics of pricing bonds and pricing equity. Finally, having established what a fundamental price for a share ought to look like in theory, we then went on to consider whether shares are priced properly in practice; i.e. are stock markets efficient? Can you beat stock markets by having a better guess of what stock prices ought to be? The evidence suggests not, unless you have insider information.

## Case study

### EFG

Source [Adapted from CIMA MAFS, May 2006 (Ogilvie 2008)]
*This case study will help you to apply what you have learned throughout the chapter.*

EFG is a South American entity specialising in providing information systems solutions to large corporate bodies. It is going through a period of rapid expansion and requires additional funds to finance the long-term working capital needs of the business.

EFG has issued one million ordinary shares, which are listed on the local stock market at a current market price of $15 per share. These currently pay a dividend of $1.40 per share. EFG also has $10 million of bank borrowings.

It is estimated that a further $3 million is required to satisfy the funding requirements of the business for the next 5-year period beginning 1 July 2006. Two major institutional shareholders have indicated that they are not prepared to invest further in EFG at the present time. The directors are therefore considering various forms of debt finance. Three alternative structures are under discussion:

- A 5-year unsecured bank loan at a fixed interest rate of 7% per annum
- A 5-year unsecured bond with a face value of $1,000 and a coupon rate of 5% per annum. The current yield to maturity on this class of bond is 6%
- A new share issue

There have been lengthy boardroom discussions on the relative merits of each instrument and you, as Finance Director, have been asked to address the following queries:

Senor A: 'The bank loan would seem to be more expensive than the unsecured bond. Is this actually the case?'

Senor B: 'Surely the share issue is better? After all we don't need to pay a dividend.'

Senor C: 'What happens if interest rates fall? Surely that will have an impact on the bond prices? How will that affect our company?'

### Required

1. Write a response to Senors A, B and C, directors of EFG, discussing the issues raised and advising on the most appropriate financing instrument for EFG. In your answer, include calculations of:
   - the impact of any interest rate rise;
   - the advantages of debt versus equity.

   Ignore tax.

2. Advise a prospective investor in the 5-year unsecured bond issued by EFG on what information he should expect to be provided with and what further analysis he should undertake in order to assess the creditworthiness of the proposed investment.

 **Questions**

1. What are debt and equity, and what is the fundamental distinction between the two?

2. What are the potential advantages of debt relative to equity for the firm?

3. Write short notes defining four money market instruments.

4. Why is company equity not issued in the money market?

5. What are the four characteristics that define a bond?

6. What is the role of credit rating agencies in financial markets?

7. What is an annuity cash flow?

8. How can the annuity factor help in the valuation of bond cash flow?

9. What is a perpetuity cash flow?

10. How does the concept of perpetuity cash flow help in the valuation of a share with a constant dividend?

11. Outline and discuss the efficient markets hypothesis with particular reference to the techniques of technical analysis and fundamental analysis.

12. Why is insider trading illegal in most countries?

13. What should be the price of a share that offers a yearly dividend of 20p if it is discounted at 20%?

14. Calculate prices for a bond with maturity of 3 years, coupon rate of 8%, annual coupon payments and a face value of £100 at the following bond interest rates (yields to maturity).

    a)   8%

    b)   10%

    c)   6%

15. How would each of the bonds (a), (b) and (c) be described relative to their par values?

 **Online resource centre**

 **Further reading**

De Bondt, W.F.M. and Thaler, R. (1985) Does the stock market overreact? *Journal of Finance*, **40**(3):793–805.

   This may be regarded as one of the seminal articles in the behavioural finance literature. It demonstrates how investors systematically overreact to unexpected and dramatic news events.

Fama, E. (1970) Efficient capital markets: a review of theory and empirical work. *Journal of Finance*, **25**:383–417.

Fama, E. (1991) Efficient capital markets: II. *Journal of Finance*, **46**:1575–1617.

Two classic articles that review the theory and evidence pertaining to the EMH.

Shiller, R.J. (2000) *Irrational Exuberance*. Princeton University Press, Princeton, New Jersey.

A very readable book which explains why bubbles might arise.

Wong, S.M.L. (2006) China's stock market: a marriage of capitalism and socialism. *Cato Journal*, **26**(3).

Available at http://www.cato.org/pubs/journal/cj26n3/cj26n3-1.pdf. A good introduction to the Chinese stock market.

# Internet references

http://www.behaviouralfinance.net/
Links to numerous papers in the area of behavioural finance.

http://www.ethicalcorp.com/
An independent company providing competitive intelligence for business sustainability.

http://www.londonstockexchange.com/en-gb/
The official home page of the London Stock Exchange.

# Suggestions for group work

Students should explore the differences in how stock prices behave between one mature stock market and one less mature stock market. Each group should prepare a report that details the main differences between the two stock markets and the reasons for these differences.

# Suggestions for presentations

Within behavioural finance, many other effects and biases have been identified such as 'Hot Hand', 'The Curse of Knowledge' and the 'Disposition Effect', to name but a few. Each student should select one effect or bias from the relevant literature and prepare a 5-minute presentation which details the effect and considers how it contradicts the EMH. Be creative and try to use appropriate visual aids (e.g. images from the internet) to encapsulate the essence of the effect.

A useful resource is http://www.behaviouralfinance.net/.

# 4 Valuation

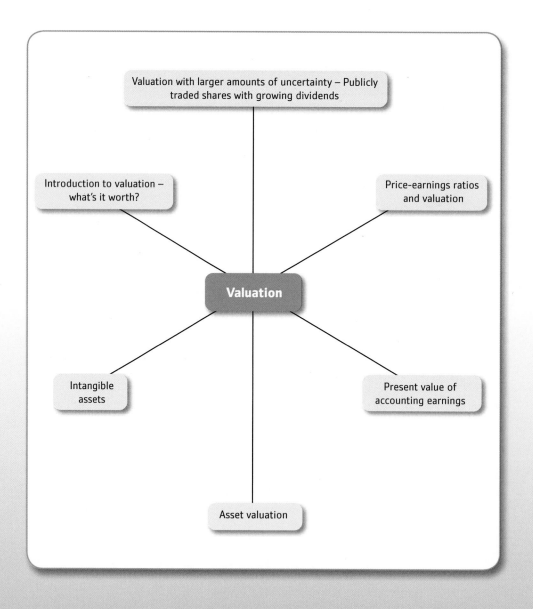

Valuation with larger amounts of uncertainty – Publicly traded shares with growing dividends

Introduction to valuation – what's it worth?

Price-earnings ratios and valuation

**Valuation**

Intangible assets

Present value of accounting earnings

Asset valuation

## Knowledge-based learning objectives

When you have completed this chapter you will be able to:

✓ Work out a price–earnings (p–e) ratio

✓ Calculate a valuation based on discounted free cash flow

✓ Estimate a market to book ratio

✓ Explain the significance of intangible assets and the difficulty involved in the measurement of intangibles

## Skills-based learning objectives development

✓ Business and financial environment consciousness: you should have developed an appreciation of valuation and how it is applicable not only on the stock market but also in business generally.

✓ Numerical skills: you should have developed the ability to calculate a p–e ratio, an estimate of free cash flow and a value to book ratio.

✓ Analytical thinking and problem-solving skills: you should have developed an understanding of the three principles of valuation, namely earnings, assets and discounted cash flow (DCF).

✓ Problem-solving skills: you should have developed the ability to apply the three principles of valuation to general valuation problems.

✓ Critical-thinking skills: you should be able to compare and contrast the three basic approaches in terms of their benefits and drawbacks.

✓ Managerial soft skills: you should have developed the ability to know how the approaches to be discussed would apply in organisations you have worked in or with which you are familiar.

✓ Interpersonal skills: you should have developed your ability to present your work clearly both verbally and in writing and to interact with others effectively upon completion of the end of chapter questions.

## Online resource centre

Visit the Online Resource Centre that accompanies this book to listen to a podcast of the authors explaining the practicalities of valuing a company coming to market for the first time.
**www.oxfordtextbooks.co.uk/marney**

### Charlie finds out that valuation is not a science

Kate and Charlie have commissioned a firm of Management Consultants, Chargealot, to advise them on how much to bid for a small privately owned company, Community Loans Ltd, who specialise in providing loans to small companies in emerging countries. Grabbing a quick coffee each, they sit down to listen to the presentation by the Chargealot's team leader. Five hundred PowerPoint slides later, Charlie feels as if his head is about to burst. He decides to start off with a simple question.

'So, just to summarise, what price exactly are you suggesting we pay for Community Loans?'

The team leader looks taken aback by this question and answers 'As I've just explained, there is no exact price. It all depends on what set of assumptions we base our analysis on, what time frame is under consideration, and what type of valuation methodology we utilise, relative negotiation power, the economic paradigm. ...'

By this point, Charlie is only hearing 'blah, blah, blah. ...' He decides to interrupt – after all, he is paying these people an absolute fortune. 'OK, OK, I appreciate all the work you have done, but let's just get down to the whole point of this meeting – can you tell me the price?'

The team leader starts to look panicked and glances at his colleagues. Unfortunately, they are all busy studying their notes and no one looks up. 'Well,' he tries again. 'It really depends on all of the factors I mentioned in my presentation. Perhaps you would like me to run through it again?'

Charlie now feels puzzled and wonders if he is missing some blindingly obvious point. 'OK,' he begins, 'taking all of the issues, assumptions, paradigms and what-have-you into account, what is the fair price to pay?'

To Charlie's astonishment, the team leader replies, 'That's the whole problem. There is no definitive 'fair price'. It all depends. ...'

Charlie cuts him off before he relaunches into some further pointless ramble. He stands up and exclaims, 'Just tell me the price! What are you recommending that we pay for Community Loan? Why can't you give me a straight answer?!'

## 4.1  Introduction to valuation – what's it worth?

### 4.1.1  The purpose of valuation

Companies are valued for a variety of purposes:

1. The valuation of companies is a basic input into takeovers, mergers and acquisitions calculations.

2. It is necessary to value firms for the purposes of initial public offering to the stock market.

3. Valuation is important from a strategic and executive point of view. How much value does each business unit create? Are there any business units that should be revamped or closed because they are creating negative value? Which strategic units are likely to contribute most in terms of growth of value? What are the drivers of value? Which units, personnel and managers are most successful at creating value?

Although there are many types of valuation approach, the main methods that we shall discuss in this chapter are:

1. Discounted cash flow (DCF).
2. Income or earnings – where the firm is valued on some multiple of accounting income or earnings or, in some cases, on some other multiple.
3. Balance sheet – where the firm is valued in terms of its assets.

We have already encountered DCF methods Chapter 2, in which we considered investment opportunities in terms of future cash flows relative to the degree to which these future cash flows should be discounted by the opportunity cost of capital. Earnings-based measures estimate value as some multiple of a company's earnings. Balance sheet or asset-based valuations are concerned with the sale or replacement value of physical or financial assets. First, though, let us consider DCF methods.

## 4.1.2 Discounted cash flow methods

As you may have gathered by now, a primary function in finance is to establish the value of assets. An important principle, which was clearly established in Chapter 2, is that the value of a project is equal to the **present value** of its future cash flows *minus* the value of any initial current investment. That is, the value of a project to a company is equal to its **net present value**. The **present value technique** which was used to establish the value of an investment project has significance well beyond the topic of investment appraisal and capital budgeting. Indeed, it is a fundamental principle of finance that the value of any financial asset can be determined as the present value of cash flows from the asset. The only drawback in using this principle is that it presupposes that we know exactly the following variables:

1. What all the cash flows are going to be in the future;
2. What risks are implied in earning these cash flows, and therefore
3. What exactly the appropriate discount rate is for the cash flows.

## Active learning activity 4.1

**Investment in yourself**

Your investment in attending a course of study can be regarded as an investment in yourself. Think about all the cash flows associated with you doing your university course. Write them down and say how certain you are about each cash flow.

For certain types of financial instrument, such as **bonds**, we do have most of the information we need with a fairly high degree of certainty. However, for other classes of financial asset much of this information is not known with the same degree of certainty. For example, there is less certainty about the value of firms with publicly quoted **shares** (also known as **equities**), because there is greater uncertainty about the relevant cash flows and risks. This observation applies with even greater force to private firms which are not publicly quoted on the stock market. In Chapter 3, we looked at the basic principles of valuing a bond and valuing a share. In the next section we look at building on this knowledge and moving up the scale of uncertainty to look at the valuation of firms with publicly quoted shares and growing dividends.

## Practical implications for managers

**Discounted cash flows – where to start**

In real life, managers will rarely face the certainties involved in the typical DCF problem. However, it is a good place to start, i.e. in a relatively predictable world, what would the value of a project, a firm or a financial instrument be? The information can always be adapted and updated as the future unfolds.

## Key concepts

- [ ] A **DCF valuation** is determined by cash flow, risk and the discount rate
- [ ] The **main valuation methods** are based on DCF, income/earnings or assets/balance sheet

## 4.2 Valuation with larger amounts of uncertainty – publicly traded shares with growing dividends

As we have seen in a previous chapter, bond valuation benefits from being a well-defined valuation with relatively small amounts of uncertainty. Share valuation as we found was less well defined and subject to greater uncertainty. We now consider share valuation with growing dividends. This, it will transpire, is even less certain and less well defined as a valuation problem.

It is a slightly more complicated matter to work out what the share price ought to be if the dividend is growing. First, we have to distinguish between dividends in different time periods. Thus the current dividend is called $d_0$ while the dividend in the next time period, i.e. next year, is $d_1$ and so on. Second, we have to incorporate an estimate for growth in dividends in our calculations. We will look at how to calculate such a figure in what follows below. However, provided that such a figure is obtainable, then the expression for the value or price of a share is as follows:

$$P_0 = d_1/(r - g)$$

where $d_1$ is the dividend in the next time period (e.g. next year), r is the discount rate and g is the rate at which dividends are growing.

You don't absolutely need to know how to derive this formula; however, for those who are curious we include it as an Appendix at the end of the chapter. It should be noted that an important assumption when using this expression is that the rate of discount is greater than the rate of growth of dividends. Thus this approach to share valuation would not be appropriate where dividends were growing rapidly. The value for the dividend in the next time period is usually estimated by taking the current dividend and the growth rate as follows:

$$d_0 = d_0 \times (1 + g)$$

Hence the expression for share price valuation with dividend growth is often written as

$$P_0 = d_0 \times (1 + g)/(r - g)$$

To illustrate the use of this formula, let's assume some numbers. Suppose that the current dividend is £10, the expectation is that dividends will grow at 5% p.a. and the discount rate is 10%. In this case, the current price is as follows:

$$P_0 = £10 \times (1 + 0.05)/(0.1 - 0.05) = 10.5/0.05 = £210$$

Note the substantial difference from the case where there is no anticipated increase in dividends. In the latter case, the value of the share is only £100. Even if it were only anticipated that dividends would be growing by 1%, the appropriate price for the share would be £112. Clearly, the assumptions that are made about future growth in dividends can have a significant effect on share price.

The question arises of how we make any assumptions about dividend growth in the first place. The most straightforward thing to do is simply to work out the growth rate based on recent dividend patterns. In order to do this, we use the simple formula for calculating returns, as returns and growth rates are really just the same thing, i.e. any return tells you how much your investment has grown, so it is a specific type of growth rate. This is illustrated in the following screenshot.

| 1 | Year | 2005 | 2006 | 2007 | 2008 | 2009 | 2010 |
|---|---|---|---|---|---|---|---|
| 2 | Time t | t - 5 | t - 4 | t - 3 | t - 2 | t - 1 | t = 0 |
| 3 | Dividend | £1.00 | £1.06 | £1.04 | £1.08 | £1.07 | £1.11 |
| 4 | | | | | | | |
| 5 | | | | | | | |
| 6 | | | | | | | |

Screenshot 4.1 Example of dividend growth

We normally concentrate on the values at the start and end of the chosen sequence, unless we have strong reason to believe that these are unrepresentative. Applying this formula we calculate the rate of growth from 2005 to 2010 as $\sqrt[5]{(1.11/1)} - 1 = 1.021 = 2.1\%$ p.a.

It should be noted of course that any growth rate estimated using this method will be an approximation. Firms are unlikely to sustain rates of growth of dividend of more than 3 or 4% for long periods. Indeed, given that in countries that have reached economic maturity, such as the UK, Japan and the US, the economy, in terms of real gross domestic product (GDP), usually grows by between 2.5% and 4% p.a., it would be impossible for any company in these countries to sustain earnings and dividend growth of more than 4% over very long periods without coming to dominate the whole economy – which of course is highly unlikely.

 Active learning activity 4.2

Infinite prices?

Suppose we have a share with a dividend of £10, growth rate of 20% and discount rate of 10%. What is the price of the share?

Suppose now that the same share has a growth rate of 10%. What is the price of the share now?

In the context of company growth, it is often the case that companies go through a life cycle of temporarily rapid growth followed by maturity and much slower growth. In this case, one must account for the abnormal growth period separately, and then add it to a valuation based on more normal growth. Suppose, for example, that the current dividend for Douglas Adams (DA) is 100p and this is expected to grow at 17% for the next 4 years, as summarised in the following screenshot.

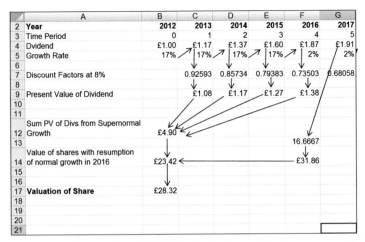

Screenshot 4.2 Dividend valuation with abnormal growth

We assume that the current year is 2012 and the dividend of £1 has just been paid. The screenshot shows the effect of extraordinary growth of 17% on the dividends for 2013–2016. Thereafter, the growth in dividend is assumed to be a more modest 2%. The valuation proceeds as follows. First of all we take the sum of the present value of dividend for the years of extraordinary growth. We assume that the appropriate discount rate for DA's risk class is 8%. This gives us a value for DA as follows:

Working to an accuracy of two decimal places, the present value of the 4 years of extraordinary growth is £1.08 + £1.17 + £1.27 + £1.38. Using the formula d/(r − g), the value of continuous growth of 2% from 2017 is £31.86. Discounting this at 8% back to 2012 gives £23.42. Thus the share is worth £28.32.[1]

Until now, we have assumed that the necessary input data, namely growth rate and discount rate, are freely available. One of the most troublesome and controversial areas involved in this kind of valuation is what exactly are the appropriate values for 'r' and 'g'. The discount rate for equity shares can be estimated from the rate of return demanded by those who supply the firm with equity. This in turn can be calculated using the Capital Asset Pricing Model (CAPM). The estimation of the CAPM is examined in Chapter 5, but we mention it at this juncture to make the point that estimation of the CAPM and hence the discount rate on equity is not without its uncertainties. However, the potential controversies surrounding potential growth rates eclipse this by an order of magnitude.

A common approach to estimating dividend growth is the one used in Screenshot 4.1, which is simple extrapolation. However, this is thought by some to be unscientific and therefore has resulted in attempts at more sophisticated analysis, such as the Gordon dividend valuation model. Gordon was a major pioneer of the method discussed in this section. However, his model advocates a particular approach to estimation of the growth rate which is as follows. The growth rate for a pure equity firm (whose capital is all raised from equity, with no debt in the capital structure) is determined as follows:

$$g = ROE \times b$$

where g is the growth rate of dividends $= \sqrt[n]{\dfrac{Last\ Year's\ Div}{Base\ Year\ Div}}$ , b is the retention ratio $(1 \geq b \geq = 0)$ and ROE is the return on equity capital.

Suppose, for example, that ROE is 20%. Therefore, net of expenses, earnings equivalent to 20% of the equity capital base would be expected every year, for an all-equity firm. Thus if equity capital is £100 million in Year 0, earnings of £20 million would be expected in Year 1. This additional equity can either be retained for future investment or distributed as dividend. If the whole £20 million is distributed as dividend in Year 1, there will be no retained earnings and no increase in the capital base. Therefore next year, earnings will also represent 20% ROE on an unchanged investment capital base of £100 million and dividends will be unchanged at £20 million Thus there is zero growth in dividends if no earnings are retained for expansion.

As we have seen if the retention ratio, b, is zero, then dividend growth, g, is also zero. Paradoxically, given the diametric opposite case, with a retention ratio, b, of 100%, dividend growth will also be zero. However, this is because no dividends are distributed and, by definition, dividend growth is zero. Suppose the retention ratio is close to 100%, however – say 90% or 0.9. Out of the £20 million earnings available at the start of Year 1, £18 million will be retained and added to invested capital. By the start of Year 2, earnings should amount to £118 million × 20% or £23.6 million. Of this £23.6 million, £21.24 million will be retained while £2.36 million is paid in dividend. This is illustrated in the following screenshot which extends the calculation to Year 3 from Year 0.

| T | | Capital Base | Earnings | Retained Earnings | Dividends | | Parameters | | |
|---|---|---|---|---|---|---|---|---|---|
| 1 | | | | | | | | | |
| 2 | 0 | 100 | 20 | 18 | 2 | | ROE | Retention b | Divs 1-b |
| 3 | 1 | 118 | 23.6 | 21.24 | 2.36 | | 20% | 0.9 | 0.1 |
| 4 | 2 | 139.24 | 27.848 | 25.0632 | 2.7848 | | | | |
| 5 | 3 | 164.3032 | 32.86064 | 29.5746 | 3.28606 | | | | |
| 6 | | | | | | | | | |
| 7 | T | GROWTH RATES OF THE ABOVE | | | | | | | |
| 8 | 1 | 0.18 | 0.18 | 0.18 | 0.18 | | | | |
| 9 | 2 | 0.18 | 0.18 | 0.18 | 0.18 | | | | |
| 10 | 3 | 0.18 | 0.18 | 0.18 | 0.18 | | | | |
| 11 | | | | | | | | | |
| 12 | | | | | | | | | |

Screenshot 4.3 Dividends and dividend growth with high retention ratio

Two points of comparison should be made between the previous situation of zero retention and the current situation of 90% retention. First, with zero retained earnings absolute dividends were bigger, but with zero growth. Second, in the current situation of 90% retention, earnings, retained earnings and dividends are all growing at the rate 18%. Thus, there is a tradeoff between absolute size of current dividend and growth of current dividend. With a much lower retention ratio, dividends would be bigger, but growth would be slower, as we can see in the next screenshot which illustrates the effect on dividend and dividend growth of a retention ratio of 0.1. As we can see, the dividends are much bigger, but dividend growth at 2% is much lower.

| T | Capital Base | Earnings | Retained Earnings | Dividends | Parameters | | |
|---|---|---|---|---|---|---|---|
| 1 | | | | | | | |
| 2 | 0 | 100 | 20 | 2 | 18 | ROE | Retention b Divs 1-b |
| 3 | 1 | 102 | 20.4 | 2.04 | 18.36 | | 20% | 0.1 | 0.9 |
| 4 | 2 | 104.04 | 20.808 | 2.0808 | 18.7272 | | | |
| 5 | 3 | 106.1208 | 21.22416 | 2.12242 | 19.1017 | | | |
| 6 | | | | | | | | |
| 7 | T | GROWTH RATES OF THE ABOVE | | | | | | |
| 8 | 1 | 0.02 | 0.02 | 0.02 | 0.02 | | | |
| 9 | 2 | 0.02 | 0.02 | 0.02 | 0.02 | | | |
| 10 | 3 | 0.02 | 0.02 | 0.02 | 0.02 | | | |
| 11 | | | | | | | | |
| 12 | | | | | | | | |

Screenshot 4.4 Dividends and dividend growth with low retention ratio

In the Gordon model, we have what would appear to be a fairly scientific approach to the determination of the growth rate of dividends, which makes use of balance sheet figures rather than simple extrapolation of previous dividends. Indeed, the approach used in the Gordon growth model is taken to much greater lengths in financial analysis, which attempts to pin down the growth rate precisely through forensic analysis of company accounts in order to determine exactly:

1. The quantity of resources retained and reinvested within the business.
2. The rate of return earned on those retained resources.

Nevertheless, financial analysis and the Gordon growth model run into the same problem:

1. The information is not precise and assumptions have to be made where there are gaps.
2. This is particularly so because financial accounts are drawn up for the purposes of accurate financial recording of the changing value of assets versus liabilities, and not for measuring incremental cash flow.

Thus any financial analysis approach will not have direct access to the process that creates value and will have to make assumptions where information is missing. Even the Gordon growth model itself makes the assumption of constant ROE over time – which is quite a strong assumption. Financial analysis often makes use of many different kinds of 'metrics' to get at the firm's underlying ability to create wealth. But again, these can be highly dependent on the underlying assumptions made.

In this sense, apparently more sophisticated approaches such as financial analysis and the Gordon growth model suffer from the same problems as the simple dividend model. In the simple dividend model, the growth rate is calculated by the use of crude extrapolation of past growth rates of dividends. In the more sophisticated approach, the extrapolation may be more subtle and sophisticated, but it remains assumption-based extrapolation with the attendant problems of this approach, viz that the assumptions are correct and not oversimplified and that what happened in the past will continue to happen in the future.

We make two final observations before we leave this section. First, we have talked mainly of **share** valuation, rather than **firm** valuation. However, it is a relatively straightforward matter to put a value on the firm itself. For example, in the case of a firm with publicly quoted equity, the value of the firm is equal to the sum of the value of the shares, i.e.

$$V_E = \text{(Price per share)} \times \text{(No. of shares issued)}$$

where $V_E$ is the value of equity

What we have calculated is the surplus value created by the firm, which in theory should equal the difference between assets and liabilities. This is the basic price that would be offered by an acquirer for the firm, though in practice a premium is often required on top of current market share price. The implicit assumption, of course, is that the acquirer adopts any debt or liabilities. Remember that the value of equity is not the same as the value of firm capital, i.e. the sum of equity *and* debt.

Second, the techniques outlined here and in the next section would also be of use to value companies whose shares were not quoted on a stock market. All that would be necessary would be to calculate future cash flow from income. Thus, for example, if we know the firm's risk and discount rate, and if there is no significant growth of earnings expected, we could value the firm on the basis of annual **free cash flow** divided by the appropriate rate of discount. Alternatively, we could use dividend valuation or price earning (p-e) valuation. However, whatever method we use, with the exception of asset-based methods, we should discount for illiquidity. This is because we have in each case essentially built up an equity value. However, equity values are more uncertain in the case of private companies with illiquid shares. Damodar (2005), for example, suggests a discount of 6% on the pure equity value of smaller companies with illiquid shares. We turn in the next section to the last mentioned of these valuation topics, p–e valuation.

## Practical implications for managers

### Dividend valuation

The most straightforward way to value the shares of a firm is using a constant dividend approach. The value of the firm is then just the aggregate value of the shares.

Extreme caution should be used when assuming growth rates for dividend valuation purposes, as small variations in the growth rate can lead to large variations in estimated value.

## Key concepts

- ☐ **Super-normal growth** – where the company and its future dividend is growing at a rate well above average, which is unsustainable in the long run
- ☐ **Steadily growing dividend** increases by a percentage amount each year
- ☐ **Dividend valuation with a growing dividend** – the formula here is slightly more involved than for simple zero growth dividend valuation
- ☐ The **Gordon assumptions** – which were an attempt to find a scientific basis for future growth in earnings and dividends

## 4.3 Price–earnings ratios and valuation

It is possible that you may never before have heard of the dividend valuation model. However, anyone even vaguely acquainted with the machinations of the stock market may well have heard of those mysterious things p–e ratios. The p–e ratio is just the ratio of share price to earnings. It is similar to the DCF approach in that the valuation of the firm's worth is based on potential future earnings and therefore future dividends. However, the critical difference is that net present value is based on **free cash flow**, while p–e ratios are based on **reported earnings in company accounts**. Basically the p–e ratio tells us how much the market is prepared to pay for each pound, dollar or yen's worth of firm earnings. The p–e ratio has the advantage of giving a more direct and simple indication of stock market evaluation than the stock price.

Suppose, for example, that Ziphead Babblebrix (ZB) is valued at £100 per share, as is S Larta Breakfast (SLB). This might cause us to assume that both firms are valued by the market as exactly the same. However, this is not the case, as the relative share prices tell us nothing about relative worth. In order to say something about relative worth, we need to have the information represented by p–e ratio. Thus, if it were to be discovered further that ZB has earnings of £25 per share, while SLB has earnings of £10 per share, this tells us something about the market's perception of the relative worth of these two shares. That is, the market is prepared to pay £10 for each £1 of SLB current earnings, while it is only prepared to pay £4 per pound for ZB's current earnings. The market's valuation of a company in terms of the worth of its current earnings is clearly related to its expectation of the company's future performance. The following factors will be taken into account by the stock market.

The first factor is potential growth in earnings and therefore growth in prospective dividend; the greater is the anticipated rate of growth of dividend, the higher would be the p–e ratio. The point was demonstrated in Section 4.2 with dividends. Faster anticipated growth in dividends led to a higher valuation of the firm's shares. For example, in the investment classic, *A Random Walk Down Wall Street*, professional investor and distinguished academic Burton Malkiel[2] illustrates the positive relationship between growth rates and p–e multiples by way of a number of examples:

> 'Thus, the company "Target" with a growth rate of 10% has a P/E [p–e] ratio of 20, while that of eBay with a growth rate of 25% has a P/E ratio of 50. eBay's earnings are valued more highly because they are expected to grow more quickly.'
>
> (Malkiel 2007, p. 113)

We will deal with risk in other chapters, but it is worth briefly stating here that the second factor that the stock market will take into account in determining price is risk, which is related to volatility of return, and is factored in to the discount rate. To refer to Malkiel once more:

> '... the bigger the swings – relative to the market as a whole – in an individual company's stock prices (or in its total yearly returns, including dividends), the greater the risk. For example, a nonswinger such as Johnson and Johnson gets the Good Housekeeping seal of approval for "widows and orphans". That's because its earnings do not decline much if at all during recessions and its dividend is secure. Thus when the market goes down 20%,

J&J usually trails with perhaps only a 10% decline. Thus the stock qualifies as one with less than average risk. Cisco Systems, on the other hand, has a very volatile past record, and it characteristically falls by 40% or more when the market declines by 20%. It is called a "flyer" or an investment that is a "businessman's risk".

(Malkiel 2007, p. 115)

A third factor in determining the p–e ratio is the dividend payout. There is no clear-cut relationship between dividend payout and p–e ratio as, for example, a high dividend payout can have advantages and disadvantages. The advantage is clearly that more cash is available now for the investor. The disadvantage is that less cash is being ploughed back into investment and therefore future growth of earnings will be low.

A fourth and final factor is the interest rate. When interest rates rise, future earnings are more heavily discounted and therefore shares are worth less. Furthermore, equities compete with bonds as a potential investment vehicle. At times of high interest rates, bonds have higher yields and therefore become more attractive to investors.

## Active learning activity 4.3

### Price–earnings ratio for Amazon.com

Find out the p–e ratios for Amazon.com from 2000 onwards. Explain what the very high p–e ratios imply.

The type of market analyst who uses p–e ratios often estimates the value of the firm using the dividend valuation technique outlined previously. That is:

$$P_0 = \frac{d_0(1+g)}{r-g}$$

This implies that the p–e ratio can be determined from the dividends–earnings ratio, a widely quoted statistic and financial ratio which can, for example, be found in the financial press. This is done as follows:

$$\frac{P_0}{E_0} = \left(\frac{d_0}{E_0}\right)\frac{(l+g)}{(r-g)}$$

or

$$\frac{P_0}{E_0} = (1-b) \times \frac{(l+g)}{(r-g)}$$

(The term $b$ is the retention ratio. The term '$(1-b)$' is the payout ratio. The discount rate, r, is sometimes written as $K_E$, as it represents the cost of equity; that is, the percentage return that must be given to those who buy the company's shares and provide equity capital.)

The p–e ratio method is in wide use in the financial community despite the possible drawbacks, which are as follows:

1. The value calculated is very sensitive to the assumption made about the growth rate, as with the techniques described in the previous section in the context of dividend as opposed to p–e valuation.

2. It is essentially a DCF technique, yet it uses accounting earnings. Accounting earnings do not represent free cash flow; however they can be adjusted to a free cash flow equivalent, as we will see below. Furthermore, the ratio of share price relative to accounting earnings may give a useful rough guide to share price relative to free cash flow.

3. Price-earnings-type analysis is often based on 'norms' for particular industries, types of firms and for the market as a whole. However, these norms are not as stable as may be thought.

As mentioned above in the context of dividend valuations, DCF-type valuations based on p–e ratios are very sensitive to assumptions about growth rates, as the following example from Malkiel (2007) illustrates. He describes the experience of Peter Williamson in trying to value an IBM share.

## Mini case study

### Growth rates for IBM

Source Peter Williamson, quoted in Malkiel 2007, p. 119

I began by forecasting growth in earnings per share of 16%. This was a little under the average for the previous ten years. ... I forecast a 16% growth rate for 10 years followed by indefinite growth at ... 3%. ... When I put all these numbers into the formula I got an intrinsic value of $172.94, about half current value.

It doesn't really seem sensible to predict only 10 years of above average growth for IBM, so I extended my 16% growth forecast to 20 years. Now the intrinsic value came to $432.66, well above the market.

1. Why is it so difficult to predict growth rates?
2. Over what time span should growth be forecast?
3. What factors do growth rates depend on?

Before leaving this section on p–e ratios, the last word must belong to Burton Malkiel:

'...The major fundamentals for these calculations are never known with certainty; they are only relatively crude estimates – perhaps one should say guesses – about what might happen in the future. ... There is I believe a fundamental indeterminateness about the value of common shares even in principle. God Almighty does not know the proper price–earnings multiple for a common stock.'

(Malkiel 2007, p.119)

In the next section we look at accounting information as a source for valuation purposes.

## Practical implications for managers

### Dividend valuation

P-e ratios are a useful shortcut to getting an approximate valuation of an unlisted company. If you have the p-e ratio of a similar listed company, you can factor in some downgrading for illiquidity of the unlisted company and multiply by earnings to get an approximate valuation.

## Key concepts

☐ The p–e ratio is the price of a share divided by its per share earnings (after tax)

☐ In general, the higher the potential growth, the higher the p–e ratio

☐ The higher the risk, the lower the p–e ratio

## 4.4 Present value of accounting earnings

Previously, we examined the standard method of valuing a share. We found that we could directly apply present value methods to come to a valuation of the share. By extension, the value of the firm could be estimated from the total value of its shares. However, not all firms have their shares listed on a stock market, and therefore it is useful to have alternative methods of valuation, based on company accounts rather than stock market valuations.

From this perspective, it might seem like almost a trivial problem to measure the value of the firm. One would simply extract the appropriate figure for accounting profit. Then it would just be a case of assessing the company's prospects and the sustainability of the accounting profit currently earned, or indeed the prospect of growth in accounting profit. It is universally recognised, however, that accounting profit may not be a good guide to underlying value for a number of reasons. First and foremost, accounting profit can vary considerably depending on the accounting conventions used. For example, consider the following mini case study.

## Mini case study

### Profit is in the eye of the beholder

Source Pratley 2002, copyright Guardian News & Media Ltd

Even now, debates rage over the accounts of FTSE 100 companies. Cable & Wireless has taken flak for the seemingly huge salary costs that are capitalised on its balance sheet rather than charged to its profit and loss account. Last year, the figure was £184m out of total capital expenditure of £1.4bn; in the previous year, the figure was £495m out of £2.4bn. ... Some conservative accountants would say that if an employee's salary is not a direct overhead then what is?

Provisions can also be made in the normal course of business, although here they have to be charged against profits. But the effect is still to flatter profits in future years. ... Cisco, for example, wrote down an astonishing $2.5bn of stock last year. When it returned to profitability this year, it collected plenty of plaudits but sceptics were not surprised – it is not hard to make a profit if you have already written down the cost of making that product.

1. Why might companies want to capitalise costs instead of charging to the profit and loss account?

2. What effects do provisions have on profits and thus on valuation?

Many companies do not adopt the same approach as Cable and Wireless in the capitalisation of wage costs. Although the accountancy world is gradually working towards standardisation, it is still the case that conventions can vary from country to country and indeed from firm to firm, and therefore accounting profit can be a variable and unreliable guide to underlying firm value.

A second problem with accounting profit is that it is relatively easy to take short-term measures to manipulate profit in order to 'boost the bottom line' in the short run, but these may be harmful to the value of the business in the long run. Thus, it can be relatively straightforward to boost profits simply by cutting back on expenditures such as marketing, advertising and training that may be critical to the survival of the business in the long run. Another well-known practice is to time the booking of cost and revenue so as to present the firm to its best advantage. An example of this way of presenting accounts can be found in the notable case of Enron. It was reported that Enron would delay reporting of any extraordinary surpluses by adding these to 'prudency reserves'. These prudency reserves could then be drawn on to flatter profits when times were less favourable, as illustrated in the following mini case study.

## Mini case study

### To be or not to be prudent?

'We made such an incredible amount of money we didn't want to recognize it all into earnings,' said the executive, who like others interviewed requested anonymity because of concern about being drawn into litigation. 'We were supposed to make $500 million in a quarter and we were doing it in a day.' Accounting experts said that the subjectivity of prudency reserves makes them susceptible to abuse. 'If you're using trading reserves as a mechanism for understating your positions in good times – and therefore not reporting profits – and later reporting the old profits in times that aren't as good, that would clearly be an abuse of the accounting rules,' said Lynn Turner, a professor at Colorado State University and the former chief accountant for the SEC.

1. Explain why Enron would not want to report making $500 million in a day.
2. What effect would wildly fluctuating earnings have on a company's valuation?

A third problem is that accounting profit does not take account of risk, unlike, for example, present value of cash flow, which does take account of risk in the discount rate. Nevertheless, the p–e ratio, discussed above, which is based on accounting earnings, does implicitly take account of risk, with a lower share price, ceteris paribus, being imputed to the same level of earnings with higher risk. Indeed income smoothing methods such as provisioning, 'prudency reserves' and cost capitalisation can have the effect of making a firm look much less volatile than it actually is, thereby concealing risk.

A fourth problem is that accounting profit does not take account of the cost of funds to shareholders. Interest payments are deducted to arrive at accounting profit, but shareholders' opportunity costs are not. Again, this is an area in which accounting profit compares unfavourably with the present value cash flow method, which takes account also of the opportunity cost of funds, as embodied in the discount rate.

Given the various points made about accounting profit, it is worth exploring methods of translating accounting profit into cash flow terms. One way to do this is to find **earnings before interest, tax, depreciation and amortisation (EBITDA)**. This can be calculated if the firm's profit and loss statement is available or if it is possible to recreate the profit and loss statement from the company accounts. The data in the next screenshot are from a company called Questular Rontok, which specialises in online role-play computer games and science fiction memorabilia.

| | A | B | C | D | E | F |
|---|---|---|---|---|---|---|
| 1 | | | | | £ | % of Sales |
| 2 | Sales Revenue | | | | £500,000 | 100% |
| 3 | Cost of Goods Sold COGS | | | | £82,500 | 17% |
| 4 | Gross Profit | | | | £417,500 | 84% |
| 5 | Selling, general and administrative expense | | | | £82,000 | 16% |
| 6 | EBITDA | | | | £335,500 | 67% |
| 7 | Depreciation and Amortization | | | | £30,000 | 6% |
| 8 | Operating Profit | | | | £305,500 | 61% |
| 9 | Interest | | | | £12,000 | 2% |
| 10 | Profit before Tax | | | | £293,500 | 59% |
| 11 | Tax | | | | £67,505 | 14% |
| 12 | Net Profit | | | | £225,995 | 45% |
| 13 | | | | | | |

Screenshot 4.5  Profit and loss for Questular Rontok

EBITDA is not always included in profit and loss statements as it is in Screenshot 4.5, but it can be calculated as gross profit – selling, general and administrative expenses (SGA). Gross profit in turn is calculated as sales revenue minus cost of goods sold (COGS). Thus we have a basis for working out free cash flow. From EBITDA of £335,500 we deduct any tax that is paid, in this case, £67,505. This gives a figure of £267,995. We do not of course deduct interest as the interest charge would eventually be covered in any discounting that was performed on the resulting cash flow. In addition, we do not of course deduct depreciation and amortisation as these are not cash flows but accounting entries. There is some justification to this approach as allowances for depreciation and amortisation can be rather arbitrary. Given a discount rate of 9.2% (we will explain below how this figure is reached) we estimate the value of the firm using the simple perpetuity approach as £267,995/0.092, which gives a figure of £2,912,989 or very nearly £3 million as a valuation for the firm.

The really tricky part now is deciding on how much to allow for investment. In practice, depreciation policies can be fairly ad-hoc and arbitrary, based as they are on standard custom and practice. **Amortisation**, which is the expenditure needed to maintain intangible assets such as goodwill, trademarks and brand awareness, can be even more subject to arbitrariness. Thus, there is a judgement call required in working out the extent to which the depreciation and amortisation figures on a firm's profit and loss statement are arbitrary and the extent to which they truly reflect the underlying need for investment. It is in making this kind of judgement that financial analysts earn their fees. We could not possibly do justice to the various techniques involved in a few paragraphs. Instead, we concentrate on a couple of simplified approaches.

One very straightforward approach is to assume that the figure for depreciation and amortisation is right and that this is the amount that needs to be reserved every year for investment in sufficient physical and intangible capital to maintain the firm at its present value. In which case, one would simply use operating profit minus tax, which gives a figure of £237,995. This would give a value for the firm of £2,586,902.

We noted above that we would need to justify our choice of discount rate. Having come up with an estimate of free cash flow, it would then be necessary to find a cost of capital in order to determine value on a present value basis. For a firm with both equity and debt, the cost of capital should include the cost of both sources of finance. In fact the correct measure is the **weighted average cost of capital (WACC)**. This is just the average of the costs of the two sources of finance, weighted by the importance of each as a source of finance. For example, suppose that the company's bank was charging 11% on the company's overdraft, while the required rate of return for shareholders was 8%. Suppose, furthermore, that out of a total capital of £1,500,000, a total of £900,000 is funded by shareholders, while £600,000 is funded from debt. The cost of capital **ignoring any tax benefit** is then $(9/15) \times 8\% + (6/15) \times 11\%$ = 4.8% + 4.4% = 9.2%. Clearly, this figure would be closer to 8% the greater the importance of equity in the capital structure, and 11% the greater the importance of debt in the capital structure. One might obtain this information from the company accounts. Failing that, one could use the CAPM, which is discussed in Chapter 5, to work out the firm's cost of equity, and the interest rate from figures available for comparable firms.

Alternatively one can strip out the figure for depreciation (D) and amortisation (A) on the grounds that the allowance for D and A is arbitrary. One might replace them with, for example, the current figures for **tangible capital expenditure** and **intangible capital expenditure**. The amount of tangible capital expenditure is familiar from day to day accounting and is just the amount of investment that is normally made in fixed capital on a year to year basis. Capital expenditure tends to be 'big and lumpy', so if you don't know when the next capital expenditure will be made you may have to go back to the last time a large capital investment was made and average it over the subsequent years before the next major capital expenditure is expected to be made. There may also be additions made to working capital over the period, so again you would have to average these out from the initial capital expenditure to the period when the next large capital investment is expected to be made.

Intangible capital is less easily defined. You could, for example, take the marketing spend, advertising, R&D and training, as proxies for intangible capital. Note that if we take the latter figures for intangible capital, we are assuming that there is a definite relationship whereby expenditure on the factors identified unambiguously adds to the value of intangible capital and thus to the value of the firm. It would be difficult to prove this beyond all reasonable doubt. However, it seems reasonable to assume that the firm would not be spending money on these items if they were not making any contribution. If this expenditure were not effective, then eventually this would probably be spotted by a venture capitalist or internal management buy-out team who could buy out the firm with the prospect of adding value and making considerable gains.

Consider the information in the next screenshot. Suppose that investment in fixed capital is made on a 5-year cycle. The last big capital expenditure was £150,000 (inflation adjusted to today's prices). This gives an average of £30,000 per year over the cycle. For the past 3 years, since the start of the investment cycle, additions to working capital have been £4,000, £3,000 and £5,000 (again inflation adjusted), giving an average of £4,000. Finally, marketing, R&D and training account for £100,000.

Thus under different assumptions we have a figure for free cash flow of £201,500. If we discount this as a perpetuity cash flow, we get £201,500/0.092 = £2,190,217. This is roughly a *third less* than our first valuation, which just goes to underline a very important point about valuation, which is that it is very much an inexact science.

| | A | B | C | D | E |
|---|---|---|---|---|---|
| 1 | EBITDA | | | | £335,500 |
| 2 | Fixed Capital Expenditure | | | | £30,000 |
| 3 | Additional Working Capital Expenditure | | | | £4,000 |
| 4 | Intangible Capital Expenditure | | | | £100,000 |
| 5 | | | | | |
| 6 | Free Cash Flow | | | | £201,500 |
| 7 | | | | | |
| 8 | Value | (as 9.2% Perpetuity) | | | £2,190,217 |

Screenshot 4.6 Valuing the firm using EBITDA

In the next section we consider valuation based on assets rather than earnings or free cash flow.

## Key concepts

- EBITDA is earnings before interest, tax, depreciation and amortisation
- Amortisation is the expenditure needed to maintain intangible assets
- WACC or weighted average cost of capital is the average of the costs of the two sources of finance, weighted by the importance of each as a source of finance
- Accounting profit can vary depending on the conventions used. The conventions used can vary for innocent reasons to do with custom and practice, to flatter the bottom line or, in the more extreme cases, to deceive and defraud

## Practical implications for managers

### Present value of accounting earnings

The comparison of firms on an accounting earnings basis can be fraught with unseen difficulties. In order to standardise accounting earnings for the purposes of comparison, firms are often compared on the basis of EBITDA. While EBITDA is neither discounted cash flow nor free cash flow, it gives a better indication of these than accounting profit.

## 4.5 Asset valuation

Often, businesses are bought and sold which are not quoted on the stock market. In order to determine a price for the business, it is necessary to have some idea of fair value. One way of arriving at a fair value would be to use the discounted cash flow described above. Another would be to look at p–e ratios for similar types of business that are publicly quoted. However, both methods are subject to considerable uncertainty concerning future cash flow, earnings, etc. Thus a third approach that is sometimes used in the valuation of the firm is in terms of its asset value or book value. The asset or book value can have a number of meanings. However, for our purposes the appropriate definition is as follows: the net asset value of a company is calculated as total assets minus intangible assets (patents, goodwill) and liabilities.

By adopting the asset-based approach, we are of course implicitly assuming that business value is equal to the 'sum of its parts', where the parts are the positive values recorded under assets and the negative contributions recorded under liabilities. The advantage of this approach is greater certainty. It is hard to argue with audited accounts. This apparent certainty is in contrast to the DCF and p–e approaches, which require the valuer to make subjective judgements about future earnings, risk and growth rate. The process of adding up firm asset values to arrive at a figure for net book value requires fewer assumptions about future performance, and it could therefore be argued to be an admirably conservative approach to valuation of the firm. However, there are drawbacks, as we will see below.

Book value or net asset value[3] is equal to the net value of tangible assets. It can also be calculated indirectly as the total value of the firm minus liabilities and intangible assets. Most assets are reported on the books of the subject company at the price at which they were acquired, net of depreciation. These values should be adjusted to fair market value wherever possible by, for example, marking to market in the case where the assets are stocks and bonds which are widely publicly traded and quoted. Suppose, for example, it is proposed to value the company Frod Perfect (FP) which has the simplified balance sheet illustrated in the following screenshot, which shows assets and liabilities at current market values.

|    | A                   | B | C            |
|----|---------------------|---|--------------|
| 1  | Fixed Assets        |   | £11,300,000  |
| 2  | Current Assets      |   | £6,600,000   |
| 3  |                     |   |              |
| 4  | Current Liabilities |   | £2,900,000   |
| 5  | Long Term Liabilities |  | £7,200,000   |
| 6  |                     |   |              |
| 7  | Net Assets          |   | £7,800,000   |
| 8  |                     |   |              |
| 9  | Owners' Equity      |   | £6,500,000   |
| 10 | Profit and Loss Acco |  | £1,300,000   |
| 11 | Shareholders' Funds |   | £7,800,000   |

Screenshot 4.7 Using net asset value

It can be seen that if there is a proposed buyer for FP, then a base figure for negotiation is the net asset value (NAV) of £7,800,000. Thus, for example, this might be the initial offer from a firm that proposed to take over FP. Of course, the acquiring firm would have to assume responsibility for the remaining liability of £10,100,000. If FP was keen to sell, perhaps because the owner was retiring, or perhaps because of liquidity problems, an offer of less than NAV might be acceptable, again provided all liabilities are assumed. Alternatively, the acquiring firm could offer a sum somewhere between £10,100,000 required to cover all liabilities and the £17,900,000 total assets figure. The latter is sometimes referred to as the total asset value (TAV).

The tangible assets approach provides a 'break-up' value of the firm in the event of liquidation of assets as well as a base point for negotiation over mergers, buy-outs and acquisitions. However, the problem with the tangible assets approach is that it misses out a large part of what businesses actually do, which is to add value by acquiring reputation, brand name, reliability, patents, etc. All of these things are intangible assets, and while it is relatively straightforward to attribute a value to buildings, plant and machinery, office equipment and so on, it is less straightforward to apply a value to intangible or invisible assets, as we discover in the next section.

Before leaving this section it is worth noting that NAV is a particularly useful approach for valuing:

- Firms in financial difficulty – after all, the firm may only be worth the wind-up value that can be realised by liquidating tangible assets and settling liabilities.

- Takeover bids – as we discussed above, NAV provides a useful starting point in this case.

- When company value is largely determined by the value of tangible assets owned or managed. Thus NAV is particularly useful in the following types of situation in which assets have a well-defined market value:
    - Property investment companies
    - Investment trusts
    - Resource-based companies

## Mini case study

### Problems with valuation

Source Jackson 2008, Copyright *Financial Times*, 'Valuation is fraught with dangers', 2008

I wrote a fortnight ago about how fundamental analysis often fails to capture the realities of markets. Let me turn to the most fundamental valuation method of all – discounted cash flow (DCF).

In formal terms, at least, DCF lies at the root of all investment decisions – whether to buy a share, acquire a company or build a factory. It is a simple three-step process: determine the sum of future cash flows, reduce them to present value through a discount rate and compare the result with today's price.

Warren Buffett, the world's most successful portfolio investor, and a noted buyer of companies, has argued repeatedly that DCF is not just the main, but the only valuation tool. Price/earnings ratios, dividend yields and even growth rates are irrelevant, except insofar as they help clarify the scale and timing of future cash flows.

But Mr Buffett is a special case. What if, for the rest of us, DCF is a fantasy?

One thoughtful if jaundiced observer of the scene, James Montier of Société Générale, effectively argues just that.

First, he says, analysts are hopeless at forecasting. And the further out they go, the more hopeless they get.

Second, the discount rate used by analysts – though not, one imagines, by Mr Buffett – is essentially subjective. Spurred on by financial theory, they use at least three components: the risk-free rate (usually the Treasury bond yield), the equity risk premium and the stock's beta. The first seems fair enough. The second is a notional figure which can be calculated all sorts of ways – by sector, by market, ex post or ex ante and so on.

More to the point, the figure arrived at is typically 3 to 4 per cent – which, given the huge risks and uncertainties in the forecast itself, is bogus precision. ...

And yet business people go on making valuation decisions every day. How come?

Part of the answer, I suspect, is that executives proceed much more cautiously than analysts. Their cash-flow projections are lower, their discount rates higher. This makes sense.

If a fund manager buys a stock on false assumptions, he can dump it. If an executive builds a plant on the same basis, he is stuck.

1. Why do you think that Warren Buffet takes the view that p–e ratios, dividend yields and even growth rates are irrelevant?

2. Are there any other ways of estimating a discount rate? How do you think Warren Buffet does it?

3. Can you explain why fund managers and executives have different discount rates?

## Key concepts

- ☐ **Asset** or **book value** is a valuation of the firm based on the value of its tangible assets. This kind of valuation may be at historical cost or market price. Clearly the latter is preferable

- ☐ **Marking to market** is the practice of updating asset values as their price changes on the market

## 4.6 Intangible assets

Intangible assets are those components of the firm's assets that have no physical presence and exist only in abstract ways. You may have come across the idea of intangible assets in a slightly different form in other business disciplines. For example, in the field of organisational design and human resource management, the term 'intellectual capital' tends to be used. Thus the terms 'intangibles' or 'human capital' refer to human capital investments in education, training and skills of the workforce, as well as investment in brand name, brand recognition, reputation and goodwill. It is true that assets we would normally think of as intangible can actually appear on the balance sheet, provided they have a clear measurable value. Thus if a firm acquires a patent or allows a sum for the acquisition of goodwill, then these are recorded on the balance sheet as assets. Nevertheless, it is widely agreed that intangible assets are difficult to value and greatly underestimated.

Intangible capital (IC) has been classified in many different ways, though the following three-way classification is broad enough to encompass most items that one would want to classify as intangible assets:

1. Human capital investments (education, training and skills of the workforce – especially that of the top management and board of directors).

2. Internal structural capital (internal governance and information systems and management practices, R&D and production systems that support product innovation and quality).

3. External structural capital (external relationships with suppliers, customers, financial reporting systems and competitive market situation including brands and market share).

It is important to try to value intangibles, as there is widespread acceptance that a large and increasing source of a company's competitive advantage stems from its investments in and the management of its various 'intangible' assets.

One of the problems that we have in identifying intangible assets is that they are often not clearly identified as such in the company accounts. Most internally generated intangibles, such as R&D, staff training costs and promotion of own brands, are treated as expenses and therefore immediately written-off in the profit and loss account. That is, there is no clear record of the ongoing accrual of benefits from these expenditures. It is natural at this point to ask why companies don't typically adopt standard procedures to provide ongoing standard valuation and reporting of intangible assets. One reason is that the firm's intangibles are the main source of its competitive advantage. Therefore corporate management are reluctant to make easily and publicly available information which may be of help to competitors. A second reason is that from the financial reporting side, fears regarding possible 'manipulation' by management and legal actions by third-parties claiming to have been misled by the information contained in the accounts appear to limit the prospects for further significant improvements in the reporting of intangibles within the framework of the audited financial statements. But the most significant reason is that there is simply not an unambiguous widely acceptable method for valuing intangible assets. They remain subject to a great deal of uncertainty. By way of attempting to measure the contribution of intangibles, a large number of proposed metrics have been offered by various different academics. However, space does not permit extended discussion of these [the interested reader is referred to Starovic and Marr (2003)], so we examine only a very common and basic measure, the market-to-book value.

## Active learning activity 4.4

### What's the value of the Coke brand name?

Find the online annual accounts of Coca-Cola Company and try to work out a value for the Coke brand name. On what assumptions do you base your analysis and how certain are you of the result?

The **market-to-book value** is the ratio of stock market valuation divided by the value of its NAV. The market-to-book value can be seen as a metric of value added. That is, a great deal of business activity consists of adding value to tangible assets such as buildings and machinery through the development of intangible assets such as brand, marketing, technology and strategic ability. This implies that a high market-to-book ratio indicates a high value of intangible assets relative to tangible assets. Stock market analysts often use market-to-book to look for value; by this they mean firms with a low market-to-book ratio, indicating that the market may have underpriced the contribution to value from intangible assets for these companies. Like any measure of value, NAV has it problems as an indicator of intangible value. International comparisons can be difficult as the NAV will vary from country to country, depending on the national or international accounting standard under which the accounts have been prepared. Also, assets values recorded under accounting convention may not reflect true market value, but may be strongly influenced by the company's specific depreciation policies, or their treatment of assets for tax purposes. In addition, when the stock market is volatile it is possible for the stock market valuation of the company to change radically over a short period of time.

## Key concepts

- [ ] **Intangibles** can refer to 'human capital' or investment in goodwill. Among the former are education, training and the skills of the workforce. Among the latter are brand name, brand recognition, reputation and goodwill
- [ ] A basic way to measure intangibles is in terms of the **market-to-book ratio** which is the market value of the firm divided by its book value

## Practical implications for managers

### Intangibles

Intangibles are very important as a source of competitiveness and value added. Yet, paradoxically, little is known about how to value them and what their precise contribution is for the average firm. Financial and managerial accounting principles were developed in the context of the manufacture and sale of undifferentiated visible goods in competitive markets. The world still awaits a new framework that fully incorporates intangibles in their own right and not just as a residual.

**Active learning activity 4.5**

Dilemma of deciding

Try to find and read the article by Johnson *et al.* (2002) 'Dilemma of deciding if a cut-price asset is a bargain'. If you are able to retrieve it, try to answer the following questions:

1. What additional information would you need before you could make a decision?
2. Is the middle of a financial crisis a good time to buy up 'bargain' assets? If not, then when?
3. What techniques might you use to establish fundamental value in order to know whether or not you have bought a bargain asset?
4. How would Warren Buffett approach the problem?

## 4.7 Summary

In this chapter we discovered that valuation is an important and central principle in the valuation of the firm, and that there are three fundamental approaches we can take: cash flow based, earnings based and asset based.

The chapter went on to build on the principle of simple share valuation, to consider the more complicated case where the dividend is growing. It was found that the calculation of discount rate, and more particularly the calculation of growth, was considerably less well defined and more uncertain a problem than our benchmark for valuation problems – basic bond valuation. Whether predicted growth is simply extrapolated from previous trends or built on Gordon's assumptions, a small error can have a multiplied effect on the valuation.

In the next section we examined the price-earnings ratio. This can be used to value a company by finding a comparable quoted company's p–e ratio and multiplying by the unquoted company's earnings. It may be advisable to reduce by a factor to allow for the relative illiquidity. The p–e ratio is based on accounting earnings, not free cash flow and, in general, the higher the potential growth, the higher the p–e ratio.

We found that accounting information can also be used for firm valuation purposes, though again a number of factors can cause problems with valuation and need to be taken into account. The particularly problematic areas are the treatment of non-cash flows such as depreciation and amortisation, in addition to corporate practices such as provisioning and capitalisation. Furthermore, conventions used in these practices can vary widely. The principle involved here was illustrated using the EBITDA approach. However, as it was pointed out, any DCF valuation based on EBITDA could vary considerably depending on what was assumed about investment.

In the next section we turned to asset valuation. In principle, this was very straightforward. The company is worth the surplus value of assets over liabilities. However, the problem with this is that it ignores intangible assets.

The valuation of intangible assets is very important because there is widespread acceptance that a large and increasing source of a company's competitive advantage stems from its investments in and the management of its various 'intangible' assets. One basic measure of the net value of intangible assets is the market-to-book value, which is represented by the ratio of the market value of the firm to the value of its tangible assets (NAV). The market-to-book value is often used by stock market analysts in addition to p–e ratios, as a measure of the scale of intangible assets.

# Questions

1. Ideally, how should firms be valued?

2. Rework the example in screenshot 4.2 with abnormal dividend growth of 15%.

3. A share in Hitchhikers' Guide (HG) yields a constant dividend of 12p and the price has recently increased from £1.50 to £1.75. What is the return on the share?

4. Assuming that the return for HG is the normal return for the class of share, what should be the price of share in Roughhikers' Guide (RG), which offers a constant dividend of £4.93?

5. What would be the share price if the dividend in RG were now expected to grow by 3% for the foreseeable future?

6. What are the critical differences between share price determination based on dividend alone and determination of p–e based on the dividend–earnings ratio?

7. Given the profit and loss account in the following screenshot, along with figures for various types of capital expenditure, formulate reasonable estimates for firm value based on earnings.

8. What is the NAV and when is NAV a particularly useful valuation method?

9. What is one of the major drawbacks of NAV?

10. Why is it important in principle to be able to value intangible assets and what makes it difficult to do in practice?

| 1 | | £ |
|---|---|---|
| 2 | Sales Revenue | £1,000,000 |
| 3 | Cost of Goods Sold COGS | £96,000 |
| 4 | Gross Profit | |
| 5 | Selling, general and administrative expense | £82,000 |
| 6 | EBITDA | |
| 7 | Depreciation and Amortization | £30,000 |
| 8 | Operating Profit | |
| 9 | Interest | £12,000 |
| 10 | Profit before Tax | |
| 11 | Tax | |
| 12 | Net Profit | |
| 13 | | |
| 14 | Fixed Capital Expenditure | £150,000.00 |
| 15 | Additional Working Capital Expenditure | £10,000.00 |
| 16 | Intangible Capital Expenditure | £112,000.00 |
| 17 | | |

Screenshot 4.8 Profit and loss account for Q7.

## Case study

## HTAT

### History

HTAT is an unquoted company that specialises in mobile phone designs. It has been trading for 4 years and is widely regarded as being the market leader in innovative design. It has also established a reputation for high quality and commitment to customer service.

Heather and Allan established the company in 2003. The company originally borrowed £200,000 (at an interest rate of 10% per annum) from the bank which is secured on the personal property of the owners. The capital is repayable in 2015.

Originally, the company operated from rented premises and leased much of its equipment. However, 2 years ago the owners decided to move premises and they have taken a 25-year lease on premises that are large enough to allow for significant expansion. They also bought new office equipment and a state-of-the-art server system.

The company now employs 10 people and is planning to recruit additional designers to handle a large contract it is hoping to obtain from a mobile phone group. It is estimated that there is a 50% chance of obtaining this contract. HTAT outsources most of the general administrative and finance functions.

### Future plans

Heather recently met the bank manager to discuss future growth and financing requirements. Mr G. Reed, the manager, asked her if the company would consider an alliance with a venture capital firm as the route to go forward. The general terms of the deal are such that the venture capital company would require a substantial proportion of the equity of the company in exchange for an injection of capital. It would also require an exit route within 4–5 years.

Allan is not convinced. He thinks that a better option is to float the company on the stock market in 2–3 years. He argues that they would be able to raise money by selling a proportion of their shares then and he thinks they would make more money (both for the company and for themselves).

Assume you have been hired by HTAT as an independent financial analyst to advise them on the value of their company should they decide to approach a venture capitalist at the present time. The following information is available.

Turnover has grown from £30,000 in the first year to £800,000 in the last year (to 31 March 2008). However, the company has made losses in the first 3 years and only made a small operating profit last year. The poor financial results seem to be due to the very high costs of research and marketing. This expenditure will continue, although Heather feels that it will not be at such high levels.

| | |
|---|---|
| Shares in issue (ordinary £1 shares) | 20,000 |
| Earnings per share | 150p |
| Dividend per share | 0 |
| Net asset value | £1,000,000 |

(The net asset value is the net book – balance sheet – value.)

The forecast turnover for the year to 31 March 2009 is £3.0 million. This depends on whether or not the company gets the mobile phone group contract. If the mobile phone group contract is secured, the forecast turnover for the year to March 2009 is forecast to be £3.0 million. Otherwise, growth will be a more modest 5%.

Operating costs, inclusive of depreciation, are expected to be 40% of turnover in the year to 31 March 2008, reducing to 25% in the following year as a result of economies of scale. Thereafter, it is expected that operating costs will remain at around 25% of turnover. Interest costs are projected to remain constant.

Tax is expected to remain at 30%.

Assume that profit after interest and tax is equal to free cash flow.

Growth in earnings in each of the years to 31 March 2010 and 2011 is expected to be 20% over 2009 levels, falling to a constant 10% per year after this time.

There are relatively few comparative companies already on the stock market. However, if we extend the definition to include all companies in electronic design and associated products, the following figures are relevant.

*p–e ratios:*

| | |
|---|---|
| Industry average | 20 |
| Range | 12–60 |

*Cost of capital:*

| | |
|---|---|
| Industry average | 15% |
| Range | 10–25% |

Share price movements in the sector are extremely volatile. Recently, two similar companies, one quoted and listed in 1999 and one unquoted, have gone into liquidation. There has been growing suspicion of 'internet-style' design companies within the business environment. There are also difficulties in securing new investment due to the recent Credit Crunch.

## Required

1. Write a two-page report to the directors of HTAT that outlines the various methods by which their company might be valued. Include the range of valuations that could be used in negotiation with a venture capitalist.

2. Reflect on any assumptions you have made and give your opinion as to the most likely valuation and justify this as far as possible. Mention any factors that have been influential in determining your most likely valuation.

3. Outline the major difficulties in arriving at a valuation for an unlisted company.

# Further reading

Boutellier, C. (undated) *The Evaluation of Intangibles: Advocating for an Option Based Approach*. Reims Management School, University of Reims Working Paper, http://www.wedb.net/download/valoracao/aula_3/bouteiller_unknowndate.pdf.

Campbell, J., Diamond, P. and Shoven, J. (2001) *Estimating the Real Rate of Return on Stocks over the Long Term*. Social Security Advisory Board (SSAB), www.ssab.gov/publications/financing/estimated%20rate%20of%20return.pdf, accessed 15 September 2009.

Damodar, A. (2005) *Marketability and Value: Measuring the Illiquidity Discount*. Stern School of Business Working Paper, July, http://pages.stern.nyu.edu/~adamodar/pdfiles/papers/liquidity.pdf.

Fernandez, P. (2007) *Company Valuation Methods: The Most Common Errors in Valuation*. Working Paper no. 449, IESE Business School, University of Navarra, www.iese.edu/research/pdfs/DI-0449-E.pdf, accessed 15 September 2009.

Malkiel, B. (2007) *A Random Walk Down Wall Street*. W.W Norton, New York.

Starovic, D. and Marr, B. (2003) *Understanding Corporate Value: Managing and Reporting Intellectual Capital*. CIMA, www.valuebasedmanagement.net/articles_cima_understanding.pdf, accessed 15 September 2009.

# Internet references

http://www.bytestart.co.uk/
A portal for small businesses in the UK which includes useful pages on valuation.

http://www.smallbusiness.co.uk/ and, in particular, http://www.smallbusiness.co.uk/channels/small-business-finance/guides-and-tips/24323/valuing-your-business-for-sale.thtml
A good article on the practical difficulties involved in valuation.

http://www.intangiblebusiness.com/brand-services/financial-services/press-coverage/why-it-is-hard-to-value-a-mystery~969.html
An interesting article on the difficulties in valuation of intangibles.

http://www.accountingweb.co.uk/ and http://www.accountingweb.co.uk/cgi-bin/item.cgi?id=157890&d=1032&h=1024&f=1026
Useful discussion on new accounting standards and valuation.

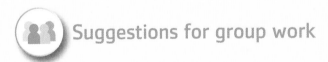

# Suggestions for group work

Students should try to calculate the value of themselves pre and post their university education. They should describe the process, the difficulties in identifying the tangible and intangible inputs to the process, and say how confident they are in their final result.

## Suggestions for presentations

Imagine you are the consultancy team, Chargealot, mentioned in the running case study. Prepare a presentation of not more than ten PowerPoint slides on the process of valuing Community Loans Ltd.

## Appendix

### Derivation of dividend pricing formula with dividend growth

The formula for price is as follows:

$$P_t = (1/(1+r)) \times d_1 + (1/(1+r)^2) \times d_2 + (1/(1+r)^3) \times d_3 + \ldots\ldots\ldots (1/(1+r)^n) \times d_n \qquad (1)$$

That is, the price of the share depends on the discounted value of the dividends from the share. The dividend in each case depends on the growth rate, i.e. each future dividend depends on the current dividend and the growth rate.

$$P_t = d_1/(1+r) + d_1 \times (1+g)/(1+r)^2 + d1 \times (1+g)^2/(1+r)^3 + \ldots d_1 \times (1+g)^{n-2}/(1+r)^{n-1}$$
$$+ d_1 \times (1+g)^{n-1}/(1+r)^n \qquad (2)$$

Multiply both sides by $(1+r)/(1+g)$:

$$P_t \times (1+r)/(1+g) = d_1/(1+g) + d_1/(1+r) + d_1 \times (1+g)/(1+r)^2$$
$$+ \ldots\ldots\ldots d_1 \times (1+g)^{n-2}/(1+r)^{n-1} \qquad (3)$$

Take Equation (2) from Equation (3):

$$P_t \times (1+r)/(1+g) = d_1/(1+g) + d_1/(1+r) + d_1 \times (1+g)/(1+r)^2$$
$$+ \ldots\ldots\ldots d_1 \times (1+g)^{n-2}/(1+r)^{n-1} \qquad (3)$$

$$P_t = d_1/(1+r) + d_1 \times (1+g)/(1+r)^2 + d_1 \times (1+g)^2/(1+r)^3$$
$$+ \ldots d_1 \times (1+g)^{n-2}/(1+r)^{n-1} + d_1 \times (1+g)^{n-1}/(1+r)^n \qquad (2)$$

The result is that

$$P_t \times (1+r)/(1+g) - P_t = d_1/(1+g) - d_1 \times (1+g)^{n-1}/(1+r)^n$$

We normally value shares on a perpetuity basis. As n, the number of time periods, approaches infinity, the term $d_1 \times (1+g)^{n-1}/(1+r)n$ approaches zero. Hence:

$$P_t \times (1+r)/(1+g) - P_t = d_1/(1+g)$$

We can use a well-known mathematical trick by which the number one can be expressed as the ratio of any number to itself, viz $1 = (1+g)/(1+g)$. Hence:

$$P_t \times (1+r)/(1+g) - P_t \times (1+g)/(1+g) = d_1/(1+g)$$

or

$$P_t \times (1 + r - 1 - g)/(1 + g) = d_1/(1 + g)$$

or

$$P_t \times (r - g)/(1 + g) = d_1/(1 + g)$$

or

$$P_t \times (r - g) = d_1$$

or

$$P_0 = d_1/(r - g)$$

# 5 Risk and the Financial Environment

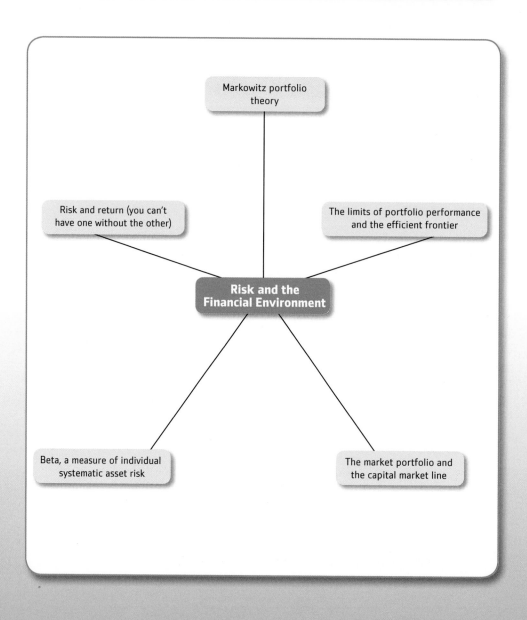

Markowitz portfolio theory

Risk and return (you can't have one without the other)

The limits of portfolio performance and the efficient frontier

**Risk and the Financial Environment**

Beta, a measure of individual systematic asset risk

The market portfolio and the capital market line

## Knowledge-based learning objectives

When you have completed this chapter you will be able to:

✓ Explain the basic nature of financial risk
✓ Explain the basic statistics necessary to appraise risk versus return
✓ Calculate these measures for individual assets, namely:
  - expected return
  - variance
  - co-variance
  - correlation
✓ Explain the conditions under which the portfolio-based approach to investment improves return relative to risk
✓ Calculate the basic statistical operational characteristics for portfolios as well as for individual assets
✓ Explain the significance of the market portfolio
✓ Explain the distinction between standard deviation as a measure of risk and beta as a measure of risk

## Skills-based learning objectives development

✓ Business and financial environment consciousness: you should have developed an understanding of the nature of risk and how this is conceptualised in basic finance.
✓ Numerical skills: you should have developed the ability to understand, manipulate and calculate standard measures of investment performance and statistics.
✓ Analytical thinking and problem-solving skills: you should have developed the ability to know how to analyse risk–return for individual assets and portfolios.
✓ Problem-solving skills: you should have developed the ability to assess risk–return and evaluate ways to adjust risk–return.
✓ Critical-thinking skills: you should have developed the ability to understand the assumptions on which investment decisions are based and to know the limitations of these techniques.
✓ Organisational skills: you should have developed your ability to organise your time and work efficiently and to gather data and information which you can translate into value-adding intelligence.
✓ Managerial soft skills: you should have developed the ability to know where judgement and interpersonal skill is needed with investment and risk management.
✓ Presentation skills: you should have developed your ability to present your work clearly both verbally and in writing.
✓ Interpersonal skills: you should have developed your ability to present your work clearly both verbally and in writing and to interact with others effectively upon completion of the end of chapter questions.

## @ Online resource centre

Visit the Online Resource Centre that accompanies this book to listen to a podcast of the authors explaining the trade-offs between risk and return in the context of investment.
**www.oxfordtextbooks.co.uk/marney**

## Fictional case study

### OrganicX and the basket of eggs

Charlie and Kate are now interested in becoming involved in project development and micro-finance in emerging economies such as India. They have taken to heart the message from the success of the Grameen Bank, namely that projects should be small, local and run on a commercial basis. With this in mind, they have now decided that they should invest some funds in micro-finance projects in the agriculture sector, but, as usual, they don't agree on the best way to proceed.

Charlie thinks that all of their available funds for this project should be invested in Nigeria, where typical returns to such projects have exceeded 20%, in contrast to the worldwide average return for similar projects of 6%.

'I know you like to bamboozle me with your fancy financial wizardry, but surely, this time, it's a no-brainer, Kate?' Charlie sits back, confident that for once he is right. Kate looks pained and he senses another of her lectures about to emerge. Before she can say a word, he pulls out a tattered newspaper clipping that starts with the headline 'Nigeria economy romps ahead'.

Kate waves it away and says, 'Charlie, did you ever hear the saying "Don't put all your eggs in one basket?"

'Of course,' Charlie replies, 'but what has that got to do with investment?'

'Well,' Kate begins, 'first of all, it's never a good idea to put all your money into one investment. What if it fails?'

Charlie looks at his newspaper clipping again and starts to speak. 'Yes, but look at the returns on offer here – 20% is not chickenfeed!'

Kate sighs. 'Okay, but that's in the past. We have no idea what will happen in the future. How many times do I need to tell you that no one can predict the future?' Before Charlie can interrupt her, she goes on, 'In any case, you are forgetting about risk. High returns are generally associated with high risk. We need to diversify across a number of markets. That will mean lower risk as a whole.'

Charlie vaguely remembers Kate going on about risk and return – round about the time he was thinking about investing in BogusBloggs (incorporated in the Cayman Islands) who were promising 50% return for a minimum investment of £1 million. Didn't he read somewhere recently that they had disappeared – along with the investors' money? Is Kate right again? She has started to explain but is using long words such as 'Markowitz portfolio theory', 'correlations' and 'the CAPM'. Charlie holds up his hand and says, 'Can't you speak in normal words for a change and just tell me what you mean in simple terms?'

'I just did,' replies Kate in an exasperated tone of voice, 'but to repeat – don't put all your eggs in one basket!'

# 5.1 Risk and return (you can't have one without the other)

### 5.1.1 Introduction

Risk and return almost always go together. That's why if someone lets you in on the ground-floor of a 'sure-fire' get rich quick scheme, you need to treat it with some scepticism. The history of financial markets is littered with the smoking ruins of products, funds and trading strategies that on a superficial level promised untold riches with no apparent downside; where apparently, 'it's just like putting out your hand to scoop up the money'. But on reflection, almost all these schemes had one flaw in common. The people or organisations involved had seriously underestimated the risks or indeed had forgotten altogether that financial return almost always goes together with financial risk.

There is no such thing as a free lunch, and there is seldom such a thing as above-average profits without above-average risk. The significance of this last statement cannot be emphasised enough. So much so that it constitutes the next secret that we are about to reveal.

The second secret (whisper it) is that risk and return are positively related. If you observe someone making abnormally high returns, either they are in possession of information that isn't available to the rest of us or they are taking very high risks.

Now, as we've said before, that may not seem like much of a secret to you, and neither does it seem like much of a secret to us, but along with secret number 1 (revealed in a Chapter 2), we have to conclude that it must be a secret, otherwise why do intelligent well-paid professional financial people appear to occasionally act as if it was unknown. Take the mini case study ('High return goes with high risk: the case of Nick Leeson') extracted from the website of Nick Leeson, the 'rogue trader'.

## Mini case study

### High return goes with high risk: the case of Nick Leeson
Source From http://www.nickleeson.com/biography/index.html, 2010

In the early 1980s, Nick Leeson landed a job as a clerk with royal bank Coutts, followed by a string of jobs with other banks, ending up with Barings, where he quickly made an impression and was promoted to the trading floor.

Before long, he was appointed manager of a new operation in futures markets on the Singapore Monetary Exchange (SIMEX) and was soon making millions for Barings by betting on the future direction of the Nikkei index. His bosses back in London, who viewed with glee his large profits, trusted the whiz kid. Leeson and his wife Lisa seemed to have everything: a salary of £50,000 with bonuses of up to £150,000, weekends in exotic places, a smart apartment and frequent parties, and to top it all they even seemed to be very much in love.

Barings believed that it wasn't exposed to any losses because Leeson claimed that he was executing purchase orders on behalf of a client. What the company did not realise is that it was responsible for error account 88888 where Leeson hid his losses. This account had been set up to cover up a mistake made by an inexperienced team member, which led to a loss of £20,000. Leeson now used this account to cover his own mounting losses.

As the losses grew, Leeson requested extra funds to continue trading, hoping to extricate himself from the mess by more deals. Over 3 months he bought more than 20,000 futures contracts worth about $180,000 each in a vain attempt to move the market. Some three quarters of the $1.5 billion he lost Barings resulted from these trades. When Barings executives discovered what had happened, they informed the Bank of England that Barings was effectively bust. In his wake Nick Leeson had wiped out the 255-year-old Baring Investment Bank, who proudly counted HM The Queen as a client. The $1.5 billion dollars of liabilities he had run up was more than the entire capital and reserves of the bank.

Eventually arrested in Frankfurt, Germany, Nick spent a few fraught months trying to escape extradition to Singapore. He failed and in December 1995 a court in Singapore sentenced him to six and a half years in prison.

1. Do you think that this kind of thing could have happened after the Nick Leeson episode? Did banks learn their lesson?

2. Why did Leeson continue trading as his losses worsened?

3. Do you think he was gambling or investing? Where would you draw the line between the two?

Nick Leeson was a star trader with Barings, making a great deal of money for the bank by betting on movements in the Japanese Nikkei index. Admittedly Barings was unaware of his mounting losses, which he had been very careful to conceal, so it wasn't clear to them that there was a great deal of risk attached to Leeson's outstanding performances. However, it might prove a lesson for the future. If a star trader is making colossal amounts of money, he or she is almost certainly doing this by taking large amounts of risk. How is this risk being managed, limited and monitored? There is a tendency in the industry to look at the bottom line. As we will argue, it's not quite as simple as that. Return has to be adjusted for risk.

The same fundamental question of risk and return applies to firms outside the financial industry. Most firms make their money by doing something risky, even when they're not dealing in exotic financial derivatives. Even by doing something very prosaic, like manufacturing bathroom fittings or selling sweets and newspapers, a firm is engaging in risk. The previous sentence may sound a little melodramatic, so at this point we should be clear about what we mean by risk. What we don't mean is that business managers are the kind of people who enjoy dangerous sports. What we mean is that in any kind of business, cash flow, sales and other financial variables such as interest rates can change and this in turn can affect profits and return. It is this potential variability in profits or financial return that is usually alluded to when defining financial risk. So risk in the financial sense then refers to variability or volatility of outcome. The more volatile or variable the possible outcome from a business or financial decision, then the more risk is said to exist. In order to explain why, we need to consider attitudes to risk, which is discussed in the next section.

## 5.1.2 Attitudes to risk

In order to simplify things, let us consider an investment decision as two possible outcomes based on the flip of a coin. Why coin-flipping? What is the value of this analogy? Coin-flipping is a useful way to think of business investment as investment that is inherently uncertain. In fact investment specifically and all business activity generally is just like that other popular human activity based on uncertainty – gambling. The difference is that gamblers choose to take unnecessary risks, because they enjoy risk. They are **risk seekers**. They would actually pay to take risk or increase their uncertainty as they prefer it that way. However, business people would typically rather not take any undue risks as they are **risk averse**. However, this does not mean that they would *never* take a risk. They are prepared to take a risk if the rewards are sufficiently high to compensate for the discomfort involved in taking that risk. Business people know that profits, cash flows, sales, etc. are inherently variable and uncertain. However, they accept this unavoidable uncertainty in the pursuit of compensatory reward. So they don't enjoy the coin-flipping game for its own sake, but they realise that it is a necessary part of their job. Let us take our coin-flipping analogy a little further to make some more specific points about attitude to risk.

Suppose we have a bet based on the outcome of a coin flip. If I win, you give me £10. If you win, I give you £10. If we took a whole series of bets of this nature, say on a daily basis, we would be interested in the expected value of the bet. An **expected value** is just a special type of average, where each value used to calculate the average is weighted by the probability that it actually occurs. In the case of the bet, the expected value is based on two possible outcomes, as illustrated in Screenshot 5.1.

| | POSSIBLE OUTCOME | Value of Outcome (V) | Probability of Outcome (P) | V*P |
|---|---|---|---|---|
| 1 | | | | |
| 2 | 1. Win | £10 | 0.5 | £5 |
| 3 | 2. Lose | -£10 | 0.5 | -£5 |
| 4 | | | | |
| 5 | | | Average or Expected Value EV | £0 |
| 6 | | | | |

Screenshot 5.1 A fair game or fair bet

The expected value is calculated as follows:

EV = (Value of Outcome 1) × (Probability of Outcome 1) + (Value of Outcome 2) × (Probability of Outcome 2) = £10 × 0.5 + (–£10) × 0.5 = £5 − £5 = 0

That is, to say, if you played this coin-toss game a lot, you would expect neither to win nor to lose from it over the long run. In fact the coin toss is a special kind of bet called a **fair game**. A fair game is a bet in which the participant, over a large series of bets is neither better nor worse off. **Risk-averse** people would not take a fair bet or indeed a business risk that was analogous to a fair bet. Though they are no worse off, they would rather live without the uncertainty, which, by definition, they dislike. However, they would be prepared to consider the coin-toss game if they would be likely to gain over a series of games of this nature. Consider now Screenshot 5.2, which shows a better-than-fair game with different possible outcomes.

| | POSSIBLE OUTCOME | Value of Outcome (V) | Probability of Outcome (P) | V*P |
|---|---|---|---|---|
| 1 | | | | |
| 2 | 1. Win | £20 | 0.5 | £10 |
| 3 | 2. Lose | -£10 | 0.5 | -£5 |
| 4 | | | | |
| 5 | | | Average or Expected Value EV | £5 |

Screenshot 5.2  A better than fair game

Now if you win, you get £20, though you can expect a loss of £10 if you lose. The expected value for this new better-than-fair game is as follows:

$$EV = £20 \times 0.5 + (-£10) \times 0.5 = £10 - £5 = £5$$

So if you played this game a lot you could expect to come out ahead, to the tune of £5 per bet, on average. Of course, given the nature of probability and uncertainty, you wouldn't always win, and you might have sustained periods of loss. But, on average, in the long run, over lots of series of games, you would come out ahead. This inducement would be enough to persuade *some*, though *not all* risk-averse individuals to take the risk. Some people would be more risk averse. For example, they might need a higher payoff, such as we find in Screenshot 5.3.

| | POSSIBLE OUTCOME | Value of Outcome (V) | Probability of Outcome (P) | V*P |
|---|---|---|---|---|
| 1 | | | | |
| 2 | 1. Win | £50 | 0.5 | £25 |
| 3 | 2. Lose | -£10 | 0.5 | -£5 |
| 4 | | | | |
| 5 | | | Average or Expected Value EV | £20 |

Screenshot 5.3  Higher payoff required for the more risk averse for taking on the same risk

Thus a *more* risk-averse person might require a higher payoff for taking the same risk, while a *less* risk-averse person would be content with a smaller reward, such as we find in Screenshot 5.4.

| | POSSIBLE OUTCOME | Value of Outcome (V) | Probability of Outcome (P) | V*P |
|---|---|---|---|---|
| 1 | | | | |
| 2 | 1. Win | £15 | 0.5 | £7.50 |
| 3 | 2. Lose | -£10 | 0.5 | -£5 |
| 4 | | | | |
| 5 | | | Average or Expected Value EV | £2.50 |

Screenshot 5.4  Lower payoff accepted by the less risk averse for taking on the same risk

The third individual represented in Screenshot 5.4 is still risk averse. However, he is *less* risk averse than either the individual in Screenshot 5.2 or the individual in Screenshot 5.3. Hence he is prepared to accept a *lower* reward for bearing the *same* risk. Nevertheless he remains risk averse, as he requires some reward for taking on risk. An important function of financial markets is to aggregate and match financial reward to financial risk in line with average risk aversion on the market. The higher the risk, the higher the reward, and vice versa. Before we pass on to a discussion of what exactly risk is, a brief word about risk-seekers is in order. If it is the case that the risk-averse people require a **reward** for taking risk, then it must logically be the case that the risk-seeking will **pay** to accept risk. As we discussed above, this is exactly why people gamble – because they enjoy risk.

On average, gamblers lose money. They must enjoy losing money otherwise why would they do it? Of course, moving away from the cold hard probabilities involved, there is often a peculiar self-deluding psychology attached to gambling situations. People have systems. They have feelings. They have insights into patterns that they've noticed; insights that haven't of course been vouchsafed to anyone else. As we have learned above, it is easy to be fooled by randomness and to attribute causalities and see patterns where there are none.

The problem with financial markets is that some traders can make a great deal of money by taking an aggressive risk-seeking approach. However, unlike in the casino situation, the risk-return trade-off may not be entirely clear until after the event. What might have appeared to be a more than a fair bet before the event may turn out to be less than fair afterwards, particularly in the murky and poorly understood worlds of derivatives and novel financial instruments. For the present, we will consider risk-seeking behaviour as something of an anomaly, and so we can normally consider business people and investors to be risk averse.

### 5.1.3 The risk averse don't like variation of outcome

Let us remind ourselves of the example of a fair bet given in Screenshot 5.1. This requires a stake of £10. If you 'call' correctly, you win £10; if you 'call' incorrectly, you lose your £10 stake. Assuming a normal unbiased coin, this is clearly a fair bet.

Imagine the same bet, the only difference being that the possible gain or loss is now £20, as illustrated in Screenshot 5.5.

| | POSSIBLE OUTCOME | Value of Outcome (V) | Probability of Outcome (P) | V*P |
|---|---|---|---|---|
| 1 | | | | |
| 2 | 1. Win | £20 | 0.5 | £10 |
| 3 | 2. Lose | -£20 | 0.5 | -£10 |
| 4 | | | | |
| 5 | | | Average or Expected Value EV | £0 |

Screenshot 5.5  A fair game or fair bet with £20 stakes

We know now that we would call these fair bets and we know that a risk-averse individual would not take such a bet or invest in a situation that resembled such a bet. Nevertheless, suppose our risk-averse individual had to choose one of the bets; which one would he choose? Even though the expected value is exactly the same for both bets, the answer would be the £10 bet. A short and simplistic answer to this question would be the size of loss involved. Clearly, risk-averse individuals would prefer to limit their losses to £10 with a probability of 0.5 rather than face a loss of £20 with the same probability of 0.5. However, that's not the whole story as although the second coin-flip offers twice as much loss, it also offers twice as much gain.

The reason is as follows. For technical reasons that we won't go into for fear of digressing too much, the prospect of losing £20 is *more than twice* as painful as the prospect of losing £10. We might therefore regard our risk-averse person as something of a pessimist, because it is also the case for technical reasons that the prospect of gaining £20 is *less than twice* as satisfying as the prospect of £10. Therefore, although the bets look exactly the same in terms of expected value, they are not regarded as the same by the risk averse. The £20 bet is less desirable because the amount of pain increases *more than proportionally* with the degree of loss, while the amount of pleasure increases *less than proportionally* with the degree of gain over the £10 bet. The technical word for satisfaction from gain is **utility** while the pain from loss is called **disutility**. Therefore, to use the technical language, the increase in **disutility** when the potential loss goes from –£10 to –£20 is greater than the increase in **utility** when the potential gain goes from £10 to £20. Thus, although the gains have doubled to offset the doubled losses, the £20 coin flip is even less desirable than the £10 coin flip.

Observe that the range of outcomes for the first bet is £10 − (–£10) = £20, while the range of outcomes in the second case is £20 − (–£20) which is £40. So we can state very roughly at this point, the wider the range or dispersion of outcomes, the less the risk-averse investor likes it. There is a little bit more to it than that, which requires more technical understanding, particularly of the statistical concepts of **standard deviation** and **variance**, but we will tackle this problem in the next section.

We noted in the previous section that an important function of financial markets is to aggregate financial risk and match this to financial reward. We now know why risk must be rewarded. It is because the typical investor is risk averse and therefore requires to be rewarded for bearing risk, in the form of variation or range of outcome. We now turn to the subject of the actual form of the relationship between risk and return. This can sometimes be the subject of some controversy. Nevertheless, there are two standard relationships that are normally taken as a basis for the risk–return relationship in finance. These are the **efficient market line (EML)**, also known as the **capital market line (CML)**, which relates return to risk for collections or **portfolios of assets**, and the **security market line (SML)** which is derived from the **Capital Asset Pricing Model (CAPM)** and relates risk to return for **individual assets** (often stocks and shares, i.e. ordinary equities). In both cases, risk is taken as some measure of variation or volatility of return in line with the preferences of the risk-averse investor described above. Remember, the less fluctuation in return, then the less risk.

## Practical implications for managers

### Attitudes to risk

The typical business person is not risk seeking. If he or she could avoid the risk in pursuit of profit then he/she would. However, almost all profit comes with risk attached. The trick is to be as clear as possible on how much risk the company is exposed to and how this is being managed. Of course, you will always have visionary entrepreneurs who see possibilities that no one else does and go with their instinct. In a sense their 'vision' takes the place of clear information. However, acting in this way is not for everyone as these people tend to be very driven, single minded and unique. And they have a *high failure rate*.

## Key concepts

- [ ] The parallel between betting and investment is that both involve risk
- [ ] The fundamental difference between betting and investment is that investment risk or business risk is unavoidable. Gambling risk is avoidable
- [ ] An expected value is an average where each value used is weighted by the probability that it actually occurs
- [ ] A fair game is a bet in which the participant, over a large series of bets, is neither better nor worse off
- [ ] Risk attitudes differ between people and generally range from risk averse to risk seeking
- [ ] We generally assume that financial managers are risk averse

## Active learning activity 5.1

### Attitudes to risk

Do a quick survey in the class. How many people:

1. Voluntarily buy insurance?
2. Save or contribute to a pension plan?
3. Regularly gamble on lottery tickets?
4. Drive a motorbike or take part in risky sports like ski-ing or mountaineering?

Are groups 1 and 2 mutually exclusive from 3 and 4? If not, explain if you consider their attitude to risk to be inconsistent and why this might be the case.

## 5.2 Markowitz portfolio theory

### 5.2.1 Introduction

Portfolio theory is derived from the work of pioneer Harry Markowitz in the 1950s. We will not dwell at length on the more technical aspects of his peerless contribution, preferring instead to get the main points of the argument across. The most important point of portfolio theory is that, unless you are risk seeking, and we would normally assume you are not, it is not a good idea to have all of your investment funds in one asset. This is because by investing your funds in two or more assets, that is to say, a **portfolio**, it is almost always possible to improve return relative to the risk being taken, or vice versa. The only proviso here is that the returns on our portfolio assets must **not be perfectly positively statistically correlated**. The technical explanations of correlation, covariance, variance and standard deviation will be given in the next section, but as a very simple example of how portfolios improve risk relative to return, let us return to our risk-averse investor who is faced with an investment that is identical to the coin-toss type fair bet discussed above.

Let's suppose that the investor has £20 to invest. Would he or she be better to stake it all on one 'coin-toss' investment, or would it be better to divide it between two or more? Perhaps unsurprisingly, the answer is that it would be better to divide the investment between two £10 coin tosses. But it's useful to examine the exact reason why. The single £20 investment would have the characteristics discussed in the previous section with two possible outcomes, each having a probability 0.5 or one half of either gaining or losing £20. Two £10 investments would spread the risk, however, by having four possible outcomes. Let's suppose that the two £10 coin-flip 'investments' are with Harry and Joe. The possible outcomes of both investments are illustrated in Screenshot 5.6.

| 1 | **POSSIBLE OUTCOME** |
|---|---|
| 2 | 1. Win Harry (+£10), Win Joe (+10) |
| 3 | 2. Win Harry (+10), Lose Joe (-10) |
| 4 | 3. Lose Harry (-10), Win Joe (+10) |
| 5 | 4. Lose Harry (-10), Lose Joe (-10) |
| 6 | |

Screenshot 5.6  Possible outcomes over two fair game bets

You will observe that there are now four outcomes rather than two. As each possible outcome is equally likely, the probability of each outcome is 0.25 or one quarter. The full calculation for expected value is given in Screenshot 5.7.

| 1 | POSSIBLE OUTCOME | Value of Outcome (V) | Probability of Outcome (P) | V*P |
|---|---|---|---|---|
| 2 | 1. Win Harry (+£10), Win Joe (+10) | 20 | 0.25 | £5.00 |
| 3 | 2. Win Harry (+10), Lose Joe (-10) | 0 | 0.25 | £0.00 |
| 4 | 3. Lose Harry (-10), Win Joe (+10) | 0 | 0.25 | £0.00 |
| 5 | 4. Lose Harry (-10), Lose Joe (-10) | -20 | 0.25 | -£5.00 |

Screenshot 5.7  Expected value over two £10 fair game bets

The really interesting thing about the two-investment portfolio approach is that although there is still a possibility of losing £20, it is now a less likely possibility. This is because the probability of losing £20 is now 0.25, as opposed to 0.5 in the previous case where £20 was staked all on one investment. Thus the allocation of the £20 fund to the two-investment portfolio is clearly less risky than the single-asset investment. This is in spite of the fact that the expected or average value of net gain in both cases is exactly the same (zero) and indeed the range of outcomes (–£20 to +£20) is also exactly the same as in the single investment case. The reason for this is that the two-investment portfolio has created two new possible outcomes which are less extreme and in the centre of the previous two existing outcomes. Consequently, it is still possible to gain £20 or to lose £20 with the portfolio approach, as it was with one single concentrated investment. But the probability of this event is now only 0.25. Furthermore, there is a new more moderate possibility now of neither gaining nor losing with probability 0.5. This new possibility might not sound terribly exciting, but it is preferable for the risk averse, who like the quiet life and prefer outcomes in the middle.

Clearly the range is no longer a reliable guide to risk, as the range in both cases is the same, yet the perception of risk is different. Hence we need to examine a more technically sophisticated measure of variation or volatility of outcome, namely variance and standard deviation.

## 5.2.2 Frequency distributions, central tendency and dispersion

We do understand that the subject of statistics is not everyone's favourite, but unfortunately it is impossible to understand portfolio theory without some basic statistical concepts, and we'll try to keep it as straightforward as possible. The basic building block for statistics is the statistical distribution otherwise known as the **frequency distribution**.

You have already come across frequency distributions in Screenshots 5.1–5.7. A frequency distribution, for our purposes, is just a description of the value of each possible outcome along with the associated probability of that outcome. Thus, Screenshot 5.7 is in effect a frequency distribution which describes four possible outcomes (20, 0, 0 and –20) with associated probabilities (0.25, 0.25, 0.25, 0.25). It is useful to be able to sum up the important characteristics of a frequency distribution. The important characteristics for our purposes are (1) where is the centre of the distribution? and (2) how spread out is the distribution?

1. **The centre of the distribution**. We want to know where the centre of the distribution is because this is usually where the most typical or frequently occurring values occur.

Therefore in order to measure this we can use the well-known concept of the mean or average, which gives us an idea of the most representative or typical value of a group of numbers. In our case, we will use a particular type of mean called the expected value, which we discussed in Section 5.1.2. The mean, expected value and other measures of 'where the centre is' are known as **measures of central tendency.**

2. **The spread of the distribution.** The other thing we need is a way of being able to summarise how spread out the distribution is about the centre. So why not just take the average distance from the centre? A quick glance back at the figures for the fair bets represented by Screenshots 5.5 and 5.6 should reveal the answer. Take Screenshot 5.5, for example, which sets out the figures for the £10 bet. The average distance would be the average of £10 and –£10 which would be zero. The same applies to Screenshot 5.6 in which one would calculate the mean distance from the centre as the average of £20 and –£20. Even if we were to take into account the probabilities, which we should, as the distance from the mean should really be calculated as an expected value, it would make no difference. In fact this problem occurs with all data sets. The way we typically get over it is to take the **expected value of the *squared* difference from the mean.**

Take, for example, the single £20 fair game investment. The calculations for this are given in Screenshot 5.8. The sequence of these calculations is as follows:

1. For each possible outcome take the distance of the associated value from the mean or expected value, i.e. 20–0 and –20–0.

2. Square this distance.

3. Multiply each squared distance by the probability of the event.

4. Take the sum of (3). This gives the variance.

5. The variance unfortunately is expressed in squared units. Therefore in order to get it back to natural units, i.e. pounds sterling, we take the square root of the variance to give us the standard deviation.

By way of further illustrating this process, in Screenshot 5.8 we have calculated variance and standard deviation for the £20 portfolio investment.

| | A | B | C | D |
|---|---|---|---|---|
| 1 | OUTCOMES | Value (V) | Probability (P) | |
| 2 | 1. Win | £20 | 0.5 | |
| 3 | 2. Lose | -£20 | 0.5 | |
| 4 | | | | |
| 5 | | | Average or EV | £0 |
| 6 | | | | |
| 7 | (1) Distance From Mean | (2) Squared Distance | (3) Sqrd Distance*Prob | |
| 8 | £20 | £400 | £200 | |
| 9 | -£20 | £400 | £200 | |
| 10 | | | | |
| 11 | | (4) Variance | 400 | |
| 12 | | | | |
| 13 | | (5) Standard Deviation | £20.00 | |
| 14 | | | | |

Screenshot 5.8 Variance and standard deviation of £20 single fair game investment

The standard deviation is normally taken as the measure of risk in finance for the reasons discussed above. As we can see, the calculations confirm what was averred earlier, namely that the portfolio approach is less risky than the single asset investment approach. The portfolio approach has reduced the amount of variation in the value of the investment.

## Active learning activity 5.2

Repeat the calculations in Screenshot 5.8 but this time use the following data – three possible outcomes to an investment, all equally weighted:

Outcome 1 = £100
Outcome 2 = £200
Outcome 3 = £300

### 5.2.3 Stock returns, volatility and correlation

It is time now to leave behind hypothetical examples involving coin tosses and to deal in some real financial assets. Let us consider that we wish to invest in a two-asset portfolio consisting of IBM ordinary shares and Coca-Cola ordinary shares. We might like to look at data on the past performance of these two stocks over the long run in order to consider how our portfolio ought to be constructed. Until fairly recently, the gathering of the necessary data might have proved wearisome and expensive.

However, nowadays such data are readily to hand. A useful resource in this respect is finance.yahoo.com, as illustrated in Screenshot 5.9. It is possible to use this site to get quotes for a large number of different assets. It is also possible, and this is the real beauty for frustrated researchers in finance, to get historical prices. In the examples that follow, we use 20-year monthly price data for Coca-Cola and IBM for the dates July 1987 to June 2008. If

Screenshot 5.9 finance.yahoo.com

you use the Yahoo website, you will be asked for 'ticker symbols' for these in order to access the data. They are easily looked up, but for the sake of information they are 'KO' and 'IBM'. You can download data from the 'historical prices' link which appears with any quote.[1]

The average monthly return for IBM is 0.61% which translates in annual terms (using the formula introduced in Chapter 1) into 7.6% [i.e. $(1 + 0.0061)12 - 1$]. Let's round it to 7.5%. For Coca-Cola, the monthly return is 1.02% which translates into an annual return of 12.95% or 13%. The standard deviation for IBM is 31.5%, while that of Coca-Cola is 25.5%. The relative volatility of IBM is clearly brought out in Figures 5.1 and 5.2, which show returns performance for the decade from the late 1980s to the late 1990s and from the late 1990s to the late 2000s, for our sample data. The Dow Jones Industrial Average (DJI) is included as a comparator.

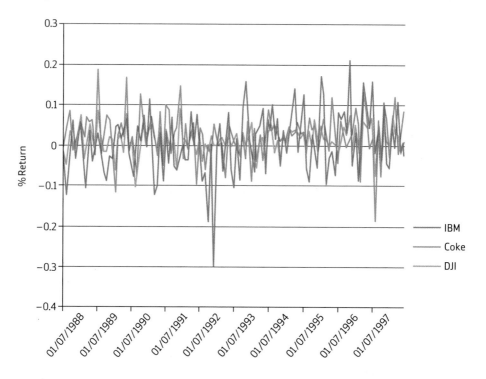

Figure 5.1 Returns for IBM, Coke and DJI 1988–1998

On an individual basis, the risk-averse investor would choose Coca-Cola and not IBM. The rejection of IBM is apparently a 'no-brainer' as it offers lower returns for higher risks (though a risk-seeking individual might be interested in the upside of the volatility of IBM – the possibility of making very high returns at certain times). However, as we discussed above, it is unwise to put your entire investment fund into one asset. So would our risk-adverse investor want to buy a portfolio consisting of both Coke and IBM? The rather surprising answer is yes, they would, thanks to the magic of portfolios. And in fact now we're going to show you a little bit of that magic. What we want to know is, what would be the return and risk of a **portfolio**

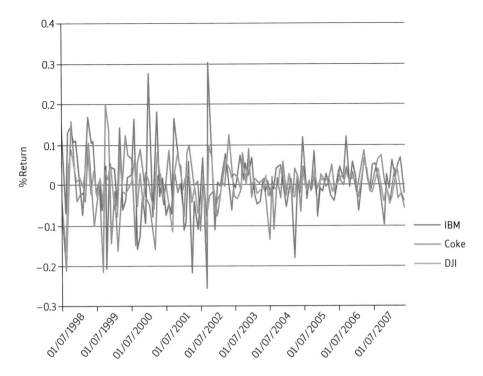

Figure 5.2  Returns for IBM, Coke and DJI 1998–2008

consisting of these two assets? In order to know that, we really need to know what the statistical relationship is between the two assets.

The statistical relationship between two assets is measured in terms of covariance or correlation. We will discuss the practical aspects of calculating these measures in the next section. However, for the moment, all we need to know is that correlation tells us something about the statistical 'fit' between two quantities. Figure 5.3 shows various scatter plots with different degrees of statistical relationship evident, depending on the correlation between the 'x' and 'y' variable. In our case of course, 'x' and 'y' would be the returns of the two assets in our portfolio.

The measure of correlation, the correlation coefficient, takes a value of between –1 and +1. If the value were –1, then the stock returns would be *perfectly* **negatively correlated**. With negative correlation, any tendency for the return on one stock to rise would be offset by a proportional decrease in the return of the other stock. Thus it would be observed that the return on Coca-Cola would tend to rise as IBM fell and vice-versa. If the value of the correlation coefficient was +1, then the stock returns would be *perfectly* **positively correlated**. With positive correlation, any tendency for the return on one stock to rise would be associated with a proportional increase in the return of the other stock. Thus it would be observed that the return on Coca-Cola would tend to rise along with any rise in IBM and vice-versa.

For most stocks the correlation is somewhere in between the two extremes of –1 and +1. The closer the correlation coefficient is to zero from either the positive or the negative side, then the weaker the statistical relationship. If the correlation coefficient takes a value of zero, there is no statistical association whatsoever. As it turns out, the correlation between the

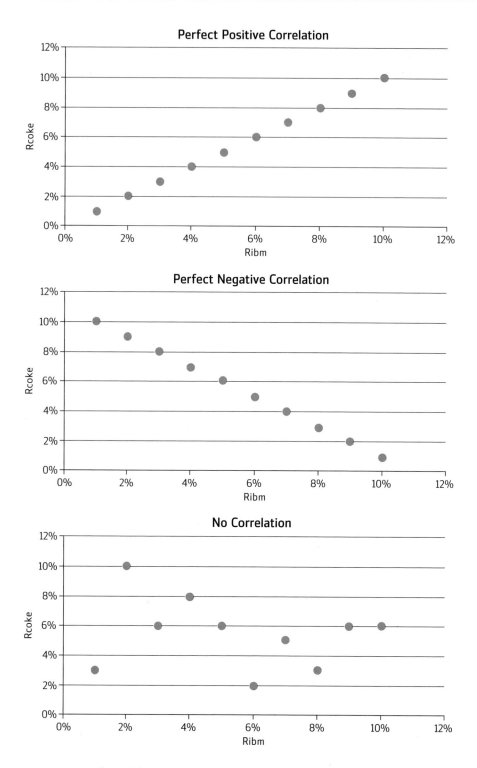

Figure 5.3 Scatter plots for different levels of correlation

stock returns for Coke and IBM is 0.04, which is not significantly different from zero. The absence of any statistical relationship can be confirmed by visual inspection of the scatterplots presented in Figures 5.4 and 5.5.

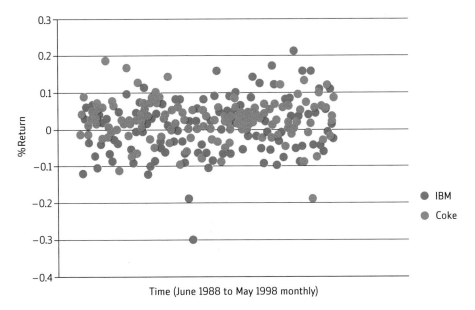

Figure 5.4 Scatterplot of stock returns for IBM and Coke 1988–1998

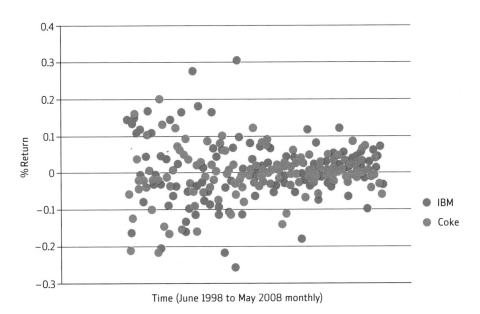

Figure 5.5 Scatterplot of stock returns for IBM and Coke 1998–2008

## Active learning activity 5.3

The following variables have been associated with success in exams. Which are likely to be positively correlated with success, which have no correlation and which have a negative correlation?

1. Going out with friends every evening
2. Attendance at tutorials
3. Number of hours of study
4. Amount of time spent on social networking
5. Length of your hair

### 5.2.4 The important statistical operating characteristics of portfolios

We are now ready to calculate the important performance characteristics of a portfolio consisting of our two ordinary shares, Coca-Cola and IBM. The calculation of the **portfolio return** is just the weighted average of the two individual stock returns and will depend on the proportion of the investment fund invested in each. For example, if we have £1,000 and decide to spend £700 on Coke shares and £300 on IBM shares, then the portfolio return will equal $0.7 \times R_{Coke} + 0.3 \times R_{IBM} = 0.7 \times 13\% + 0.3 \times 7.6\% = 11.38\%$. So, in an average year, we would expect that our investment in Coke would be worth £700 (1 + 13%) = £791 at the end of the year, while our investment in IBM would be worth £300 (1 + 7.6%) = £322.8. The sum of £791 and £322.8 is £1,113.8. So the value of our £1,000, assuming that next year is an average year, should grow to £1113.8. That is, it grows by 11.38%.

More generally, if a portfolio contains two assets, asset a and asset b, the return is as follows:

$$R_p = S_a R_a + S_b R_b$$

where $R_p$ is the portfolio return, $S_a$ is the share of asset a in the portfolio (e.g. in the example, $S_{Coke} = S_a$), $R_a$ is the return on asset a (e.g. in the example, $R_{Coke} = R_a$), $S_b$ is the share of asset b in the portfolio (e.g. in the example, $S_{IBM} = S_b$) and $R_b$ is the return on asset b (e.g. in the example, $R_b = R_b$).

As the averages taken are usually expected returns, this is often expressed as follows:

$$E(R_p) = S_a E(R_a) + S_b E(R_b)$$

where E(R) represents the expected or average value of return, R.

You can see then that the calculation of the portfolio **return** is really very straightforward. The calculation of portfolio **risk**, on the other hand, is slightly more involved. The variance of the portfolio is as follows:

$$Var_p = S_a^2 Var_a + (1 - S_a)^2 Var_b + 2S_a(1 - S_a)Corr_{ab} Stdev_a Stdev_b$$

where Var is variance, Stdev is standard deviation and Corr is correlation.

The standard symbol for standard deviation is the Greek symbol lower-case sigma ($\sigma$), while that for correlation is the Greek symbol lower-case rho ($\rho$). Hence, the expression for the portfolio variance is sometimes written:

$$\sigma_p^2 = S_a^2\sigma_a^2 + (1 - S_a)^2\sigma_b^2 + 2S_a(1 - S_a)\rho_{ab}\sigma_a\sigma_b$$

Once you've got the variance, the portfolio risk or standard deviation is just the square root of your figure:

$$\sigma_p = \sqrt{\sigma_p^2}$$

Returning to our example, assume that the correlation between the return on Coca-Cola and the return on IBM is zero. This is because it allows us for the moment to ignore the third term of our spectacular equation for portfolio variance, $2S_a(1 - S_a)Corr_{ab}Stdev_aStdev_b$. Now, remember that the variance is just the square of the standard deviation. So our variances for individual returns are as follows:

$$Var_{coke} = (Stdev_{coke})^2 = (23.5\%)^2 = (0.235)^2 = 0.0552 = 5.52\%$$

$$Var_{IBM} = (Stdev_{IBM})^2 = (31.5\%)^2 = (0.315)^2 = 0.0992 = 9.92\%$$

Now put it all together:

$$Var_p = S_a^2Var_a + (1 - S_a)^2Var_b = 0.7^2 \times (5.52\%) + 0.3^2 \times (9.92\%) = 3.60\%$$

The 70% Coke, 30% IBM is just one of many portfolios that we could have created. We could have split our investment fund an infinite number of ways. Screenshot 5.10 shows a number of possible portfolios between the two extremes of portfolio A, where the fund is 100% invested in Coke, and portfolio K, where the fund is 100% invested in IBM. Two things are worth observing here. First, portfolios B through K, which consist of an investment of between 10% and 70% of the fund, have a lower standard deviation and therefore a lower risk than portfolio A, consisting of 100% investment in Coke and nothing in IBM. Second, however, is the really surprising thing about the portfolio that is brought out in the column to the right of the column

| | | Rcoke | RIBM | Var coke | Var IBM | Corr coke-IBM | Improvement in return per unit of risk over 100% investment in Coke – Portfolios B to E |
|---|---|---|---|---|---|---|---|
| 1 | PERFORMANCE CHARACTERISTICS OF PORTFOLIO | | | | | | |
| 2 | | | | | | | |
| 3 | | Rcoke | RIBM | Var coke | Var IBM | Corr coke-IBM | |
| 4 | | 13.00% | 7.60% | 5.52% | 9.92% | 0 | |
| 5 | | | | | | | |
| 6 | Porfolios | Scoke | SIBM | Rp | Varp | Stdevp | Return per Unit of Risk |
| 7 | A (All Coke) | 1 | 0 | 13.00% | 5.52% | 23.50% | 0.553191489 |
| 8 | B | 0.9 | 0.1 | 12.46% | 4.57% | 21.38% | 0.582698043 |
| 9 | C | 0.8 | 0.2 | 11.92% | 3.93% | 19.83% | 0.601185036 |
| 10 | D | 0.7 | 0.3 | 11.38% | 3.60% | 18.97% | 0.599857816 |
| 11 | E | 0.6 | 0.4 | 10.84% | 3.58% | 18.91% | 0.573256179 |
| 12 | F | 0.5 | 0.5 | 10.30% | 3.86% | 19.65% | 0.524171331 |
| 13 | G | 0.4 | 0.6 | 9.76% | 4.46% | 21.11% | 0.462372341 |
| 14 | H | 0.3 | 0.7 | 9.22% | 5.36% | 23.15% | 0.398278641 |
| 15 | I | 0.2 | 0.8 | 8.68% | 6.57% | 25.63% | 0.338605554 |
| 16 | J | 0.1 | 0.9 | 8.14% | 8.09% | 28.45% | 0.286143834 |
| 17 | K (All IBM) | 0 | 1 | 7.60% | 9.92% | 31.50% | 0.241269841 |

Screenshot 5.10 Performance characteristics of Coke–IBM portfolios. Zero correlation

of portfolio standard deviations. In this column, the portfolio return is divided by the portfolio standard deviation to get the amount of return per unit of standard deviation; in other words, the amount of **return per unit of risk**. It is evident that portfolios B, C, D and E, where between 10% and 40% of the fund is invested in IBM, provide a better return relative to risk than a 100% investment in Coke, despite the fact that Coke has better average return and lower risk than IBM. Now that's portfolio magic!

It's not just the fact that the portfolio improves the risk–return relationship which is so useful about portfolios. It's also the fact that the portfolio allows much finer adjustment of risk relative to return in line with investor preferences and attitudes, as the following risk–return diagram (Figure 5.6) shows. This is sometimes known as the **opportunity set** as it shows the opportunities available to the investor in terms of return relative to risk.

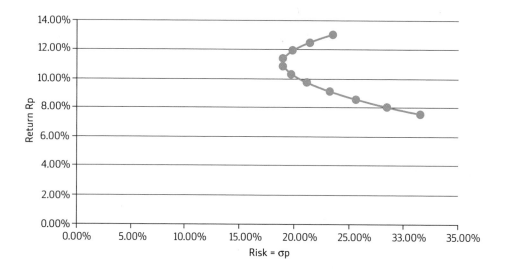

Figure 5.6  Risk–return relationship/opportunity set

In fact we could have done even better if the correlation between the two stocks had happened to be negative, as we can see in Screenshot 5.11 in which it is assumed that the correlation coefficient is –1.

An interesting feature of the relationship between risk and return when the returns are perfectly negatively correlated is that there is the possibility of reducing risk to zero, as we can see with the **zero risk portfolio** which lies between portfolio E and portfolio F. To be honest, this is more of an interesting theoretical point than a practical possibility, but it is useful to know. Figure 5.7 shows the relationship between the risk and return in this case.

You will notice two things about the relationship in this case. First, the relationship is much more angular, rather than being in the shape of a curve as was the case previously. Second, the relationship comes in much more towards the vertical axis; that is, much more risk reduction (and improvement of return relative to risk) is possible with perfect negative correlation. This illustrates a general principle. The further towards –1 the correlation coefficient is, the greater the possibility of risk reduction. The futher towards +1 the correlation coefficient is, the smaller the possibility of risk reduction.

| 19 | PERFORMANCE CHARACTERISTICS OF PORTFOLIO | | | | | | |
|---|---|---|---|---|---|---|---|
| 20 | | | | | | | |
| 21 | | $R_{coke}$ | $R_{IBM}$ | Var coke | Var IBM | Corr coke-IBM | |
| 22 | | 13.00% | 7.60% | 5.52% | 9.92% | -1 | |
| 23 | | | | | | | |
| 24 | **Porfolios** | $S_{coke}$ | $S_{IBM}$ | Rp | Varp | Stdevp | Return per Unit of Risk |
| 25 | A (All Coke) | 1 | 0 | 13.00% | 5.52% | *23.50%* | *0.553191489* |
| 26 | B | 0.9 | 0.1 | 12.46% | 3.24% | 18.00% | 0.692222222 |
| 27 | C | 0.8 | 0.2 | 11.92% | 1.56% | 12.50% | 0.9536 |
| 28 | D | 0.7 | 0.3 | 11.38% | 0.49% | 7.00% | 1.625714286 |
| 29 | E | 0.6 | 0.4 | 10.84% | 0.02% | 1.50% | 7.226666667 |
| 30 | **Zero Risk** | 0.573 | 0.427 | 10.69% | 0.00% | 0.02% na | |
| 31 | F | 0.5 | 0.5 | 10.30% | 0.16% | 4.00% | 2.575 |
| 32 | G | 0.4 | 0.6 | 9.76% | 0.90% | 9.50% | 1.027368421 |
| 33 | H | 0.3 | 0.7 | 9.22% | 2.25% | 15.00% | 0.614666667 |
| 34 | I | 0.2 | 0.8 | 8.68% | 4.20% | 20.50% | 0.423414634 |
| 35 | J | 0.1 | 0.9 | 8.14% | 6.76% | 26.00% | 0.313076923 |
| 36 | K (All IBM) | 0 | 1 | 7.60% | 9.92% | *31.50%* | *0.241269841* |
| 37 | | | | | | | |

Screenshot 5.11  Performance characteristics of Coke–IBM portfolios.
Perfect negative correlation = −1

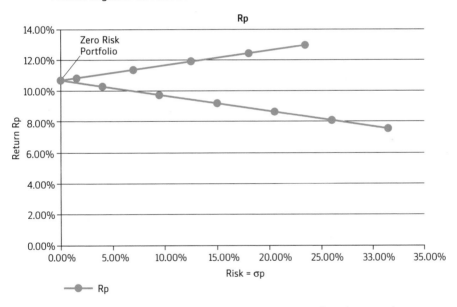

Figure 5.7  Risk–return relationship/opportunity set. Correlation = −1

We have talked at length about portfolio correlation as it is a very important concept. We now turn to the full calculation of portfolio risk including correlation/covariance.

### 5.2.5 How to do portfolio arithmetic and how to calculate covariance and correlation

In real life, we would typically calculate the performance characteristics of the portfolio using what are called **time series data**. That is to say, we would gather daily or weekly or possibly even hourly data and calculate the relevant characteristics using the appropriate spreadsheet functions, such as var(), correl(), etc. However, it is useful to know what these functions actually do, so in what follows we present a simplified version of our data, so that we can practise calculating the fundamental performance characteristics from scratch. In most simplified portfolio problems, the performance of the portfolio is typically examined over various phases of the business cycle. See if you can spot any cyclical behaviour in the annual returns data for Coke, IBM and the DJI in Figure 5.8.

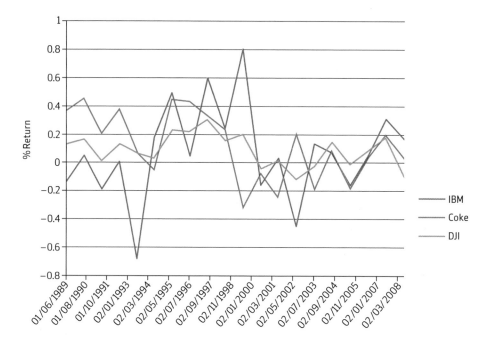

Figure 5.8 Annual returns data for Coke, IBM and the DJI

Four phases are evident:

1. A time of middling performance from 1989 to 1994.

2. A time of exceptional performance from 1995 to 1999.

3. A time of poor performance from 2000 to 2004.

4. A time of modest recovery from 2005 to 2008.

We will call these phases:

1. Normal growth.                    3. Recession.

2. Boom.                             4. Recovery.

The average return for each of the four phases is presented in Screenshot 5.12. You will notice that we have also calculated probabilities. We arrived at these figures by just taking the number of years that returns were in a particular phase and dividing by the total number of sample years which was 12. So, for example, there were 4 years in phase 1, 3 years in phase 2 and so on. Screenshot 5.12 shows the expected values for Coke, IBM and the DJI. This is calculated in the way explained in Section 5.1.3.

| 1 | STATES OF THE WORLD | PROBABILITY | RETURNS | | |
|---|---|---|---|---|---|
| 2 | | | Coca-Cola | IBM | Dow-Jones |
| 3 | 1. Normal Growth | 0.3 | 23.79% | -1.79% | 8.77% |
| 4 | 2. Boom | 0.25 | 22.32% | 43.50% | 22.15% |
| 5 | 3. Recession | 0.25 | -4.11% | -7.65% | -1.00% |
| 6 | 4. Recovery | 0.2 | 3.01% | 8.33% | 10.01% |
| 7 | | | | | |
| 8 | E(R) | | 12.29% | 10.09% | 9.92% |
| 9 | | | | | |

Screenshot 5.12 Expected returns for Coke, IBM and the DJI

We now need to find variances and standard deviations for Coke and IBM. These are found in the stages (described above in Section 5.2.4) by:

1. Taking each deviation.
2. Squaring each deviation.
3. Multiplying each square deviation by probability.
4. Taking the sum of (3) to get the variance.
5. Taking the square root of (4) to get the standard deviation.

This is demonstrated in Screenshots 5.13 and 5.14.

You will notice that our estimated standard deviations are significantly smaller than previously. With the full data set we have estimated a standard deviation of 31.5 for IBM and 23.5 for Coke. The figures are now 20.02 and 12.22 respectively. Clearly we have lost a lot of information by summarising and aggregating the data in the way we have. In real life, we would do things the long way, taking data based on as frequent an interval as possible. However, this is long, complicated and messy, so for the pedagogic purposes of constructing a simpler hypothetical example which illustrates the basic principles involved, we will stick with our data from Screenshots 5.13 and 5.14 despite our misgivings.

In order to calculate the important portfolio characteristics, we also need a statistical measure of how the returns relate to each other. We can do this calculating the **covariance** or **correlation**, which was introduced earlier. Let us consider the **covariance** first of all. The covariance is calculated in a very similar fashion to the **variance**. The difference is that instead of squaring one individual set of deviations, we multiply one set of deviations by the other set of deviations to see how the two sets of returns co-vary with each other. So the process for covariance is as follows:

1. For each stock return take the deviation from the mean.
2. Multiply one set of deviations by the other set.
3. Multiply each co-deviation by probability.
4. Take the sum of (3) to get the co-variance.

| 1 | | Coca-Cola | | | | | |
|---|---|---|---|---|---|---|---|
| 2 | | | | | | | |
| 3 | SOW | Prob | Returns | Exp Retn. | (1) Deviation | (2) Sq Dev | (3) Sq Dev*Pr |
| 4 | 1. Normal Growth | 0.3 | 23.79% | 12.29% | 11.50% | 1.32% | 0.40% |
| 5 | 2. Boom | 0.25 | 22.32% | 12.29% | 10.03% | 1.01% | 0.25% |
| 6 | 3. Recession | 0.25 | -4.11% | 12.29% | -16.40% | 2.69% | 0.67% |
| 7 | 4. Recovery | 0.2 | 3.01% | 12.29% | -9.28% | 0.86% | 0.17% |
| 8 | | | | | | | |
| 9 | | | | | | (4) Var | 1.49% |
| 10 | | | | | | (5) St Dev | 12.22% |

Screenshot 5.13  Variance and standard deviation for Coke returns

| 14 | | IBM | | | | | |
|---|---|---|---|---|---|---|---|
| 15 | | | | | | | |
| 16 | SOW | Prob | Returns | Exp Retn. | (1) Deviation | (2) Sq Dev | (3) Sq Dev*Pr |
| 17 | 1. Normal Growth | 0.3 | -1.79% | 10.09% | -11.88% | 1.41% | 0.42% |
| 18 | 2. Boom | 0.25 | 43.50% | 10.09% | 33.41% | 11.16% | 2.79% |
| 19 | 3. Recession | 0.25 | -7.65% | 10.09% | -17.74% | 3.15% | 0.79% |
| 20 | 4. Recovery | 0.2 | 8.33% | 10.09% | -1.76% | 0.03% | 0.01% |
| 21 | | | | | | | |
| 22 | | | | | | (4) Var | 4.01% |
| 23 | | | | | | (5) St Dev | 20.02% |

Screenshot 5.14  Variance and standard deviation for IBM returns

So the only real difference from the variance is step (2) and even that is fairly obviously analogous to stage (2) from the variance process. The whole procedure is demonstrated in Screenshot 5.15.

The correlation coefficient is closely related to the covariance measure. Covariance is in certain respects unsatisfactory as it does not come in standard units. Thus it is difficult to compare the outcome of one covariance with another in terms of which gives the closer statistical fit. The correlation coefficient gets over this by providing an absolute scale between –1 and +1. The correlation coefficient is defined as:

$$\rho_{ab} = (\text{Cov}_{ab}/[\sigma_a \sigma_b]).$$

That is, the covariance is divided by the product of the two standard deviations to get a standard range of correlation. We should note a particular point about the correlation coefficient we have calculated for our simplified example using four aggregated averages from 20 points of annual data. This is that it is very different from the result using 240 values from monthly data. Again, it highlights the issue that in real life one must be careful not to over-aggregate when performing this kind of analysis. However, the figure will do for the moment for our hypothetical example.

| 26 | COVARIANCE OF COCA-COLA WITH IBM | | | | | |
|---|---|---|---|---|---|---|
| 27 | | | | | | |
| 28 SOW | | Prob | (1a) Deviation | (1b) Deviation | (2) DevCk*DevIBM | (3) DevCk*DevIBM*Pr |
| 29 1. Normal Growth | | 0.3 | 11.50% | -11.88% | -1.37% | -0.41% |
| 30 2. Boom | | 0.25 | 10.03% | 33.41% | 3.35% | 0.84% |
| 31 3. Recession | | 0.25 | -16.40% | -17.74% | 2.91% | 0.73% |
| 32 4. Recovery | | 0.2 | -9.28% | -1.76% | 0.16% | 0.03% |
| 33 | | | | | | |
| 34 | | | | | (4) Cov Coke-IBM | 1.19% |
| 35 | | | | | (5) Correlation | 0.4856655 |
| 36 | | | | | | |

Screenshot 5.15  Covariance of Coke and IBM returns

The next thing would be to construct expected returns and risk for our portfolio. We dealt with the calculation of these in Section 5.5.4. However, it is worth restating the equation for risk.

$$\sigma_p = \sqrt{\sigma_p^2} = \sqrt{(S_a^2\sigma_a^2 + (1 - S_a)^2\sigma_b^2 + 2S_a(1 - S_a)\rho_{ab}\sigma_a\sigma_b)}$$

As the correlation coefficient is defined as the covariance divided by the product of the two standard deviations, the expression for risk can also be written as follows:

$$\sigma_p = \sqrt{\sigma_p^2} = \sqrt{(S_a^2\sigma_a^2 + (1 - S_a)^2\sigma_b^2 + 2S_a(1 - S_a)\sigma_{ab})}$$

where $\sigma_{ab}$ is the covariance of asset a with asset b.

Tackle the calculation by breaking it down into its constituent parts. These are as follows:

1. The calculation of the direct contribution of asset a to portfolio variance: $S_a^2\sigma_a^2$

2. The calculation of the direct contribution of asset b to portfolio variance: $(1 - S_a)^2\sigma_b^2$

3. The calculation of the interaction term: $2S_a(1 - S_a)\sigma_{ab}$

4. Sum (1) to (3) to get portfolio variance

5. Take the square root to get portfolio standard deviation or risk

This sequence of calculations is demonstrated in Screenshot 5.16.

| 1 | | Coca-Cola | IBM | | | | | |
|---|---|---|---|---|---|---|---|---|
| 2 E(R) | | 12.29% | 10.09% | | | | | |
| 3 Var | | 1.49% | 4.01% | | | | | |
| 4 Covar | | | 1.19% | | | | | |
| 5 | | | | | | | | |
| 6 PORTFOLIO RISK CALCULATION | | | | | | | | |
| 7 Portfolios | Scoke | SIBM | (1) | (2) | (3) | (4) | (5) | |
| 8 A | 1 | 0 | 0.01492 | 0 | 0 | 0.014924 | 0.12216 | |
| 9 B | 0.75 | 0.25 | 0.00839 | 0.0025 | 0.004453595 | 0.0153526 | 0.12391 | |
| 10 C | 0.5 | 0.5 | 0.00373 | 0.01002 | 0.005938126 | 0.0196861 | 0.14031 | |
| 11 D | 0.25 | 0.75 | 0.00093 | 0.02254 | 0.004453595 | 0.0279246 | 0.16711 | |
| 12 E | 0 | 1 | 0 | 0.04007 | 0 | 0.040068 | 0.20017 | |
| 13 | | | | | | | | |

Screenshot 5.16  Sequence of calculations necessary to calculate portfolio risk

We will come back to the calculation of portfolio risk when we tackle some examples in the exercises below, but hopefully you now have a clear idea how the important operational characteristics are calculated.

## Practical implications for managers

### Markowitz portfolio theory and portfolio arithmetic

In theory, the best way to run a business would be to take a portfolio approach as this would maximise return relative to risk. This might be more difficult for most small- to medium-size businesses which tend to be very concentrated in one type of business or in one geographical area. Nevertheless, if possible try to diversify or spread the risk. One of your authors had a friend who had a successful business supplying lasers for cosmetic treatment. At one point it was valued at £2 million. It was at this stage that he should have diversified the risk and locked in some of the value in cash terms by selling a stake in the business and holding a portfolio of 49% cash and 51% stake in the business. The business got into some trouble and eventually was worth nothing.

## Key concepts

- [ ] A **frequency distribution** is a description of the value of each possible outcome along with the associated probability of that outcome
- [ ] **Statistical correlation** measures the degree to which two variables move together and ranges from +1 to −1
- [ ] For stocks with **negative correlation**, any tendency for the return on one stock to rise would be offset by a proportional decrease in the return of the other stock
- [ ] For stocks with **positive correlation**, any tendency for the return on one stock to rise would be offset by a proportional increase in the return of the other stock
- [ ] **Return per unit of risk** is calculated by portfolio return divided by the portfolio standard deviation
- [ ] An **opportunity set** is a risk–return diagram which shows the opportunities available to the investor in terms of return relative to risk
- [ ] **Portfolio return** is the average of the individual stock returns weighted by the proportion of the investment fund invested in each
- [ ] The **mean of a distribution** is the average
- [ ] The **portfolio standard deviation** is a measure of the risk of the portfolio investment

**Active learning activity 5.4**

## Portfolio calculations

Go to finance.yahoo.com and download price data for two different popular stocks, then calculate monthly returns. Remember when calculating the return to allow for stock splits and dividends. For a demonstration of how this was done for the case of IBM and Coke, please see the spreadsheet online. Once you have calculated monthly returns along with the variance and adjusted these to the average annual equivalent, calculate the expected return and risk of portfolios comprising your two assets.

## 5.3 The limits of portfolio performance and the efficient frontier

### 5.3.1 Introduction – the limits of portfolio performance

We return now to the portfolios calculated using the more detailed data in Section 5.2.3. We saw that with zero correlation, portfolio improved risk versus return, while the portfolio with perfect negative correlation improved risk versus return even more, giving the maximum possible improvement in return relative to risk. Just to complete this analysis, we might also look at perfect positive correlation. The portfolio characteristics are given in Screenshot 5.17.

As you can see from risk, return and return per unit of risk, there would be absolutely no point in holding a portfolio under these circumstances. Any move towards investment in IBM from 100% investment in Coke would **increase risk** and **reduce return**. The position is summarised in Figure 5.9.

| 41 | | $R_{coke}$ | $R_{IBM}$ | Var $_{coke}$ | Var $_{IBM}$ | Corr $_{coke\text{-}IBM}$ | |
|----|----|----|----|----|----|----|----|
| 42 | | 13.00% | 7.60% | 5.52% | 9.92% | 1 | |
| 43 | | | | | | | |
| 44 | **Porfolios** | $S_{coke}$ | $S_{IBM}$ | **Rp** | **Varp** | **Stdevp** | **Return per Unit of Risk** |
| 45 | A (All Coke) | 1 | 0 | **13.00%** | 5.52% | *23.50%* | *0.553191489* |
| 46 | B | 0.9 | 0.1 | **12.46%** | 5.90% | 24.30% | 0.512757202 |
| 47 | C | 0.8 | 0.2 | **11.92%** | 6.30% | 25.10% | 0.474900398 |
| 48 | D | 0.7 | 0.3 | **11.38%** | 6.71% | 25.90% | 0.439382239 |
| 49 | E | 0.6 | 0.4 | **10.84%** | 7.13% | 26.70% | 0.405992509 |
| 50 | F | 0.5 | 0.5 | **10.30%** | 7.56% | 27.50% | 0.374545455 |
| 51 | G | 0.4 | 0.6 | **9.76%** | 8.01% | 28.30% | 0.344876325 |
| 52 | H | 0.3 | 0.7 | **9.22%** | 8.47% | 29.10% | 0.316838488 |
| 53 | I | 0.2 | 0.8 | **8.68%** | 8.94% | 29.90% | 0.290301003 |
| 54 | J | 0.1 | 0.9 | **8.14%** | 9.42% | 30.70% | 0.26514658 |
| 55 | K (All IBM) | 0 | 1 | **7.60%** | 9.92% | *31.50%* | *0.241269841* |
| 56 | | | | | | | |

Screenshot 5.17  Portfolio in which Coke returns and IBM returns are perfectly correlated

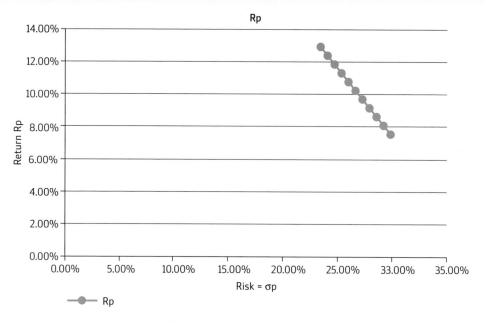

Figure 5.9  Perfect positive correlation = +1

In fact the only point in holding a portfolio under the circumstances that returns were perfectly positively correlated would be for the purpose of adjusting the amount of risk being tak-
en in order to closely match investor preference. Even that would only work if the asset with
the lower return also had lower risk, **unlike in the present case**. For example, if the return
on variance of the IBM return were less than the variance of the Coke return, for example, 1%
instead of 9%, then Figure 5.10 would represent the risk–return combinations possible.

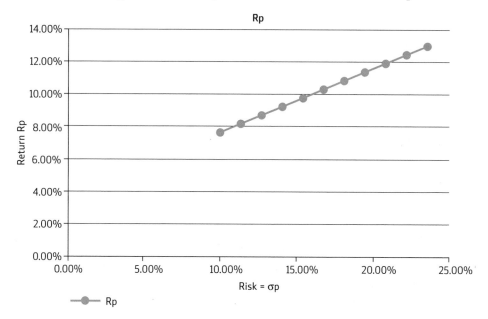

Figure 5.10  Perfect correlation – benefit to portfolio from adjusting risk, but no
other portfolio benefits

Accordingly, investors could at least adjust the amount of risk taken between 10% and 23% depending on their taste for risk. However, there is no benefit in terms of improved return relative to risk.

The case of perfect correlation sets a bound on the ability of portfolio managers to gain improved return per unit of risk. If correlation is +1, there will be very little or no improvement. This is in contrast with the other extreme boundary case, where correlation is perfectly negative. In this case, as we have seen, there is a maximal ability to improve return relative to risk. The opportunity set relationship between risk and return for these two extreme positions along with the relationship for zero correlation are shown in Figure 5.11. In practice the relationship for most pairs of assets will look more like the zero correlation case than the two extreme cases.

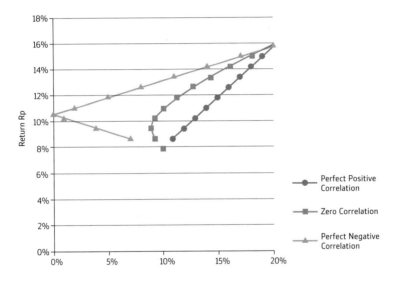

Figure 5.11 The boundaries on risk–return possibilities

## 5.3.2 Portfolios of portfolios

It is possible to hold portfolios of portfolios. It is feasible to do this without any loss of return relative to risk provided portfolio characteristics are scalable downwards. Thus, for example, in theory a £100 investment should have exactly the same risk–return portfolio characteristics as a £1,000 investment. In practice, we might have one or two problems in buying and making fine adjustments to portfolios if we were dealing in such small sums. However, given that most portfolio investments are typically in quite large sums, it is not unrealistic to suppose that say a £10,000 investment had exactly the same characteristics as a £100,000 investment for the same given proportional investment. So, for example, £7,000 invested in Coke and £3,000 in IBM should have the same portfolio performance in terms of risk and return as £70,000 and £30,000, respectively. Given this scalability, one could improve investment performance further by dividing one's fund between more assets or portfolios. The idea of investing in more portfolios allows us to investigate the possibility of going beyond the two-asset portfolio and extending our portfolio to any number of assets. Take the following example in Screenshot 5.18 using data for four stocks, A, B, C and D. [The figures for this example are taken from Benninga (2000).]

| 9 | | A | B | C | D |
|---|---|---|---|---|---|
| 10 | E(R) | 6.00% | 8.00% | 10.00% | 15.00% |
| 11 | Var | 10.00% | 30.00% | 40.00% | 50.00% |
| 12 | Std Dev | 31.62% | 54.77% | 63.25% | 70.71% |
| 13 | | | | | |
| 14 | Cov(A,B) | 1.00% | | Cov(C,D) | 2.00% |
| 15 | Corr(A,B) | 5.77% | | Corr(C,D) | 4.47% |

Screenshot 5.18 Performance characteristics for assets A, B, C and D

Imagine we had constructed two portfolios already. Portfolio 1 consists of assets A, B, C and D in the proportions, 20%, 30%, 40% and 10%. Portfolio 2 is in the proportions 20%, 10%, 10% and 60%. Each portfolio has a mean and expected return. Therefore, in effect, we can treat the two portfolios in exactly the same way as we would treat two individual assets. Screenshot 5.19 shows performance characteristics for portfolio 1 (0.2, 0.3, 0.4, 0.1) and portfolio 2 (0.2, 0.1, 0.1, 0.6).

| 17 | Portfolio 1 | | | Portfolio 2 | |
|---|---|---|---|---|---|
| 18 | E(R) | 9.10% | | E(R) | 12.00% |
| 19 | Var | 12.16% | | Var | 20.34% |
| 20 | | | | | |
| 21 | Cov(A,B) | 0.0714 | | | |
| 22 | Corr(A,B) | 0.4540 | | | |

Screenshot 5.19 Performance characteristics for portfolios 1 and 2

The performance characteristics of the new portfolio, portfolio X-Z which are themselves portfolios of portfolios 1 and 2, are given in Screenshot 5.20.

| 25 | Portfolios | S port1 | S port2 | Rp | Stdevp | |
|---|---|---|---|---|---|---|
| 26 | | 1 | 0 | 9.10% | 34.9% | |
| 27 | Y | 0.95 | 0.05 | 9.25% | 34.2% | |
| 28 | | 0.9 | 0.1 | 9.39% | 33.7% | |
| 29 | | 0.85 | 0.15 | 9.54% | 33.3% | |
| 30 | | 0.8 | 0.2 | 9.68% | 33.0% | |
| 31 | W | 0.75 | 0.25 | 9.83% | 32.8% | |
| 32 | X | 0.7 | 0.3 | 9.97% | 32.8% | |
| 33 | | 0.65 | 0.35 | 10.12% | 33.0% | |
| 34 | | 0.6 | 0.4 | 10.26% | 33.3% | |
| 35 | | 0.55 | 0.45 | 10.41% | 33.7% | |
| 36 | Z | 0.5 | 0.5 | 10.55% | 34.2% | |
| 37 | | 0.4 | 0.6 | 10.84% | 35.6% | |
| 38 | | 0.3 | 0.7 | 11.13% | 37.5% | |
| 39 | | 0.2 | 0.8 | 11.42% | 39.7% | |
| 40 | | 0.1 | 0.9 | 11.71% | 42.3% | |
| 41 | | 0 | 1 | 12.00% | 45.1% | |

Screenshot 5.20 Performance characteristics for portfolio Y–Z (which are themselves composed of 1 and 2)

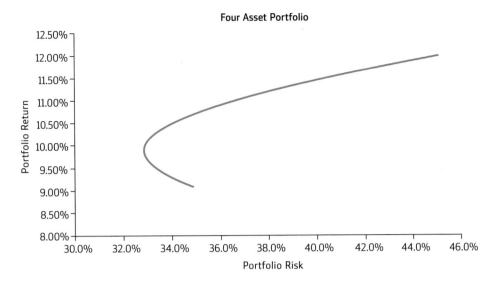

Figure 5.12  Opportuniy set for two portfolios of four risky assets

The risk–return characteristics of the opportunity set are summarised in Figure 5.12. You will notice that the graph has the same general shape as in the two-asset case. So, in general, for any amount of risky assets with imperfect correlation, the shape is always roughly the same. Note that the investor would not choose portfolios on the bottom part of the opportunity set. This is because it is always possible to do better on the upper section of the line than the lower section. This point is brought out in more detail in Figure 5.13 , where the portfolios underlined and italicised have the same risk but lower returns than the portfolios highlighted in bold. Thus, for example, portfolio Z with a return of 10.55% and a risk of 34.2% is superior to portfolio Y with the same risk but a return of only 9.25%. By the same token, X

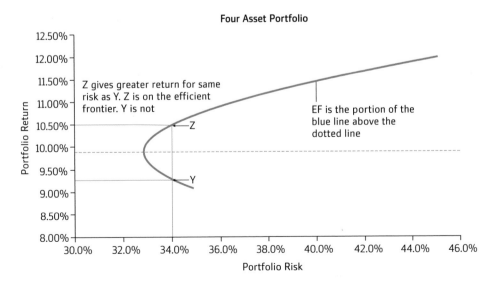

Figure 5.13  An efficient versus an inefficient portfolio

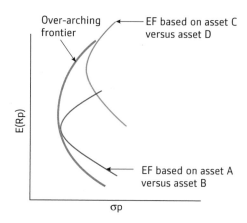

Figure 5.14 Multi-asset efficient frontier composed of two-asset efficient frontiers

(9.97%, 32.8%) would be preferred to W (9.83%, 32.8%). No portfolios would be chosen by the rational investor in the lower section of the opportunity set, as they offer a lower return for the same amount of risk as we can see in Figure 5.13.

The part of the opportunity set above the horizontal line in Figure 5.14 is called the **efficient frontier**.

We could have taken a slightly different approach in dealing with more than two assets. This would have two efficient frontiers representing two sets of assets, for example, 'A' versus 'B' and 'C' versus 'D'. The diagram shows that we could combine these in an over-arching frontier which combined the two. As you can see, risk–return improves along the over-arching frontier which represents the possibilities available with four assets. This exercise could be pursued further with more assets, which would improve risk–return up to a limit.

### 5.3.3 Choice of portfolio on the efficient frontier

Provided the efficient frontier represents a number of assets in a fully diversified portfolio, it indicates the returns relative to risk that are **possible** for the investor. In other words, the efficient frontier is the **supply of investment return**. The price of investment return is the risk that has to be borne to achieve a particular return. The **demand for investment return** depends on the investor's preferences with regard to risk and return. This demand in turn is derived from the investor's attitude to risk, a topic that was discussed in the first section of this chapter. Economic theory suggests that if the investor's attitude to risk is well defined, it is possible to construct **indifference curves** for return relative to risk, which show the combinations of return relative to risk that are regarded as equivalent by the investor. In theory, then, it is possible to find the precise portfolio that will match the investor's preferences.

Recall the example in Section 5.1 of various kinds of better-than-fair games. Clearly it would be possible to rank these in terms of their relative attractiveness. Those with higher expected gain relative to possible loss would be preferred to those with lower expected gain relative to possible loss. Indifference curve analysis does exactly the same kind of thing. The main difference is that indifference curves take the form of lines rather than points. Lines higher up on the diagram represent return relative to risk which is more desirable for the risk-averse investor. Thus in Figure 5.15, which illustrates a number of indifference curves, as far as the risk-averse investor is concerned $IC_1 > IC_2 > IC_3$. It is straightforward enough to demonstrate this point. For a given risk, $E(R_1) > E(R_2) > E(R_3)$, or for a given return, $\sigma_1 < \sigma_2 < \sigma_3$.

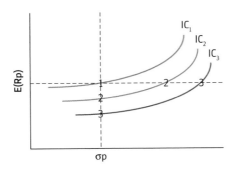

Figure 5.15 Plot of investor's preferences between return and risk. The higher indifference curve represents greater utility

Each line in itself represents different risk–return possibilities which are equally acceptable to the investor. Notice that the lines are convex. This is because each successive increase in risk will require a proportionally higher increase in return to be equally acceptable to the risk-averse investor. In Figure 5.16, the increments in risk are equal, but each successive unit increase in risk requires successively larger increases in required return as compensation for risk. This is for the reasons we discussed in Section 5.1 about risk-averse investors and their attitude to gain-versus-loss.

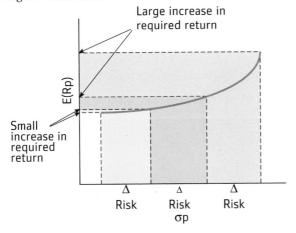

Figure 5.16 Each successive unit increase in risk requires successively large amounts of return compensation

If we could construct these indifference curves in real life, then it would be possible to find a unique point of equilibrium which would give the investor the highest possible

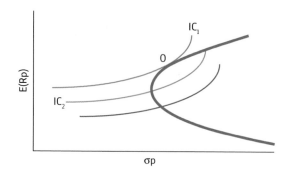

Figure 5.17  The optimal portfolio 'O'. $IC_1$.represents the highest utility attainable by the investor given the constraint imposed by the available return-risk trade-off represented by the efficient frontier (EF)

satisfaction given the constraints imposed by what is technically feasible, as represented by the efficient frontier (Figure 5.17).

In practice, of course, investors' attitudes are usually vaguer and less well-defined than is strictly necessary for the construction of indifference curves. Thus investors would face a choice of, roughly, where they want to be in terms of risk–return on the efficient frontier. In addition, some investors, particularly personal investors, may not be familiar with the concept of the efficient frontier. The way that personal investment advisers get over this is as follows. First, they deal in a few broad portfolio categories, rather than an almost infinite set of possibilities. This is illustrated in Figure 5.18.

**Recommended Asset Allocation for a Long Term Investment with a Moderately Adventurous Attitude to Risk**

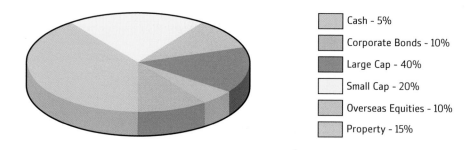

Cash - 5%

Corporate Bonds - 10%

Large Cap - 40%

Small Cap - 20%

Overseas Equities - 10%

Property - 15%

The asset allocation models relating to these risk categories have been prepared by AKG consulting actuaries. Whilst every care has been taken in their preparation it is important to note that individual circumstances may differ. The precise make up of the underlying funds will also affect the efficiency of these models.

It is important that your affairs are reviewed on a regular basis to ensure that your attitude to risk has not changed and that the portfolio continues to meet your requirements.

Figure 5.18  Example of a broad category portfolio type used by investment managers for practical purposes. (From Arch Financial Planning website http://www.arch-fp.co.uk/asset_allocation.php)

Second, attitude to return-relative-to-risk is determined using a survey such as that demonstrated on the Arch Financial Planning website (http://www.arch-fp.co.uk/asset_al-location.php).

So, in short, theoretically, it is possible to find exactly the portfolio that would suit an investor's preferences. In practice, the choice of 'best' portfolio is vaguer and less precise.

## Practical implications for managers

### The efficient frontier

Although diversification may not always be possible for small- to medium-size businesses, it is useful to have some idea of the return relative to risk for the business compared to other businesses. If possible, get someone from outside the business to review this information as well as a diverse group of individuals within the company. Is return relative to risk acceptable? Does it match investors', employees' and managers' preferences for risk?

## Key concepts

- ☐ The **efficient frontier** shows the return-risk trade-off for portfolios. Its shape depends on the correlation between the underlying portfolio asset returns
- ☐ **Return-risk and correlation** – the limits imposed on return-risk portfolio improvement depend on the nature of correlation between the underlying assets
- ☐ **Two-asset portfolio** – simple portfolio used for purposes of teaching
- ☐ **Multi-asset portfolio** – portfolios of portfolios and many asset portfolios
- ☐ **Investor preference** and how investors choose where they want to be on the efficient frontier

## Active learning activity 5.5

### The efficient frontier

Have a quick internet search for 'efficient frontier'. You should find pages on a number of investment sites detailing efficient frontiers and asset classes they have constructed. Based on your findings, try to match these to investor preferences.

## 5.4 The market portfolio and capital market line

### 5.4.1 The risk-free asset, choice of portfolio and market portfolio

So far we have considered portfolios of risky assets, typically ordinary shares in companies. The well-diversified risk-averse investor will usually hold some less risky assets such as bonds and cash. The consideration of how to incorporate bonds into a portfolio of risky assets is another 'portfolio of portfolios' type of problem. Take, for example, the 10-year bond quoted on the opening page of finance.yahoo.com. Unlike the quotes on this website for equities, bonds are quoted in terms of their percentage return. The specific bond in question is a US government 10-year Treasury Note. We downloaded historical data between July 1998 and June 2008 and found that the average return for this type of bond was 4.73% while the standard deviation was 0.73%. As we can see, the standard deviation of the return was about one fifth of the return itself. This compares very favourably with the stock data we dealt with above, where the standard deviation was many times the actual return. This is because bond returns, particularly those of stable sovereign governments, tend to be very stable. For theoretical purposes, government bonds such as the 10-year Treasury Note are often treated as **risk-free assets (RFAs)**. While they are not entirely risk-free, the low standard deviation of return and the low risk of default of high quality government bonds means that the assumption that these asset are risk-free is not an unacceptable oversimplification. Thus we assume in what follows that the **risk-free rate** is 5%, while the standard deviation of the RFA is 0%. We should point out that the risk free asset is more usually seen as a government treasury *bill* rather than a government treasury *note*, which is a type of bond. Our reasons for choosing the latter over the former was so that the interested reader can easily download the date we used and replicate our calculations.

Now let's consider combining the RFA with the risky portfolios Z (10.55%, 34.2%) and X (9.97%, 32.8%) from Section 5.3.6. We simplify slightly by rounding; thus our portfolios are now Z (10.5%, 34.%) and X (10%, 33%). Assuming that Z and X are scalable in the way that was discussed in Section 5.3.2, we could hold a portfolio consisting of Z or X and the RFA. Screenshot 5.21 shows the possible portfolios.

| 1 | Portfolio | RFA | S x | $R_P$ | $Stdev_P$ |
|---|---|---|---|---|---|
| 2 | 1 | 1 | 0 | 5.00% | 0.00% |
| 3 | 2 | 0.75 | 0.25 | 6.25% | 8.25% |
| 4 | 3 | 0.5 | 0.5 | 7.50% | 16.50% |
| 5 | 4 | 0.25 | 0.75 | 8.75% | 24.75% |
| 6 | 5 | 0 | 1 | 10.00% | 33.00% |
| 7 | | | | | |
| 8 | Portfolio | RFA | S z | $R_P$ | $Stdev_P$ |
| 9 | 6 | 1 | 0 | 5.00% | 0.00% |
| 10 | 7 | 0.75 | 0.25 | 6.38% | 8.50% |
| 11 | 8 | 0.5 | 0.5 | 7.75% | 17.00% |
| 12 | 9 | 0.25 | 0.75 | 9.13% | 25.50% |
| 13 | 10 | 0 | 1 | 10.50% | 34.00% |

Screenshot 5.21 Portfolios of X with RF

It should be noted that the calculation of risk for portfolios 1–5 is very simple. Given that the risk of the RFA is zero, risk or standard deviation for the portfolio is just equal to the proportion invested in X times the risk of X.

It is worth examining the risk–return relationship in more detail. Take portfolios 1–5, which consist of portfolio X and the RFA. The extreme points in this relationship are given by the portfolios 1 and 5. Starting at 1, where we are fully invested in the RFA, we note that each 1.25% increase in return is matched by an 8.25 increase in risk, i.e. the relationship is straightforward and linear. Similar observations could be made about portfolios 6–10 consisting of investments in Z and the RFA. Figure 5.19 shows the effect of the new portfolio choices available.

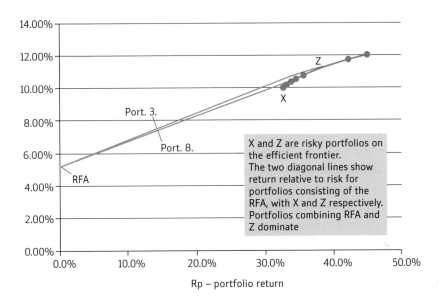

Figure 5.19   Portfolios of risky and risk-free assets

The portfolio choices 1–5 lie on the lower straight line, while the choices 6–10 lie on the upper straight line. Notice that the investor would always choose portfolios on the upper straight line as they offer higher return per unit of risk. In fact one could repeat this experiment, improving on return relative to risk until one found the best possible. This would be at the point where the straight line risk–return opportunities were just tangential to the efficient frontier. This is illustrated for a different set of portfolios in Figure 5.20.

The point of tangency of the straight line RFA portfolio choice represents a particular portfolio, 'M'. In theory, portfolio M would be the only risky portfolio held by investors as any other risky portfolio on the efficient frontier would offer inferior risk–return possibilities when combined with the RFA. In principle, this 'gets us off the hook' with the problem of detailed consideration of the problem of detailed choice of portfolio by the investor. There need not be any consideration of choice of risky asset, as only one risky asset would be held, namely the portfolio M, known as the **market portfolio**. The choice facing investors then would be how far they would wish to venture along the line CML. The abbreviation CML

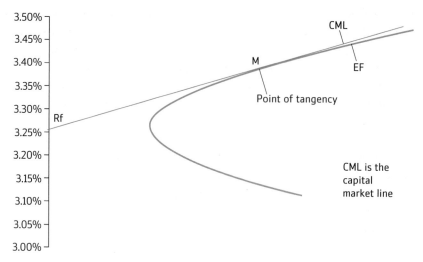

Figure 5.20  Portfolios of risky and risk-free assets – the tangent portfolio M

stands for the **capital market line**. The CML represents relative proportions invested between the RFA and the market portfolio. The idea that only one portfolio needs to be considered is known as the **separation theorem**.

Note that it is possible to go beyond 100% investment in the market portfolio. The investor is able to do this by borrowing at the risk-free rate in order to invest even more than is allowed by the investment fund in the market portfolio. This is an example of a leveraged investment, which on the one hand improves returns, but on the other hand also increases risk as can be seen in Figure 5.21.

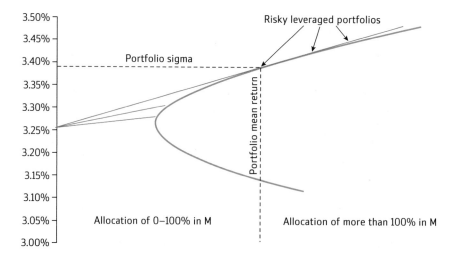

Figure 5.21  Going beyond 100% investment in M

Portfolio M has a special significance in all sorts of ways. First, in theory, all risky assets must be in this portfolio. We know that the rational risk-averse investor would be unlikely to hold any other risky portfolio, such as X or Z, as these would give inferior returns relative to risk. Thus, all risky assets must form part of portfolio M, the market portfolio. If any risky assets were not held as part of the market portfolio, there would be no demand for them. So, for example, all of the equities quoted on the stock market must be held as part of the market portfolio. In fact, one could go further to say that all risky assets, including all equities quoted throughout the world, riskier bonds of lower quality than the RFA, and even people's houses should be treated as part of the market portfolio. (In the UK, though not so much in other countries, houses are treated as investment vehicles.) This is of course in theory. In practice, the market portfolio is usually taken as any well-diversified portfolio, or as a stock index, such as the DJI, the FTSE 100 and the Nikkei. This raises the question of how representative stock indices are, as they only measure the value of larger blue chip well-capitalised firms. Indeed there has been some academic controversy on this point. Nevertheless, most commentators agree that as a rough index of the market portfolio, it is acceptable to use a stock index.

## Mini case study

### Fund managers and index tracker funds

Source *Economist*

Historically, the appeal of fund managers has been due to two things: risk reduction through diversification, and an ability to pick the right assets. Think back to the nineteenth century. Victorian investors faced specific risk because they usually held only a handful of securities in their portfolios. To avoid this risk, they often sought the help of their accountants or solicitors. Those professionals soon found themselves with a lucrative sideline in investment advice. Investment trusts (which still exist today) were set up because it was more efficient to bundle together clients' assets into pooled portfolios. Mutual funds were built on similar principles; by agglomerating the assets of a whole range of clients, it was possible to vastly reduce specific risk.

However, since the development of index-tracking funds in the 1970s, the business of diversification has become commoditised. Clients can get access to a broad portfolio, such as the shares in the S&P 500 index, for fees of a fraction of a percentage point of the assets a year. Indeed, the widespread use of indices has dramatically changed the fund-management business.

Originally, indices were devised (often by newspapers) as a means of assessing the stock market's mood. Then it occurred to investors that they could use the indices as a means of judging whether their fund manager was doing a good job. As they became more sophisticated, they realised that fund managers would be able to beat the index, in the long run, by taking more risks, and started to move to risk-adjusted performance measures that combined returns with volatility. These led to the development of alpha, a measure of a fund manager's skill, defined as the ability to produce superior risk-adjusted returns.

1. What are the advantages and disadvantages of using index tracker funds, such as the FTSE 100, to monitor investment performance?

## Mini case study

### It's all Greek

Source *Economist* 2008b

In recent years there has been a move to separate the effect of alpha from that of beta, which is the portion of an investor's return that comes straight from the market. Thus, if the S&P 500 index rises 8% and an American equity-fund manager delivers a 10% return, the investor gets eight percentage points of beta and two of alpha. Arguably, the client should pay top dollar only for the two additional points, not the eight he could have received even from a low-cost index-tracking fund.

1. Are fund managers necessary? What does the empirical evidence have to say about their long-term performance?
2. Where would their 'alpha' advantage come from?
3. What would be the advantage of holding a stock index tracker fund, as opposed to an actively managed fund?
4. Would there be any disadvantages?
5. What do you think beta is?

## Key concepts

☐ The **risk-free asset** is an asset with no variation in returns

☐ The **capital market line** represents relative proportions invested between the RFA and the market portfolio

☐ The **market portfolio** is a portfolio of all risky assets

☐ The **separation theorem** is the somewhat academic idea that there is no need for investors to pick specific assets for their portfolio. All they need to do is to make a decision on the proportions of the RFA and the market portfolio they wish to hold

## Active learning activity 5.6

### The efficient frontier

If you undertook the previous learning activity on calculating your own portfolio characteristics, try to find roughly where the market portfolio would be by drawing a line tangential to the efficient frontier from the risk-free rate. You could, for example, take the US Treasury 10-year rate as your risk-free rate. What problems lie with choosing a different risk-free rate?

## 5.5 Beta, a measure of individual systematic asset risk

### 5.5.1 Individual risk is relative to a diversified portfolio

We saw earlier that it is possible to improve return relative to risk by holding two or more assets in a portfolio. In fact, as a general rule, provided the assets involved are sufficiently diverse, it is possible to show that risk will be reduced as additional assets are added. This phenomenon of risk reduction has a limit, which is reached when the portfolio contains between 20 and 20 assets. This limit is known as the **limit of diversification**.

Figure 5.22 shows that additional assets when added to the portfolio reduce portfolio risk, up to a limit, beyond which no further reduction is possible. Provided the assets are as diverse and uncorrelated as possible, this limit is usually reached at 20–30 assets. Risk reduction can be even further improved if international as opposed to domestic diversification is possible.

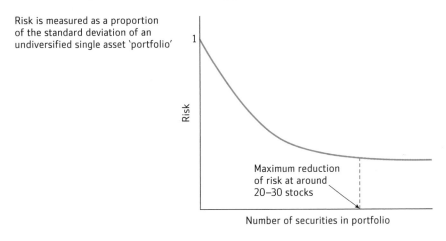

Figure 5.22 Portfolio risk is reduced by diversification

It is normally assumed that the rational risk-averse investor would hold such a portfolio, as it is possible to improve risk without reduction in return, and indeed in some cases, as we have demonstrated, while improving return at the same time. This brings us to a key point in finance. The market **does not reward undiversified risk**. So, for example, we saw in a Section 5.2 that the returns for IBM had a very high standard deviation, despite the fact that it had a relatively low return. Specifically, and rounding up, the return for IBM was 7.5% as against a risk of 31.5%, while the return for Coke was 13% with a risk of only 25.5%. That is, the return of Coke is bigger while the individual risk is smaller. This is because it is assumed on the market that investors can easily and cheaply diversify their portfolios and therefore should not be in a position where they are fully exposed to the risk of an individual stock, such as IBM. Indeed, we saw in Section 5.2 how much better IBM could be as an investment proposition once it was held in a portfolio with Coke. Hence, the market does not reward diversifiable risk, but it does reward undiversifiable risk.

This raises the question of what undiversifiable risk is. Undiversifiable risk is the risk that arises from the fact that all firms face uncertainty because of macroeconomic factors beyond their control, and in particular the business cycle. Thus firms face unforeseen downturns in demand because of recessions and interest rate rises, pressure on costs from inflation, falling competitiveness from overvalued exchange rates and so on. These types of macroeconomic factor tend to have a cyclical nature, with sustained booms in demand and economic activity eventually triggering inflation and high interest rates, followed by retrenchments and corrections and the slide into recession, with lower levels of economic activity and higher levels of unemployment. The cyclical nature of the overall economy is brought out in Figure 5.23, which shows annual returns data for Coke and IBM between 1989 and 2008, in which it is possible to discern boom, bust and recovery. As a basic point of comparison, we take the performance of the DJI (Dow Jones Index) as a representative market portfolio.

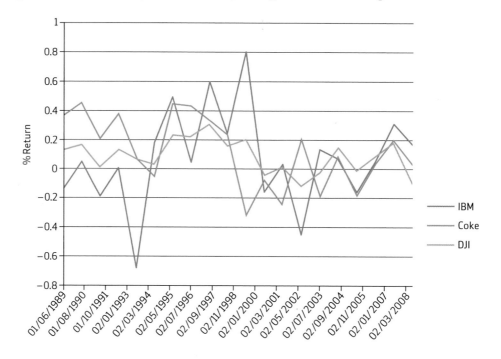

Figure 5.23 Annual returns data for Coke, IBM and the DJI

It can be seen that the IBM returns vary more over the cycle than the DJI, whereas the Coke returns more closely follows the DJI returns over the cycle. Of course visual inspection lacks precision, and what is really needed is a precise measure of how individual returns vary with the market index. An obvious candidate is the **covariance** measure, which was introduced in Section 5.2. The only problem with covariance is that it is difficult to compare one set of covariances with another as they don't come in standardised units. Hence in order to examine how much returns over the business cycle compared to the market index, we use beta, which is essentially still the covariance of the individual stock with the market portfolio, but which is then standardised by dividing by the covariance of the market return with itself. Thus **beta** measures market or undiversifiable risk by comparison with the market portfolio. The formula is as follows:

$$B_i = Cov(r_i, r_M)/Cov(r_M, r_M)$$

As the covariance of the market return with itself is just the variance of the market return then the formula is normally written as:

$$B_i = Cov(r_i, r_M)/Var(r_M)$$

Clearly, the beta of the market portfolio, which is $B_i = Cov(r_M, r_M)/Cov(r_M, r_M)$, will be equal to one. This serves as a point of reference for other betas. Stocks with a beta of more than one are known as **aggressive stocks**, because their returns tend to vary more than the market return over the business cycle. Stocks with a beta of less than one are known as **defensive stocks** as their returns tend to vary less than the return on the market portfolio over the business cycle.

### 5.5.2 The causes of low and high beta

Beta risk is caused by vulnerability to factors associated with the business cycle. The most obvious examples of high beta companies are those that have demand that is highly sensitive to the business cycle. Makers of luxury goods and providers of leisure services will do well in prosperous boom times, but will often find that demand falls off quite sharply during recessions. The mini case study below ('Gambling and beta') shows that even Las Vegas is susceptible to economic downturns.

### Mini case study

#### Gambling shares and beta

Source *Economist* 2008c

**Las Vegas' casinos have been on a roll. Is their luck about to run out?**

After a long boom, the industry faces a rare slowdown and belts are tightening across Sin City. Gambling has long been considered all but recession-proof. Only twice have overall revenues on the Las Vegas Strip fallen since it took over from the downtown as America's gambling hotspot in the late 1980s – most recently after the attacks of September 11th 2001 – and both dips were short and shallow. Gamblers, they say, will keep betting as the economy slows, still hoping for that big win.

But Vegas is less about gambling than it used to be. Today only 41% of its revenues come from betting, down from 58% in 1990. These days people are as likely to come for shopping, shows and fine dining as for blackjack or baccarat; the Forum Shops, at Caesar's Palace, has the highest sales per square foot of any American mall. Today's visitors are more likely to be worried by broader economic woes than the punters who used to flock to the city were, says Bill Lerner of Deutsche Bank.

The housing slump and high petrol prices do seem to be taking their toll. In the year to April, gaming revenue across Vegas was down by 3.3% from the year before. A dip in occupancy, usually an impressive 90–95%, has prompted hotels to cut room rates, reversing a steady rise in recent years to more than $135 a night on average. Sub-$100 deals at prominent Strip hotels have proliferated in recent weeks.

Nor can the city fall back on convention business, which has boomed in recent years. Attendance fell by 7.1% in the first quarter compared with a year earlier – a worrying sign because conference-goers spend twice as much per trip as pleasure-seekers do, though things picked up a bit in April. Las Vegas Sands Corp, the most convention-oriented of the big operators, posted an unexpected loss in the first quarter. Occupancy at its latest mega-hotel, the Palazzo, was a mere 79%. Harrah's dipped into the red too. Global gambling firms' share prices have fallen sharply this year because of fears over Vegas and signs that revenue growth in Macau, Asia's booming gambling capital, will slow.

All this coincides with the industry's biggest-ever building spurt, raising the spectre of over-supply. Wynn Resorts is building a $2.2 billion follow-up to Wynn Las Vegas, the Encore, and MGM is spending $9.2 billion on a 76-acre project called CityCenter. More than 40,000 new rooms will become available in the next four years, triple the number Beijing is providing for the Olympics – and in a city that already has 7% of America's hotel rooms.

1. In the past how did Las Vegas gambling companies perform relative to the market?

2. How do they perform now?

3. What factors do you think have caused the change?

Other types of business that one would expect to be hit hardest by economic downturn would be jewellery and fashion. And of course, construction and related industries are also very dependent on the stage of the economic cycle. For example, in 2008 it was reported that 4,000 estate agent businesses will close in the UK as a result of the housing downturn.

## Mini case study

### Estate agents and beta

As your authors have observed before, British people are rather obsessed with the notion that their house, apart from being a place to live is also their primary investment vehicle. The booming house market in the UK which spluttered to a halt in 2008, following the credit crunch of 2007, led to large scale redundancies in estate agency and the closure of many estate agents' branches.[2]

1. What would you expect the beta for property and construction companies to be? Try to confirm what typical betas are. Various databases can be found at www2.ntu.ac.uk/llr/library/betavalues.htm.

2. Try again, this time for power and water companies.

3. How about telecoms? Do their betas suggest they are more of the nature of utilities or technology companies?

On the other hand, we would expect the betas of utilities companies which supply water, gas and electricity to be much lower as demand for these products is much more constant.

As well as cyclical demand, the other main factor that can boost a firm's beta is the extent to which a firm's profits and returns are affected by high fixed cost. If a firm's production cost is mainly fixed as opposed to variable then there is a high level of **operational gearing**. Clearly a high proportion of fixed to variable cost can work to a firm's advantage in times of strong demand. This is because larger volumes of production and sales can be spread over a given amount of fixed cost, thus reducing the amount of fixed cost per unit, e.g. if fixed costs are £10,000 and we sell 1,000 units, then per unit fixed cost is £10. If we sell 100,000 units, then it is 10p. Manufacturing and industrial companies, particularly those in industries such as mining and heavy engineering, tend to have high fixed costs. Take the steel industry, for example. They are hit by a double whammy, as the fixed costs of steel-making plant are very high, while demand for steel is very dependent on cyclical demand from construction and industry, which depends in turn on the level of economic activity.

In high-technology industries, such as electronics and pharmaceuticals, both demand and supply conditions can be highly volatile. New products are constantly being developed. For example, 10 years ago, no one had ever heard of Google, iPods or USB drives. In addition, the conditions under which these items are produced and the nature of competition in these industries is constantly shifting. Thus, high technology generally makes returns more volatile across the cycle, as we have seen with IBM.

### 5.5.3 Some beta calculations – the Capital Asset Pricing Model

For our 20 years of data, the figures for the covariances of IBM and Coke with the market are 0.187% and 0.119% respectively. The figure for the variance of the DJI is 0.159%. Hence the betas are 1.176 and 0.748 respectively. Thus we can say that IBM has more risk than the typical market portfolio consisting of the DJI, while Coke has relatively less risk. The other benefit of knowing beta is that once we know it, we are able to calculate the return we should expect for particular securities using the **Capital Asset Pricing Model (CAPM)**. The CAPM relates return-risk to the following three variables: risk, as measured by beta ($\beta_i$), the risk-free rate ($r_f$), and the rate of return on the market, $r_m$. The equation that links all these together is known as the **security market line (SML)**. The SML is as follows:

$$E(r_i) = r_f + \beta_i(E(r_m) - r_f)$$

In graphical terms, the SML is just a straight line relating return on an individual security to the beta of that security. The intercept of the line will be at $r_f$, the risk-free rate, as by definition this is where risk and beta are equal to zero. The other point that allows us to find the line on a graph is where beta is equal to one. The corresponding point to this is $r_m$ as the beta of one at the corresponding point on the SML is the value of beta for the market portfolio. The slope of the line is equal to the term in parentheses, $(E(r_m) - r_f)$, which is known as the **market premium**. The market premium measures the additional return available from the market portfolio over the risk-free rate for taking on market risk. The SML is illustrated in Figure 5.24.

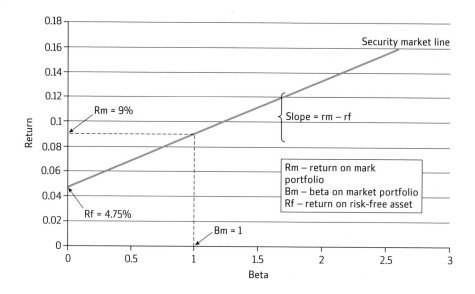

Figure 5.24 The security market line of the CAPM – beta versus return

Beta then weights the amount of premium earned on a particular security in proportion to the market risk represented by a particular security. Clearly, high beta stocks would be expected to have a higher return and low beta stocks would be expected to have a lower return. We have already estimated the risk-free return at 4.75%. From our monthly data, we estimate $r_m$ as the return on the DJI, which is 9%. The market premium is 4.25%. Thus the expected returns are as follows:

$$E(r_{coke}) = r_f + \beta_{coke}(E(r_m) - r_f) = 4.75\% + 0.748 \times (9\% - 4.75\%) = 7.96\%$$

$$E(r_{IBM}) = r_f + \beta_{IBM}(E(r_m) - r_f) = 4.75\% + 1.14 \times (9\% - 4.75\%) = 9.79\%$$

This suggests that the return on Coke (13%) is higher than we would expect from beta, while the return on IBM (7.5%) is lower than we would expect from beta. What should happen in the long run is that arbitrage should push both shares towards the equilibrium return. Before we explain how this happens we should point out that the CAPM is a one period model which determines return between one period and the next. Also, we should point out that we are going to define return here simply as $(P_{t+1} - P_t)/P_t$. Now, let us consider the future price $P_{t+1}$ to be a given, determined perhaps by the prospect of future dividends. At the moment, an IBM share is overpriced. Hence demand for this stock will fall, because it is underperforming, and trading in this stock will push the current price $P_t$ down. As the stock price falls, the percentage gain of the future price over the current price increases. That is to say, return increases. It will increase to the point where equilibrium is restored at 9.79%.

For example, suppose the current price of an IBM share is $93, and the expected future price in a year's time is $100. If there is not expected to be any dividend, then the investor will make 7.5% by holding this share. However, this is less than is required for the risk represented by the stock's beta, which as we saw is 9.79%. Hence, investors will sell rather than buy this share, pushing the current price down. The current price should fall from $93 to $91.08 in order for return to increase to the appropriate level and for equilibrium to be restored.

A similar line of reasoning would apply to the share in Coke. Suppose that the current price of a share in Coke is $88.5 and the expected future price in a year's time is $100. The Coke share will yield a return of 13% which is higher than is strictly justified by its beta risk. With no dividend, the return on Coke which is justified by its beta risk is 7.96%. Investors will want to buy this share. As they do so, the current price of the share will increase, pushing the return $(P_{t+1} - P_t)/P_t$ down. This process will come to an end when the price reaches approximately $92.63, when the equilibrium return of 7.96% is restored, as we show in Figures 5.25 and 5.26.

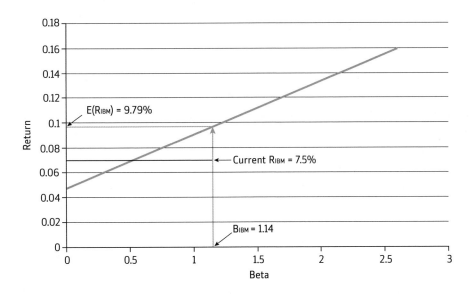

Figure 5.25 Return on IBM is too low. Price falls, return increases and equilibrium is restored

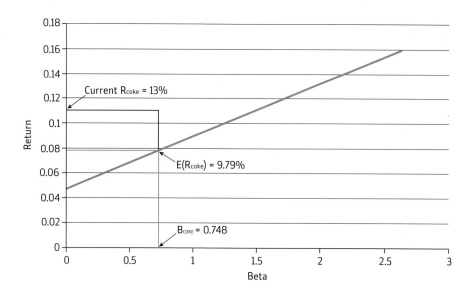

**Figure 5.26** Return on Coke is too high. Price increases, return falls and equilibrium is restored

### 5.4.4 Some final observations on beta

We have now spent some time considering beta as a way of measuring risk. Beta we argued is an appropriate way to measure the risk of an individual asset as opposed to a portfolio of assets. It would be wrong to use standard deviation of asset or stock return in this context as standard deviation does not distinguish between diversifiable risk, which can easily be reduced to zero by holding a diversified portfolio, and undiversifiable risk, which cannot. Beta is an accurate measure of diversifiable risk as it measures volatility relative to the market portfolio (usually a stock exchange index) over the business cycle. Thus we would appear to have cracked the problem of measuring risk for both portfolios of risky assets and individual risky assets. It is worth bearing in mind though that beta is only a model and, as such, it has limitations. The limitations of the model are as follows.

First, the theory underpinning beta is similar to a lot of financial theory in that it is based on the theory of perfectly competitive markets from economics. Thus it is assumed that there are many buyers and sellers in asset markets, that no one has market power, that there is perfect information and so on. This is not really a major criticism of the CAPM as financial markets come closer than the market for any other type of product to fulfilling the ideal of perfect competition.

Second, the empirical evidence isn't completely supportive of the CAPM. The consensus is that while earlier studies were generally in line with the idea of the SML, later studies suggest that the intercept is higher than would be expected given the risk-free rate, while the slope is lower than expected given the market premium. However, it is still the best measure of individual risk that we have at the present time, as work on other measures such as arbitrage pricing theory is somewhat inconclusive at the present time.

## Key concepts

- ☐ **Diversifiable risk** can be removed by choosing different investments
- ☐ The market only rewards **undiversifiable risk**
- ☐ The degree to which an investment moves relative to the market portfolio is known as **beta** and is measured as $B_i = Cov(r_i, r_M)/Var(r_M)$
- ☐ The **security market line (SML)** is a straight line relating return on an individual security to the beta of that security
- ☐ The **Capital Asset Pricing Model (CAPM)** gives us the required return on a security using the formula $E(r_i) = r_f + \beta_i(E(r_m) - r_f)$

## Active learning activity 5.7

### Beta

Go to the following web link: http://www2.ntu.ac.uk/llr/library/betavalues.htm. Investigate some of the beta databases. Find beta for a couple of companies. Find an RFA in the way suggested above to calculate the risk-free rate. Find a market index to calculate the market return. Calculate the appropriate return for your companies.

## 5.6 Summary

In this chapter, we have explained the basic nature of financial risk which can be broadly defined as variation in expected outcomes. There are a range of attitudes to risk, from risk seeking to risk averse, but we normally assume that a rational investor is risk averse.

There are several relevant measures used to appraise risk versus return. Expected return is calculated based on past returns, so we must bear in mind that the past is not necessarily an indicator of what to expect in the future. A simple measure of risk is variance, or the much more commonly used square root of variance, the standard deviation. The standard deviation gives us a measure of how much the investment asset has varied away from the expected return (again based on observations from the past). Correlation, the degree to which two assets vary in relation to each other, is also useful, as any correlation less than +1 between asset returns will lead to diversification benefits to portfolio investment. It should be noted that the risk–return trade-off when measured in terms of expected return relative to standard deviation of return applies only to **portfolios**. When we consider return relative to risk for individual securities, the relevant measure of risk is beta risk. This is because standard deviation of return includes both diversifiable and undiversifiable risk.

The market portfolio is of considerable relevance when we consider that there should be no reward for diversifiable risk. Investors should only be rewarded according to how much risk an investor takes on in relation to the market portfolio. The market portfolio can be considered as a benchmark for return versus volatility, will all other assets measured against this benchmark. Stocks with higher volatility than the market portfolio are considered to have a high beta, and demand higher return than the market portfolio. The risk on any individual stock in relation to the market portfolio is known as beta.

## Case study

### Charity investing could become cutting edge

Source Grene 2008, Copyright, *Financial Times*, 2008

Charities have the freedom to be the most interesting investors around, but are hesitant to break the bounds of tradition, says a new report from Sarasin & Partners, which manages money for 175 of them. The report, *Sarasin & Partners Compendium of Investment for Charities*, looks at current trends in endowment investing – globalisation and alternative asset classes are key terms here – and describes the ideal process for setting investment policy.

'While trustees and investors are perhaps more able than ever to create portfolios that match their particular circumstances, agreeing and implementing investment policy still represents a major challenge,' says the foreword to the report, written by Richard Maitland, Edward Campbell-Johnston and Henry Boucher.

Guy Monson, Sarasin's chief investment officer, points out that the UK's Trustee Act 2000 says: 'A trustee may make any kind of investment that he could make if he were absolutely entitled to the assets of the trust', with the exception of direct purchase of land. Once the statutory duty of care is fulfilled, which Mr Monson interprets to mean diversification, and a risk process should be in place, 'you can do anything you like'.

Charities have traditionally been the poor relation of investing in the UK, says Mr Monson. They have not been adventurous in their investment policies, even though in the US endowment funds such as those of Harvard and Yale Universities have been exemplars of innovative and successful investment. 'But things are changing here very, very fast,' says Mr Monson. The changes highlighted in the report include the increased use of pooled vehicles, a move away from measuring performance against peers to using bespoke benchmarks, a tendency to aim for returns higher than cash or higher than inflation instead of beating indices, and increasing willingness to allow derivatives to be used in investment management.

While these techniques have become mainstream in pension fund investing, they still count as new for charities. Charity investing has different requirements and objectives than pension funds, however. While each charity has different objectives, as a group they are likely to have an investment horizon at perpetuity and need to generate a regular income stream, which is not dependent on variables such as longevity.

Endowments therefore can approach the task of setting their investment policy on different terms than other investors. For a start, their investment horizon is likely to be much longer than most investors. On its own, this can make a difference to the basic assumptions used in setting investment policy, especially when it comes to asset allocation, deciding what proportions of the fund to put into equities, bonds and other asset classes.

The classic analysis looks at various combinations of two asset classes, usually equities and bonds, to find the proportions that offer the highest returns for an acceptable level of risk. This produces a curved line called the efficient frontier, the furthest right on the graph below. It shows, for the UK market, that although holding the whole portfolio in government bonds is slightly riskier than including a small allocation to equities, beyond that, more equities means more risk.

The limitation of this useful exercise is that it only applies over a 12-month period. If the same calculation is done over a longer period, it turns out that bonds in the long run are more volatile than equities.

If UK charities take on board this kind of investment thinking and combine it with increasing the range of asset classes they use, as is already happening, they could find themselves at the cutting edge of investment innovation, like their US counterparts.

1. Why would charities be 'more interesting investors'? Interesting investors compared to whom?

2. Why is there less of a tradition of dynamic and visionary investment among UK charity investors compared to US investors?

3. Try to find out what the following terminology means: 'pooled vehicles', 'measuring performance against peers', 'using bespoke benchmarks'.

4. Do you think it wise for charity investors to engage in derivatives investment? Do some research and try to find out what derivatives vehicles are available for more conservative investors.

5. We reproduce some US data provided by Ibbotson,[3] who along with Sinquefield is celebrated for this kind of exercise. Does the information suggested in the following tables suggest that '... bonds in the long run are more volatile than equities'? If not, what can the author mean?

## Stocks, Bonds, Bills and Inflation
Summary Statistics 1926–2005

| | Compound annual return | Arithmetic annual return | Risk (standard deviation) | |
|---|---|---|---|---|
| Large company stocks | 10.4% | 12.3% | 20.2% | |
| Small company stocks | 12.6% | 17.4% | 32.9% | * |
| Government bonds | 5.5% | 5.8% | 9.2% | |
| Treasury bills | 3.7% | 3.8% | 3.1% | |
| Inflation | 3.0% | 3.1% | 4.3% | |

−90 ————————— 0 ————————— 90

* The 1833 small company stock total return was 142.8%

6. The information contained in the Ibbotson table is over the very long run. How would the same data look over a time horizon of 3 months to 5 years?

# ? Questions

1. Define the opportunity set and explain how it differs from the efficient frontier.

2. What is the market portfolio and how is it possible to be more than 100% invested in the market portfolio?

3. If an individual security return is not consistent with beta and the security market line, what should happen to bring it into line?

4. For the following coin-toss games, if the initial 'investment' is £10, are the games, 'fair', 'less than fair' or 'more than fair'. In each case what would be the expected value of gain or loss over ten 'investments'?

| Probability of win | Value of win |
|---|---|
| 0.1 | £100 |
| 0.4 | £15 |
| 0.5 | £10 |
| 0.5 | £5 |
| 0.8 | £2 |
| 0.9 | £3 |

5. Shares A and B have been observed to behave in the following way:

| State of the world | Probability | Return A | Return B |
|---|---|---|---|
| Boom | 0.2 | 10% | 2% |
| Normal | 0.4 | 8% | 4% |
| Recession | 0.4 | −2% | 5% |

a) Calculate the expected return and standard deviation for A and B.

b) Calculate the covariance and correlation between the two shares.

c) Find the portfolio return and risk for the following portfolios:

| Portfolio | Investment in A |
|---|---|
| 1 | 100% |
| 2 | 90% |
| 3 | 75% |
| 4 | 60% |
| 5 | 50% |
| 6 | 40% |
| 7 | 25% |
| 8 | 10% |
| 9 | 0% |

Construct the opportunity set and the efficient frontier.

6. Depending on outcomes a, b and c below, returns on a share issued by the Docklands Umbrella company will vary respectively between 25%, 10% and 2%. What is the expected return and standard deviation for this share?

   a) The probability of a very wet winter is 0.3.

   b) The probability of a moderately wet winter is 0.4.

   c) The probability of a dry winter is 0.3.

7. Business at the East Spam five-a-side pitches during the winter also depends on the amount of rain. Using the same probabilities in Question 6, returns on a share in East Spam will vary respectively between 5%, 12% and 20% depending on the weather. What is the expected return and standard deviation for this share?

8. Now calculate the covariance between the returns for Docklands Umbrella and East Spam. From your data, calculate also the correlation coefficient.

9. Calculate portfolio expected return, variance and standard deviation for the following portfolios consisting of Docklands Umbrella (DU) and East Spam (ES): 75% DU 25% ES, 60% DU 40% ES, 15% DU 85% ES.

10. Consider the following information:

    Expected market return 7%
    Standard deviation of market return 10%
    Risk-free rate 3%
    Correlation coefficient between:
    Stock A and the market 0.5
    Stock B and the market 0.3
    Standard deviation for stock A 15%
    Standard deviation for stock B 20%

    a) Calculate the beta for stock A and stock B.

    b) Calculate the required return for each stock.

11. Suppose $E(r_m)$ = 12% $r_f$ = 8%. Which of the following shares have a return justified by the CAPM and which do not? For those that do not, what should happen next?

    | Firm | Beta | Current rate of return (%) |
    |------|------|----------------------------|
    | A    | 0.7  | 7                          |
    | B    | 1.3  | 13                         |
    | C    | 0.9  | 9                          |

12. The shares of firm A have a beta of 1.2, $r_f$ = 5% and the risk premium is 8%.

    a) What is $E(r_a)$?

    b) What is $E(r_a)$ if the risk premium is 10%?

13. What is the equation of the security market line and what does it tell us about risk–return?

14. The CAPM is an equilibrium model. What happens if return is greater than is justified by beta risk? What if it is less?

15. What is the implication of the CAPM for the percentage required return on equity?

# Further reading

Elton, E.J. and Gruber, M.J. (1997) Modern portfolio theory, 1950 to date. *Journal of Banking and Finance* 21:1743–1759.

Faff, R.W., Brooks, R.D. and Kee, H.Y. (2002) New evidence on the impact of financial leverage on beta risk: a time-series approach. *North American Journal of Economics and Finance* 13(1):1–20.

Fama, E.F. and French, K.R. (2003) The Capital Asset Pricing Model: theory and evidence. *Journal of Economic Perspectives* 18(3):25–46.

Graham, J.R. and Harvey, C.R. (2001) The theory and practice of corporate finance: evidence from the field. *Journal of Financial Economics* 60(2–3):187–243.

Morelli, D. (2007) Beta, size, book-to-market equity and returns: a study based on UK data. *Journal of Multi-national Financial Management* 17(3):257–272.

Schubert, R., Brown, M., Gysler, M. and Brachinger, H.W. (1999) Financial decision-making: are women really more risk averse? *American Economic Review* 89(2):381–385.

# Internet references

finance.yahoo.com
Useful for stock prices around the world.

www2.ntu.ac.uk/llr/library/betavalues.htm
Good resource for looking up beta values from databases. (A particularly well-known database is the London Business School Database.)

www.diehards.org
General information, recommendations and discussions based on MPT.

www.travismorien.com
Many excellent articles on investment.

www.altruistfa.com/readingroom.htm
Thoughtful articles which also include practical implications.

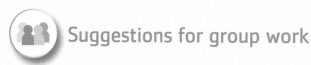

# Suggestions for group work

1. Each group should construct one portfolio consisting of ten stocks randomly chosen from the FT100. Assume an investment of £1 million pounds evenly split over the ten stocks. Over a 4-week period, use Excel to calculate the returns and standard deviation of your portfolio on a weekly basis. Compare against the FT100. What factors explain the differences between the performance of your portfolio and the performance of the FT100?

2. Each group should choose just one stock from the FT100. Go to finance.yahoo.com and download a chart of your stock over the past year in comparison to the FT100. In your group, discuss the main issues in stock selection and try to find out the reasons for your stock's performance over the past year. Are there any circumstances where you would consider putting all your money into one stock?

 ## Suggestions for presentations

1. In a group, devise a presentation that outlines the risk and expected returns available to investing in emerging stock markets over the next 5 years. You can choose one particular country or a selection.

2. Imagine that you have to persuade an institutional investor to buy extra equity in one of the banks affected by the credit crisis. Make a presentation that outlines the key risks and expected returns from investing in such a bank.

# 6

# Risk and the International Environment

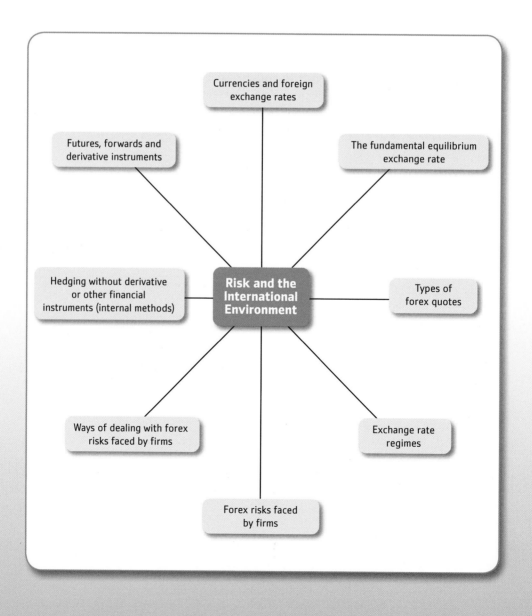

## Knowledge-based learning objectives

When you have completed this chapter you will be able to:

- ✓ Explain the uses of derivatives
- ✓ Explain the differences between forwards, futures and options
- ✓ Describe the different types of currency exchange rates
- ✓ Explain economic, transaction and translation risks and be able to formulate strategies to minimise risks in the international financial environment
- ✓ Understand internal hedging methods
- ✓ Calculate the financial outcomes of simple hedging strategies

## Skills-based learning objectives development

- ✓ Business and financial environment consciousness: you should have developed an appreciation of the risks in the international financial environment and how international risks can affect businesses.
- ✓ Numerical skills: you should have developed the ability to calculate the outcome of a hedging strategy.
- ✓ Analytical thinking and problem-solving skills: you should have developed an understanding of the merits, limitations and dangers of derivative use.
- ✓ Problem-solving skills: you should have developed the ability to apply your knowledge to recommend suitable hedging strategies.
- ✓ Critical-thinking skills: you should be able to compare and contrast the basic approaches in terms of their benefits and drawbacks.
- ✓ Managerial soft skills: you should have developed the ability to know how the strategies would apply in organisations you have worked in or with which you are familiar.
- ✓ Interpersonal skills: you should have developed your ability to present your work clearly both verbally and in writing and to interact with others effectively upon completion of the end of chapter questions.

## Online resource centre

Visit the Online Resource Centre that accompanies this book to listen to a podcast of the authors explaining the dangers of derivatives when used for speculative purposes.
**www.oxfordtextbooks.co.uk/marney**

## Fictional case study

### Charlie cuts his hedges ...

Kate stomps into Charlie's office waving the ever ominous spreadsheets. 'Did I, or did I not, ask you to check that we had a forward contract for the Nigerian payable to our supplier in Port Harcourt?'

Charlie breathes a sigh of relief – for once he is confident that he has made a good decision. 'Yes you did, Kate. And I have to confess that I haven't. But just calm down and I'll explain'. Kate looks very annoyed but sits down, arms crossed, and nods her head for Charlie to continue. 'OK, you know the currency is called the naira? Well, the last time we were due to make a payment of 50 million naira to our Nigerian customer, I looked up a currency conversion website and discovered that the naira had lost well over 20% of its value in the time we entered into the contract until the time we were paid. It was 170 naira to the £ when we signed the contract and 230 when the money was paid. So we contracted to sell pounds for naira at 170 – that's about £294,117 and we were locked in because of this forward contract you insisted on. But if we had just taken the rate on the day the money was due, it would only have cost us £217,391. Unless my brains have turned to scrambled eggs, that means we lost over £75,000! Obviously, this seems a long-term trend so we don't want to miss out again. Surely?'

Charlie looks rather triumphant. However, far from looking relieved, Kate looks even fiercer. 'Would you like some toast with your scrambled eggs?' she says sarcastically. ' Do you realise the amount of risk you have exposed us to? This payment is not due for 6 months. What happens if the naira falls to 100 naira to the pound? I'll tell you – we would have to pay £500,000!'

'That's not very likely' says Charlie. 'In the last 5 years it's not fallen bellow 150, and right now it's at 250 – saving us even more!'

'That's not the point, Charlie,' replies Kate, 'we now have an unknown future liability which could cost us hundreds of thousands more. And what happens if the Nigerian government changes its economic policies?'.

Charlie sighs, 'No doubt you are going to explain it to me in gruesome detail. ...'

## 6.1 Futures, forwards and derivative instruments

### 6.1.1 Why derivatives are useful

Let's take a look back to the American 'Wild West' where cowboys lived a simple life, eating beans round the campfire at night and herding cattle during the day. But where were they taking the cattle? The answer is Chicago. Chicago was the nearest city in the Mid West and it had a railhead. As a result, a huge meat-packing industry developed in the area in the nineteenth century. And because of the meat-packing industry, eventually other food processing industries also tended to locate in the area. However, food processing companies had a problem. The price of food commodities can be volatile. This is because supply depends on natural conditions which vary from year to year, and it is very difficult to know in advance whether in the forthcoming year the harvest will be good or bad. As a consequence, the problem for food processors was that their costs could vary considerably from year to year as a result of this uncertainty.

## Active learning activity 6.1

### Feast or famine?

Think about the consequences for food production if prices are very volatile. What would happen to production if prices were very low one year? What would happen to production if prices were very high one year? What are the unique features that make farmed produce more prone to volatility than manufactured goods?

However, as a way of dealing with this volatility, the Chicago food processors came up with a remarkable innovation. The Chicago Board of Trade (CBOT) was established in 1848 and started trading an early form of **forward contract** in 1849. A commodities forward contract is a contract in which the counterparties agree to exchange a commodity at some date in the future but at a price decided *now*. Consequently, food processing companies were able to know in advance what they would be paying for basic inputs such as wheat and were able to plan accordingly. Farmers could also lock in a selling price.

A further innovation at CBOT was the **futures contract**. A futures contract is different from a forward contract in that it comes in a variety of standardised forms and is exchange traded. A forward contract by comparison is a private tailor-made contract between two counterparties, normally arranged by an intermediary known as a broker. The advantages offered by a futures contract over a forward contract are as follows. First, it is easier to find a counterparty to a standardised market traded contract. As a consequence, the futures contract cuts down on **search** and **information** costs. Second, the terms and conditions of the futures contract are already known and there is no need to draw up a contract from 'scratch'. Hence the futures market cuts down on **transaction** cost. Third, any change in value of a futures contract is known rapidly because of continuous market trading. A futures contract can change in value before the delivery date. This is because as the future unfolds and more information becomes known or changes, the counterparties will have a better idea of what the actual market price is going to be and whether they have bought or sold at a favourable or foolish price. Clearly if it emerges that the contracted price is favourable, the contract will become more valuable, while if it begins to appear that the contract was a foolish bargain, it will become less valuable.

The problem with a forward contract is that it may be difficult to know precisely how valuable the contract is, given that it is private and not traded. Because futures contracts are exchange traded, the value of the contract is always precisely known. That is, there is what is called **price discovery**. Given that the decision with futures is a simple one of price and number of contracts, you may wonder then why anyone would want a forward contract. The reason is that, as we have already learned, it may be difficult to get precisely the contract you desire with futures as they come in a limited number of standardised varieties.[1] A forward contract also allows a tailor made to specific circumstances contract and is often used by smaller companies.

Moving on from specific points about types of contract, a much more fundamental point about the origins of derivatives in the Chicago commodities market is that it was the start of attempts by business to conduct formalised **risk management** through **derivative instruments** (explained below). Participants in the market began to observe that it was possible to offset or **hedge** risk. For example, the main risk traditionally faced by farmers is that market price is lower than expected by the time the harvest is brought to market. However, the new commodity markets provided a way of hedging against this by allowing famers to purchase contracts to sell at a pre-known contract price. However, notice that by purchasing forward contracts in order to hedge, they had discarded the potential benefit of not hedging and facing the risk. They would no longer gain above-normal profits in the event of a poor harvest and high prices. If price had soared after they pre-agreed to sell forward at the contract price, they missed out on the additional profit (provided of course their own crops hadn't catastrophically failed!). But on the other hand, they avoided the risks associated with a price collapse. In short, the risk of receiving low prices was offset by buying into the opposite risk of missing out on high prices and the two opposite risks cancelled, leaving the farmer with a predictable normal average yearly profit. We see once more a relationship between lower and more stable returns or higher and more volatile ones.

In addition to the concept of risk management, the other important new idea which emerged from the Chicago commodities markets was that of the **derivative instrument**. A derivative instrument is one that is derived from some underlying asset. In the case of a commodities futures contract, the value of the contract is derived from the exchange of commodities which is to take place at some point in the future. This future exchange is what gives the contract value. And of course, the potential value from that exchange at a future date can go up and down as information emerges and the market becomes clearer about what the actual market price or **spot price** is likely to be forward or futures contract to sell at the long-run average market price then your contract will become much more valuable if news starts to filter through that there has been a bumper harvest and that the price is likely to be very low. Conversely, your contract would lose value and might even be worthless, if news started to emerge that crops had been bad and prices were expected to be very high.

The exact opposite would apply if you had a contract to **buy** at the average market price. If it began to look as if the spot price was going to be very high on the expiry date, then the contract would start to become very valuable. However, if the market expectation increasingly was that the price was likely to be low, then the contract would lose value and again might even become worthless.

Of course to realise the value of your contract you would have to sell it on in the secondary market. The original hedgers on the mercantile exchanges would probably have kept theirs as they were committed to the exchange of the underlying commodity at the specified price. However, the principal of risk management by buying into an offsetting price movement was established.

A major innovation in derivatives instruments was when this basic insight from the commodities market was applied to financial instruments. The principles of risk management discovered on the mercantile markets all those years ago were transferred to the financial markets when the first foreign currency futures were traded on the International Monetary Market (IMM), an offshoot of the Chicago Mercantile Exchange (CME) in 1971. This was the start of what we would normally think of as **financial derivative instruments**. IMM followed up in 1976 with another key financial derivative – a 90-day US Treasury Bill. Note that unlike commodities contracts where actual physical delivery of **the underlying** (asset on which the contract is based) might be a very important part of the contract, physical exchange is rarely a consideration in financial derivatives. The point is to use price movements for risk management. Hence, if, like a farmer, you face the risk that the price might fall, you buy into the opposite risk. As we saw in our example, a farmer who had taken forward contracts to sell at an average price would face the risk with the contract of the spot price being well above average. However, this was offset by the risk that his physical produce had to be sold at a very low price. Thus the hedged position achieved a stable price which would be seen as a result of the two offsetting risks cancelling each other out.

It is this basic feature that appeals to investors, risk managers and businesses. They often face risk from adverse price movements. Hence they can hedge that risk by buying into the opposite price movement. This is why the 90-day Treasury Bill (also referred to as TBills) futures have value. Many businesses and financial investors can be badly affected by adverse changes in the interest rate. Therefore, it is useful for them to be able to buy into the opposite interest rate risk.

Suppose, for example, a US firm has a relatively large amount of debt, and therefore a high **gearing ratio**.[2] It could be very badly affected by a large increase in the interest rate and in its debt servicing costs. One way to deal with this risk would be to take out 90-day TBill derivatives. The 90-day TBill rate is a key rate which will have a big influence on other rates throughout the whole interest rate structure. Accordingly, if the firm does suffer large cost increases from increases in the interest rate, it can buy into the opposite risk if it has taken out futures contracts to sell 90-day TBills. The interest rate increases, the price of TBills falls, and the firm makes a profit by selling at the previously agreed **strike** or **exercise** price. If we call the new lower spot price $S$ and the pre-agreed exercise price $E$, the firm will make a profit equal to the difference between the relatively high exercise price and the now relatively low spot price, i.e. $E - S$. The profit on the derivatives should more or less offset the loss from the increase in interest rates, leaving the firm no better or worse off. If the interest rate had fallen, it is likely that the spot price would have been greater than the exercise price and the firm would have made a loss equal to $S - E$. But this is offset by the gain from paying reduced interest costs. Again the firm is not better or worse off.

Financial derivatives now come with a wide variety of 'underlying' assets, including individual equities such as IBM, stock indices such as the Nikkei and a variety of bond-based instruments. As we discussed above, two of the basic varieties are forward contracts and futures contracts. The former it will be remembered are bespoke or 'tailor-made' private contracts, while the latter are standardised market traded contracts which are marked to market daily. A third main type of financial derivative is the **option**. An option gives the purchaser the right but not the obligation to buy or to sell at the exercise price. An option to buy at the exercise price is called a **call**, while an option to sell is called a **put**. A call option will only be exercised if the spot price is above the exercise price, while a put will only be exercised at a price below the exercise price.

A fourth way in which firms attempt to control price and interest rate volatility is in terms of swaps. We reserve discussion of this topic until we can illustrate the concept in the context of foreign currency exchange.

Finally, it should be noted that with financial derivatives such as futures and options, actual delivery seldom takes place. The point of these contracts for a business is to take a position on the price movement of the underlying in order to hedge against adverse price or interest rate movements.

 ## Practical implications for managers

### Costs and benefits

It must be remembered that there is no such thing as a free lunch. The added flexibility of an option comes at a price. You can think of an option as an insurance policy. You have to pay a premium up front. Whether you exercise the option or not, the premium is a sunk cost. So whilst options seem like an attractive option, they come at a price. In reality, futures and options are mainly used by large companies, and smaller companies tend not to hedge at all or only use simple forward contracts or swaps.

Potentially one of the most volatile of economic variables that firms face is the foreign currency exchange rate. We examine some basic facts about foreign exchange (or forex) in the next section, then we consider how we can apply the lessons learned in this section on derivatives to the management of forex risk. By way of considering how forex and other risks are controlled using derivative instruments, read the following mini case study ('CSN: Brazil steelmaker rolls out fresh strategy').

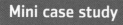 ### Mini case study

### CSN: Brazil steelmaker rolls out fresh strategy
Source Rumsey 2008, Copyright *Financial Times*, 2008

CSN's shares have been affected by investor mood swings on commodities and in mid-July it launched a total return swap (the company swaps dividends and capital appreciation in return for a cash flow) on its own shares worth 3.5 per cent of outstanding capital.
'We wanted to reposition our capital structure so as to benefit from the interest in commodi-

ties and reduce unnecessary volatility,' says Mr Lazcano, the finance director.

Until this latest move, CSN had kept its use of derivatives relatively simple – although with total nominal value of contracts in the hundreds of millions of dollars, the portfolio is already sizeable.

The company controls their use, limiting its activities to reducing risk and volatility, says Mr Lazcano. CSN uses primarily forex and interest rate futures and swaps through the local exchange and over the counter markets to hedge exposure stemming from borrowing and currency transactions. The company occasionally uses options, but with specific aims. CSN also hedges exposure to commodities that it uses, such as zinc and aluminium.

Laying off risk has become easier over the years, thanks to deeper Brazilian capital markets, says Mr Lazcano. Investment horizons among Brazilian businesses are much longer than they used to be and the government has been working to build out a liquid government and corporate yield curve to act as a benchmark, he says.

That has promoted the rapid development of capital and derivatives markets and means CSN does not face liquidity or product constraints – a problem common in the rest of Latin America. Indeed, Mr Lazcano sees the Brazilian derivatives market as deep, well-legislated and sophisticated and goes so far as to call it 'the mirror image of Wall Street'.

At the same time as the Brazilian derivative markets have been opening wide, CSN has been rapidly expanding and reshaping its business in line with many commodities companies in Latin America. Both these changes will see CSN step up its use of financial markets and derivatives significantly in coming years.

'CSN may raise funds in euros, yen and who knows what other currencies. The volumes of our derivatives transactions will have to increase to square with our foreign exchange and interest rate exposures,' says Mr Lazcano.

1. Why do you think that CSN only uses options for 'specific aims'?

2. How do derivatives reduce volatility?

3. Is Mr Lazcano correct to say that the Brazilian derivatives market is the 'the mirror image of Wall Street'?

## Key concepts

- [ ] A **derivative** instrument is one that is **derived** from some underlying asset
- [ ] **The underlying asset** is the asset from which the contract is derived
- [ ] A **forward contract** is a bespoke over-the-counter contract that can be tailored to the exact amount
- [ ] A **futures contract** is a standardised market traded contract which is marked to market daily
- [ ] An **option** gives the purchaser the right but not the obligation to buy or to sell at the exercise price
- [ ] A **call** option gives the right (but not the obligation) to **buy** the underlying at the pre-agreed **exercise** price
- [ ] A **put** option gives the right (but not the obligation) to **sell** the underlying at the pre-agreed **exercise** price

## Practical implications for managers

### Derivative instruments

Derivative instruments are a good servant, but a poor master. When carefully managed and controlled, they can effectively manage price risk. However, if poorly controlled or if used to take on more risk, downside loss can be very high indeed.

## 6.2  Currencies and foreign exchange rates

Every currency has a value relative to another currency and these values fluctuate according to supply and demand, which in turn is determined by macroeconomic and political factors.

'Changing money is the central point of financial contact between nations and the indispensable vehicle of world trade, e.g. Dollar, Euro or the Gambian dalasi or Haitian gourde, has a value in terms of other currencies. The relative or exchange values of the world's major currencies now fluctuate continuously, to the delight or misery of currency traders, and are reported daily in the financial columns of the newspapers. Fortunately, widespread convertibility now permits easy exchange between most of the world's major currencies. ... [There are now very few] restrictions on buying and selling national currencies.'

(From the International Monetary Fund website, About the IMF, www.imf.org)

## Active learning activity 6.2

### Volatility in currencies

Go to www.yahoo.com and click on the finance section. Find the 5-year chart for the British Pound (GBP) against the American dollar (USD). Why did the GBP fall against the USD during the credit crisis? What factors do you think influence the exchange rates between countries?

After the Second World War, many government authorities worldwide decided that they wanted to avoid the serious economic problems and instability that were associated with the interwar years. Following the Bretton Woods conference of 1944, the International Monetary Fund was set up in order to oversee a new global system of **fixed exchange rates**. This system lasted until 1971, when it became apparent that it lacked the flexibility to cope with the increasing volatility of world markets and was abandoned. Most of the world's major trading economies moved to a system of **floating exchange rates**, with a price for currencies established by inflows and outflows of the currency in terms of other currencies; that is to say, supply and demand. Indeed this is precisely the reason why Milton Friedman, who had pioneered the idea of floating exchange rates, was so influential in the development of foreign exchange futures such as on the Chicago Mercantile Exchange.

However, forex rates can be surprisingly volatile, much more volatile than was envisaged when it was first proposed to change from fixed to floating exchange rates. This is demonstrated clearly in Figure 6.1 which shows the bilateral rates of the three main trading currencies, the dollar, the yen and the euro.

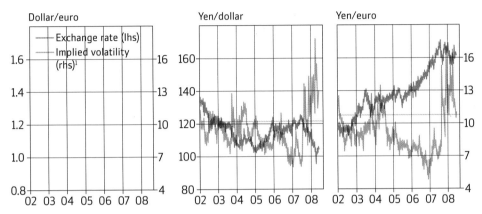

[1]One-month, in percent. The horizontal line refers to the January 1999-April 2008 average.

Figure 6.1 Exchange rate volatilities

*Sources*: Bloomberg; national data

We can see, for example, that it is not unusual for the USD to fluctuate in the range ¥100 to ¥160, i.e. 60% from the lower to the higher figure. For many companies, volatility of this magnitude in revenues or costs for their business could make all the difference between profit and loss. We look at some methods of coping with this volatility in the sections that follow, but for the present we concentrate on familiarising ourselves with some of the basic background information concerning the forex markets.

The City of London Information service, 'The City', has this to say about the foreign exchange markets:

'Globally, average daily turnover in traditional foreign exchange market transactions totalled $2.9 trillion in April 2009, down nearly a quarter on the previous year's record total. Including non-traditional foreign exchange derivatives and products traded on exchanges, turnover averaged around $3.1 trillion a day.'

(IFSL Research 2010, p.15, Figure 6.2)

The UK was the main geographic centre for foreign exchange trading with 36% of the global total in April 2009 (Figure 6.3). The US was the second largest centre with 14% of the global total. Japan and Singapore were the next largest centres with around 6% each. Most of the remainder was accounted for by Germany, Switzerland, Australia, Canada, France and Hong Kong (IFSL Research 2010, p.15).

US dollars, (billions)[1]

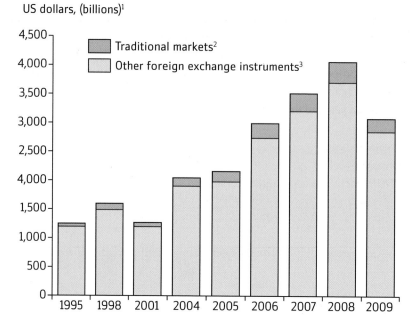

[1] April; [2] spot transactions, outright forwards and fx swaps
[3] currency swaps and options & exchange traded contracts

Figure 6.2  Average daily turnover of global forex

*Source*: Bank for International Settlements; IFSL estimates based on FXJSC, FXC, SFEMC, TFEMC data

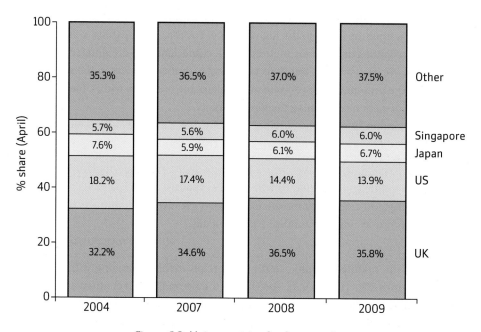

Figure 6.3  Main countries for forex trading

*Source*: Bank for International Settlements; IFSL estimates based on FXJSC, FXC, SFEMC, TFEMC data

Different types of participant in the forex market have different levels of access, and are therefore quoted at different prices. At the bottom of this pyramid is the retail forex buyer usually purchasing for the purposes of foreign business trips and vacations. The percentage difference between buy and sell prices (known as **bid** and **offer** rates) can be eye-watering. At the top, in terms of access is the forex interbank market, spreads between bid and offer rates at this level are usually very low. The interbank market is used by banks both to cover their commercial forex transactions on behalf of customers and to trade and speculate on their own account. The Bank for International Settlements (BIS) estimates that the interbank market accounts for 60% of spot exchange rate transactions, and therefore has a predominant influence. Other major participants include Central Banks, hedge funds, investment managers, non-bank forex brokers and money remittance companies such as Western Union.

This concludes our description of some of the basic key features of the foreign exchange markets. In the next section we look at a basic theory of how forex rates are determined.

## Key concepts

- A **fixed exchange rate** is when a currency is fixed in value relative to other currencies
- A **floating exchange rate** is when a currency is freely floating and its value is determined purely by supply and demand on foreign exchange (**forex**) markets
- **Exchange rate volatility** is the tendency for the prices of freely traded currencies on forex markets to show large amounts of variation in value
- The **London forex market** is the largest in the world

## Practical implications for managers

### Foreign currency trading

Most of the world's currency trades involve the dollar on one side. Therefore if you have a lot of different currency transactions, you may find it easier to charge in dollars. This is not unacceptable for many trade transactions and indeed oil is priced in dollars in the world market.

## 6.3 The fundamental equilibrium exchange rate

In this section, we consider only a bilateral market where one currency is traded against another. (In real life, there are many currencies and a change in one bilateral value will probably impact on all sorts of other bilateral values.) The exchange rate is a price that is determined on a highly competitive market and as such it should be the outcome of the forces of supply and demand.

- The **demand** for GBP on the €/£ forex market could come from many sources. For example, Italians who want to holiday in Scotland, or Belgian banks buying specialist financial services from the 'square mile' financial district in London. As with any normal goods, as the forex price of sterling increases, demand for sterling declines.

- The lower the GBP exchange rate is relative to any currency, the cheaper are British goods and services, plus physical and financial assets from the point of view of the overseas country.

## Practical implications for managers

### Is it better to have a strong or weak home currency?

If you work for an importing business, a weaker pound makes the goods more expensive. In contrast, if you work for an export orientated business, then your goods are relatively more attractive to foreign buyers.

In addition, to trade in goods and services, another important component in the demand for sterling consists of long-term investment. Long-term investment includes companies who want to carry out real investment in Britain, investment managers and sovereign wealth funds that wish to invest in long-term portfolio financial assets in the UK, and foreign companies which wish to acquire British companies.

## Active learning activity 6.3

### Imagine you had 10 million ...

... Indian Rupees (INR) and were an Indian citizen. You wish to invest outside of the domestic environment (if you want to know how much this is in GBP, check with an online currency convertor). What are the key factors that would induce you to invest in a foreign country?

A final component of the demand for sterling in exchange for euros comes from revenues received from abroad from the ownership of assets overseas. The incomes receivable can vary from rent receivable from the ownership of holiday homes in Spain, dividends from German shares and coupon payments on Dutch corporate bonds. When this net income from abroad is added to exports of goods and services, it is counted as an inflow on the **current account** of the national accounts. Longer-term capital flows would be counted in the **capital account**.

- The **supply** of sterling is provided by all those holders of sterling who wish to acquire euros, for example, importers who buy Bosche dishwashers or big institutional investors who want to acquire euro-area government bonds.

- The higher the €/£ exchange rate, the cheaper are purchases of European goods, services, physical assets and financial assets.

An example is illustrated in Figure 6.4.

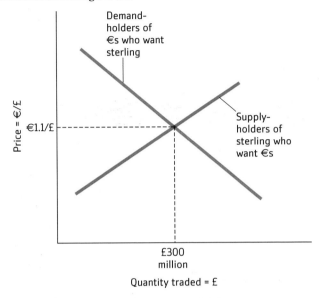

Figure 6.4  Equilibrium price of forex, where equilibrium price is €1.1/£ and quantity traded is £300 million per day

Traditionally it was thought that the exchange rate was determined mainly by these longer-terms factors, which are relatively stable, though they do respond to changes in exchange rates.

Supply and demand in these terms was measured in terms of the balance on the current account, i.e. the balance on trade plus income payments from abroad, in addition to long-term real investment from abroad.

The **fundamental equilibrium exchange rate (FEER)** is the exchange rate that is consistent with a balance of supply and demand measured on this basis, namely exports minus imports plus net capital flows. This is probably true in the long term, but the exchange rate in the long to medium term can be very volatile and unpredictable and it will vary considerably from the FEER. Furthermore, trade balances, current account balances and capital account balances are subject to a large amount of statistical error, making it very difficult to calculate the FEER on this basis in the first place.

There are a number of alternative approaches to the determination of the equilibrium rate of exchange. The first, **purchasing power parity (PPP)**, is based on the idea that the equilibrium exchange rate can be seem as the equilibrium ratio of currencies, and that this ratio can be established on the basis of relative prices. For example, if a Dell Inspiron 10 mini laptop costs £200 in the UK and the same computer is $400 in the US, *and* if there is the same ratio between sterling and dollar prices for all other goods and services, then the PPP exchange rate should be $2/£1. If this is *not* the current exchange rate, then there will be an **arbitrage opportunity** which will push the exchange rate back to equilibrium.

For example, if the exchange rate were at parity of $1/£1, then the dollar would be over-valued and the pound would be undervalued. Entrepreneurs and arbitrageurs would spot the opportunity of buying up laptops in the UK for $200 (£200 × $1/£1) and reselling them in the US for $400 – making $200 with each computer or a mark-up of 100%. This would increase demand for sterling and decrease demand for dollars, pushing up the value of sterling and lowering the value of dollars. Eventually the whole process would come to a halt when equilibrium was restored at the PPP value of $2/£1.

If, on the other hand, the exchange rate was at $4/£1, then the dollar would be under-valued and the pound would be overvalued. Entrepreneurs and arbitrageurs would spot the opportunity of buying up laptops in the US for £100 ($400 × £1/$4) and reselling them in the UK at £200 – making £100 with each computer or a mark-up of 100%. This would increase demand for dollars and decrease demand for sterling, pushing up the value of dollars and lowering the value of sterling. Eventually the whole process would come to a halt when equilibrium was restored at the PPP value of $2/£1.

In short, PPP theory argues that currency ratios or foreign exchange rates should be in the same proportion as the ratio of foreign prices (quoted in foreign currency) to domestic prices (quoted in domestic currency). However, as we will find out in the case study at the end of the chapter, PPP in this **absolute** form does not always hold. Nevertheless, relative PPP does tend to hold. This predicts that the exchange rate will change in line with relative rates of inflation. So, for example, if US inflation was 5% while that in the UK was 3%, we would expect the $/£ exchange rate to increase by 2%. That is, in this situation, the US dollar would be losing value 2% more quickly than sterling and hence 2% more dollars would be needed to buy sterling at the end of the year.

Of course, at shorter time horizons, longer-term trends in trade flow are swamped by shorter-term capital flows which respond to changes in the interest rate and expectations about changes in the exchange rate. Therefore it makes more sense in some circumstances to base one's theory on relative interest rates rather than the relative prices of goods and traded services. **Covered interest parity (CIP)** theory is similar to PPP in that it is an **arbitrage-based** theory. Basically it states that returns on interest-bearing assets in one country should equal those in other countries. If not, then there is an arbitrage opportunity and the exchange rate should adjust accordingly. The scope of this chapter does not really allow us to expand on this rather more complex theory of exchange rate determination.

In the next section we look at the ways in which forex rates are quoted.

## Key concepts

- The **supply** of currency on a **bilateral forex market** is the amount of domestic currency made available by holders of domestic currency in exchange for foreign currency. The *higher* the price in terms of forex per unit domestic currency, the *greater* is the supply

- The **demand** for currency on a **bilateral forex market** is the amount of domestic currency that holders of foreign currency wish to purchase in exchange for foreign currency. The *higher* the price in terms of forex per unit domestic currency, the *smaller* is the demand

- The **fundamental equilibrium exchange rate** or **FEER** is the exchange rate consistent with long-term supply and demand factors

- **Purchasing power parity** is the theory that currency exchange rates should be in the same ratio as relative prices between countries. Relative PPP is the theory that the percentage change in exchange rate represents the difference in inflation rates between the two countries

- **Covered interest parity** is the theory that the exchange rate should adjust to equalise risk free interest-bearing returns between countries

## 6.4 Types of forex quotes

Table 6.1 illustrates a quote for $/ ¥ from the www.yahoo 'Finance' website.

Table 6.1 Quote for yen per dollar including the bid–offer rates per dollar

| (CCY: USDJPY=X)Last Trade: | 99.325 |
|---|---|
| Trade Time: | 1:44pm ET |
| Change: | ↑ 0.680 (0.69%) |
| Prev Close: | 98.645 |
| Open: | 98.660 |
| Day's Range: | 98.360 – 99.930 |
| 52wk Range: | 87.110 – 110.700 |
| Bid: | 99.325 |
| Ask: | 99.350 |

*Source*: Reproduced by kind permission of yahoo.com

Exchange rates can be quoted in one of two ways. First, foreign currencies can be priced in terms of foreign currency. When forex is priced in this way, it is known as the **direct exchange rate**. So, for example, it is pounds sterling that matter to your authors and hence for them the direct exchange rates against the dollar, euro and yen would be £/$, £/€ and £/¥. Conversely, the **indirect** rates would be $/£, €/£ and ¥/£, expressing the foreign currency price of domestic currency. Obviously the indirect rate is simply the inverse of the direct rate, and vice versa. In the UK, the general public are more familiar with indirect rates, though it may be different in your own country. We often tend to think of foreign currency being quoted as a single price. However, those who deal in foreign currencies quote two prices, **bid** and **offer** prices, depending on whether they are buying or selling.

### Active learning activity 6.4

#### Direct or indirect?

The discussion on PPP above was framed in terms of the indirect $/£ rate (from the point of view of your sterling-valued authors). Can you reframe the whole discussion in terms of the direct exchange rate?

Most of the rates above are **central rates**. That is to say, they are averages of bid/offer rates. However, as we can see at the bottom of the table, there is a difference between the bid and ask rates. Dealers will **buy** dollars from you at the **bid** price of 99.325 and **sell** dollars to you at the **ask** price of 99.35. Their profit is the **spread** between the selling and buying price which is equal to 99.35 − 99.325 = 0.025 ¥/$. Table 6.2 shows bid–offer rates in various currencies. It is important to note here that quotes are expressed in indirect terms, despite the labels in the leftmost column. Consequently, the rate GBP/USD is actually in terms of $/£ while that for USD/JPY is actually expressed in terms of ¥/$. This can often happen in real life forex markets. What the first quote really means is that the market is currently buying pounds at $1.4715 and selling pounds at $1.4719.

Table 6.2  Bid–offer rates

| Currency | Bid | Ask |
|---|---|---|
| EUR/USD | 1.3453 | 1.3456 |
| GBP/USD | 1.4715 | 1.4719 |
| USD/JPY | 99.49 | 99.52 |
| USD/CHF | 1.1342 | 1.1345 |
| AUD/USD | 0.7156 | 0.7159 |
| USD/CAD | 1.2391 | 1.2395 |
| NZD/USD | 0.5778 | 0.5783 |

*Source*: Reproduced by kind permission of easy-forex.com.

Of course these kinds of spreads are only available to the very large traders on the forex interbank market. If you buy foreign currency for your holidays or even if you deal in what you think are relatively large amounts of currency for business purposes, the spread will be much larger, as we can see in the following mini case study ('Where was the risk in converting my humble fee?').

## Mini case study

### Where was the risk in converting my humble fee?

Source Winpenny 2008, Copyright *Financial Times*, 2008

Sir, Your edition of June 23 featured complaints from both buyers and sellers of euros ('Why must our holiday euros cost so much?', Christopher Johnson, Comment; and 'A nice earner on foreign exchange', Nigel Foster, Letters). May I add a complaint of my own as to the scandalous hidden commissions banks impose on this risk-free routine transaction?

As a small independent consultant I recently received a fee payment of €7,350. NatWest removed £7 commission from this, which I believe is very reasonable, and a further £153 hidden commission, being the difference between the exchange rate applied (1.2932) and the spot rate in the FT of that day (1.2594). This is both unreasonable and indefensible.

As an economist, I understand the reasons for the spread in buying and selling rates, which reflect risks of holding volatile currencies. What I cannot understand is where the risk lies in the conversion of my humble fee. A transfer is made from a bank in Paris and an amount in euros lands on the trading desk of NatWest HQ, which can, if it is risk-averse, sell it for sterling instantaneously at the market rate at that second on that day. At this wholesale level, spread margins should be tiny, and I would then be credited with the sterling proceeds, minus a transparent commission. If the bank chooses to hold the euros, thereby incurring a theoretical, but surely small, forex risk, then it should not make me suffer for its decision to take a view on the forex market.

It does not improve my humour to note that on my Visa statement, a recent euro hotel bill was debited to my account at 1.2183, an equally bad rate in the opposite direction. It seems that in banking, 'heads they win, tails I lose'.

Although Mr Johnson has my sympathies, I find it ironic that he, as a distinguished former chief economic adviser to a leading bank and therefore implicated in this conspiracy, is unable to explain the rationale for forex margins of 2 to 5 per cent, and is himself now suffering from this furtive practice.

1. Are NatWest charging 'unreasonable and indefensible' fees?

2. Is it true that in forex transactions 'heads they win, tails I lose'? If so, why might this be the case?

## Active learning activity 6.5

### A nice little earner?

The next time you are passing a money changer look at the bid–ask rates for a currency of your choice. Take a note of these rates and compare with the rates quoted in the *Financial Times*. Why are these rates different? Why do you think that airport money changers often have worse rates than a bank just outside the airport?

Until now, we have considered only the **spot rate** on the foreign currency markets. This is the rate that applies to exchanges of currency taking place now. Another important foreign exchange rate is the **forward rate**. We explained the concept of forward markets in Section 6.1, so the reader should have no difficulty in grasping the fact that the forward rate is the exchange rate applicable *now* for exchanges of currency to take place in the *future*. Table 6.3 shows currency rates quoted in the *Financial Times*.

Table 6.3  Currency rates

## POUND SPOT FORWARD AGAINST THE POUND

| Apr 15 | | Closing mid-point | Change on day | Bid/offer spread | Day's mid High | Day's mid Low | One month Rate | One month %PA | Three month Rate | Three month %PA | One year Rate | One year %PA | Bank of Eng. Index |
|---|---|---|---|---|---|---|---|---|---|---|---|---|---|
| **Europe** | | | | | | | | | | | | | |
| Czech Rep. | (Koruna) | 28.6984 | 0.2495 | 724-244 | 28.6990 | 28.3960 | 28.7101 | -0.5 | 28.7349 | -0.5 | 28.7532 | -0.2 | - |
| Denmark | (Danish Krone) | 8.5031 | 0.0590 | 002-059 | 8.5059 | 8.4284 | 8.5039 | -0.1 | 8.5051 | -0.1 | 8.5134 | -0.1 | - |
| Hungary | (Forint) | 300.231 | 2.3592 | 961-500 | 300.800 | 297.140 | 301.374 | -4.6 | 303.394 | -4.2 | 310.442 | -3.3 | - |
| Norway | (Nor. Krone) | 9.0816 | 0.0074 | 765-867 | 9.1012 | 9.0376 | 9.0932 | -1.5 | 9.1188 | -1.6 | 9.2329 | -1.6 | 106.0 |
| Poland | (Zloty) | 4.4059 | 0.0263 | 034-084 | 4.4157 | 4.3720 | 4.4155 | -2.6 | 4.4343 | -2.6 | 4.5060 | -2.2 | - |
| Russia | (Rouble) | 44.9728 | 0.1736 | 609-847 | 44.9847 | 44.7170 | 45.0928 | -3.2 | 45.3224 | -3.1 | 46.6124 | -3.5 | - |
| Sweden | (Krona) | 11.0558 | 0.0219 | 506-610 | 11.0812 | 11.0097 | 11.0530 | 0.3 | 11.0486 | 0.3 | 11.0603 | 0.0 | 79.2 |
| Switzerland | (Fr) | 1.6383 | 0.0094 | 375-391 | 1.6386 | 1.6260 | 1.6375 | 0.6 | 1.6360 | 0.6 | 1.6296 | 0.5 | 124.4 |
| Turkey | (New Lira) | 2.2799 | -0.0038 | 790-807 | 2.2903 | 2.2746 | 2.2908 | -5.7 | 2.3145 | -6.0 | 2.4405 | -6.6 | - |
| UK | (£) | 1.0000 | - | - | - | - | - | - | - | - | - | - | 79.4 |
| Euro | (Euro) | 1.1425 | 0.0079 | 421-428 | 1.1425 | 1.1324 | 1.1422 | 0.2 | 1.1418 | 0.2 | 1.1411 | 0.1 | 99.0 |
| SDR | - | 1.0158 | 0.0035 | - | - | - | - | | - | | - | | - |
| **Americas** | | | | | | | | | | | | | |
| Argentina | (Peso) | 6.0075 | 0.0094 | 013-136 | 6.0159 | 5.9663 | 6.0314 | -4.8 | 6.0932 | -5.6 | 6.6339 | -9.4 | - |
| Brazil | (Real) | 2.6967 | 0.0024 | 955-979 | 2.7094 | 2.6853 | 2.7127 | -7.1 | 2.7493 | -7.7 | 2.9448 | -8.4 | - |
| Canada | (Canadian $) | 1.5483 | 0.0061 | 476-489 | 1.5493 | 1.5385 | 1.5480 | 0.2 | 1.5478 | 0.1 | 1.5567 | -0.5 | 113.7 |
| Mexico | (Mexican Peso) | 18.9210 | 0.0836 | 164-255 | 18.9272 | 18.8073 | 18.9776 | -3.6 | 19.1026 | -3.8 | 19.7621 | -4.3 | - |
| Peru | (New Sol) | 4.3946 | 0.0132 | 931-961 | - | - | 4.3950 | -0.1 | 4.3992 | -0.4 | 4.4208 | -0.6 | - |
| USA | (US $) | 1.5499 | 0.0039 | 496-501 | 1.5523 | 1.5387 | 1.5496 | 0.2 | 1.5492 | 0.2 | 1.5478 | 0.1 | 83.7 |
| **Pacific/Middle East/Africa** | | | | | | | | | | | | | |
| Australia | (A$) | 1.6599 | 0.0058 | 593-605 | 1.6618 | 1.6518 | 1.6652 | -3.8 | 1.6765 | -4.0 | 1.7315 | -4.1 | 102.8 |
| Hong Kong | (HK $) | 12.0288 | 0.0303 | 264-311 | 12.0476 | 11.9428 | 12.0240 | 0.5 | 12.0141 | 0.5 | 11.9793 | 0.4 | - |
| India | (Indian Rupee) | 68.8754 | 0.1170 | 565-942 | 68.8960 | 68.2310 | 69.0692 | -3.4 | 69.4616 | -3.4 | 71.0961 | -3.1 | - |
| Indonesia | (Rupiah) | 13960.3 | 26.9490 | 415-640 | 13978.5 | 13863.7 | 14031.9 | -6.1 | 14193.6 | -6.6 | 14955.2 | -6.7 | - |
| Iran | (Rial) | 15343.5 | 30.3850 | 970-900 | 15367.8 | 15248.5 | - | | - | | - | | - |
| Israel | (Shekel) | 5.7259 | -0.0005 | 219-299 | 5.7631 | 5.6961 | 5.7273 | -0.3 | 5.7301 | -0.3 | 5.7607 | -0.6 | - |
| Japan | (Yen) | 144.322 | -0.0976 | 268-376 | 145.040 | 143.280 | 144.269 | 0.4 | 144.155 | 0.5 | 143.382 | 0.7 | 151.8 |
| Kuwait | (Kuwaiti Dinar) | 0.4455 | 0.0012 | 452-457 | 0.4512 | 0.4426 | 0.4457 | -0.8 | 0.4459 | -0.4 | 0.4469 | -0.3 | - |
| Malaysia | (Ringgit) | 4.9557 | 0.0077 | 510-603 | 4.9606 | 4.9145 | 4.9634 | -1.9 | 4.9792 | -1.9 | 5.0480 | -1.8 | - |
| New Zealand | (NZ $) | 2.1772 | 0.0106 | 761-783 | 2.1783 | 2.1588 | 2.1812 | -2.2 | 2.1897 | -2.3 | 2.2394 | -2.8 | 102.2 |

*Source*: *Financial Times*, 2010

There are two points of note about forward rates. First, there are many currencies with no forward market. Second, forward currency rates tend to be quoted for a limited number of maturities, namely 1 month, 3 months, 6 months and 1 year.

As can be seen from Table 6.3, the forward rate is not the same as the spot rate. Take the Turkish lira, for example. The spot rate for the lira is 2.2799L/£. The 1-month forward rate is 2.2908L/£. Hence the lira is expected to fall in value relative to the pound (more lira will be needed to buy a pound) over this time horizon. The 1-month forward lira is said to be at a **discount** to the pound, the discount being around 0.01 L/£. In fact, as can be ascertained from Table 6.3, the lira is expected to continuously lose value against the pound, with the amount of lira needed to purchase £1 eventually expected to reach a value of 2.4405 in 1 year's time.

In the next section, we look at different kinds of regimes that countries can put in place to manage their currency relative to foreign currencies.

## Practical implications for managers

### Watch out for indirect currency quotes

If you live in a country like the UK, where foreign currency is normally quoted in indirect terms, it is easy to be confused over currency value unless your mental arithmetic is very sharp. For example, a current quote for retail UK residents who want to buy dollars is shown in Figure 6.5.

| | US Dollar | |
|---|---|---|
| 9 September 2009 | Buy | Sell |
| Interchange fx | 1.7134 | 1.6220 |

Figure 6.5  Dollar exchange rate quote for the UK retail market

One would have to divide each of these into the number one to get the actual price per dollar in sterling of 0.5836 buy and 0.6162 sell. It's at this point that the more absent-minded of your authors momentarily imagines that he's spotted an arbitrage opportunity – then he remembers. The institution will give you 58.36p for each dollar they buy from you and will charge you 61.62p for each dollar they sell to you. Bang goes the arbitrage. Doh!

## Key concepts

- ☐ A **bid rate** is the price at which the market is prepared to *buy* a nominated currency (or any other financial asset)
- ☐ An **ask (or offer) rate** is the price at which the market is prepared to *sell* a nominated currency (or any other financial asset)
- ☐ A **central rate** is an average of the bid and ask rates
- ☐ A **spot rate** is the current market price for currency exchanges taking place *now*, or indeed any other financial exchange taking place now)
- ☐ A **forward rate** is the current market price for currency exchanges taking place at some predetermined point in the future (or indeed any other financial exchange taking place in the future). Different forward rates are normally quoted for different future exchange dates

## 6.5  Exchange rate regimes

In this section we will be mainly concentrating on the **freely floating** or **flexible** exchange rate, in which the exchange rate is determined by the free play of supply and demand. However, sometimes there are limits to the extent to which the rate is allowed to vary. In this case, the exchange rate will be a **managed float** or a **dirty float**. The limits on a currency's upper and lower value against foreign currency will be set as a result of government economic policy and will be kept in place through intervention by the Central Bank. If the value of domestic currency gets 'too high', it may be felt by the government that this will make exports uncompetitive. Thus the Central Bank will intervene, selling domestic currency and buying foreign currency. If the rate gets 'too low', the government may anticipate that the cost of imports will rise, and this will cause inflation. In this case, the Central Bank will attempt to 'prop up' domestic currency by buying it on the forex markets using its foreign exchange reserves. However, given the size of global currency flows, governments may find it difficult to make their preferred currency rates 'stick' if the markets strongly disagree with them, as the following mini case study illustrates ('Rupiah plunges after forex changes').

## Mini case study

### Rupiah plunges after forex changes

Source Aglionby 2008, Copyright *Financial Times*, 2008

The rupiah fell 3.6 per cent on Thursday to a 7½-year low as investors took the view that a new Indonesian central bank regulation restricting some foreign exchange purchases might be a precursor to currency controls.

Miranda Goeltom, the Bank Indonesia senior deputy governor, told the *Financial Times* such concerns were baseless. She said the regulation, issued late on Wednesday, was targeted at improving liquidity in the market, not determining the rupiah's exchange rate and that capital controls were not envisaged.

The regulation states that for amounts greater than $100,000 a month foreign currency buyers must submit documentation of an underlying transaction and, for Indonesian residents, a tax number.

But bankers described the timing of the move as 'poor' considering the global aversion to emerging market risk and fragile sentiment towards Indonesia. They warned that since the regulation did not address the underlying selling pressure on the rupiah, it was unlikely to reverse it.

'Indonesians themselves now don't trust the central bank to preserve the rupiah's value,' said Tim Condon of ING. 'The authorities were doing a good job until mid-October but then they blinked and the markets got them on their heels. The risk [of further significant depreciation] is elevated now.'

The rupiah fell to 11,998 to the US dollar on Thursday, a 32 per cent drop since early August, before rallying to 11,800, according to Bloomberg. Its all-time low was 17,000, hit during the financial crisis a decade ago.

Ms Goeltom said the regulation was 'not related to any intervention measures'. 'We just want to discourage people who don't have any need to buy foreign currency,' she said. 'If you have a legitimate need, there's no limitation on how much you can buy.'

1. Why do investors dislike currency controls?

2. What impact would a '32 percent drop since early August' have on (a) importers and (b) exporters?

In a freely floating exchange rate system, a fall in currency value is conventionally called a **depreciation**, whereas a rise in a currency's international value will be called an **appreciation**.

The alternative to a floating exchange rate system is a **fixed exchange rate system**. A loss of value of a currency's value in this system, usually forced by the market or a change in government policy, is called a **devaluation**, whereas an increase of domestic currency value against foreign currency is a **revaluation**.

The most stable fixed exchange regimes are backed by an international agreement. The most extensive historical exchange rate system in history was the Bretton Woods system mentioned above. This kind of formal exchange rate system often imposes a formal obligation of loans among Central Banks in case of necessity.

A **currency crisis** is the breakdown of fixed exchange rates with an unwilling devaluation or even the end of that regime in favour of a floating exchange rate.

A **currency board** is where the domestic currency is issued in some fixed ratio relative to net reserves of foreign currency at the Central Bank, usually the dollar. In this kind of arrangement, the Central Bank does not engage in money creation, but allows the supply of domestic currency to rise and fall in line with foreign currency reserves. Well-known currency board systems include Hong Kong which maintains the Hong Kong dollar at a value in line with the US dollar, Lithuania, Estonia and Bosnia who have anchored the local currency to the euro and many Caribbean states who maintain the Caribbean dollar against the US dollar via currency board arrangements. Argentina had a currency board (anchored to the US dollar) up until 2002.

## Active learning activity 6.6

### Would a global currency be good for business?

Suppose all the countries in the world decided to adopt one currency. Let's call it the Guru. What advantages would arise for business if all trading was carried out in Gurus? What problems would arise for countries? (Hint: think about the arguments for and against adoption of the euro.)

So far we have talked in very general terms about foreign exchange as a macroenvironmental factor. In the next section, we look at some of the specifics of how this affects firms.

## Key concepts

- [ ] A **freely floating** or **flexible** exchange rate is an exchange rate that is determined purely by the free play of supply and demand

- [ ] A **managed float** or a **dirty float** is one in which there is a limit by the issuing authority on the extent to which a currency is allowed to float. Buying or selling, respectively, by the monetary authority will take place as the currency approaches lower or upper limits in value against other countries

- [ ] A **currency crisis** is the breakdown of a fixed exchange rate and subsequent devaluation. This is often associated with concurrent macroeconomic and political problems

- [ ] A **currency board** is where the domestic currency is issued in some fixed ratio relative to net reserves of foreign currency at the Central Bank, usually the dollar

## Practical implications for managers

### Which type of forex regime is riskier – floating or fixed?

There isn't actually an easy answer to this question. Floating exchange rates can be very volatile. Fixed, on the other hand, can change in sudden, large and discontinuous ways if the fixed exchange rate is strongly out of line with fundamentals. The currency can suddenly 'blow up' like a steam boiler exploding. An example is the UK's disastrous experience with the European fixed exchange rate mechanism on 'Black Wednesday' in 1992. Also remember that some of the world's countries are on fixed or quasi-fixed exchange rate systems.

## 6.6  Forex risks faced by firms

### 6.6.1 Transaction risks

There are three types of forex risk faced by firms. First, there is **transaction risk**. This is the risk that business transactions involving foreign currencies will have a variable value measured in domestic currency. So, for example, imagine that a US multinational burger joint has an operation in the UK in 2008. Let's call it Burger Don's. Every year, Burger Don's expects to receive £100 million from its UK operation. Since 2004 the pound sterling has been worth, roughly and on average, $2. Therefore every year they're fairly confident of receiving $200 million, as this is what has happened in 2004, 2005, 2006 and 2007. But the summer of 2008 brings very bad news indeed. The pound plunges by a quarter of its value. Each pound is now only worth $1.50. Total revenues from the UK only amount to $150 million. As we have observed before, a 25% decline is a very big change for any business and could easily mean the difference between substantial profit and substantial loss. Figure 6.6 charts the decline in the pound.

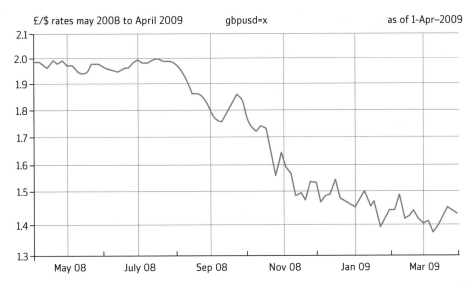

£/$ rates may 2008 to April 2009        gbpusd=x        as of 1-Apr–2009

Figure 6.6  £/$ rates May 2008 to April 2009

Copyright 2009 Yahoo! Inc. http://finance.yahoo.com/

*Source*: Reproduction by kind permission of yahoo.com

## 6.6.2 Translation risk

**Translation risk** is the impact on a company's balance sheet and profit and loss account from having operations reporting in various different currencies. When accounts are consolidated in a single home currency, there can be considerable variation from financial statement to financial statement and what looks like a very successful foreign venture can look like a failure when translated back for accounting purposes – even though, in real life, there has been no actual attempt to convert foreign currency earnings, assets and liabilities into domestic currency.

Take the example of Burger Don's above. Suppose that Burger Don's was a multinational, which tended to treat foreign operations as stand-alone, and only rarely actually 'cashed in' and repatriated foreign earnings. At present, Burger Don's is looking at a 25% fall in earnings and a 25% write-down in asset value in the UK. Furthermore, if the capital used to finance the UK operation was raised in the US, it is also looking at a 33% increase in the value of liabilities! These figures are enough to swamp anyone's accounts in red ink. However, the figures remain purely paper figures until there is actual repatriation of earnings. In terms of assets versus liabilities, again, the effect would be purely theoretical until the UK operation was wound up and actual net asset value was realised.

As we can see in the next mini case study ('Mothercare to push on with plans to expand', Mothercare, a firm previously based solely in the UK, faces increasing risk, both in transaction and translation terms.

## Mini case study

### Mothercare to push on with plans to expand

Source Pearson and O'Doherty 2009, Copyright *Financial Times*, 2009

Mothercare, the UK baby products retailer, plans to push ahead with international expansion, despite warning gross margins would come under pressure because of sterling weakness.

The company said it would continue with its plan to open 100 stores abroad annually after a trading update yesterday that showed total international sales had risen 40 per cent in its final quarter, down from 49 per cent in the previous quarter.

Ben Gordon, chief executive, blamed the slight slowdown on seasonal holidays and said the Middle East, Russia, Eastern Europe and China offered huge opportunities for growth. 'We've got 21 stores in India and that's going to grow dramatically over the next two or three years,' he added.

But most of Mothercare's products are made with components bought in dollars in south-east Asia and, as such, he warned sterling's weakness would mean a drop in gross margins.

David Stoddart, an analyst at Altium, said: 'The fundamental story remains intact but the currency impact means a larger forecast change for 2010 than I think any of us expected.'

While the currency weakness has been partly offset by sales abroad, a large majority of the company's revenue still comes from its UK stores. UK sales were better than expected, rising 3.7 per cent, while total group sales rose 5.6 per cent in the 11 weeks to March 28.

Mr Gordon said the group was well-positioned given it was debt-free and operating in a resilient industry.

'People continue to spend on their babies after they've stopped spending on discretionary items for themselves,' he said.

In the full year to March 28, total group sales rose 6.9 per cent and UK sales rose 1.4 per cent like-for-like. International sales were up 44.5 per cent, mainly because of new store openings. The shares fell 4½p to 391½p.

Mothercare has been nurtured in the past six years by Ben Gordon, who has reformed it since the days of falling sales and profit warnings. International expansion has continued at an impressive rate and the identification of geographically diverse markets will afford greater resilience. But sterling weakness poses a threat to the bottom line and, as such, the stock – trading at 12 times prospective earnings – looks fairly priced.

1. Most of Mothercare's products are made with components bought in dollars in south-east Asia. As a UK-based company, why would Mothercare buy in dollars instead of pounds?

2. Can Mothercare do anything to counteract the weakness of the pound?

3. What impact does international expansion have on Mothercare's revenue and what are the key factors in determining profitability in overseas markets?

## 6.6.3 Exchange rates and economic risk

**Economic risk** is the risk associated with the overall conditions of the economy of the country. It includes changes such as major political changes and changes to major economic variables such as inflation and growth rates. In the long run, such changes will affect the trend in exchange rates and hence the competitivity of firms operating in non-domestic environments. Generally, a fall in the value of domestic currency is good for exporters, while a rise in the value of foreign currency is bad. Of course, exporters could always absorb the higher value of currency, by lowering the domestic price they aspire to achieve abroad and maintaining the foreign currency price at a constant level. However, this would then put pressure on profits, so there will be a limited extent to which exporters are able to do this. In the mini case study below ('Yen soars despite Japan's troubles'), we examine the more common scenario of currency strength causing business problems.

### Mini case study

### Yen soars despite Japan's troubles

Source Whipp and Garnham 2009, Copyright *Financial Times*, 2009

Economic weakness is no barrier to a strong currency these days. Just ask Japan.

The yen stormed to a series of multi-year highs this week, hitting a 13½-year high against the dollar, a seven-year peak against the euro and a record high against sterling.

This is in spite of the fact that Japan's export-dependent economy continues to suffer from the global economic downturn. The Bank of Japan warned this week that the country could expect its economy to contract in the current fiscal year, ending on March 31, and the next one.

But rapidly deteriorating economic data, including a record drop in exports for December, and a lengthening list of exporters that expect steep annual losses have done nothing to weaken the currency.

One reason for this is that the yen is seen as a haven at a time of extreme nervousness in global markets and when the US, eurozone and the UK are all in recession or heading there.

Analysts say the yen is benefiting from increasing concerns about a spill-over from the credit crisis to the financial system. Financial shares in Europe and the US have come under renewed pressure this week.

The strength of the yen could not have come at a worse time for Japan's exporters. Global demand is slumping and the stronger yen, which makes Japanese products more expensive and eats into repatriated earnings, has generated shocks. Toyota's announcement that it was likely to post its first loss in 70 years was one such shock.

When the dollar slid to fresh 13-year lows of ¥87.10 against the yen this week, discussions about the possibility of intervention by Japan's ministry of finance increased.

Japan has not intervened in currency markets for five years.

Derek Halfpenny, at Bank of Tokyo-Mitsubishi UFJ, said he expected Japan to intervene to buy dollars against the yen if the greenback lurched down through ¥85.

'There must be an increasing risk that the authorities are growing concerned – especially about the deflationary impetus from a surge in the yen,' he said.

1. Given the weaknesses of the Japanese economy, why is the yen regarded as a 'safe haven'?

2. What can the Japanese government do to weaken the yen and how would this help Japanese businesses?

In the next section we look at methods that firms can use to deal with these risks.

 **Key concepts**

- ☐ **Transaction risk** is the most direct and immediate risk from foreign currency fluctuation. It is the risk that moneys receivable denominated in foreign currency will lose value before they can be exchanged for domestic currency, or, conversely, that money payable in a foreign currency will rise in value before domestic currency can be exchanged for foreign currency

- ☐ **Translation risk** is the risk that adverse currency movements, while not actually realised in cash value, will strongly affect the company's accounting performance and, in particular, its **net asset value**

- ☐ **Economic risk** is the risk associated with the overall conditions of the economy of the country. It may include the political risks such as sudden takeover by a hostile government or economic risks such as rampant inflation.

 **Practical implications for managers**

### The time frames of forex risk

Roughly, transaction risk is an immediate risk in forex transactions, translation risk is a medium-term risk and economic risk is a long-term risk

## 6.7 Ways of dealing with forex risks faced by firms

### 6.7.1 Traditional forward contract

Forward contracts are the most commonly used method of dealing with exchange rate risk. We examined forward contracts in Section 6.1 above. We saw that the counterparties to a **traditional currency forward contract** would enter into an exchange rate agreed now for a currency exchange some time in the *future*. For example, suppose you were a manufacturer based in Thailand and you had a special deal to buy oil from Qatar in Qatar riyals (QAR) (oil is usually priced in US dollars). The exchange rate at the time of writing is as follows:

| | | |
|---|---|---|
| 1.00 THB | = | 0.102869 QAR |
| 1 QAR | = | 9.72114 THB |

Your next consignment will be delivered in 5 months, but you worry that the baht may lose value against the riyal before this date, driving up the baht price of a fundamental input. Your budget for oil is THB1 million. In order to make sure of completely hedging this risk, and being able to buy the oil you require for THB1 million, you have to enter into a contract to purchase 102,889.158 QAR now at a forward price of 9.71920 THB/QAR:

| | | |
|---|---|---|
| 1,000,000.00 THB | = | 102,889.158 QAR |
| 1 THB = 0.102889 QAR | | 1 QAR = 9.71920 THB |

There are two ways of entering into this type of forward contract. One way is to find a counterparty who wants to take the exact opposite position over the same time horizon and maturity. You can arrange things through a broker, who will try to match your specific requirements against a counterparty with the equal and opposite requirements. The alternative method is to find a bank or other financial institution willing to act as counterparty.

Table 6.4  Colombian peso versus the US dollar

| Financial Institution | Limits | | | Requests |
|---|---|---|---|---|
| | Date of quote | Length of contract | Minimum amount | Pricing (%) |
| ABN Amro | 1/29/04 | 2 years | | 9.2% |
| Citibank | Forward 2/26/2004 | 1 year | $10,000 | 9.0% |
| BcoOccidente | 2/18/04 | 6–9 months | $US20,000 | |

Note: Most banks offer Non-deliverable forwards for the same tenor as their Forward offering. Most banks seem to offer Euro forwards and swaps similar to US$ parameters.

*Source*: Holden & Holden 2004.

Table 6.4 has an applied example from the forward market for the Colombian peso versus the US dollar. It is taken from Holden and Holden (2004).

As can be seen from Table 6.4, a forward contract is not something to enter into lightly, as the premium, in this case around 9%, can be substantial; also, there are a limited number of counterparties and a limited number of maturities. As Holden and Holden observe:

'More generally, the disadvantages of forward transactions are that a substantial deposit is generally required at the time the contract is entered into and default on the contract often results in a heavy penalty. Furthermore, the contract must be of a size that interests the dealer. As we have seen, there is generally a premium to be paid with a forward contract, and that premium might exceed the costs imposed in the event of a disadvantageous change in the currency involved. While there is flexibility in establishing delivery dates initially, once they are established there is no way to change them. Therefore, if circumstances change for the buyer, there is no way to liquidate the contract without incurring a penalty. Forward contracts also generally require a form of collateral security.'

(Holden and Holden 2004, p. 22)

## 6.7.2 Non-deliverable forward contract

There are of course a number of alternatives to traditional forwards. For example, one could engage in a non-deliverable forward contract in which there is no actual exchange of currencies, but simply a net exchange in a nominated currency from the loser to the gainer in terms of any price movement that has taken place.

For example, suppose a Colombian business called ConQuesos has to pay out $500,000 in 6 months' time. It finds that it is able to buy these dollars forward at a rate of COP 2,450/$1 from BEMbank (where COP is the Colombian peso). The deal will cost a total of COP 1,225,000,000.

Consider the following scenarios when the contract matures in 6 months' time. First, if the spot price is COP 2,450/$1 at maturity, neither party has gained or lost. Second, if the Colombian peso has risen in value relative to the dollar, say to COP 2,400/$1, then ConQuesos has made a loss while BEMbank has made a profit. The $500,000 can now be bought for COP 1,200,000,000 at the spot rate. But ConQuesos is committed to buying at the forward price of COP 2,450/$1, or a total transaction cost of COP 1,225,000,000, resulting in a loss of COP 25,000,000. In dollar terms, COP 1,225,000,000 would now buy $510,417. Hence the dollar loss for ConQuesos would be $10,417. Final settlement would be in terms of the price difference – a transfer of $10,417 from ConQuesos to BEMbank.

Conversely, if the spot price had gone to COP 2,500 by maturity, $500,000 would now cost COP 1,250,000,000 at the spot rate. This is considerably more than ConQuesos has paid forward for $500,000 (i.e. COP 1,225,000,000), resulting in a gain of COP 25,000,000. In dollar terms, COP 1,225,000,000 would now only buy $490,000. Thus the dollar loss for BEMbank would be $10,000. Final settlement would be in terms of the price difference – a transfer of $10,000 from BEMbank to ConQuesos.

### 6.7.3 Currency futures contract

Another variation on a theme is the use of currency futures, which we examined in Section 6.1. Their main distinction from forwards, as we discussed, is that they are continuously market traded and come in a limited number of varieties.

Parties to futures contracts also have to provide the broker with an initial margin and pay variation margin if the price moves against them. For companies in the emerging economies, a performance bond is generally required, in the form of either a government security or a letter of credit, which can be for either the full value of the contract or some lesser percentage.

The advantages are as follows:

- Since there is an active market in the currencies traded on the exchange, they are very liquid and can be sold at any time.

- They are of a standardised size, so they are easy to obtain and have much lower transaction costs than forward contracts.

- Contracts are also standardised, and are for standardised amounts, so they are easy to understand.

However, it may be difficult to hedge precisely, given the standardised nature of futures. Furthermore, although it may be relatively easy to find futures contracts in currency pairs involving US dollars, euros, yen, British pounds and Swiss francs, it may be very difficult to find a contract in many currencies outside this select group of frequently traded currencies.

### 6.7.4 Currency swaps

Currency swaps are similar in some ways to forward agreements, though they usually have much longer maturities. They normally involve companies dealing in a number of currencies, but having a preferred currency for most working purposes. The reason why a company would rather work in a particular currency is usually for the practical reason that it is easier to deal in the home currency.

However, another strong motivation for companies dealing in currency swaps is usually that they have a comparative advantage in borrowing in one currency, typically the home currency, but may need to borrow foreign currency for the purposes of foreign business and investment. For example, a Malaysian company has a comparative advantage for borrowing in the Malaysian bond market rather than in the UK, but needs to finance a sterling investment in a UK project. What it may try to do is to find a UK company that can borrow on favourable terms in the UK, but which needs to fund investment in Malaya. It would make sense for the Malayan company to swap its ringgits for the UK company's sterling.

A swap agreement involves a simultaneous spot purchase of foreign exchange along with an offsetting forward purchase of domestic currency. The re-exchange of the currencies at a future date allows for the conversion of a stream of cash flows in one currency into another at a defined exchange rate. It is a form of barter. Because swaps allow for a temporary exchange of currencies and they are often used to make investments, the arrangement can be set to have a maturity that coincides with the maturity of an investment. The currency is then returned at that time. The exchange rate for the forward delivery is fixed upon signing the contract and thereby avoids the risk of currency fluctuations over the life of the investment. As Holden and Holden observe:

> 'Swap markets are available not only in main trading currencies, but also in newly emerging economies such as Korea, India, Indonesia, the Philippines, Thailand, the Czech Republic, Hungary, Poland, Slovakia, Mexico and South Africa. (In these markets, long-term swaps between dollars and the local currency are available.) The cost of hypothetical transactions (investigation did not reveal any actual transactions between microfinance institutions and foreign lenders that had already occurred) indicates that the annual cost would be in the range of 18% on swaps with a maturity of up to 10 years.'

(Holden and Holden 2004)

## Practical implications for managers

### Using currency instruments for forex risk management

For small- or medium-sized businesses this can be expensive and difficult. An alternative is not to hedge the risk – at least you might gain on the upside – or to borrow or lend forex in anticipation of needing it in the future. This is discussed next.

## Key concepts

- A **traditional currency forward contract** is one in which the counterparties agree to swap currencies at a predetermined point in the future but at an exchange rate agreed now
- A **non-deliverable forward contract** is similar to a traditional currency forward contract with the exception that no exchange of currencies takes place. The counterparties settle the contract in terms of an exchange between the 'winner' and the 'loser'
- For a **currency futures contract** the comparison is the same as it would be between any forward and futures contract. The forward contract is usually private and difficult to value or sell on. The futures contract is market traded. Hence it is clear what the value of the contract is. Furthermore, it is easily 'closed out'
- **Currency swaps** are much like currency futures contracts. The main difference is that swaps usually have small to medium firms as both counterparties, rather than a large financial institution as one of the counterparties, as it is based on a swap of normal business cash flow

## 6.8  Hedging without derivative or other financial instruments (internal methods)

### 6.8.1 Leading and lagging

This is an option that is available to larger more internationally diversified companies, typically multinational corporations (MNCs). The various divisions within an MNC deal in a variety of currencies all the time between divisions in different countries. Rather than treating each transaction involving a foreign currency in isolation, the MNC will aggregate intercompany forex transactions so that they can time intercompany payments in such a way as to maximise the advantage to the company as a whole. Therefore the strategy involves leading or prepaying intercompany invoices when the payer's currency is at risk of devaluing against the payment currency and lagging those payments if the payer's currency is likely to appreciate. Accordingly the strategy avoids local currency loss when a currency is devaluing and maximises local currency gain when a currency is appreciating.

### 6.8.2 Netting

Again, **netting** is an option that is available to larger more internationally diversified companies, typically MNCs. The idea is that the overarching corporation minimises forex volatility by aggregating intercompany forex transactions and working out the **net amount** that is to be transferred from one division to another. The exposure that remains – net payments to payees – can be hedged in the forward market if desired.

### 6.8.3 Foreign currency borrowing

From a conceptual point of view, perhaps the simplest approach to forex risk management is to borrow or lend foreign currency ahead of need. For example, suppose your company has to make a payment of $1 million in 6 months' time and you are worried that the domestic currency might devalue, substantially increasing your domestic currency costs of making the $1 million payment. What you could do is to borrow $1 million at current exchange rates and place it on deposit. That way, you have guaranteed that the dollar funds will be available to make the payment. Simple as this strategy is, there are costs associated with it in the sense that there may well be a gap between interest payable on the loan and interest receivable on the deposit. In fact the gap can be fairly substantial given that most deals in forex markets are much larger than the sums involved in small to medium sized enterprise transactions. A sum of $25 million is considered relatively small in the forex wholesale markets, while for small to medium size businesses this could be a very large sum indeed. Therefore it may be difficult to raise the necessary funds in the first place without incurring substantial transaction costs.

An additional problem would be the exact form in which the company would hold a large foreign currency deposit. Holding a large sum of currency in a current account or as a short-term deposit would imply foregoing a substantial amount of interest. On the other hand, it may be difficult to place the funds in some kind of bill-type instrument with an exactly matching maturity. Costs of raising foreign currency can be particularly costly for companies in newly emerging countries.

## Key concepts

- **Leading** and **lagging** refers to the practice of delaying or bringing forward payments and receipts in such a way as to minimise loss from currency swings
- **Netting** is when MNCs aggregate intercompany forex transactions and settle the net amount between international divisions
- **Foreign currency borrowing** is foreign currency that is borrowed or loaned ahead of need

## 6.9 Summary

This chapter opened with a discussion of derivative instruments, that is to say financial instruments that are derived from ordinary **underlying** instruments such as agricultural contracts, bonds or even stock indices. These instruments had their origin in the huge food products market of Chicago in the middle of the nineteenth century. It was found that both farmers and food processors could better manage their exposure to these risks by buying and selling **forward**. That is, they could take out a contract to **exchange** something in the *future*, but at a **price** determined *now*. Later variants on this approach were **futures contracts** which were standardised and exchange traded and options that give the **right** but **not the obligation** to buy or sell the underlying.

We then went on to discuss the major shift of world forex regime from fixed to floating exchange rates in the 1970s. Despite the many advantages over fixed exchange rate systems, one of the unexpected drawbacks was **exchange rate volatility**. Exchange rate volatility continues to be a problem today, which is why firms need techniques of dealing with **exchange rate risk**. We argued that exchange rates are fundamentally determined by long-run supply and demand factors. This approach to the determination of the exchange rate is known as the **fundamental equilibrium exchange rate (FEER)**. However, given the limitations of FEER as a practical approach, other approaches in common use are **purchasing power parity (PPP)** and **covered interest parity (CIP)**. We then went on to examine some facts and figures on the key trading currencies (dollar, yen and euro) and the main forex trading centre (London). We also made the distinction between **bid**, **ask**, **spot** and **forward** rates on the foreign currency markets. We finally examined some of the ways in which a firm could manage transaction risk. These included external methods such as **traditional forward currency contract**, **non-deliverable forward contract**, **currency futures contract** and **currency swaps**. We also looked at internal methods such as **leading** and **lagging**, **netting** and **foreign currency borrowing**.

# ? Questions

1. What is a forward contract and why would a forward contract be used?

2. What are the main differences between a futures and forward contract? What are the main advantages of a futures contract over a forward contract?

3. Why are forwards, futures and options called derivative instruments?

4. Why do forwards, futures and options allow firms to manage risk?

5. Many of the world's countries moved from a fixed to a floating exchange rate system in the early 1970s. What was the most unexpected feature of floating exchange rate systems?

6. Which are the main trading currencies in terms of market share and which was the biggest forex trading centre in terms of turnover in 2009?

7. What is the difference between a bid and offer rate?

8. What does the acronym FEER stand for and what concept of exchange rate determination does it represent?

9. Outline and discuss the various exchange rate risks faced by firms.

10. Compare and contrast the various financial instruments that are available for managing exchange rate risk, with particular reference to a small to medium sized company in one of the emerging economies.

11. Outline and discuss the various *internal* options that are available for the management of forex risk, with particular reference to a small to medium sized company in an emerging economy.

## Case study

### Attacks on China's cheap currency are overdone

Source *Economist* 2009

CHINA has been accused of 'manipulating' its currency by Tim Geithner, America's new treasury secretary, and this week Dominique Strauss-Kahn, the managing director of the IMF, said that it was 'common knowledge' that the yuan was undervalued. You would assume that such strong claims were backed by solid proof, but the evidence is, in fact, mixed.

Of course China manipulates its exchange rate – in the sense that the level of the yuan is not set by the market, but influenced by foreign-exchange intervention. The real issue is whether Beijing is deliberately keeping the yuan cheap. From July 2005, when it abandoned its fixed peg to the dollar, Beijing allowed the yuan to rise steadily, but since last July it has again been virtually pegged to the greenback. And there are concerns that China may allow the yuan to depreci-

ate to help its exporters. But American politicians are wrong to focus only on the yuan's dollar exchange rate. Since July the yuan has risen in real trade-weighted terms [see Figure 6.7]. So how much further should it rise?

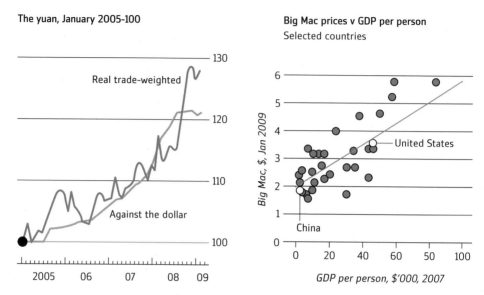

Figure 6.7 Food for thought
*Sources: Economist* 2009

Those who argue that the yuan is still too cheap point to three factors: China's foreign-exchange reserves have surged; it has a huge trade surplus; and prices are much cheaper in China than in America. Start with official reserves. If China had not bought lots of dollars over the past few years, the yuan's exchange rate would have risen by more. However, in the fourth quarter of 2008, China's reserves barely rose, despite a record current-account surplus. This suggests that private capital is now flowing out of China.

Charles Dumas, an economist at Lombard Street Research, argues that outflows of hot money could become a flood if China did not have capital controls. Currency 'manipulation' amounts to more than foreign-exchange intervention; China also has strict capital controls which, although leaky, keep private savings at home. If Beijing scrapped those controls firms and households would want to invest abroad to diversify their assets. In other words, if the value of the yuan was not 'manipulated' and instead was set entirely by the free market, it might fall, not rise.

### Beefing up the argument

An alternative way of defining the 'fair' value of a currency is purchasing-power parity (PPP): the idea that, in the long run, exchange rates should equalise prices across countries. The Economist's Big Mac index offers a crude estimate of how far exchange rates are from PPP. Our January update found that a Big Mac cost 48% less in China than in America, which might suggest that the yuan is 48% undervalued against the dollar. But by this gauge, the currencies of virtually all low-income countries are undervalued, since prices are generally lower in these countries than in rich ones.

PPP is a long-term concept. However, the relationship between prices and GDP per head can be used to estimate the short-term fair value of a currency relative to others. Using a simple model, which adjusts the Big Mac index for differences in countries' GDP per head and relative labour costs, gives the result that the yuan is now less than 5% undervalued.

The evidence that the yuan is significantly undervalued is hardly rock-solid. It probably is still a bit too cheap, and it would certainly be a mistake for Beijing to allow it to fall, not least because this would risk a protectionist backlash from abroad. In the longer term, the yuan needs to keep rising against a basket of currencies. But for now, some of the accusations being thrown at China are wide of the mark.

1. Why would the Chinese yuan have a 'fixed peg' to the dollar?

2. What are the risks to the country itself in doing this?

3. What are the forex risks of an exporter to China? What are the forex risks of an importer?

4. Would the forex risks of a foreign-owned venture in China differ from the above?

5. Why would a rise in the Chinese Treasury's foreign exchange reserves have prevented the yuan from rising more?

6. The article suggests that by focusing on trade flows, critics such as the US are missing an important point about how the fundamental exchange rate or FEER works and how it is calculated. What other types of flow should be taken into account?

7. And if these other types of flow were not controlled, what could happen to the Chinese yuan?

8. You should be able to find the Big Mac Index on *The Economist* website at www.economist. com. Download this and explain how exactly PPPs are calculated by *The Economist* using a Big Mac in the US as a standard of comparison.

9. Are there any factors in this kind of PPP comparison of exchange rates that may have been overlooked?

 ## Further reading

Berg, A. and Pattillo, C. (1999) Predicting currency crises: the indicators approach and an alternative. *Journal of International Money and Finance* **18**:561–586.

Besembinder, H. (1994) Bid–ask spreads in the interbank foreign exchange markets. *Journal of Financial Economics* **35**:317–348.

Faff, R.W. and Marshall, A. (2005) International evidence on the determinants of foreign exchange rate exposure. *Journal of International Business Studies* **36**:722–724.

Ghosh, A.R., Gulde, A.M. and Wolf, H.C. (1998) *Currency Boards: The Ultimate Fix?* IMF Working Paper 8. IMF, Washington, DC.

Holden, P. and Holden, S. (2004) *Foreign Exchange Risk and Microfinance Institutions*. Microfinance Gateway, Washington, DC.

IFSL Research (2010) *International Financial Markets in the UK*. TheCityUK, London.

Jorion, P. (1995) 'Predicting volatility in the foreign exchange market. *Journal of Finance* **50**:507–528.

Marshall, A.P. (2000) Foreign exchange risk management in UK, USA and Asia Pacific multinational companies. *Journal of Multinational Financial Management* 10(2):185–211.

# Internet references

There are some very good 'meta' sites in this area, i.e. international business or international finance sites that point to other sites. Two of these are:

http://globaledge.msu.edu/resourcedesk/
http://www.internationaleconomics.net/bizfinance.html#finance
We culled the following very interesting sites from the former:

### Barclays International: Business Banking

Barclays, an offshore banking firm, provides a number of reports for its customers. Economic reports include the European Economics Quarterly Forecast, UK Economic Quarterly Insights and Prospects, Euro Weekly, and Foreign Exchange Weekly. It also provides industry reports for the construction, manufacturing and services sectors.

### Bloomberg Online: Foreign Exchange

The Bloomberg website offers a wide range of tools and information about financial markets. Real time rates, financial news and currency converters are available for more than 200 currencies.

### International Finance Theory & Policy Analysis

The International Economics Study Center website is provided by an academic from George Washington University and includes a textbook online format, so the site contains a vast amount of information for those interested in international finance and cross-country transactions. It also includes a good deal of international trade information and news on the main page.

### International Swap and Derivatives Association (ISDA)

This website is the home to a global financial trade association whose members trade negotiated derivatives, covering trades and options in fields such as interest rates, currency, commodities, energy and credit.

### Valore International Finance

This website features articles on issues shaping the world of the international executive with a focus in finance. Some of the featured financial articles on the site are a few years old, but the user can find current value in the World at a Glance, Landmarks and Connections pages.

# Suggestions for group work

Suppose you were part of the finance team in a firm based in India. Your main supplier is Malayan while your main market is in the US. As a group, try to find out if it would be possible to use the risk management instruments discussed in this chapter in order to guard against the risks of a strong Malaysian ringgit and a weak US dollar. What would be the relative fixed and variable cost for each instrument, which markets or institutions would provide them and what would be the relative advantages and disadvantages? Include a final recommendation on what hedging strategy should be adopted by the company, if any.

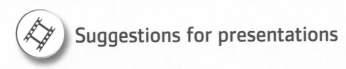 Suggestions for presentations

1.  Is the Chinese yuan deliberately undervalued?
2.  Exchange rate volatility – can it really be 'managed'?

# 7 Capital Budgeting

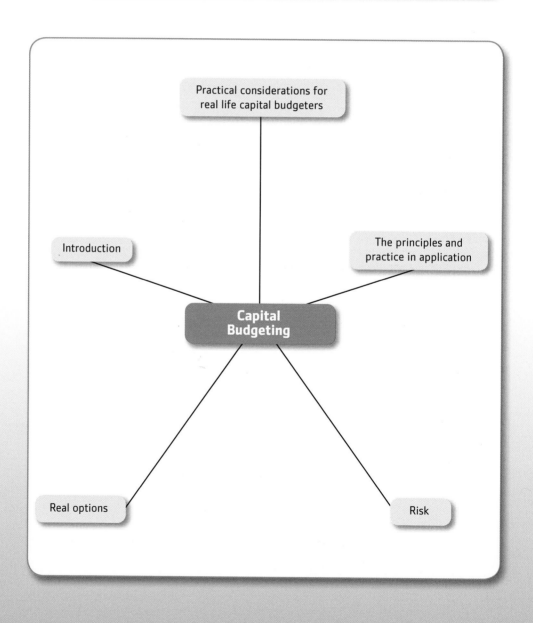

- Practical considerations for real life capital budgeters
- Introduction
- The principles and practice in application
- **Capital Budgeting**
- Real options
- Risk

## Knowledge-based learning objectives

When you have completed this chapter you will be able to:

✓ Realise that past costs are forever sunk
✓ Understand the effects interest, tax and unequal project time spans can have on net present value
✓ Comprehend the main practical issues involved in capital budgeting
✓ Be aware of the treatment of risk in capital budgeting decisions
✓ Understand how real options analysis may change investment decisions

## Skills-based learning objectives development

✓ Business and financial environment consciousness: you should have developed an understanding of the nature of capital budgeting and the types of decisions that need to be taken to support capital budgeting projects.
✓ Numerical skills: you should have developed the ability to understand, manipulate and calculate standard metrics for capital budgeting decisions.
✓ Analytical thinking and problem-solving skills: you should have developed the ability to know how to analyse capital budgeting projects.
✓ Problem-solving skills: you should have developed the ability to assess how to evaluate a capital budgeting decision.
✓ Critical-thinking skills: you should have developed the ability to understand the assumptions on which capital budgeting techniques are based and to know the limitations of these techniques.
✓ Organisational skills: you should have developed your ability to organise your time and work efficiently and to gather data and information which you can translate into value-adding intelligence.
✓ Managerial soft skills: you should have developed the ability to know where judgement and interpersonal skills are needed within a capital budgeting framework.
✓ Presentation skills: you should have developed your ability to present your work clearly both verbally and in writing.
✓ Interpersonal skills: you should have developed your ability to present your work clearly both verbally and in writing and to interact with others effectively upon completion of the end of chapter questions.

## Online resource centre

Visit the Online Resource Centre that accompanies this book to listen to a podcast of the authors discussing the difficulties in making capital budgeting decisions in practical situations.
**www.oxfordtextbooks.co.uk/marney**

## OrganicX considers its options

Charlie and Kate are in the boardroom discussing their expansion plans. Given the popularity of their investments in Shanghai, they are wondering whether or not to open an office there. 'I think we should go ahead,' says Charlie. 'The market research we did at such an enormous cost will be wasted otherwise. In addition, we are already paying Lee Lei a fortune to look after our clients over there.'

Kate sighs, 'Charlie, the market research is a sunk cost so forget about it – it's gone, in the past, already spent. It doesn't matter what we decide now – we can't time travel to get it back. As for Lee Lei, we are paying him anyway, whether we like it or not, so that's not relevant either.'

Charlie frowns but decides not to follow up and instead tries a different argument. 'If we open up a full office the costs will be tremendous – the property market is really overheated in Shanghai.'

Kate smiles because she has done her research on office space. 'We can get prime property on a lease with an option to expand our floor space, at the same price, within 3 years if we want. So we won't be spending too much up front.'

'What about revenues?' asks Charlie. 'How much more is a fancy office going to bring us in?'

Kate explains the increase in projected revenues and other extra variable costs, although she admits that the figures are only a forecast based on the market research and her own estimates. However, Charlie is worried about the extra risk. He is well aware that the credit crunch has caused a downgrade in growth rates for China and that the stock market has been very volatile. He thinks the revenue estimates should also be more conservative.

'How can we take account of all the risk involved?' he asks.

Kate replies, 'We can do some sensitivity analysis – basically looking at how the cash flows change according to how the key variables change – but I'm sure we should still invest. The intangible benefits alone are worth it.'

'Intangible benefits?' queries Charlie. 'What do you mean by that?'

'Well,' begins Kate, 'the prestige of having an office there, the value of having a physical presence, the opportunities that will arise just by going forward with the initial investment – all of these will increase our future options. In fact, I can't think of one reason not to go ahead.'

Charlie thinks hard and replies, 'If we do go ahead in Shanghai, can we still open the office in Indonesia? Or do the same boring rules apply there!'

# 7.1 Introduction

In Chapter 2 we introduced the basic methods of investment appraisal and, in particular, discounted cash flow methods such as internal rate of return (IRR) and net present value (NPV). In this chapter we delve into some of the more practical applications of these techniques and some of the problems that may be encountered when the company attempts to apply these techniques. We also take cognisance of the strategic background against which these decisions tend to be made. As part of the conceptual framework which it is necessary to have in order to appreciate the wider application of these techniques, it is useful at this point to remind ourselves that company investment appraisal is often also known as **capital budgeting**. That is to say, most companies usually have a number of projects that are competing for funds from the investment budget.

## Mini case study

### Damning UK defence equipment review criticises 'infinite demand'

Source Lemer *et al.* 2009, Copyright *Financial Times*, 2009

A damning official report has exposed Britain's defence equipment programme as an unaffordable 'fiction', prompting ministers to order a radical shake-up at the Ministry of Defence.

The review by Bernard Gray, a former ministerial adviser, concludes that a 'sclerotic' culture has been unable to check 'infinite demand' from the armed forces, leaving an equipment programme that is more costly than 'any likely projection of future budgets'.

The 296-page study was set to be published in July but was delayed after Downing Street balked at its devastating conclusions. On average, the current equipment programme is expected to overrun by almost £35bn and slip by about five years. Meanwhile, the cumulative cost of delaying projects approaches £2.2bn a year.

The report underscored the wrenching budget decisions facing the next government. In Mr Gray's worst-case scenario, Britain will only be able to afford about half of the equipment programme by 2020, with the MoD having only £5bn to spend on £10bn of commitments.

The government welcomed the report's 'directness', while admitting that significant cuts would soon need to be made.

Lord Drayson, the minister in charge of defence acquisition reform, told the *Financial Times* that 'under any realistic scenario the defence equipment plan is overheated'. He pledged to implement most of Mr Gray's recommendations 'within six months'.

Reforms will include a review every four or five years to rebalance spending plans, a 10-year budget for the MoD in keeping with the long-term nature of defence projects and an annual audit to ensure affordability.

Still, Lord Drayson said the MoD had rejected one of Mr Gray's most significant conclusions – that the government organisation that buys and supports military kit should be outsourced in order rapidly to improve delivery. Defence insiders said the move could cost more money than it saved.

1. What problems can poor capital budgeting create?
2. What solutions are suggested by this case study?

When evaluating company investments, a company has an investment or capital budget and it will attempt to allocate this in such a way as to maximise shareholder wealth. Until now, we have tended to assume, as does the core theory, that the company will maximise shareholder wealth by using the following decision criteria for investment projects considered in isolation:

Accept *all* projects where NPV $\geq$ 0; IRR $\geq$ k
where k is the cost of capital.

In real life of course, firms often face the situation that *not* all projects can be taken as there will be a *fixed* capital budget.

Now let us suppose that we have a number of projects, and we wish to allocate capital in such a way as to make best use of our capital resources. Theory suggests that we can still allocate the budget in such a way as to maximise value/shareholder wealth by maximising NPV and IRR **subject to the budget constraint.** Suppose we have a budget of £10 million and five business projects labelled A to E, as in Screenshot 7.1.

| 1 | Project | Investment Required | |
|---|---------|---------------------|---|
| 2 | A | £5m | |
| 3 | B | £2m | |
| 4 | C | £1m | |
| 5 | D | £3m | |
| 6 | E | £1m | |

Screenshot 7.1 Capital investment projects with cost of investment

Clearly the budget precludes the adoption of all projects. One approach we might take is to rank projects by NPV or IRR. We present this ranking in Screenshot 7.2.

| 9 | Project | NPV | IRR | Investment Required |
|----|---------|--------|------|---------------------|
| 10 | E | £2.10m | 78% | £1m |
| 11 | C | £1.71m | 56% | £1m |
| 12 | B | £0.81m | 25% | £2m |
| 13 | A | £0.57m | 17% | £5m |
| 14 | D | £0.32m | 16% | £3m |
| 15 | | | | |

Screenshot 7.2 Capital investment projects with NPVs and IRR

Given our use of NPV/IRR it is clear that the order in which the firm should invest its capital would be E, C, B, A, D. Thus we would invest in projects E, C, B, A. This would absorb £9 million of capital, leaving only £1 million to invest in D. If D is divisible, then we could use up the remainder of the capital budget by investing in one third of project D. However, physical investment projects, unlike financial portfolio investment, are often not divisible, so fractional investment may not be possible. The other main point of note here is that we have been fortunate in that normal NPV/IRR criteria allow us to properly rank these projects. This is not always the case when capital is **constrained** or **rationed**, and we would more usually use an approach based on incremental benefit *relative* to incremental cost. Capital may either be rationed internally (soft rationing) or externally (hard rationing). For example, we might construct a **profitability index**, which divides PV of future cash flow by initial investment. The results are presented in Screenshot 7.3. By great good luck, the index gives the same ranking as NPV for projects A to E, as we can see from the screenshot.

| | A | B | C | D | E | F | G |
|---|---|---|---|---|---|---|---|
| | PROJECT | INITIAL INVESTMENT | NPV | PROJECT RANK BY NPV | PVFC (NPV + IN. INV.) | PROFITABILITY (PVFC / INITIAL INVESTMENT) | PROJECT RANK BY PROF. |
| 1 | | | | | | | |
| 2 | A | 5 | 0.57 | 4 | 5.57 | 1.114 | 4 |
| 3 | B | 2 | 0.81 | 3 | 2.81 | 1.405 | 3 |
| 4 | C | 1 | 1.71 | 2 | 2.71 | 2.710 | 2 |
| 5 | D | 3 | 0.32 | 5 | 3.32 | 1.107 | 5 |
| 6 | E | 1 | 2.10 | 1 | 3.10 | 3.100 | 1 |

Screenshot 7.3 Ranking by NPV and profitability index for projects A to E

It is not normally the case that NPV/IRR, which measures financial benefit in absolute terms, will give the same rankings as an incremental benefit approach such as profitability index. Consequently, when capital is rationed, it can make more sense to look at investment projects in terms of their efficiency rather than their absolute NPV. As you will recall, with normal NPV, provided we have a conventional cash flow consisting of an initial outlay in period zero, followed by a series of revenues, we simply subtract the current outlay from the discounted value of the future revenues. However, when looking at investment efficiency, we are less interested in the present value of cash flows (or PVCF) *minus* initial outlay than in PVCF *relative to* initial outlay. That is, we're taking a more 'bangs per buck' approach in terms of output per unit of input. Take the following figures in Screenshot 7.4 for projects P through U. We can find the NPV of each project quite simply by taking the initial cost from the PV revenue of each project.

| | | Initial Cost | PV Revenue |
|---|---|---|---|
| 17 | | | |
| 18 | P | 40 | 56.5 |
| 19 | Q | 50 | 67 |
| 20 | R | 30 | 48.8 |
| 21 | S | 45 | 59 |
| 22 | T | 15 | 22.4 |
| 23 | U | 20 | 30.8 |

Screenshot 7.4 Initial costs versus present value of revenue for projects P–U (millions)

We could assess these projects in terms of their absolute NPV. However, this would be misleading in the event of capital rationing, as we can see when we take the ratios of PV of revenue to initial cost.

As you can see in Screenshot 7.5, the ranking order of projects is quite different under the two schemes. For example, project Q ranks second in terms of absolute NPV, but only fifth in terms of profitability. In short then, if capital is unlimited, we would take on all projects P through U, as they are all wealth enhancing having NPVs greater than zero. However, if capital has an upper limit then we must carefully assess each project in terms of the return/cost ratio, which tells us something about project efficiency in terms of the use of capital and the benefit that the incremental capital produces.

|  | Ranked by NPV | | Ranked by Profitability Index | |
| --- | --- | --- | --- | --- |
| P | 3 | 16.5 | 1.4125 | 4 |
| Q | 2 | 17 | 1.34 | 5 |
| R | 1 | 18.8 | 1.62667 | 1 |
| S | 4 | 14 | 1.31111 | 6 |
| T | 6 | 7.4 | 1.49333 | 3 |
| U | 5 | 10.8 | 1.54 | 2 |

Screenshot 7.5  Profitability index for projects P–U (millions)

For example, if the capital budget were £110 million, we would invest in projects R, U, T and P. This would cost £105 million and would yield a PV of £158 million in future revenue, or £53 million NPV. If projects were **divisible**, the remaining funds could be deposited in one-tenth of project Q. If projects were strictly **indivisible**, but it was necessary to keep the capitals budget liquid and free from risk, then the remaining funds could be placed on deposit (probably at an interest rate less than the cost of capital and therefore, in a long term situation, the extra funds should, theoretically, be returned to shareholders). Also note that PI is only strictly appropriate when projects are divisible and is most suitable when projects are of equal duration and risk. If projects are indivisible, it is more appropriate to consider combined NPVs for combinations of projects.

## Active learning activity 7.1

### The effect of increased capital

Try the same calculations for a capital budget of £100 million. What are the results?

The assumption of project divisibility is a potentially controversial one assuming as it does that the project would be 'scalable', allowing the firm to invest in fractions of a project. In the real world unlike the world of theory, things are messy and lumpy. In most cases, projects tend to be 'all or nothing'. That is to say, you either have to undertake the whole investment expenditure or forget the project. In concluding this topic, we should point out that we have only considered **single period** capital rationing. The amount of capital may fluctuate over the lifetime of the various projects, thus giving rise to **multi-period** capital rationing. The latter is a much more complicated problem which is outside the scope of this book.

Having considered the problem of capital rationing, in the next section we look at how we decide what to include as costs and benefits from an investment project.

## Mini case study

### Capex caution

Source Hahn 2008 (from CFO Publishing)

Capital spending generally goes as the economy goes – which means it's currently in the doldrums. Growth of U.S. capital expenditures (capex) has slowed from a robust 21 percent in 2006 to 13 percent in 2007 to nominal growth projected for 2008, according to business consultancy The Hackett Group. According to finance chiefs (both here and abroad) polled in Duke University/*CFO Magazine's* latest Global Business Outlook survey, capital spending will rise a paltry 3 percent this year.

Company after company has announced that it will tighten the purse strings in 2008. For example, department store chain J.C. Penney will open fewer new stores, while specialty retailers from Ann Taylor to Zales are scaling back capex plans. Meanwhile, skyrocketing fuel prices have forced airlines like Delta and American Airlines to throttle back on capex, too.

JX Enterprises/Peterbilt of Wisconsin, a privately owned chain of truck dealerships that had planned to open one new dealership per year, has suspended its 2008 expansion, says CFO Mark Muskevitsch. 'Last year we had an aggressive capital-spending plan,' he says. 'So far this year we have done only things we have to do, such as replacing computer hardware, but not facility upgrades or refinishing lots.' Computer-software upgrades will have to wait until sales pick up, he adds.

Still, says Muskevitsch, trucking demand usually begins to recover before other sectors, which means business may pick up in the second half of the year. If so, the company will consider a modified expansion plan – leasing rather than buying a new facility.

### Power spenders

To a large extent capex strategies depend on what industry you play in. Companies in some sectors, such as biotechnology and telecommunications, still have solid growth prospects and have to invest, points out Roger Wery, director of the operational strategy practice at consulting firm PRTM. 'Some companies can't stop investing, because they are in a ruthless, competitive environment,' he adds. Yahoo, for example, is spending large amounts on capex even though its EBITDA (earnings before interest, taxes, depreciation, and amortization) has slowed. 'They feel pinched, but they have to continue to invest,' says Wery.

1. Why can't Yahoo cut back on their capital expenditure?
2. Think of at least three types of expenditure that cannot be cut back in times of recession.

## Practical implications for managers

### How can projects be valued?

Far from being a simple decision of accepting all projects with a positive NPV, capital budget-ing decisions are often complex in practice. The challenge facing managers is being aware of valuation tools available and their drawbacks. The old adage of 'garbage in, garbage out' should always be remembered.

## Key concepts

- ☐ **Capital budgeting** is the method by which companies appraise investment decisions
- ☐ **NPV** is the net present value of a project
- ☐ **IRR** is the internal rate of return on a project
- ☐ **Constrained** or **rationed capital** occurs when there is not enough capital available to invest in every positive NPV project
- ☐ A **profitability index** is the ratio of PVFC to initial cost
- ☐ If projects are **indivisible** they cannot be broken down into smaller projects to make better use of constrained capital

## 7.2  Practical considerations for real life capital budgeters

### 7.2.1 Sunk costs are forever sunk

Consider the following example. When you were in Jaipur, India, you took part in a vintage car rally. You so enjoyed yourself that you have bought a vintage Rolls Royce for investment pur-poses at a price of INR 5 million which you paid cash. Suppose you are now in great need of liquidity, but since the date of purchase, the vintage car market has turned down, so the price you can now achieve from the resale of your asset is only INR 2 million. Would you accept this price? The answer is that as a rational economic agent, you would. As the owner of the car, and also a rational economic agent, in the event that the market got significantly worse, you would accept any price greater than zero, even a very low one such as INR 1 million.

Obviously, as with much economic theory, there is considerable abstraction. For exam-ple, you may well hang on to your car in the expectation that the market might recover. In addition, there would be certain emotions that would come into play. You may be more highly motivated to improve the situation if you are angry about the deficit and grudge the 'lost' money; or are ashamed of being such a fool. But you may well have no choice with assets such as vintage cars (or works of art or similar investments) which have few alternative uses. The same applies of course to materials and machinery that are very specialised, such as steel-making plants and equipment.

Thus, there is more than a grain of truth in the principle of sunk costs from economics provided it is not taken to extremes. There really is no point in chasing losses. If it is only INR £2 million that is on offer and that situation is unlikely to change, and we have a pressing need for money, then we will, reluctantly, take the INR £2 million. This is an important principle in capital budgeting. We *ignore* **sunk** or **historical cost**. That is to say, the historical cost of assets that we bought in the past or the market price they may have commanded is entirely irrelevant.

 ## Practical implications for managers

### Learn to let go

As a manager, or indeed as anyone making a decision, it can be difficult to ignore past costs when considering future choices. Gamblers may decide to keep gambling on the basis of trying to recoup past losses when they should merely take into account the current odds of winning. Making a decision with a project is similar; historical costs should be ignored and only the present situation should be taken into consideration.

## Mini case study

### Beware the pressure of sunk costs

Source Bazerman 2009 (from Harvard Business Publishing)

'Ignore sunk costs,' accounting professors and economists tell us. The amount of money and effort we've invested in the past, they say, is irrelevant to our future investments.

This advice is easy to follow in the classroom, but much harder in the real world. Logically, you know that the purchase price of your home has little bearing on its current value. But when you've poured all of your energy and savings into a piece of property, especially one as personal as a home, you're likely to have trouble putting the purchase price out of your head.

In one negotiation simulation, Kristina Diekmann, an associate professor of management at the University of Utah, and her colleagues, found that when appraising a property, both sellers and buyers are affected by the price the seller originally paid for it. This purchase price did not affect assessments of the property's value, but it did affect both buyers' and sellers' bid expectations and reservation points (the reservation point is the point at which the BATNA, or the best alternative to a negotiated agreement, becomes preferable to starting or continuing a negotiation).

During slumps in the housing market, few of us will accept the possibility that our investment has failed to appreciate much, or has even declined in value. Homes can remain vacant for months, even years, while sellers stubbornly refuse to lower their asking price. Psychologically, further escalating our commitment to our initial investment seems like the only option. Our sunk costs – and those that others have made – weigh on us and set us up for the escalatory trap. This is true in many negotiation settings, including salary disputes and contract talks with long-term clients.

1. Think of three real life situations in which you may be tempted to consider sunk costs when making a financial decision.

2. Why should sunk costs be considered irrelevant in those situations?

### 7.2.2 Only count actual marginal cash flows

So you're stuck with this vintage Rolls-Royce in Jaipur, India, and you're in despair about the drop in its value from INR 5 million to INR 2 million. But then you discover that the price in the UK market is rather higher at £37,000 or INR 3 million. However, it will cost you 0.5 million rupees to modify the car to meet UK emission standard and for shipping to and marketing in the UK. The sale will take place in around 1 year's time.

What is the correct way of assessing the value of this project? Clearly it wouldn't be right if we took into account the historical cost. On the other hand, you are foregoing the opportunity to sell right away in India at INR 2 million. In which case, the INR 2 million is known as the **opportunity cost**. The opportunity cost, another concept imported from economics, is defined as any benefit that we forego by committing a resource to a particular use, thereby making it unavailable for any alternative uses.

For example, the reason why we apply interest rates and discount rates is that money is a scarce resource with alternative uses. If a project does not earn at least enough to cover the cost of capital, then the capital would be better left in the bank to earn interest. The interest foregone is the opportunity cost of the capital.

Thus, taking into account sunk cost would be erroneous, but it is necessary to consider the cash alternatives that would be possible with a given resource. Let's consider two alternative ways of doing the calculation, one wrong and one right as demonstrated in Table 7.1.

Clearly the cash flow A calculation is *wrong* as it takes into account historical sunk cost. Also, it does not take into account opportunity cost. Cash flow B is the right approach.

**Active learning activity 7.2**

### The cost of opportunities

Create a cash flow assuming the Indian sale price is INR 1 million, the modification cost is INR 1 million and the UK sale price is INR 2.5 million.

Table 7.1 Capital budgeting and opportunity costs

| Time | Item | Cash flow A (INR 000,000) | Time | Item | Cash flow B (INR 000,000) |
|---|---|---|---|---|---|
| 0 | Historical cost | −5 | 0 | Opportunity cost | −2 |
| 0 | Repairs, etc. | −0.5 | 0 | Repairs, etc. | −0.5 |
| 1 | Sale price in UK | 3 | 1 | | 3 |
| | NPV@ 10% | −2.77 | | NPV@ 10% | 0.23 |

## Practical implications for managers

### Opportunity costs

Managers should remember that the alternative to investing in a project is almost never to leave the cash inactive. It could be earning interest in a bank account (this would only be a short-term solution for large cash balances as you would not be maximising shareholder wealth if you only earned interest) or be invested in another project. Thus it is important to take into account the alternative uses of the cash that the business is foregoing by investing when considering a project.

The yearly **depreciation** expense from writing off a firm's buildings, computers, equipment and so on is an important example of an item that appears as an accounting expense which does not represent actual cash expenditure. The actual cash outflow associated with the purchase of a depreciable asset takes place when the asset is purchased. The asset is then depreciated over its useful life.

However, this depreciation is a notional expenditure intended to provide for the replacement of the asset at the end of its economic life. As it does not represent real cash expenditure, we do not include it in any cash flow calculation. As you will often be using data from company accounts and, in particular, concepts such as accounting income or accounting profit, you will need to remember to add back depreciation to these to get a true picture of actual cash flow. This is because accounting earnings are usually reported after tax, interest and depreciation. You will also need to add back interest, as we explain below.

Let's take the example of an Egyptian entrepreneur, EF, who has just started her own mobile phone hire business. In order to fund the purchase of 20 phones at 500 Egyptian pounds each, she takes out a microfinance loan at a hefty commercial rate of 15%. The business is intended to supplement her family's income. The figures for her reportable annual income are shown in Table 7.2.

Note that the initial cost of the 20 mobile phones does not appear. This is a **capital cost** and appears only implicitly as depreciation. Now this is how income is recorded for financial recording purposes. However, if we were to assess EF's project on an NPV basis, we would add the depreciation back. Before we do this, there are two other matters we need to take into account, namely interest and tax.

Table 7.2  EF phone company – income statement

| | EGP |
|---|---|
| *Annual reportable net income* | |
| Income from phone rental | 17,000 |
| *Expenses* | |
| Miscellaneous – phone batteries, etc. | –500 |
| Depreciation | –500 |
| Interest at 15% | –1,500 |
| Reportable income | 14,500 |
| Taxes at 30% | 4,350 |
| Net income after expenses, depreciation, tax and interest | 10,150 |

First, there is the matter of interest payments, which we normally deduct before arriving at a figure for accounting income. However, we should not leave in interest costs when calculating NPV, as this would be **double counting**, given that interest costs are already included in the WACC, which is, of course, the appropriate rate of discount. Thus we would treat interest payments the same way as depreciation.

However, slightly bizarrely, we actually leave these items in at first, then deduct them at the end. The reason for this is that the interest and depreciation reduce taxable profit as they are normally allowable as deductions for tax purposes. Thus interest and depreciation provide a **tax shield**. Hence we would have the situation depicted in Screenshot 7.6. i.e. net income is arrived at in exactly the same way as was demonstrated in Table 7.2. We then add back interest and depreciation to arrive at a recurring annual cash flow of EGP 12,500. This is an annuity cash flow as it recurs over 20 years, so we can use the annuity factor of 6.26 to arrive at a present value of EGP 76,050.88 and NPV of 66,050.88. Note that we are using a discount rate of 15% which is the rate of interest on EF's loan. This implies that EF's implied cost of equity is also 15%.

Depreciation and interest payments together amount to EGP 2,000 and this reduces taxable income by the same amount. The cash saving is the 30% of EGP 2,000 that would otherwise have to be paid. In other words, there is a **tax shield** worth EGP 600 and this is the difference between cash flow with the tax benefit and cash flow without the tax benefit.

Another practical problem that often crops up is that mutually exclusive projects may have different life spans, making comparisons between them more difficult. Consider the following two projects A and B in Screenshot 7.7.

| | A | B | C | D | E | F | G |
|---|---|---|---|---|---|---|---|
| 1 | T | | | | T | Grand Total | |
| 2 | 0 | Cost of twenty mobile phones | -10,000 | | | -10,000.00 | |
| 3 | | | | | | | |
| 4 | 1 to 20 | | | | 1 to 20 | 76,050.88 | |
| 5 | | Income from Phone Rental | 17,000 | | | | |
| 6 | | Expenses | | | NPV of Project | 66,050.88 | |
| 7 | | Miscellaneous - Phone Batteries et | -500 | | | | |
| 8 | | Depreciation | -500 | | | | |
| 9 | | Interest at 15% | -1,500 | | (Annuity Factor - 15% over 20 Years) | | |
| 10 | | | | | 6.2593315 | | |
| 11 | | Reportable Income | 14,500 | | | | |
| 12 | | | | | | | |
| 13 | | Taxes at 30% | 4,350 | | | | |
| 14 | | | | | | | |
| 15 | | Income after Tax | 10,150 | | | | |
| 16 | | | | | | | |
| 17 | | Add back depreciation | 10,650 | | | | |
| 18 | | | | | | | |
| 19 | | Add back Interest | 12,150 | | | | |

Screenshot 7.6  Net present value of cash flow, taking account of the tax benefit

| | A | B | C | D |
|---|---|---|---|---|
| 1 | T | Cashflow A | Cashflow B | |
| 2 | 0 | -£10,000 | -£10,000 | |
| 3 | 1 | £1,000 | £5,000 | |
| 4 | 2 | £2,000 | £5,000 | |
| 5 | 3 | £3,000 | £5,000 | |
| 6 | 4 | £4,000 | | |
| 7 | 5 | £3,500 | | |
| 8 | 6 | £4,000 | | |
| 9 | 7 | £4,000 | | |
| 10 | | | | |
| 11 | NPV@12% | £2,667 | £1,794 | |

Screenshot 7.7  Capital budgeting and unequal life spans

You may have the impression that project A is superior and should be accepted in preference to project B. However, project A is twice as long as project B. If it were possible to reinvest in project B when it terminated, and in effect run project B *twice* over the time it takes to run project A *once*, it will prove to have a more attractive NPV, as we can see in Screenshot 7.8.

| | A | B | C | D |
|---|---|---|---|---|
| 13 | T | Cashflow A | Cashflow B | |
| 14 | 0 | -£10,000 | -£10,000 | |
| 15 | 1 | £1,000 | £5,000 | |
| 16 | 2 | £2,000 | £5,000 | |
| 17 | 3 | £3,000 | £5,000 | |
| 18 | 4 | £4,000 | -£10,000 | |
| 19 | 5 | £3,500 | £5,000 | |
| 20 | 6 | £4,000 | £5,000 | |
| 21 | 7 | £4,000 | £5,000 | |
| 22 | | | | |
| 23 | NPV@12% | £2,667 | £2,934 | |

Screenshot 7.8 Capital budgeting and reinvestment

Of course it is not usually as simple as this to do the comparison. When projects have different maturities, it is possible to use the **annual equivalent** approach. This involves replicating the shorter project so that the lives of the two investments have the same time span. The technique consists of simply dividing the NPV of each project by the **annuity factor** to get an annual equivalent for each cash flow. Annuity factors can be found in table 2 at the back of the book.

To give a specific example, the appropriate annuity factor for the 7-year project A is $A_{n=7, r=12\%}$ which is 4.56, while that for the 3-year project B is $A_{n=3, r=12\%}$ which is 2.4. We adjust each of the NPVs by taking the ratios $NPV_A/A_{n=7, r=12\%}$ and $NPV_B/A_{n=3, r=12\%}$ which gives £584.30 and £1,221.54; this is the annual equivalent value for each project respectively. We can now see that B is the superior project and that the same principle could be applied to any number of projects of unequal length.

A final point that needs to be taken into consideration is inflation. When setting out expected expenditure and income from an investment, you will need to decide how much to build in as a cost escalator. A straightforward way of doing this is simply to adjust costs into the future by the rate of inflation – in exactly the same way that we might apply interest to convert a present value into a future value. For example, in Screenshot 7.9 we show a very simple adjustment of cost on the assumption of 3% inflation for the foreseeable future.

| A | B | C | D | E | F |
|---|---|---|---|---|---|
| Year | 1 | 2 | 3 | 4 | |
| | | | | | |
| Estimated Costs | 100 | 100 | 100 | 100 | |
| Costs plus inflation | 103 | 106.09 | 109.273 | 112.551 | |

Screenshot 7.9 Incorporating the effects of general inflation

However, you may want to build in differential rates of price increase for various items of cost and revenue. For example, prices for commodities such as oil, copper and zinc can rise by considerably more than the general rate of inflation at times of high global demand. In addition, staff costs have an automatic tendency to rise faster than general price inflation. Finally, if you are selling into a highly competitive market, the price you can charge may rise more slowly than general price inflation. Hence you may want to build in a higher price escalator for costs than revenues. Again, it is simply a case of multiplying by 'one plus percentage increase in price' and compounding this over the relevant time period. We demonstrate this in Screenshot 7.10 for the following assumptions: materials costs rising at 2%, wage costs rising at 3% and revenues rising at 1%.

| | A | B | C | D | E | F |
|---|---|---|---|---|---|---|
| Year | | 1 | 2 | 3 | 4 | |
| Materials | | | | | | |
| | | 102 | 104.04 | 106.121 | 108.243 | |
| Labour | | 103 | 106.09 | 109.273 | 112.551 | |
| Revenues | | | | | | |
| | | 303 | 309.06 | 315.241 | 321.546 | |
| | | | | | | |
| Net | | | | | | |
| Income | | 98 | 98.93 | 99.8477 | 100.752 | |

Screenshot 7.10  Differential increases in input prices

Net income barely increases. And indeed, given general inflation, the real value of net income is declining over time. For example, if inflation is 1%, we can find real net income by deflating at 1%. (In effect we are 'discounting' using the inflation rate.) This would give figures of 97.95, 97.88 and 97.79 for years 2, 3 and 4 compared to year 1 (a very slow fall). However, we do not actually need to explicitly deflate. It will be recalled that the discounting process takes into account risk, time impatience and inflation, so present values already account for inflation. Therefore it is only necessary to adjust for specific inflation. The alternative would be to strip out inflation, forecast the cash flows in real terms and discount with real discount rates.

## Mini case study

### Tata halts Bangladesh investment

Source BBC 2006[1]

Indian industrial giant Tata has said it is suspending work on a $3bn investment in Bangladesh because of delays by the government.
  Tata planned to build a power plant, steel mill and fertiliser factory in the country, making it the single biggest investment in Bangladesh. On Sunday, senior Bangladesh ministers said gen-

eral elections due in January made it hard to accept the proposals.

A government spokesman said they hoped Tata would return to Bangladesh. The announcement by Tata was made after a meeting between its negotiators and officials of Bangladesh's Board of Investment.

'We are extremely disappointed and frustrated ... we thought the projects were good for the country's economy, for the people and the balance of payment,' Alan Rosling, executive director of Tata Sons, told journalists in Dhaka.

He said they had discussed the issue with senior ministers and key officials for the past two days. 'All of them appreciated our proposals, but they could not go beyond politics,' Mr Rosling is quoted as saying by Reuters.

### Politics

The BBC's Waliur Rahman in Dhaka says the government is hesitant about reaching an agreement on a big investment plan ahead of the elections. Reports say some politicians and economists have said that Bangladesh should not rush to accept Tata's proposals because they may eventually go against Bangladesh's interests. But ministers say the delay is not due to any 'anti-India' bias.

Bangladesh has however found it hard to attract money – total foreign direct investment (FDI) in Bangladesh since 1972 has totalled $3bn. The World Economic Forum (WEF) said in a 2004 report that Bangladesh was one of the most uncompetitive places to do business.

1. What non-financial criteria should be taken into account when making capital budgeting decisions?

## Active learning activity 7.3

### Hyperinflation

After the First World War Germany suffered from inflation. In January 1921, there were 64 marks to the dollar. By November 1923 this had changed to 4,200,000,000,000 marks to the dollar. How would you incorporate such a high rate of inflation into a capital budgeting calculation?

## Key concepts

☐ **Sunk** or **historical costs** are costs that have already been incurred and cannot be recovered

☐ An **opportunity cost** is any benefit that we forego by committing a resource to a particular use, thereby making it unavailable for any alternative uses

☐ **Depreciation** is a non-cash expense incurred from the devaluation of assets over time

- [ ] **Capital costs** are the necessary costs of initiating and maintaining a project
- [ ] **Double counting** is the act of counting costs or revenues twice
- [ ] A **tax shield** reduces the taxation liabilities the company incurs
- [ ] The **annual equivalent** approach is a way to compare projects of different maturities by replicating the shorter project so the two investments have the same time span

## Practical implications for managers

### Academic studies and use of discounting techniques

A summary of results from academic studies shows that:

1. discounted cash flow (DCF) techniques are used, but a significant minority of firms do not do so;
2. larger firms are more likely to use DCF techniques; and
3. when these techniques are used, they are used in conjunction with other techniques that are both theoretically deficient and redundant such as ARR and Payback.

Now that we have examined some important general principles of incremental cash flow, we look at how these principles are specifically applied in the next section.

# 7.3 The principles and practice in application

## 7.3.1 Identifying the relevant cash flows

We will now go through a small-scale exercise to demonstrate some of the principles we have discussed and to elaborate on some further ones that we have not. OK, so here are some rules that you're already familiar with.

First, we should identify **free cash flow**, not accounting income or accounting profit. Second, we should only consider **incremental cash flows**. This of course raises the question of what free cash flow actually is. Free cash flow is more or less identical to the concept of the surplus cash that is left either to be retained by the firm or to be distributed to the owners of the firm's capital whether they own equity or debt.

Free cash flow is defined as follows:

$$
\begin{aligned}
\text{Free cash flow} \ = \ &\text{after-tax operating income} \\
&+ \text{depreciation} \\
&+ \text{interest} \\
&- \text{capital expenditures} \\
&- \text{change in net working capital}
\end{aligned}
$$

We have met all of these concepts before although we need to expand on working capital, which we mentioned in Chapter 2.

**Working capital** can be defined informally as the money needed by the firm as a 'float' to meet day-to-day expenses. More formally, working capital represents the difference between current assets and current liabilities. This of course raises the question of what exactly are current assets and current liabilities. Current assets are non-interest-bearing liquid assets. Liquid assets are assets whose cash value could be realised in the short term, say within a year at the very maximum, without heavy discounting, 'haircuts' or 'fire sales'. Current assets would include cash, accounts receivable, inventory, marketable securities, prepaid expenses, etc. Current liabilities, on the other hand, mean a company's debts or obligations that are due within 1 year. This would include, for example, short-term debt, accounts payable, accrued liabilities and other debts.

Having said all that, what matters from the point of view of capital budgeting and project assessment is the *change* in working capital, i.e. any increase in working capital specifically associated with a new project. Now that we have acknowledged the need to include working capital, let us review the other components of free cash flow:

1. **Cost of fixed assets**. Most projects require initial investment in fixed investment assets.

2. **Scrap value**. We have not previously mentioned this, but the concept is a simple enough one. Many assets will have a resale value at the end of the project's life and this should also be included in the calculation of free cash flow. Scrap value may be estimated as the starting value of capital minus the various depreciation charges over the project's life. The residual value is the scrap value.

3. **Continuation value**. Sometimes a project will continue to produce income after the project has ended. Unless there is good reason to know what the life of this post-project income will be, this is normally discounted as a perpetuity after the terminal year of the project.

4. **Working capital**. There will be a need to invest in working capital. This will appear as a negative cash flow in the initial year of investment. As, by definition, working capital is not used up in the process of production, the working capital will be returned the year after the terminal year of the project. Note that the calculation of working capital could be a deal more complicated if there is expected to be a substantial variance in inventory and accounts payable and receivable over the course of the project. However, for most projects the difference between these should be fairly constant over the project's life. At

the end of the project, inventories will be sold and accounts received, and so working capital will be released from the project.

5. **Terminal value.** Items (2) scrap value, (3) contamination value and (4) working capital, taken together constitute the terminal value cash flows.

6. **Non-cash charges.** For our purposes, this is the depreciation cost that we 'add back in' after we have taken account of the tax shield.

7. **Interest expenses.** As we have already pointed out these would not be included as this would amount to double counting. Another way of thinking of this is in accounting terms. We are interested in the free cash flow which is available to distribute to the providers of the firm's capital. This includes the providers of interest-bearing capital. Nevertheless we may want to 'count this in' and 'count it out' again to estimate the value of the tax shield.

## 7.3.2 The basic principles of incremental cash flow

**Incremental cash flow** is the difference between (1) the firm's cash flows if it doesn't undertake the project and (2) the cash flows if it does undertake the project. As discussed above, it is important in the context of incremental cash flow that we *do not* take account of (1) sunk costs and that we *do* take account of (2) opportunity costs. A further important category in the context of incremental cash flow is (3) **externalities**.

Very often, a new project will have an impact on other aspects of the firm's operations. Suppose, for example, your company decides to acquire plastic moulding machinery in order to make outdoor garden furniture. As the machinery will not be run at maximum capacity this will also benefit the toys division which would be able to use the spare plastic moulding machinery. Or suppose your project is mainly concerned with finding oil, but there is also a good chance that you may also find natural gas with a significant market value. Or imagine a new project might require that employees be trained in a new technical skill which will improve their effectiveness and productivity for the firm beyond the life of the project.

There may also be *negative* externalities. The classic example would be if the project is to launch a new brand which may have the adverse side effect of cannibalisation of existing brands. For example, when Cold Guinness was launched as a new type of draft beer, it would have taken business from the existing 'ordinary' Guinness brand. Other negative externalities would be if the new project made severe demands on the firm's existing resources.

## Practical implications for managers

### Negative externalities

When introducing a new product line negative externalities should be taken into close consideration. As with the Guinness example, new products may draw market share away from previous products if they are not differentiated sufficiently.

### 7.3.3 Putting it all together – an exemplary case

4G is a new-start gaming-software company. It consists of the sole proprietor, Mr Ginger, who has already had some small-scale successes programming games. He intends to launch a new product called 'Drive-By Vampires versus Zombie Flesh Eaters' (DrByVZFE).

The required equipment such as state-of-the-art computers, large video screens and specialist animation equipment and software would cost £500,000, plus an additional £30,000 for shipping and installation. In addition, inventories would rise by £50,000 worth of unsold games. (Inventories will remain at this level until year 4 when inventory will be run down.) All of these costs would be incurred at t = 0. As computer and electronic equipment falls in value very rapidly, fixed capital will be depreciated at 50% per year.

The project is expected to operate for 4 years, as the PC games industry is very fast-moving and fashion driven, so at this time the project will be terminated. In those 4 years £100,000 of staff costs will be paid by 4G. This will consist of £50,000 to Mr Ginger himself as a skilled programmer in his own right and £50,000 for part-time admin and occasional IT help. He intends to keep programming, marketing and distributing the game by producing new versions. However, by year 5, he estimates that the market will have moved on. There will be a modest fee into the foreseeable future from licensing to 'retro' discount game distributors.

The cash inflows are assumed to begin 1 year after the project is undertaken, or at t = 1, and to continue out to t = 4. At the end of the project's life (t = 4), the equipment is expected to have a salvage value of only £31,250 given that computer equipment loses value very quickly. There will also be the terminal income to consider.

Mr Ginger expects 4G to sell 100,000 games per year. However, he is aware of the strong influence of product life cycle in this kind of market. Therefore he plans to vary the price over time and keep quantity sold fairly constant. Thus, the year 1 version of the game will be sold to distributors at an introductory price of £10, the year 2 version will have a premium price of £20 and years 3 and 4 versions will have increasingly discounted prices of £10 and £5. He estimates that he can licence his game to vintage game discounters for a post-project income of £25,000 p.a.

Cash operating costs for the project (total operating costs less depreciation) are just equal to the flat £100,000 wage cost per year. 4G corporate tax rate is 35% and its estimated cost of capital is 15%. It is important to note though that Mr Ginger has no real data for the riskiness of previous projects as they were done on an ad-hoc and amateur basis. He is using the percentage cost he was quoted by the bank to borrow funds. However, he is actually going to fund half the project using money he has inherited in a legacy.

Your job is to put the project data together and come up with a recommendation. Here is a summary of the main data that we need:

*Initial costs*
Equipment: £500,000
Shipping and installation: £30,000

*Changes in net working capital (WC)*
Inventories: £50,000

*Other key data*
Capital is depreciated at 50% per year
Expected unit sales: 50,000
Price per unit: £10, £20, £10, £5
Operating costs: flat £100,000
Tax rate: 35%
Discount rate: 15%

*Terminal values*
Expected salvage value: £31,250
Continuation income: £25,000

Repayment of working capital: £50,000

Screenshot 7.11 contains the information presented roughly as it would be in a normal income statement.

| | A | B | C | D | E | F |
|---|---|---|---|---|---|---|
| 9 | *Operating Cash Flows* | | | | | |
| 10 | Unit Sales | | £50,000 | £50,000 | £50,000 | £50,000 |
| 11 | Price per Unit | | £10 | £20 | £10 | £5 |
| 12 | Total Revenues | | £500,000 | £1,000,000 | £500,000 | £250,000 |
| 13 | Expenses - Wage Costs | | -£100,000 | -£100,000 | -£100,000 | -£100,000 |
| 14 | Depreciation | | -£250,000 | -£125,000 | -£62,500 | -£31,250 |
| 15 | Interest | | -£43,500 | -£43,500 | -£43,500 | -£43,500 |
| 16 | Total Costs | | -£393,500 | -£268,500 | -£206,000 | -£174,750 |
| 17 | | | | | | |
| 18 | *Operating Income* | | £106,500 | £731,500 | £294,000 | £75,250 |
| 19 | Tax | | -£37,275 | -£256,025 | -£102,900 | -£26,338 |
| 20 | *After Tax Operating Income* | | £69,225 | £475,475 | £191,100 | £48,913 |

Screenshot 7.11 Capital budgeting for 4G (income statement)

As you can see, we derive the operating cash flow at the end of the statement for each year of operation. Screenshot 7.12 shows how depreciation and interest are added back to get operating cash flow including the tax shield. This, along with the initial investment outlay, is what we need to put together the cash flows necessary for NPV purposes, as shown in Screenshot 7.13.

So it's fairly obvious that Mr Ginger should go ahead with the project. Let's just go back over our checklist to see how 4G's project fits with what we said. (1) The cost of fixed assets is fairly obvious. (2) Scrap value is the residual remaining as the £500,000 halves in value every year for 4 years. (3) Continuation value is £25,000 in year 5 plus £25,000 discounted as a perpetuity in year 5, then further discounted back to year 0. (4) Working capital is very simple:

| | A | B | C | D | E | F |
|---|---|---|---|---|---|---|
| 24 | **After Tax Operating Income** | | £69,225 | £475,475 | £191,100 | £48,913 |
| 25 | Depreciation | | -£250,000 | -£125,000 | -£62,500 | -£31,250 |
| 26 | Interest | | -£43,500 | -£43,500 | -£43,500 | -£43,500 |
| 27 | **Operating Cash Flow** | | £362,725 | £643,975 | £297,100 | £123,663 |
| 28 | | | | | | |
| 29 | | | | | | |
| 30 | Value of Tax Shield | | £102,725.00 | £58,975.00 | £37,100.00 | £26,162.50 |
| 31 | (Calculated seperately as 35% of interest and depreciation) | | | | | |

Screenshot 7.12  Cash flow for 4G including the tax shield

£50,000 in at the start, then £50,000 back at the end. Thus we have (5) terminal values. Item (6) non-cash charges represents the depreciation that was subtracted to calculate operating income then added back again. Item (7) interest was treated in exactly the same way. The tax shield value of these items is listed separately in Screenshot 7.12. Suppose now that he borrows half the initial outlay of £580,000 from the bank at an interest rate of 15%. If none of the capital sum advanced is repaid until the project is finished, then there will be £43,500 of interest to pay every year. If the corporate tax rate is 35%, this will save £13,050 of tax every year. Screenshot 7.13 shows the effect of the tax shield on the project.

| | A | B | C | D | E | F | G | H |
|---|---|---|---|---|---|---|---|---|
| 33 | | Year | | | | | | |
| 34 | | 0 | 1 | 2 | 3 | 4 | 5 | |
| 35 | Cost of Computers, Equipment and Software | -£500,000 | | | | | | £191,667 Continuance Income |
| 36 | Delivery and Installation | -£30,000 | | | | | | £31,250 Scrap Value |
| 37 | Increase in Inventory | -£50,000 | | | | | | £50,000 Decrease in Inventory |
| 38 | Project Future Net Cash Flows | | £362,725 | £643,975 | £297,100 | £123,663 | | |
| 39 | | | | | | | | |
| 40 | *Investment Outlay* | -£580,000 | | | | | | £272,917 *Terminal Values* |
| 41 | | | | | | | | |
| 42 | *Discounted Cash Flow* | -£580,000 | £315,413 | £486,938 | £195,348 | £70,704 | £135,688 | |
| 43 | | | | | | | | |
| 44 | NPV@15% | £624,091 | | | | | | |
| 45 | | | | | | | | |
| 46 | | 15% | | | | | | |
| 47 | | | | | | | | |
| 48 | Discount Factors | 1.0000 | 0.8696 | 0.7561 | 0.6575 | 0.5718 | 0.4972 | |

Screenshot 7.13  Discount cash flow and NPV for 4G

Finally, Mr Ginger should really consider the discount rate he is using. The rate of 15% is what the bank charges on its loan. His own cost of equity, which he is not sure of, must be higher. As a ball-park figure he tries a WACC (and therefore a discount rate) of 25%.

|  | A | B | C | D | E | F | G | H |
|---|---|---|---|---|---|---|---|---|
| 33 |  | Year |  |  |  |  |  |  |
| 34 |  | 0 | 1 | 2 | 3 | 4 | 5 |  |
| 35 | Cost of Computers, Equipment and Software | -£500,000 |  |  |  |  | £125,000 | Continuance Income |
| 36 | Delivery and Installation | -£30,000 |  |  |  |  | £31,250 | Scrap Value |
| 37 | Increase in Inventory | -£50,000 |  |  |  |  | £50,000 | Decrease in Inventory |
| 38 | Project Future Net Cash Flows |  | £362,725 | £643,975 | £297,100 | £123,663 |  |  |
| 39 |  |  |  |  |  |  |  |  |
| 40 | Investment Outlay | -£580,000 |  |  |  |  | £206,250 | Terminal Values |
| 41 |  |  |  |  |  |  |  |  |
| 42 | Discounted Cash Flow | -£580,000 | £290,180 | £412,144 | £152,115 | £50,652 | £67,584 |  |
| 43 |  |  |  |  |  |  |  |  |
| 44 | NPV@25% | £392,675 |  |  |  |  |  |  |
| 45 |  |  |  |  |  |  |  |  |
| 46 |  | 25% |  |  |  |  |  |  |
| 47 |  |  |  |  |  |  |  |  |
| 48 | Discount Factors | 1.0000 | 0.8000 | 0.6400 | 0.5120 | 0.4096 | 0.3277 |  |

Screenshot 7.14 The impact of a higher WACC (25%)

Even at this high cost of capital, the project still looks very attractive. In fact, he could go further and calculate the IRR for the project, which is around 60%. Given that he has now decided to borrow half of the funds from the bank at 15%, his own cost of equity would have to be around 105% to exceed this.

Before leaving this section, it is worth considering how incremental cash flow principles have been applied. In terms of some of the basic principles, i.e. marginal cash flow *ignoring* sunk cost, *including* opportunity cost and allowing for externalities, what of them? Well, there are no real issues in our case study concerning sunk cost or externalities. However, there *was* an issue over opportunity cost. Mr Ginger is a skilled programmer and could earn a decent wage in industry. Or he could set up the company and employ someone else to programme. Mr Ginger might have chosen not to 'pay himself a wage'. However, this would have been neglecting an important opportunity cost.

A final issue that has arisen is uncertainty. Mr Ginger doesn't actually know what his WACC is. There may well also be a certain amount of uncertainty over other key parameters such as costs and selling price. This is the subject of the next section.

## Key concepts

- Free cash flow is surplus cash that is left either to be retained by the firm or to be distributed to the owners of the firm's capital, whether they own equity or debt
- Working capital is the difference between current assets and current liabilities and is needed to meet day-to-day expenses
- Cost of fixed assets is the initial investment in fixed investment assets
- Scrap value is the value of starting value of capital minus the various depreciation charges over the project's life

- ☐ **Continuation value** is the income produced after the project has ended
- ☐ **Terminal value** is the scrap value, continuation value and working capital taken together
- ☐ **Incremental cash flow** is the difference between the firm's cash flows if it doesn't undertake the project and the cash flows if it does undertake the project
- ☐ **Externalities** are costs (negative) or benefits (positive) arising from a defined economic activity that affects others outside the defined economic activity and which are not reflected fully in the direct monetary costs or prices

## 7.4 Risk

Although we have spoken a great deal of risk in the context of financial investments such as portfolios of shares, we have mentioned it very little in the context of capital budgeting and 'real' investment in business projects. This is partly for pedagogic reasons. That is, it greatly simplifies matters when teaching these already complicated techniques to behave as if the cash flows are a 'given'.

Furthermore, in classical finance theory, the element of risk is already accounted for by the discount rate. However, the whole area of investment, risk and uncertainty is still one of ongoing development, and it may be that the discount rate is an imperfect measure of risk, particularly in the case of a firm not quoted on the capital markets and therefore not subject to the scrutiny of the market who come to a collective judgement on what the firm's discount rate ought to be when assessing the correct price of the firm's securities. Thus unquoted firms are particularly vulnerable to this kind of risk, as indeed are those participants in any firm who are not 'perfectly hedged' by holding a perfectly diversified portfolio such as the market portfolio. Furthermore, even for quoted firms, markets have been known to get it wrong and their imputed WACC may be very badly out of date.

Finally, the project may be very different from the kind of thing the firm has tackled before and there may consequently be many more 'unknown unknowns' than the firm would normally face with a project.

We have talked a lot in previous examples about capital budgeting as if the information was readily to hand. However, the information will in fact probably have to be collated across many sources, including a number of departments across the firm. And then this information has to be aggregated into basic data for the proposed investment and projected into the future. Hence there is a need to establish the uncertainty over the assumptions made and how these impact on the project's cash flows and its NPV.

A well-known approach is to do a **sensitivity analysis**, where we vary each assumed input over a range of values in terms of the possible percentage variation round a central value, in order to assess the impact on project NPV. This is possible in a number of ways on Excel, for example, see Screenshot 7.15 of (unknown) WACC versus NPV using Excel's Data Table function.

| WACC | NPV |
|------|-----|
| 15% | £534,586 |
| 20% | £418,818 |
| 25% | £325,869 |
| 30% | £250,544 |
| 35% | £188,996 |
| 40% | £138,337 |
| 45% | £96,371 |
| 50% | £61,407 |

Screenshot 7.15 Data table analysis of changing the assumed WACC

One could also use sensitivity analysis in Excel. In Screenshot 7.16 we have used this function to examine the consequences of weaker demand than anticipated, resulting in lower sales and 50% lower cash flows in column E. We also examine the alternative scenario with 50% higher cash flows in column F. The comparator is column D, which contains the original assumptions for yearly cash flow.

| A | B | C | D | E | F |
|---|---|---|---|---|---|
| **Scenario Summary** | | | | | |
| | | | Current Values: | Low Prices Weak Demand | High Prices Strong Demand |
| **Changing Cells:** | | | | | |
| | | $C$73 | £360,550 | £186,800 | £534,300 |
| | | $D$73 | £641,800 | £327,425 | £956,175 |
| | | $E$73 | £294,925 | £153,988 | £435,863 |
| | | $F$73 | £121,488 | £67,269 | £175,706 |
| **Result Cells:** | | | | | |
| | | $B$71 | £325,868.97 | -£21,785.43 | £673,523.37 |
| Notes: Current Values column represents values of changing cells at time Scenario Summary Report was created. Changing cells for each scenario are highlighted in gray. | | | | | |

Screenshot 7.16  Excel scenario analysis of sales revenue assumptions

Sensitivity analysis measures the effect of changes in a particular variable, say revenues, on a project's NPV. To perform a sensitivity analysis, all variables are fixed at their expected values except one. This one variable is then changed, often by specified percentages, and the resulting effect on NPV is noted. One could go a lot further than the very simple analyses that we have performed here. Furthermore one could do multidimensional analyses by allowing more than one variable to change at a time. A multidimensional analysis is known as a **scenario analysis**. However, it is beyond the scope of this book to go further into this subject. Nevertheless we do expand on the use of scenarios and how unfolding events might change underlying assumptions in the next section.

**Key concepts**

A **sensitivity analysis** involves varying every assumed project input over a range of values to assess their impact

## 7.5 Real options

Basic capital budgeting and investment theory tends to proceed on the basis that the project's basic parameters are a 'given'. That is, we have a given set of cash flows and a cost of capital, and the project either proceeds or it doesn't depending on NPV/IRR. However, at various stages of an investment project's life, the outcome is not necessarily preordained, and in actual fact there is usually more than one path that could be taken with the project as the future unfolds. Real options are a way of looking at investments as an unfolding process.

At various stages of the project there may be options to continue, expand or abandon the project. For example, one of your author's favourite places is the Keelman, Newburn, Newcastle upon Tyne. This is an inn which started life as a brewery in an abandoned mine building. The owners bought the surrounding gap site as well. Then they built a pub. Then they opened a restaurant. Then they opened accommodation block 1, followed by accommodation block 2. This was done on a sequential basis over a period of years. Clearly it would have been foolish as small business people to try to bring all of this capacity online at once. However, there was always the option for the future. Hence we might set out the process of buying the building and the site as in Figure 7.1.

When the business started with the brewery, there was a lot that could be done with the site. In fact, as it turned out, there were four options on further investment projects. Thus if the proprietors had decided to sell the site on they might have added on a premium for the various options that went with the site. They might have pointed out that outline planning permission had already been granted or that there was a lack of such facilities in the locale. Nevertheless, it would probably have taken quite a bit of convincing at the start of the project to get any kind of significant price for option D, something that remained far in the future and highly uncertain.

On the other hand, once the pub had opened, the ability to price option B on the restaurant would have been greatly helped by the fact that the pub had started to provide meals and that they were 'doing a roaring trade'. The prospect was now much more concrete. Again, the ability to value option D on further accommodation would be greatly helped by the success of the first phase of accommodation which was often fully booked. The main point then about the real options approach is as follows:

1. That a project should take account not only of the NPV of cash flows but also of the options associated with the project that may become available, i.e. the options to choose a course of action or change direction have value in themselves.

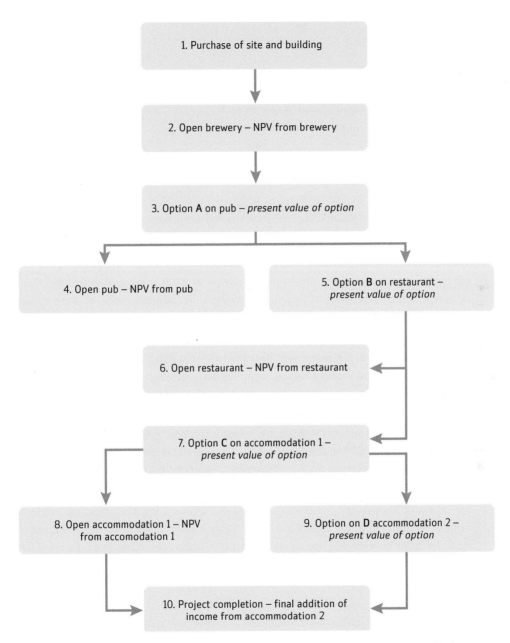

Figure 7.1 An illustration of the potential for applying real options valuation at the Keelman inn

2. That the value of a project very much depends on your time perspective. At the start of the project, it might have been possible to have a clearer idea on prospects for the pub than the prospects for accommodation. Towards the middle and end of the project, it is the accommodation possibilities that are providing the main option value.

**Practical implications for managers**

**Projects can evolve**

Over time it is necessary to evaluate the current options available to the company. A manager should not just be content with evaluating the value of a project at its inception, as more profitable avenues may open through real options as the project matures.

### 7.5.1 Types of option

According to Amram and Kulatilaka (1999), the main types of option are as follows:

- **Timing options.** Sales of low-fat ice cream are surging. Operating at full capacity, the Healthy Cow Creamery is considering whether to expand its plant. Launching the expansion would require a big up-front investment, and the company's managers can't be sure that the sales boom will persist. However, they have the option of delaying the investment until they learn more about the strength of demand.

- **Growth options.** Friend-to-Friend, a company that sells cosmetics through a network of independent sales people, is trying to decide whether to enter the vast Chinese market. The initial investment to build a manufacturing and sales organisation would be large, but it may lead to the opportunity to sell a whole range of products through an established sales network and create growth.

- **Staging options.** International Widget is looking at a new manufacturing system. The proposal calls for a full, multimillion-dollar rollout at all factories over the next 2 years. But the business benefits of the project remain uncertain. The company has the option to invest in the new system in stages rather than all at once.

- **Exit options.** Molecular Sciences has a patent for a promising new chemical product, but it is worried about the size of the market opportunity and it is unsure whether the manufacturing process will meet government regulations regarding toxic chemicals. If the company does begin an effort to commercialise the product, though, it will have the option to abandon the project if demand doesn't materialise or if there is environmental liability.

- **Flexibility options.** Cell Incorporated needs to decide how to best manufacture its latest cellular telephone. Demand for the new product is uncertain, although forecasts indicate that sales will be spread across two continents. A traditional manufacturing analysis indicates that a single plant would be much cheaper to build and operate than two plants on two continents. But the analysis fails to take into account the flexibility of the option to shift production from continent to continent in response to shifts in demand, exchange rates or production costs.

- **Operating options.** Bright Light Software has long contracted with other companies to produce and package its CD-ROMs. Its sales have grown rapidly in recent years, however, and now the company is trying to decide whether it makes sense to build its own plant. If it goes ahead, it would gain a number of operating options.

- **Learning options.** Learning options are similar to timing options. By doing things on a small scale and in a limited way, it is possible to gather more information about the right way ahead, when a number of different ways are possible. The example Amram and Kulatilaka (1999) give, concerns a film company that is unsure which of three different Christmas films to concentrate on for marketing purposes, so it distributes all three on a limited basis early in the season to see which does best.

You can now get a chance to apply the concept of real options in the following mini case study ('Major plant expansion for precision injection molding company').

## Mini case study

### Major plant expansion for precision injection molding company

Source Azom[2]

Vision Technical Molding LLC, a manufacturer of precision injection molding components, today announced a major 27,000-sq-ft facility expansion to provide world-class capabilities and services to the medical device industry. The company, which has achieved double-digit growth during each of the last four years, made this strategic investment to meet increasing customer demand for the rapid turnaround of complex medical devices often requiring post-molding operations. The 57,000-sq-ft facility now features a new ISO Class 8 clean room; a new material drying and conveying system; additional quality control lab space; a dedicated metrology department, and a full service tool-room. The new facility is currently in full operation 24 hours a day, seven days a week.

'The demand for high-quality, injection molded single and multi-use medical devices is increasing,' said Steven Arnold, president, Vision Technical Molding. 'To meet this growing need, we invested in a significantly larger and more comprehensive state-of-the-art facility. Our customers will benefit from the latest technologies and value-added operations, as well as our enhanced ability to handle multi-component molding and assembly. This project further underscores our commitment to the medical industry.'

1. What type of options did Vision Technical Molding LLC use?
2. What options are not available to Vision Technical Molding LLC for this project?

## Active learning activity 7.4

### Real options

There are many real options associated with buying an oil field. How many can you think of?

## Key concepts

- ☐ **Real options** are the opportunities that can arise over a project's time frame. It may become more profitable to expand, cut back or shut down the project over time
- ☐ **Timing options** give the option to wait until an unknown variable becomes clearer
- ☐ **Growth options** give the option to use the project's assets in more projects later
- ☐ **Staging options** give the option to invest in stages rather than all at once
- ☐ **Exit options** give the option to abandon the project if its assumed variables are less favourable than projected
- ☐ **Flexibility options** give the option to shift output between assets to gain competitive advantages
- ☐ **Operating options** give the option to control operations centrally or distribute them locally
- ☐ **Learning options** give the option to limit the project until more information on the correct implementation is researched

## 7.6 Summary

This chapter has examined the theory and practical applications of capital budgeting. We began by examining the core theory of accepting all projects where NPV ≥ 0 and IRR ≥ k. This is not possible when capital is rationed, however, so we discussed ways of ranking projects in terms of value. When projects are divisible, this is best done with use of a profitability index, constructed using the ratios of PV of revenue to initial cost. When projects are not divisible, we can consider combinations of NPVs.

Next we discussed the practical considerations that must be taken into account when making capital budgeting decisions. First, we introduced the rule that sunk costs are entirely irrelevant. Second, we discussed the importance of including opportunity costs. Third, we explained why depreciation should be added back in NPV calculations. Fourth, we considered why interest should not be included as it is already included in the discount rate, and how the tax shield it can create should be included. Finally, the annual equivalent approach was discussed as a means to compare projects with differing life spans.

We worked through an example and explained several concepts that readers may not have been familiar with. Free cash flow was defined as after tax operating income + depreciation – capital expenditures – change in net working capital. Working capital was explained as the money needed to meet day-to-day expenses. The other components of free cash flow were discussed: cost of fixed assets, scrap value, continuation value, terminal value, non-cash charges and interest expenses. Externalities were also explained as the impact the project will have, negative or positive, on other company projects. We then worked through an example to illustrate the concepts first hand.

Risk was briefly examined next. This section noted that while our understanding of risk and uncertainty is currently evolving, financial theory holds that the discount rate accounts for the riskiness of the project. Practically, however, the information a company bases its assumptions on may not be entirely accurate and this may not be reflected in the discount rate. One way to mitigate this problem is to run a sensitivity analysis, varying assumed inputs. This allows us to assess the impact of a change in variables to check the robustness of a capital budgeting decision.

Finally we mentioned real options. They are alternatives to merely passively investing in a project. Often it will be more profitable to expand, shut down or otherwise manipulate the project during its life span. Timing, growth staging, exit, flexibility, operating and learning options are all examples of real options.

# Questions

1. List the conditions under which NPV and IRR can give conflicting results.

2. Why is NPV held to be superior to IRR for investment appraisal? Does this mean IRR is redundant?

3. A company with a cost of capital of 8% has the following investment opportunities:

| Year (£ million) | Project A | Project B | Project C | Project D |
|---|---|---|---|---|
| 0 | (10) | (8) | (7.5) | (8) |
| 1 | | 2 | 3 | 1.5 |
| 2 | | 3 | 3 | 1.5 |
| 3 | | 4 | 3 | 7 |
| 4 | | 4 | 2 | |
| 5 | | | 1 | |
| 6 | 30 | | | |

What projects should the company invest in if:

a) the company is not capital rationed;

b) the company has a capital budget of £20 million and the projects are divisible;

c) the company has a capital budget of £20 million and the projects are not divisible.

4. Identify and discuss the relevant cash flows for a capital budgeting decision.

5. Explain in terms of financial theory why risk needs to be separately considered in capital budgeting decisions and discuss the relevance of sensitivity analysis in this context.

6. Use examples to explain the effect of real options on capital budgeting decisions.

7. See Figure 7.2. UK annual inflation measured by the retail price index (RPI) went negative in March 2009 for the first time since 1960, to −0.4%. How would you incorporate deflation into capital budgets?

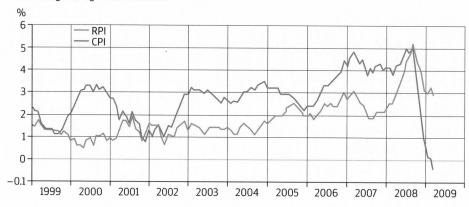

Figure 7.2  UK inflation 1999–2009 (percentage change over 12 months)

*Source: ONS*

## Case study

### Sorting out the relevant from the non-relevant costs

Source ACCA http://www.accaglobal.com/students/student_accountant/archive/2004/47/1163453

The managing director of Parser Ltd, a small business, is considering undertaking a one-off contract. She has asked her inexperienced accountant to advise on what costs are likely to be incurred so that she can price at a profit. The following schedule has been prepared:

| Costs for special order | Notes | £ |
|---|---|---|
| Direct wages | 1 | 28,500 |
| Supervisor costs | 2 | 11,500 |
| General overheads | 3 | 4,000 |
| Machine depreciation | 4 | 2,300 |
| Machine overheads | 5 | 18,000 |
| Materials | 6 | 34,000 |
| | | 98,300 |

## Notes

1. Direct wages comprise the wages of two employees, particularly skilled in the labour process for this job. They could be transferred from another department to undertake the work on the special order. They are fully occupied in their usual department and sub-contracting staff would have to be brought in to undertake the work left behind. The sub-contracting costs to replace the two employees would be £32,000 for the period of the work. Alternatively, new sub-contractors could be brought in directly for the duration of the contract. The costs associated with this would amount to £31,300.

2. A supervisor would have to work on the special order. The cost of £11,500 is made up of £8,000 normal payments plus £3,500 additional bonus for working on the special order. Normal payments refer to the fixed salary of the supervisor. In addition, the supervisor would lose incentive payments in his normal work amounting to £2,500. It is not anticipated that any replacement costs relating to the supervisor's work on other jobs would arise.

3. General overheads comprise an apportionment of £3,000 plus an estimate of £1,000 incremental overheads.

4. Machine depreciation represents the normal period cost, based on the duration of the contract. It is anticipated that £500 will be incurred in *additional* machine maintenance costs.

5. Machine overheads (for running costs such as electricity) are charged at £3 per hour. It is estimated that 6,000 hours will be needed for the special order. The machine has 4,000 hours' available capacity. The further 2,000 hours required will mean an existing job is taken off the machine, resulting in a lost contribution of £2 per hour (before overheads are charged).

6. Materials represent the purchase costs of 7,500 kg bought some time ago. The materials are no longer used and are unlikely to be wanted in the future except for the special order. Although the complete stock of materials (amounting to 10,000 kg), or part thereof, could be sold for £4.20 per kg, it is recorded at historical cost of £34,000. The replacement cost of material used in the project would be £33,375.

Because the business does not have adequate funds to finance the special order, a bank overdraft of £20,000 would be required for the project duration of 3 months. The overdraft would be repaid at the end of the period. The company uses a cost of capital of 20% to appraise projects. The bank's overdraft rate is 18%.

The managing director has heard that for special orders such as this, relevant costing should be used that also incorporates opportunity costs. She has approached you to create a revised costing schedule based on relevant costing principles.

## Required

Produce a revised costing schedule for the special project based on relevant costs. Fully explain and justify each of the costs included in the revised schedule. In addition, explain what non-financial factors should be taken into account.

# Further reading

Amram, M. and Kulatilaka, N. (1999) Disciplined decisions: aligning strategy with the financial markets. *Harvard Business Review*, January–February.

Dudley, L. (1972) A note on reinvestment assumptions in choosing between net present value and internal rate of return. *Journal of Finance* **27**(4):907–915.
Looks at the causes of conflict between NPV and IRR.

Geisbeek, W., Schall, L. and Sundem, G. (1978) Survey and analysis of capital budgeting methods. *Journal of Finance* **33**(1):281–287.
A later survey which finds an increased number of companies were using even more complex capital budgeting techniques.

Klammer, T. (1972) Empirical evidence of the adoption of sophisticated capital budgeting techniques. *Journal of Business* **45**(3):387–397.
An early survey on the use of capital budgeting techniques in companies.

Leslie, K. and Michaels, M. (1997) The real power of real options. *McKinsey Quarterly* **3**.
Looks at applying real options to company decisions.

Luehrman, T. (1998) Investment opportunities as real options: getting started on the numbers. *Harvard Business Review* **76**(July–August):3–15.
Looks at attaching numbers to real options.

# Internet references

ftp://ftp.cba.uri.edu/classes/dash/isida/capitalbudgtingevaluation.pdf
An excellent case study analysis of the role of formal evaluation techniques in the decision making process.

http://sunk-cost.behaviouralfinance.net/
Contains links to several informative resources on sunk costs.

http://www.investopedia.com/terms/c/capitalbudgeting.asp
A basic entry on capital budgeting.

http://www.real-options.com/overview_intro.htm
Contains information on real options.

http://www.realoptions.org/abstracts.html
Collects the papers submitted to the Annual International Real Options Conference.

http://apotso.wordpress.com/2006/09/30/evaluation-of-the-merits-and-drawbacks-of-the-use-of-the-internal-rate-of-return-as-an-investment-criterion%E2%80%A6/
Goes into detail on the benefits and drawbacks of the IRR method.

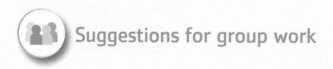

# Suggestions for group work

1. Students should discuss the investment decision they have made in the context of their decision to enter higher education. What are the main costs and benefits?

2. Consider and discuss what externalities may arise in the following projects:

   a)  Coca-Cola creates a new flavour of soft drink and sets up a factory to accommodate its production.

   b)  A government decides to allow companies to dump waste products into the sea.

 Suggestions for presentations

1. Assume the role of a consultant asked to explain why relying on IRR for capital budgeting decisions is not a good idea. Create a presentation of your arguments.

2. Imagine you are employed in a company that is unsure of whether to invest in a new factory on the basis of NPV valuation. Create a presentation that explains the real options that may be available for such a project.

# 8 Capital Structure

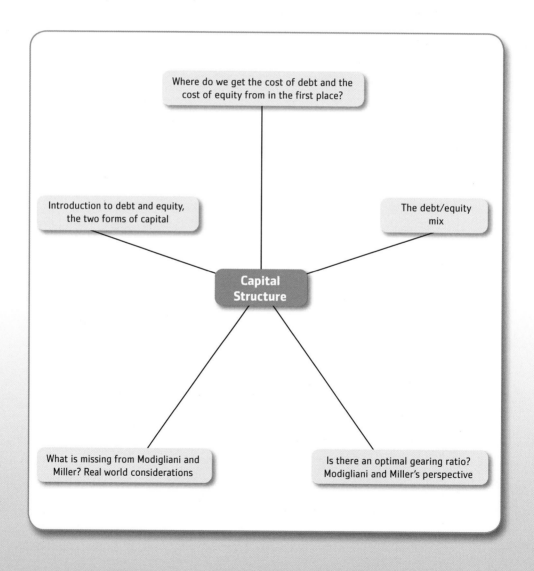

Where do we get the cost of debt and the cost of equity from in the first place?

Introduction to debt and equity, the two forms of capital

The debt/equity mix

Capital Structure

What is missing from Modigliani and Miller? Real world considerations

Is there an optimal gearing ratio? Modigliani and Miller's perspective

## Knowledge-based learning objectives

When you have completed this chapter you will be able to:

✓ Define the weighted average cost of capital (WACC)

✓ Understand what gearing and leverage are and how they affect the WACC

✓ Discern the difference between operational risk caused by operational gearing and financial risk caused by financial gearing

✓ Understand the difference between pure financial risk and the risk of financial distress

✓ Explain Modigliani and Miller's important contributions to the concept of optimal gearing

✓ Appreciate why the pecking order approach may capture a subtle truth missed by both Modigliani and Miller and the traditional approach

## Skills-based learning objectives development

✓ Business and financial environment consciousness: develop further understanding of how the discount rate is a key factor in the financial environment and how changes in capital structure can affect the survival of businesses.

✓ Numerical skills: develop the ability to understand, manipulate and interpret the cost of equity, debt and WACC.

✓ Analytical thinking and problem-solving skills: develop the ability to critically assess the main theories of capital structure and enumerate leveraged beta, which takes account of both operational and financial risk.

✓ Organisational skills: further develop your ability to organise your time and work efficiently and to gather data and information that you can translate into value-adding intelligence.

✓ Presentation skills: further develop your ability to present your work clearly both verbally and in writing.

## Online resource centre

Visit the Online Resource Centre that accompanies this book to listen to a podcast of the authors explaining the concept of the cost of capital.
**www.oxfordtextbooks.co.uk/marney**

### Charlie gets a WACC to the head

Kate enters Charlie's office, her arms full of spreadsheets. Dumping the spreadsheets on Charlie's desk, she lets out a huge sigh of frustration. 'Our cost of capital seems to be much higher than the average,' she says. Charlie senses he is about to be treated to yet another explanation of some anarchistic financial theory and waits for Kate to continue. He nearly falls off his chair at what Kate says next. 'We need more debt!'

'More debt? More debt? We'll be at the mercy of the banks then. Why don't we just issue some more shares if we're a bit short of cash?' responds Charlie.

'That's not quite the point,' says Kate. 'The fact is that debt is much cheaper.'

This really surprises Charlie. Surely debt, where interest has to be paid, is much more expensive than shares? Sure, the issue costs can be high, but after that surely share capital is pretty cheap – dividends are just 5% per year, and the last time he looked, interest rates for corporate debt were around 15%.

However, Kate continues: 'They're only happy with 5% just now in the expectation of much bigger dividends once the company has stopped growing so fast. Plus, debt has a lot of advantages. First, the interest is tax deductible so we can benefit from the tax break, but, more importantly, it lowers our overall cost of capital. In fact, some people think the more debt, the better!'

'How can that be?' asks Charlie. He can appreciate the bit about saving tax but can't see why debt would be cheaper than shares, which seem to him to be basically free money apart from the dividends (and, in bad times, dividends don't absolutely have to be paid). 'How can that possibly be?' he asks.

'Well, it's quite simple really,' replies Kate. 'Modigliani and Miller, a pair of very famous economists, showed that a company should take on as much debt as possible ...'

'Economists live on a different planet!' interrupts Charlie.

Kate rolls her eyes and continues. 'Nevertheless, the problem with share capital is its very high cost – around 20% for OrganicX. We really need more debt to bring our overall cost of capital down.' Kate smoothes out the spreadsheets and passes them to Charlie. His eyes glaze over as he sees Greek letters – alphas and betas – and complicated looking formulae. He could tell this was going to be a long afternoon.

'Go on then, explain to me why debt is so good and why we need more of it? And what do all these Greek letters have to do with share capital?'

## 8.1 Introduction to debt and equity, the two forms of capital

In previous chapters, the discount rate has featured fairly prominently. This is because investment decisions often involve discounting the value of future cash flow, which in turn is necessary to take account of risk. The question arises of where this rate of discount comes from. The **rate of discount** that is appropriate to apply to a firm's future cash flows from projects should be based on the cost of funds to the firm. The technically correct way to measure this is to use the **weighted average cost of capital (WACC)**. We can then make comparisons between different companies, projects and risk levels.

You should be aware by now that firms raise capital under two broad headings, equity and debt. **Equity** is the capital of those who own the firm. It can be internal in the case where the company is privately owned, or raised externally from shareholders who have nothing to do with the day-to-day running of the company. The rewards that go to the owners of equity capital are determined as a residual after all other payments have been made; specifically, fixed and variable operating costs, tax, depreciation and interest. What is left over is available to be ploughed back as investment, distributed as a dividend to the owners of equity or carried forward as accumulated reserves which belong to shareholders, i.e. the owners of the equity.

The required return to equity tends to be relatively high because equity is inherently risky – from the point of view of the investor. Equity holders get paid last, and only if a surplus is available. Furthermore, the value of equity depends on the future prospects of the firm and the future value of the firm. As we have seen in previous chapters, these are subject to a great deal of uncertainty, and therefore equity is risky from the point of view of the investor. From the point of view of the firm, equity is less risky as in principle the dividend can be varied to suit the firm's financial position and ability to pay out to shareholders. Indeed, the firm can opt not to pay a dividend at all if trading conditions are particularly demanding. In practice, in normal times, firms rarely suspend dividends or radically alter payouts because of the negative signalling effect and the potential to upset incumbent shareholders.

However, in the immediate aftermath of the credit crunch, times are far from normal, and dividends are indeed being suspended by many companies throughout the world. For example, in the UK in 2008, it was reported in the press that a quarter of FTSE companies are cutting dividends next year. Many investors rely on dividends for income and, in addition, dividends may provide more than a third of annualised total return. Hence in less exceptional times British companies do not willingly alienate 'coupon clippers' (dividend payees).[1]

To sum up, equity is more risky for the investor but less so for the firm compared to the alternative, which is debt.

**Debt** is held by those who have lent money to the company but have no participation in the ownership of the company. Debt can vary in nature from the basic bank overdraft to bonds and other sophisticated financial instruments available on the capital market. Debt interest is determined as a series of defined fixed or floating interest payments, which must be honoured by the company. Failure to honour debt obligations, or breaching **covenants** (conditions applied by the lender to the borrowers), can result in the company becoming financially distressed, lapsing into insolvency and being taken into administration, or even being declared bankrupt. Thus, while debt tends to be cheaper for the firm, it is also riskier. Debt is less risky for the investor, as it is very clear exactly how much the investor should receive in return for the loan, and the firm will be in serious trouble should it fail to make interest or principal payments as they are due.

However, as illustrated by Active learning activity 8.1, in times of liquidity crisis (credit crunch), debt may prove even more risky for the firm, especially if debt cannot be refinanced.

## Active learning activity 8.1

### Debt and the credit crunch

Go online and look up a reputable financial database such as www.ft.com or www.economist.com. Look for stories about firms that have closed because of high debt levels or have radically reduced their levels of debt. Is there any mention of the difficulties of re-financing post credit crunch?

A primary source of debt capital for most firms is bank borrowing. The interest is charged on the basis of some reference rate. For example, the reference rate could be based on any of the following depending on the maturity and risk profile of the loan:

1. Cost of bank funds:
   - Discount rate – the rate that a Central Bank charges on loans made to commercial banking institutions is known as the discount rate.
   - Commercial paper rate – commercial papers are short-term discount bills issued by established corporate borrowers. These bills mature in 6 months or less. Commercial paper (this is typically not expressed as a plural) along with certificates of deposit are important sources of primary short-term funds for banks; hence the rate on these instruments serves as a basis for the ultimate rate charged to business borrowers.

2. The risk-free rate:
   - Treasury bill rate – a Treasury bill is a short-term (1 year or less) risk-free bond issued by many governments, including the US and UK governments. Treasury bills are made available to buyers at a price that is less than its redemption value upon maturity.
   - Treasury bond rate – unlike short-term Treasury bills, Treasury bonds are bonds that do not mature for at least 1 year, and most of them have a duration of 10–30 years. The interest rates on these bonds vary depending on their maturity.

3. Rates charged on similar loans:
   - Corporate bond rate – the interest rate on long-term corporate bonds can vary depending on a number of factors, including the time to maturity and risk classification.

Thus shorter-term loans might take the commercial paper rate or the Treasury bill rate as the reference rate, longer-terms loans would be based on the Treasury bond rate, and riskier lending propositions might be based on the corporate bond rate. Larger borrowings by more internationally focused companies might be based on the London Interbank Offered Rate (LIBOR) (first discussed in Chapter 3). In the UK, the reference rate is often the minimum lending rate set by the Bank of England. Once the reference rate is established, a mark-up is then added to reflect the risk of the lending proposition from the lending bank's point of view. Businesses often use a mixture of business overdraft and longer-term commercial borrowing which are usually secured on the company's assets. In the case of a small business, the borrowings may be secured on the proprietor's personal assets. Other forms of debt-type finance include:

- **Invoice factoring**: this is where a finance house or other financial institution takes over a company's outstanding invoices at a discount. This would typically be done by small- to medium-size companies.
- **Commercial paper**: this was mentioned in Chapter 3. The Commercial Paper Market is part of the money markets, i.e. the market for short-term wholesale finance. Commercial paper is typically issued by large financially strong companies with good credit ratings.
- **Debentures**: these are a form of bond issued by businesses. They are normally unsecured in the US, but in the UK debentures refer to secured debt.

Having considered the two forms of capital, we discover in the next section how we form an overall cost of capital, based on the cost of both types of capital. It is also useful to understand that there are differences in capital ratios across countries, as you will discover by doing the following Active learning activity.

## Active learning activity 8.2

### Where do firms get their funds?

The proportion of debt to equity and of bonds to bank debt varies widely from country to country. Look online and find some international comparisons. Why does the proportion of debt to equity vary across countries?

There are also practical implications for private companies who may find it difficult to work out a cost of capital.

## Practical implications for managers

### The cost of debt and equity

It is necessary to be clear about what the cost of capital is exactly for the organisation. There may be no equity as you may conventionally think of it – i.e. publicly traded or private shares. However, there will probably be internal equity, such as owners' capital and firm reserves. A company with no traded shares would need to work out the opportunity cost of this capital.

## 8.1.1 Introducing weighted average cost of capital

There are no companies with 100% debt and it is uncommon for a company to be completely equity funded, for reasons which we will discuss below. Therefore the overall cost of capital will be a weighted average somewhere between the cost of debt and the cost of equity capital. So, for example, if the cost of debt is 9%, the cost of equity is 15% and the weightings are 2/3 equity and 1/3 debt, the WACC equals $(1/3) \times 9\% + (2/3) \times 15\% = 13\%$.

With **no tax**, the expression for the WACC is as follows:

$$WACC = R_D(D/V) + R_E(E/V)$$

where $R_D$ is required return on debt, $R_E$ is required return to equity, D is market value of debt, E is market value of equity, and $V = D + E$ is the total value of all the debt plus equity.

In the context of the WACC, we tend to talk of cost of equity and cost of debt. Thus, we would more normally write the WACC as follows:

$$WACC = K_D(D/V) + K_E(E/V)$$

where $K_D$ is the cost of debt and $K_E$ is the cost of equity. This is how the WACC will be written in everything that follows.

In the example above, we assumed that the weights were already known. But in most circumstances we have to calculate the weights in the first place. So, by way of illustration, assume the following: equity is worth £150 million, debt is worth £50 million, the cost of debt ($K_D$) is 10% and the cost of equity ($K_E$) is 15%. In which case, debt represents 1/4 of the capital structure and equity represents 3/4. The WACC would be 13.75%. It is important to note that when we are calculating the weights of each part of debt and equity that we use current market values and not book values as book values will not reflect the current situation. We can also expand the WACC equation to take into account other forms of capital such as preference shares and different classes of debt. In fact, the WACC can take account of all potential components of overall capital.

A final point about the WACC is that under the tax regimes of most countries, interest payments reduce taxable profit. Thus, suppose the rate of corporation tax was 30%. Every £100 of interest payment would reduce taxable profit by £100. Given the tax rate, every £100 of taxable profit is entitled to have £30 worth of tax deducted. Thus a reduction of taxable profit by £100 reduces tax payable by £30. The deductibility of interest for tax purposes is known as a tax shield. For example, suppose the original loan was for £1,000 and the interest rate was 10%. The interest payment, gross, would be £100. However, each £100 worth of interest saves £30 of tax. So the interest payment net of the tax benefit is £70. In percentage terms, the cost of debt capital including the tax shield is expressed as follows:

$$(1 - T)K_D$$

where T is the rate of corporation tax.

The WACC will now be:

$$WACC = (1 - T)K_D(D/V) + K_E(E/V)$$

or

$$WACC = K_{DAT}(D/V) + K_E(E/V)$$

where $K_{DAT}$ is the after tax cost of debt capital $(1 - T)K_D$

where g is the growth rate of dividends, $P_0$ is the price in $t = 0$, and $d_0$ is the dividend in $t = 0$.

In summary then, the WACC is a relatively straightforward concept in which we establish the cost of debt and equity. Once the costs of debt and equity, and their relative importance as sources of capital, have been established we are then in the position of being able to derive the WACC. And once we have derived the WACC, we know the opportunity cost of capital, the appropriate discount rate for the firm's investments and the appropriate discount rate for the purposes of valuing the firm itself. Of course, it goes without saying that the return on the firm's investments should be greater than or equal to the WACC.

$$IRR \geq WACC$$

A practical implication of the WACC concept is that it should only be used under normal circumstances. In cases where the risk of new projects is very different from the usual or where the capital structure will be changed by undertaking a particular project, we would need to use a marginal cost of capital.

But where did we get the figures for $K_D$ and $K_E$ in the first place? We consider this question in the next section.

## Practical implications for managers

### Weighted average cost of capital

It is important to note that the WACC is a long-term concept, and that it should apply to all of the firm's projects, unless they are exceptional and very different from the firm's normal business. Thus the WACC is a key consideration in the assessment of the success or failure of the firm's projects, operations and divisions. Can you think of any circumstances where the WACC would *not* be applicable?

## Key concepts

☐ The **weighted average cost of capital (WACC)** is the expected rate of return on the company's after tax cost of debt and the cost of equity. The weights are the fractions of each type of debt and equity in the company's capital structure

☐ **Equity** is the capital of those who own the firm, such as shareholders

> ☐ **Debt** is held by those who have lent money to the company but have no participation in the ownership of the company
>
> ☐ **Covenants** are conditions applied on a loan by the lender to the borrowers. Breach of them can result in harsh repercussions
>
> ☐ **Invoice factoring** is the process by which business can sell on, at a discount, unpaid invoices for collection
>
> ☐ **Debenture** is a type of business debt instrument. The precise form a debenture takes can vary widely, depending on the context

## 8.2 Where do we get the cost of debt and the cost of equity from in the first place?

In the foregoing discussion, we have rather begged the question of how we calculated costs of debt and equity. However, we have pretty much covered this in the concepts discussed in previous chapters. To recap, consider the **cost of equity** which, if unknown, can be determined from the CAPM, or from the dividend valuation model. That is, we can use either technique to produce a required ROE. Thus for firm ZoNits (ZN) the cost of equity is as follows:

$$K_E = R_f + \beta_{ZN}(R_m - R_f)$$

Alternatively we could have used the dividend pricing model, ignoring growth:

$$K_E = d/P$$

We could of course have used other variants of the DCF share pricing model, such as dividend pricing with growth:

$$K_E = d_1/P + g$$

where g is the growth rate of dividends.

Second, consider the **cost of debt**. Most firms will rely to a greater or lesser extent on bank finance. The rate that they pay on bank finance will be based on some **reference rate** which represents the bank's cost of capital. The cost of debt is normally determined as a percentage mark-up on the bank's cost of funds, which will usually be determined with regard to some reference rate, as discussed in Section 8.1. So, for example, a bank may lend to a large international firm and use the 3-month LIBOR as its reference rate. This is the rate at which the bank borrows money on the interbank market in order to fund its loan book. Suppose the current LIBOR rate is 5%. The bank adds a mark-up to this which will vary directly with the perceived risk of the firm as a borrower. Thus the bank may add 4% in the light of the borrowing firm's perceived risk, and arrive at a figure of 9%.

If the rate is fixed, then this will apply throughout the life of the loan. If it is floating, then there will be review periods built into the loan agreement, when the interest rate may change. In short, calculation of the cost of debt is relatively straightforward.

Two further points are worth noting. First, the cost of debt, just like the cost of equity, may itself be a weighted average as there may be more than one source of debt just as there may be more than one source of equity. For example, most firms have an overdraft facility for shorter-term cash-flow purposes and a longer-term borrowing facility for investment purposes. Strictly speaking, only long-term debt should be counted for the purposes of WACC. However, many firms make constant use of the overdraft facility on a rolling basis and if the overall balance on the overdraft facility is significant over periods of time over a year then it should be counted with long-term debt.

Suppose the value of the overdraft facility fluctuates considerably over the cycle but has an average value of £0.5 million. Furthermore, let us suppose that long-term debt had a value of £0.75 million. The interest rates payable are, respectively, 9% and 7%. Hence the overall cost of debt would be $(2/5) \times 9\% + (3/5) \times 7\%$ which is 3.6% plus 4.2% which is 7.8%.

The other point is that when a firm relies on plain vanilla bond funding, the bond interest rate, or yield to maturity, may have changed since the date of issue, and the coupon rate may no longer equal the current yield to maturity. Nevertheless if the current rate is unclear, it can be inferred by taking the internal rate of return from the bond's cash flows.

The mechanics of working out the cost of debt or equity are usually relatively straightforward for a quoted company. However, we assume that any model we use for calculation is in fact relevant. The following practical implication box highlights some potential problems.

## Practical implications for managers

### How do we calculate the cost of debt and the cost of equity?

From a practical point of view, the calculation of debt is relatively straightforward for a company that relies on a few bank loans. It can get more complicated if bonds of various maturities and rates are involved.

The cost of equity may be more difficult if firms are not publicly quoted. However, one way to do this is to consider a publicly quoted competitor's cost of equity and adjust for the risk of the non quoted company.

## Key concepts

- ☐ The **cost of equity** is the return required by the owners on their equity
- ☐ The **cost of debt** is the return required by the lenders on their loan
- ☐ A **reference rate** is the rate used by a bank or other lender as a basis for the interest charged to a borrower. The reference rate will usually reflect the bank's cost of funds

## 8.3 The debt/equity mix

A key decision for many firms is the proportion in which debt and equity should be mixed. The proportion is measured as the ratio of debt to equity, or the proportion of debt to total capital, and is known as the gearing or leverage ratio. As we have seen above, the weighting affects the cost of capital. If we assume that costs of debt and equity remained *constant* as the debt/equity mix *changed*, a higher weighting in equity would mean a higher WACC, while a lower weighting in equity/higher weighting in debt would mean a lower WACC.

So what determines the mix? Should the firm adopt a small proportion of debt and a large proportion of equity, or vice versa? In fact, an even more natural question that arises at this point is why might the firm not have an all-debt structure, as this would minimise the cost of capital? The answer to this last question is that a 100% debt structure would mean that lenders to the company would bear all the risk and in effect they would own the company – so 100% debt would not be feasible or logical.

However, a more pertinent question would be, why not take the proportion of debt in the capital structure close to 100%? The short answer to this is that things are not as simple as they might seem, and that, in particular, debt and equity costs are not necessarily constant as we change the debt/equity ratio. We spend the rest of this section discovering precisely why.

### 8.3.1 More debt leads to higher gearing and adds to the volatility and risk of equity return

The gearing ratio itself is usually defined as either

D/E

where D is long-term debt and E is shareholders' funds.

or

D/(D + E)

both ratios are multiplied by 100%

The way in which the gearing ratio affects the risk of equity is as follows. As the gearing ratio increases, the firm's commitment to fixed interest payments increases. In other words, fixed cost will increase. Any increase in fixed cost will increase the volatility of the firm's performance. The following profit–loss diagrams illustrate this principle. Figure 8.1 shows a firm with a high proportion of fixed to variable costs, while Figure 8.2 shows a firm with a lower proportion of fixed to variable costs.

Gearing is also known as leverage.[2] Hence Figure 8.1 illustrates the effect of higher gearing or leverage, while Figure 8.2 represents the effect of low gearing/leverage. Thus with higher gearing, losses and profits are higher. Consequently, higher gearing may be attractive as it may improve bottom line performance. However, it also has a higher downside risk. Note that over a business cycle there would be larger profits and losses for the more geared firm and hence more volatility and variability in performance.

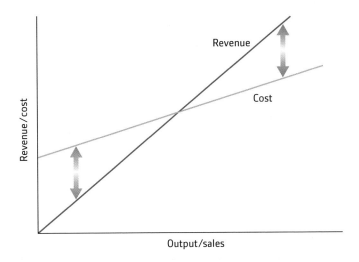

Figure 8.1  High ratio of fixed to variable cost

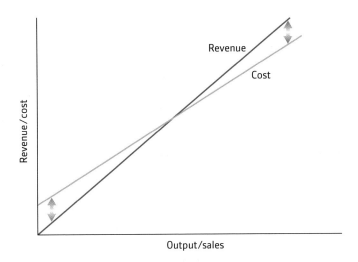

Figure 8.2  Low ratio of fixed to variable cost

The gearing which is represented by adding debt to the firm's capital mix is known as **financial gearing**. This is distinguished from **operational gearing**. Operational gearing refers to the magnitude of fixed production costs in the firm's day-to-day operations, and the variability in performance caused by this. Financial gearing is the *addition* to operational fixed cost arising from the fixed cost of debt finance. We also make the distinction between operational risk and financial risk. Operational risk is just the risk arising from the firm's day-to-day activities. It would be measured, for example, by beta, assuming the firm is 100% equity financed. Financial risk is the additional risk or additional **beta** that results from financial gearing. To illustrate these concepts, let's take an example.

The following possible financial structures are proposed for AcmeFireBang (AFB), a novelties company:

- 0% debt/all equity – 20 million shares sold at a nominal value of £1.

- 20% debt – £4 million debt (carrying a 7% interest cost after tax) and £16 million equity.

- 40% debt – £8 million debt (also carrying a 7% interest cost after tax) and £12 million equity.

It is important to note at this point that the increase in financial gearing from 20% to 40% does not increase the cost of debt – that is, there is not perceived to be any increase in risk by debt-holders as a result of the increase in financial gearing at this point. We expand on this point below.

Imagine that the company does not know how much it will earn before profits, interest and tax in the future. However, it estimates that it will be one of the following three possible outcomes:

1. Modest £0.5 million.

2. Good £3 million.

3. Excellent £4 million.

| 19 | Structure 1 (0 Debt) | Structure 2 (20% Debt) | Structure 3 (40% Debt) |
|---|---|---|---|
| 20 *Modest* | | | |
| 21 Revenues | 0.1 | 0.1 | 0.1 |
| 22 Interest Payments | 0 | 0.28 | 0.56 |
| 23 Earnings Distributed to Shar | 0.1 | -0.18 | -0.46 |
| 24 ROE | 0.50% | -1.13% | -3.83% |
| 25 | | | |
| 26 *Good* | | | |
| 27 Revenues | 3 | 3 | 3 |
| 28 Interest Payments | 0 | 0.28 | 0.56 |
| 29 Earnings Distributed to Shar | 3 | 2.72 | 2.44 |
| 30 ROE | 15.00% | 17.00% | 20.33% |
| 31 | | | |
| 32 *Excellent* | | | |
| 33 Revenues | 7 | 7 | 7 |
| 34 Interest Payments | 0 | 0.28 | 0.56 |
| 35 Earnings Distributed to Shar | 7 | 6.72 | 6.44 |
| 36 ROE | 35.00% | 42.00% | 53.67% |

Screenshot 8.1 Return on equity across the cycle for different capital structures

There are two things to observe about Screenshot 8.1. The first is that the variability of the firm's performance is greater the more highly geared it is. This can clearly be seen in the range of fluctuation in ROE over the cycle. With a zero debt structure, the ROE fluctuates in the range 0.5% to 35%, for the 20% debt structure it is –1.13% to 42%, while for the 40% structure it is –3.83% to 53.67%. This obvious increase in variability with increasing gearing would not change if we were to use a more formal measure of variability such as the standard deviation.

The second point to observe is that increased variability is, as we have seen before, a 'two-edged sword'. On the one hand, it is possible to achieve more impressive looking results for the average ROE by increasing gearing. On the other hand, the increase in gearing increases the magnitude of potential downside losses. The possibility of more impressive looking results for shareholders comes of course at a cost, which is greater *risk* to equity and therefore a greater *cost* of equity.

We can get a feel for the extent of the increase in the cost of equity by looking at the impact of gearing on beta. First of all, we calculate the standard deviation of the return to equity for each capital structure across the cycle. These values for standard deviation are given in Screenshot 8.2.

| 49 | | Structure 1 (0 Debt) | Structure 2 (20% Debt) | Structure 3 (40% Debt) |
|---|---|---|---|---|
| 50 | *Modest* | | | |
| 51 | ROE | 0.50% | -1.13% | -3.83% |
| 52 | | | | |
| 53 | *Good* | | | |
| 54 | ROE | 15.00% | 17.00% | 20.33% |
| 55 | | | | |
| 56 | *Excellent* | | | |
| 57 | ROE | 35.00% | 42.00% | 53.67% |
| 58 | | | | |
| 59 | Standard Deviation of ROE across the cycle | 14.14% | 17.68% | 23.57% |
| 60 | | | | |

Screenshot 8.2  Standard deviation of ROE across the cycle

Let us assume that the correlation of the ROE on AcmeFireBang with the market portfolio is +1, i.e. perfect and positive. Let us further assume that the standard deviation of the market return is 0.1 or 10%. We are now in a position to calculate the variance of the market return and the covariance of the AFB return. Therefore we can calculate beta from these data. For example, for the all-equity structure the variance of the market return, $\sigma^2_M$, is 1% or 0.01. The covariance ($\sigma_{M \text{ with AFB}}$) can be found from the product of the correlation coefficient with the respective standard deviations. Thus we have $\rho_{M \text{ with AFB}} \times \sigma_M \times \sigma_{AFB}$ which is equal to $1 \times 0.1 \times 0.141$. Divide this figure (0.0141) by the variance (0.01) to get 1.41. In fact, in this specific case, given our assumption that $\rho_{M \text{ with AFB}} = 1$, the beta can be stated as $\sigma_{AFB}/\sigma_M$ and it can easily be seen how we arrived at the figures for the other betas that are presented in the next screenshot.

| 60 | | Structure 1 (0 Debt) | Structure 2 (20% Debt) | Structure 3 (40% Debt) |
|---|---|---|---|---|
| 61 | | | | |
| 62 | Standard Deviation of ROE across the cycle | 14.14% | 17.68% | 23.57% |
| 63 | | | | |
| 64 | Beta | 1.41 | 1.77 | 2.36 |
| 65 | | | | |
| 66 | % Change Beta/KE | | 25.00% | 66.67% |
| 67 | | | | |
| 68 | | | | |

Screenshot 8.3  Beta and the percentage change in beta with leverage

As a result of our calculations we can now see that in this particular case, if the company goes from an all-equity structure to 20% debt, beta and the cost of equity increase by roughly one quarter (25%). If the company goes from an all-equity structure to 40% debt, beta and the cost of equity will increase by two thirds (66.67%). Note that only the first beta for the all-equity structure is a pure beta, i.e. beta is normally defined in such a way as to measure the firm's day-to-day operational risk. Hence conventional or **fundamental beta** measurement is based on the implicit assumption of an all-equity capital structure. The two other betas calculated here are **leveraged betas**. That is, they measure both operational risk and the additional risk that is derived from leverage. In fact, we have inadvertently discovered what is known as the 'Hamada formula' for leveraged beta, which in the absence of tax is as follows:

$$\beta_L = (1 + D/E)\beta_{UL}$$

where $\beta_L$ is leveraged beta and $\beta_{UL}$ is unleveraged or fundamental beta.

It should be noted that the Hamada formula is more normally written as follows to take account of the tax shield:

$$\beta_{UL} = (1 + (1 - T)D/E)\beta_L$$

The Hamada formula raises an interesting point. We need not have gone through all the rigmarole of calculating ROEs and standard deviations of ROEs for the leveraged capital structures. All that was necessary was to multiply fundamental beta of 1.41 by $1 + D/E$. This is clearly brought out in Screenshot 8.4, as the first multiple would be $1 + 0.2/0.8$ or 1.25 and the second would be $1 + 0.4/0.6$ or 1.67. Notice, given the Hamada formula, how quickly leverage increases equity volatility and multiplies the cost of capital. Screenshot 8.4 shows how beta increases with leverage.

| 1 | Unlevered | Levered | | | | | | | | | |
|---|---|---|---|---|---|---|---|---|---|---|---|
| 2 | All Equity | D/(D+E) | | | | | | | | | |
| 3 | | 0 | 0.1 | 0.2 | 0.3 | 0.4 | 0.5 | 0.6 | 0.7 | 0.8 | 0.9 |
| 4 | | | | | | | | | | | |
| 5 | Unlevered | Levered | | | | | | | | | |
| 6 | All Equity | D/E | | | | | | | | | |
| 7 | | 0 | 0.11111 | | 0.25 | 0.42857 | 0.66667 | 1 | 1.5 | 2.33333 | 4 | 9 |
| 8 | | | | | | | | | | | |
| 9 | Unlevered | Levered | | | | | | | | | |
| 10 | Beta | Beta | | | | | | | | | |
| 11 | | 1 | 1.11111 | | 1.25 | 1.42857 | 1.66667 | 2 | 2.5 | 3.33333 | 5 | 10 |
| 12 | | | | | | | | | | | |

Screenshot 8.4 The impact of leverage on beta

As can be seen, the effect of increasing the ratio of debt to total capital $[D/(D + E)]$ has a disproportionate non-linear effect on the D/E ratio and consequently levered beta, which is multiplied by 3.3 for a 70% debt structure, by 5 for an 80% debt structure and by 10 for a 90% debt structure. Thus the volatility and risk, and the cost of equity, will increase sharply beyond a 50/50 structure, though in real life the effect will be mitigated slightly by the tax shield, as can be seen in the following screenshot, where it is assumed that the rate of corporation tax is 30%.

The figure shows there is some mitigation, but the basic disproportionate increase in volatility beyond 60% debt remains. Thus gearing is still associated with higher volatility and equity risk.

| | | | | | | | | | |
|---|---|---|---|---|---|---|---|---|---|
| **Unlevered All Equity** | **Levered D/(D+E)** | | | | | | | | |
| 0 | 0.1 | 0.2 | 0.3 | 0.4 | 0.5 | 0.6 | 0.7 | 0.8 | 0.9 |
| **Unlevered All Equity** | **Levered (1-T)D/E** | | | | | | | | |
| 0 | 0.07778 | 0.175 | 0.3 | 0.46667 | 0.7 | 1.05 | 1.63333 | 2.8 | 6.3 |
| **Unlevered Beta** | **Levered Tax Adjusted Beta** | | | | | | | | |
| 1 | 1.07778 | 1.175 | 1.3 | 1.46667 | 1.7 | 2.05 | 2.63333 | 3.8 | 7.3 |

Screenshot 8.5 The effect of gearing on levered and tax-adjusted beta. Rate of corporation tax (T) is 30%

Let us cast our minds back to the start of the present analysis of why increased gearing causes increased volatility. One of the things that strike the reader on inspecting Screenshot 8.1 is the possibility of greater and greater loss as the amount of gearing increases. Quite apart from any concerns about volatility in itself, large losses could cause the firm serious problems. Thus far in this section, we have assumed that all that matters is volatility and that if the firm with a 40% debt structure did make a negative ROE of –3.83%, it would make good the loss and 'bounce back', i.e. recover quickly. This is not an unreasonable assumption with such a small proportional loss.

However, as we have seen, volatility quickly increases beyond about 60% debt/capital, and hence the magnitude of any losses will also start to rapidly increase at this point. As they do, the assumption that the firm will bounce back from very poor negative ROE to very high positive ROE becomes more difficult to sustain. When there is a large shortfall in income available to pay interest, there may not be sufficient even in shareholders' reserves to meet the liability.

At this point the firm will be in **financial distress**, and the prospect of recovering sufficiently to earn once more the large positive returns that go with high volatility is greatly diminished. Thus, the high volatility associated with high gearing can be a problem in itself by increasing beta and raising the cost of equity. However, it also creates an additional problem by making the possibility of financial distress more likely. Financial distress can result in the company enacting cost-cutting measures such as firing employees, so a high volatility also reduces job security.

We can appreciate the effects of high leverage and thus the potential for financial distress by completing Active learning activity 8.3.

## Active learning activity 8.3

Replicate the spreadsheets above. Try different leverage factors and confirm that leverage does have the effect we have suggested. What happens when leverage is increased to very high levels?

### 8.3.2 Higher leverage increases the risk of financial distress

Consider the following example. While Dr Weevil is in cryogenic suspension, No. 3 has decided to use the time profitably by setting up a company to look after the assets from Dr Weevil's business empire. A corporation called Virtuclon is to be established. It will be capitalised 50% by debt and 50% by equity. Hence one half of its £2,000 million (£2 billion) of capital will be obtained from lenders, who require a 10% return to debt, while one half will be obtained from shareholders, who require a 16% return to equity. If the corporation tax rate is 30% then the post-tax cost of debt is 7%. The basic data required are as follows:

Cost of debt $K_{DAT} = 7\%$
Cost of equity $K_E = 16\%$
Weight of debt $V_D/(V_D + V_E)$ £1 billion/£2 billion $W_D = 0.5$
Weight of equity $V_E/(V_D + V_E)$ £1 billion/£2 billion $W_E = 0.5$
WACC $= (16 \times 0.5) + (7 \times 0.5) = 11.5\%$

Thus, every year Virtuclon aims to produce enough income to pay 11.5% of £2 billion, or £230 million. Of this £230 million, £70 million net of the tax shield (7% of £1 billion debt) will be paid as interest, while £160 million (16% of £1 billion equity) will be paid as dividends every year from its day-to-day operations involving 'cable companies, steel mills, shipping and a factory in Chicago that makes ... miniature factories'. A point that is of considerable importance and has been stressed in the foregoing discussion is the nature of the payments that have to be made to holders of debt and holders of equity.

Although in net terms the company pays £70 million of interest after taking into account the tax shield, it must in the first instance pay £100 million before claiming the tax allowance. This £100 million *must* be paid. If it is not, the firm faces the possibility of legal action, administration and foreclosure. The £160 million does not necessarily have to be paid. Few firms would willingly upset their shareholders, and there may be longer-term consequences to reductions in dividend or suspension of dividend. However, it is, at least in principle, within the firm's rights to lower or suspend the dividend should income after depreciation, tax and interest be insufficient to meet dividend payments. But, as we intimated, holders of debt must be paid their interest, or else the firm risks financial distress.

Now let's suppose that Dr Weevil is scheduled to return from sabbatical within the next year, and that No. 3 wants to make a big impression, by making the business performance numbers look as impressive as possible. He plans to buy back equity from current shareholders Mustapha, Frau Farber and Scott Weevil by borrowing more interest-bearing capital. There is also a sub-plot here. Being a controlling kind of guy, No. 3 wants to liquidate all the other equity, so that control is vested in his own and Dr Weevil's equity stake which is worth £200 million. If he borrowed to buy back the shareholdings of the others, this would take the capital structure to a much more highly geared 10% equity/90% debt mix. Even if the cost of debt remained the same, Virtuclon would now have to make at least £180 million in profit before interest and tax. That is, debt would now be worth £1,800 million and 10% interest would have to be paid before the tax allowance could be reclaimed later.

Not achieving this sum would be unthinkable, as this would lead to financial distress. So, by wanting to look more impressive and having ambitions to take control, No. 3 has increased the pressure on himself and his company to perform. Furthermore, the cost of debt is likely to substantially increase as lenders will recognise the greater probability of financial distress and default.

We can see then why the risk of financial distress is usually thought to increase with gearing or debt/equity. Financial distress is where the firm cannot fully meet its obligations to creditors. What exactly is the cost of financial distress? Well, it's the possibility of costly, time-consuming and morale-sapping financial insolvency, or even the irrevocable loss of the firm altogether in the event that losses are so great as to render the firm bankrupt. The costs are various and include:

- Loss of company focus as managers crisis-manage and firefight, which in turn can lose valuable customers, who may not be getting the attention they require, and also key suppliers.
- Loss of trade credit from suppliers who may be reluctant to supply when there is so much financial uncertainty.
- Legal costs, professional costs and opportunity cost of management time.
- Fire sales of valuable assets in order to restore liquidity.

The likelihood of additional financial risk derived from gearing to have a high probability of pushing the company into insolvency depends on similar factors to the causes of beta risk, viz:

- The sensitivity of the company's revenues to the general level of economic activity.
- The proportion of fixed to variable costs.
- The liquidity and marketability of the firm's assets.
- The cash-generative ability of the business.

Take, for example, the steel industry. The demand for steel is a derived demand from businesses that use it for construction and manufacture. Therefore demand is very closely correlated to the business cycle and it can be substantially reduced when there is a downturn in the economy. Steel-making plants, on the other hand, represent very expensive and highly specialised (physical) capital which would probably be of little interest to most other businesses. Thus there is a very high fixed cost of (physical) capital. When there is a downturn in the economy, this type of heavy manufacturing is faced with a 'double-whammy' of substantially reduced demand along with substantially increased unit cost, resulting from lower capacity usage of large-scale and expensive physical capital. This is illustrated in the following extract from the *Financial Times* in the mini case study 'A firm that is vulnerable to financial leverage'.

## Mini case study

### A firm that is vulnerable to financial leverage

Source Marsh 2008, Copyright *Financial Times*, 'Mittal fatigue', 2008

Lakshmi Mittal next week faces the biggest test of his career. The Indian metals magnate will try to convince investors that his vision of the steel industry still has merit, in spite of the battering the sector has received amid the global financial crisis.

When he presents the third-quarter results of ArcelorMittal on Wednesday, speaking to analysts and investors in telephone conversations from his company's imposing headquarters in the centre of Luxembourg, Mr Mittal will do his best to put a brave face on a 72 per cent decline in the share price of the world's biggest steelmaker over the past four months.

Slides in the market value of most large steel businesses have exceeded the falls incurred at many of the industrial companies that are their biggest customers. Since late June, as can be seen in the figure below, steel shares have underperformed the Datastream composite index of all quoted companies worldwide by 52 per cent.

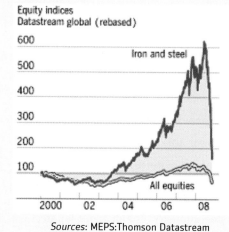

*Sources*: MEPS:Thomson Datastream

1. Are there any measures that the steel industry can take to alleviate the risks arising from financial leverage?

Clearly then, the steel manufacturing sector is very susceptible to beta-type risk and therefore equity should be used more liberally and debt more sparingly in order to avoid various risks, including the risk of financial distress. The risk of financial distress for steel-making at a given gearing ratio is much greater than, say, for a chain of betting shops like William Hill. The capital involved here are the shops and the fittings. The shops can be leased rather than bought outright, and in normal times the shops will have plenty of alternative uses, even if they are owned. The other main form of fixed capital deployed is the shop-fitting, which is a small expense relative to the firm's overall value. In addition, betting is a cash business that does not seem to be badly affected by downturns and recessions. Hence, there is less risk of financial distress at a given gearing ratio than say a steel company, and a betting company should be able to achieve a higher gearing ratio than a manufacturing company without undue risk. This is illustrated in the mini case study 'A company that is more suited to leverage'.

## Mini case study

### A company that is more suited to leverage

Source Urry 2008, Copyright *Financial Times*, 'William Hill confident in spite of profits', 2008

William Hill's new chief executive on Wednesday said he was confident that the bookmaker would prove resilient in the face of a downturn in consumer spending, as he presented lower profits for 2007.

Ralph Topping, who was promoted from within the group to the job last week, said, 'I'm not concerned about a consumer downturn. We weathered the last recession well.'

1. In what circumstances would William Hill suffer from the effects of financial leverage?

In the next section we consider the practical implications of increased leverage.

## Practical implications for managers

### The effect of increasing gearing/leverage

Debt is an indispensible part of most firms' capital. However, when a decision is taken to increase leverage, it is important to be aware of not only how this affects the firm now, but also how it is likely to affect the firm in the event of a severe downturn. Think about the recent credit crunch and how many firms went out of business due to being unable to service debt costs.

## Key concepts

- **Financial gearing** is the gearing that is represented by adding debt to the firm's capital mix
- **Operational gearing** refers to the fixed production costs in the firm's day-to-day operations, and the variability in performance caused by it
- **Leveraged betas** measure both operational risk and the additional risk that is derived from leverage
- **Financial distress** is a state a company can find itself in when it is unable to meet its obligations to its creditors. It can lead to bankruptcy

## 8.4 Is there an optimal gearing ratio? Modigliani and Miller's perspective

### 8.4.1 Modigliani and Miller's proposition 1

The extent to which the gearing ratio can be or should be increased has been the subject of considerable controversy in the world of finance. There are basically two views. First, the traditional view, based on an eclectic assembly of pragmatic reasons, which is very broadly as follows. Few companies are 100% equity financed. This is because debt is generally cheaper than equity, particularly because of the tax shield, and it makes no sense therefore to deny oneself access to this cheaper form of capital. Nevertheless, there is a limit to the amount of debt that can be taken on, because, for example, as we have seen, as leverage increases, the cost of equity increases as well. This directly increases the volatility of the ROE and therefore the required ROE, $K_E$, eventually starts to increase dramatically. In addition, as gearing increases, the risk of financial distress increases. The increased risk of financial distress may not be very significant at lower levels of gearing, but there comes a point where it begins to be regarded as an important risk and so the required return on debt will also eventually start to increase.

Eventually, then, with increased gearing we reach a point where the benefit of switching from increasingly expensive equity to cheaper debt will be outweighed by the additional costs of both types of capital at higher levels of leverage. This is illustrated as a possibility in Figure 8.3.

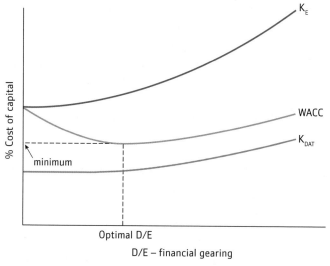

Figure 8.3 Traditional view that there is a theoretical optimal gearing ratio that minimises the WACC and therefore maximises the firm's value

The possibility of an optimal capital gearing ratio was refuted, however, by Modigliani and Miller (1958) who proposed that there is *no* optimal gearing ratio. This contrasting position is shown in Figure 8.4.

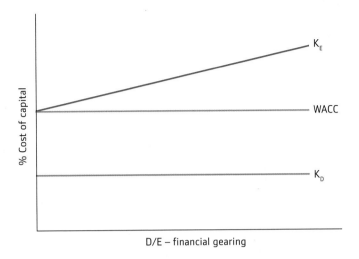

Figure 8.4 Modigliani and Miller's view that there is no optimal gearing ratio that minimises the WACC

This came as something of a surprise to financial professionals. Before the 1960s, it was taken for granted that there was an optimal mix of debt and equity. To be frank, the subject was not much debated and argued, as the academic discipline of corporate finance was then in its infancy. However, all that changed with the publication of the seminal work of Modigliani and Miller. There are basically two versions of M and M on this subject, and it is to the first classic M and M model that we turn.

Modigliani and Miller in their original guise (1958) argued that the firm's decision on the proportion of debt to equity should have no impact on the firm's WACC. It should not make the slightest difference if the firm is using a mix of 90% equity and 10% debt or the converse 10/90 mix. The proposition basically boils down to this. If the value of the WACC could be manipulated and more importantly lowered by selecting a particular gearing ratio, then the value of the firm could similarly be boosted by selecting a particular gearing ratio. Consider a simple model of firm value as the sum of discounted cash flow from its projects, i.e.

V = CF/WACC

where V is the value of the firm, CF is the firm's perpetuity cash flows from various projects and WACC is the appropriate discount rate given the risk class of the firm.

The value of the WACC should depend on the appropriate discount rate, given the risk of the firm's projects. The value of the firm in turn should depend on the value of the cash flows from its investment projects discounted at a rate appropriate to the risk of these projects. Value should depend fundamentally on day-to-day business ability and not on the way the firm is financed. Otherwise, firm value could be manipulated through financial engineering, with nothing fundamental changing.

Furthermore, Modigliani and Miller express the traditional economist's suspicion of 'free-lunches' or, to give it its proper name, **costless riskless gain**. They supply a complicated arbitrage argument which is well outside the scope of this book, but the intuitive sense of what they say is as follows. In an efficient world with scarce resources of capital, why should such a boost to firm value be available for nothing? That is, capital, whether in the form of debt or equity, is a scarce resource. If it were not a scarce resource, it should be available very cheaply, or possibly for nothing. However, as is well known, capital does not come cheap. If it was possible that one form of capital, such as debt, would produce an instant and costless benefit, then there would be an instant and extensive increase in demand for this capital, which would drive up the price of debt relative to equity and negate the benefit. Thus, the proportion of debt and equity should make no difference to underlying fundamental value.

It should be pointed out that M and M were using an approach that is fundamental in much economic theory, which is to imagine a frictionless world of **perfect competition**. By imagining this world and making explicit assumptions about the way people and institutions behave in this world, it is possible to come to conclusions that follow by strict logic from what has been assumed in the first place. Among the assumptions that M and M made were the following:

1. There are no taxes.

2. There is **perfect information**. All information that *needs* to be known to value the firm or the firm's projects *is* known. That is, information is either known with certainty or, in the case where the information is uncertain, it can be precisely quantified.

3. There are no costs of financial distress and liquidation. This is an important assumption, as we will see below.

4. Firms can be classified into distinct risk classes. This is related to assumption 2, i.e. we know precisely how risky the firm and its projects are.

5. There are **perfect capital markets**, in which it is possible to borrow and lend at the risk-free rate. This seems rather a strong assumption when we consider our own ability to borrow as individuals. However, large financial institutions can borrow at rates much closer to the risk-free rate, so this assumption is not quite as unrealistic as some of the others. If we now consider each of the assumptions in turn as an Active learning activity, we can reflect on the usefulness of the assumptions.

## Active learning activity 8.4

### Reflecting on Modigliani and Miller

Go through each of Modigliani and Miller's assumptions. Do you think each is a reasonable assumption to make? If not, how unrealistic do you think it is? How radically would M and M have to be revised if the assumption was very unrealistic?

Modigliani and Miller's propositions follow by logical necessity from their assumptions. It is up to us to judge how reasonable these assumptions are. It is not easy to get across some of the more subtle and complex aspects of proposition 1 of M and M. However, perhaps we can convince ourselves of the possible theoretical truth of M and M if we revisit the example summarised in Screenshot 8.1. This showed the effect on the ROE from increasing gearing. We now show these figures again, in Screenshot 8.6, but this time with the WACC calculated as well.

| | A | B | C | D |
|---|---|---|---|---|
| 19 | | Structure 1 (0 Debt) | Structure 2 (20% Debt) | Structure 3 (40% Debt) |
| 20 | *Modest* | | | |
| 21 | Revenues | 0.1 | 0.1 | 0.1 |
| 22 | Interest Payments | 0 | 0.28 | 0.56 |
| 23 | Earnings Distributed to Share | 0.1 | -0.18 | -0.46 |
| 24 | ROE | 0.50% | -1.13% | -3.83% |
| 25 | WACC | 0.50% | 0.50% | 0.50% |
| 26 | | | | |
| 27 | *Good* | | | |
| 28 | Revenues | 3 | 3 | 3 |
| 29 | Interest Payments | 0 | 0.28 | 0.56 |
| 30 | Earnings Distributed to Share | 3 | 2.72 | 2.44 |
| 31 | ROE | 15.00% | 17.00% | 20.33% |
| 32 | WACC | 15.00% | 15.00% | 15.00% |
| 33 | | | | |
| 34 | *Excellent* | | | |
| 35 | Revenues | 7 | 7 | 7 |
| 36 | Interest Payments | 0 | 0.28 | 0.56 |
| 37 | Earnings Distributed to Share | 7 | 6.72 | 6.44 |
| 38 | ROE | 35.00% | 42.00% | 53.67% |
| 39 | WACC | 35.00% | 35.00% | 35.00% |
| 40 | | | | |

Screenshot 8.6 Modigliani and Miller's proposition 1 – the WACC does not change with capital structure

As can be seen, while the ROE can vary considerably over various capital structures, WACC always remains the same. It should be noted that this is not a substantial logical proof such as was offered by M and M. Rather the result is definitional, following from the way in which the ROE is defined as the residual left over after interest is paid. In our particular example, the WACC must necessarily be constant across capital structures given the way we have set the problem up. Nevertheless, it can be seen that regardless of capital structure, any benefit of reduced debt cost is exactly outweighed by the increase in the cost of equity and therefore the **WACC remains the same.**

## 8.4.2 Modigliani and Miller's proposition 2

In a revised (1963) version of their proposition which allowed for the possibility of taxation, they said something rather different. Given that interest payments on debt are tax-deductible, the firm's overall value should increase as it substitutes debt for equity. This is because the firm is in effect now in a position of receiving a 'free lunch' in the form of free money from the government. The larger the proportion of debt it uses in the capital structure, the lower the WACC. This modified position of M and M is represented in Figure 8.5.

As an article in *The Economist* (2005) observed:

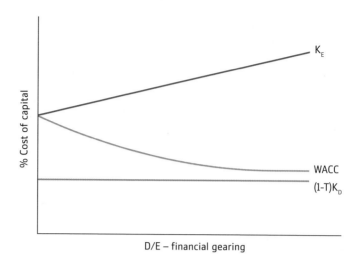

Figure 8.5 Modified Modigliani and Miller's proposition 2 view that the optimal gearing ratio is close to 100% if interest payments are tax deductible

'... this suggests that many firms in the 1950s and 1960s had too much equity and not enough debt. However, it is clear that over the past couple of decades they have been trying to rectify that.

But not, perhaps, as vigorously as might be expected. As Mr Miller cheerfully conceded, his and his colleague's proposition implied that firms should be financed almost entirely with debt. Yet many big companies still think that their weighted average cost of capital – the total mix of debt and equity – would be cheaper in the long term if they maintained a solid credit rating.'

('Debt is good for you', *The Economist*, 25 January 2001)

This quote neatly brings out the extreme nature of the proposition derived by M and M's proposition 2. While it may be strictly logical, it is not really practical. This alerts us to the fact that although M and M have now taken account of taxes, there is still something vital missing from their account of firms and how they reach a capital structure decision.

## Practical implications for managers

### Modigliani and Miller – are there lessons for business?

Modigliani and Miller have stimulated a great deal of research in this area and forced businesses to be much more careful and coherent about this kind of decision.

Moreover, they were drawing logical conclusions which followed of necessity from their assumptions. Under different circumstances this can be a useful approach. It is up to us to judge where reality starts and the model ends. The implication from proposition 2, that a company should gear up as much as possible, became pervasive in modern times. What were the consequences of this perspective?

## Key concepts

- A **costless riskless gain** or 'free lunch' creates value at no cost or risk to the company
- A world of **perfect competition** is one of the assumptions Modigliani and Miller make in their theories. It assumes the lack of taxes, market barriers and financial distress costs. It also assumes there are perfect capital markets and perfect information
- **Perfect capital** markets are markets where capital is borrowed and lent at the risk-free rate
- **Perfect information** means that information necessary to value companies either is known with certainty or can be precisely quantified

## 8.5 What is missing from Modigliani and Miller? Real world considerations

### 8.5.1 Practical reasons why Modigliani and Miller's models might not be the 'whole story'

Modigliani and Miller were without doubt very distinguished scholars – it's hard to argue with a Nobel Prize! However, they were very much men of their time, using a style of theorising that was regarded as the correct way to proceed. We have talked about this theoretical world in the previous section.

Let us consider two of the potential problems with the theoretical financial economics of the time. First, it tended to be assumed that shareholder value was automatically maximised, without any real consideration of the mechanics involved. After all, it would be highly illogical if shareholders were to permit anything less, given the implicit assumption of no barriers to maximisation. Nevertheless, the development of agency theory suggested a very good reason why income for shareholders can be less than optimal. This is because, given the classic divorce of ownership and control, shareholders employ agents on their behalf. And those agents may or may not act on the shareholder's behalf, particularly in the light of the second problem, **information**.

Clearly, insiders, i.e. the managers of the firm, know more about what is going on in the firm than outsiders do. As we have mentioned in previous chapters, this is why **insider trading** is illegal in most countries, because it is considered that managers have an unfair informational advantage which they should not be allowed to exploit. However, when it comes to the day-to-day relationship between managers and shareholders, it is less easy to legislate against managers not working as hard as they might, or against managers pursuing their own objectives rather than the owners of the firm's equity. Hence, given the imbalance in information, or what is known technically as **asymmetric information**, there is an '**agency problem**'. That is, the investor cannot always be sure that the agents employed on his or her behalf to run the company may not exploit the informational advantage to pursue their own agenda. The equity/debt decision can help control these informational and agency problems, as we discover in the next section.

## 8.5.2 Practical reasons why a high debt ratio might be beneficial

One benefit of high gearing is that a large amount of debt reduces free cash flow through interest payments and keeps it out of the hands of managers, who may have a tendency to overinvest in vanity projects which in retrospect are of dubious value. Take the sorry example of GEC-Marconi.

It is almost a cliché in this kind of corporate finance textbook to rehearse the story of this British firm and the large cash pile that it had once accumulated under long-time chief executive and presiding genius Lord Weinstock. Nevertheless, it is worth repeating this story once more, just to remind ourselves of the awesome ability of managers to destroy value by pursuing poorly conceived investments and takeovers. Following Lord Weinstock's retirement, this cash pile was systematically destroyed by a new generation of managers who regarded such cash hoarding as old fashioned. See the mini case study 'Managerial overinvestment: how managers can destroy value' for more details.

## Mini case study

### Managerial overinvestment: how managers can destroy value

Source *Economist* 2005

At the height of dotcom madness in 2000, it [GEC-Marconi] was a company worth £35 billion. Before then, as GEC, it had been one of Britain's top manufacturers, run by the redoubtable industrialist Arnold Weinstock. But on 25 October, the bulk of Marconi was bought by Ericsson, a Swedish telecommunications group, for a piffling £1.2 billion.

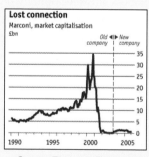

*Source*: Thomson Datastream

The sale closes an ignominious episode in British commercial history. All that remains of the industrial giant that Lord Weinstock assembled is a small telecoms-services company. Called, uninspiringly, Telent – Ericsson has purchased the Marconi brand – it had sales of only £336 million in the last financial year.

1. What are the problems of holding large cash balances?

Thus, an argument for high levels of debt, or rather an argument against excessively high levels of equity, is that it helps to control the agency problem by ensuring that cash is not freely available to managers and is effectively rationed, as much of it will already be earmarked for interest payment. Lord Weinstock was an exceptional manager who kept tight control of finance. However, where there is less stringent managerial control, shareholders' interest might be best served by having high debt ratios. This would guard against careless **reinvestment risk**.

Another reason why debt might help to overcome agency and information problems is in motivating managers not to neglect their duties. As we have stressed in many of the previous sections, interest has to be paid. It is not optional. Therefore high debt levels will motivate managers to perform. There is an old saying in business, 'Debt is a dagger. Equity is a pillow'. Thus high debt ratios can help with managerial motivation.

Another reason why high debt ratios can be useful to the firm is when it is felt by core shareholders that the equity base is so diffuse that it has diluted control of the firm, to the point where it is felt that the firm has lost its focus on the core business. For this reason it may be strategically imperative to buy back shares and concentrate equity in a few hands. This is often what venture capital companies do. They will buy out existing shareholdings in order to concentrate ownership in their own hands so that they can gain the benefits of the radical restructuring they undertake in target companies. If the finance to buy out existing shareholders is raised through the use of junk bonds, for example, then this will obviously increase the debt/equity ratio. Nevertheless, an alternative which may well be used is the replacement of publicly quoted external equity with privately owned internal equity. This maximises the gains, assuming the *concentration* of equity is successful.

These various control benefits of lower equity and higher debt would of course have to be balanced against more risky returns to equity and the risk of financial distress.

Apart from the control benefits of a high debt ratio, there may also be benefits to the firm from announcing an increase in the debt ratio, as it is generally taken by investors and the capital markets that the firm is confident that the cash flows from its current projects will be enough to pay the interest on the debt. A new issue of public equity, on the other hand, can be taken as a sign that future revenues are uncertain and that the firm wants the equity market to share in the risk. Thus an increase in the debt ratio can be seen as an important signal.

### 8.5.3 Practical reasons why firms may opt for lower debt ratios

Managers exert a great deal of day-to-day control over the firm and therefore may not wish high debt ratios for the agency reasons discussed above. However, apart from that, managers may wish to minimise debt because they are more exposed to risk than the typical owner/investor with a diversified portfolio. The income and human capital of the typical manager may be much more specific to the firm and much less diversifiable. Hence managers may be, for good reasons, much more reluctant to expose the firm to additional financial risk from leverage than shareholders.

As well as **managerial preferences**, another reason for not maximising the debt ratio is for the purposes of maintaining **operational slack**. That is, the firm may maintain spare borrowing capacity so that if an attractive investment opportunity does come up, it can quickly raise funds to take advantage of the opportunity.

A final reason why firms may not maximise leverage as they theoretically should is that there are limits on the amounts they can borrow. These limits are imposed by (1) the physical limit of the assets that the firm has to offer as security and (2) the intangible limits imposed and the increasingly stringent conditions and covenants imposed by lenders as the firm becomes more indebted. Thus, firms who prefer to maintain full freedom to operate may prefer lower debt levels. There may also be other factors to consider, as suggested in the next Active learning activity.

## Active learning activity 8.5

### Differences in debt/equity ratios across industries

Gather aggregate data on debt/equity ratios for two sharply contrasting industrial sectors. Can you explain the differences in terms of the theories that we have advanced?

Just to briefly summarise Sections 8.5.2 and 8.5.3, the main reason to expect an optimal gearing ratio is that there comes a point when the advantage of cheaper debt, particularly the tax advantage, is offset by the increasing risk of financial distress. However, there are also many other advantages and disadvantages of increasing debt. Taken together, these factors strengthen the argument for optimal gearing. However, in the next section we examine a very different idea from the notion that the gearing ratio is reached as a result of fine adjustments between equity and debt to find an optimum.

### 8.5.4 Pecking order theory – perhaps we're looking at the whole problem from the wrong angle

Let us return to Lord Weinstock who we first met in Section 8.5.2. At GEC, Lord Weinstock was well known for being a very 'hands on' manager. All capital investment projects involving free cash flow had to be carefully justified to him before they could go ahead. Clearly, he must have been quite forbidding given that he was sitting on top of what was perceived by the new generation of managers as an excessive and needless cash pile. In fact his approach may have been much more sensible than it looked at the time in that he had a strong preference for internal capital over external capital – whether debt or equity. He had a tendency to hoard internal capital. This is consistent with a well-known theory of capital allocation, known as the **pecking order** theory.

The pecking order theory suggests that there are actually **three types of capital**, which are, in order of preference, internal funds, debt and external equity. Internal funds is cheaper and much easier to deploy than the other two. Of course, in a perfect capital market this distinction between internal and external capital would make no sense. If the firm had excess internal funds these would be invested in projects that yielded the market equilibrium rate of ROE. If no such projects were available, the money would be returned to the firm's investors who would be able to invest at the market rate in, depending on their taste for risk, either the debt or the equity of other firms, realising the *same* theoretical risk-adjusted return.

However, there are a number of problems with this traditional view of corporate investment. First, it suggests that firms are clear on exactly what *future* returns to investment are going to be. Second, it implies that the firm is fairly clear on what its future investment projects are going to be in the medium to long term. Third, it infers that the information known to the firm about future returns can be costlessly conveyed to debt and equity markets in order to secure the appropriate investment funds.

Clearly all of these conditions are regularly breached in real-life markets as opposed to perfect markets. First, estimates of investment returns may be highly speculative, and full of unknowns, and not at all to the tastes for risk of debt and equity markets. Second, investment opportunities may appear suddenly and have to be seized quickly using funds that can be easily and flexibly deployed – again something that might be difficult using external funding. However, perhaps the most important point is the third one. Firms, particularly innovative entrepreneurial firms, may have a very different view of the likely prospects of investment based on their own private internal information than do the capital markets, and the direct financial and indirect managerial time costs of trying to overcome the information asymmetry to convince external capital markets may be prohibitive. Furthermore, firms may be reluctant to reveal too much of their internal private information for fear of losing their competitive advantage.

Hence many firms may prefer to keep a cushion of internal capital and only resort to the markets when this is strictly necessary. Note the critical difference here from the previous sections. The firm does not 'select an optimal gearing ratio'. Rather, the gearing ratio follows from the strategic priorities and history of the firm, as the mini case study 'Pecking order theory – a subtly different approach' seems to imply.

## Mini case study

### Pecking order theory – a subtly different approach

Source *Economist* 2001

Managers prefer this kind of theory to the Modigliani–Miller one because it does not imply categorically that they are doing the wrong thing. But does it give them much guidance on what, in fact, they should be doing? Some would argue that in a way it does; that firms 'target' a credit rating they are happy with – according to the business they are in – and stick to it. Rick Escherich, an analyst at J.P. Morgan, has looked at a sample of 50 companies taken from *Fortune* magazine's list of 'most admired companies', and found that only four of them have been downgraded by more than one notch over the past ten years. Most of them have the same rating now as they did a decade ago.

However, Stephen Kealhofer of KMV says that, according to his firm's research, firms do not target credit ratings, indeed quite the opposite: 'We find that firms engage in anti-targeting behaviour.' Generally, they are more interested in their business plans than in what the rating agencies say. If they get into trouble, they increase their liabilities to enable them to carry out these plans, as the telecoms firms have done. 'Only when they get close to default do they reduce them,' he points out.

Mr Kealhofer prefers a third explanation of firms' behaviour, dubbed 'the pecking-order theory'. The central plank of this theory, first propounded by Stewart Myers in 1984, is that outside investors in a firm know less about the health of a firm than its managers do. That can be a problem when the company wants to issue equity: investors may believe, rightly or wrongly, that the company is doing this because it thinks its shares are overpriced, and may respond by selling them. Issuing debt generally has a much less dramatic effect, but external finance is still costly. That is why the vast majority of new capital raised by firms comes from retained profits.

The pecking-order theory might help to explain why many big firms hold large cash reserves. If they find that these are insufficient, they often take another route: to delay paying their bills. In effect, when they need to borrow, the first place they look to is their trade creditors. Only when that route becomes difficult do they turn to external lenders – i.e., banks or the bond market – and only as a last resort to the equity markets. That helps to explain why companies with stable profits often borrow a lot less than unprofitable ones.

1. Given the recent events in financial markets, do you think that the Pecking Order Theory is relevant to FTSE 100 companies?

There are two important points of note. First, it may not be as simple as a two-way split between external debt and equity. Rather it is very probable that the firm faces a three-way choice between external debt, external equity and internal funds. The fact that there has been a trend for stock market delisting and that venture capital companies tend to 'take companies private' for example, suggests that internal funds may be preferable to external capital.

Second, firms may not select a point on a graph that is the optimal gearing ratio. Rather, pecking order theory suggests that the gearing ratio follows from and does not determine other strategic decisions. Thus the gearing ratio is a result of the historical investment decisions and capital needs rather than fine-tuning between debt and equity. There are also practical considerations to take into account, as highlighted in the next Active learning activity.

## Active learning activity 8.6

### Higher or lower?

There are almost always reasons both for and against higher gearing. There is probably no well-defined optimal level. List the key considerations that a finance manager might take into account.

## Key concepts

- **Asymmetric information** refers to an imbalance in the information known by two parties
- An **agency problem** occurs when a conflict of interest arises between the owner of the business and the agents hired to run the business on his or her behalf
- **Reinvestment risk** is the risk that capital will be reinvested at a lower potential rate of return than the WACC
- **Operational slack** is a reason for companies to maintain a non-maximised debt ratio. It is spare borrowing capacity that can be used if an attractive investment opportunity reveals itself
- **Pecking order** theory suggests that there are three types of capital. Ranked in order of preference they are internal funds, debt and external equity

## 8.6 Summary

This chapter has explained the main component parts of the capital structure of a company. The cost of debt is the market return demanded by debt-holders and the cost of equity is the expected rate of return demanded by the company's shareholders. The proportions of each type of debt or equity are weighted in their respective proportions, multiplied by their respective costs, and this calculation results in the weighted average cost of capital – the WACC.

Gearing, or leverage, is the proportion of debt to equity in the capital structure. The traditional perspective is that there is some optimal gearing ratio. However, Modigliani and Miller argue that, under certain assumptions and in the absence of tax, capital structure is irrelevant. In a later paper, tax is introduced, and the tax shield effect means that they advocate a high level of debt to maximise company value.

Operational risk is caused by operational gearing and financial risk is caused by financial gearing. Operational gearing refers to the magnitude of fixed cost in the firm's day-to-day operations, and the variability in performance caused by this. The financial gearing effect is the addition to operational fixed cost arising from the fixed cost of debt finance.

We also set out arguments as to why the pecking order approach may capture a subtle truth missed by both Modigliani and Miller and the traditional approach. The pecking order theory suggests that there are actually three types of capital, which are, in order of preference, internal funds, debt and external equity.

We close by observing that pecking order theory, though interesting and useful to know, is by no means a part of the orthodox theory of capital structuring decisions. The 'consensus', if we may call it such, is that there is an optimal capital debt/equity mix at the point where the benefit of the tax shield on cheaper debt starts to be offset by higher required return on debt because of the increasing risk of financial distress. When taken together with the other practical and empirical reasons for lower or higher gearing, there probably is an optimal gearing range, though there may not be a single point ratio for leverage.

# Questions

1. Outline and discuss the main differences between debt and equity.

2. Consider a five year 12% bond issued by firm A, which is presently selling at £1,037. Using the internal rate of return, work out the return on the bond and hence the cost of the firm's debt capital.

3. The beta of firm A is 1.5, the risk-free rate is 3% and the return on the FTSE all-share index is 12%. What is the firm's cost of equity?

4. If shares in firm A have an annual dividend of 10p with no prospect of growth, what is the value of a share in A?

5. If firm A has issued one thousand bonds and one million shares and the tax rate is 20%, what is its cost of capital?

6. What are the main differences between:

   a) operational and financial risk?

   b) operational and financial gearing?

   c) leveraged and unleveraged beta?

7. What kinds of factors make a firm more vulnerable to financial distress with increased leverage?

8. In which ways does pecking order theory differ from the conventional M and M versus orthodoxy debate on gearing?

9. In both their dividend irrelevancy hypothesis (discussed in the next chapter) and the capital structure irrelevancy hypothesis, Modigliani and Miller base their argument on a particular view of what determines firm value. With particular respect to Modigliani and Miller's concept of firm value, outline and discuss this concept.

10. The following possible financial structures are proposed for AcmeFireBang, a novelties company. Tax is ignored.

    - Structure 1: all-equity – 10 million shares sold at a nominal value of £1

    - Structure 2: 30% debt – £3 million debt (carrying 10% interest) and £7 million equity

    - Structure 3: 50% debt – £5 million debt (carrying 11% interest) and £5 million equity

      The company does not know how much it will earn before profits, interest and tax in the future. However, it estimates that it will be one of the following:

    - Modest £0.5 million

    - Good £3 million

    - Excellent £4 million

    a) Complete the calculations (i) to (v) on the following spreadsheet for ROE and WACC under these three scenarios for all three proposed capital structures.

|  | Structure 1 (0 debt) | Structure 2 (30% debt) | Structure 3 (50% debt) |
|---|---|---|---|
| **Modest** |  |  |  |
| Profit before interest (£ million) | 0.5 | 0.5 | 0.5 |
| Less interest payments (£ million) | 0 | 0.3 | 0.55 |
| ROE (%) | 5.00 | 2.86 | (iii) |
| WACC (%) | (i) | 5.00 | 5.00 |
| **Good** |  |  |  |
| Profit before interest (£ million) | 3 | 3 | 3 |
| Less interest payments (£ million) | 0 | 0.3 | 0.55 |
| ROE (%) | 30.00 | (ii) | (iv) |
| WACC (%) | 30.00 | 30.00 | 30.00 |
| **Excellent** |  |  |  |
| Profit before interest (£ million) | 4 | 4 | 4 |
| Less interest payments (£ million) | 0 | 0.3 | 0.55 |
| ROE (%) | 40.00 | 52.86 | (v) |
| WACC (%) | 40.00 | 40.00 | 40.00 |

b) With reference to the table above, indicate and elaborate on the effect of financial gearing.

## Case study

### Morrison steals a march on rival Tesco

Source Braithwaite and Urry 2008, Copyright *Financial Times*, 2008

Wm Morrison cemented its position as the fastest growing of the listed supermarkets with a third-quarter trading update that left rivals in the shade. The grocery chain recorded like-for-like sales growth of 8.1 per cent, excluding petrol, and announced it would buy 38 stores from the Co-operative Group as it invested in expansion.

The trading update, which beat analysts' expectations, followed an anaemic performance by Tesco, the UK's biggest retailer, which this week reported 2 per cent like-for-like sales growth during its third quarter and gambled on winning over cash-strapped customers with its 'discount brands' strategy.

Describing Tesco as 'the world's best retailer', Marc Bolland, chief executive of Morrison, nonetheless noted that he was 'enjoying the challenge'.

'Once again we have grown our like-for-like sales well ahead of the market,' he said. 'We are continuing to do particularly well in London, the south and Scotland ... We don't always take customers in from Tesco; we gain customers from all our major competitors.'

Morrison's total sales in the 13 weeks to November 2 rose 14.9 per cent, or 9.5 per cent excluding fuel. Tesco has said that its numbers were dragged down by the decision to introduce cheaper brands, although that strategy would prevail in the medium term.

'We are following carefully what happens at Tesco,' said Mr Bolland. 'Our own price offer is so strong. ... we would not do [something similar] now.'

Morrison said that its numbers still contained some inflation but that most of the increase came from new customers and that inflation had peaked.

The UK's fourth-largest supermarket group, Morrison said it was buying 38 stores from the Co-op for £223m, plus costs of £98m. Along with the acquisition of a distribution centre, Morrison is to spend £403m.

John Kershaw, analyst at Merrill Lynch, said the transaction showed, 'Morrison's ambition but at a price'. He reckoned the deal, which involves smaller stores than the average Morrisons supermarket, 'only just covers its weighted average cost of capital'.

The move is the first big expansion by Morrison since it acquired Safeway in 2004, a deal that took longer than expected to integrate successfully. The Co-op deal would be earnings enhancing in the 2010–11 financial year, the company said.

Morrison added it would now curtail its planned share buy-back to finance the £403m of investments. Shares in Morrison fell 5¾p to close at 244¾p.

1. What is the minimum return a company should make on any investment?

2. Discuss whether there are problems if the deal – Morrisons buying the Co-op stores – 'only just covers its WACC'.

3. Why did the price of Morrison's shares fall on announcement of the deal?

# Further reading

Bancal, F. and Mittoo, U. (2004) Cross-country determinants of capital structure choice: a survey of European firms. *Financial Management* 33(4). Available at http://ssrn.com/abstract=594781.
This paper considers the factors that determine capital structure across various European countries.

Barclay, M., Smith, J. and Clifford, W. (2005) The capital structure puzzle: the evidence revisited. *Journal of Applied Corporate Finance* 17(1):8–17.
This paper attempts to reconcile the different theories of capital structure and considers the capital structure puzzle.

Huang, G. and Song, F.M. (2006) The determinants of capital structure: evidence from China. *China Economic Review* 17(1):14–36.
This paper analyses the determinants of capital structure in China.

Modigliani, F. and Miller, M.H. (1958) The cost of capital, corporation finance and the theory of investment. *American Economic Review* 48(3):261–297.
The classic paper that explains M and M proposition 1.

Modigliani, F. and Miller, M.H. (1963) Corporate income taxes and the cost of capital: a correction. *American Economic Review* 53(3):433–443.
The classic paper that explains M and M proposition 2.

## Internet references

http://online.wsj.com/article/sb124027187331937083.html
An article detailing some of the history of the effects of capital structure and its contribution to recent recessions.

http://thatswacc.com/
An online tool that calculates the WACC of any company listed on the NYSE, AMEX or NSDQ stock exchanges.

## Suggestions for group work

Students should try to calculate the appropriate WACC for a listed company. They should describe the process, the difficulties in identifying the inputs to the process and the confidence that they have in their final result.

## Suggestions for presentations

1. Students should be divided into teams of two. Each team should take an opposing view on the merits of low debt versus high debt and be prepared to argue their case with reference to practical examples.

2. With regard to Modigliani and Miller propositions 1 and 2, students should prepare either group or individual presentations on the implications of both M and M propositions for modern businesses.

# 9 Dividend Policy

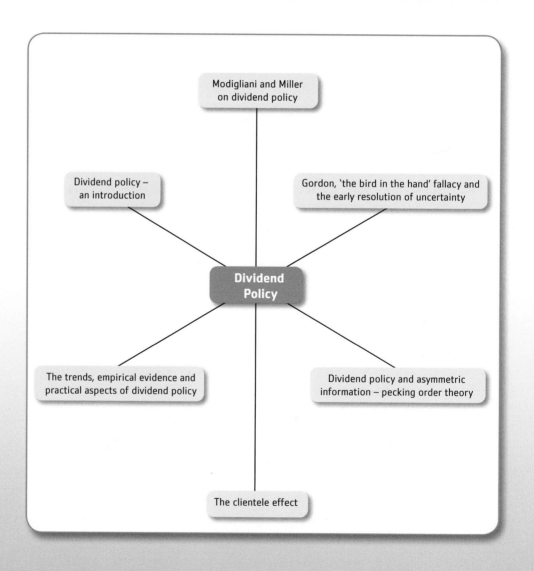

- Modigliani and Miller on dividend policy
- Dividend policy – an introduction
- Gordon, 'the bird in the hand' fallacy and the early resolution of uncertainty
- Dividend Policy
- The trends, empirical evidence and practical aspects of dividend policy
- Dividend policy and asymmetric information – pecking order theory
- The clientele effect

## Knowledge-based learning objectives

When you have completed this chapter you will be able to:

✓ Understand why a clear statement on dividends is important for investors
✓ Understand the theoretical position of Modigliani and Miller in relation to dividend policy
✓ Discern why dividend irrelevance still holds, whether or not investors have a rate of discount equal to the firm's rate of return on capital
✓ Appreciate Gordon's dividend theory and why it is considered by most informed commentators to be a 'bird in the hand' fallacy
✓ Understand the pecking order hypothesis and the theoretical conditions under which it might hold
✓ Appreciate the reasons why, contrary to Modigliani and Miller, there may well be a clientele effect
✓ Appreciate the practical issues involved in dividend policy

## Skills-based learning objectives development

✓ Business and financial environment consciousness: you should have developed an appreciation of the effects of different dividend policies risks in the international financial environment.
✓ Numerical skills: you should have developed the ability to calculate the amount of dividends to be paid under different policies.
✓ Analytical thinking and problem-solving skills: you should have developed an understanding of the merits and limitations of the various theories of dividend policies.
✓ Problem-solving skills: you should have developed the ability to apply your knowledge to recommend suitable dividend policies.
✓ Critical-thinking skills: you should be able to understand the practical implications of different dividend policies.
✓ Managerial soft skills: you should have developed the ability to know how the strategies would apply in organisations you have worked in or with which you are familiar.
✓ Interpersonal skills: you should have developed your ability to present your work clearly both verbally and in writing and to interact with others effectively upon completion of the end of chapter questions.

## Online resource centre

Visit the Online Resource Centre that accompanies this book to listen to a podcast of the authors discussing the dividend policy of a selection of FT100 companies.
www.oxfordtextbooks.co.uk/marney

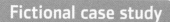

## Fictional case study

### OrganicX find that dividend policy matters

Kate is poring over the projected financial statements for the coming year. As usual, she is surrounded by spreadsheets. Charlie enters her office full of news about the latest opportunities available to OrganicX and launches into a glowing description of growth opportunities in China.

Kate looks up, a frown on her face. 'It's perhaps not such a good time to be thinking about expansion, Charlie ...' she begins, but Charlie jumps right in.

'How can you say that, Kate? Demand for our products is huge! We need to expand now – first mover advantage and all that!'

Kate sighs. As usual, she has to be the 'bad guy' and rein in Charlie's exuberance. 'You know the debt markets are very tight just now, Charlie – it's not a good time to be looking for more money to expand. Besides, our institutional investors are expecting a big increase in dividend payments this year. We did promise a target rate of 20% of profit after tax each year and that's what they will be expecting. With profits at record levels, we have to make good on our commitment to pay up. We just won't be able to invest in all the projects you want to do this year once we pay the dividends.'

Charlie waves his hand dismissively. 'Surely they will be the first to realise that they stand to make more in the long run if we invest more now? Let's just do it. These investors work in the city – they understand better than anyone that you need to invest in order to grow.'

'It's not quite so simple,' replies Kate, 'and it could affect our share price quite badly if we suddenly change our dividend policy at the last minute.'

Charlie thinks for a minute and comes up with what he thinks is the perfect counter-argument to Kate's worries. 'What about companies such as Google? They have never paid a dividend and yet the stock price doesn't seem to suffer. In fact, Google do exactly what I want to do – reinvest to grow.'

'Yes', replies Kate, 'but Google never made any promises to pay dividends to their investors in the near future. The point is that you can't suddenly change your dividend policy.'

'But why?' asks Charlie, puzzled as to why one company can get away without paying dividends and yet his company appears to be obliged to pay out money which, as far as he is concerned, makes no sense when opportunities to invest abound.

As usual, Kate has an answer, and she begins, 'Quite apart from the ethics of going back on our word, there is also the clientele effect. ...'

## 9.1 Dividend policy – an introduction

This chapter examines the theories that underpin a firm's **dividend policies** and the realities that are observed in the market. Traditionally the ability to pay a dividend has been seen as a marker of company well-being, but, matters are not so simple. For example, it was reported in November 2008 that well-known British companies such as DSG International, owner of the Currys and PC World chains, and Mitchells & Butlers, the pubs group, had both scrapped their dividends. This is by no means normal everyday behaviour on the part of companies, which in more conventional times would usually try to keep the dividend as stable as possible. However, the times were not normal. Companies needed to retain cash to shore up their depleted balance sheets following the high cost and sheer unavailability of debt finance post credit crunch. The most interesting point to come out of all of this was that despite the fact that the 15% fall in dividends for UK companies was higher than the 5% fall observed during the recession of the 1990s, companies were not punished by markets. They themselves recognised that the times were extraordinary and that firms' need to cope with debt problems came before the requirement to pay dividend.[1]

As these particular examples suggests, company dividends were only radically altered because of the abnormal situation in which the companies found themselves. Company dividends are normally very steady and only changed after very careful consideration by companies. In particular companies are very reluctant to lower dividends as this is not usually well received by the market and tends to have a very adverse effect on the share price, as Punch Taverns found to its cost. Yet a few weeks later, Mitchell and Butler, a very similar type of company, cut their dividend without any kind of adverse effect. This reaction to changes in dividend does not fit very well with both of the theoretical models that we have of why firms pay dividends and what equity holders expect in terms of dividends and capital gains.

The view that a cut in the dividend is bad news and will lead to a fall in share price, while the converse applies in the case of an increase in the dividend, is so commonplace that it might almost be referred to as the 'commonsense' view of dividend policy. The reason for this is that the investor lives in a world of unknowns and uncertainty.

Therefore a change in the dividend may signal information previously known only to the firm and unknown to the market. When, as in this case, there is a cut in dividend, the market quickly revises down its expectation of future income and future dividends. As in the previous chapter on capital gearing, clearly **imperfect information** and **information asymmetry** potentially play a big part in the relationship between firms and their equity investors. Changes in dividend, by sending out a particular signal, can have a significant impact. However, many companies are not very forthcoming about their dividend policy, as we discover in the mini case study 'Firms and their dividend policies'.

## Mini case study

### Firms and their dividend policies

Source Lee 2008, Copyright *Financial Times*, 2008

With falling interest rates making cash on deposit increasingly unattractive, one would have expected that historically high equity dividend yields would be a factor in changing market sentiment. But the reason that few investors are buying into these yields is because they doubt their maintainability – fearing savage dividend cuts as companies struggle with falling orders and high borrowings.

My contention is that more companies could reassure shareholders if they were more open.

Too many seem to be members of 'Dividends Anonymous' – their attitude is to say as little as possible on dividend policy, keeping shareholders guessing until the payout is announced in a two-line statement in the preliminary results.

For example, I was shocked when Christie Group, the business/leisure industry services company, slashed its interim dividend by two-thirds – in spite of being debt-free – with hardly a word of explanation nor indication of what future dividend policy might be. Rest assured, I made my views known!

Three other purchases – T Clarke, the electrical contractor; Marshalls, the building industry supplier; and Vitec, the broadcasting equipment provider – have all issued trading statements in the past few weeks but none has given any indication on dividends. I am optimistic that T Clarke and Vitec will at least maintain their dividends – both yielding around double figures. But I haven't a clue what Marshalls will do given its difficult trading environment – its shares currently yield approaching 20 per cent.

There seems to be a collective neurosis among some boards that any indication of future dividends amounts to a 'forecast' which could result in them all being clapped in irons.

Some companies have no inhibitions. Primary Health Properties says in its interim statement: 'The Group remains dedicated to a strong, increasing dividend yield.' Severfield-Rowen, the structured steel specialist, said: 'Following consultation with share-holders, the board has decided to adopt a prudent dividend policy designed to support a more sustainable dividend across the economic cycle, whilst also delivering a progressive dividend during periods of growth.'

With many equities on double-figure but uncertain yields, the maintenance of that dividend can clearly significantly affect a share price. So the overall message to boards is: please share with us your thoughts on dividend policy – more comprehensively and more frequently.

1. What are the advantages to firms of being clear about their future plans for dividends in the medium to long run?
2. What are the disadvantages?
3. Do you think there are commercial reasons why many firms seem reluctant to commit themselves to a clear statement on dividend policy?

Given the strong signal that a dividend change can send out, it is surprising that not all companies clearly communicate their dividend policy.

There are a number of possible explanations for this. The first is that many companies are not keen on making any information public, lest they inadvertently give away competitive advantage to their rivals. Companies are thus naturally secretive, and publicly quoted companies always have to 'walk a tightrope' between their duty of public disclosure to their investors and the need for commercial secrecy. Thus they may reveal the minimum necessary. Second, it may be that some companies are unwilling to relinquish control of important information as this dilutes the power of management and passes it to 'outsiders', i.e. investors. In other words, what we have here is another aspect of the principal-agent problem.

A third reason is that, contrary to what might be expected from economic theory, some management teams are better than others and have different skills and abilities, such as the ability to communicate and persuade. Nevertheless, at least some shareholders may be happy to look beyond the management team's ability to 'put a spin on things' and recognise that they have other abilities that are value-adding.

Finally, we turn to the world of theory for explanation. There are two main theories of dividend policy and both suggest, surprisingly, that large variation in dividends, at least in the short to medium run, should not matter either because capital markets are close to perfect, or for the practical reason that firms carefully plan dividends to ensure smoothness and continuity.

Hence, it behoves us to set dividend policy within a proper analytical framework so that we can be more informed about the impact of changes in dividend.

As with capital gearing theory, much of the original dividend literature was developed by Modigliani and Miller in a celebrated seminal article (Miller and Modigliani 1961). This is the subject of the next section.

## Practical implications for managers

### How much should be revealed to shareholders?

In this section we have explored the idea that shareholders can become frustrated if little or nothing is revealed about how much exactly the firm plans to invest and how much will be distributed to shareholders in the medium to long term. The manager must 'walk a tightrope' between the requirements of 'due disclosure' and the extra information needed to reassure the market (sometimes known as 'signalling') and the discretion necessitated by not revealing too much to competitors.

## Key concepts

- **Imperfect information** is when market participants do not know all the relevant facts about their investment choices
- **Information asymmetry** is when one party in a relationship (such as the agency relationship between company managers and shareholders) holds an information advantage over the other
- **Dividend policy** describes how a company decides on both the amount and form of dividend payment to distribute to shareholders.

# 9.2 Modigliani and Miller on dividend policy

## 9.2.1 Modigliani and Miller's assumptions

Modigliani and Miller (1961) are nothing if not consistent, and apply the same principles to dividend theory that they apply to capital gearing policy. These are as follows:

1. The value of the firm should depend on the value of cash flow from its investment projects discounted at a rate appropriate to the risk of these projects.

2. Value should depend fundamentally on day-to-day business ability and not on the way the firm is financed.

3. Otherwise, firm value could be manipulated through financial engineering without any change in the firm's fundamental business activities and investment projects.

In this case, the choice is not one between debt and equity, but between retained earnings and dividend payout. According to Modigliani and Miller in this case, it should not matter whether the firm's projects are financed from the retention of dividends or from a fresh issue of equity, as they are entirely equivalent. This may sound like something of a strong statement, but bear in mind that we are back again in the theoretical world of neoclassical economics and the **frictionless** world of **perfect competition**. The assumptions that Modigliani and Miller made were the following:

1. There are no taxes.

2. There is perfect information. All information that needs to be known to value the firm or the firm's projects is known. That is, information is either known with certainty or, in the case where the information is uncertain, it can be precisely quantified.

3. Firms can be classified into distinct risk classes. This is related to assumption 2 as this assumption implies that we know precisely how risky the firm and its projects are.

4. There are perfect capital markets, in which it is possible to borrow and lend at the risk-free rate. An additional and very controversial assumption concerning capital markets is that it is possible to raise fresh equity without incurring substantial transactions costs such as merchant bankers' management fees and underwriting costs.

5. Capital is perfectly divisible into any size of unit. For example, £2 million of capital can be reduced to £100,000 worth of capital without any disruption to the firm's business or any reduction in percentage return. All that happens is that operations are scaled down proportionally.

6. By the same token, capital can be scaled up by any amount without disruption to the firm or any change in the firm's percentage return.

 **Active learning activity 9.1**

### Fictional frictionless?

Explore the concept of the perfect frictionless market. Do you think financial markets come closer to being frictionless markets than other markets? Are financial markets frictionless enough to warrant being called perfect markets?

Again, Modigliani and Miller's position can be summarised as the idea that there are no 'free lunches' or costless riskless gain. If it were possible to boost the firm's value by altering the dividend payout, then surely it would be done? If investors preferred to maximise the growth of their incomes, and therefore would pay more for shares with greater future income, then surely most firms would pay out low or no dividends in order to retain profits for investment?

If, on the other hand, investors preferred the certainty of dividends now as opposed to the uncertainty of dividends in the future then surely all firms would be maximising payouts while retaining the minimum necessary to keep the firm in business? The answer to this is, from Modigliani and Miller's point of view, that investors, *assuming* that they have perfect information, will already know what current and future dividends are sustainable by the firm. Their reasoning follows in the next section.

### 9.2.2 The conditions under which current cash flow and future cash flow are equivalent, and therefore the timing of dividends is irrelevant

Recall the dividend pricing model of share valuation in which, provided there is no expected growth in the firm's revenues, the value of a firm and its shares can be represented as a simple problem in perpetuity valuation.

$P_t = d/r$

Let us suppose that the share pays a dividend of £100 per share, which in percentage terms is 10% of capital employed per share. All earnings are paid out as dividends. Capital employed per share is £1,000. The price of the share is of course as follows:

£1,000 = £100/0.1

Imagine that shareholders now clamoured for an increase in dividend. The only way to bring this about would be to eat into capital. Thus if it were decided to double next year's dividend to £200, this would reduce capital employed by £100 to £900 in Year 1. Given that capital is returning 10%, earnings from the capital invested would be reduced to £90 per year. The price of the share would now be equal to the sum of the following components: (1) the discounted cash flow from the double dividend next year; plus (2) the prospect of a perpetuity cash flow worth £90 continuing from Year 2, as follows:

Pt = (1) £200/1.1 + (2) (£90/0.1) × (1/1.1)

or

Pt = £200/1.1 + £900/1.1

which is the equivalent of

Pt = 181.82 + 818.18 = £1000

Note that the £90 is discounted as a perpetuity starting in Year 1, then it is further 'discounted back' to Year 0. As we can see, the value per share is still £1,000 in present value (PV) terms.

As has been demonstrated, the investor is also no better or worse off if the firm brings the dividend forward. The PV of future income remains the same.

A similar argument would apply if the investors were more parsimonious and wanted to postpone the dividend in order to add to capital employed. Suppose now that investors wanted to forego £50 worth of dividend in order to augment capital invested. Capital employed would rise to £1,050. This would return a cash flow of £105 in perpetuity. The requisite valuation of the share would be the sum of (1) the discounted value of the new lower dividend next year, plus (2) the perpetuity value of the new higher level of capital in Year 1, discounted back to Year 0. That is:

$$Pt = £50/1.1 + (£105/0.1) \times (1/1.1)$$
$$Pt = £50/1.1 + £1050 \times 1/1.1$$
$$Pt = £45.45 + £954.55 = £1000$$

An analogous line of reasoning could be applied to the value of the firm, as was applied to the value of the firm's shares. If shareholder value does not change, then neither does the value of the firm. The value of an all-equity firm is just equal to the value per share times the number of shares. Thus if the firm had issued 10,000 shares, the equity value of the firm would be £1,000,000 and would be unaffected by dividend policy for precisely the reasons that apply in the case of individual shares.

This then is Modigliani and Miller's fundamental proposition. The value of the firm is fundamentally determined by the net present value (NPV) from its investments and is not in any way dependent on the timing of dividends. It makes *no* difference whether large amounts of dividend are paid now, or large amounts are retained to provide larger future dividends – provided the rate of return on the firm's investments equals the investors' discount rate.

It is worth bearing in mind the precise condition under which this is true. It is when the firm's rate of return on equity capital is precisely the same as the discount rate applied by investors which allows them to translate future value into present. Any current income sacrificed by investors earns a percentage return at exactly the right discount rate to make it equivalent to current income. Any future income sacrificed by investors will be losing only the future return which would have made it exactly equivalent to current income.

The condition that the rate of return on capital is *exactly* equal to the return required by investors could be seen as a little restrictive. Would dividend irrelevance still hold if they had a different required return from the one on offer? This is the subject of the next section.

### 9.2.3 Dividend irrelevance still holds when required return does not equal return on capital (for a minority of investors)

From time to time, of course investors will find that their circumstances have changed. In particular, the amount they can save to invest and their need for current income will change, depending on their circumstances and their stage in the lifecycle.

So, for example, older people who have been saving for retirement will want to start to free up savings and investment in order to be able to spend freely in their old age. If the firm had a substantial minority of this type of investor, should it bring the dividend forward in the manner suggested in the example on the doubling of the dividend in Section 9.2.2? After all, the other investors would not mind, given that the discount rate they are applying is 10%.

However, this is unlikely to satisfy a minority clientele who have developed a need for cash. This is because, desiring a higher cash to future income ratio, they are now more time impatient than the average investor, and, in effect, their discount rate has increased well beyond 10%.

If their personal rate of discount has increased beyond 10%, the PV of the future income stream from dividends is now worth less than the current cash value of the shares for the impatient investor. For example, if the need for cash pushes their discount rate to 20% as that cash is at a premium for them, then the PV of the dividends is now only worth £916.67 to these individuals.

However, they can make an immediate gain by selling for £1,000 per share something that they only value at £916.67 per share. That is, they can make 'home-made' dividends to meet their cash needs. They can sell stock until their cash needs are alleviated and their personal cash becomes more abundant relative to future income. Consequently, they will become less time impatient and their personal discount rate will fall back in line with return on offer from the firm's investments (10%).

By the same token, the firm need not postpone dividends if there is a substantial minority of investors who are more time patient than the majority. For example, there may be a significant fraction of investors who are young, affluent and childless. They don't spend all their income and are looking for ways of channelling their surplus funds into saving, investment and future income. Indeed, their relative time patience may be such that their personal rate of discount is lower than the average rate for investors of 10%. What they should do according to Modigliani and Miller is to 'mop up' their surplus funds by buying more shares. As they do this, their surplus funds will fall relative to the income necessary for current expenditure. Thus they will become more time impatient and their personal discount rate will rise once more to 10%.

In all of the examples above, there was no change in the composition of the firm's investment projects. Is this a critical omission? Let us suppose now that the firm wished to invest in a positive NPV project. In order to do this, it needs to raise more capital.

This introduces an important additional point that Modigliani and Miller make in the context of dividend policy. It makes no difference whether **additional capital** is raised from existing shareholders by withholding the dividend or whether it is raised by issuing a new set of shares. Clearly, rational shareholders would be willing to forego the dividend as the return on the firm's new investment project is, by definition, greater than the average investor's rate of discount, given that the NPV on the proposed new project is greater than zero.

However, if there were a substantial (but noisy) minority who would object to dividend retention, then the firm could raise the equity through the issue of more shares, e.g. a **rights issue**, so that those investors who did have discount rates of 10% could take advantage of the new wealth-creating opportunity. We sum up Modigliani and Miller's valuable insights in the following section.

### 9.2.4 Some conclusions on Modigliani and Miller and on their use of assumptions

In short then, we can conclude the following from Modigliani and Miller.

First, if all investors have the same time preference and discount rate, and that this is equal to the firm's return on equity, it makes no difference when investors receive their dividend. Whether it is now, next year or 10 years hence; all that matters is that the PV is in each case the same, which it should be given the assumption that the rate of return on equity capital is equal to the rate of discount of investors.

Second, if personal discount rates are different for a minority of investors, those who feel that the current dividend is too low or who would be unwilling to forego dividend for further investment can make **home-made dividends** by selling stock. Those who feel that the dividend is more than they need can reinvest it in the company's stock. There is no need for the company to compromise its dividend policies to accommodate these minority clienteles.

Notice the way in which the 'no free lunch' principle runs through all of this. There is no point in either bringing dividends forward or postponing them, as the NPV of dividends is always the same – provided all investors have the *same* discount rate. Even those investors who do not have the same discount rate as the majority and who would benefit from bringing forward or delaying dividend can solve their problem themselves, by selling or buying shares on the frictionless capital market. They do not need the company to do it for them.

Third, it does not matter to the firm whether new positive NPV projects are financed by dividend retention or by a new issue of shares, as new equity can be issued on the frictionless capital market at exactly the same cost, namely, the required return on equity.

Finally, it should be noted that again Modigliani and Miller rely on arbitrage to keep their propositions in place. For example, if there were perfect information and frictionless markets, the issue of shares would be a simple process of issuing certificates of ownership. If it were more costly to issue new shares, firms would retain dividends beyond the preferences of investors. They would therefore have to offer higher returns on existing shares. Returns would be bid up to the point where there was no difference between the cost of equity on existing shares and the cost of equity on new share issue.

 **Active learning activity 9.2**

#### Assumptions and conclusions

Suggest some ways in which the relaxation of Modigliani and Millers' assumptions would affect their conclusions.

What happens if there are differential taxes for dividends and capital gains?

## Practical implications for managers

**How do practical people draw conclusions from abstract models?**

There are at least two reasons why the models discussed above may not hold. First, what are called **transactions costs** mean that the 'costless' adjustments to accommodate the dividend-investment decisions suggested by Modigliani and Miller are actually very costly and inconvenient. Rights issues and shareholder reinvestment/home-made dividends may not allow the flexibility implied in the Modigliani and Miller model when we step outside the 'perfect frictionless market'. Also, as well as being costly, transactions may be subject to much more unquantifiable uncertainty because of asymmetric information.

## Key concepts

- **Frictionless** markets are ones that have no taxes and transaction costs
- **Perfect competition** is a market state in which there are many buyers and sellers, perfect information, homogeneous goods and no transaction costs
- The **'no free lunch'** principle states that you cannot create additional value in finance without taking on increased risk
- **Home-made dividends** can be made by selling stock to raise capital, essentially simulating a dividend payout
- **Transactions costs** are expenditures that must be paid when transaction with a third party occurs, such as buying shares or issuing equity
- A **rights issue** is an issue of stock by a firm which is already established on the stock market (newcomers usually issue stock through an Initial Public Offering)

## 9.3 Gordon, 'the bird in the hand' fallacy and the early resolution of uncertainty

The alternative view of dividends is that they are a highly uncertain residual. That is, dividends are paid from earnings after expenses, tax, interest and depreciation. In other words, shareholders come at the end of a fairly long queue waiting for payment, after suppliers, employees of the company, the government and investors in company debt. Only after all of the forgoing have been paid can the firm determine whether there is a surplus or not. And even if there is a surplus, there is no obligation on the part of the firm to make this surplus over to shareholders. They can if they wish retain the surplus for reinvestment purposes.

Of course the firm should not arbitrarily retain profits. In making the decision to retain earnings or pay the dividend, the firm should compare the return on earnings versus the shareholders' required return, or cost of equity (shareholders required return), and only retain earnings if there are positive NPV projects with return greater than the cost of equity. If return is less than the cost of equity and projects have negative NPV, then clearly the firm should reduce investment and retained earnings, and return greater amounts of dividends to the shareholders. None of this of course is inconsistent with Modigliani and Miller and the standard view of efficient markets in which wealth maximising firms automatically allocate shareholders' capital efficiently.

However, consider real-life issues which may cause the everyday 'here and now' firm's actions to diverge from this idealised view. One possible problem is the problem of **'hubris'** and overinvestment, particularly when it comes to takeovers of other firms. The potential gains from takeovers are notoriously difficult to value, given that much of the information about the target firm may be in the form of private and tacit information which it is difficult for the acquiring firm to properly uncover. In addition, new investments such as takeovers are often predicated on the assumption of 'all other factors remaining equal'.

Take, for example, the radical revision in fortunes of the Royal Bank of Scotland over the course of one year which we have mentioned before. It had seemed to be 'riding the crest of a wave' with its takeover of the Dutch bank ABN Amro in 2007. However, the following year information began to emerge that the bank was badly exposed to sub-prime losses and also that it had paid too much for ABN Amro. In fact the market value of RBS's assets dropped so dramatically that the bank had to be rescued by the UK government. In 2008, the bank's shares had fallen to £0.22, in contrast with their value 1 year earlier of more than £3.[2]

The main point here is of course unpredictable and difficult-to-quantify uncertainty. If you had been an investor in RBS shares in 2006, could you possibly have foreseen the extent of the subsequent problems with this company? For example, many of the problems with ABN Amro's financial health only became apparent after the takeover by RBS. Thus, arguably, much of the requisite information was not publicly available and therefore there was a problem of asymmetric information. Again, RBS had been expanding rapidly by takeover until this expansion terminated with the takeover of ABN Amro. Prior to the ABN Amro takeover, how could you have told whether RBS's takeovers had been motivated by **hubris**, but with very fortunate outcomes, or by contrast, whether it was just very successful deal making? Furthermore, how was any investor to foresee the problems with sub-prime mortgages which greatly exacerbated problems in the banking sector, given that banks themselves did not foresee problems of this magnitude? Finally, given that mortgage-backed securities had been traded between banks in private and complex ways, even the banks themselves did not know the extent of their rivals' exposure to these instruments at the time of the credit crunch. How then was the average investor to know which banks were exposed?

In short, ex-ante or before the event, there was a great deal of asymmetric information; private information that the investor may not have been aware of, the risk of which may have been difficult to quantify using the standard approach based on discounting and normal distribution-based conventional statistics. First, because the information was not available to those outside the banks; second, because even those inside the banks did not have a full picture; and third, because those inside the banks were unaware of just how mistaken they

raising of debt capital can also be time consuming and expensive and may result in restraints on management's freedom of action in the form of covenants. Nevertheless, the problem of overcoming information asymmetry is less arduous in the case of debt than of equity, given the lower risk to the investor, though the least costly form of capital for the firm in terms of transaction cost would be internal equity from retained earnings. Therefore pecking order theory suggests that internal capital is preferred to debt, which is preferred to external equity.

It should be pointed out that pecking order theory, like Gordon's 'bird in the hand theory', remains controversial. Nevertheless, it is also consistent with the theory of agency and asymmetric information in that the form of capital with the greatest information asymmetry has the highest transaction cost and is therefore least preferable to the firm. A classic article that expands on the ideas that asymmetric information is positively associated with transaction cost is 'The market for lemons' by Akerlof (1970). Akerlof observed that in the second-hand car market, there were two types of cars – jewels, which were above-average cars which had been well maintained and were relatively problem-free, and lemons, which were problematic. The puzzle faced by car-buyers, however, was that there was no way of knowing which was which without undertaking significant additional cost. For example, prospective buyers could pay a mechanic to go along with them.

However, this relative cost of ascertaining the car's quality would be large relative to the difference in value between a 'jewel' and a 'lemon'. Furthermore, if other buyers were there at the same time, they would be able to know, without cost, about the car's quality as well (a problem known as the **free-rider problem**). Therefore, many buyers would not go to this trouble and the quality of the car would remain unknown. Thus the average price on the market would reflect the probability of buying a jewel versus buying a lemon. The price would be on the low side for owners of 'jewels' who would be reluctant to part with their cars on the market. On the other hand, owners of lemons would have a strong incentive to part with their cars, and therefore there would be a high proportion of lemons to jewels and a high probability of making a poor 'investment' in a second-hand car.

Akerlof's 'jewels and lemons' car market has strong parallels with the market for finance. This is because his representation of the used car market is one in which there is an *incomplete* market in which transactions may not go ahead because of *incomplete* information.

When firms are trying to borrow money, either in the form of equity or in the form of debt, it is not clear to the market whether they are 'jewels' or 'lemons'. Furthermore, the financial market faces a problem additional to that of the car market. This is because they are not buying an inanimate object such as a car. In essence they are buying the promise by the buyer that the debt or equity contract will be honoured. The performance of this contract in turn depends on the behaviour of the individuals who are seeking funds.

There are two possible problems. The first is that those who need funds in the first place may be those who are profligate and not good at managing money. This is the ex ante or 'before the event' problem of **adverse selection**. Those who typically want to borrow money from you are usually not those to whom you would care to lend. The other problem is the ex-post (after the event) problem of **moral hazard**. Once borrowers are in receipt of the money, they may relax and just fritter the money away, rather than trying their utmost to ensure the borrowed capital is used efficiently to achieve the agreed returns.

Thus there could be a strong preference on the part of firms for retaining dividends and using internal capital. The firm itself knows its capabilities and how investments are likely to perform. However, this information is private and it may be very costly to convey to external providers of capital. To some extent, financial intermediaries such as banks get over this problem. They have various techniques to guard against risk such as requiring borrowers to keep a certain minimum balance or requiring collateral. Furthermore, the bank may have an informational advantage over other external bodies if the firm is a long-standing customer.

Hence, a case can be made for the pecking order proposition, both in terms of the stylised facts – most firms still use internal capital or intermediated capital rather than disintermediated external capital, whether equity or bond-type debt, and from a theoretical perspective as well. It could be that for most firms the informational disadvantages are too costly to overcome. The implication of this version of the **pecking order theory** is that it would be difficult to arbitrage between the different forms of capital which should in principle have the same percentage cost on a risk-adjusted basis. Therefore, when firms do issue equity, they may have strong preferences for dividend retention given how expensive it is to issue more equity or debt. Investors may indeed have strong preferences for earlier dividends to resolve information problems and uncertainty. This is the subject of the next section.

## Practical implications for managers

### The pecking order

Consider your own firm. Who owns the equity in the firm? Is there a single owner? Would external equity be difficult to raise? For example, would you have to approach a venture capitalist and lose effective control of the firm? Would it be feasible to list on a small less-regulated exchange like the UK's AIM? Are you in a position to issue bonds? Unless your firm was fairly large, this is unlikely. How difficult and costly would it be to raise external debt?

## Key concepts

- ☐ The **free-rider problem** is when a profit can be made through the actions of another party, disincentivising the action happening in the first place
- ☐ **Adverse selection** occurs when the least suitable applicants are the most likely to apply for financial help
- ☐ A **moral hazard** occurs if there is an incentive to act contrary to a financial agreement
- ☐ **Pecking order theory** suggests that companies value certain kinds of financing over others once the agreement is in place

## 9.5 The clientele effect

In addition to the possibility that firms may have preferences for dividend retention greater than would be predicted by Modigliani and Miller because of the pecking order, the **clientele effect** argues that shareholders may gravitate to firms with particular patterns of dividend payout, contrary to what was predicted by Modigliani and Miller. In their view of things, it did not matter what clientele the firm attracted, in terms of shareholders' preferences for dividends now versus dividends in the future. If shareholders wanted more or fewer current dividends than was currently on offer from the firm, they could make 'home-made dividends' or reinvest – according to time preference.

However, in real life, the purchase and sale of shares is not a costless process. Therefore shareholders may gravitate towards company shares with dividends that match their time preference.

We talked earlier of individuals who had different preferences of dividends depending on their stage in life. **Institutional investors**, who often represent a far larger proportion of share purchasers than individuals, may also have strong preferences between shares based on the timing of dividends.

For example, pension funds and insurance companies have to closely match cash flow receivable from assets with cash flow payable on liabilities over time. As pensions become due for payment, it is imperative that the cash from investments is available at the right time to make these payments.

While pension funds as large investors probably have lower percentage dealing costs than most, actual dividends tend to have more stable values than 'home-made dividends', or share sales, which will depend unavoidably on selling into potentially volatile markets. Another type of institutional investor, investment trusts, are often divided into growth funds, which rely on low dividends and high capital gains from growth stocks, and income funds, which are looking for a steady stream of relatively high dividends. Again, they will have differing needs and preferences for dividend payout versus dividend retention.

Another reason for clientele effects is to do with the **tax treatment of dividends** versus changes in capital value (i.e. percentage gain or loss in the value of the investment). Dividends are treated as income and taxed at the same rate as income, while capital gains are sometimes taxed at a separate and usually lower rate. Furthermore, the tax system may discriminate between short-term capital gains and long-term capital gains, the former usually being taxed more highly than the latter. These observations apply broadly to the US, and thus there are strong reasons in the US context to believe that there could be strong preferences between dividends now and dividends in the future.

In the UK, by contrast, there is now little difference between taxes on dividends and capital gains for the individual investor. In both cases, tax is payable at the investor's marginal tax rate. On this basis, there is no strong tax benefit reason for individuals for preferring dividends now or dividends later. However, there is still one modest reason for preferring dividends later. This is because capital gains tax can be deferred until the capital gain is actually realised. Thus investors are able to wait until the most advantageous time when they have little or no other declared income and tax allowances to use up.

The preference for dividends versus capital gains will probably be determined to at least some extent by the prevailing tax system within a particular country. It is also the case that institutions may pay either no tax or be subject to quite different taxation rates from individuals.

## Mini case study

### Special dividend at Hargreaves

Source Stafford 2009, Copyright *Financial Times*, 2009

Hargreaves Lansdown is to pay shareholders a special dividend for a second consecutive year as the UK's largest independent financial adviser reported a 20 per cent rise in profit for the year to June 30.

But the group warned investors not to count on the continuation of special pay-outs, as it expected income from interest to be 'materially reduced'.

'It's not guaranteed,' said Stephen Lansdown, executive chairman and co-founder of the group which floated in 2007. 'It's important that people don't take it as read, as we may need the cash to support the business in other ways in the future.'

Peter Hargreaves, chief executive and co-founder of the Bristol-based group, highlighted the difficult market conditions. 'The FTSE 100 Index at the financial year end, June 30 2009, was approximately 40 per cent lower than its peak at the beginning of the millennium nine-and-a-half years prior.'

Revenue from interest over the year climbed from £16.7m (€19m, $27.1m) to £31.1m, more than offsetting a decline in fees and commission income from £102.3m to £99.6m.

The special dividend of 2.807p a share comes on top of an increase in the final dividend from 2.42p to 4.229p, giving an overall pay-out of 10.101p a share. This represents a rise of almost 30 per cent over the previous year. Earnings per share were 11.1p (9p).

Revenues rose 10 per cent to £132.8m while pre-tax profit rose from £60.9m to £73.1m.

1.  Why did Hargreaves Lansdown pay a special dividend?

2.  Is this decision reinforced by any financial theory?

Institutional investors may well have clientele-type preferences as they are often tax exempt on dividends. Indeed, a preference for dividends by institutions based on their tax position is precisely what is suggested in some recent empirical evidence, such as Moser and Puckett (2009).

In conclusion, the common theme of the last three sections on 'early resolution of uncertainty', 'pecking order' and 'clientele effects' has been that it is possible to find some sense in them as a basis of a theoretical alternative to Modigliani and Miller, namely, asymmetric information and Akerlof's 'jewels and lemons'. Therefore, theoretically, dividend policy may make a difference to firm value. In the next section by contrast we confine ourselves to practical considerations and empirical evidence concerning dividend decisions.

## Practical implications for managers

### The clientele effect

Consider your own firm. How many shareholders are there? Are they known or unknown? Do you have shareholders meetings? Who attends? Do you think that the influential shareholders who attend these meetings are representative of the shareholders as a whole? Do they have particular policies on investment, reinvestment and dividend payout?

## Key concepts

- [ ] The **clientele effect** is the theory that a company can attract or deter shareholders based upon their dividend and financing policies
- [ ] **Institutional investors** are large organisations that can use their substantial finances to buy large amounts of shares
- [ ] **Tax treatment of dividends** differs between countries and can be an important factor leading to the clientele effect

## 9.6 The trends, empirical evidence and practical aspects of dividend policy

### 9.6.1 Dividend management in practice

## Active learning activity 9.3

### Dividend policy research

Go on a reputable financial database such as www.ft.com and key in the words 'dividend policy'. Do any of the companies' dividend policies seem to follow any particular policy?

As we suggested at the start of this chapter, firms do not change their dividend very quickly in the short term. This is most probably because of the strong signalling effect that is involved.

Firms would not typically talk of signalling, agency theory and asymmetric information as such. They are more likely to frame any discussion of dividend in terms of the confidence of shareholders. Shareholders will be reassured to find company statements affirming that 'current levels of dividend will be sustained for the foreseeable future'. Hence a dividend is fixed by the company not so much as the NPV from projects or the maximum payout current earnings; they are more likely to determine a minimum level that can be paid even in a 'worst-case' scenario when current investments have gone badly wrong.

Firms may, in effect, do the following:

1. They forecast surplus cash flow (earnings minus retained earnings) for the medium to long term (e.g. 5 years).

2. They set the dividend as a conservative proportion of surplus cash flow – certainly below the maximum that could be paid out every year. Any surplus will be retained against future dividends.

3. In bumper years, when there is a clear excess, a special dividend may be paid. If earnings continue to be realised at a higher level, the dividend will be cautiously increased.

4. If earnings are low, dividends will be paid from previous years' retained earnings. If there are insufficient retained earnings, the money will be borrowed against future earnings. If the downturn in earnings proves to go on for longer than anticipated, the firm will have to do what no firm wishes to do in normal times – declare a cut in dividend.

Normally the only time a firm does not pay a dividend at all is when it is going through a period of rapid growth. The reader is reminded of the equation for pricing shares when the dividend is expected to grow:

$$P_0 = \frac{d_0(1 + g)}{(r - g)}$$

That is, share price depends on next-period dividend divided by r − g (the discount rate, r, minus the growth rate of dividends, g).

This can be rearranged to give an expression for the discount rate which is also the cost of equity:

$$K_E = \frac{d_0(1 + g)}{P_0} + g$$

The impact of the dividend on the return is ambiguous. On the one hand, an increase in next-period dividend will increase the return. On the other hand, it will reduce retained earnings and the capital available for investment and growth in earnings. Clearly there is a trade-off between the next dividend and the growth rate. In fact in most cases the trade-off is such that it is normally accepted by the market that rapidly growing new companies need not pay a dividend until the initial rapid growth phase is over.

Examples include 'budget airlines' such as Ryanair[3] and Easyjet and computer technology companies such as Dell and Microsoft pre-2004. Low-price air travel is a relatively new concept in Europe and has only been around since the 1990s, though it is longer established in the US. The market for personal computers has been growing rapidly for many years, and until fairly recently showed no sign of slowing down. All of the aforementioned companies had a policy of ploughing back all earnings into capital in order to expand their market and to consolidate and maintain their lead over their rivals. It will be interesting given the current slowdown in world growth whether these firms start to pay a dividend as demand growth slows down. By 2004 Microsoft realised that growth had slowed and that they were sitting on excessive amounts of cash, so they started to pay a dividend. Whether or not to pay a dividend is the subject of the next mini case study ('To pay or not to pay? That is the (dividend) question').

## Mini case study

### To pay or not to pay? That is the (dividend) question
Source *Economist* 2002

#### Should technology companies pay dividends?

Dividends have long been shrinking; ever fewer companies are bothering with them at all. According to Standard & Poor's, only 72% of companies in its S&P 500 index paid a dividend last year, down from 94% in 1980. Last year, the average dividend payment shrank by 3.3%, the biggest drop in 50 years. Barely one-fifth of all listed American companies paid a dividend in 1999.

What about companies that have never paid a dividend? Surely initiating dividends must work wonders for share prices. Actually, no. Steve Milunovich of Merrill Lynch recently looked at three high-technology outfits: Intel, Computer Associates and Compaq. In two of the three, launching a dividend scheme was followed by a decline in price/earnings ratios relative to their competitors.

This result is hardly scientific, but it confirms the intuition of many managers who think that introducing dividends at fast-growing companies might be bad for share prices. To understand why, go back to the signal theory. Just as a dividend might signal stability to some investors, to others it might suggest that the company has run out of good investment ideas. Presumably, that is why dividend-free shares have become the club tie of America's high-growth companies.

Dividends are still an unsolved puzzle for financial economists, eluding any single theory. At the same time, however, managers have devised other ways of returning cash, ones that often better suit a company's (or even shareholders') needs.

1. Why do you think there was a long-run tendency for fewer companies to pay dividends in the US at this time?

2. Why did the initiation of a dividend lead to a downgrading of hi-tech company valuation?

3. What other ways might companies have of returning cash?

### 9.6.2 Trends and empirical evidence for dividend practices

In section 9.6.1, the mini case study based on an excerpt from *The Economist* suggested, somewhat surprisingly, that investors would appear to prefer growth companies *not* to pay a dividend – the commencement of dividend would appear to signal that the firm has run out of rapid growth opportunities.

The other theme that comes out in this mini case study is that dividend policy should be set against the external context of time and place. That is, in the US at this time there was a fashion for retaining dividend. This is confirmed by Fama and French (2001) who found that the proportion of US companies paying cash dividends fell from 66.5% in 1978 to only 20.8% by 1999.

In addition, Benito and Young (2002) examined a sample of US corporations for the period 1974–1999. They found, on the one hand, an increasing tendency for US companies to pay no dividend. However, on the other hand, they found that the average value of dividend payments had increased. This is because the high dividend payers in 1999 were paying twice as much relative to sales revenue compared with 1977. Thus of those firms that still chose to pay dividends, there was a much higher payout.

A similar phenomenon was observed by Baker and Wurgler (2004) who found that dividends were paid by a high proportion of listed companies in the 1960s, before starting a long decline from about 1978.

All this evidence relates to the US. There is less evidence for Europe and Asia; this is for a number of reasons. First, these blocs are not necessarily culturally homogeneous and therefore an aggregation of this kind may not be so meaningful. Second, many countries in these blocs, such as the Eastern bloc countries of Europe, or the South East Asian countries are more recently emergent in economic terms, and therefore long-run data may not exist. Nevertheless, some observations can be made about Europe. This is done in the following mini case study ['To pay or not to pay? That is the (dividend) question, part 2'] which is a continuation of the extract examined in the previous mini case study.

## Mini case study

### To pay or not to pay? That is the (dividend) question, part 2
Source *Economist* 2002

**Should technology companies pay dividends?**
The long-term decline of the dividend tracks another trend. More companies have been using spare cash to buy back their own shares. This provides a boost to share prices, and means that each remaining share gets a bigger slice of profits.

In Europe, where dividends have played a bigger role than in America, companies have greatly increased their use of buy-backs in the past decade. CFO Europe, a sister publication of *The Economist*, found in a study of 127 large European companies that buy-backs have grown from nothing in 1993 to a 15% share of all cash returned to investors in 2000. This growth occurred as the fraction of all profits paid out remained unchanged, suggesting that buy-backs are, as in America, starting to supplant dividends.

1. Why do you think that more companies in Europe have been using buy-backs?

2. What are the alternatives to buy-backs?

Nevertheless, the trend to buy-backs rather than dividends in Europe appeared to go into reverse in 2005, as the following excerpt (mini case study 'Why cash has become king once again') from the *Financial Times* suggests.

## Mini case study

### Why cash has become king once again

Source London 2005, Copyright *Financial Times*, 2005

After 20 years in decline, dividends are making a comeback. Companies – including Microsoft, Federal Express and Viacom – have started making cash payments for the first time. Others, such as BP, which last week increased its dividend by 26 per cent, have made a step-change in the amount they distribute to shareholders.

1. Why do you think that dividends are making a comeback?

So far we have talked about dividend policy in terms of trends and fashions. This is hardly scientific, but the reasons for the fall in dividends in the 1980s and 1990s in the US, followed by a reversal in 2005, are not entirely clear. Explanations for both the downward trend and revival that have been forwarded include the following:

1. The **maturity hypothesis** (as outlined in Fama and French, 2001), is the hypothesis that many firms in the first two decades of their study were small and fast growing (and thus had many investment opportunities), and that they were coming to maturity by the middle of the third decade and therefore now in a position to pay a dividend. However, this was not a complete explanation as, even adjusting for size and maturity, there was still a tendency to lower dividends from 1978 to 1999.

2. Tax: in the US at this time, up to 2003, dividends were taxed at a less favourable rate than capital gains. Thus dividends might have been minimised and only paid out to satisfy those clienteles who needed a regular predictable income. However, Julio and Ikenberry (2004) found that the trend back to dividends started in 2001, long before changes in the tax status of dividends relative to capital gains were considered.

3. Discipline: dividends impose an important discipline on managers, forcing them to focus on free cash flow. This is the '**corporate governance**' hypothesis, whereby, follow-

ing the business scandals of 2001, such as Enron and Worldcomm, businesses switched back to dividend payment to reassure investors.

4. **Signalling mechanism**: the increased payout from 2005 could be a sign that managers expect good times ahead. However, this is not always the case, as Aviva found out to its cost.

5. The spread of **stock options**, which might be expected to encourage senior managers to boost stock prices by retaining earnings to increase growth.

6. The **declining influence of private investors** who often rely on stocks for regular income.

7. **Cycles of bullish/bearish sentiment**: that is, trends and fashions which could affect the attitude of investors towards 'safe' dividend-paying stocks.

Having examined various potential explanations for observed empirical trends in dividend policy, we come finally to the last part of our discussion, which is on the practical alternatives to share dividends.

### 9.6.3 Alternatives to dividends

- **Share repurchase/buy-backs**: at their own discretion, firms can offer to purchase share from current shareholders at a premium to market price. We discussed above that in many, if not all, tax regimes, capital gains are taxed at a lower rate than the income from dividends. Therefore, share buy-backs can be more tax efficient than dividends for the investor. Buy-backs give companies greater flexibility as they enable companies to return cash to shareholders when they are cash rich and there are few investment opportunities, or to retain it when profitable projects arise.

- **Special dividend**: a 'one-off' extraordinary dividend. This has the flexibility of share repurchase but not the tax advantage.

- **Scrip dividend**: additional shares are offered to shareholders in lieu of the normal cash dividend.

We also talked, in the context of Modigliani and Miller, about a **rights issue**, which represented the offer of additional shares at a price to existing shareholders. This is not really comparable to dividend payment, and is normally used when the firm needs to raise new equity capital quickly. Nevertheless, it is a part of the array of policy instruments which are available in the pursuit of shareholder wealth.

## Practical implications for managers

### Know your investors

Managers need to consider their investors and understand how changes in dividend policy can affect them.

**Key concepts**

- The **maturity hypothesis** is the hypothesis that dividends are increased as smaller and fast growing firms become mature. Basically as firms become mature, they have fewer growth opportunities available and therefore pay dividends rather than invest in growth

- The **'corporate governance'** hypothesis states that the need to pay dividends disciplines managers into focusing on free cash flow

- **Signalling theory** states that the actions a company takes regarding dividend can have important informational content. This is due to information asymmetry

- **Stock options** are a remuneration technique which grants a manager a call option on the company's stock, giving the manager an incentive to increase the share price

- **Market sentiment** is how the market generally feels about the direction of the share price. It can be **bullish** (upwards expectant) or **bearish** (downwards expectant)

- A **share repurchase** (or **buy-back**) is when a firm offers to purchase shares from current shareholders at a premium to market price

- A **special dividend** is a one-off event used to avoid the increased future expectations a raised normal dividend would create

- A **scrip dividend** is when a firm offers shares instead of the normal cash dividend

## 9.7 Summary

This chapter has examined the theory behind a firm's dividend policies, the reality observed in the market, and the contrast between them.

Traditionally the ability to pay a dividend has been seen as a marker of company well-being. A cut in dividend therefore was seen as a signal that the company was faring worse than expected and tended to lead to a drop in share price. This is due to the problems of imperfect and asymmetrical information: investors do not know everything there is to know about the firm they are investing in, and a company insider will know more. This had led to companies traditionally being vague when communicating the reasoning behind their dividend policy and has created substantial amounts of literature examining dividend policy decisions.

The principal theoretical work in this area is Miller and Modigliani (1961). Their assumptions and reasoning are examined in detail in this chapter. Assuming a frictionless world of perfect competition, Miller and Modigliani argue that there is no need for the firm to adjust dividend policy to accommodate clienteles with specific time preferences. Impatient investors who want more dividend can sell shares (to create an immediate 'home-made dividend'). By contrast, more than usually patient investors can buy more shares with their dividend. Similarly the decision to finance projects through either retaining the dividend or other means such as a rights issue should not make any difference, as a positive NPV project will create wealth for shareholders in either case.

However, Miller and Modigliani's model is highly abstract and firms often do have specific dividend policies, so we examined alternative theoretical frameworks in addition to the evidence on actual practice. From the theoretical point of view, asymmetric and imperfect information may mean that investors may prefer immediate dividends over later dividends or reinvestment as they cannot be sure the company is in competent hands. This is the argument of Gordon (1959). It is important to note that Gordon was refuted by the academic community as being a 'bird in the hand' fallacy; the market has already discounted future cash flows at the risk level they perceive the company to have. Further discounting future dividends is irrational. However, there is some evidence that indicates that this built-in discount factor may not be sufficient in times of high market volatility, and recent real options research has been attempting to model scenarios to better account for this uncertainty.

Pecking order theory is also investigated as an alternative to Miller and Modigliani's theory. Because not all financing options are equal in reality (due to transaction costs and debt covenants, for example), pecking order theory suggests that companies prefer using existing internal capital first, then debt, then external equity to finance projects. This means that earnings being retained rather than paid as a dividend may be preferred as it would leave internal cash reserves available.

It was also argued that dividend policy may indeed have real and important effects because of it being interpreted as a signal to the market, given imperfect, asymmetrical information. We outlined a theoretical framework taking account of asymmetric information using Akerlof's 'jewels and lemons' approach.

The clientele effect was also examined. This is the theory that a company can attract or deter shareholders based upon its dividend and financing policies. This is because several of Miller and Modigliani's assumptions, such as no taxes and the ability to create equivalent home-made dividends, do not hold true in capital markets. This can lead to preferences among investors for certain dividend policies.

Finally, the chapter concluded by outlining practical dividend policy, surveying some empirical evidence on dividend policies, and looked at some alternatives to dividends.

 Questions

1. Under which of the following circumstances would Modigliani and Miller's dividend irrelevance theory hold true?

   a) Shareholders can create home-dividends according to their own preferences.

   b) Gains from dividends are certain, capital gains are not.

   c) Shareholders choose companies on the basis of the dividend policy.

   d) Tax treatment of dividends and capitals gains is different.

   e) Investors believe in signalling theory.

2. Outline the reasons why companies might not always be as clear on their dividend policy as they could be.

3. What are the assumptions underlying the Modigliani and Miller model?

4. Assume an all-equity firm with capital employed per shareholder equal to £900, a yearly dividend equal to £81 and a discount rate of 9%.

   a) Calculate the PV of capital and dividends per shareholder.

   b) Calculate the PV per shareholder if it were decided to double next year's dividend to £162.

   c) As far as Modigliani and Miller are concerned, what does this exercise demonstrate concerning dividend policy?

   d) What critical assumption concerning discount rates was necessary to reach this conclusion?

5. Repeat Q4 for a cut in dividend to £40.50.

6. What factors affect time impatience and personal discount rates?

7. Explain why Modigliani and Miller's dividend irrelevance proposition is unaffected by the fact that investors may have different time horizons and therefore different discount rates from each other and the firm.

8. How can Gordon's 'bird in the hand' theory be linked to asymmetric information and 'non-standard' random events?

9. Outline Akerlof's 'jewels and lemons' theory.

10. In what way does this theory explain why external equity capital has high transaction costs and that therefore there may be a 'pecking order'?

11. How might the costs of overcoming asymmetric information lead to clientele effects?

Please read the two following case studies and answer the questions at the end of the second case study.

## Case study

### Cautious dividend policies are getting easier to justify
Source Copyright *Financial Times*, 2009

Aviva's Andrew Moss has discovered there's something worse than the stigma of cutting your dividend when everybody expects you to go on raising it: it's the stigma of maintaining the dividend when everybody thinks you should cut it.

The insurer's chief executive would have been damned either way. He kept the 2008 dividend at the conservative end of Aviva's policy and still received a raspberry. His only other option would have been to junk the policy. Hardly a sign of his confidence in the future. As it is, though, the sharp drop in Aviva's shares yesterday suggests many investors don't believe his forecasts of business and capital strength. Hardly a sign of their confidence in Mr Moss.

So, is the dividend a sacred symbol of corporate solidity, to be slaughtered only as a last resort? Or is it a handy (and cheap) first resort when wondering how to conserve or top up cash balances?

As the recession deepens, it can be either. It depends what you (and your investors) think of your company. ITV's Michael Grade, dragged over the coals for cutting programming budgets, would have been burnt alive by investors (and employees) had he clung on to the dividend. Yet if Tony Hayward of BP had hinted earlier this week at a dividend cut rather than a freeze, the reaction would have made yesterday's aversion to Aviva look like a mere blip.

What's clear is that on the priority list of legitimate reasons to tinker with historic dividend policy, safety is catching up with survival. The techniques for deciding what to do are the same, though. First, consider what the company can afford in the short term (hint: if you have to borrow to pay shareholders, you're on the wrong track). Second, examine what a 'progressive' policy means for group finances over a longer period, when the black magic of compound interest can undermine promises. Only then, judge the impact of the decision on shareholders themselves.

Yes, there are plenty of investors for whom a dividend cut or suspension, however it's dressed up, is a surefire sign of distress. Yes, mass 'divicide' would reduce institutions' cash, possibly exacerbate market falls and even jeopardise wider capital raising. But when all but a lucky few companies are under strain, it surely cannot be wrong to be careful.

## Mini case study

### Ferrexpo dividend policy sends out mixed messages

Source Hill 2009, Copyright *Financial Times*, 2009

When it comes to the dividend, there used to be only four decisions directors could take: raise it, freeze it, cut it, or cancel it. Ferrexpo's board has, however, discovered a fifth: wait and see.

The company yearns to be seen as a conventional UK corporate citizen. It has blue-chip City advisers in JP Morgan Cazenove and Deutsche Bank. It was (briefly) part of the FTSE 100 and longs to return there. Its chief executive boasts that Ferrexpo's governance accords with 'best western practices'.

Yet the Ukrainian iron ore producer somehow keeps finding itself in situations that are unconventional – even in the context of a London market that is far less homogeneous than it used to be.

Ferrexpo will never be ICI. The chief executive – Kostyantin Zhevago – is a youthful Ukrainian billionaire, who founded and is still majority shareholder of the group. He only recently fought off an attempted coup by two other super-rich east Europeans, who remain substantial investors through their respective vehicles. The other large shareholder is a company owned by a Czech coal mining tycoon.

Still, the board's decision to 'defer' the declaration of its interim dividend until October is unorthodox. If Ferrexpo believes it would have to stretch to pay the $20m (£11.7m) it has regularly dispensed to shareholders since flotation, why not just cancel or cut the dividend? The rest of the Ferrexpo statement is all about cash conservation, after all, and peers have not hesitated to rein in dividends given the uncertain conditions in commodities. Alternatively, if Ferrexpo has confidence in the second half – when it says it should be trading more profitably – why not follow the route mapped yesterday by F&C Asset Management and pay an interim dividend (uncovered by earnings in F&C's case) while reserving the right to reduce the final pay-out if markets do not improve?

Mr Zhevago prides himself on the consistency with which Ferrexpo is meeting its obligations as a listed UK company. It may be that the size of the dividend is so minimal that minority investors, more interested in the group's long-term growth prospects, don't mind much when it's paid. But if its consistency Mr Zhevago is after, he and his board should think about regularity of payment. Having deferred the decision on an interim dividend once, Ferrexpo could presumably postpone it again. And having made minority investors wait, the directors will send a far worse signal if they decide, come October, that they'd be better not paying an interim at all.

1. Why did investors react negatively when Aviva chose to maintain their dividend instead of cutting it?

2. The writer believes that, had ITV chosen to maintain their dividend, 'ITV's Michael Grade ... would have been burnt alive by investors', but if BP had chosen to cut their dividend, 'the reaction would have made yesterday's aversion to Aviva look like a mere blip'. What would have caused the different reaction?

3. Why might borrowing to pay investors dividends be a bad idea?

4. Why do you think Ferrexpo chose to 'wait and see' regarding their dividend policy rather than raise, freeze, cut or cancel it?

5. Do you think that that was a poor decision? Why?

 # Further reading

Akerlof, G. (1970) The market for 'lemons': quality uncertainty and the market mechanism. *Quarterly Journal of Economics* **84**(3):488–500.

Baker, M. and Wurgler, J. (2004) A catering theory of dividends. *Journal of Finance* **59**(3):1125–1165.
An important paper that examines trends in dividend payment.

Benito, A. and Young, G. (2002) *Financial pressure and balance sheet adjustment by UK firms*. Banco de España Working Paper No. 0209. Banco de España, Madrid.
Examines how a variety of factors can affect dividend policy.

Fama, E. and French, K. (2001) Disappearing dividends: changing firm characteristics or lower propensity to pay? *Journal of Financial Economics* **60**:3–43.
This paper also looks at trends in dividend payouts but is more modern in scope.

Julio, B. and Ikenberry, D. (2004) *Reappearing Dividends, Working Paper. College of Business, University of Illinois*.
This paper investigates the maturity hypothesis and corporate governance as reasons for the recorded swing in dividend trends.

Miller, M. and Modigliani, F. (1961) Dividend policy, growth and the valuation of shares. *Journal of Business* **34**(4).
An extremely important paper that shaped much of modern dividend theory.

# Internet references

http://www.direct.gov.uk/en/moneytaxandbenefits/taxes/taxonsavingsandinvestments/dg_4016453
Contains information on the tax rate of dividends in the UK.

http://www.investopedia.com/articles/03/011703.asp
An article on why and how companies pay dividends.

http://www.dividend.com/historical/
A tool to look up the historical dividends of US companies.

http://www.fionaallan.plus.com/results%2020081115.xls
A spreadsheet containing FTSE share information, including dividend yields.

http://bespokeinvest.typepad.com/bespoke/2007/09/historical-di-1.html
A graphical representation of dividend yields on the S&P 500 from 1925–2007.

# Suggestions for group work

1.  Students should discuss Miller and Modigliani's (1961) work. How likely are their assumptions to hold true in a real life market? How does that affect the value of their research?

2.  Students should consider their own dividend preferences. They should examine and discuss the tax rules of their own countries, their own lifestyle and any other pertinent factor that would affect their preferences, and whether or not they could address these using 'home-made' dividends.

# Suggestions for presentations

1.  Assume the role of a manager in a FTSE 100 listed company of your choice. Investigate the dividend decisions over the past 3 years and prepare a presentation on the type of dividend decision your company has followed and why.

2.  Imagine you are employed as a consultant to a company where the CEO has read Gordon's (1959) theory and now wants to pay immediate dividends in the belief that this will please shareholders. Create a presentation explaining the opposition to Gordon's theory.

# 10 Working Capital Management

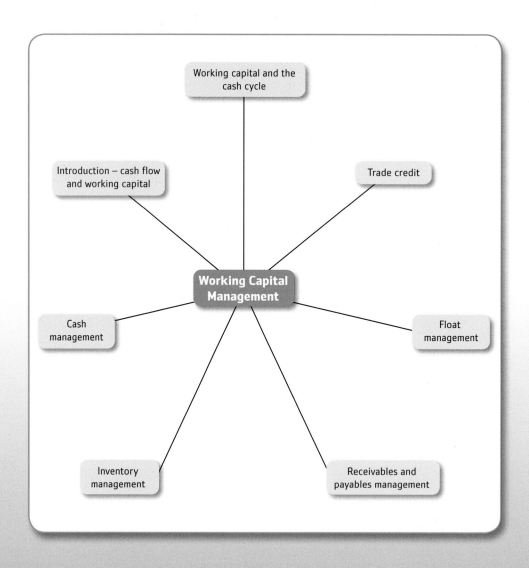

- Working capital and the cash cycle
- Introduction – cash flow and working capital
- Trade credit
- Cash management
- Float management
- Inventory management
- Receivables and payables management

**Working Capital Management**

## Knowledge-based learning objectives

When you have completed this chapter you will be able to:

✓ Understand cash flow and **working capital**

✓ Understand the concept of net current assets

✓ Recognise the difference between permanent and non-permanent assets

✓ Understand the **cash cycle**

✓ Understand **trade credit**

✓ Recognise the difference between float, receivables and accounts payable

✓ Recognise the main models of cash management

✓ Understand the terminology involved in trade credit

## Skills-based learning objectives development

✓ Business and financial environment consciousness: develop understanding of how short-term finance can be just as critical as longer-term financial considerations.

✓ Numerical skills: develop the ability to understand, manipulate and interpret current assets, working capital, the cash cycle, trade credit, the optimal ordering quantity and the optimal amount of cash for the business to hold.

✓ Analytical thinking and problem-solving skills: develop the ability to critically assess the business's short-term financial efficiency and the trade-offs that characterise short-term financial management, including inventory cost minimisation versus stock availability, minimising credit terms offered while taking full advantage of credit from vendors, and minimising unproductive surplus cash versus the need to keep some available for unforeseen eventualities.

✓ Organisational skills: further develop your ability to organise your time and work efficiently and to gather data and information that you can translate into value-adding intelligence.

✓ Presentation skills: further develop your ability to present your work clearly both verbally and in writing.

## Online resource centre

Visit the Online Resource Centre that accompanies this book to listen to a podcast of the authors discussing working capital.

**www.oxfordtextbooks.co.uk/marney**

## Fictional case study

### Can OrganicX recycle its cash?

Charlie is poring over the latest management accounts and, as usual, feeling increasingly frustrated by the amount of jargon, and the fact that no two pieces of paper seem to be in agreement. In particular, he is trying to reconcile the fact that OrganicX – according to all the measures he knows about – is a very profitable company, and yet there appears to be what looks like a huge overdraft appearing in the balance sheet. He is well aware that the business has been expanding at a phenomenal rate in recent months, most notably in countries where the start-up costs have been higher than normal, and that Kate has been involved in long (and most probably terribly boring) talks with their bankers. In fact, now that he thinks about it, she has been looking a bit worried recently, despite all the new business coming their way. He decides to call in to her office. Sure enough, there she is, deep in her spreadsheets.

'Kate, just when I thought I was getting the hang of all this accounting stuff, I have a found something strange. We appear to owe the bank a huge amount of money on an overdraft, in addition to all those long-term loans, which I did not know about. Surely this must be wrong? After all, you were saying just the other day that our profits are increasing by 10% every quarter.'

Kate frowns, and Charlie notices that she does indeed look very stressed. 'We are making a lot in profits, Charlie,' she begins, 'but unfortunately we have two big problems. One, we need a lot of cash up front to open all the new offices and take on new staff. Two, we don't get actual money in for quite some time after opening a new office. These two factors are making the cash position very tight at the moment and, to be honest, it's not been easy to get the banks to finance us. You know how difficult things are at the moment in the financial markets. Basically, we need more cash than we have to finance the day-to-day operations of the business, so I didn't have any other option but to practically beg for an overdraft'.

Charlie is appalled. He is well aware (from a rather unfortunate episode in his student days) that an overdraft usually carries huge costs in interest, and can also be recalled at short notice. 'Surely we can take the profits from one part of our business and use this money to finance our new offices? Kind of recycle it through the business?' he asks.

'Unfortunately not,' replies Kate. 'You need to understand that profit in no way equals cash and, to be frank, we are at a crisis point. If we cannot raise more cash soon, we may be in serious trouble. It's not a good time to go back to the stock market and sell more shares, and it's really very difficult to raise any more by way of loans'. Charlie frowns deeply. How has this happened when profits seem to be so good?

## 10.1  Introduction – cash flow and working capital

In this chapter we consider some shorter-term and more immediate financial issues than we have typically considered in the rest of the book. This is not to downplay the importance of cash flow management and the immediate relevance of the short-term net cash position. It is a commonplace fact of entrepreneurship studies that many new businesses fail, and a frequent reason for this failure is not that the underlying business strategy is unsound, but because the business has run into cash flow problems, perhaps exacerbated by overly rapid expansion, leading to a lack of **liquidity** and thence to insolvency.

As a result, it is almost a cliché to aver that cash is the lifeblood of the business, but it is nonetheless true. One of the jobs of the financial manager is to ensure that cash flows regularly and predictably through the body corporate, ensuring the health of the firm. A substantial part of day-to-day cash flow is normally financed from **working capital** which is defined as that part of investment capital which is *not* used up in the process of production. Thus working capital associated with a particular project is returned intact when the project is ended.

The main requirements for short-term working capital management are that cash is available to the business when needed to meet day-to-day expenditures, that cash is not tied up in unproductive and excessive inventory and, in the last resort, that the business is not 'awash with cash' – suggesting an excess of liquidity which could be put to more productive use such as paying off loans. We must admit that to many small business owners, this last scenario will seem highly unlikely, but it is not entirely unknown.

In the next section, we consider more explicitly the position between cash flow, net **working capital** and **net current assets**.

## 10.1. Short-term funding, working capital and net current assets

As we implied above, the importance of working capital is to ensure the availability of cash and near-cash equivalents. Cash equivalents are highly liquid short-term investments that (1) are readily convertible to cash and (2) have little risk of any fluctuation in value. The availability of these liquid assets allows the company to avoid cash flow constraints, so that it is in a position to continue trading without any hitches and to take advantage of expansion opportunities as and when they arise. For many small businesses these liquid assets would simply consist of the money held in any bank accounts belonging to the firm, accounts receivable (i.e. money owed by debtors) and stock held in inventory.

However, for large companies, the meaning of cash and cash equivalents can get much more sophisticated than this. Accordingly, they might also consist of money market instruments, treasury bills and commercial paper. There may also be a further distinction between **cash equivalents** defined as having a maturity of less than 3 months and **short-term investments** defined as having a maturity of between 3 months and 1 year.

The reason why working capital in the form of cash and liquid assets normally needs to be available is to meet short-term obligations, such as purchasing inventory or advertising. As working capital, it should (like all the other firm's assets) be managed in such a way as to maximise profit. The 'trick' is to minimise its use while making sure cash is always available when needed.

Working capital management can be particularly demanding at times of new investment and rapid expansion. Clearly, when the business expands, there are more unknowns than usual and there will in addition be greater cash demands. A particularly apposite question is 'Can current project business cash requirements be financed internally or will the firm have to turn to a bank and take on debt?'

A very basic way in which a firm's working capital management and short-term financial position is often assessed is in terms of its net current assets, which is equal to **current assets** minus **current liabilities**. Both current assets and current liabilities are of shorter maturities of anything up to a year. Current assets consist of cash held by the firm or other short-term liquid assets such as accounts receivable and inventory. Current liabilities again are short term in nature and consist of, for example, accounts payable to other firms, unpaid taxes and short-term credit such as temporary overdraft facilities, or indeed any short-term loans (maturity less than a year). In addition, current liabilities may include items such as dividends and interest payable, and any repayment of principal on bonds or loans that will fall due in the current year.

The value of **net current assets**, if positive, indicates the extent to which business activities are generating working capital or, if negative, the extent to which the firm is using up working capital. It can *also* be thought of as the net cash position of the company if it realised the monetary value of short-term resources, and used them to pay off its short-term liabilities. It is often the most reliable indicator of the company's financial position, and the usual metric that is used to assess the net current position is either the **current ratio** or the **quick ratio**. The **current ratio** is as follows:

$$\text{Current Ratio} = \frac{\text{Value of Current Assets}}{\text{Value of Current Liabilities}}$$

So, for example, if current assets are £15 million while current liabilities are £5 million, then the current ratio has a value of 3. As a general rule, the current ratio should be at least 1.5 to meet current cash flow needs. A high current ratio, say of 2 or higher, can suggest that the company is hoarding assets and not using them efficiently. Of course another important standard which should be considered in this kind of analysis is the industry norm. In highly cyclical industries with large amounts of capital tied up in inventory, for example, luxury goods, it makes sense to hoard cash in the upward part of the cycle as a bulwark against the downswing.

Sometimes it is useful to strip out inventory. This is particularly the case for a company that is in financial trouble and may be going out of business. The reason for this is it takes time to find buyers for inventory, even if incentives are offered such as discounts, before an actual cash value is realised. Take the example of Borders bookshops. Both your authors used to like nothing better than an hour or two browsing the Borders branch in Glasgow, with its comfy armchairs and large handsome premises dating back to Victorian times. In December 2009, however, Borders went into administration. Before closing their shops they had to advertise sales featuring discounts of over 50% for almost a month to attempt to sell all their inventory. Even afterwards it is likely that there was leftover stock.

Therefore a current ratio for Borders would be misleading; analysis of working capital would be more reliable if inventory were stripped out and the quick ratio were used instead. The **quick ratio** (sometimes known as the **acid test**) is simply current assets *minus* **inventories** divided by **current liabilities**. In cases such as these where it may take a long time to sell inventories, the quick ratio gives a more reliable guide to whether or not the company has sufficient liquid assets to meet short-term operating needs.

The quick ratio may also exclude any prepayments made. Prepayments are a current asset as they represent a payment the company has already made. They are excluded as firms cannot usually claim this money back in the event of financial distress.

Now you may imagine that companies would typically operate by closely matching current assets with current liabilities and longer-term assets with longer-term liabilities over the cycle. However, this is not always necessarily the case and in order to explain this point, we are going to have to make some additional fine distinctions between types of asset and liability.

An important subcategory of current asset is **permanent assets**. Permanent assets are the assets that the firm needs to continue in operation. These take two forms. First, there are assets such as inventory and accounts receivable from customers. If these assets fall to zero, cash flow dries up and the business is effectively finished. Thus the assets are *permanent* as they must continually be replaced if the business is to continue. The other type of permanent current asset consists of rapidly depreciating capital items such as computers which quickly become virtually worthless. However, we are mainly concerned with the former rather than the latter.

On the other hand, an important category of liability that we need to define is a type of liability known as **spontaneous sources of funds**. Spontaneous funds arise in the natural course of business. Spontaneous finance is defined as the sum of trade credit and other payables and accruals that arise spontaneously in the firm's day-to-day operations. For most practical purposes spontaneous finance *is* trade credit.

Now we have got the definitions out the way, it's possible to observe that in principle **permanent current assets** would normally require **permanent working capital**. We can see an example of this in Figure 10.1.

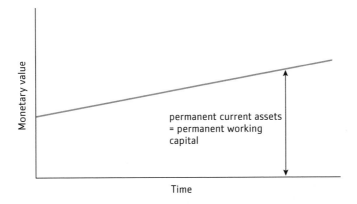

Figure 10.1 Permanent working capital matched to permanent current assets

Of course not all current assets are permanent. Some current assets are temporary. For example, in the months before Christmas, European and American retailers will be holding far larger inventories than they normally keep. Following Christmas, any excess will be sold off in the January sales. Thus inventory will have a seasonal component, peaking around December and rapidly receding again in January. This seasonal increase in inventory represents an increase in temporary current assets requiring a temporary increase in working capital, as shown in Figure 10.2.

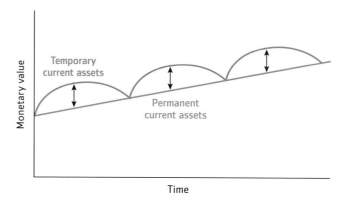

Figure 10.2 Temporary working capital matched to temporary current assets

Temporary current assets would normally be covered by temporary working capital, such as short-term bank loans or overdraft facilities. The two principles of covering temporary current assets with short-term financing, while covering permanent current assets and fixed capital with long-term funding, is a particular working capital strategy known as **matching**. This is illustrated in Figure 10.3, where we add in fixed assets as well as current assets.

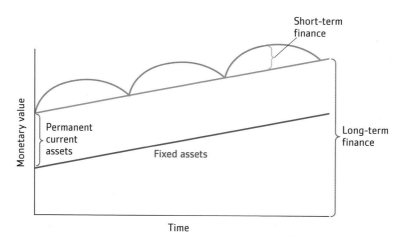

Figure 10.3 Matching finance maturity to capital maturity – conservative strategy

From the point of view of maximising profit, the matching strategy is typically at the con-servative end of things, in terms of return relative to risk. Thus we might engage more short-term finance covering some or all of current permanent assets with short-term finance rather than long-term finance, as shown in Figure 10.4.

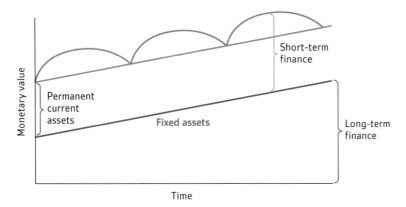

Figure 10.4  Making greater use of short-term finance – aggressive strategy

Greater use of short-term finance has the advantage that, given the standard yield curve, short-term interest rates will be lower than long-term interest rates. Of course the strategy carries greater risk, as credit will have to be rolled over on a frequent basis. The risks are that the credit may simply not be there and even if it is that the interest rate has risen substan-tially. Short-term rates tend to be more volatile than long-term ones. Clearly this kind of strategy would appeal to the less risk adverse or to businesses with more certainty and less volatility.

If the firm is really focused on increasing return relative to risk, the other possibility is to economise on current assets. This can be done, for example, by holding lower inventory or reducing the credit terms available to customers while delaying payment to vendors. One method of measuring return, the return on investment (ROI) equation is as follows:

$$ROI = \frac{Net\ Profit}{Total\ Assets}$$

Total assets are the sum of current and fixed assets. Thus ROI can be redefined as follows:

$$ROI = \frac{Net\ Profit}{Current\ Assets + Fixed\ Assets}$$

Thus ROI would increase if current assets were cut, as shown in Figure 10.5.

But of course this strategy is very risky. The risks are of alienating customers by running out of stock and offering stingy credit terms while simultaneously upsetting suppliers by delaying payments. Eventually day-to-day business could get very difficult indeed! Some aspects of working capital policy are illustrated in the next mini case study ('Working capital strategy').

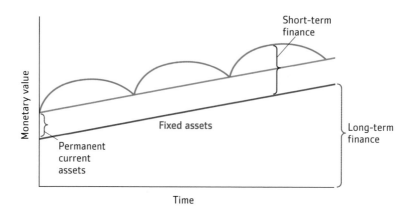

Figure 10.5 Making greater use of short-term finance and minimising net short-term assets – very aggressive strategy

## Mini case study

### Orders at Hightex to raise the roof

Source Blackwell 2009, Copyright *Financial Times*, 2009

An AIM-quoted company that in April had a market capitalisation of less than £3m has notched up orders for the next couple of years worth more than €45m (£40.5m) for roofing large sports stadiums.

Hightex joined the junior market in September 2006, raising £1.5m at 10p a share. But in spite of winning the contract for the retractable roof at Wimbledon, the shares tumbled to a low of 1.56p in April this year.

A recovery began after the announcement in August that the company would supply the roof for the new national stadium in Warsaw, to be used for the UEFA 2012 European Football Championship. It was helped by news of a maiden interim profit of €147,000 on revenue of €7.3m.

The Polish deal, worth €13m, was followed in October with winning the €18.9m contract to supply the roof for the Olympic Stadium in Kiev, also being built for UEFA 2012. A few weeks later the company was able to raise £2.5m through a placing at 7p a share in order to provide working capital to fuel the growth.

Then just before Christmas the company won a C$20.9m (£12.3m) contract to supply the retractable roof of the BC Place Stadium, home of the BC Lions American Football team in British Columbia. Charles DesForges, executive chairman, said at the time the contract would reinforce Hightex's 'reputation as a world leader in specialist retractable roof systems'.

The company arrived on AIM as a second-generation family business, but has been turned round by Mr DesForges and Charles Sebag-Montefiore. Mr Sebag-Montefiore said on Tuesday that the process had been like turning round a supertanker, but now the company was in a position to market itself aggressively.

The roofs are constructed from a Teflon-type fabric strengthened with glass fibre. Hightex buys the material, but specialises in precision cutting. It employs about 50 people.

1. What would you judge Hightex's policy to be with respect to short-/long-term finance?
2. Is the working capital raised likely to be liquidated and returned in the foreseeable future?

The case study concludes this introductory section. In the next section we examine an important concept in working capital management – the cash cycle.

## Practical implications for managers

### Working capital strategy

The manager is faced with a number of trade-offs in this area and as is always the case in finance there is a trade-off between risk and return. Only so many of the key decision factors can be quantified. A great deal rests on managerial judgement.

## Key concepts

- **Liquidity** measures how easily an asset can be turned into cash. A liquid company is one that can easily access cash

- **Working capital** is that part of investment capital which is not used up in the process of production. **Working capital** associated with a particular project is returned intact (in nominal terms) when the project is ended

- **Cash** and **near-cash equivalents**. Cash equivalents are highly liquid short-term investments that (1) are readily convertible to cash and (2) have little risk of any fluctuation in value

- There may also be a further distinction between **cash equivalents** defined as having a maturity of less than 3 months and **short-term investments** defined as having a maturity of between 3 months and 1 year

- **Current assets** are assets of less than 1 year's maturity. They consist of assets such as cash held by the firm or other short-term liquid assets such as accounts receivable and inventory

- **Current liabilities** are liabilities of less than 1 year's maturity. They consist of obligations such as accounts payable to other firms, unpaid taxes and short-term credit

- **Net current assets**, if positive, indicates the extent to which business activities are generating working capital or, if negative, the extent to which the firm is using up working capital. The value of net current assets can also be thought of as the net cash position of the company

- The **current ratio** is as follows:

  $$\text{Current Ratio} = \frac{\text{Value of Current Assets}}{\text{Value of Current Liabilities}}$$

- The **quick ratio** (or **acid test**) is simply current assets minus inventories divided by current liabilities

- **Permanent assets** are the assets that generate cash flow and which the firm needs to continue in operation

- **Spontaneous sources of funds** consist of liabilities that arise in the natural course of business, such as trade credit and other payables and accruals

# 10.2 Working capital and the cash cycle

## 10.2.1 The cash cycle

It has long been a fact of business that it relies on circulating or working capital that does not get used up in the process of production, and the importance of this factor was noted as long ago as 1776 by Adam Smith. In fact it was only with the advent of the industrial age that fixed capital investment became a significant part of financial calculation. The elementary components of working capital are as follows:

Working capital = the sum of cash + liquid assets + money owed by debtors + money tied up in inventory – money owed to creditors.

We might think of the second half of this definition, as the part that causes a cash cycle in the first place. That is, take the components:

Money owed by debtors + money tied up in inventory – money owed to creditors.

For most companies, the sum of these components will vary over the cash cycle and will typically be negative at least part of the time; hence the need in the first place for cash and liquid assets to bridge the gap.

The components of the cash cycle are: **accounts receivable, accounts payable** and **inventory. Accounts receivable** represent invoices to customers who have not yet paid; accounts payable represents invoices that we must ultimately settle with suppliers, and inventory represents raw materials, finished goods and goods held in warehouses, office supply consumables, goods for sale held in store and in stock by retailers, and so on. In terms of the effect these have on the business, we might say that ideally we would like accounts receivable to be paid as soon as possible, we ourselves would like to hold off as long as possible in settling accounts payable and we would aim as far as possible to hold a minimum of inventory subject to maintaining business efficiency and being able to meet customer demand.

However, the fundamental business conditions do not usually allow us to reach this ideal state and so some firms such as high-tech manufacturing and pharmaceuticals would have cash tied up in expensive stock and consumables for relatively long periods of time before their goods can be sold on. By contrast, online merchant Amazon has a *negative* cash cycle. It charges customers for purchases when they are made but can delay paying its suppliers.

This is an enviable position to be in, actually having other companies lend you their own working capital, which then acts effectively as an interest free loan. Clearly most firms are not in this position, and will actually have to incur the need for positive working capital. That is to say, they have to put money out now in the hope of getting it back in the future. We could think of it as follows: normally there is a significant space of time between delivery of order and receipt of payment, particularly when one is involved in a business to business transaction. This can be seen in Figure 10.6.

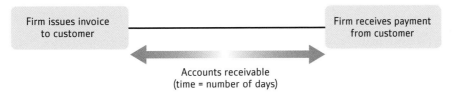

Figure 10.6 Delays in payment to the firm

The longer is the red arrow, the longer the time between the invoicing of goods and services and the actual receipt of cash and the more working capital that is needed to fill the gap.

Your authors can fully appreciate the downside of this part of the cycle. As young postgraduate research students, we frequently did part-time tutoring work at various universities. Tuition time with classes could not be invoiced until the end of the month and all universities seem to have a policy of paying 1 month in arrears, giving an average time to payment of one and a half months – no fun at all when you have holes in your shoes and you're subsisting on a diet of baked beans! The analogy with the firm is of course that they will already necessarily have incurred expenditure prior to the issue of the invoice. This is not entirely a bad thing as the firm itself will receive credit from suppliers in the form of a facility to pay in arrears (alas not something normally granted to postgraduate students). We could see this as a blue time arrow where, in effect, suppliers are lending us their working capital in Figure 10.7. Putting these together gives us Figure 10.8.

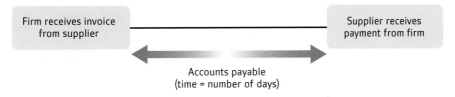

Figure 10.7 Delays in payment to suppliers

We can see then that the firm enjoys a credit-free grace period, in effect borrowing working capital from suppliers. In turn, the firm must extend the same courtesy to its own customers, necessitating the use of its own working capital. There will be in many cases a 'red-bracket gap' between cash-out and cash-in, necessitating the use of working capital.

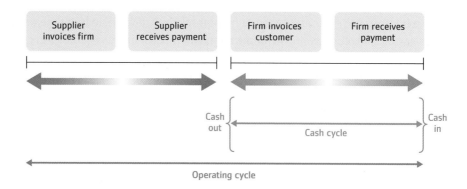

Figure 10.8 The operating cycle

It is evidently in the interest of business to try to minimise working capital in the ways that have been suggested in the previous paragraphs, such as speeding payments from customers and slowing payments to suppliers – in effect, shortening the red arrow and lengthening the blue arrow.

Note the two cycles identified in Figure 10.8. First, we have the operating cycle, identified in green, which is the number of days between the purchase of necessary inputs for production and final receipt of payment from the customer. Second, and probably more importantly, is the cash cycle identified in red which represents the length of time between cash-in and cash-out. Note, however, that the various stages in payment and credit we have suggested in Figure 10.8 need not occur in the strict sequence we have suggested. Thus it is entirely plausible that the firm can phase payments in time such that the 'red bracket' gap between cash-in and cash-out is minimised, as can be seen in Figure 10.9.

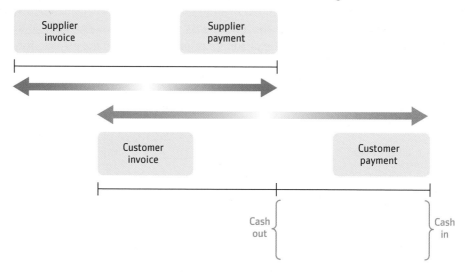

Figure 10.9 Minimised 'red-bracket' gap

And indeed if you are astute enough and lucky enough to have the right business operating conditions, it is perfectly possible to have a 'blue bracket' gap where cash comes in before it is actually spent! This would appear to be the case for the example of Amazon, discussed previously. This can be seen in the Figure 10.10.

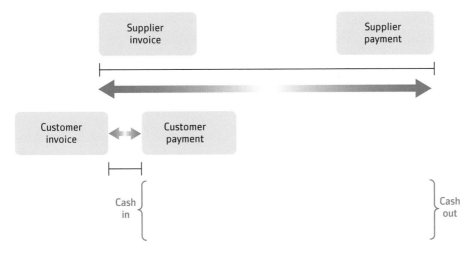

Figure 10.10  A blue-bracket gap (negative cash cycle)

Consequently, from a cash flow point of view, the perfect business is one in which cash comes in before it goes out. However, realistically, it may be difficult or impossible to reduce the use of working capital and the gap between cash-out and cash-in given that it is a zero-sum game, i.e. most businesses are attempting to do the same thing. A firm's suppliers want to get paid more quickly at the same time as its business customers are attempting to pay more slowly. Furthermore, it can potentially be controversial if there is an imbalance of bargaining power between the two parties involved. Take the mini case study concerning the UK's retail giant, Tesco ('Payment terms for suppliers: the special case of very large buyers').

## Mini case study

### Payment terms for suppliers: the special case of very large buyers

Source Rigby 2008, Copyright *Financial Times*, 2008

Tesco is asking all its non-food suppliers to wait an extra 30 days for payment of goods, as Britain's biggest retailer looks for ways to free up millions of pounds as it enters the all-important Christmas trading season.

The retailer wrote to all its general merchandise suppliers this month saying it had decided to change its payment terms from 30 to 60 days, effective from December 1, according to a letter seen by the Financial Times.

'We have written to suppliers to seek their agreement to the change and hope to implement it before the end of the year.'

The timing of the payment terms will leave Tesco with millions of pounds extra in working capital in the run-up to Christmas.

Its non-food sales in the UK stood at £8.3bn in the year to April representing just over a fifth of its turn-over in its home market.

Tesco insisted last night that the move was part of a global review.

The timing of the decision means that the supermarket chain will be able to use that cash due to suppliers on price cuts and promotions in the fierce battle for Christmas spending.

But the decision will provoke anger from suppliers who will now have to wait for longer to be paid from Tesco. It made nearly £3bn in profit last year.

1. The effect on the cash cycle for Tesco's non-food suppliers is fairly obvious. Can you suggest ways in which you might quantify the precise financial impact on the suppliers affected?

2. It would be natural for suppliers to claim that Tesco was 'being unfair'. However, how might they make a proper case for this claim? What metrics would they use?

3. Is the strong bargaining ability of large retailers with suppliers beneficial to consumers in the long run?

We are sure that the intention at Tesco was to maximise financial efficiency in order to maximise shareholder value, but the inadvertent effect has been to generate adverse publicity, and to further fuel the ongoing controversy in the UK concerning the relationship between Britain's big powerful supermarkets and their often much smaller suppliers.

## 10.2.2 Measurement of the cash cycle

The cash cycle (or cash conversion cycle) can be measured as follows:

CCC = Inventory days + Accounts Receivable Days – Accounts Payable Days

In other words, what we're interested in is the length of time that working capital is tied up. The longer this time, the greater the opportunity cost of financing. Inventory days is the average length of time it takes to sell your inventory. Accounts receivable days is the average length of time it takes to collect money from customers, and accounts payable days is the average length of time it takes to pay suppliers. The individual calculations are:

$$\text{Inventory Days} = \frac{\text{Value of Inventory}}{\text{Average Daily COGS}}$$

$$\text{Accounts Payable Days} = \frac{\text{Value of Accounts Payable}}{\text{Average Daily COGS}}$$

$$\text{Accounts Receivable Days} = \frac{\text{Value of Accounts Receivable}}{\text{Average Daily Sales}}$$

where COGS is the cost of goods sold. This is often extracted on an annual basis from company accounts and divided by 365 to allow calculation in days.

## Practical implications for managers

### The cash cycle

A key role for the financial manager in terms of the cash cycle is to look for ways of minimising inventory days and accounts receivable days, while increasing amounts payable days. Nevertheless, there may be limits to, for example, improving net account days given that other companies are trying to do much the same thing. Inventory days may be more amenable to improvement given the amount of work that has been done in this area with techniques such as 'just in time' and 'Kanban'.

## Key concepts

- ☐ The **cash cycle** is the time gap between the necessary outlay of cash for items such as supplies and employees' wages and the receipt of cash from customers, that is, the gap between **accounts payable** and **accounts receivable**. Also known as the **cash conversion cycle** it can be calculated by taking the average number of days working capital is tied up in inventory and accounts receivable minus working capital returned from accounts payable. This is usually calculated on a monthly or yearly basis

- ☐ **Accounts payable** is money owed *by* the firm to its creditors

- ☐ **Accounts receivable** is money owed *to* the firm by its debtors

- ☐ The **operating cycle** is the number of days between the purchase of necessary inputs for production and final receipt of payment from the customer

## 10.3 Trade credit

### 10.3.1 The need for trade credit

The question arises of course as to why trade credit is used in the first place. Surely if firms got their act together they could just pay each other on time and avoid the game of 'beggar my neighbour' by trying to stretch their accounts payable (creditor) days while reducing their accounts receivable (debtor) days? However, as we saw above, there is necessarily time involved in both the operating and cash cycle, and therefore necessarily an outlay of working capital. Nonetheless, a valid question that does arise in this context is the following. Does this working capital necessarily have to be borrowed from other firms in terms of trade credit? Could it not be borrowed from a bank?

The answer must lie in the fact that capital markets are imperfect and that small businesses often struggle to obtain debt finance from banks on reasonable terms. That is to say, the market is imperfect because of asymmetric information. A vendor who sells regularly to a small firm is probably better placed to know how creditworthy a small firm is than a bank, because the vendor deals with the firm frequently and has a good idea of how the firm tends to do business. Therefore, from the vendor's point of view, the extension of credit is necessary to attract and retain business customers. Business customers, particularly the smaller ones, gain a valuable source of working capital which rivals bank lending in importance. And of course, the vendor can always repossess any goods supplied, which can subsequently be resold to other customers and therefore has collateral value.

## 10.3.2 The cost of trade credit

As we have pointed out before, if the company must tie up cash as working capital then this has an opportunity cost. The opportunity cost in monetary terms is simply the value of the cash flow involved.

Suppose that, on average, the outstanding balance for accounts receivable is £500,000. This represents a present value of £500,000 in working capital permanently on loan in order to provide credit to customers. The percentage cost of extending this credit will be the firm's cost of capital, i.e. the WACC. Thus, it should be fairly clear to the finance department that a benefit worth more than the WACC is received from the extension of this facility.

Of course this cost would be lower if the working capital needed to extend credit were not permanent working capital. Thus if the sum involved was £500,000, the WACC was 15% and it was intended to sell the business after 6 years, the cost would be as shown in Screenshot 10.1.

| | T | CF | DF@15% | DCF |
|---|---|---|---|---|
| 1 | T | CF | DF@15% | DCF |
| 2 | 0 | -£500,000 | 1 | -£500,000 |
| 3 | 1 | | | |
| 4 | 2 | | | |
| 5 | 3 | | | |
| 6 | 4 | | | |
| 7 | 5 | | | |
| 8 | 6 | £500,000 | 0.4323276 | £216,164 |
| 9 | | | | |
| 10 | | | NPV | -£283,836 |

Screenshot 10.1 Cost of working capital

It is a considerable sum of money given that it represents more than half of the value of working capital. In other words, although the nominal value of working capital is returned at the end of the project, there may be a substantial reduction in the real value, particularly if the firm's discount rate is high and if working capital must be committed for long periods of time. Even if the working capital were only needed for a year, the DCF would be as follows;

$$-£500,000 + \frac{£500,000}{1.15} = -£65,217$$

Hence, at 15% discount, £65,217 (around 13%) of £500,000 working capital is used up, even if it is only committed for a year. Although £500,000 in nominal terms is returned to us at the end of a year, there is a high opportunity cost of committing the working capital to trade credit.

### 10.3.3 The specifics of credit terms

The actual credit terms used, though easy enough in principle to understand, are rather jargon ridden, so it is worth taking some time to understand the terminology involved. One of the most commonly used terms is **net 30**. All that this means is that the vendor expects payment within 30 days after the service has been rendered. In the case of trade good suppliers, this would be 30 days after the goods have been dispatched to the buyer; in the case of an accountant, this would mean that payment would be expected from firm X within 30 days of the completion of firm X's audit. There will often be a discount for early payment. Thus the invoice might contain the statement *5/7 net 30*. This means that a discount of 5% will be given for full payment within 7 days. Failing that the account must be settled in 30 days. If the debtor does not pay in full within the specified **net time**, he/she normally starts to accrue interest penalties.

It is worth restating that net terms for the purchase of goods are from the date of dispatch. Time in transit is counted as part of the time over which credit is extended even if, for example, the goods are late in arriving. However, vendors may set their terms out more favourably by quoting credit terms **ROG**, i.e. time to repay starts from the receipt of goods. For example, *3/15 ROG 40* means that full payment is due within 40 days from the receipt of goods, but that a 3% discount will be given if full payment is received within 15 days. A final variation on this theme is **EOM**. This means that the invoice must be settled by the end of the month, e.g. April invoices must be settled by the end of April. There are numerous variations on these basic rules. A much used rule is '10th and 25th' which grants half-month credit and specifies that all invoices issued before the 16th must be paid by the 25th of the month, while any invoice dated 16th to month end must be paid by the 10th of the following month.

## Practical implications for managers

### Trade credit

It is a key role of the financial manager to know how much it is costing your organisation to extend trade credit, while being able to quantify the benefit of cash settlement versus trade credit with vendors.

## Key concepts

- Extending **trade credit** to your customers builds goodwill but comes at a cost
- **x/y Net z** means that the x% discount will be granted for payment within y days. Otherwise payment is due within z days
- If a credit term is quoted as **ROG** it means the time to repay starts from the **receipt of goods**. **EOM** means the account must be settled by the **end of the month**

## 10.4 Float management

The cash balance shown by a firm on its books is called the book or ledger balance (1) whereas the balance shown in its bank account is called the available or collected balance (2). The difference (2) minus (1) is defined as the float.

### 10.4.1 Disbursement float

This is the amount of money which is available to the firm in the time before payment to vendors actually affects the firm's cash balance. It includes the process of postage and delivery of cheques, cheque clearing and the time at the other end between receipt of cheques or other forms of payment and processing. Take the following example from the website of the Indian Chartered Accountants Institute (ICAI) (http://www.icai.org/post.html?post_id=2935):

> 'Suppose that ABC Company has a book balance as well as available balance of Rs. 4 Lac [Lac is a unit in the Indian numbering system equal to 100,000] with its bank, State Bank of India, as of March 31. On April 1 it pays Rs. 1 Lac by cheque to one of its suppliers and hence reduces its book balance by Rs. 1 Lac.
>
> The State Bank of India, however, will not debit ABC's account till the cheque has been presented for payment on, say, April 6. Until that happens the firm's available balance is greater than its book balance by Rs. 1 Lac. Hence, between April 1 and April 6 ABC Company has a disbursement float of Rs. 1 Lac.
>
> Disbursement float = Firm's available Bank balance – Firm's book balance = Rs. 4 Lac – Rs. 3 Lac = Rs. 1 Lac'

### 10.4.2 The collection float

The collection float is more or less the opposite of the disbursement float. It is the amount of money that needs to be in place in the time that it takes the firm to actually acquire the cash once the buyer has approved the payment of the invoice by cheque or other means. Again we can find a useful example from the ICAI website:

'For example, suppose that XYZ Company has a book balance as well as an available balance of Rs. 5 Lac as of April 30. On May 1 XYZ Company receives a cheque for Rs. 1.5 Lac from a customer which it deposits in the bank. It increases its book balance by Rs. 1.5. Lac. However, this amount is not available to ABC Company until its bank presents the cheque to the customer's bank on, say, May 5. So, between May 1 and May 5 ABC Company has a collection float of (–) Rs. 1.5 Lac.

The collection float = the firm's available bank balance − Firm's book balance = Rs. 5.0 Lac − Rs. 6.5 Lac = (–) Rs. 1.5 Lac. The collection float is the negative of the disbursement float.'

### 10.4.3 The net float

The net float is just the difference between the collection float and the disbursement float. A firm with a positive net float can use it to its advantage and maintain a smaller cash balance. A firm with a negative net float will need to tie down higher amounts of working capital, however, because its collection period is longer than its disbursement period.

### 10.4.4 The future

The idea of the float will eventually become a thing of the past with the increasing use of real-time electronic transfer. For example, in the UK, business cheque use peaked in 1997 at 1.2 billion transactions and had fallen to 692 million by 2008 (UK Payments Administration 2009). Nevertheless it remains a significant means of payment for businesses in some parts of the world.

## Practical implications for managers

### Float management

The size of float needed by most firms is likely to decline with the increased adoption of electronic payment systems.

## Key concepts

- A **disbursement float** is the amount of money that will be available in the time before payment to vendors actually affects the firm's cash balance, such as the process of postage and delivery of cheques and cheque clearing
- A **collection float** is the amount of money that will be needed to bridge the gap between the buyer approving the payment of the invoice and the firm actually receiving cash
- A **net float** is just the difference between the collection float and the disbursement float

## 10.5  Receivables and payables management

### 10.5.1  Accounts receivable

You may remember that accounts receivable (AR) represents the total amount that has been invoiced but not yet paid by customers. As we have seen, we would ideally have as short a time as possible between providing goods and services and getting paid. However, the provision of credit may be a very necessary part of the competitive process. Therefore there is something of a trade-off involved in setting a credit period for customers. The main factors to take into account are the industry standard for trade terms and the interest costs of extending credit.

Clearly the industry standard will have to be observed unless the company is in a particularly strong competitive position. The trick is to avoid 'slippage' in the sense of letting the credit period grow beyond what was agreed or what was expected. Consequently, the financial controller will need to keep a close eye particularly on large accounts that are due for payment and on 'delinquency' – that is, customers who habitually pay at a later date than the agreed date.

In Section 10.1 we looked at how to calculate accounts receivable days. This will be a key calculation for the management of accounts receivable.

Another common technique that is often used is the accounts receivable aging schedule. This consists of a listing of the customers making up the total accounts receivable balance and is usually prepared at the end of each month. The idea is to compare whether average days to payment of accounts receivable is deteriorating or improving. Clearly if there is deterioration this means higher working capital costs and may lead to cash flow problems.

There are various ways in which we could summarise accounts receivable in a form that would allow analysis and management of the situation. Screenshot 10.2 shows a possible table for a very small company. It identifies individual companies by amount owed and the time period over which money is owed.

| | A | B | C | D | E | F |
|---|---|---|---|---|---|---|
| | | | | | | |
| 2 | | | Chabenezer Marney Loans | | | |
| 3 | | | December 24, 2012 | | | |
| 4 | | Total | | 1 to 30 | 31 to 60 | Over |
| 5 | | Accts. | | Days | Days | 60 Days |
| 6 | | Rec. | | Past | Past | Past |
| 7 | Customer Name | | Current | Due Date | Due Date | DueDate |
| 8 | Tiny Tim Orange Sellers | £2,200 | £400 | £700 | £900 | £200 |
| 9 | Bob Cratchit's Christmas Pud Co. | £5,800 | £2,800 | £3,000 | ---- | ---- |
| 10 | Jacob Marley Ghost Tours | £6,000 | £1,000 | £5,000 | ---- | ---- |
| 11 | Fezziwig Wig Copany | £2,600 | ---- | £1,600 | ---- | £1,000 |
| 12 | Fred and Nephew - Party Organisers | £2,000 | £1,100 | £500 | £400 | ---- |
| 13 | Old and Past - Family History Co. | £400 | ---- | £400 | ---- | ---- |
| 14 | Present Concerns | £5,600 | £600 | ---- | £5,000 | ---- |
| 15 | FutureBright | £1,200 | £1,200 | ---- | ---- | ---- |
| 16 | Total | £25,800 | £7,100 | £11,200 | £6,300 | £1,200 |

Screenshot 10.2  Chabenezer Marney loans

However, this kind of table may be impractical for companies with many customers. In which case, they will want to use summary information rather than personally identifying individual customers, as in Screenshot 10.3.

| | SUMMARY ACCOUNTS OUTSTANDING – MICKLEMUCKLECORP | | |
|---|---|---|---|
| 40 41 | | | |
| 42 43 44 | Days Outstanding | Amount Outstanding (£) | Percentage |
| 45 | | | |
| 46 | "1–10 | £118,900 | 21.37% |
| 47 | "11–30 | £111,000 | 19.95% |
| 48 | "31–40 | £225,639 | 40.55% |
| 49 | "41–50 | £60,363 | 10.85% |
| 50 | "51–60 | £27,892 | 5.01% |
| 51 | "60 + | £12,598 | 2.26% |
| 52 | Total | £556,392 | |

Screenshot 10.3 Micklemucklecorp accounts outstanding

This kind of report can easily be generated from MS Access or other software or can even be done on Excel using the data functions. This allows the 'interrogation' of the data to pinpoint exactly which customers are in arrears and which customers are likely to fall into arrears.

## 10.5.2 Collections policy

But what are you going to do when people don't pay? Whichever policy you choose should be the result of careful forethought and considered policy rather than reactionary and ad-hoc.

A sensible approach is to keep it very light and amiable until the strategy has been shown clearly not to work. After all, you don't want to alienate customers and lose repeat business. But there may come a point, which you have clearly defined beforehand, at which you realise that you still haven't been paid. Thus, in terms of policy, you may want to consider the following stages:

The steps usually taken are (1) letters, including reminders, to expedite payment; (2) telephone calls for personal contact; (3) personal visits; (4) assistance of collection agencies; and finally (5) legal action.

You also may want to differentiate in terms of the speed with which you go through the various stages. Hence an old and valued customer should probably be given the benefit of the doubt for at least a while if he/she claims to be going through hard times. However, it's probably not a good idea to be too understanding with a persistent offender. Indeed you may want to consider if you really need to do business with a customer who habitually abuses your trust.

Going to law is very serious and you may want to think long and hard before you undertake it. In many cases the legal costs will more than outweigh the sums owed. Better perhaps to expect a certain percentage of bad debt every year and make provisions accordingly.

### 10.5.3 Credit policy and credit standards

How much credit do you want to extend? If possible, none whatsoever, as the extension of credit involves the costly use of working capital and constitutes additional business risk. But that's unlikely to be possible in many industries. Therefore, you need to decide what the minimum is that you have to extend in order to retain customers.

The easiest way to do this would be to have the same terms and conditions as the rest of the industry or of comparable industries. However, if you wish to capture market share from competitors, extending more generous credit terms may be a means of doing this. However, before this is ventured, you should have a clear idea of the potential monetary benefit of this as there will be costs involved, viz collection cost, working capital cost and provision for bad debt. Realistically, how much is it all going to cost? For example, you might employ someone full-time as a credit controller at a salary of £30,000, expect to have bad debt of 5% of sales and use the company's cost of capital of 15% for the average of 1 month's credit sales. Hence your costs will be as shown in Screenshot 10.4 for a projected range of total sales.

| 1 | COST OF CREDIT POLICY | | | | |
|---|---|---|---|---|---|
| 2 | | | | | |
| 3 | SALES | CREDIT CONTROLLER | COST OF CAPITAL | COST OF BAD DEBT | COSTS AS % OF SALES |
| 4 | £100,000 | £30,000 | £1,250 | £5,000 | 36.25% |
| 5 | £500,000 | £30,000 | £6,250 | £25,000 | 12.25% |
| 6 | £1,000,000 | £60,000 | £12,500 | £50,000 | 12.25% |
| 7 | £5,000,000 | £60,000 | £62,500 | £250,000 | 7.45% |
| 8 | | | | | |

Screenshot 10.4   Cost of credit policy

(We have assumed that once you reach sales of £1 million, you will need a second credit controller.) You might want to ask yourself questions such as, 'Can I justify this level of cost? Would it be cheaper and more effective to use a collections agency rather than full-time credit control staff? Should I insure my credit risk – adding to cost but reducing the uncertainties? Will I get benefits equivalent to 7.45% of sales from my credit policy with £5 million of sales? For example, in the absence of my credit policy would sales decline by more than 7.45%? Will I get benefits worth 36.25% of sales should sales decline to £100,000? (This is highly unlikely!)

The other thing you may want to undertake is marginal analysis. That is, is it possible to establish the effect of an increase in the credit period on sales? What will be the effect of extending the credit period on cost? What is the net effect likely to be – positive or negative?

### 10.5.4 Credit analysis

In principle, the firm should gather as much information as possible about the firm wishing credit. Thus firms specialising in financing large amounts of trade credit typically look for one or more of the following: financial statements, a credit bureau report, a bank reference and a personal guarantee. If you are supplying trade credit worth a great deal of money to another firm, it may not be unreasonable to ask for a bank reference and a trade reference. The latter is a statement of confidence from other businesses that the credit buyer deals with. However, it may be difficult to get this kind of detailed information. In fact, the available public evidence suggests that simple trade credit limits are the most common tool in credit management. As Scherr (1996) observes:

> 'Over 85% of large firms use this tool, and they typically assign credit limits to more than 80% of their customers (Beranek and Scherr, 1991, and Besley and Osteryoung, 1985). While such a widely-used technique must have practical value, practitioners and researchers have little understanding of how it can enhance shareholder wealth.
>
> By far the most popular method of setting credit limits is the analyst's judgement (Besley and Osteryoung, 1985). This may or may not lead to wealth maximization, depending on the analyst's skills and biases. Further, while practitioners almost always cite "risk control" as the primary motivation for using credit limits (Beranek and Scherr, 1991, and Besley and Osteryoung, 1985), there is little agreement among them as to what type of risk is controlled, although there appears to be a strong connection between credit limits policy and credit investigation expenses'

(Scherr 1996).

Consequently, it may or may not be possible to obtain *external* information about the firm requesting trade credit which reduces the risk of trade credit. Or, as Scherr (1996) suggests, the firm supplying the trade credit may simply take a pragmatic 'trial and error' approach where a relatively small value of trade credit is granted at first, followed by increasingly larger amounts as the firm builds up trust and develops a relationship with the credit customer. Indeed a long, continuous and well-documented history with a credit customer is likely to be the firm's greatest asset in this context. This is often how banks assess creditworthiness. They have long relationships with customers, providing them with insider information and allowing them to overcome information asymmetry.

## Practical implications for managers

### Receivables management

One of the most reliable methods for establishing the creditworthiness of business customers is the private information that the firm has from previous dealings, possibly over many years. However, this information may not be a great deal of use at times of expansion when new customers must be sought. This is one of the many sources of uncertainty which makes periods of growth much more risky than normal trading conditions.

### 10.5.5 Payables management

Accounts payable represent money owed *by* the firm to its creditors. Payables management is slightly easier than receivables management. The trick here is really to take full advantage of any credit offered by comparing the discount offered for early payment with the effective value of the boost to working capital from waiting until the final day in order to pay.

For example, suppose the terms offered are 3/7 net 40. This means that a 3% discount will be offered if the account is settled within 7 days. Otherwise the firm has 40 days to pay. If the firm decides not to take the discount, it incurs an opportunity cost by so doing. That is, in effect by not taking the credit, the firm has decided to take a loan of £97 per £100 invoice for 33 days. The present value of this loan is the £3 in the £100 that has been given up. At present, we don't know what this is costing us in annualised percentage terms, so we will call this X% for the moment. The present value of the loan is:

$$£3 = £97 \times X\% \times \frac{33}{365}$$

Thus X, the unknown annualised percentage, is calculated as follows:

$$X\% = \left(\frac{3}{97}\right) \times \left(\frac{365}{33}\right) = 34.21\%$$

Note that the percentage cost of not taking a discount varies negatively with the length of the credit period. Thus if the terms offered had been 3/7 net 60, the calculation would have been as follows:

$$X\% = \left(\frac{3}{97}\right) \times \left(\frac{365}{53}\right) = 21.3\%$$

The rates paid for trade credit should, of course, be subtracted from the WACC to find the overall percentage gain (or loss) on trade credit. Nevertheless, some of the percentage values involved here are surprisingly high and, one would have thought, greater than the WACC for many firms. It is a reflection of the imperfection of the market for short-term capital and perhaps also the volatility of short-term interest rates that many firms will actually take the credit rather than the discount. If no discount has been offered, then the benefit of trade credit is just equal to the WACC.

## Practical implications for managers

### Payables management

As a financial professional, you need to be able to quantify the benefits of immediate settlement versus trade credit.

## Key concepts

- [ ] A **collections policy** is necessary to deal with customers who do not pay the firm on time. It can involve letters, telephone calls, personal visits, the assistance of collection agencies and even legal action to expedite payment
- [ ] A **credit policy** is necessary for the firm to set conditions on when credit is extended and under what conditions
- [ ] Before extending credit a **credit analysis** should be undertaken to check the credit worthiness of the potential customer

## 10.6 Inventory management

The basic principle of inventory management is relatively straightforward. It is the art of maintaining a minimum acceptable level of stock consistent with minimising the risks associated with 'stock-out'. Too much cash tied up in stock and inventory is a waste of working capital. Too little stock, on the other hand, risks disrupting production or adversely affecting customers.

There are two basic approaches to inventory. One approach is the comparatively informal approach of a service business which keeps relatively low-value stocks of consumables and materials. An office-based industry such as an accountancy firm would have stocks of paper, printer cartridges and so on. The business of managing stock will be a relatively low-level routine administration job, and standard orders will be placed at preset intervals. The costs of being 'stock-out' are relatively low as the customers are fellow members of staff who may be able to manage for a day or two without their pens and pads. (The big risk is, of course, that it's the boss who's been affected by stock-out!)

To take another example of the informal approach, smaller retailers will have stocks of goods for sale which they will keep an eye on and replenish from time to time when they take a trip to their wholesaler. Stock-out can be an important risk for the small retailer as it could adversely affect customer loyalty. Nevertheless this kind of inventory management will probably be done intuitively by the proprietor on the basis of past experience of what is likely to sell and with an eye to the bottom line.

Regardless of the size of the operation there are three basic costs of inventory. These are:

1. The cost of the material (plus freight and other costs associated directly with a particular replenishment shipment).

2. The carry cost of inventory.

3. The cost of issuing a replenishment order and processing the stock receipt.

This classification of basic cost suggests a number of fairly simple principles when managing inventory, for example:

- Make sure you are only ordering what is strictly needed or what is likely to sell.

- Do not hold too much inventory – this is eating up working capital (and risks of obsolence increase).

- On the other hand, don't make orders so meagre that you are constantly having key employees using their valuable time to place rush orders, which may come at considerable additional cost.

So, for certain types of enterprise inventory, management is relatively straightforward. However, for manufacturing companies and large retailers, a great deal is at stake with inventory management. The sums tied up in inventory are large and a good supply chain system which integrates inventory and distribution can give the firm a significant competitive edge.

The **economic order quantity** is that quantity of a product that will minimise the total cost of inventory per item in stock. It 'balances' the costs you incur as you buy and maintain the stock of a product. In this way it determines the point at which the level of inventory minimises total inventory cost. The EOQ is typically applied to items with recurring usage, that is items sold or used on a regular basis. The result is the most cost effective quantity to order. In purchasing this is known as the order quantity.

The EOQ model is the standard way of determining the cost minimising level of inventory. It is based on the assumptions that the firm will have a relatively stable and well-known demand for inventory, based on relatively stable demand from customers; that the costs of ordering and holding inventory are relatively constant; and that the firm has maintained a constant time gap between ordering, receipt of inventory and need for inventory. It is a 'robust' model in the sense that there can be a considerable amount of departure from these assumptions without entirely negating the usefulness of the model.

Figure 10.11 is a representation of the order process throughout the year. The diagram has **order quantity** on the vertical axis with **time** on the horizontal axis. In this case, an order cycle is represented in which a quantity equal to Q is ordered. This is run down and re-ordered, twice. The termination point of the diagram on the time axis is at Y where 1 year has elapsed. Over the course of the year the cycle has repeated once and starts once again just as the year ends. At the termination point, three orders of magnitude Q have been placed. The symbol A is used for total orders over the year.

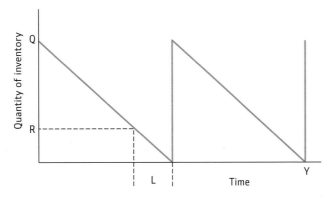

Figure 10.11 EOC order process over time

Therefore, in this case:

$$A = 3 \times Q$$

For example, if the average order quantity was Q = 100 items, cumulative orders over the year would be A = 300 items.

Two other points on the figure are indicated. R is the quantity at which stocks are sufficiently run down that a new order needs to be placed, e.g. R might equal 20 items. The letter L on the time axis represents the time from order to delivery.

Note that the stock arrives 'just in time' as inventory goes to zero. The order cycle in this case must be 6 months. The year starts with a full inventory. This is run down to zero and replenished half way through the year, and once again by the end of the year. There are two costs associated with inventory. First, there is the storage cost of holding inventory. This will include both 'warehousing' cost and the opportunity cost of funds tied up in inventory. Storage costs will vary directly with average level of inventory held. Average level of inventory, in turn, will be the average between the start of the cycle, Q, and at the end of the cycle, 0. Thus the average inventory is (Q+0)/2 or Q/2. Storage cost can be calculated as:

$$\text{Storage Cost} = \frac{Q}{2} \times C_h$$

where $C_h$ is the cost per unit per year of holding inventory.

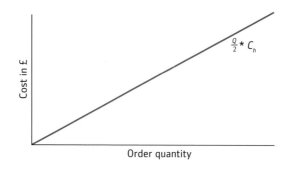

Figure 10.12 Storage cost varies directly with order quantity

Clearly this cost will vary directly and linearly with the amount of inventory held, as shown in Figure 10.12.

The other cost involved here is the ordering cost. This is also known as purchase cost or set-up cost, and is the sum of the fixed costs that are incurred each time an item is ordered. Unlike inventory cost, this cost does not vary directly with the quantity ordered. It is primarily associated with the staff time needed to process the order. This would include incoming quality inspection, invoice processing and vendor payment, in addition to the paperwork involved in processing the transaction as well as physical activities such as unloading and delivery to other departments. The ordering cost will depend on the number of times that orders are made, as follows:

$$\text{Ordering Cost} = \frac{A}{Q} \times C_p$$

where $C_p$ is the cost per order and $\frac{A}{Q}$ is the number of orders per year (total yearly order $A$ divided by average order quantity $Q$).

The relationship between ordering cost and order size is very similar to the relation between average fixed cost and volume or output. The greater the order size, the lower the order cost, as shown in Figure 10.13.

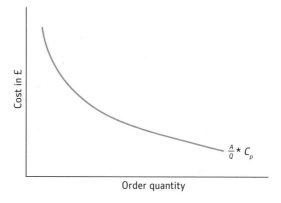

Figure 10.13 Ordering cost is like a fixed overhead cost. Ordering cost per unit falls as ordering cost is spread over more units

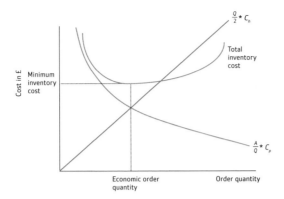

Figure 10.14  Total inventory cost and the EOQ

Putting these together, we can find **total inventory cost** and the EOQ, as demonstrated in Figure 10.14.

$$Optimal\ Order\ Quantity\ Q^* = \sqrt{\frac{2 * A * C_p}{C_h}}$$

## Mini case study

### Make sure you have your Christmas stock in

Source Maitland 2005, Copyright *Financial Times*, 2005

Predicting demand for Christmas trees, crackers and men's socks is usually not too difficult at this time of year. But forecasting sales of the hottest new electronic gadget or the must-have Christmas toy is quite another matter.

Every year, much-hyped products disappear from the shelves long before most people have done their Christmas shopping, leaving fashion-conscious consumers and frazzled parents wallowing in disappointment and frustration.

This year, Microsoft's Xbox 360 game console sold out soon after its late November launch in the US and its early December launch in Europe. Its scarcity has been reflected on eBay, with consoles selling for as much as $1,000 (£565) at auction, compared with the official price of about $400. Even Steve Ballmer, Microsoft's chief executive officer, has said he has had problems obtaining one for his children.

Last year, it was Robosapiens toys and iPods that failed to appear under the solidly predictable tree. Supplies of Sony PlayStations got held up in a supertanker in the Suez Canal and the company had to charter Russian cargo aircraft to make deliveries.

Supply disruptions are not confined to toys and consumer goods. UK supermarkets stopped taking orders online for Christmas grocery deliveries in mid-December this year because of extraordinarily high demand.

Even festive specialities can run out because of spikes in demand, as happened when Delia

Smith, the celebrity television cook, used cranberries in her *Winter Collection* series. Her chocolate truffle torte also caused a European shortage of liquid glucose.

The persistence of pre-Christmas sell-outs, despite the use of sophisticated forecasting tools, has led to suspicions that companies ration or withhold hot goods to feed the consumer frenzy.

Yossi Sheffi, director of Massachusetts Institute of Technology's Centre for Transportation and Logistics, says it is not uncommon for companies to announce expected shortages when launching a new product. 'People want more of something that is scarce. Most manufacturers will feed newspapers with these stories because they help future sales.'

The danger is that actual shortages, especially in the run-up to Christmas, will alienate customers, as well as lose potential sales.

1. List the sort of problems that could be caused by these kinds of 'stock-out' problems.

2. Outline three or four possible solutions to the problem.

3. If you were a retailer, would it generally be a better long-run strategy to do nothing and expect stock-outs or to greatly increase orders with the prospect of excess stock left in January?

## Practical implications for managers

### Inventory management

This can be a highly technical area and techniques of inventory control can be very sophisticated. However, in essence it is a case of managing the trade-off between the costs of holding too much inventory versus the cost of over-frequent ordering and running out of stock.

## Key concepts

☐ **Economic order quantity** is that quantity of inventory that minimises the total cost of inventory per item in stock

☐ **Total cost of inventory** consists of storage cost plus ordering cost

## 10.7 Cash management

### 10.7.1 Reasons for holding cash – the demand for money

Cash is the lifeblood of the firm and it is critical to hold cash and highly liquid assets which are sufficient to cover the firm's needs – taking account of the inevitable fluctuations due to seasonality, stage of the business cycle and the ever-present unseen random factors. A useful framework which is widely used in finance is the motives for holding money identified by distinguished economist John Maynard Keynes. These are the transactions motive, the precautionary motive and the speculative motive. In addition to these, for firms there is also the compensation balance.

1. **Transactions motive** – one reason why we hold cash as individuals is that we get a big 'lump' of cash when we are paid. Thereafter, this is slowly depleted as we make payments straight from our account or withdraw money for small day-to-day expenditures. To use the technical language, there is a mismatch of cash inflow and cash outflow. The same thing happens for business. Cash arrives in discrete 'wedges' and at different intervals from the times when payments have to be made. Thus, it is necessary to hold a positive cash balance to cover all expenditures before the next 'wedge' of cash arrives.

2. **Precautionary motive** – this is cash that we hold back against unexpected expenditure. For example, if you've missed the bus and you're running late you're going to have to unexpectedly find the money for a taxi. Even though business finance is done on a more formal and managerial basis, it is still perfectly possible to have unexpected expenditures, e.g. an unexpectedly high level of custom may necessitate the unexpected disbursal of overtime payments.

3. **Speculative motive** – this is the need to keep free cash flow available to be deployed quickly in the event of an investment opportunity. Of course there will always be disagreements between shareholders and managers over how large this 'war chest' ought to be, given the agency problems involved with extensive management access to free cash flow.

4. **Compensation balance** – this is not one of the classic motives for holding money. Nevertheless it is of practical importance for many businesses to hold positive bank balances as these are often a condition of the bank providing commercial loans or other financial services.

Traditional cash management involves making sure that a system is set up to ensure that invoices are paid as and when they are due, usually in cooperation with the bank, that payments approvals are controlled and managed efficiently, and that surplus cash is swept on a regular basis into an interest-bearing account. As far as possible these activities should be centralised within the organisation in order to take advantage of routinised processes, specialised staff and any bargaining leverage that may be gained with the bank for handling large volumes of cash.

However, in addition to this, another important part of the job is liquidity forecasting to identify working capital gaps and the financing required to support the organisation. Furthermore, cash management has a medium- to long-term aspect in that it is necessary to anticipate the need for cash availability to service debt obligations, pay dividends and ensure taxes are paid. Moreover, cash may have to be made available at regular intervals for investment projects. Cash management is increasingly a proactive business function. We saw this in the mini case study on the International Accounts Payable Professionals (IAPP) ('Accounts-payable professionals'). Another notable organisation is Treasury Management International which publishes articles by treasury employees for treasury employees.

## 10.7.2 Cash management

Effective cash management requires reasonably accurate cash flow forecasting. The steps in cash flow forecasting are as follows:

1. Forecast the anticipated cash inflows.

2. Forecast the anticipated cash outflows.

3. Determine net cash flow for each period.

4. Calculate the cumulative cash flow.

In principle it is a practical rather than a heavily theoretical exercise and the most straightforward way to demonstrate the principles involved is in terms of an exemplary spreadsheet. The specimen spreadsheet shown in Screenshot 10.5 is provided by the UK government for the use of small businesses.

| | A | B |
|---|---|---|
| 1 | Monthly Cash Flow Projection | |
| 2 | Explanation of Data to Enter | |
| 3 | | |
| | 1. CASH ON HAND | |
| 4 | [Beginning of month] | Cash on hand same as (7), Cash Position Previous Month |
| 5 | 2. INCOME | |
| 6 | (a) Cash Sales | All cash sales.  Omit credit sales unless cash is actually received. |
| 7 | (b) Collections from Credit Accounts | Amount to be expected from all credit accounts. |
| 8 | (c) Loan or Other Cash Injection | Indicate here all cash injections not shown in 2(a) or 2(b) above. |
| | 3. TOTAL CASH RECEIPTS | |
| 9 | [2a + 2b + 2c=3] | Self-explanatory |
| | 4. TOTAL CASH AVAILABLE | |
| 10 | [Before cash out] (1 + 3) | Self-explanatory |
| 11 | 5. OUTGOINGS | |
| 12 | (a) Purchases (Merchandise) | Merchandise for resale or for use in product [paid for in current month] |
| 13 | (b) Gross Wages (excludes withdrawals) | Base pay plus overtime [if any] |
| 14 | (c) Payroll Expenses (Taxes, etc.) | Include paid vacations, paid sick leave, health insurance etc |
| 15 | (d) Outside Services | This could include outside labor and/or materials for specialised overflow work |
| 16 | (e) Supplies (Office and operating) | Items purchased for use in the business [not for resale] |
| 17 | (l) Utilities | Water, heat, light, and/or power |
| 18 | (m) Insurance | Coverages on business property and products, e.g., fire, liability; |
| 19 | (n) Taxes | Property taxes plus inventory tax, sales tax, excise tax, if applicable |
| 20 | (r) Subtotal | This subtotal indicates cash out for operating costs |
| 21 | (s) Loan Principal Payment | Include payment on all loans, including vehicle and equipment purchases on time payment |
| 22 | (t) Capital Purchases [Specify] | Non-expensed [depreciable] expenditures such as equipment, building, vehicle purchases, |
| 23 | (u) Other Start-up Costs | Expenses incurred prior to first month projection and paid after the "start-up" position |
| 24 | (v) Reserve and/or Escrow [Specify] | Example:  insurance, tax, or equipment escrow to reduce impact of large periodic payments |
| | 6. TOTAL CASH PAID OUT | |
| 25 | [Total 5a thru 5w] | Self-explanatory |
| | 7. CASH POSITION | |
| 26 | [End of month]  (4 minus 6) | Enter this amount in (1) Cash on Hand following month – See "A" of "Analysis" |

Screenshot 10.5  Cash forecast specimen spreadsheet

*Source*: www.businesslink.gov.uk/Finance_files/Cash_Flow_Projection_Worksheet_v2.xls.

©Crown copyright 2010

Thus, given a forecast period of a month, it is a case of taking any **cash** available at the start of the month (1) and adding to this **total cash receipts** (3) [which itself is the result of summing various expected sources of **income** (2)]. This gives the sum of positive cash flows or **total cash available** (4). In order to get an idea of expected negative cash flow, one then itemises **outgoings** (5). The sum of outgoings yields **total cash paid out** (6). The forecast net cash position is then just **total cash available** (4) – **total cash paid out** (6).

When the expected cash position is likely to be negative, the financial manager would release cash from liquid assets to make up the difference. In fact, the firm will normally have a target positive balance which it aims to have every month (explained in the next section), so liquid assets will also be used to 'top this up' to the normal positive cash balance. When net cash flow is positive, it may well be carried forward as suggested in this example. However, if positive cash flow is significantly in excess of the target balance, it is a good idea to invest it in a liquid short-term interest-bearing asset. For example, the University of Hawaii has the following rules regarding cash management:

> '... Idle cash from all operating funds will be pooled and invested by the Treasury Office. Interest earned will be prorated based on average weekly cash balances. (3) Temporary idle cash shall be fully invested to obtain maximum yield consistent with safety, liquidity and diversification. (4) Short-term investments of operating funds may be made in U.S. Treasury bills, U.S. Treasury notes and bonds, U.S. Government Agency obligations, Banker's acceptance, certificate of deposit, commercial paper, money market funds, repurchase agreements, savings accounts, and student loan resource securities.'[1]

Cash flow forecasting tells us what the cash flow position is likely to be. However, it gives no guidance as to what the cash flow position *ought* to be. What might constitute an optimal, sufficient or even minimally acceptable cash balance?

### 10.7.4 Determination of acceptable cash balance

The determination of sufficient cash balance will usually be based on past experience. Thus one might simply take the average of past monthly balances, adjusting for seasonality and allowing for differences, such as an expansion in the business and much greater calls on cash in the future. However, this is rather vague and it is useful to have more definite metrics to at least provide a 'ballpark' figure. One way of doing this is to use the Baumol model. Baumol's insight was that the formula for optimal inventory could be applied to cash holdings. The formula is as follows:

$$Z = \sqrt{\frac{2FT}{k}}$$

where $Z$ is the target cash balance, $F$ is the fixed cost of selling assets to replenish cash, $T$ is total amount of cash needed over a year and $k$ is the opportunity cost of holding cash (annual rate).

Suppose, for example, that Fizzel Fireworks disburses £1 million per year. The cash interest rate is 4% and Fizzel's broker charges £50 per transaction. We can calculate the required cash balance as:

$$\sqrt{\frac{2 \times 50 \times 1m}{0.04}} = \sqrt{2500m} = £50,000$$

The interpretation of this result is as follows. The company should hold the bulk of its planned expenditure of £1m in 'an interest bearing account or interest bearing securities while drawing down £50,000 in 20 lots in order to replenish the current account as it goes to zero. Of course, if there was no transaction cost involved in selling securities and there was no delay on receiving the proceeds of securities' sales, then the firm should hold all of its cash in the form of interest bearing securities and simply sell them whenever cash was required.

The problem with the Baumol model is that it is based on relatively stable cash inflows and outflows. Cash flows may not be very predictable. Furthermore, money managers and treasurers are a cautious lot. They may want a safety margin in addition to a minimum necessary efficient balance.

An alternative to the Baumol model which allows for variability in cash flow is the Miller–Orr model. An example can be seen in Figure 10.15.

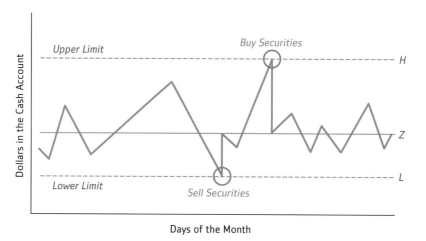

Figure 10.15 The Miller–Orr model graph.
*Source*: Fred Thompson www.willamette.edu/~fthompso/lectures/cashbud.ppt

This provides a formula for determining the target cash balance (Z). However, given its somewhat random nature, cash is allowed to fluctuate until it reaches one of two 'trigger points' which prompt intervention. When the lower trigger point is reached (lower limit L), this prompts the firm to sell securities in order to raise the cash level back to the amount Z. When the upper trigger point, H, is reached the firm should lower cash holdings back to the average Z by investing excess cash in securities. The main difference from the Baumol model is that it incorporates uncertainty in the form of the variance of cash flow. In the Miller–Orr model the cash balance is determined as follows:

$$Z = \sqrt[3]{\frac{3FV}{4k}} + L$$

where V is the daily variance of the cash flow and L is the absolute lowest level of cash that must be available.

For example: suppose that short-term securities yield 5% per year and it costs the organisation $50 each time it buys or sells securities. The daily variance of cash flows is 1,000 (V) and your bank requires $1,000 minimum checking account balance (L), where L is the lower limit.

$$Z = \sqrt[3]{\frac{3 \times 50 \times 1000}{4 \times \frac{.05}{360}}} + 1,000 = 1646.33$$

Note that in this case, we are using the *daily* rate of interest. We restore cash balance to the value Z, or 1646.33 by buying or selling securities once the upper or lower limit has been reached.

Once we know the ideal cash balance, we can determine the upper limit as a function of this quantity and the lower limit; the upper limit for the cash account (H) is determined by the following equation:

$$H = 3Z - 2L$$

where U is the upper limit of the cash balance.

Thus the upper limit is determined as follows:

$$H = 3\,(\$4,939) - 2(\$1,000) = \$2,939$$

## Practical implications for managers

### Cash management

In the absence of the information needed for sophisticated money balance management, small and medium sized businesses often need to make a judgement call. The choice is between hoarding cash and keeping reserves or trusting that bridging finance will always be available externally. It is for this reason that companies of this size often rely on reserves or internal equity given the risk and uncertainty of raising finance externally.

## Key concepts

- ☐ The **motives for holding cash** include the transactions motive, the precautionary motive, the speculative motive and the compensation balance
- ☐ The **transactions motive** states that cash is held because there is a mismatch between cash inflows and cash outflows, i.e. if cash inflow is in one large payment at the beginning of the month and the cash outflows are smaller and spread out

- ☐ The **precautionary motive** states that cash is held in case of unexpected expenditures
- ☐ The **speculative motive** states that cash is held in case of an unexpected investment opportunity
- ☐ A **compensation balance** is cash held by a firm to meet conditions for loans or other financial services
- ☐ **Baumol's inventory model** of optimal cash holding is as follows: $Z = \sqrt{\dfrac{2FT}{k}}$, where Z is the target cash balance, F is the fixed cost of selling assets to replenish cash, T is the total amount of cash needed over a year and k is the opportunity cost of holding cash (annual rate)
- ☐ The **Miller–Orr model** of cash flow management is as follows: $Z = \sqrt[3]{\dfrac{3FV}{4k}} + L$, where V is the variance of the cash flow and L is the absolute lowest level of cash that must be available. The main difference from the Baumol model is that it incorporates uncertainty in the form of the variance of cash flow

## 10.8 Summary

This chapter has been subtly different from all the other chapters in this book as it is slightly less theoretical and rather more concerned with shorter-term rather than longer-term decision making. In particular it was concerned with the management of day-to-day cash flow, liquidity and working capital.

Working capital as we found out was capital which was not used up in the course of production and, in principle, could be returned at the end of a particular investment project. Because of the highly cyclical nature even over the shorter time perspective of days weeks and years, the level of working capital would tend to rise and fall depending in the behaviour of current assets relative to current liabilities. The factors that were particularly influential in the ebb and flow of net current assets were payables (–), receivables (+) and inventory (+). As a result of the effect of these on working capital it is necessary to carefully manage these areas with particular respect to their impact on the availability of cash. In the last section we considered how cash itself might be managed in order to cope with variation in this item.

## ? Questions

1. How would you define working capital?
2. In what situations would you use the quick ratio rather than the current ratio?
3. Distinguish between permanent assets and non-permanent assets. Why is it important to maintain permanent assets and permanent working capital?

4. Why does Amazon allegedly have an enviable cash cycle? Describe the typical cash cycle for less fortunate firms.

5. Compare and contrast short-term and longer-term strategies for working capital management.

6. What does 2/10 net 28 mean in terms of trade credit?

7. Distinguish between the three different types of float.

8. What issues should you consider when extending trade credit to business customers?

9. How would you explain the economic order quantity?

10. What is the percentage opportunity cost if you accept trade credit at 2/6 net 20?

11. FW confectionery company is considering how much cash it should hold. Suppose that it typically pays out £3 million over the year. The cash interest rate is 2.5% and FW's bank charges £3 per transaction to convert its short-term investments into cash. What average cash balance should FW hold on EOQ principles?

## Case study

### Getting to grips with working capital

Source Clar 2009[2]

In January 2008, PPG made their largest-ever acquisition by purchasing the Dutch-based Sigma-Kalon from financial sponsor Bain Capital. This acquisition differed from previous M&A activity as the two organisations were of comparable size in Europe, but with very different business models (Fig 10.16). However, in order to leverage the full potential of the new organisation, and optimise cash concentration for the repayment of corporate debt, Treasury needed to combine the cash management activities of PPG and SigmaKalon in an efficient manner. This article outlines some of the challenges and considerations in achieving this.

| Key differences | PPG legacy | SigmaKalon legacy |
|---|---|---|
| ERP | Oracle | SAP |
| Business model | Business-to-business | Business-to-customer |
| Cash position | Cash rich (prior to acquisition) | Highly leveraged |
| Financial process centralisation | Segregation of collections and payments | Cash management organised in clusters |
| Cash management | Physical pooling-Ireland | Notional pooling-The Netherlands |
| Shared services | Pan-European SSC | Some local SSCs |
| Transaction volume | 277,000 transactions per annum | 880,000 transactions per annum |

Figure 10.16  PPG and SigmaKalon business models

## Business organisation

In addition to the company's organisational complexity and geographical diversity, most of the 13 business units are organised around a Principal Structure. Essentially, a Principal Structure is a corporate business model where raw materials are purchased by a principal entity, delivered to local warehouses owned by the principal, then processed by consignment manufacturers (factories) on a toll fee basis. Finished goods are then sold by local Sales companies at cost plus a fee. To facilitate this business model, the company's principal is located in Switzerland. However, PPG Finance BV, its in-house bank, is located in the Netherlands, a country with the most extensive network of tax exemption treaties, but also where notional pooling is well established and where the provision of security confined to a right of set-off instead of general cross-guarantees is also accepted.

## Summary

In summary, PPG Treasury faced two challenges: firstly, combining two cash management structures managed by two very different organisations, and secondly, maximising cash concentration to reduce corporate debt to the bare minimum. To achieve this, PPG implemented a cross-currency notional pool in 20 countries in just nine months. This has proved to be a highly efficient and convenient mechanism, but a strong understanding of the tax and legal implications was necessary, together with close involvement alongside IT teams from start to finish to facilitate the changes to the business.

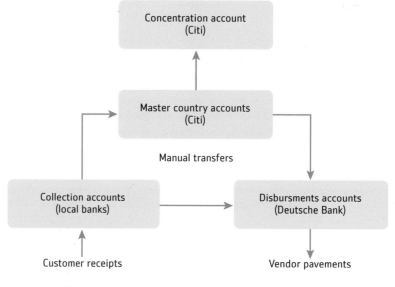

Figure 10.17 Former PPG cash management structure

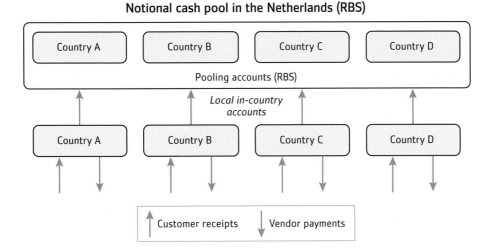

Figure 10.18  Former SigmaKalon cash management structure

## Cash management harmonisation

From a treasury perspective, to enable cash management operations to be centralised efficiently and to maximise the amount of cash available to the group, PPG needed to streamline and harmonise the former PPG and SigmaKalon cash management structures. PPG Treasury now has responsibility for all treasury and cash management activities of the combined group in 36 countries across 145 locations, incorporating 75 legal entities, 27 currencies and more than 700 bank accounts.

## Former PPG model

The PPG legacy cash management model was initially designed to be monitored from the US in a cash-rich B2B environment. Local accounts were maintained in key countries for collections and non trade disbursements, and the European SSC based in the Czech Republic managed most European trade payments, primarily through disbursement accounts (Fig 10.17). These accounts were funded either from local liquidity or cash held on deposit with a treasury centre located in Dublin. In addition to the payments and collections accounts was an overlay pooling structure in euros only, established with an overlay bank. Liquidity was zero balanced manually to local concentration accounts held with the overlay bank on a daily basis, and then swept automatically to a euro master account in Ireland. Any FX positions arising from non-euro denominated inter company current accounts were typically hedged using numerous FX swaps.

## Former SigmaKalon cash management structure

In contrast, the SigmaKalon cash management organisation had been established on the basis of its pan-European B2C business model and a highly leveraged structure. The company operated a notional cash pool with ABN Amro in the Netherlands, now The Royal Bank of Scotland (RBS). With a few exceptions, SigmaKalon entities maintained local accounts, either with a branch of ABN Amro or a local bank, with pooling accounts in the Netherlands. The local in-country accounts were zero balanced on a daily basis to the respective pooling accounts in the necessary currencies. Payables and receivables were processed locally through the in-country accounts and liquidity was concentrated in the cross-currency cash pool.

PPG Treasury faced the challenge of combining these two cash management structures, with the following objectives:

1. Optimise the funding of working capital with a 'zero float' structure
2. Provide parent company with visibility on cash generation on a daily basis
3. Reduce costs by minimising bank costs, standardising and automating processes

To achieve these objectives, PPG paid particular attention to fixed costs (such as account maintenance and zero-balancing costs), ensured that the structure would refund the full cash pool benefit, streamlined the payment processes with as few exceptions as possible (e.g. for tax reasons, as in Italy and Turkey) by notably overhauling the existing payment factory and the inter-company netting process. PPG also leveraged the RBS banking network inherited from ABN Amro in order to enhance cash visibility on more than 500 bank accounts, with the exception of a few local entities (e.g., equity ownerships) in which Treasury has no control over liquidity.

The new structure combined elements of the former PPG structure, such as a centralised SSC maintaining a payment factory, and of SigmaKalon, an in-house bank at the heart of a cross-currency notional cash pool. The group's headquarters in Pittsburgh was supportive of the project as Treasury was able to outline and to quantify how these objectives would be achieved.

1. What two challenges were faced by PPG Treasury?
2. Would you describe their cash management operation as simple or complex?
3. What were the objectives of PPG in combining the two cash management structures?
4. Given that PPG is a multinational company, what function was needed here in addition to the conventional cash management schemes?
5. Look up the definitions of the following:
   - Overlay account
   - Sweep account
   - Concentration account
   - Compensated balance

 # Further reading

Chiou, J.R., Cheng, L. and Wu, H.W. (2006) The determinants of working capital management. *Journal of American Academy of Business* **10**(1):149–155.

Deloof, M. (2003) Does working capital management affect profitability of Belgian firms? *Journal of Business Finance and Accounting* **30**(3&4):573–587.

Edward, A. (2002) Simple way to find order quantities subject to an aggregate constraint. (Statistical data included.) *Production & Inventory Management Journal*, December.

Filbeck, G. and Krueger, T.M. (2005) An analysis of working capital management results across industries. *American Journal of Business* **20**(2).

Filbeck, G., Krueger, T.M. and Preece, D. (2007) *CFO Magazine* Working Capital Survey: do selected firms work for shareholders? *Quarterly Journal of Business & Economics* **46**(2):5–22.

Hassim, S., Kadir, M.R.A., Lew, Y-L and Sim, Y-C (2003) Estimation of minimum working capital for construction projects in Malaysia. *Journal of Construction Engineering and Management* **129**(4):369–374.

Visemith, W.M. (2004) Determining the optimum level of working capital in the Cameroon business environment. *African Journal of Finance and Management* **13**(1).

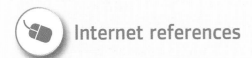

## Internet references

www.cfo.com
*CFO* (Chief Financial Officer) magazine website.

www.treasury-management.com
*Treasury Management International* magazine website.

http://www.iappnet.org/
International Accounts Payable Professionals (IAPP) website.

http://www.planware.org/workingcapital.htm#2
A good basic source of working capital information.

http://www.icai.org/post.html?post_id=2935
Cash Management – Institute of Chartered Accountants of India. An Indian look at cash management.

## Suggestions for group work

1. Discuss the importance of liquidity both in firms and in your everyday life.
2. Discuss how important credit and credit collections policy is to a customer and compare it with their importance to a company.

## Suggestions for presentations

1. Give a presentation from the perspective of Kate from the running case study on the difference between profit and cash.
2. Choose an industry and create a presentation on what considerations firms in that industry must take into account when managing their cash cycle. What are their motivations for holding cash? How much should they hold compared to other industries?

# 11 Mergers and Acquisitions

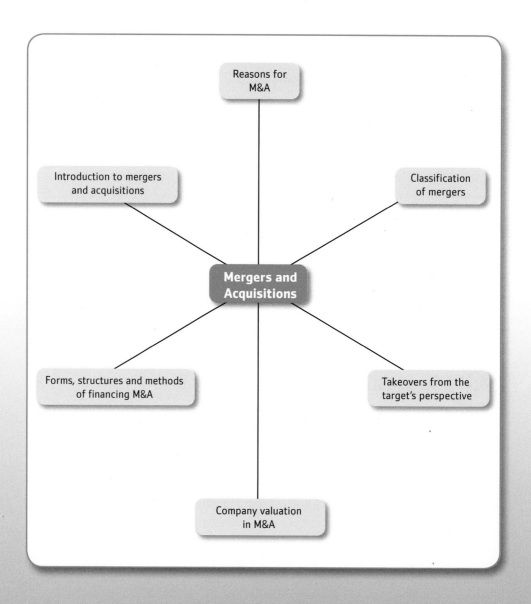

Reasons for M&A

Introduction to mergers and acquisitions

Classification of mergers

**Mergers and Acquisitions**

Forms, structures and methods of financing M&A

Takeovers from the target's perspective

Company valuation in M&A

## Knowledge-based learning objectives

When you have completed this chapter you will be able to:

✓ Understand what mergers and acquisitions (M&A) are

✓ Explain the difference between vertical, horizontal and conglomerate integration

✓ Be aware of the reasons behind undertaking M&A

✓ Understand the agency problem and why M&A may not increase shareholder wealth

✓ Explain the different types of M&A and their advantages and disadvantages

✓ Understand the potential tax benefits from M&A

## Skills-based learning objectives development

✓ Business and financial environment consciousness: you should appreciate how there can be various reasons for M&A, and why a company may not always make it clear why it is going ahead with M&A.

✓ Numerical skills: you should be able to value a company to come to an initial offer, while understanding why the final bid price may be above or below this.

✓ Analytical thinking skills: you should be able to apply this knowledge to examine M&A announcements and the rationale behind them.

✓ Interpersonal skills: you should have developed your ability to present your work clearly both verbally and in writing and to interact with others effectively upon completion of the end of chapter questions.

✓ Managerial soft skills: you should have developed the ability to know how the approaches to be discussed would apply in organisations you have worked in or with which you are familiar.

## Online resource centre

Visit the Online Resource Centre that accompanies this book to listen to a podcast of the authors discussing recent M&A decisions and the reasons behind them.

**www.oxfordtextbooks.co.uk/marney**

## Fictional case study

### OrganicX feels threatened

Charlie leans back in his chair and thinks about the phone call he has just received. In the past few days, the share price of OrganicX has jumped up by 10%. It seems that another company, Exploitalot Plc, has been buying up shares in OrganicX. His advisors have just called to say that it may be that Exploitalot is preparing a takeover bid. Charlie is horrified, as this company is well known for poor labour policies and there have been whispers in the City about unethical practices involving secret deals in developing countries.

As usual, it is not long before Kate appears and it is obvious by her frown that she too has heard the news. 'Over my dead body,' are the first words to emerge from Kate. 'Everything we have worked for will be for nothing if Exploitalot get their grubby hands on us.'

'Why us?' asks Charlie. 'It's not their usual line of business.'

'It's obvious.' replies Kate. 'They want to use OrganicX to clean up their image. Nowadays, shareholders are becoming more concerned with reputation. If Exploitalot succeed, they can certainly use our brand name to clean up their image. It would be worth a lot to them.'

For a moment, Charlie has thoughts about all his shares being bought up for a premium. The share price of OrganicX had declined due to the credit crunch and Charlie has some fleeting thoughts of yachts and long lazy days … but … no! He realises that he just couldn't sell out (or at least not to Exploitalot). Fighting down his feelings of guilt for having even briefly considered such a course of action, he turns to Kate and says, 'Okay, so what can we do about it? Surely, they can't just take us over?'

Kate looks worried and replies, 'It depends on how much they offer the shareholders. I would hope that the shareholders share our vision – but throw enough money at them and they might be tempted.'

'So what can we do about it?' asks Charlie, sure that Kate will, as usual, have a master plan.

Kate looks thoughtful. 'We need to contact all our major shareholders and make sure they are on-side first, and then we need to look at defence strategies.' However, Kate looks very worried indeed and Charlie realises that they may be in for a very tough time.

# 11.1 Introduction to mergers and acquisitions

## 11.1.1 Mergers and acquisitions – some definitions

**Mergers and acquisitions**, often known as just **M and A**, or **M&A**, is the process by which two or more separate businesses are combined into one enterprise, with a single top management and common ownership. The term 'merger' is often loosely used in the media and can be taken to cover both.

However, there is a difference between a **merger** and an **acquisition**. Suppose we wish to merge two companies, 'M' and 'N' for example. Strictly, in a **merger** transaction, the two companies M and N will pool all their assets and liabilities; and shareholders exchange their shares in M or N for shares in a new holding company MN. An example of a genuine merger is that between British Airways and Iberia. By contrast, in an **acquisition** (or '**take over**'), company M would buy all (or most) of the equity shares, or the net assets, in N. A good example is US food giant Kraft's takeover of UK confectioner Cadbury. Another was the proposed but ultimately unsuccessful acquisition by UK insurance company Prudential of US Insurer AIG's Asian division.

In the case of an acquisition, the purchase price normally consists of cash or shares offered by company M (the **acquirer**) to company N (the **target**). The deal may also be done in terms of some combination of cash and shares. Thus M buys out the previous ownership's stake in N and extinguishes N as an independent firm; though for marketing or strategic reasons the identity of company N may be kept on as a brand. Sometimes the offer by the acquirer to take over the share capital of the target will be in exchange for the loan stock of the acquiring company rather than cash or shares. Loan stock is essentially company debt instruments such as bonds. It is less likely to feature in typical merger, though it is not entirely unknown as a means of payment.

The reason why any acquiring company would wish to make a bid for a target company in the first place is in principle the same reason that companies make any finance decision – to maximise firm value. Thus, when an acquiring firm makes a bid for a target firm, the senior management of the acquirer or bidder should be strongly convinced that the new combined entity will represent greater value for shareholders than the sum of values for the bidder and target taken individually. There must be added value created from the merger. One might therefore expect M&A activity to occur on a case by case basis as firms discover opportunities to add value for shareholders through acquisition and merger. However, surprisingly, there is rather a lot of evidence to suggest that M&A activity tends to occur in waves and is strongly influenced by macroeconomic and other external factors, as we shall see in the next section.

## Practical implications for managers

### Value adding or value destroying?

It can often be difficult in reality to be certain of the value of an M&A decision. There are many potential advantages and disadvantages to undertaking M&A. Managers must be reasonably certain that their valuations are accurate and their assumptions are sound. Otherwise they may find that the merger has actually harmed shareholder wealth.

## Key concepts

- [ ] A **merger** is when two companies combine into a new entity
- [ ] An **acquisition**, or **takeover**, is when one company buys all, or most, of the assets of another company

### 11.1.2 The current merger climate

## Mini case study

### Mergers and acquisitions activity – decline or temporary pause?
Source *Economist* 2008d

Like every other business activity nowadays (except bankruptcy-advisory work) merging and acquiring companies (M&A) is in a deep slump. Last week BHP Billiton, a mining giant, withdrew from its planned hostile acquisition of Rio Tinto. This is part of a trend of corporate grooms abandoning their would-be wives at the altar. According to Thomson Reuters, that takes the total value of cancelled mergers so far in this quarter to $322 billion, a two-year high and almost as much as the value of completed mergers in this quarter ($362 billion).

1.  What do you understand by the term, 'mergers activity'?
2.  Why was there such a downturn in merger activity in 2008?
3.  What are the wider implications of this downturn in M&A for the global economy?

The reason for the sudden downturn, the article in the mini-case study ('Mergers and acquisitions activity – decline or temporary pause?') suggests, is that just before the credit crunch, M&A were driven by 'financial engineering' considerations. Thus we might infer that the downturn was perhaps the tail-end of an excessive time of M&A boom, characterised by irrational enthusiasm and deal-making for its own sake.

The article goes on to give a cautious welcome to continued M&A in pharmaceuticals, utilities, engineering, etc. involving US pharmaceutical companies Pfizer and Wyeth, Merck for Schering-Plough; Canadian oil companies Suncor and Petro-Canada; RWE, a Germany utility company, and Holland's Essent, also a utility company. We can therefore see that M&A continues, though at a much reduced level and in a qualitatively different manner.

One of the main differences from the past identified in the Economist article is the suggestion that in future there will be less emphasis on 'financial engineering' and much more emphasis on M&A based on a sound business case and with strong balance sheet justification. Nevertheless, the inescapable fact at the moment is that M&A activity is at its lowest for some time and may take a while to recover, certainly in the US and the UK. However, apart from the recent downturn, one of the more notable aspects of recent merger history has been the fact that merger activity, once almost exclusively a US phenomenon, has now gone global.

---

**Mini case study**

## Mergers and acquisition activity outside the West

Source Song 2009, Copyright *Financial Times*, 'Mergers & Acquisitions'. Ambitious companies with war-chests look for value', 2009

South Korea's merger and acquisition market is showing signs of recovery following months of inactivity.

Bankers expect deal flow to revive with economic recovery and moves by the government to resume its privatisation plans.

South Korea enjoyed growth in M&A reaching double-digits in percentage terms in the past three years as the government and creditors sold companies acquired in the wake of the 1997–8 financial crisis, while Korean companies looked for growth through M&A.

The country saw the number of transactions grow from 772 in 2007 to 1,153 in 2008 although the combined value fell from $64.48bn to $41.93bn, according to Thomson Reuters.

But the market has been frozen since last September's collapse of Lehman Brothers, as sellers have been discouraged by lower valuations, local banks remain reluctant to provide finance, and an uncertain economic outlook made purchasers wary.

Bankers expect the M&A market to shrink this year. However, they are optimistic as markets stabilise and local banks with liquidity become active in financing.

'There is a sense that the market may slowly be recovering,' says John Kim, head of Korea Investment Banking at Goldman Sachs.

1. List reasons why M&A activity in South East Asia (Korea, China, Japan, etc.) may recover independently of what is happening elsewhere.

2. What are the counter-arguments?

---

Even with M&A activity at a low point in some nations it remains an important business decision, one that must be understood. Section 11.2 explains many of the reasons behind M&A and their implications.

# 11.2 Reasons for M&A

## 11.2.1 The broad motives

A **strategic** takeover is when a company acquires a target company in order to forward its strategic objectives. These may result in staff losses or cost-cutting at the target company. The intention is that the merged entity is more strategically competitive than either the target or the acquiring company individually and that the takeover is a true permanent merger of the two companies. For example, Prudential's unsuccessful bid for AIG Asia in 2010 would appear to be based on a decision to make the Asian market a priority, which it was not previously.

A **financial** takeover is when an acquiring company, usually a private equity or buy-out firm, takes over a target firm with the intention of radically improving the target company's financial performance. Usually the acquirer will then sell the target company on. In any event the acquirer will continue to operate as a stand-alone independent company.

Beyond these broad motives, the acquiring company will be likely to have specific goals in mind, such as those discussed below.

### 11.2.1.1  *Economies of scale and scope*

An **economy of scale** is an advantage of large size. That is, a large organisation often has lower costs per unit of production or per unit transaction cost than a smaller organisation.

There are many reasons for economies of scale and scope and these have been covered exhaustively in the economics literature. For example, high fixed costs of running a large organisation may not increase in proportion to size. Thus the fixed cost can be spread over a larger number of sales or spread over a greater number of units of output. One way by which corporations spread high fixed costs when contemplating a takeover is by removing duplication. They may intend to run the merged entity with the same levels of staffing and expenditure for departments and functions such as headquarters, admin, senior management, marketing and advertising. Even if they plan to expand these functions in the acquiring company in order to cope with the enhanced size of the organisation, the expansion will be much more modest than the overall increase in firm size, creating efficiency savings for the post-merger company.

As well as getting the maximum throughput across high fixed cost functions, another important source of scale advantage is in the nature of production itself. In manufacturing, there is a 'square-cube' rule which governs physical production and implies that physical output can be increased exponentially relative to the increase in input. In order to increase output significantly to get the advantage of scale economies, it may be necessary to increase the size of the firm though M&A. For example, in the pharmaceuticals industry, with the recent purchase of Ratiopharm from Merckle, the acquiring company Teva aimed to lift Ratiopharm's operating profit margin by cutting costs and by a better utilisation of the company's production capacity.

A more subtle source of scale economy in service industries, such as finance, is the advantages that accrue to financial intermediaries in being able to aggregate many transactions. This allows them to overcome informational and contractual problems, by standardising and regularising many basic financial transactions. Furthermore, they gain private informational advantages by having long-term relationships with customers which allow them to overcome otherwise costly problems of information asymmetry.

Another advantage that large organisations have is the ability to buy inputs much more cheaply. Steel producers, for example, use a lot of electricity and can negotiate discounts compared to very small users such as domestic households. Also, as you may recall, in

Chapter 6 we talked of how large wholesale foreign exchange dealers were able to negotiate much lower transaction costs for forex dealing than small firms or holiday-makers.

An **economy of scope** is a slightly more subtle thing. It is the ability to put an existing resource to a novel productive use with little or no additional cost. One example that appeared many years ago in the British press was when it was announced that ASDA, the UK retail giant, was considering using its car parks as drive-in movie theatres at night after stores were closed. This plan never came to fruition, however. A more common example of an economy of scope would be the acquisition of another company's product line that complements an existing product and allows revenue synergies from selling them together.

### 11.2.1.2 *Synergy*

**Synergy** is a word that is often used in the context of mergers and the term can be rather loosely applied at times. However, strictly speaking, the word synergy applies to operational or marketing advantages that are completely **unrelated to size**, but which make the merged organisation more efficient in some way. For example, a merger between a bank and an insurance company might be justified on the basis of 'cross-selling'. If the acquirer were the bank, it would be possible for bank staff to cross-sell insurance to customers as part of their everyday activities. Synergy and economies of scope are roughly equivalent terms. However, just to confuse matters, the word synergy is often taken to mean the additional value from the merger, i.e. that the value of a successful merger is greater than the sum of the values of the merged companies.

### 11.2.1.3 *Vertical integration*

This is the idea that by integrating every stage of production within one organisation important economies of scale are realised. The classic example is oil production. Most oil companies do everything 'in-house', from the actual physical extraction of oil to the sale of petrol at garage forecourts (or, as one might say in the US, the sale of gas at gas stations).

In past times, tight vertical integration was an important source of competitive advantage for large firms in many industries. For example, the ability to combine the distillation and brewing of alcoholic drinks at one end of the production process while maintaining control of distribution through dominance of pubs at the other has been an important part of the drinks industry strategy in the UK for the last century. Even comparatively recently, according to Knowles and Egan (2001), there was still 'rapid consolidation of the brewing sector in an attempt to achieve economies of scale in production, distribution and marketing'.

Thus, the possibility of vertical integration can be a major motivator for M&A, as the combination of cost reduction through vertical integration with dominance of distribution can yield very powerful advantages over disintegrated competition.

### 11.2.1.4 *Rapid growth*

'Organic' growth through the build-up of customer base and brand recognition can be a slow and painstaking process. A company seeking a hastier alternative may attempt to grow rapidly through acquisition. This is a risky strategy as the management may overlook problems and overvalue their M&A. It has been argued that the Royal Bank of Scotland (RBS) overvalued ABN Amro when it acquired it in 2007, and that this had a significant bearing on RBS's subsequent problems.

A point related to rapid growth is that the acquisition can allow the company to satisfy key strategic objectives immediately by obtaining valuable staff, brands, markets, client base, technology, etc. by means of acquisition. The alternative of starting from 'the ground up' would in most cases be much slower.

### 11.2.1.5  *Reduction of competition/acquisition of monopoly power*

M&A can also be used to reduce the costs of competition or to create a monopoly rent. **Monopoly rent** is the added value that can be extracted from a market when the company has sole control over it. Due to its illegality in most countries the stated objective of M&A will never be 'the acquisition of monopoly power' as this would attract the opprobrium of the public and the attention of government regulatory departments. Anti-competitiveness is a legitimate concern on the part of government and the public, so it has often featured as a reason for blocking M&A in a number of high-profile cases. However, competition reduction may often be the genuine reason, or act as an additional incentive, for many M&A proposals.

## Mini case study

### NHS computer merger blocked
Source Hencke 2003, Copyright Guardian News & Media Ltd

A judge has prevented the £337m merger of two British computer software companies to prevent them dominating the planned national electronic patient record system for the NHS.

The merger would have given them a near monopoly in the provision of computer software for a medical record system for every person in England, accessible anywhere a patient receives treatment.

The two companies, iSOFT and Torex, already had dominant positions in the NHS. iSOFT had sales of £74m a year in the UK and EU, mainly as a supplier to hospitals. Torex supplied software to GPs, laboratories and hospitals, with £65m of sales. A merger would have given the two companies a 44% share of the existing electronic patient record market, compared with the 14% share of McKesson, their nearest rival. Their share of hospital laboratory software market would have been 56%. In Scotland and Wales, the new company would have had a monopoly.

1. Why do you think this merger was proposed?

2. Why was it blocked, and are there any counter-arguments?

### 11.2.1.6  *Efficiency gains*

Another reason for M&A is that management in the acquiring firm are confident that they could run the target company more efficiently than it is currently being run by the incumbent management.

The signal that management is inefficient can be found, for example, in the fact that the share price is lower than it ought to be. Thus, if the price/earnings (P/E) ratio for a company is lower than for comparable companies (such as those in the same industry), this may indicate that value added by management is less than the stock market expects. Normally if this is the case then shareholders of the target company would be expected to remove the inefficient managers through a vote. The problem is that such a vote may be dominated by a few large 'block' shareholders and many individual shareholders outside the main power grouping may have little real leverage with the board.

Managers may be **entrenched** in the company through their own shareholdings or agreements with other powerful shareholders. Therefore shareholders who are unhappy with current management may have no option but to sell their shares, leaving the management inefficiencies in place and making a takeover bid more likely because of the depressed share price.

### 11.2.1.7 *Tax advantages of loss-making divisions*

Taxes are only payable when a positive profit is actually made. Therefore it may be worthwhile acquiring a loss-making division in order to reduce taxable profit. However, these beneficial effects are to some extent mitigated by the ability to use loss carryback and carryforward, tax rules that allow a company to reduce tax liabilities by applying tax credits from current operating loss to previous or future years.

### 11.2.1.8 *Risk reduction*

Larger companies with diversified holdings will usually be less risky than smaller companies concentrated in fewer business areas. An increase in the size of the company through M&A should therefore reduce the idiosyncratic risk of the business operation as a whole.

However, this ought not to provide any benefit to the risk-averse shareholder who will hold a properly diversified portfolio in the first place. Nevertheless it may be a strong unspoken motive for management and staff to support takeovers. Their income and employment are much more exposed to the idiosyncratic risk. Furthermore, they may have much greater exposure to investment risk in the firm as the company's share schemes and other equity-based incentives encourage concentration in the company's own shares.

Note that owner-managers of smaller family companies may have more valid reasons for seeking mergers as they are in much the same position as salaried managers in terms of having an undiversified wealth portfolio. Thus, selling a stake in the business can make good sense for a small family firm as it diversifies the risk to which the family owners are exposed.

A further risk benefit of diversification may be that through diversification and reduction of idiosyncratic risk, the firm's vulnerability to financial distress may be reduced. Therefore the firm may comfortably take on higher levels of indebtedness and/or reduce the cost of debt and the cost of capital.

### 11.2.1.9 *Expropriation and shutdown*

Although we value firms on a perpetuity basis as if they were infinitely lived, in reality they rarely are. Eventually when a firm has gone through a period of maturity with little growth and steady returns, it may start to show signs of decline. In this case further investment would be inadvisable as it is likely to subtract rather than add value. There may have come a terminal point where the firm should be liquidated, and the net asset value built up and accumulated over the years should be finally cashed in before it is irrevocably lost. It is easier for a new management group to do this than existing management.

In addition, a 'new broom' takeover would probably find it easier to deal with privileges, benefits and conditions accumulated over the years that the company can no longer afford. For example, the US 'big three' motor firms have been severely disadvantaged by enormous pensions liabilities. Unfortunately, these firms are so large and the US legal system so aggressively litigious that M&A is unlikely to offer a solution as it would be very risky to take them over in the expectation of being able to avoid pensions liability.

### 11.2.1.10  *Hubris and empire building*

**Hubris** is when managers believe that their judgement is better than it actually is. This can result in poor M&A decisions being made as managers believe they can see an opportunity to create value where there is none. This results in value being lost, as even if the merger itself is value-neutral there are numerous costs associated with undertaking M&A. **Empire-building** managers are driven to acquire more companies to fulfil their own egotistical desires. This kind of reason for taking over companies will only rarely coincide with the objective of maximisation of shareholder value. However, it cannot be neglected as it can be a powerful motivation for the executives of the acquiring company. We expand on the topic in the section below on the **agency problem**.

### 11.2.1.11  *Critical mass*

Most business is now conducted in an increasingly globalised world. Hence it may be important to achieve a 'critical mass' for technical, scientific or marketing reasons. For example, for decades there has been ongoing restructuring and merger activity in the pharmaceuticals industry and this shows no sign of abating. This is necessary because pharmaceuticals require extensive laboratory work which is very expensive.

Furthermore, even after careful and extensive development, a certain proportion of drugs will inevitably fail. Therefore the pharmaceutical firm has to be large enough to be able to absorb the losses and have a diversified portfolio of different drugs. Finally, the marketing and distribution of drugs is also very expensive. An important part of the marketing of drugs involves personal selling – never the cheapest of marketing options. For all these reasons the size of pharmaceutical companies continues to grow and there have been no obvious examples yet of pharmaceutical companies that are 'too big'.

Another reason for gaining 'critical mass' is that in the business-to-business world, companies may be reluctant to deal with other companies that are small and therefore have a higher probability of failure. This could create considerable problems if the failed company was a key supplier.

The critical mass argument helps to explain the willingness of some target companies to cooperate with divestiture or outright sale. For example, a UK company, Fisons, agreed to outright sale to French pharmaceutical giant Rhône-Poulenc in 1995. In fact what happened subsequently is rather instructive, as in January 1999, Rhône-Poulenc merged with Hoechst AG to form Aventis. In 2004, Aventis went on to merge with Sanofi-Synthélabo forming Sanofi-Aventis, the third largest pharmaceutical company in the world.[1] The move to ever bigger companies in the pharmaceuticals industry continues at the time of writing with Merck's $41 billion takeover of Schering Plough and Pfizer's $68 billion takeover of Wyeth.[2]

It should be noted that size can also bring important drawbacks, including remoteness of management control, extra layers of overhead cost and rigid bureaucracy.

### 11.2.1.12 *To obtain a stock market listing*

Rather than go to the trouble and expense of an initial public offering, a way for a large unlisted firm to get a stock market listing is to buy a smaller publicly quoted company. When the target publicly quoted company's shares are withdrawn in favour of the shares issued by the newly merged entity, the private acquiring company would have ownership – provided of course it had safeguarded majority ownership of the shares.

### 11.2.1.13 *Desire to avoid government interference*

There may be a desire to avoid outside control: it is much harder for governments to interfere with intra-group transactions than with 'visible' market deals between autonomous companies. This may be an important reason for international combinations.

## Active learning activity 11.1

### M&A reasons

Do a quick survey of M&A news stories online. Which reasons are most often cited as justification for M&A?

While this section has covered the most likely reasons a company may undertake M&A there can be other reasons. Section 11.2.3 summarises the main motives that have been identified in the business and academic literature for M&A. In the following section we briefly consider a potential problem of M&A, which is that this activity may be more motivated by managerial ambition than a real desire to add value for shareholders.

## Practical implications for managers

### Consider your options

Managers must keep all the potential advantages of an M&A decision in mind. While merging with one company may create economies of scale and critical mass, merging with another may create greater efficiency gains. The expense inherent in M&A means that these decisions should not be taken lightly.

## Key concepts

- An **economy of scale** is an advantage created through size
- An **economy of scope** is the ability to use resources to create value in a new way at low cost
- **Monopoly rent** is the premium a company can charge when there is insufficient competition to maintain a fair price
- An **entrenched manager** is one who is difficult to remove due to his or her shareholdings or connections within the company
- **Hubris** is when managers believe that their judgement is better than it actually is
- **Empire building** is the act of conducting M&A for reasons of personal prestige
- **Agency theory** describes the difficulties that arise when an agent (such as a manager) does not have the same interests as the principal (in this case, the shareholders)
- **Synergy** can be considered equivalent to an economy of scope

### 11.2.2 The agency problem: management versus shareholders

We mentioned previously that two of the reasons for merger can be risk reduction and empire building – both of which benefit management rather than shareholders. In other words, we re-encounter the agency problem. The area of M&A is one where there may be the most serious conflict of interests between the managers who make the decisions and the shareholders who largely bear the costs (in terms of share price reactions) of these decisions. Managers are likely to have a relatively undiversified wealth portfolio. Most or all of their income and a high proportion of their wealth is held in the form of shares and options on the shares of their employing firm. Thus they will be anxious to diversify away most of their company's 'unique risk'.

Getting into new areas of business may be beneficial for managers, but it may also involve the risk of overpaying. On average, acquiring groups have to pay a 25% premium on the vendor's (pre-bid) share price. This may absorb nearly all the economic gains from the merger, leaving little if any reward for shareholders in the acquiring group. Certainly, the empirical evidence suggests that the shareholders of the acquiring firm tend not to gain from mergers, though the shareholders of the target group often do very well. [3]

Though there are no gains for acquiring firm shareholders, managers may welcome size for its own sake as executive pay levels and measures of firm size are highly positively correlated.

However, apart from the agency problems, M&A activity provides one agency *benefit* for shareholders as poor managers, who fail to maximise shareholder wealth, ought in the end to be vulnerable to a takeover bid for control of their company. That is, the market for corporate control should ensure managerial efficiency. A successful bid for an underperforming company could yield large profits for those who organise such a bid. They could either run the business better themselves or split it up and sell parts of it off. This argument applies with less force to private unquoted companies, however, which may not be easy to take over; hence they are high-risk investments, certainly for minority shareholders. Before we leave this section on the reasons for M&A, we present a summary of the many and varied reasons in the next and final subsection.

## Practical implications for managers

### Examining motives

Managers do not always place the creation of shareholder wealth above the creation of personal wealth. Any M&A proposal should be examined for potential agency issues.

### 11.2.3 Summary of reasons for acquisition

Production

- Expanding capacity
- Economies of scale and scope
- Acquiring technology
- Vertical integration, for quality control or supply reasons

Marketing

- Expanding market share
- Extending product range
- Gaining entry to new markets
- Eliminating competition
- Vertical integration, for distribution reasons

Miscellaneous

- Target company's shares or assets 'under-priced' (in the opinion of the acquirer)
- Applying superior management skills to the acquiree's business
- Acquiring management skills to apply to the acquirer's business
- Preventing a competitor from acquiring the target company
- Making the acquiring company itself less attractive to a predator
- Tax benefits
- Avoiding government interference (perhaps by buying in a different country)
- Diversifying business risk (although the shareholder can do this for themselves)
- Empire building and hubris

As you can see the reasons for M&A are many and complicated. Great caution should be exercised when a business is considering activity of this nature, as it can be possible for firms to lose sight of clear-cut and absolute reasons for M&A, relying on a vague mixture of some or all of the above. As far as possible, clear-cut quantifiable benefits under distinct headings should always be established where possible. That is to say, a process of **due diligence** should be undertaken whenever a merger is proposed. Due diligence means that the acquiring management team should conduct checks so that they are reasonably confident of the potential value of the merger or acquisition. This is an ethical duty of any management team before a purchase goes ahead. We look at ways in which values can be arrived at later in the chapter. In the next section we look at forms of M&A.

## Key concepts

- ☐ A large **premium** is usually paid over the firm's actual value in M&A. This can result in no gains to the bidder whatsoever
- ☐ **Due diligence** is the process of investigation of all material facts in relation to potential investment

# 11.3 Classification of mergers

### 11.3.1 Conventional 'majority stake' M&A

Mergers are often classified in terms of the relation of either firm to each other in terms of the stage of production.

We have mentioned **vertical integration** above. This is where the merger combines firms at different stages of production in the same 'industry'. They may aim to control quality, or to ensure sources of supply or retail outlets. Thus a producer of soft drinks might combine 'upstream' with fruit growers or a company making containers, or 'downstream' with a food and drink chain.

Many mergers are **horizontal**, combining firms in the same business: for example, a daily newspaper merging with a Sunday newspaper would be a horizontal merger. Horizontal mergers are the most likely kind to lead to economies of scale and the advantages from spreading high fixed costs that we discussed above.

**Conglomerate mergers** combine firms in different industries, perhaps with no obvious connection: for example, a cigarette maker and an insurance company, or a drinks manufacturer and a chain of opticians. Conglomerate mergers were very common in the 1960s and 1970s when the received wisdom was that management was a generic skill that was transferrable across industries. Therefore a well-managed company could expand by acquiring companies even in unrelated areas by applying the same organisational and managerial skill that had led to success in the past. This view is no longer deemed to be a strong basis for merger and such conglomerate mergers are now fairly rare. Though there are some notably successful conglomerates such as French company LVMH, which owns Luis Vuitton among many other fashion brands, and German giant, Siemens. Economic benefits for conglomerate mergers might stem from tax savings, management skills in the centre or financial efficiencies.

### 11.3.2 Joint ventures and 'minority stake' M&A

So far we have been discussing M&A on the basis that they involve controlling the majority of the target company's equity shares. But share deals between partners in a joint venture (JV) may involve less than 100% of the equity, especially when the JV is a cross-boundary international venture. For example, if a company wishes to expand into a foreign country, it may make sense to proceed by way of JV or minority interest. The participants to a JV continue to exist as separate firms with the JV as a separate entity. The JV usually has a limited life span and has been set up with a specific purpose in mind; for example, the development of a new technology or the testing of a new strategic approach at 'arms length'.

It is not unknown for a JV stake to be a minority one. Why would a company choose to own only a minority interest, rather than a majority stake or 100% of the equity? Such an arrangement does, of course, reduce the amount it needs to invest in an enterprise of any given size. More important, however, is the possibility of benefiting from the foreign partner's local knowledge and connections. There may be dangers of course. Not all cultures may see such relationships in the same light. British Aerospace sold its 80% interest in Rover to the German company BMW, which came as something of a shock to the Japanese company Honda who owned 20% of Rover's equity.[4] British Aerospace would appear to have regarded its 80/20 'partnership' with Honda as mainly financial, to be sold on if and when a 'better deal' came along; whereas Honda believed its 20% interest in Rover was a long-term arrangement.

In one sense, a minority interest, or investment in a JV may resemble a real 'option'. It may give an investing company a springboard for developing 100% interests in the country (or industry) concerned, when it has learned enough and when it has begun to establish a local reputation of its own. On the other hand, the local partner may be gaining access to foreign technology. With this view, joint ventures and minority interests may often turn out not to be long-term arrangements.

## Mini case study

### Enel and EDF plan nuclear joint venture

Source Boland 2009, Copyright *Financial Times*, 2009

Enel and Electricité de France have created a joint venture to assess the feasibility of building at least four nuclear power plants in Italy, marking the latest stage in the relaunch of the country's nuclear industry more than 20 years after it was rejected by the public.

The new venture, known as Sviluppo Nucleare Italia, will be based in Rome and follows the signing of an agreement between the heads of government of the two countries in February to restart nuclear power production in Italy.

The country ended nuclear power production at home after a referendum in 1987 – a year after the accident at the Chernobyl nuclear power plant in Ukraine – opting to import nuclear-generated energy from France.

But public opinion in Italy has followed a trend seen across Europe and shifted towards greater acceptance of nuclear energy as a cleaner alternative to oil or coal-powered stations and as an opportunity to reduce a reliance on eastern European energy supplies.

Italy's parliament approved a law last month that opened the door to the relaunch of the domestic nuclear industry.

The new venture is owned equally by the two utilities, which will nominate four directors each. Enel will nominate the chief executive and EDF will nominate the chairman and vice-chairman.

The task of the venture, the two companies said on Monday, was to study the feasibility of building at least four advanced European pressurised reactor nuclear plants. Once the studies have been completed, contracts to build, own and operate each plant would be awarded to individual companies.

1. Why did Enel and Electricité de France choose to create a joint venture instead of financing expansion on their own?

2. What problems can occur with joint ventures?

### 11.3.3 Other forms of restructuring

#### 11.3.3.1 *Demerging*

Changes to company law and tax law, as well as in corporate management fashions, or other good reasons may lead to 'demergers'. There are three main versions: trade sales, spin-offs and management buy-outs.

*Trade sales*

From time to time a group may want to sell one of its divisions. This may be because:

1. Another firm has offered an attractively high price.

2. To avoid the need to finance heavy future investment or to dispose of a loss-making business with poor prospects under existing management.

In such cases, selling to another company in the same industry may make a lot of sense. A parent company may have to make large write-offs in order to leave a poorly performing business viable; but selling it relieves the parent of future losses without the costs inherent in winding it up. When selling previously nationalised Jaguar and British Airways to the public, the UK government wrote down their fixed assets. This made it easier for them to report accounting profits afterwards, though it did not affect the cash flows of the businesses. In the state sector, a number of small privatisations were sales to trade buyers, rather than public offers for sale: for example, British Rail Hotels and British Coal.

## Active learning activity 11.2

### Tata for now

In 2008 car manufacturer Ford sold its Jaguar and Land Rover brands to an Indian company, Tata. Students should assume the perspective of a Tata manager before the purchase and consider the case for acquiring these brands.

### Spin-offs

With a spin-off, the holding company distributes shares in a subsidiary pro rata to its own shareholders. This may be a substantial business in its own right, and thereafter have a separate stock market listing. Recent examples from the UK include Courtaulds Textiles (Courtaulds), Vodafone (Racal Electronics) and Zeneca (Imperial Chemical Industries). Some international examples include Seahawk Drilling (Pride International) and Madison Square Garden (Cablevision).

Spin-Offs may make sense where two businesses are not closely related and enjoy few if any economies of scale. The arrangement that first joined the two businesses together may even have been a mistake. The most notable recent example was the merger between Time Warner and AOL, which turned out to be disastrous. There was some talk in the financial press that Time Warner would like to demerge but could not find a buyer for AOL.

### Management buy-outs

A holding company wishing to sell a business may seek a trade buyer, or for large companies it may consider a spin-off. But sometimes the best offer may come from its existing managers. They may recognise its potential better than outside parties. In a management buy-out (MBO) the management team arranges to buy an equity stake in the business. Venture capitalists back them by putting up the rest of the purchase price. This is partly equity and often mostly loan capital.

Because the new company is often highly geared, such deals are called leveraged buy-outs (LBOs) in the US. This makes them risky, but it also pressures the management team to perform as most of the company cash flow will be needed to service the debt. If they do so, they can make large capital gains from their equity stake. This may not be a large proportion of the company's total capital, but it will nearly always represent a substantial part of their personal wealth.

There is an obvious moral hazard here for managers of a subsidiary company. They may be tempted to do less than their best while part of a larger group, in order to benefit themselves by buying an equity stake cheap. The danger may be even stronger if a management team plans to buy out the whole group, rather than just a part of it. In a variant, a management buy-in, a management team from outside an enterprise offers to buy it. Venture capitalists may back the team, as in MBOs. In such cases there is no moral hazard, but outsiders will not know the business as well as inside managers.

## Mini case study

### Management buy-out 'close to completion' at retailer Robert Dyas

Source Mathiason 2009, Copyright Guardian News & Media Ltd

Lenders to Robert Dyas today backed a management buy-out (MBO) of the high street hardware retailer in a last-ditch move that will save 1,200 jobs and prevent the 105-shop chain collapsing.

The deal is expected to be concluded over the Easter weekend and means the financial interest of private equity firm Change Capital in the business, thought to be in the region of £10m, will be completely wiped out.

Robert Dyas, an ironmonger turned home and garden convenience store chain, will be run by the former Kingfisher and MFI director Stephen Round and corporate turnaround specialist Ian Gray, both recruited recently.

The retailer last night said in a statement: 'The directors can confirm constructive talks have been ongoing with the company's bankers and as a result we are close to completing an MBO.'

Lloyds and Allied Irish Banks, the chain's principal lenders, may at some point convert their debt into equity, though there are no immediate plans to do so. Directors of Robert Dyas have put their own cash into the MBO.

Bankers and the private equity owners of Robert Dyas have for the past seven months been involved in a standoff over the terms of refinancing the 130-year-old business. Though it has grown sales by 3% in the most recent quarter, the chain has suffered from an onerous debt repayment schedule.

1.  List the advantages and disadvantages of MBOs.
2.  What disadvantage is likely to be most prominent in the case of Robert Dyas?

So far we have largely viewed things from the point of view of the acquiring company. In the next section we examine the M&A from the perspective of the target company.

## Key concepts

- [ ] **Joint ventures** are collaborations between two or more companies. They afford several advantages to companies seeking to explore new markets
- [ ] A **demerger** is when a company sells part of its assets as an entity in its own right

# 11.4 Takeovers from the target's perspective

## 11.4.1 Reasons for wanting to sell

Many commercial assets are for sale if 'the price is right', even if the owners were not planning to sell. People who have founded a business, or inherited it, may want either to retire or to spread their investment risk. They can defer any capital gains tax bill by receiving shares rather than cash; and if they accept shares in a listed company, they can dispose of them whenever they choose as the shares of listed companies are highly liquid.

Another reason for selling a business may be management problems, due to either succession or a lack of ability to manage a larger business following a period of growth. The death or retirement of one or two key people can often reveal a need for new management. Sometimes selling an ailing business may simply be a better alternative to bankruptcy. Sale as a going concern will normally produce a better price than winding a firm up; and it will avoid many human and legal problems.

Selling a division of a group of companies may make *strategic* sense if it no longer fits with the core business, or if the group needs extra finance for the rest of its business. It may also make the vendor company less attractive to a predator. As with the reasons for buying a firm, there are also many reasons for selling.

## 11.4.2 Summary of reasons for selling

Ownership

- Owner wants to diversify risk
- Owner wants to cash out

Management

- Manager(s) about to retire, with no obvious successor
- Poor business prospects under control of present management, possibly following expansion or a change of direction

Part of a group

- Needs extra source of finance
- No longer fits with core business or strategy of vendor group
- Make vendor less attractive to a predator

Miscellaneous

- Needs economies of scale from specilisation
- Managers know that company shares or assets are 'over-valued'

Even when there are sound reasons for seeking the sale of a business, at least some of the company's owners or the company's management may not want to sell at all. If the bidding company has identified poor management in the target company its first act will usually be to replace them. Even if the target managers and employees are capable they may be surplus to requirements after the merger or acquisition. In the next section we look at some defence tactics often used to deter aggressive M&A.

### 11.4.2  Defence tactics

#### 11.4.2.1  *Defences to takeover*

There are numerous ways in which a targeted company can guard against takeover. In this section we examine some of the more popular and effective techniques.

- **Greenmail:** this is where the target company buys back its own shares at a premium from the company that plans to make an acquisition. Without a majority ownership in the target company the takeover cannot proceed.

- **Golden parachute**: excessively generous severance terms are built into the contracts of senior managers to be triggered in the event of a takeover. The prospective payments are so excessive that they threaten the viability of the merged company should a takeover go ahead.

- **Scorched earth**: scorched earth defences involve the target company making itself as unattractive as possible by selling or destroying key assets. **Crown jewels** is a variant on scorched earth in which specifically the target firm's most valuable assets are sold off.

- **Staggered board**: this is when only a fraction of the board can be replaced every year. Normally one-third of all directors stand for election every year, and each director is re-elected roughly once every 3 years. Thus it is difficult for the acquiring company to use any recent shareholding it has built up to elect its own nominees to the board and ensure that the merger is not opposed.

- **Poison pills**: there are shareholders' rights that give target shareholders the right to acquire stock in the merged company or in the target company at a 50% discount.

Note that this short list of defence tactics largely applies to the US. This is for two reasons. Firstly, because the US is far and away the most mature and biggest M&A market. Secondly, most of these defences have been found to be permissible by the American legal system. In the UK, by contrast, there is a general presumption against what is called 'frustrating action' by the British Takeover Panel. Moreover, there are conditions under which frustrating action can be considered unacceptable by the Australian Takeover Panel. In many other countries, the history of M&A is much shorter, and it may not be clear which, if any, anti-takeover defences are acceptable. Nevertheless, outside the English-speaking world there is much more ambivalence about the benefits of the market for corporate control on the part of national governments and this in itself may act as an anti-takeover defence.

## Active learning activity 11.3

### Terms of defence

Find out what the following terms mean in the context of defence against takeover: Pac Man, Nancy Reagan, Grey Knight, Killer Bees, Macaroni.

Of course this kind of activity is rarely consistent with maximising shareholder wealth. In most developed economies, regulations exist that govern takeover practice and require the target's directors to provide full details of any offer to enable the target's shareholders to make an informed decision.

## Practical implications for managers

### When to sell, and when not to sell

Managers must realise when it is in the company's best interest to sell defunct assets, and when it is best to employ defensive tactics to deter the bidder. However, as managers are often replaced when M&A take place, this can give rise to an agency problem.

## Key concepts

- ☐ **Succession** refers to the replacement of employees of a firm. It can be due to death, retirement, removal or several other causes. When it involves key roles, delays in succession can be critical
- ☐ A **hostile takeover** is an M&A offer that does not have the support of the target company's board

## 11.5 Company valuation in M&A

### 11.5.1 Introduction

An acquiring company may regard an acquisition as a capital investment 'project'. The value of the investment is basically as follows:

Purchase price + Any extra amount the acquirer plans to invest in the business – The disposal proceeds of any surplus assets.

The following main considerations apply to the valuation process:

1. The assets being acquired may be equity shares in the holding company of a group, the assets of the group or the assets of part of a group.

2. Specified liabilities may also be taken over.

3. Estimates of the acquisition project's future cash flows should allow for synergy, or other expected changes, as well as for any future investment.

4. The acquirer may also wish to allow for some terminal value at the horizon date.

From previous chapters, you should recall that there are a number of valuation techniques that can be used to find the maximum purchase price payable. In the next section, we briefly examine the two most commonly used methods:

- Valuation by calculating the P/E ratio multiple.

- Valuation by discounting the estimated future cash flows arising from the acquisition to present value. The discount rate should represent the rate of return commensurate with the riskiness of the business being acquired (which may not be the same as the acquirer's discount rate).

## 11.5.2 The price/earnings ratio multiple

The easiest way to explain the P/E ratio approach is to illustrate with an applied example using the kind of data that an acquiring company would typically be faced with.

Arthur plc is negotiating with the three owner-directors of Parthia Limited for the purchase of their company. Parthia's profits are as follows:

|  | Previous year (actual) | Current year (estimate) |
| --- | --- | --- |
| Profit before interest and tax | £700,000 | £850,000 |
| Profit after tax (earnings) | £500,000 | £600,000 |

Profits are calculated after deducting Parthia's directors' remuneration of £300,000. Arthur's finance director has estimated that using Arthur's own depreciation policies, the annual depreciation charge would be £50,000 higher. Arthur plc's shares are currently priced in the stock market on a P/E ratio of 15. Its ratio of market capitalisation to profit before interest and tax (PBIT multiple) is 11.5. The average P/E ratio for Arthur's industrial sector is 14.

So how would we tackle this particular kind of valuation problem?

1. We need to consider what adjustments should be made to the earnings of Arthur prior to applying the P/E ratio multiple. At this point we might conclude that there would be no need to increase the number of directors' posts at Arthur, while at the same time losing existing directors' posts at Parthia. Thus £300,000 of extra PBIT, or alternatively of profit before tax, should become available. On the other hand, we would have to reduce the figure for profit after tax by £50,000 to reflect the difference between Arthur and Parthia's depreciation processes. Thus, the new figures for Parthia are:

|  | Previous year (actual) | Current year (estimate) |
|---|---|---|
| Profit before interest and tax | £1,000,000 | £1,150,000 |
| Profit after tax (earnings) | £750,000 | £850,000 |

2. It is also necessary to calculate the value of Parthia using a 'plausible' P/E ratio multiple. Average PBIT is equal to the average of £1 million + £1.15 million which is £1.075 million. Using the industry PBIT ratio gives £12.36 million. Average profit after tax is the average of £750,000 + £850,000 which is £800,000. Using the industry P/E ratio (as the most conservative one) gives £11.20 million. We would take the latter as the prospective value of the merged entity if we were being cautious, careful and conservative.

3. We also need to be clear that these are 'ballpark', 'back of the envelope' figures. However, the underlying weaknesses are just the same as any much more sophisticated statistical extrapolation method. That is, in common with any extrapolation technique, we assume that the underlying parameters represent stable relationships and that these relationships will continue to hold in the future. Also, it is quite a simplification of a much more complicated process. In the next section we consider the other main technique used – discounted cash flow (DCF).

## 11.5.3 Discounted cash flow valuation

By this stage you should be aware that the most 'scientific' method of valuation in common use is the discounted cash flow (DCF) method. DCF is a financial technique to evaluate the financial costs and benefits of long-term investments, or to estimate the value of an investment (such as a long-term acquisition). It can be used to make a company valuation, based on the anticipated free cash flows of the company over a number of years. There are quite a few occasions when it is not used because of the uncertainty in every takeover about future cash flows. It would be most suitable for the valuation of target companies that own product rights with a limited life span, such as patents on medical products, and books.

### 11.5.3.1 *Making a DCF valuation*

To make a DCF valuation, the following steps are taken:

- Construct a profile of the anticipated 'free cash flows' of the target company over the chosen investment period/payback period. (Free cash flow can be estimated as earnings after tax but before interest and depreciation; i.e. net operating profit after tax. From the latter, subtract any likely capital expenditure.)
- Estimate, in cash flow terms, the expected benefits from synergies, economies of scale, cost savings, etc.
- Allow for any anticipated rationalisation costs, or new investments that would be required in fixed assets (new equipment) or working capital (stocks and debtors).
- Allow for any anticipated benefits from the resale of a part of the acquired company.

- Decide what the maximum payback period should be to establish the duration of our DCF calculations
- Decide on the appropriate discount rate
- Make the present value calculation.

### 11.5.3.2 *Estimating cash flows*

Estimating the cash flows from an investment is inevitably subject to some uncertainty, especially since the cash flows need to be projected several years into the future. A reasonable estimate of the extra cash flows from acquiring a company would be:

| The pre-tax profits of the company | +A |
|---|---|
| Annual depreciation | +B |
| Additions to profits from synergy benefits | +C |
| Less taxation on profits | –D |

Additional cash flows from acquisition = A+B+C–D

In addition, however, the cash flows should provide for any cost of post-acquisition rationalisation measures. These should include the cost of redundancies and the revenue from the disposal of unwanted assets or business units. By discounting the expected net cash flows from an acquisition, at the required investment rate of return, a valuation can be obtained for the target company. The valuation is simply the present value of the future cash flows, up to the end of the purchasing company's maximum payback period.

For example, imagine that one company, Erchie plc, wishes to take over another, Foxtrot plc. It is expected that the extra cash flows from the acquisition will be as follows, after allowing for synergy benefits and corporate taxation:

| Year | Cash flows (£ million) |
|---|---|
| 1 | 10 |
| 2 | 15 |
| 3 | 20 |
| 4 | 25 |
| 5 | 25 |

There will be reorganisation costs after the takeover, estimated at £6 million soon after the acquisition and £12 million about 1 year later. There will also be a requirement early in Year 1 to invest a further £5 million in new equipment for Foxtrot. Erchie plc expects all of its acquisitions to earn an investment return of 8% per annum. The maximum payback period for Erchie's investments is 5 years.

| 1 | | | Discount Rate | | 8% | |
|---|---|---|---|---|---|---|
| 2 | | | | | | |
| 3 | Year | Positive Cashflow | Negative Cashflow | DF | | DCF |
| 4 | T | £m | £m | | | |
| 5 | 0 | na | | -6 | 1 | -6 |
| 6 | 1 | | | -12 | 0.92593 | -11.1111 |
| 7 | 1 | | | -17 | 0.92593 | -15.7407 |
| 8 | 1 | 10 | | | 0.92593 | 9.25926 |
| 9 | 2 | 15 | | | 0.85734 | 12.8601 |
| 10 | 3 | 20 | | | 0.79383 | 15.8766 |
| 11 | 4 | 25 | | | 0.73503 | 18.3757 |
| 12 | 5 | 25 | | | 0.68058 | 17.0146 |
| 13 | | | | | | |
| 14 | | | | | SUM DCF | 40.5345 |
| 15 | | | | | | |

Screenshot 11.1  Present value of the Foxtrot acquisition

As you can see from Screenshot 11.1, we reach an estimated value in this case of £40.5 million or £40,534,500.

## Active learning activity 11.4

### Foxtrot Delta Charlie Foxtrot

Calculate the PV of the Foxtrot acquisition using DCF methodology but with the following cash flows:

| Year | Cash flow (£ million) |
|---|---|
| 1 | 20 |
| 2 | 25 |
| 3 | 25 |
| 4 | 30 |
| 5 | 35 |

As a check on valuations reached in this way, it may be useful to employ other valuation methods too, such as P/E ratios or even book values of assets. Whatever the valuations reached, in listed companies it has been common for the purchase price to average some 25% more than the pre-bid market price per share, as we have noted previously in the chapter. This may often leave a demanding task for the acquirer's management to earn a profit on top of that premium. Of course, as with many techniques in finance, the figures may be difficult to establish precisely and less formal intuitive skill may be necessary. It is to this we turn to in the next section.

## Practical implications for managers

### Only an estimate?

In reality the figure reached using this method can be very different from the offer made. Managers must be aware of the weaknesses of any valuing technique and that there are also intangible factors to consider.

### 11.5.4 Bargaining

Valuation techniques, particularly those involving DCF, work best where there is a minimum of uncertainty. There may, however, be less formal aspects of the valuation process that are more intuitive and based on business instinct. In a 'friendly' deal, an acquirer (A) will try to find out why the seller (S) wants to sell. Is S aware of adverse future factors which A does not know about? Or are there personal reasons for selling? S will similarly try to discover A's motives. Does A value some aspect of the business more highly than S? If so, why? And how much is it worth to A?

Both A and S should take care throughout to keep an eye on possible alternatives. A will be comparing S with other possible purchases, or with internal growth. S will be looking around for other possible buyers or at continuing ownership. If there seems to be no feasible alternative, it will be hard to drive much of a bargain from S's point of view.

Given the potential ambiguity in firm value outside the theoretical world of perfect information, both buyer and seller may have in mind a range of suitable prices that would be acceptable. If they overlap, a deal should be possible.

Of course the range may alter during the bargaining. Empirical evidence in both the US and the UK suggests that on average the post-acquisition performance of merged entities is somewhat disappointing and that the risk-adjusted returns to the shareholders of the acquiring firm tend to be negative [see Agrawal and Jaffe (2000) and Weston *et al.* (2004) for a summary of this research]. This should not be too surprising, particularly when there is more than one suitor for a target company, since the eventual winner in any competitive bidding situation is usually the participant with the most optimistic assessment of the asset's worth.

In the excitement of an auction, a 'successful' buyer can end up paying far more than he or she planned and/or far more than the acquired asset is worth. Though in a friendly takeover situation this may be rationalised as being the price of keeping a deal 'friendly', in reality it is simply an instance of the all-too-common problem of the '**winners curse**'. Thus the ability to walk away from a deal that is costing too much may not win much glory, but perhaps it serves the interests of shareholders better than over-expensive 'triumphs'.

In the next section we discuss some of the factors that can significantly impinge on M&A and which need to be taken into explicit consideration when considering the structure of a deal.

## Key concepts

☐ The **winner's curse** refers to the evidence that when bidding for a company using incomplete information (as is the case to some extent in any acquisition) there is a tendency to overpay

## 11.6 Forms, structures and methods of financing M&A

### 11.6.1 Financial structure of takeover

We concentrate largely on the acquisition of **publicly quoted** companies. Much more has been written about this than has been written about the acquisition of private companies, particularly in the academic literature.

Usually, the offer to buy or takeover a company will involve a bid for ownership of existing shares. Occasionally, the offer will be in terms of some of the target company's assets. The reason for this kind of offer is often to be able to strip out productive assets while avoiding excessive future liabilities, for example, pension liabilities. This kind of activity does not always receive very favourable press, and is sometimes characterised as 'cherry picking' or 'asset stripping'. However, a case can be made that it is a very necessary part of the economic process of freeing up productive resources from declining organisations in order to redistribute them to growing organisations.

When an acquiring firm makes an offer to buy stock from shareholders of a target company, the offer is known as a tender offer. The nature in which this offer is made can be **friendly** or **hostile**. In the former case, the offer is acceptable to the board of the target company and they will recommend it to their shareholders. In the latter case, the bid is not acceptable to the board of the target company. In the case of a hostile or unsolicited bid, the bidder must appeal to the target company's shareholders directly to get them to accept.

A **leveraged buy-out** is when the acquisition of the target company is funded largely from debt. That is, the acquiring company acquires the wherewithal to pay the target shareholders by borrowing the money. Leveraged buy-outs are often used for financial takeovers and for management buy-outs. The obvious advantages are that the acquirer need only raise a fraction of the price necessary. The debt is secured on the assets of the target company which then assumes the liability.

## 11.6.2 Principal methods of paying for M&A

- Share exchange
- Cash

In most deals, these will be the principal form of payment on offer. The advantage of a cash offer over shares is that it avoids transaction costs and allows the acquiring firm to move quickly when an opportunity comes up. However, for most companies there will be a limit to the value of purchases that can realistically be made in this way.

In a share offer, shares on the **target company** will usually be acquired in exchange for shares in the **acquiring company** which will then represent shares in the merged entity. Additional equity is also sometimes sought by the acquiring firm pre-bid in a **pre-bid equity issue**. The equity is bought by investors on the understanding that it will be paid off from future cash flows. The firm may also envisage being able to pay off the purchase cost using assets acquired; however, this is prohibited under a number of legal codes.

Less commonly, loan stock may be offered – namely bonds, convertible loans or preferred shares. Bonds may be acceptable to target shareholders as they combine the advantage of shares in offering the possibility of the deferral of capital gains tax, while at the same time offering a less risky more certain monetary prospect than shares. Convertibles are a relatively less common approach. Typically in a loan stock after the target shareholder will be offered preferred stock or bonds plus options on the shares of the newly merged firm.

Finally the acquiring firm may make the offer in terms of **deferred payment**. Deferred consideration financing is sometimes known as **earn-out**. It involves the immediate payment of cash or shares plus deferred payment contingent on the target achieving certain predetermined performance in terms of either sales or profits. The advantages and disadvantages for the acquirer are as follows:

Advantages to acquirer:

- It may avoid 'winner's curse' whereby all surplus value is extracted by the target shareholders.
- The talents of target employees are retained, but the acquirer valuation risk is reduced, as the valuation is now contingent on performance.
- There is a smaller need for 'up-front' finance.
- The target remains a separate legal entity for liability purposes, which reduces liability risk. For example, this can provide a hedge against warranty and indemnity claims.

Disadvantages to acquirer:

- There may be a conflict of motives between the target and the bidder, unless the target has strong incentives to maximise value for the bidder.
- The target needs to be given autonomy to meet the targets and the buyer's integration plans are delayed.
- The target may lack motivation after becoming rich through the up-front payment.
- There is an incentive for the target to focus on short-term goals.

### 11.6.3 The choice of financing method – some considerations

Among the various considerations determining the financing method would be the following.

#### 11.6.3.1 *Control*

There are various pros and cons to the different methods of acquiring a target firm. For example, one of the main reasons for acquiring a target firm is to gain control of the firm. However, different methods of payment imply different amounts of control. The principal difference is that when paying with shares, the bidder loses a certain amount of control, and target shareholders maintain a voting interest in the newly merged firm. In all other cases, the target firm shareholders are completely bought out.

Other forms of compensation leave bidder shareholders in control, as target shareholders are no longer owners. Nevertheless, there may be some control issues with the increase in indebtedness associated with a loan stock offer, as the bond owners may well impose covenants, and it will be difficult to raise further the indebtedness of the newly merged firm should the need arise.

### Practical implications for managers

#### The importance of control

While the financial advantages of each financing method are important to consider, managers must also evaluate the level of control they are willing to concede. While one option may be more financially viable it may result in unexpected consequences due to a lack of control available to the bidding company.

#### 11.6.3.2 *Capital gains tax*

Capital gains tax (CGT) can generally be deferred by target shareholders when payment is made on a non-cash basis.

This is not a consideration for pension funds, charitable trusts and unit or investment trusts, which don't normally pay CGT. However, CGT may be a consideration for other target shareholders. They may prefer to defer or rollover CGT by accepting shares rather than cash. CGT becomes payable when the shares are sold and the gain in value is realised.

In some cases, when bonds are received by the target shareholder, the capital gains are frozen and carried forward and the shareholder must pay tax on them when the loan is disposed of, i.e. when the bond matures. This could be unattractive to shareholders if the acquirer has a low credit rating.

There are also tax advantages to acquiring firms through using bonds as the main form of finance. As we observed earlier, when using bonds, the acquiring firm receives a tax deduction on interest payments, while target shareholders may be liable for income tax on the interest.

## Key concepts

- A **strategic takeover** is when a company acquires a target company to forward its strategic objectives
- A **financial takeover** is when an acquiring company takes over a target firm with the intention of improving the target company's financial performance
- **Publically quoted companies** are those that are listed on the stock market
- A **leveraged buy-out** is when the acquisition of the target company is funded largely from debt
- There are **financial** and **tax implications** to any financing decision, including M&A

## 11.7 Summary

This chapter has examined mergers and acquisitions in detail. A merger is when two companies combine into a new entity. An acquisition, or takeover, is when one company buys all, or most, of the assets of another company. The goal of M&A is to create value, but this may not always be the case in reality.

We discussed the main reasons for M&A, including economies of scale and scope, vertical integration, rapid growth, reduction of competition, efficiency gains, tax advantages, risk reduction, expropriation and shutdown, hubris, empire building, synergy, critical mass, obtaining a listing and avoiding government interference.

The agency problem was also discussed in great detail and how it pertains to M&A decisions. It is the difficulties that arise when a manager does not have the same interests as the shareholders. Some empirical evidence argues that agency issues are at the heart of observed losses after M&A activity, due to hubris and empire building.

The classification of M&A was examined and explained in terms of horizontal, vertical and conglomerate mergers, with examples given. The reasons behind joint ventures were discussed in detail, along with the converse of M&A, demergers. Three main examples of demergers were given. Trade sales are a sale of one part of the company. Spin-offs create new business entities whose shares are offered pro-rata to the holding company's shareholders. Management buy-outs involve the internal management team raising capital to buy the company from current shareholders.

Of course, M&A involves more than one company so the perspective of the target company was also considered. Possible reasons for wanting to sell include risk diversification and reduced tax complexities for the owner, succession issues, poor business prospects under present management, the desire for extra group finance, lack of fit with the rest of the group, to deter predator companies from the group, to acquire economies of scale, or the seller's belief that the assets are overvalued. Various defensive tactics for those reluctant to sell were detailed, such as greenmail, golden parachutes and scorched earth and staggered board techniques.

DCF and P/E ratio techniques provide a valuable basis for target company valuation and were discussed in detail with examples given. Bargaining is a more intuitive and less formal way of valuing companies and can complement more precise techniques.

Finally the mechanics of financing an M&A attempt were examined. The advantages of each method of finance were discussed in both taxation of control terms. A tender offer is when the acquiring company makes an offer to the target company's shareholders. A leveraged buy-out is when an acquisition is funded mostly or entirely from debt. The offer can be made in cash, shares, loan stock or any combination of these three. This payment can be deferred until target goals are met. The level of control achieved after a merger or acquisition is important to consider. The tax benefits of a financing decision are also a major factor to consider and it was therefore examined closely. Non-cash offers may be made so that target shareholders can defer capital gains tax. Bonds may be offered so the predator company can deduct interest payments from its tax liabilities.

 Questions

1. List some of the main reasons for mergers and acquisitions. Which of these seem more compelling to you and why?

2. Are there reasons for merger activity that could be positively harmful for shareholder wealth? If so, what are they?

3. List the differences between horizontal, vertical and conglomerate integration.

4. As well as the purchase of one company by another, what are the other main forms of restructuring?

5. What reasons might a business have for selling to a bidder?

6. What considerations should a bidding company take into account when considering how to finance its bid?

7. What are some of the more conventional defence tactics? You may wish to investigate this topic on the internet.

8. Outline and discuss the main ways in which payment for a target company may be made, with particular reference to the relative advantages and disadvantages.

9. Longfellow has agreed to acquire Sherman Brothers. The following information relates to the two firms prior to the merger:

|                     | Longfellow | Sherman Brothers |
|---------------------|------------|------------------|
| Earnings            | $600,000   | $900,000         |
| Shares outstanding  | 400,000    | 250,000          |
| Earnings per share  | $1.50      | $3.60            |
| P/E ratio           | 21         | 21               |

The merger terms provide that two shares of Longfellow will be issued for every share of Sherman Brothers.

### Required

a) Josh owns 100 shares of Longfellow. If the P/E ratio of the combined firm is estimated to be 19, will he gain or lose from the transaction?

b) Are synergistic benefits evident?

10. Lamoureux Engine is evaluating four possible targets, which have the following financial data:

|                    | P        | Q        | R        | S        |
|--------------------|----------|----------|----------|----------|
| Benefits           | $2.8m    | $3.9m    | $3.1m    | $4.5m    |
| Shares outstanding | 200,000  | 300,000  | 100,000  | 400,000  |
| Price per share    | $10      | $18      | $30      | $7       |
| Expected earnings  | $400,000 | $600,000 | $700,000 | $600,000 |

Lamoureux currently has 800,000 shares outstanding, its share price is $14 and its expected earnings are $1.6 million without any merger. Assume that the target firms have no debt, no premium is paid and cash is used to finance the mergers.

### Required

a) Calculate the NPV of the four proposed mergers. Are any of the mergers infeasible?

b) Calculate the post-merger EPS for the feasible merger candidates.

c) If only one merger can be undertaken, which one should it be and why?

## Case study

### Some practical examples from IT and Home Entertainment

Source Moulds 2009 (from *The Daily Telegraph*)

#### Yahoo!/Microsoft

Commentators have picked through both companies' earnings statements to find evidence of an imminent deal. They were not disappointed. Yahoo! chief executive Carol Bartz praised Microsoft's new search engine Bing and – in an obvious thawing of relations – highlighted the need to scale up on search, something that could be achieved by partnering with Microsoft.

Any deal will come under immense scrutiny. Microsoft sought a search and online advertising deal only after Yahoo! rejected its $47.5bn (£29bn) takeover bid. History suggests it may have got a lucky break.

Technology companies have a spectacularly bad record where it comes to mergers and acquisitions. Often established companies use their deep pockets to get exposure to the supposed 'next big thing'. In these cases, deals tend to be struck just at the point where the hype around the new company is at its most feverish.

Once the buyer has paid whatever inflated price is finally agreed, it finds itself under immense pressure to squeeze profitability out of its acquisition, ultimately destroying the asset.

Not all tech M&A is disastrous. In 2003, Google bought a little-known software company called Applied Semantics for $102m for its Adsense programme, which now generates the majority of the search giant's revenues.

1. Why did Microsoft get a lucky break when its bid for Yahoo! did not succeed?

2. Why should Microsoft still be interested in Yahoo! now it has its own search engine?

3. What is the colloquial name for a successful bid for an overpriced asset?

### AOL/Time Warner (January 2000)

But more often than not, the large deals, announced with great fanfare, prove to be immensely destructive. Thought to be one of the worst mergers ever, the AOL/Time Warner deal epitomised the dotcom era. When the merger was announced, the two companies had a combined market value of more than $300bn (£180bn). By the time the deal closed in 2001 that had fallen more than $100bn as internet stocks plunged. Today, the combined market cap of Time Warner and Time Warner Cable is just over $40bn. The unhappy marriage finally unravelled in May this year, when Time Warner finally admitted defeat and said it would spin off AOL.

1. What factors could have caused such a drastic reduction in value? (You may need to do some additional research to answer this question.)

### eBay/Skype (September 2005)

In another bizarre fit, online auction house eBay paid a staggering $2.6bn (£1.58bn) for web phone company Skype back in 2005. The idea was that buyers and sellers could talk to each other via Skype.

eBay should perhaps have undertaken a little more research. eBay sellers say the idea that they have time to talk to buyers was always ridiculous.

In 2007, the company made a tacit admission that it had massively overpaid with a shock $1.4bn write-down on the acquisition.

eBay is now looking to dispose of Skype with an IPO set for the first half of next year. It is thought that it could raise close to $2bn.

1. What factors could have led managers at eBay to make such an expensive mistake?

### Google/YouTube (October 2006)

The jury is out on this deal. YouTube has caused considerable grief for its wealthy parent with a barrage of lawsuits for copyright infringement from content providers. Viacom led the way with a $1bn (£608m) claim in 2007, which fast developed into a class action suit, including the Premier League, that is ongoing.

YouTube is losing money despite Google's expertise in search advertising. A Credit Suisse analyst famously estimated in May that it would haemorrhage $470m this year. That figure has now been widely discredited with more realistic assessments at around $170m, but the company is still clearly in the red.

On the other hand, YouTube is growing, with more than 400,000 viewers in May, watching hundreds of millions of videos a day and uploading hundreds of thousands.

The whole area of online media is still in a state of flux.

Adam Daum, an analyst at research house Gartner, says: 'There has been a massive growth of consumption in video and media in general online, but nobody has really worked out a good, profitable business model.'

News Corp, NBC Universal and Disney launched a video-on-demand service in the US to compete with YouTube. Content is free and funded with advertisements but there is already talk of introducing a version where viewers have to pay for their content.

Daum says: 'Over the next year or two, the idea that everything on the internet is free could go out the window. At that point if YouTube's got the audience, it will be in a very good position indeed.'

Ultimately, Google has deep enough pockets that YouTube has plenty of time to develop a profitable business.

1. Was YouTube a bad buy? If not, what might it be described as?

2. Would it have been a bad buy for a different kind of company?

3. Do you think due diligence has been exercised properly?

 # Further reading

Agrawal, A. and Jaffe, J. (2000) The post-merger performance puzzle. In: Cooper, C. and Gregory, A. (eds) *Advances in Mergers and Acquisitions*, Vol. 1. Elsevier, Amsterdam, pp. 7–41.
  An important look at post-merger performance.

Bruner, R. (2001) *Does M&A Pay? A Survey of Evidence for the Decision Maker*. Working Paper, Darden Graduate School of Business, University of Virginia.
  An informative review of literature on the value of M&A.

Fama, E.F. (1980) Agency problems and the theory of the firm. *Journal of Political Economy* **88**:288–307.
  The defining research on agency theory and how it pertains to companies.

Knowles, T. and Egan, D. (2001) The changing structure of UK brewing and pub retailing. *International Journal of Wine Marketing* **13**:59–72.
  This article explains how the distilling and brewery industry gained economies of scale through vertical integration.

Sudarsanam, P.S. (1995) The role of defensive strategies and ownership structure of target firms: evidence from UK take-over firms. *European Financial Management* **1**(3):223–240.
  An important look at the effectiveness of some takeover defence strategies in the UK.

# Internet references

http://www.statistics.gov.uk/statbase/product.asp?vlnk=72
The UK National Statistics page on M&A decisions.

http://www.ft.com/indepth/m&a

http://www.guardian.co.uk/business/mergers-and-acquisitions
News sources on recent M&A announcements and developments.

http://investopedia.com/university/mergers/
A basic introduction to M&A for students unfamiliar with the subject.

http://www.econlib.org/library/enc1/takeoversandleveragedbuyouts.html
A history of the development of the M&A corporate culture.

http://www.rba.co.uk/sources/manda.htm
A selection of links to news feeds services and databases concerning M&A.

# Suggestions for group work

1. In hindsight it can be argued that Royal Bank of Scotland's takeover of ABN Amro in 2007 was a mistake, but there was also compelling reasons to do so. Students should split into two groups, one to represent the Board of RBS while the other represents the Board of ABN Amro at the time of the takeover. Students should discuss the advantages and disadvantages of the proposed acquisition from their assumed perspective and try to come to a mutual agreement on its efficacy.

2. The takeover of HBOS by Lloyds TSB in 2008 also involved two large banks, but under very different circumstances. Students should use a similar framework to question 1 to consider the differences between the takeovers.

# Suggestions for presentations

1. Students should choose two listed companies and explain why they should merge or acquire the other. Calculations are not necessary, but students should consider the reasons that drive M&A.

2. Find a recent example of a hostile takeover attempt. Assume the role of a manager in the target company and create a presentation detailing possible defensive strategies that could be used.

# 12 Interest and Future Values

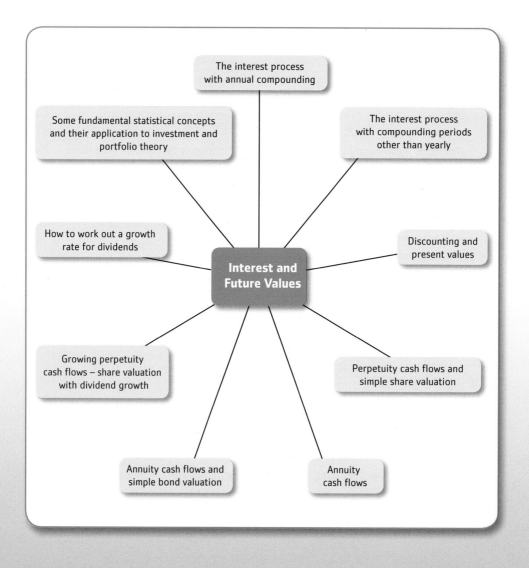

The interest process with annual compounding

Some fundamental statistical concepts and their application to investment and portfolio theory

The interest process with compounding periods other than yearly

How to work out a growth rate for dividends

**Interest and Future Values**

Discounting and present values

Growing perpetuity cash flows – share valuation with dividend growth

Perpetuity cash flows and simple share valuation

Annuity cash flows and simple bond valuation

Annuity cash flows

A fundamental technique for the purposes of discounting and finding the present value (PV) is the simple interest process. This is such an intuitive process one might be tempted to take it as read. However, it is worth considering formally. Suppose, as in Chapter 1, we start with £100 and then apply 10% interest each year for 2 years. We could represent this process as described below.

## 12.1 The interest process with annual compounding

See Screenshot 12.1.

| | A | B | C | D | E | F |
|---|---|---|---|---|---|---|
| 1 | Year | 0 | | 1 | | 2 |
| 2 | Value of | | | | | |
| 3 | Deposit | 100 | | 110 | | 121 |
| 4 | | | Add interest after 1 year | | Add interest after 1 year | |
| 5 | | | | | | |
| 6 | | | 100*(1+10%) | | 110*(1+10%) | |
| 7 | | | | | | |
| 8 | | | | | | |

Screenshot 12.1  Simple interest process

In Year 1, our £100 would have become £110 as a result of the following process:

$$£110 = (1 + 0.1) \times £100$$

or

$$£110 = (1 + 10\%) \times £100$$

Now if we were to write the same thing in symbols, it would say

$$FV_1 = (1 + r) \times PV \tag{1}$$

The future value of your deposit ($FV_1$) in **one time period from now** is the result of the application of one plus some interest rate $(1 + r)$ to the amount you have now (PV). Using actual numerical units, we will have £110 ($FV_1$) in 1 year's time as a result of applying 10% interest to our **present sum** or **PV** of £100.

We can apply similar reasoning to the Year 2 calculation, in which the interest rate of 10% will now be applied twice, as follows:

$$£121 = (1 + 0.1) \times (1 + 0.1) \times £100$$

$$£121 = 1.1 \times 1.1 \times £100$$

$$£121 = 1.1^2 \times £100$$

Now if we were to write this equation in symbols, it would say

$$FV_2 = (1 + r)^2 PV \tag{2}$$

Thus over 3 years the £100 deposit would become £133.1. Formally:

$$FV_3 = (1 + r)^3 PV \tag{3}$$

And so on.

## 12.2 The interest process with compounding periods other than yearly

Typically in finance, unless otherwise stated, the interest rate is understood to be the annual interest rate. We look at how to compare interest rates over many periods in a later section. However, given that interest may be applied over other periods than a year, it is necessary to understand how this affects the interest process. The answer is that we take the annual rate as the standard rate and adjust accordingly. For example, suppose we were now entitled to 10% **simple** or **nominal interest**, but that the interest was to be compounded at 6-monthly intervals. Halfway through the year, half of the required interest would be applied; in this case it would be 5%, or $(10\%/2)$. So in 6 months' time, we would have £105 as follows:

£105 = $(1 + (0.1 \div 2))$

or

£105 = $(1 + 0.05) \times £100$

Now if we were to write the same thing in symbols, it would say

$$FV_{0.5} = \left(1 + \frac{r}{2}\right) \times PV \tag{4}$$

In other words, assuming that 1 year is our standard time unit, the future value halfway through the year is found by applying half the interest after six months.

The interest rate of 5% would be applied again at the end of the year, as follows:

£110.25 = £1.05 × £105

or, in terms of the overall process from the beginning,

£110.25 = £1.05 × £1.05 × £100

or

£110.25 = £1.05² × £100

Again, if we were to write the same thing in symbols, it would say:

$$FV_1 = \left(1 + \frac{r}{2}\right)^2 PV \tag{5}$$

Six-month compounding is known as **semi-annual compounding**. Thus in order to calculate interest semi-annually the interest rate is halved while the compounding period is doubled. Note that the net result is that we get a little more than the £110 that resulted from annual compounding because of the greater frequency of compounding.

The same principle could be applied to any time period. For example, monthly compounding would be as follows:

$$£110.47 = 1.0083^{12} \times £100$$

$$FV_1 = \left(1 + \frac{r}{12}\right)^{12} PV \tag{6}$$

As we can see, the compounding period is multiplied by 12 while the rate applied is divided by 12 ($0.1/12 = 0.0083$). Again we note that the end result (£110.47) is a little more than would be the case with annual (£110) or semi-annual (£110.25) compounding. For very short-term deposits, interest might be applied daily. It should now be fairly evident that the compounding period would be 365, while the annual rate would be divided by 365, thus:

$$£110.516 = 1.0027^{365} \times £100$$

$$FV_1 = \left(1 + \frac{r}{365}\right)^{365} PV$$

It is important to note that a common convention in finance is actually to calculate daily interest on the basis of a **360 day year**. Compounding would be applied as appropriate.

Finally we come to the notion of **continuous compounding**. Continuous compounding is based on the idea that the compounding process does not take place at discrete intervals such as a day, a week or a year. Rather, the process is ongoing and continuous. This being the case, we can use a mathematical constant called the **natural exponent** to work out the value of our deposit after a year. The natural exponent has a value of 2.718 ... etc. and is symbolised as the constant e. We can use it to apply continuous interest by multiplying the initial sum by $e^r$, where r is the interest rate. Thus with continuous compounding we receive

$$£110.517 = e^{0.1} \times £100$$

or

$$FV_1 = e^r PV$$

As we can see, there is very little difference between daily compounding and continuous compounding. One final point of note is that the expression $e^r$ is just the limit of $(1 + r/n)^n$ as n gets very large and approaches infinity. We have in fact pretty much demonstrated this by showing what happens when n goes from 1 to 2 to 12 to 365.

One final point is that in order to use continuous compounding for any period other than a year, one multiplies the subscript r by the appropriate time period. Thus 10% p.a. applied over 2 years would be as follows:

$£122.14 = e^{0.2} \times £100$

$FV_2 = e^{2 \times r} \, PV$

over 3 years

$£134.986 = e^{0.3} \times £100$

$FV_3 = e^{3 \times r} \, PV$

and over 6 months

$£105.127 = e^{0.05} \times £100$

$FV_{0.5} = e^{0.5 \times r} \, PV$

## 12.3 Discounting and present values

The calculation of PV from future values is just the reverse of calculating the future value from the PV. For example, if £110 is the result of applying 10% interest to £100 for 1 year, then £100 is the PV of £110 receivable in 1 year's time. When we reverse the interest process for the purposes of discounting and calculating PV, the interest rate used is known as the **discount rate**. Clearly an important underlying assumption in our calculation is that the interest rate or discount rate is 10% compounded annually. Thus:

if

$£110 = (1 + 0.1) \times £100$

$£100 = \dfrac{£110}{1.1}$

or

$£110 = £110 \times \dfrac{1}{11}$

and finally

$£100 = £110 \times 0.91$

The number 10% or 0.1 is the **discount rate**. The number 1/1.1 or 0.91 is the **discount factor**. (Note: we have abbreviated this number – it is actually 0.90909. ...)

Now if we were to write the same thing in symbols, it would say:

if

$FV_1 = (1 + r) \times PV$

$PV = \dfrac{FV_1}{(1 + r)}$

$PV = FV_1 \times \dfrac{1}{(1 + r)}$

or

$PV = FV_1 \times DF_1$

where $DF_1$ is the *one* period discount factor, $1/(1 + r)$.

Exactly the same thing can be said for the future value in Year 2. Thus:

if

$£121 = (1 + 0.1)^2 \times £100$

$£100 = \dfrac{£121}{1.1^2}$

$£100 = £121 \times \dfrac{1}{1.1^2}$

and finally

$£100 = £121 \times 0.816$

Now if we were to write the same thing in symbols, it would say:

if

$FV_2 = (1 + r)^2 \times PV$

$PV = \dfrac{FV_2}{(1 + r)^2}$

$PV = FV_2 \times \dfrac{1}{(1 + r)^2}$

and finally

$PV = FV_2 \times DF_2$

where $DF_2$ is the *two* period discount factor, $1/(1 + r)^2$.

And so on. Screenshots 12.2 and 12.3 show the discount factors for time periods $T = 0$ to 5 for a discount rate of 10% (compounded annually).

| | A | B | C | D |
|---|---|---|---|---|
| 1 | T | DF | r | |
| 2 | | | 10% | |
| 3 | 0 | 1 | | |
| 4 | 1 | 0.90909 | | |
| 5 | 2 | 0.82645 | | |
| 6 | 3 | 0.75131 | | |
| 7 | 4 | 0.68301 | | |
| 8 | 5 | 0.62092 | | |

Screenshot 12.2  Discount factors at 10%

| | A | B | C |
|---|---|---|---|
| 1 | T | DF | r |
| 2 | | | 0.1 |
| 3 | 0 | =1/(1+$C$2)^A3 | |
| 4 | 1 | =1/(1+$C$2)^A4 | |
| 5 | 2 | =1/(1+$C$2)^A5 | |
| 6 | 3 | =1/(1+$C$2)^A6 | |
| 7 | 4 | =1/(1+$C$2)^A7 | |
| 8 | 5 | =1/(1+$C$2)^A8 | |

Screenshot 12.3  Spreadsheet formulae for discount factors at 10%

As we can see, the discount factor declines the further we go into the future. That is to say, the further away in time a cash flow is, the more heavily discounted it is, because the less valuable it is in PV terms.

One of the important assumptions we have made is that interest is compounded annually. Clearly different amounts of compounding will be appropriate for different compounding periods. For example, the interest on residential mortgages is charged on a monthly basis. Thus, a monthly compounded discount rate would be appropriate for working out the value of a mortgage. Or, for example, the interest on bonds is paid semi-annually, so a 6-month compounding would be appropriate. Six-monthly compounded discount factors for a nominal annual rate of 10% are illustrated in Screenshot 12.4.

| | A | B | C | D |
|---|---|---|---|---|
| 1 | T | DF | r | |
| 2 | | | 10% | |
| 3 | 0 | 1 | | |
| 4 | 0.5 | 0.952381 | | |
| 5 | 1 | 0.9070295 | | |
| 6 | 1.5 | 0.8638376 | | |
| 7 | 2 | 0.8227025 | | |
| 8 | 2.5 | 0.7835262 | | |

Screenshot 12.4  Discount factors at 10% – semi-annual compounding

Again we include the Excel formulae for sake of reference in Screenshot 12.5.

| | A | B | C |
|---|---|---|---|
| 1 | T | DF | r |
| 2 | | | 0.1 |
| 3 | 0 | =1/(1+$C$2)^(A3*2) | |
| 4 | 0.5 | =1/(1+$C$2/2)^(A4*2) | |
| 5 | 1 | =1/(1+$C$2/2)^(A5*2) | |
| 6 | 1.5 | =1/(1+$C$2/2)^(A6*2) | |
| 7 | 2 | =1/(1+$C$2/2)^(A7*2) | |
| 8 | 2.5 | =1/(1+$C$2/2)^(A8*2) | |

Screenshot 12.5 Spreadsheet formulae for discount factors at 10% – semi-annual compounding

As we can see in each case, the nominal annual discount rate is divided by two, while the compounding period is multiplied by two. Now let's see what a discounted cash flow would look like. First of all, suppose there is a cash flow of £100 every year receivable for 5 years starting in 1 year's time and the discount rate is 10% compounded annually (see Screenshot 12.6). 'CF' stands for cash flow and 'DCF' for discounted cash flow. As we can see, the PV of the cash flow would be £376.67.

| | A | B | C | D | E |
|---|---|---|---|---|---|
| 1 | T | DF | r | CF | DCF |
| 2 | | | 10% | | |
| 3 | 0 | 1 | | | |
| 4 | 1 | 0.907029 | | 100 | 90.70295 |
| 5 | 2 | 0.822702 | | 100 | 82.27025 |
| 6 | 3 | 0.746215 | | 100 | 74.62154 |
| 7 | 4 | 0.676839 | | 100 | 67.68394 |
| 8 | 5 | 0.613913 | | 100 | 61.39133 |
| 9 | | | | | |
| 10 | | | | SUM = PVCF | 376.67 |
| 11 | | | | | |

Screenshot 12.6 Value of £100 per year receivable over 5 years discounted at 10%

Suppose now that we received a **nominally equivalent** sum, but this time it amounted to £50 every 6 months starting in 6 months and ending at the start of Year 5. In this case, as we can see in Screenshot 12.7, the PV of the cash is £377.

| | A | B | C | D | E | F | G |
|---|---|---|---|---|---|---|---|
| 1 | T | DF | r | CF | DCF | | |
| 2 | | | 10% | | | | |
| 3 | 0 | 1 | | | | | |
| 4 | 0.5 | 0.952381 | | 50 | 47.619 | | |
| 5 | 1 | 0.9070295 | | 50 | 45.3515 | | |
| 6 | 1.5 | 0.8638376 | | 50 | 43.1919 | | |
| 7 | 2 | 0.8227025 | | 50 | 41.1351 | | |
| 8 | 2.5 | 0.7835262 | | 50 | 39.1763 | | |
| 9 | 3 | 0.5644739 | | 50 | 28.2237 | | |
| 10 | 3.5 | 0.7106813 | | 50 | 35.5341 | | |
| 11 | 4 | 0.6768394 | | 50 | 33.842 | | |
| 12 | 4.5 | 0.6446089 | | 50 | 32.2304 | | |
| 13 | 5 | 0.6139133 | | 50 | 30.6957 | | |
| 14 | | | | | | | |
| 15 | | | | SUM = PVCF | 377 | | |

Screenshot 12.7 Value of £50 per 6 months receivable over 5 years discounted at 10%

The difference is not big, but it does remind us that five lots of £100 receivable at yearly intervals has a different time value from ten lots of £50 receivable at 6-monthly intervals.

## 12.4 Perpetuity cash flows and simple share valuation

A perpetuity cash flow is a **recurring cash flow** (exactly the same cash flow occurring at exactly the same regular interval) that goes on to infinity. An example of the use of perpetuities is to be found in share valuation. Most firms' shares are valued on a perpetuity basis. The reason for this is that the firm is expected to go on for such a long time that, in effect, it is infinitely lived. Therefore ownership of the share represents a claim to a regular stream of dividends for, in effect, an infinite period of time. The **recurring cash flow** is shown in Screenshot 12.8.

| | A | B | C | D | E | F | G | H | I |
|---|---|---|---|---|---|---|---|---|---|
| 1 | t | 1 | 2 | 3 | 4 | 5 | 6 ........ | ∞ | |
| 2 | d | 10 | 10 | 10 | 10 | 10 | 10 | | 10 |
| 3 | | | | | | | | | |

Screenshot 12.8 Annual £10 perpetuity

With a finite cash flow, we could offer a finite solution, by using the fundamental principle that the value of almost any financial asset should be equal to the PV of the cash flow from the asset. Thus the price that should be offered should equal the PV of the cash flow from the dividends. However, how do you put such a value on an infinite sum like the following?

$$P_t = d \times \frac{1}{1+r} + d\frac{1}{(1+r)^2} + d\frac{1}{(1+r)^3} + \ldots \ldots \ldots \ldots d\frac{1}{(1+r)^\infty}$$

$$P_t = d \times \left(\frac{1}{1+r} + \frac{1}{(1+r)^2} + \frac{1}{(1+r)^3} + \ldots \ldots \ldots \ldots \frac{1}{(1+r)^\infty}\right)$$

where P is the share price, d is the constant dividend and r is the discount rate.

It looks an impossible problem, but it isn't. We can make progress here by trying a moderately large number rather than an impossibly large number like infinity. Suppose the discount rate was 10% and we assumed that the firm will pay a dividend every year for 50 years. The price of a share in the firm would be as follows:

$$P_t = d \times \left(\frac{1}{1+r} + \frac{1}{(1+r)^2} + \frac{1}{(1+r)^3} + \ldots \ldots \ldots \ldots \frac{1}{(1+r)^{50}}\right)$$

If you do all of the 50 calculations involved, you will find that the price can be expressed as

$$P_t = 9.915 \times d$$

Now let's suppose the firm will pay a dividend over the next 100 years. The price would be as follows:

$$P_t = 9.999274 \times d$$

In other words, the longer the period over which the firm pays a constant dividend every year, the closer the price gets to ten times the dividend. There is a sound technical reason for this. The longer the time over which a regular repeated cash flow is discounted, the closer the sum of all discount factors, $\left(\frac{1}{1+r} + \frac{1}{1+r^2} + \frac{1}{1+r^3} + \ldots \ldots \ldots \ldots \frac{1}{1+rn}\right)$ gets to 1/r. For example, if the discount rate is 10%, 1/r = 1/0.1 = 10. This is the requisite factor required to discount a perpetuity at 10%.

Just to prove the point, suppose we took a discount rate of 20% and found the sum of all the discount factors for a 100-period cash flow. We would find that $\left(\frac{1}{1+0.1} + \frac{1}{1+0.22} + \frac{1}{1+0.23} + \ldots \ldots \ldots \ldots \frac{1}{1+0.2100}\right)$ is very close to 5, which is the same thing as 1/20% or 1/0.2. So, the value of a share with constant dividend is easy to work out in DCF terms. Just multiply the constant dividend divide the constant dividend by the discount rate as follows:

$$P_t = d/r$$

Just to remind the reader, a perpetuity cash flow is an amount fixed in monetary terms that recurs at regular intervals. The concept of the perpetuity cash flow is useful and crops up quite a lot in finance. For example, it can be used to work out the value of another kind of **recurring cash flow (RCF)**, the annuity cash flow.

## 12.5  Annuity cash flows

Like the perpetuity cash flow, the annuity cash flow is a recurring cash flow. The difference is that the annuity is a recurring cash flow over a **fixed time period**. For example, Screenshot 12.9 shows an annuity payment of £10 over 5 years.

| | A | B | C | D | E | F | G |
|---|---|---|---|---|---|---|---|
| 1 | t | 1 | 2 | 3 | 4 | 5 | |
| 2 | Payment | 10 | 10 | 10 | 10 | 10 | |

Screenshot 12.9  Five-year £10 annuity

However, annuities can be much longer than 5 years, and it can be very tedious to calculate the PV of the annuity. For example, to calculate the value of a 20-year annuity the long way involves 20 different calculations. A shortcut method is available, however.

To find the shortcut method, we start by noting that the 5-year annuity is the equivalent of the difference between two perpetuities, one starting in 1 year's time and another starting in 6 year's time, as we can see in Screenshot 12.10.

| | A | B | C | D | E | F | G | H | I |
|---|---|---|---|---|---|---|---|---|---|
| 1 | t | 1 | 2 | 3 | 4 | 5 | 6 .............. | | 7 |
| 2 | Start Year 1 | 10 | 10 | 10 | 10 | 10 | 10 | 10 | 10 |
| 3 | Start Year 6 | ............ | ............ | ............ | ............ | ............ | 10 | 10 | 10 |
| 4 | | | | | | | | | |
| 5 | Difference | 10 | 10 | 10 | 10 | 10 | | | |
| 6 | | | | | | | | | |

Screenshot 12.10  An annuity as the difference between two perpetuities

If the interest rate is 10%, the **value of the first perpetuity** is RCF/r or £10/0.1 which is the equivalent of £100. If we were already in Year 5, waiting for the second perpetuity to start in Year 6, then the value of the second perpetuity would also be £100. But we are of course still in Year 0 and therefore the second perpetuity (starting in Year 6) must be less valuable as the cash flow benefits don't start until much later. To find a value for this second perpetuity, we must discount its Year 5 value back 5 years. Therefore the calculation is a two-stage one as shown in Figure 12.11.

| | A | B | C | D | E | F | G | H | I |
|---|---|---|---|---|---|---|---|---|---|
| 1 | t | 1 | 2 | 3 | 4 | 5 | 6 ............ | | 7 |
| 2 | Start Year 1 | 10 | 10 | 10 | 10 | 10 | 10 | 10 | 10 |
| 3 | Start Year 6 ............ | ............ | ............ | ............ | ............ | ............ | 10 | 10 | 10 |
| 4 | | | | | | | | | |
| 5 | Difference | 10 | 10 | 10 | 10 | 10 | | | |

Figure 12.11 The value of a perpetuity which will commence in 5 years

At a discount rate of 10%, the 5-year discount factor $1/(1 + r)^5$ is 0.621. Therefore the **value of the second perpetuity** is equal to $(1/0.1) \times £10 \times 0.621$ or £62.1.

Now returning to the original point of interest, namely the **value of the 5-year annuity**, this will be equal to the **difference between the two perpetuities** or £100 − £62.1 = £37.9. Let's just check this is right by doing it the long way, as shown in Screenshot 12.11.

| 6 | | | | |
|---|---|---|---|---|
| 7 | | | 0.1 | |
| 8 | t | CF | DF@10% | DCF |
| 9 | 1 | 10 | 0.90909 | 9.09091 |
| 10 | 2 | 10 | 0.82645 | 8.26446 |
| 11 | 3 | 10 | 0.75131 | 7.51315 |
| 12 | 4 | 10 | 0.68301 | 6.83013 |
| 13 | 5 | 10 | 0.62092 | 6.20921 |
| 14 | | | | |
| 15 | | | Sum DCF | 37.9079 |
| 16 | | | | |

Screenshot 12.11 Doing the calculation the long way!

As we can see, the approach works. Formally the difference between the two annuities is

$$RCF \times \frac{1}{r} - RCF \times \frac{1}{r} \times \frac{1}{(1 + r)^5}$$

or

$$RCF \times \frac{1}{r} \times \left( \frac{1 - 1}{(1 + r)^5} \right)$$

$$\frac{1 - \frac{1}{(1 + r)^5}}{r}$$

We can confirm this last equation by plugging in the numbers.

$$\frac{1 - \frac{1}{1.1^5}}{0.1} = \frac{0.379}{0.1} = 3.79$$

This is the discount factor to be applied to the annuity RCF of £10, and again we have the answer of £37.9. More generally for an annuity commencing in 1 year's time and ending in n years' time, the formula is:

$$\frac{1 - \frac{1}{(1+r)^n}}{r}$$

$$\frac{1 - DF_n}{r}$$

That is, the **annuity factor** for an n-period annuity is equal to 1 minus the appropriate **discount factor** divided by the **discount rate**.

## 12.6  Annuity cash flows and simple bond valuation

As we have discussed at length in the book, most financial assets can be valued on the basis of the PV of the cash flows from the asset. And so a bond can be valued as the **PV of the cash flow from the bond**. When a bond is issued, it pays a coupon based on the coupon rate. At issue, the bond coupon rate is equal to the relevant interest rate, which for bonds is called the yield to maturity. So, for example, suppose a bond is issued that has a face value of £1,000 and that will pay an annual coupon at a rate of 6%. This means that the bond will pay £60 per year until the year of maturity. At maturity it will pay a last coupon of £60 plus the initial sum borrowed, i.e. the face value of £1,000, will be redeemed.

If we assume that the bond has a 5-year life, then on a **DCF** basis, at a discount rate of 6%, the bond is worth £1,000, as shown in Screenshot 12.12.

| | A | B | C | D | E | F | G | H |
|---|---|---|---|---|---|---|---|---|
| 1 | 6% Bond with Five Year Maturity and Annual Coupons | | | | | | | |
| 2 | Cashflow for the Bond Investor | | | | | | | |
| 3 | | | | | | | | |
| 4 | Time | 1 | 2 | 3 | 4 | 5 | 5 | |
| 5 | Cashflow | 60 | 60 | 60 | 60 | 60 | 1000 | |
| 6 | *Discount factors @ 6%* | 0.9434 | 0.89 | 0.83962 | 0.79209 | 0.74726 | 0.74726 | |
| 7 | Discounted Cashflow | 56.6038 | 53.3998 | 50.3772 | 47.5256 | 44.8355 | 747.258 | |
| 8 | | | | | | | | |
| 9 | Price = Sum DCF | 1000 | | | | | | |
| 10 | | | | | | | | |
| 11 | | | | | | | | |
| 12 | | | | | | | | |

Screenshot 12.12  Discount rate = coupon rate. Bond is at par

When a bond's price is equal to its face value, it is said to be at **par.** Par value will occur when the coupon rate equals the discount rate. Of course, the way that we have calculated the price of the bond is the long way of doing this kind of DCF calculation. What we could have done is to split it into two parts: part one would be the calculation of the annuity cash flow from the coupon; part two would be to add the discounted value of the final repayment of the face value. The calculation would be as follows:

$$Price = Sum(DCF) = Coupon \times AF_{r=6\%}^{t=5} + Face\ Value \times DF_{r=6\%}^{t=5}$$

or

$$Price = Sum(DCF) = Coupon \times AF_{r=6\%}^{t=5} + 1000 \times DF_{r=6\%}^{t=5}$$

We can read off the discount factor $DF_{r=6\%}^{t=5}$ from Screenshot 12.12 as 0.74726. Thus the annuity factor, $\dfrac{1 - DF_n}{r}$ is equal to $\dfrac{1 - 0.74726}{0.06}$ or 4.2133 ... The value of the bond then is $60 \times 4.2133 + 1000 \times 0.74726 = 1000$

Now if the interest rate and hence the discount rate should happen to rise after the bond is issued, the future cash flow will be more heavily discounted and the bond will be worth less. Suppose, for example, the interest rate rose from 6% to 8%. The bond price will fall from £1,000 to £920.14. This can be seen in Screenshot 12.13.

| | A | B | C | D | E | F | G | H |
|---|---|---|---|---|---|---|---|---|
| 1 | 6% Bond with Five Year Maturity, £1000 Face Value and Annual Coupons | | | | | | | |
| 2 | Cashflow for the Bond Investor | | | | | | | |
| 3 | | | | | | | | |
| 4 | Time | 1 | 2 | 3 | 4 | 5 | 5 | |
| 5 | Cashflow | 60 | 60 | 60 | 60 | 60 | 1000 | |
| 6 | **Discount Factors @ 8%** | 0.92593 | 0.85734 | 0.79383 | 0.73503 | 0.68058 | 0.68058 | |
| 7 | Discounted Cashflow | 55.5556 | 51.4403 | 47.6299 | 44.1018 | 40.835 | 680.583 | |
| 8 | | | | | | | | |
| 9 | Price = Sum DCF | 920.146 | | | | | | |
| 10 | | | | | | | | |

Screenshot 12.13 Discount rate > coupon rate. Bond value below par

The bond is no longer at **par** but is now said to be at a **discount** to face value. As we already know, the technical reason why this is the case is of course because the cash flow from the bond is now more heavily discounted. However, we might also explain the discount as follows. The 6% bond with its £60 coupons can no longer compete with bonds now being issued at 8% and offering £80 coupons. Hence those investors now holding 6%/£60 coupon bonds would have to offer an added inducement to potential buyers in the form of a discount in price sufficient to make the old 6% coupon bond equivalent to the newer 8%/£80 bond for investors seeking to buy. For technical reasons which we won't go into at this point, the discount on price is just sufficient to offset the disadvantage of the lower coupons of the 6% bond, making the overall return equal to 8%.

This point is brought out more clearly if we do the equivalent shortcut calculation:

$$Price = Sum(DCF) = 60 \times AF_{r=8\%}^{t=5} + 1000 \times DF_{r=8\%}^{t=5}$$

We can read off the discount factor $DF_{r=8\%}^{t=5}$ from Screenshot 12.13 as 0.68058. Thus the annuity factor $\frac{1 - DF_n}{r}$ is equal to $\frac{1 - 0.68058}{0.08}$ or 3.9927. The value of the bond then is $60 \times 3.9927 + 1000 \times 0.68058 = 920.14$

We can see directly now that both the annuity factor and the discount factor have declined.

Of course, the opposite could happen after issue and the interest rate could fall after the 6% bond is issued. For example, if the interest rate fell from 6% to 4% after the 6% bond was issued, the bond price would rise from £1,000 to £1,089, as illustrated in Screenshot 12.14.

| | A | B | C | D | E | F | G | H |
|---|---|---|---|---|---|---|---|---|
| 1 | 6% Bond with Five Year Maturity, £1000 Face Value and Annual Coupons | | | | | | | |
| 2 | Cashflow for the Bond Investor | | | | | | | |
| 3 | | | | | | | | |
| 4 | Time | 1 | 2 | 3 | 4 | 5 | 5 | |
| 5 | Cashflow | 60 | 60 | 60 | 60 | 60 | 1000 | |
| 6 | *Discount Factors @ 4%* | 0.96154 | 0.92456 | 0.889 | 0.8548 | 0.82193 | 0.82193 | |
| 7 | Discounted Cashflow | 57.6923 | 55.4734 | 53.3398 | 51.2883 | 49.3156 | 821.927 | |
| 8 | | | | | | | | |
| 9 | Price = Sum DCF | 1089.04 | | | | | | |
| 10 | | | | | | | | |
| 11 | | | | | | | | |

Screenshot 12.14  Discount rate < coupon rate. Bond value above par

Using the shortcut formula

$$Price = Sum(DCF) = 60 \times AF_{r=4\%}^{t=5} + 1000 \times DF_{r=4\%}^{t=5}$$

we can read off the discount factor $DF_{r=4\%}^{t=5}$ from Screenshot 12.14 as 0.82193. Thus the annuity factor $\frac{1 - DF_n}{r}$ is equal to $\frac{1 - 0.82193}{0.04}$ or 4.4518. The value of the bond then is $60 \times 4.4518 + 1000 \times 3 \times 0.82193 = 1089.04$

The rise in price is of course because the bond's cash flows are now *less* heavily discounted, as we can see from the shortcut calculation. Or, to put it more intuitively, those investors now holding 6% bonds are in possession of a fixed income instrument that offers bigger coupons than the 4% bonds now being issued. Thus, if they wish to sell, they can put the price up a bit and sell at a premium. Again for technical reasons which we won't go into at this point, the premium on price is just sufficient to offset the advantage of the higher coupons, making the overall return equal to 4%.

Notice that we have now established the inverse relationship between bond yield and bond price. The yield, or yield to maturity to give it its full name, is just the bond's rate of return, or indeed the bond's rate of interest. When general interest rates go up, bond yields usually go up and bond prices fall. And of course, falling interest rates usually mean falling yields and rising prices.

## 12.7 Growing perpetuity cash flows – share valuation with dividend growth

Of course the dividend for many companies may actually be expected to grow over the years. Let us return to the example in Screenshot 12.8, in which the RCF dividend is £10 and the discount rate is 10%. Let us now also assume an expected growth of dividends of 5% into the foreseeable future and, in effect, in perpetuity. The symbol 'g' is often used for the growth rate. Thus the valuation problem now is as follows:

$$P_t = d_1 \times \frac{1}{1+r} + d_2 \times \frac{1}{(1+r)^2} + d_3 \times \frac{1}{(1+r)^3} + \text{... ... ...} \; d_\infty \frac{1}{(1+r)^\infty}$$

Note the introduction of time subscripts. These were not necessary in simple share valuation, as the dividend in that case was a simple recurring cash flow and did not vary with time. However, given growth rate 'g', the dividend in any time period can now be expressed as follows:

$$d_t = (1+g)^t d_1$$

Thus, for example, if the rate of growth of dividends is 5% then the dividend in Year 2 is as follows:

$$d_2 = (1 + 0.05) \times d_1 = 1.05 \times £10 = £10.50$$
$$d_3 = (1 + 0.05) \times d_2 = (1 + 0.05)^2 \times d_1 = 1.1025 \times £10 = £11.25$$

And so on. In order to solve the problem of an **infinite** dividend series with growth we must first consider a **finite** dividend series with growth:

$$P_t = d_1 \times \left( \frac{1}{1+r} + \frac{1+g}{(1+r)^2} + \frac{(1+g)^2}{(1+r)^3} + \frac{(1+g)^3}{(1+r)^4} \text{... ... ...} \frac{(1+g)^{n-1}}{(1+r)^n} \right) \qquad (7)$$

where P is the share price, d is the constant dividend or recurring cash flow, r is the discount rate, g is the growth rate and n is the last period in which a dividend will be paid (i.e. the limit to the finite series).

Thus we have an equation that allows us to value a share with finite dividends, but no easy solution to the infinite dividend problem in sight – just yet. Now let us multiply Equation (7) by $\frac{1+g}{1+r}$. This results in the following equation:

$$P_t \times \frac{1+g}{1+r} = d_1 \left( \frac{1+g}{(1+r)^2} + \frac{(1+g)^2}{(1+r)^3} + \frac{(1+g)^3}{(1+r)^4} \text{... ... ...} + \frac{(1+g)^{n-1}}{(1+r)^n} + \frac{(1+g)^n}{(1+r)^{n+1}} \right) \qquad (8)$$

If you compare the two equations, you can see that there are a lot of common terms and that they are *almost* identical.

If we take Equation (8) from Equation (7) we are left with:

$$P_t\left(1 - \frac{1+g}{1+r}\right) = d_1\left(\frac{1}{(1+r)} - \frac{(1+g)^n}{(1+r)^{n+1}}\right)$$

This is for a finite stream of dividends. Now as 'n', the last time period in which a dividend is received, gets bigger and bigger, so big in fact that it approaches infinity, then the term $\frac{(1+g)^n}{(1+r)^{n+1}}$ will become very small (**provided the growth rate 'g' is less than the discount rate 'r'**). So small in fact that it can be ignored. In formal mathematical terms:

$$\lim_{n\to\infty} \frac{(1+g)^n}{(1+r)^{n+1}} = 0$$

Thus for an infinite dividend stream

$$P_t\left(1 - \frac{1+g}{1+r}\right) = d_1 \times \frac{1}{(1+r)}$$

Now we can use the common and useful mathematical trick that the number one can be expressed as the quotient of any other number divided by itself, e.g. $1 = \frac{1+r}{1+r}$

$$P_t\left(\frac{1+r}{1+r} - \frac{1+g}{1+r}\right) = d_1 \times \frac{1}{(1+r)}$$

Multiply by the common denominator $(1 + r)$

$$P_t(1 + r - 1 - g) = d_1$$

Finally

$$P_t(r - g) = d_1$$

or

$$P_t = \frac{d_1}{r - g}$$

observing of course the necessary condition that $r > g$. This must hold or the equation has no solution and we are in the twilight zone. Indeed Sornette (2003) attributes potentially catastrophic bubbles in asset prices, inter-alia, to excessive speculation in the markets to such an extent that anticipated growth rate of dividends 'g' gets very close to the discount rate 'r', causing the price to go to infinity.

You may also see the formula for dividend valuation written as follows:

$$P_t = \frac{d_0(1 + g)}{r - g}$$

That is, the formula is expressed in terms of the current dividend rather than the dividend anticipated next period. The other way in which you may see this formula written is in terms of the discount rate or **cost of equity capital** rather than the price:

$$r = k_E = \frac{d_1}{P_t} + g = \frac{d_0}{P_t}(1 + g) + g$$

## 12.8 How to work out a growth rate for dividends

In order to work out the growth rate, we use the simple formula for calculating returns introduced in Chapter 1 as returns and growth rates are really just the same thing, i.e. a return tells you how much your investment has grown, so it is a specific type of growth rate. Take the example shown in Screenshot 12.15.

| | A | B | C | D | E | F | G | H |
|---|---|---|---|---|---|---|---|---|
| 1 | Year | 2005 | 2006 | 2007 | 2008 | 2009 | 2010 | |
| 2 | Time t | t - 5 | t - 4 | t - 3 | t - 2 | t - 1 | t = 0 | |
| 3 | Dividend | £1.00 | £1.06 | £1.04 | £1.08 | £1.07 | £1.11 | |
| 4 | | | | | | | | |
| 5 | | | | | | | | |
| 6 | | | | | | | | |

Screenshot 12.15 Example of dividend growth

We normally concentrate on the values at the start and end of the chosen sequence, unless we have strong reason to believe that these are unrepresentative, so in a sense the values in between are irrelevant. Applying this formula we calculate that the rate of growth from 2005–2010 is $\sqrt[5]{(1.11/1)} - 1 = 1.021 = 2.1\%$ p.a.

The alternative to simple extrapolation from past data is to use the Gordon assumptions, which at one time were considered to be more scientific. We can make a useful start by recalling that in all firms, dividends depend on earnings and that the growth of dividends will depend critically on the growth of earnings. Earnings in turn depend on the capital put in place by the firm in the first place, and the growth in earnings will be given by the return on capital. Recall that a return is very similar to a growth rate, and that a growth rate is a very similar thing to a return. Thus the extent to which earnings will grow, '$g_E$' is equal to the return on capital, 'r'. In an all-equity firm, $g_E = r = ROE$. Thus earnings grow at a rate given by return 'r', or more specifically the return on equity, ROE. The *maximum* rate at which dividends can grow will depend of course on the maximum rate at which earnings grow, 'r' or ROE.

The other factor that determines the growth of dividends is the balance reached by the firm between retaining earnings for further investment and paying out current earnings to shareholders, thereby reducing the amounts available for investment and the growth of future earnings. The proportion of retained earnings is usually given the symbol 'b'. The net result of all of this is the following formula for the growth of dividends:

$$g = r \times b = ROE \times b$$

where b, the retention ratio, is defined as the ratio of retained earnings/total earnings.

The parameter 'b' is the converse parameter to the parameter $(1 - b)$, the latter representing the payout ratio as it is the proportion of earnings not retained and therefore paid out as dividend.

The Gordon formula can look slightly anomalous to the untutored eye as it states that the higher the retention ratio (and therefore the *lower* the proportional dividend payout), the *higher* the growth of dividends. However, consider the extreme position b = 0, $(1 - b)$ = 1, that is, all earnings paid out as dividend and no earnings retained. The growth of dividends would be zero and this would be because no earnings were being set aside for investment and future growth.

To take some examples: suppose the retention ratio was 40%, while the ROE was 15%. That would make growth in dividends = 0.4 × 0.15 = 0.06 = 6%. However, if the retention ratio was increased to 80%, then the growth rate of dividends would be 0.8 × 0.15 = 12%.

## 12.9 Some fundamental statistical concepts and their application to investment and portfolio theory

### 12.9.1 Expected return, variance and standard deviation

Investment theory deals in values that are not known with certainty and therefore it is fundamentally bound up with the science of analysing uncertain outcomes, namely statistics. All statistical work is based on the concept of the **frequency distribution**. A frequency distribution consists of an exhaustive list of possible outcomes, the value of each outcome and the associated probability of each outcome. We are familiar with frequency distributions from everyday games involving coin tosses and dice throwing. Thus, for example, the frequency distribution for coin tossing consists of the values (Heads, Tails). This represents the two possible outcomes. The associated probabilities are $\left(\frac{1}{2}, \frac{1}{2}\right)$. Thus the frequency distribution is simply a way of linking each possible outcome to its associated probability.

Another familiar distribution is that which belongs to the simple die, used in many board games such as backgammon. The outcome of throwing a die will be one of six possibilities (1, 2, 3, 4, 5, 6) with associated probabilities $\left(\frac{1}{6}, \frac{1}{6}, \frac{1}{6}, \frac{1}{6}, \frac{1}{6}, \frac{1}{6}\right)$. Note that these familiar distributions are called uniform distributions. A uniform distribution is one in which each outcome is equally probable and has the same probability. In many investment problems the distribution will not be uniform.

In what follows, we are going to examine two central questions in statistics. These are: (1) Where is the centre of the distribution? and (2) How spread out is the distribution? In order to do so, we make use of two hypothetical investment opportunities. **Investment 1** consists of four potential outcomes (20, 5, 0, −5) with associated distributions $\left(\frac{4}{10}, \frac{3}{10}, \frac{2}{10}, \frac{1}{10}\right)$. **Investment 2** consists of the same four potential outcomes (20, 5, 0, −5) but with different associated probabilities $\left(\frac{1}{4}, \frac{1}{4}, \frac{1}{4}, \frac{1}{4}\right)$. (What kind of distribution is Investment 2?) Screenshot 12.16 represents the frequency distribution of each investment in tabular form.

| | A | B | C | E | F | G | H | I | J |
|---|---|---|---|---|---|---|---|---|---|
| 1 | *Investment 1* | | | | | | | | |
| 2 | Outcome | Return | Probability | | | | | | |
| 3 | 1 | 20 | 0.4 | | | | | | |
| 4 | 2 | 5 | 0.3 | | | | | | |
| 5 | 3 | 0 | 0.2 | | | | | | |
| 6 | 4 | -5 | 0.1 | | | | | | |
| 7 | | | | | | | | | |
| 8 | | | | | | | Expectd Value = Sum (R*P) = | | |
| 9 | | | | | | | | | |
| 10 | *Investment 2 (Uniform Distribution)* | | | | | | | | |
| 11 | Outcome | Return | Probability | | | | | | |
| 12 | 1 | 20 | 0.25 | | | | | | |
| 13 | 2 | 5 | 0.25 | | | | | | |
| 14 | 3 | 0 | 0.25 | | | | | | |
| 15 | 4 | -5 | 0.25 | | | | | | |
| 16 | | | | | | | | | |
| 17 | | | | | | | Sum R*P = E(R) | | |
| 18 | | | | | | | | | |

Screenshot 12.16  The frequency distribution of two investments

The first task is to find the **location** for the distribution of each investment opportunity. That is, where would we consider the distribution to be located, centred or anchored? What would be a representative value for our investment? We can do this by using the well-known concept of the mean or average. In fact, we will go slightly further by using a particular type of mean called the **expected value**, which is just the same as the average, only with each value weighted by its probability or frequency of occurrence. The mean, expected value and other measures of 'where the centre is' are known as **measures of central tendency**.

The formula for the **expected value** is as follows:

$$E(X) = \sum_{i=1}^{n} p_i X_i = p_1 \times X_1 + p_2 \times X_2 + \dots p_n \times X_n$$

where X is the value for each outcome and E(X) is the expected or average outcome. Therefore for each investment, the calculation will be:

$$E(X) = \sum_{i=1}^{4} p_i X_i = p_1 \times X_1 + p_2 \times X_2 + p_3 + X_3 + p_4 \times X_4$$

So, for example, for Investment 1 the calculation will be

$$E(X) = \frac{4}{10} \times 20 + \frac{3}{10} \times 5 + \frac{2}{10} \times 0 + \frac{1}{10} \times (-5)$$

$$= \frac{80}{10} + \frac{15}{10} + \frac{0}{10} + \frac{-5}{10} = 8 + 1.5 + 0 - 0.5 = 9$$

and for Investment 2 it would be

$$E(X) = \frac{1}{4} \times 20 + \frac{1}{4} \times 5 + \frac{1}{4} \times 0 + \frac{1}{4} \times (-5)$$

$$= \frac{20 + 5 + 0 - 5}{4} = \frac{20}{4} = 5$$

Note that in the case of Investment 2 we could just have used the simple mean, as all possible values have the same probability and are uniformly distributed. Clearly the expected value for Investment 1 is greater than that for Investment 2 because there is more probability of positive outcomes and less of zero or negative outcomes.

As well as specifying some measure of location or central tendency, we would normally also want to know how spread out the possible investment outcomes are. Ideally we might use average distance from the mean. However, it is worth considering why this would be a logical impossibility. Take Investment 1. Suppose we find the distance from the mean in each case, then find the probability-weighted average (i.e. **expected value**) of the distances. Each of these distances is called a **deviation** and the expected value of the deviations would be as follows:

$$E(X - E(X)) \times E(X - E(X)) = \sum_{i=1}^{4} p_i(X_i - E(X))$$

$$= \frac{4}{10} \times (20 - 9) + \frac{3}{10} \times (5 - 9) + \frac{2}{10} \times (0 - 9) + \frac{1}{10} \times (-5 - 9)$$

$$= \frac{4}{10} \times (11) + \frac{3}{10} \times (-4) + \frac{2}{10} \times (-9) + \frac{1}{10} \times (-14)$$

$$= \frac{44 - 12 - 18 - 14}{10} = \frac{0}{10} = 0$$

Just in case you think that it's a 'trick of the numbers', we could do the same thing for Investment 2.

$$E(X - E(X)) = \sum_{i=1}^{4} p_i(X_i - E(X)) =$$

$$= \frac{1}{4} \times (20 - 5) + \frac{1}{4} \times (5 - 5) + \frac{1}{4} \times (0 - 5) + \frac{1}{4} \times (-5 - 5)$$

$$= \frac{15 + 0 - 5 - 10}{4} = \frac{0}{4} = 0$$

Clearly another method is needed and the standard approach is to calculate the **variance**. The method for the variance is exactly the same as above except that each of the deviations is **squared**. So, for example, we take Investment 1:

$$E(X - E(X))^2 = \sum_{i=1}^{4} p_i(X_i - E(X))^2$$

$$= \frac{4}{10} \times (11)^2 + \frac{3}{10} \times (-4)^2 + \frac{2}{10} \times (-9)^2 + \frac{1}{10} \times (-14)^2$$

$$= \frac{4}{10} \times 121 + \frac{3}{10} \times 16 + \frac{2}{10} \times 81 + \frac{1}{10} \times 196$$

$$= \frac{484 + 48 + 162 + 196}{10} = \frac{890}{10} = 89$$

Screenshot 12.17 shows the same calculations on a spreadsheet.

| | A | B | C | D | E | F |
|---|---|---|---|---|---|---|
| 10 | **Investment 1** | | | | | |
| 11 | Outcome | Deviation (D) | Deviation Squared (D^2) | Probability (P) | D(^2)*P | |
| 12 | | 1 | 11 | 121 | 0.4 | 48.4 |
| 13 | | 2 | -4 | 16 | 0.3 | 4.8 |
| 14 | | 3 | -9 | 81 | 0.2 | 16.2 |
| 15 | | 4 | -14 | 196 | 0.1 | 19.6 |
| 16 | | | | | | |
| 17 | | | | Variance = Sum (D(^2)*P) = | 89 | |
| 18 | | | | | 9.434 | |
| 19 | | | | | | |
| 20 | | | | | | |
| 21 | Outcome | Deviation | Probability | | | |
| 22 | | 11 | | 0.4 | 48.4 | |
| 23 | | -4 | | 0.3 | 4.8 | |
| 24 | | -9 | | 0.2 | 16.2 | |
| 25 | | -14 | | 0.1 | 19.6 | |
| 26 | | | | | | |
| 27 | | | | | 89 | |

Screenshot 12.17  Variance of return – Investment 1

So we now have our variance, a measure of how spread out the data are about the expected value of 9. However, one problem remains. Our original investment would be expressed in terms of monetary values. So, for example, the original investments could have been expressed in GBP or British pounds. On average then we expect to make £9 by investing in Investment 1. However, the variance produces output in **squared units**. In this case, the variance is 89 **GB pounds squared**, which makes no sense at all. We convert back to natural units by finding the **standard deviation**, which is defined as the **square root of the variance**. The square root of 89 is 9.43. Thus, for investment 1, standard deviation is 9.43. When we write the standard deviation in symbols, the Greek letter sigma (lowercase) is used. Thus, the standard deviation is $\sigma_1 = 9.43$, while the variance is $\sigma_1^2 = 89$. For Investment 2 the calculations are:

$$E(X - E(X))^2 = \sum_{i=1}^{4} p_i (X_i - E(X))^2$$

$$= \frac{1}{4} \times (20 - 5)^2 + \frac{1}{4} \times (5 - 5)^2 + \frac{1}{4} \times (0 - 5)^2 + \frac{1}{4} \times (-5 - 5)^2$$

$$= \frac{1}{4} \times (-15)^2 + \frac{1}{4} \times (0)^2 + \frac{1}{4} \times (-5)^2 + \frac{1}{4} \times (-10)^2$$

$$= \frac{225 + 0 + 25 + 100}{4} = \frac{350}{4} = 87.5$$

Again, see the spreadsheet in Screenshot 12.18.

| | A | B | C | D | E | F | G |
|---|---|---|---|---|---|---|---|
| 10 | Investment 2 | | | | | | |
| 11 | Outcome | Deviation | Deviation | Probability (P) | D(^2)*P | | |
| 12 | 1 | 15 | 225 | 0.25 | 56.25 | | |
| 13 | 2 | 0 | 0 | 0.25 | 0 | | |
| 14 | 3 | -5 | 25 | 0.25 | 6.25 | | |
| 15 | 4 | -10 | 100 | 0.25 | 25 | | |
| 16 | | | | | | | |
| 17 | | | Variance = Sum (D(^2)*P) = | | 87.5 | | |
| 18 | | | | | 9.35414 | | |
| 19 | | | | | | | |
| 20 | | | | | | | |
| 21 | Outcome | Deviation | Probability | | | | |
| 22 | | 15 | 0.4 | 90 | | | |
| 23 | | 0 | 0.3 | 0 | | | |
| 24 | | -5 | 0.2 | 5 | | | |
| 25 | | -10 | 0.1 | 10 | | | |
| 26 | | | | | | | |
| 27 | | | | 105 | | | |
| 28 | | | | | | | |

Screenshot 12.18 Variance of return – Investment 2

And again to convert our variance for Investment 2 into natural units we have to find the standard deviation, which is 9.35. Thus, the standard deviation is $\sigma_2 = 9.35$, while the variance is $\sigma_1^2 = 87.5$.

Notice that Investment 1 has the higher standard deviation, and hence a higher risk but also a higher return. However, Investment 1 with 0.95% return per 1% of standard deviation offers a better risk-adjusted return than Investment 2 with 0.53% per 1% return. If there were no opportunities to hold a diversified portfolio, the investor would clearly choose Investment 1. However, in order to appreciate a portfolio consisting of both investment opportunities, we need to know the statistical connection between the two investments. This is measured using covariance and correlation.

## 12.9.2 Covariance and correlation

In order to illustrate the concepts of covariance and correlation, we introduce a new investment scheme – **Investment 3**. This particular investment scheme has the following payoffs $(-5, 0, 5, 20)$ with associated distributions $\left(\frac{4}{10}, \frac{3}{10}, \frac{2}{10}, \frac{1}{10}\right)$. In other words, it is the reverse of

Investment 1, as we can see from Screenshot 12.19.

| | A | B | C | D | E | F | G | H |
|---|---|---|---|---|---|---|---|---|
| 1 | | | **Investment 1** | **Investment 3** | | | | |
| 2 | Outcome | Probability | Return | Return | | | | R*P |
| 3 | 1 | 0.4 | 20 | -5 | | | | 8 |
| 4 | 2 | 0.3 | 5 | 0 | | | | 1.5 |
| 5 | 3 | 0.2 | 0 | 5 | | | | 0 |
| 6 | 4 | 0.1 | -5 | 20 | | | | -0.5 |
| 7 | | | | | | | | |
| 8 | | Expected Value | 9 | 1 | | | | |
| 9 | | | | | | | | |
| 10 | | | | | | | | |
| 11 | **Investment 2 (Uniform Distribution)** | | | | | | | |
| 12 | Outcome | Return | Probability | R*P | | | | |
| 13 | 1 | 20 | 0.25 | 5 | | | | |
| 14 | 2 | 5 | 0.25 | 1.25 | | | | |
| 15 | 3 | 0 | 0.25 | 0 | | | | |
| 16 | 4 | -5 | 0.25 | -1.25 | | | | |
| 17 | | | | | | | | |
| 18 | | Expected Value = Sum (R*P) = | | 5 | | | | |

Screenshot 12.19  Expected return for Investments 1 and 2

With a return of 1, as opposed to 9 for Investment 1, Investment 3 has a much lower expected return. However, it could have very useful offsetting properties when held as part of a diversified portfolio. We leave it as an exercise for the reader to confirm that the variance and standard deviation of Investment 3 is 74 and 7.38.

Now suppose we wanted to know the statistical relation between the two. We could start by taking the covariance. As its name suggests, the method of calculation for the covariance is very similar to the method of calculation for the variance itself. When calculating the variance, we found each deviation from the mean and multiplied it by itself. For example, in calculating the **variance** for Investment 1, we calculated the following:

$$E(X - E(X))^2 = \sum_{i=1}^{4} p_i (X_i - E(X)) \times (X_i - E(X))$$

$$= \frac{4}{10} \times (20 - 9) \times (20 - 9) + \frac{3}{10} \times (5 - 9) \times (5 - 9) + \frac{2}{10} \times (0 - 9) \times (0 - 9)$$

$$+ \frac{1}{10} \times (-5 - 9) \times (-5 - 9)$$

By analogy, and if we attach the label 'X' to Investment 1 and 'Y' to Investment 3, the formula for **covariance** is as follows:

$$E(X - E(X)) \times E(Y - E(Y)) = \sum_{i=1}^{4} p_i (X_i - E(X)) \times (Y_i - E(Y))$$

$$= \frac{4}{10} \times (20 - 9) \times (-5 - 1) + \frac{3}{10} \times (5 - 9) \times (0 - 1) + \frac{2}{10} \times (0 - 9) \times (5 - 1)$$

$$+ \frac{1}{10} \times (-5 - 9) \times (20 - 1)$$

$$= \frac{4}{10} \times (11) \times (-6) + \frac{3}{10} \times (-4) \times (-1) + \frac{2}{10} \times (-9) \times (4) + \frac{1}{10} \times (-14) \times (19)$$

$$= \frac{4}{10} \times (-66) + \frac{3}{10} \times 4 + \frac{2}{10} \times (-36) + \frac{1}{10} \times (-266)$$

$$= \frac{-264 + 12 - 72 - 266}{10} = \frac{-590}{10} = -59$$

We now have a measure of the statistical relation between the returns of Investment 1 and Investment 3. The problem, however, is the same as the problem we had with the variance. The solution is not expressed in recognisable units. To get over this we convert the covariance to the regression coefficient by dividing the covariance by the product of standard deviation 1 and standard deviation 3. Formally,

$$\rho_{13} = \frac{Cov_{13}}{\sigma_1 \times \sigma_3} = \frac{\sigma_{13}}{\sigma_1 \times \sigma_3} = \frac{-59}{9.43 \times 7.38} = -0.85$$

where the Greek letter rho, $\rho$, represents the correlation coefficient.

Now this figure of –0.85 represents a negative relationship and a fairly significant one at that, because the strongest negative statistical correlation one can get is –1, which represents **perfect negative correlation**. If there were no statistical relation at all, the correlation would be zero. As the figure is closer to –1 than to zero, it indicates a strongly negative relationship. A strongly positive statistical relation would be close to +1. As we know, the reason why we are reviewing this concept is that it comes into portfolio theory, and in particular the hideous formula for two-asset portfolio variance, viz

$$\sigma_p^2 = W_a^2 \sigma_a^2 + (1 - W_a)^2 \sigma_b^2 + 2W_a(1 - W_a)Cov_{ab}$$

$$= W_a^2 \sigma_a^2 + (1 - W_a)^2 \sigma_b^2 + 2W_a(1 - W_a)\sigma_{ab}$$

where 'a' and 'b' are the two portfolio assets, $\sigma_p^2$ is the variance of the portfolio (percentage) return, $W_a$ is the proportion of the total fund invested in asset 'a', $\sigma_a^2$ is the variance of (percentage) return 'a', $\sigma_b^2$ is the variance of (percentage) return 'b' and $\sigma_{ab}$ is the covariance of return 'a' with return 'b'.

We observed above that the correlation coefficient between return 'a' and return 'b' is defined as:

$$\rho_{ab} = \frac{Cov_{ab}}{\sigma_a \times \sigma_b}$$

Therefore

$$Cov_{ab} = \sigma_a \times \sigma_b \times \rho_{ab}$$

And the formula for portfolio return variance can be rewritten as:

$$\sigma_p = W_a^2 \sigma_a^2 + (1 - W_a)^2 \sigma_b^2 + 2W_a(1 - W_a) \times \sigma_a \times \sigma_b \times \rho_{ab}$$

See chapter five for more details on portfolio calculations.

# Appendix

Table 1 Present Value of £1 at compound interest $(1 + r)^{-n}$

| Periods of n | Discount rate as a percentage | | | | | | | | | | |
|---|---|---|---|---|---|---|---|---|---|---|---|
| | 1% | 2% | 3% | 4% | 5% | 6% | 7% | 8% | 9% | 10% | 11% |
| 1 | 0.9901 | 0.9804 | 0.9709 | 0.9615 | 0.9524 | 0.9434 | 0.9346 | 0.9259 | 0.9174 | 0.9091 | 0.9009 |
| 2 | 0.9803 | 0.9612 | 0.9426 | 0.9246 | 0.9070 | 0.8900 | 0.8734 | 0.8573 | 0.8417 | 0.8264 | 0.8116 |
| 3 | 0.9706 | 0.9423 | 0.9151 | 0.8890 | 0.8638 | 0.8396 | 0.8163 | 0.7938 | 0.7722 | 0.7513 | 0.7312 |
| 4 | 0.9610 | 0.9238 | 0.8885 | 0.8548 | 0.8227 | 0.7921 | 0.7629 | 0.7350 | 0.7084 | 0.6830 | 0.6587 |
| 5 | 0.9515 | 0.9057 | 0.8626 | 0.8219 | 0.7835 | 0.7473 | 0.7130 | 0.6806 | 0.6499 | 0.6209 | 0.5935 |
| 6 | 0.9420 | 0.8880 | 0.8375 | 0.7903 | 0.7462 | 0.7050 | 0.6663 | 0.6302 | 0.5963 | 0.5645 | 0.5346 |
| 7 | 0.9327 | 0.8706 | 0.8131 | 0.7599 | 0.7107 | 0.6651 | 0.6227 | 0.5835 | 0.5470 | 0.5132 | 0.4817 |
| 8 | 0.9235 | 0.8535 | 0.7894 | 0.7307 | 0.6768 | 0.6274 | 0.5820 | 0.5403 | 0.5019 | 0.4665 | 0.4339 |
| 9 | 0.9143 | 0.8368 | 0.7664 | 0.7026 | 0.6446 | 0.5919 | 0.5439 | 0.5002 | 0.4604 | 0.4241 | 0.3909 |
| 10 | 0.9053 | 0.8203 | 0.7441 | 0.6756 | 0.6139 | 0.5584 | 0.5083 | 0.4632 | 0.4224 | 0.3855 | 0.3522 |
| 11 | 0.8963 | 0.8043 | 0.7224 | 0.6496 | 0.5847 | 0.5268 | 0.4751 | 0.4289 | 0.3875 | 0.3505 | 0.3173 |
| 12 | 0.8874 | 0.7885 | 0.7014 | 0.6246 | 0.5568 | 0.4970 | 0.4440 | 0.3971 | 0.3555 | 0.3186 | 0.2858 |
| 13 | 0.8787 | 0.7730 | 0.6810 | 0.6006 | 0.5303 | 0.4688 | 0.4150 | 0.3677 | 0.3262 | 0.2897 | 0.2575 |
| 14 | 0.8700 | 0.7579 | 0.6611 | 0.5775 | 0.5051 | 0.4423 | 0.3878 | 0.3405 | 0.2992 | 0.2633 | 0.2320 |
| 15 | 0.8613 | 0.7430 | 0.6419 | 0.5553 | 0.4810 | 0.4173 | 0.3624 | 0.3152 | 0.2745 | 0.2394 | 0.2090 |
| 16 | 0.8528 | 0.7284 | 0.6232 | 0.5339 | 0.4581 | 0.3936 | 0.3387 | 0.2919 | 0.2519 | 0.2176 | 0.1883 |
| 17 | 0.8444 | 0.7142 | 0.6050 | 0.5134 | 0.4363 | 0.3714 | 0.3166 | 0.2703 | 0.2311 | 0.1978 | 0.1696 |
| 18 | 0.8360 | 0.7002 | 0.5874 | 0.4936 | 0.4155 | 0.3503 | 0.2959 | 0.2502 | 0.2120 | 0.1799 | 0.1528 |
| 19 | 0.8277 | 0.6864 | 0.5703 | 0.4746 | 0.3957 | 0.3305 | 0.2765 | 0.2317 | 0.1945 | 0.1635 | 0.1377 |
| 20 | 0.8195 | 0.6730 | 0.5537 | 0.4564 | 0.3769 | 0.3118 | 0.2584 | 0.2145 | 0.1784 | 0.1486 | 0.1240 |
| 21 | 0.8114 | 0.6598 | 0.5375 | 0.4388 | 0.3589 | 0.2942 | 0.2415 | 0.1987 | 0.1637 | 0.1351 | 0.1117 |
| 22 | 0.8034 | 0.6468 | 0.5219 | 0.4220 | 0.3418 | 0.2775 | 0.2257 | 0.1839 | 0.1502 | 0.1228 | 0.1007 |
| 23 | 0.7954 | 0.6342 | 0.5067 | 0.4057 | 0.3256 | 0.2618 | 0.2109 | 0.1703 | 0.1378 | 0.1117 | 0.0907 |
| 24 | 0.7876 | 0.6217 | 0.4919 | 0.3901 | 0.3101 | 0.2470 | 0.1971 | 0.1577 | 0.1264 | 0.1015 | 0.0817 |
| 25 | 0.7798 | 0.6095 | 0.4776 | 0.3751 | 0.2953 | 0.2330 | 0.1842 | 0.1460 | 0.1160 | 0.0923 | 0.0736 |

| Periods of n | Discount rate as a percentage | | | | | | | | | | | | | | |
|---|---|---|---|---|---|---|---|---|---|---|---|---|---|---|---|
| | 12% | 13% | 14% | 15% | 16% | 17% | 18% | 19% | 20% | 25% | 30% | | | | |
| 1 | 0.8929 | 0.8850 | 0.8772 | 0.8696 | 0.8621 | 0.8547 | 0.8475 | 0.8403 | 0.8333 | 0.8000 | 0.7692 | | | | |
| 2 | 0.7972 | 0.7831 | 0.7695 | 0.7561 | 0.7432 | 0.7305 | 0.7182 | 0.7062 | 0.6944 | 0.6400 | 0.5917 | | | | |
| 3 | 0.7118 | 0.6931 | 0.6750 | 0.6575 | 0.6407 | 0.6244 | 0.6086 | 0.5934 | 0.5787 | 0.5120 | 0.4552 | | | | |
| 4 | 0.6355 | 0.6133 | 0.5921 | 0.5718 | 0.5523 | 0.5337 | 0.5158 | 0.4987 | 0.4823 | 0.4096 | 0.3501 | | | | |
| 5 | 0.5674 | 0.5428 | 0.5194 | 0.4972 | 0.4761 | 0.4561 | 0.4371 | 0.4190 | 0.4019 | 0.3277 | 0.2693 | | | | |
| 6 | 0.5066 | 0.4803 | 0.4556 | 0.4323 | 0.4104 | 0.3898 | 0.3704 | 0.3521 | 0.3349 | 0.2621 | 0.2072 | | | | |
| 7 | 0.4523 | 0.4251 | 0.3996 | 0.3759 | 0.3538 | 0.3332 | 0.3139 | 0.2959 | 0.2791 | 0.2097 | 0.1594 | | | | |
| 8 | 0.4039 | 0.3762 | 0.3506 | 0.3269 | 0.3050 | 0.2848 | 0.2660 | 0.2487 | 0.2326 | 0.1678 | 0.1226 | | | | |
| 9 | 0.3606 | 0.3329 | 0.3075 | 0.2843 | 0.2630 | 0.2434 | 0.2255 | 0.2090 | 0.1938 | 0.1342 | 0.0943 | | | | |
| 10 | 0.3220 | 0.2946 | 0.2697 | 0.2472 | 0.2267 | 0.2080 | 0.1911 | 0.1756 | 0.1615 | 0.1074 | 0.0725 | | | | |
| 11 | 0.2875 | 0.2607 | 0.2366 | 0.2149 | 0.1954 | 0.1778 | 0.1619 | 0.1476 | 0.1346 | 0.0859 | 0.0558 | | | | |
| 12 | 0.2567 | 0.2307 | 0.2076 | 0.1869 | 0.1685 | 0.1520 | 0.1372 | 0.1240 | 0.1122 | 0.0687 | 0.0429 | | | | |
| 13 | 0.2292 | 0.2042 | 0.1821 | 0.1625 | 0.1452 | 0.1299 | 0.1163 | 0.1042 | 0.0935 | 0.0550 | 0.0330 | | | | |
| 14 | 0.2046 | 0.1807 | 0.1597 | 0.1413 | 0.1252 | 0.1110 | 0.0985 | 0.0876 | 0.0779 | 0.0440 | 0.0254 | | | | |
| 15 | 0.1827 | 0.1599 | 0.1401 | 0.1229 | 0.1079 | 0.0949 | 0.0835 | 0.0736 | 0.0649 | 0.0352 | 0.0195 | | | | |
| 16 | 0.1631 | 0.1415 | 0.1229 | 0.1069 | 0.0930 | 0.0811 | 0.0708 | 0.0618 | 0.0541 | 0.0281 | 0.0150 | | | | |
| 17 | 0.1456 | 0.1252 | 0.1078 | 0.0929 | 0.0802 | 0.0693 | 0.0600 | 0.0520 | 0.0451 | 0.0225 | 0.0116 | | | | |
| 18 | 0.1300 | 0.1108 | 0.0946 | 0.0808 | 0.0691 | 0.0592 | 0.0508 | 0.0437 | 0.0376 | 0.0180 | 0.0089 | | | | |
| 19 | 0.1161 | 0.0981 | 0.0829 | 0.0703 | 0.0596 | 0.0506 | 0.0431 | 0.0367 | 0.0313 | 0.0144 | 0.0068 | | | | |
| 20 | 0.1037 | 0.0868 | 0.0728 | 0.0611 | 0.0514 | 0.0433 | 0.0365 | 0.0308 | 0.0261 | 0.0115 | 0.0053 | | | | |
| 21 | 0.0926 | 0.0768 | 0.0638 | 0.0531 | 0.0443 | 0.0370 | 0.0309 | 0.0259 | 0.0217 | 0.0092 | 0.0040 | | | | |
| 22 | 0.0826 | 0.0680 | 0.0560 | 0.0462 | 0.0382 | 0.0316 | 0.0262 | 0.0218 | 0.0181 | 0.0074 | 0.0031 | | | | |
| 23 | 0.0738 | 0.0601 | 0.0491 | 0.0402 | 0.0329 | 0.0270 | 0.0222 | 0.0183 | 0.0151 | 0.0059 | 0.0024 | | | | |
| 24 | 0.0659 | 0.0532 | 0.0431 | 0.0349 | 0.0284 | 0.0231 | 0.0188 | 0.0154 | 0.0126 | 0.0047 | 0.0018 | | | | |
| 25 | 0.0588 | 0.0471 | 0.0378 | 0.0304 | 0.0245 | 0.0197 | 0.0160 | 0.0129 | 0.0105 | 0.0038 | 0.0014 | | | | |

Table 2 Annuity table: The present value of £1 received or paid per year at a compound rate of interest $1/r - \{1/[r(1+r)^n]\}$

| Periods of n | Discount rate as a percentage | | | | | | | | | | |
|---|---|---|---|---|---|---|---|---|---|---|---|
| | 1% | 2% | 3% | 4% | 5% | 6% | 7% | 8% | 9% | 10% | 11% |
| 1 | 0.990 | 0.980 | 0.971 | 0.962 | 0.952 | 0.943 | 0.935 | 0.926 | 0.917 | 0.909 | 0.901 |
| 2 | 1.970 | 1.942 | 1.913 | 1.886 | 1.859 | 1.833 | 1.808 | 1.783 | 1.759 | 1.736 | 1.713 |
| 3 | 2.941 | 2.884 | 2.829 | 2.775 | 2.723 | 2.673 | 2.624 | 2.577 | 2.531 | 2.487 | 2.444 |
| 4 | 3.902 | 3.808 | 3.717 | 3.630 | 3.546 | 3.465 | 3.387 | 3.312 | 3.240 | 3.170 | 3.102 |
| 5 | 4.853 | 4.713 | 4.580 | 4.452 | 4.329 | 4.212 | 4.100 | 3.993 | 3.890 | 3.791 | 3.696 |
| 6 | 5.795 | 5.601 | 5.417 | 5.242 | 5.076 | 4.917 | 4.767 | 4.623 | 4.486 | 4.355 | 4.231 |
| 7 | 6.728 | 6.472 | 6.230 | 6.002 | 5.786 | 5.582 | 5.389 | 5.206 | 5.033 | 4.868 | 4.712 |
| 8 | 7.652 | 7.325 | 7.020 | 6.733 | 6.463 | 6.210 | 5.971 | 5.747 | 5.535 | 5.335 | 5.146 |
| 9 | 8.566 | 8.162 | 7.786 | 7.435 | 7.108 | 6.802 | 6.515 | 6.247 | 5.995 | 5.759 | 5.537 |
| 10 | 9.471 | 8.983 | 8.530 | 8.111 | 7.722 | 7.360 | 7.024 | 6.710 | 6.418 | 6.145 | 5.889 |
| 11 | 10.368 | 9.787 | 9.253 | 8.760 | 8.306 | 7.887 | 7.499 | 7.139 | 6.805 | 6.495 | 6.207 |
| 12 | 11.255 | 10.575 | 9.954 | 9.385 | 8.863 | 8.384 | 7.943 | 7.536 | 7.161 | 6.814 | 6.492 |
| 13 | 12.134 | 11.348 | 10.635 | 9.986 | 9.394 | 8.853 | 8.358 | 7.904 | 7.487 | 7.103 | 6.750 |
| 14 | 13.004 | 12.106 | 11.296 | 10.563 | 9.899 | 9.295 | 8.745 | 8.244 | 7.786 | 7.367 | 6.982 |
| 15 | 13.865 | 12.849 | 11.938 | 11.118 | 10.380 | 9.712 | 9.108 | 8.559 | 8.061 | 7.606 | 7.191 |
| 16 | 14.718 | 13.578 | 12.561 | 11.652 | 10.838 | 10.106 | 9.447 | 8.851 | 8.313 | 7.824 | 7.379 |
| 17 | 15.562 | 14.292 | 13.166 | 12.166 | 11.274 | 10.477 | 9.763 | 9.122 | 8.544 | 8.022 | 7.549 |
| 18 | 16.398 | 14.992 | 13.754 | 12.659 | 11.690 | 10.828 | 10.059 | 9.372 | 8.756 | 8.201 | 7.702 |
| 19 | 17.226 | 15.678 | 14.324 | 13.134 | 12.085 | 11.158 | 10.336 | 9.604 | 8.950 | 8.365 | 7.839 |
| 20 | 18.046 | 16.351 | 14.877 | 13.590 | 12.462 | 11.470 | 10.594 | 9.818 | 9.129 | 8.514 | 7.963 |
| 21 | 18.857 | 17.011 | 15.415 | 14.029 | 12.821 | 11.764 | 10.836 | 10.017 | 9.292 | 8.649 | 8.075 |
| 22 | 19.660 | 17.658 | 15.937 | 14.451 | 13.163 | 12.042 | 11.061 | 10.201 | 9.442 | 8.772 | 8.176 |
| 23 | 20.456 | 18.292 | 16.444 | 14.857 | 13.489 | 12.303 | 11.272 | 10.371 | 9.580 | 8.883 | 8.266 |
| 24 | 21.243 | 18.914 | 16.936 | 15.247 | 13.799 | 12.550 | 11.469 | 10.529 | 9.707 | 8.985 | 8.348 |
| 25 | 22.023 | 19.523 | 17.413 | 15.622 | 14.094 | 12.783 | 11.654 | 10.675 | 9.823 | 9.077 | 8.422 |

## Discount rate as a percentage

| Periods of n | 12% | 13% | 14% | 15% | 16% | 17% | 18% | 19% | 20% | 25% | 30% |
|---|---|---|---|---|---|---|---|---|---|---|---|
| 1 | 0.893 | 0.885 | 0.877 | 0.870 | 0.862 | 0.855 | 0.847 | 0.840 | 0.833 | 0.800 | 0.769 |
| 2 | 1.690 | 1.668 | 1.647 | 1.626 | 1.605 | 1.585 | 1.566 | 1.547 | 1.528 | 1.440 | 1.361 |
| 3 | 2.402 | 2.361 | 2.322 | 2.283 | 2.246 | 2.210 | 2.174 | 2.140 | 2.106 | 1.952 | 1.816 |
| 4 | 3.037 | 2.974 | 2.914 | 2.855 | 2.798 | 2.743 | 2.690 | 2.639 | 2.589 | 2.362 | 2.166 |
| 5 | 3.605 | 3.517 | 3.433 | 3.352 | 3.274 | 3.199 | 3.127 | 3.058 | 2.991 | 2.689 | 2.436 |
| 6 | 4.111 | 3.998 | 3.889 | 3.784 | 3.685 | 3.589 | 3.498 | 3.410 | 3.326 | 2.951 | 2.643 |
| 7 | 4.564 | 4.423 | 4.288 | 4.160 | 4.039 | 3.922 | 3.812 | 3.706 | 3.605 | 3.161 | 2.802 |
| 8 | 4.968 | 4.799 | 4.639 | 4.487 | 4.344 | 4.207 | 4.078 | 3.954 | 3.837 | 3.329 | 2.925 |
| 9 | 5.328 | 5.132 | 4.946 | 4.772 | 4.607 | 4.451 | 4.303 | 4.163 | 4.031 | 3.463 | 3.019 |
| 10 | 5.650 | 5.426 | 5.216 | 5.019 | 4.833 | 4.659 | 4.494 | 4.339 | 4.192 | 3.571 | 3.092 |
| 11 | 5.938 | 5.687 | 5.453 | 5.234 | 5.029 | 4.836 | 4.656 | 4.486 | 4.327 | 3.656 | 3.147 |
| 12 | 6.194 | 5.918 | 5.660 | 5.421 | 5.197 | 4.988 | 4.793 | 4.611 | 4.439 | 3.725 | 3.190 |
| 13 | 6.424 | 6.122 | 5.842 | 5.583 | 5.342 | 5.118 | 4.910 | 4.715 | 4.533 | 3.780 | 3.223 |
| 14 | 6.628 | 6.302 | 6.002 | 5.724 | 5.468 | 5.229 | 5.008 | 4.802 | 4.611 | 3.824 | 3.249 |
| 15 | 6.811 | 6.462 | 6.142 | 5.847 | 5.575 | 5.324 | 5.092 | 4.876 | 4.675 | 3.859 | 3.268 |
| 16 | 6.974 | 6.604 | 6.265 | 5.954 | 5.668 | 5.405 | 5.162 | 4.938 | 4.730 | 3.887 | 3.283 |
| 17 | 7.120 | 6.729 | 6.373 | 6.047 | 5.749 | 5.475 | 5.222 | 4.990 | 4.775 | 3.910 | 3.295 |
| 18 | 7.250 | 6.840 | 6.467 | 6.128 | 5.818 | 5.534 | 5.273 | 5.033 | 4.812 | 3.928 | 3.304 |
| 19 | 7.366 | 6.938 | 6.550 | 6.198 | 5.877 | 5.584 | 5.316 | 5.070 | 4.843 | 3.942 | 3.311 |
| 20 | 7.469 | 7.025 | 6.623 | 6.259 | 5.929 | 5.628 | 5.353 | 5.101 | 4.870 | 3.954 | 3.316 |
| 21 | 7.562 | 7.102 | 6.687 | 6.312 | 5.973 | 5.665 | 5.384 | 5.127 | 4.891 | 3.963 | 3.320 |
| 22 | 7.645 | 7.170 | 6.743 | 6.359 | 6.011 | 5.696 | 5.410 | 5.149 | 4.909 | 3.970 | 3.323 |
| 23 | 7.718 | 7.230 | 6.792 | 6.399 | 6.044 | 5.723 | 5.432 | 5.167 | 4.925 | 3.976 | 3.325 |
| 24 | 7.784 | 7.283 | 6.835 | 6.434 | 6.073 | 5.746 | 5.451 | 5.182 | 4.937 | 3.981 | 3.327 |
| 25 | 7.843 | 7.330 | 6.873 | 6.464 | 6.097 | 5.766 | 5.467 | 5.195 | 4.948 | 3.985 | 3.329 |

Table 3: Future Value of £1 at compound interest $(1 + r)^n$

| Periods of n | Discount rate as a percentage | | | | | | | | | | |
|---|---|---|---|---|---|---|---|---|---|---|---|
| | 1% | 2% | 3% | 4% | 5% | 6% | 7% | 8% | 9% | 10% | 11% |
| 1 | 1.010 | 1.020 | 1.030 | 1.040 | 1.050 | 1.060 | 1.070 | 1.080 | 1.090 | 1.100 | 1.110 |
| 2 | 1.020 | 1.040 | 1.061 | 1.082 | 1.103 | 1.124 | 1.145 | 1.166 | 1.188 | 1.210 | 1.232 |
| 3 | 1.030 | 1.061 | 1.093 | 1.125 | 1.158 | 1.191 | 1.225 | 1.260 | 1.295 | 1.331 | 1.368 |
| 4 | 1.041 | 1.082 | 1.126 | 1.170 | 1.216 | 1.262 | 1.311 | 1.360 | 1.412 | 1.464 | 1.518 |
| 5 | 1.051 | 1.104 | 1.159 | 1.217 | 1.276 | 1.338 | 1.403 | 1.469 | 1.539 | 1.611 | 1.685 |
| 6 | 1.062 | 1.126 | 1.194 | 1.265 | 1.340 | 1.419 | 1.501 | 1.587 | 1.677 | 1.772 | 1.870 |
| 7 | 1.072 | 1.149 | 1.230 | 1.316 | 1.407 | 1.504 | 1.606 | 1.714 | 1.828 | 1.949 | 2.076 |
| 8 | 1.083 | 1.172 | 1.267 | 1.369 | 1.477 | 1.594 | 1.718 | 1.851 | 1.993 | 2.144 | 2.305 |
| 9 | 1.094 | 1.195 | 1.305 | 1.423 | 1.551 | 1.689 | 1.838 | 1.999 | 2.172 | 2.358 | 2.558 |
| 10 | 1.105 | 1.219 | 1.344 | 1.480 | 1.629 | 1.791 | 1.967 | 2.159 | 2.367 | 2.594 | 2.839 |
| 11 | 1.116 | 1.243 | 1.384 | 1.539 | 1.710 | 1.898 | 2.105 | 2.332 | 2.580 | 2.853 | 3.152 |
| 12 | 1.127 | 1.268 | 1.426 | 1.601 | 1.796 | 2.012 | 2.252 | 2.518 | 2.813 | 3.138 | 3.498 |
| 13 | 1.138 | 1.294 | 1.469 | 1.665 | 1.886 | 2.133 | 2.410 | 2.720 | 3.066 | 3.452 | 3.883 |
| 14 | 1.149 | 1.319 | 1.513 | 1.732 | 1.980 | 2.261 | 2.579 | 2.937 | 3.342 | 3.797 | 4.310 |
| 15 | 1.161 | 1.346 | 1.558 | 1.801 | 2.079 | 2.397 | 2.759 | 3.172 | 3.642 | 4.177 | 4.785 |
| 16 | 1.173 | 1.373 | 1.605 | 1.873 | 2.183 | 2.540 | 2.952 | 3.426 | 3.970 | 4.595 | 5.311 |
| 17 | 1.184 | 1.400 | 1.653 | 1.948 | 2.292 | 2.693 | 3.159 | 3.700 | 4.328 | 5.054 | 5.895 |
| 18 | 1.196 | 1.428 | 1.702 | 2.026 | 2.407 | 2.854 | 3.380 | 3.996 | 4.717 | 5.560 | 6.544 |
| 19 | 1.208 | 1.457 | 1.754 | 2.107 | 2.527 | 3.026 | 3.617 | 4.316 | 5.142 | 6.116 | 7.263 |
| 20 | 1.220 | 1.486 | 1.806 | 2.191 | 2.653 | 3.207 | 3.870 | 4.661 | 5.604 | 6.727 | 8.062 |
| 21 | 1.232 | 1.516 | 1.860 | 2.279 | 2.786 | 3.400 | 4.141 | 5.034 | 6.109 | 7.400 | 8.949 |
| 22 | 1.245 | 1.546 | 1.916 | 2.370 | 2.925 | 3.604 | 4.430 | 5.437 | 6.659 | 8.140 | 9.934 |
| 23 | 1.257 | 1.577 | 1.974 | 2.465 | 3.072 | 3.820 | 4.741 | 5.871 | 7.258 | 8.954 | 11.026 |
| 24 | 1.270 | 1.608 | 2.033 | 2.563 | 3.225 | 4.049 | 5.072 | 6.341 | 7.911 | 9.850 | 12.239 |
| 25 | 1.282 | 1.641 | 2.094 | 2.666 | 3.386 | 4.292 | 5.427 | 6.848 | 8.623 | 10.835 | 13.585 |

| Periods of n | 12% | 13% | 14% | 15% | 16% | 17% | 18% | 19% | 20% | 25% | 30% |
|---|---|---|---|---|---|---|---|---|---|---|---|
| 1 | 1.120 | 1.130 | 1.140 | 1.150 | 1.160 | 1.170 | 1.180 | 1.190 | 1.200 | 1.250 | 1.300 |
| 2 | 1.254 | 1.277 | 1.300 | 1.323 | 1.346 | 1.369 | 1.392 | 1.416 | 1.440 | 1.563 | 1.690 |
| 3 | 1.405 | 1.443 | 1.482 | 1.521 | 1.561 | 1.602 | 1.643 | 1.685 | 1.728 | 1.953 | 2.197 |
| 4 | 1.574 | 1.630 | 1.689 | 1.749 | 1.811 | 1.874 | 1.939 | 2.005 | 2.074 | 2.441 | 2.856 |
| 5 | 1.762 | 1.842 | 1.925 | 2.011 | 2.100 | 2.192 | 2.288 | 2.386 | 2.488 | 3.052 | 3.713 |
| 6 | 1.974 | 2.082 | 2.195 | 2.313 | 2.436 | 2.565 | 2.700 | 2.840 | 2.986 | 3.815 | 4.827 |
| 7 | 2.211 | 2.353 | 2.502 | 2.660 | 2.826 | 3.001 | 3.185 | 3.379 | 3.583 | 4.768 | 6.275 |
| 8 | 2.476 | 2.658 | 2.853 | 3.059 | 3.278 | 3.511 | 3.759 | 4.021 | 4.300 | 5.960 | 8.157 |
| 9 | 2.773 | 3.004 | 3.252 | 3.518 | 3.803 | 4.108 | 4.435 | 4.785 | 5.160 | 7.451 | 10.604 |
| 10 | 3.106 | 3.395 | 3.707 | 4.046 | 4.411 | 4.807 | 5.234 | 5.695 | 6.192 | 9.313 | 13.786 |
| 11 | 3.479 | 3.836 | 4.226 | 4.652 | 5.117 | 5.624 | 6.176 | 6.777 | 7.430 | 11.642 | 17.922 |
| 12 | 3.896 | 4.335 | 4.818 | 5.350 | 5.936 | 6.580 | 7.288 | 8.064 | 8.916 | 14.552 | 23.298 |
| 13 | 4.363 | 4.898 | 5.492 | 6.153 | 6.886 | 7.699 | 8.599 | 9.596 | 10.699 | 18.190 | 30.288 |
| 14 | 4.887 | 5.535 | 6.261 | 7.076 | 7.988 | 9.007 | 10.147 | 11.420 | 12.839 | 22.737 | 39.374 |
| 15 | 5.474 | 6.254 | 7.138 | 8.137 | 9.266 | 10.539 | 11.974 | 13.590 | 15.407 | 28.422 | 51.186 |
| 16 | 6.130 | 7.067 | 8.137 | 9.358 | 10.748 | 12.330 | 14.129 | 16.172 | 18.488 | 35.527 | 66.542 |
| 17 | 6.866 | 7.986 | 9.276 | 10.761 | 12.468 | 14.426 | 16.672 | 19.244 | 22.186 | 44.409 | 86.504 |
| 18 | 7.690 | 9.024 | 10.575 | 12.375 | 14.463 | 16.879 | 19.673 | 22.901 | 26.623 | 55.511 | 112.455 |
| 19 | 8.613 | 10.197 | 12.056 | 14.232 | 16.777 | 19.748 | 23.214 | 27.252 | 31.948 | 69.389 | 146.192 |
| 20 | 9.646 | 11.523 | 13.743 | 16.367 | 19.461 | 23.106 | 27.393 | 32.429 | 38.338 | 86.736 | 190.050 |
| 21 | 10.804 | 13.021 | 15.668 | 18.822 | 22.574 | 27.034 | 32.324 | 38.591 | 46.005 | 108.420 | 247.065 |
| 22 | 12.100 | 14.714 | 17.861 | 21.645 | 26.186 | 31.629 | 38.142 | 45.923 | 55.206 | 135.525 | 321.184 |
| 23 | 13.552 | 16.627 | 20.362 | 24.891 | 30.376 | 37.006 | 45.008 | 54.649 | 66.247 | 169.407 | 417.539 |
| 24 | 15.179 | 18.788 | 23.212 | 28.625 | 35.236 | 43.297 | 53.109 | 65.032 | 79.497 | 211.758 | 542.801 |
| 25 | 17.000 | 21.231 | 26.462 | 32.919 | 40.874 | 50.658 | 62.669 | 77.388 | 95.396 | 264.698 | 705.641 |

Discount rate as a percentage

# References

Agarwal, A. and Jaffe, J. (2000) The post-merger performance puzzle. In: Cooper, C. and Gregory, A. (eds) *Advances in Mergers and Acquisitions*, Vol. 1. Elsevier, Amsterdam, pp. 7–41.

Aglionby, J. (2008) Rupiah plunges after forex changes. *Financial Times*, 13 November.

Akerlof, G. (1970) The market for 'lemons': quality uncertainty and the market mechanism. *Quarterly Journal of Economics* **84**(3):488–500.

Amram, M. and Kulatilaka, N. (1999) Disciplined decisions: aligning strategy with the financial markets. *Harvard Business Review*, January–February.

Anda, J.N. (2007) The analytics of climate change. Letter to the editor. *Financial Times*, 4 December.

Barboza, D. (2002) Former officials say Enron hid gains during the crisis in California. *New York Times*, 23 June.

Bar-Hillel, M. (2008) Fear of closure for 4000 estate agents. *London Evening Standard*, 14 April.

Bazerman, M. (2009) *Beware the pressure of sunk costs*. Blog entry on Harvard Law School Program on Negotiation, 6 October.

BBC (1999) *Are you ready to rock'n'roll?* BBC News, 9 February. http://news.bbc.co.uk/1/hi/business/the_economy/275760.stm.

BBC (2006) *Tata halts Bangladesh investment*. BBC News, 10 July, news.bbc.co.uk/1/hi/world/south_asia/5164926.stm.

Benito, A. and Young, G. (2002) Financial pressure and balance sheet adjustment by UK firms. *Banco de España Working Paper No. 0209*. Banco de España, Madrid.

Benninga S. (2000) *Financial modelling*, 1st edn. Massachusetts Institute of Technology Press, Cambridge.

Birchall, J. (2007) An onus on retailers to keep their hands clean. *Financial Times*, 16 January.

Blackwell, D. (2009) Orders at Hightex to raise the roof. *Financial Times*, 29 December.

Boland, V. (2009) Enel and EDF plan nuclear joint venture. *Financial Times*, 3 August.

Braithwaite, T. and Urry, M. (2008) Morrison steals a march on rival Tesco. *Financial Times*, 4 December.

Clapper, T.M. (2007) Corporate social responsibility: spotlighting companies that give back. From blog at http://www.associatedcontent.com/article/172494/corporate_social_responsibility_spotlightinghtml?cat=3, accessed 19 March.

Clar, A. (2009) Getting to grips with working capital. *Treasury Management International* online magazine, November, http://www.treasury-management.com/show-article.php?article=1279.

Damodar, A. (2005) Marketability and value: measuring the illiquidity discount. *Stern School of Business Working Paper*, July, http://pages.stern.nyu.edu/~adamodar/pdfiles/papers/liquidity.pdf.

Dvorak, P. (2007) Finding the best measure of 'corporate citizenship'. *Wall Street Journal*, 2 July, http://online.wsj.com/article/sb118332860213454548.html.

*Economist* (2001) Debt is good for you. *The Economist*, 25 January.

*Economist* (2002) Dividends' end: should technology companies pay dividends? *The Economist*, 10 January.

*Economist* (2005) Business past, business future: the takeover of Marconi. *The Economist*, 27 October.

*Economist* (2007) Hints, tips and handcuffs: American regulators have declared war on insider trading. *The Economist*, 8 March.

*Economist* (2008a) Desperately seeking a cash cure. *The Economist*, 20 November. Martin Wolf's blog: http://blogs.ft.com/crookblog/2008/08/adam-smith-on-csr/.

*Economist* (2008b) Better than beta? Managers' superior skills are becoming harder to prove. *The Economist*, 28 February.

*Economist* (2008c) A cut in the wages of sin. Las Vegas's casinos have been on a roll. Is their luck about to run out? *The Economist*, 26 June.

*Economist* (2008d) The urge to merge: mergers and acquisitions could boom again next year. *The Economist*, 2 December.

*Economist* (2009) Burger-thy-neighbour policies: attacks on China's cheap currency are overdone. *The Economist*, 5 February.

Esty, D. (2007) Is China turning green? *Fortune Magazine*, 4 May. http://www.law.yale.edu/news/5070.htm.

Fama, E. and French, K. (2001) Disappearing dividends: changing firm characteristics or lower propensity to pay? *Journal of Financial Economics* **60**: 3–43.

Farrow, P. (2010) Why millions are sharing BP's pain. *Daily Telegraph*, 5 June.

*Financial Times* (2008a) BP raises oil price assumptions. *Financial Times*, 5 February.

*Financial Times* (2008b) Buying sports stars. *Financial Times*, 1 February.

Fisher, I. (1929) *The Stock Market Crash of 1929*. http://history1900s.about.com/od/1920s/a/stockcrash1929.htm.

Friedman, M. (1962) *Capitalism and Freedom*. University of Chicago Press, Chicago.

Friedman, M. (1970) The social responsibility of business is to increase profits. *New York Times Magazine*, 13 September, p. 6.

Fyfe, C., Marney, J.P. and Tarbert, H.F.E. (1999) Technical analysis versus market efficiency – a genetic programming approach. *Applied Financial Economics* **9**(2):183–191.

Fyfe, C., Marney, J.P. and Tarbert, H.F.E. (2005) Risk adjusted returns from technical trading: a genetic programming approach. *Applied Financial Economics* **15**(15):1073–1077.

Galbraith, K. (2007) Sustainable maths: environmental reporting for companies needs teeth. *The Economist*, 15 November.

Gordon, M.J. (1959) Dividends, earnings, and stock prices. *Review of Economics and Statistics* **41**(2), Part 1:99–105, http://www.wiso.uni-hamburg.de/fileadmin/sozialoekonomie/bwl/bassen/lehre/international_finance_i/assignments/1959_gordon.pdf.

Grene, S. (2008) Charity investing could become cutting edge. *Financial Times*, 10 March.

Hahn, A.L. (2008) Capex caution. *CFO Magazine*, 1 June.

Hencke, D. (2003) NHS computer merger blocked. *The Guardian*, 8 December.

Hill, A. (2009) Ferrexpo dividend policy sends out mixed messages. *Financial Times*, 6 August.

Hill, A. and Gresser, C. (2009) Cautious dividend policies are getting easier to justify. *Financial Times*, 5 March.

Hirshleifer, D. and Shumway, T. (2003) Good day sunshine: stock returns and the weather. *Journal of Finance* **58**(3):1009–1032.

Holden, P. and Holden, S. (2004) Foreign exchange risk and microfinance institutions. Mimeo, *Economic Research Institute and Microrate*, July.

IFSL Research (2010) *International Financial Markets in the UK, May 2010*. CityUK, http://www.thecityuk.com/media/154873/ifm%20in%20the%20uk%2005%202010.pdf.

International Accounts Payable Professionals (2010) *Definition of Accounts Payable*. http://www.theiapp.org/apdefinition.

Jackson, T. (2008) Valuation is fraught with dangers. *Financial Times*, 14 September.

Jensen, M.C. (1978) Some anomalous evidence regarding market efficiency. *Journal of Financial Economics* **6**(2/3):95–101.

Johnson, R., Gordon, N., Dow, J. and Osborne, C. (2008) Dilemma of deciding if a cut-price asset is a bargain. *Financial Times*, 8 October.

Julio, B. and Ikenberry, D. (2004) *Reappearing dividends*. Working Paper, College of Business, University of Illinois, Champaign.

Knowles, T. and Egan, D. (2001) The changing structure of UK brewing and pub retailing. *International Journal of Wine Marketing* **13**:59–72.

Lee, J. (2008) My portfolio. *Financial Times*, 5 December.

Lemer, J., Barker, A. and Blitz, J. (2009) Damning UK defence equipment review criticises 'infinite demand. *Financial Times*, 16 October.

Lo, A.W. Mamaysky, H. and Wang, J. (2000) Foundations of technical analysis. *Journal of Finance* **LV**(4).

London, S. (2005) Why cash has become king once again. *Financial Times*, 14 February.

Maitland, A. (2005) Make sure you have your Christmas stock in. *Financial Times*, 18 December.

Malkiel, B. (2007) *A Random Walk Down Wall St.* W.W. Norton, New York.

Marney, J.P., Tarbert, H., Koetsier, J. and Guidi, M. (2008) The application of the self-organizing map, the k-means algorithm and the multi-layer perceptron to the detection of technical trading patterns. *Applied Financial Economics* 18(12):1009–1019.

Marsh, P. (2008) Mittal fatigue. *Financial Times*, 30 October.

Mathiason, N. (2009) Management buyout close to completion at retailer Robert Dyas. *The Guardian*, 5 April.

Miller, M. and Modigliani, F. (1961) Dividend policy, growth and the valuation of shares. *Journal of Business*, **34**(4):411–433.

Modigliani, F. and Miller, M.H. (1958) The cost of capital, corporation finance and the theory of investment. *American Economic Review*, **48**(3):261-297.

Modigliani, F. and Miller, M.H. (1963) Corporate income taxes and the cost of capital: a correction. *American Economic Review* 53(3):433–443.

Moser, J. and Puckett, A. (2009) Dividend tax clienteles: evidence from tax law changes. *Journal of the American Tax Association* **31**(1).

Moulds, Y. (2009) Technology tie-ups have a habit of crashing: Microsoft and Yahoo! continue to thrash out the terms of a multi-billion dollar search and online advertising deal. *The Telegraph*, 24 July.

Ogilvie, J. (2008) *CIMA Official Learning System: Management, Accounting, Financial Strategy*. CIMA–Elsevier, Amsterdam, pp 562–563.

Patrikarakos, D. and Shyamantha, A. (2008) Role models from banking and finance. *Financial Times*, 23 June.

Pearson, S. and O'Doherty, J. (2009) Mothercare to push on with plans to expand. *Financial Times*, 2 April.

Pratley, N. (2002) The cookbook any firm can follow. *The Guardian*, 28 June.

Rigby, E. (2008) Tesco to change payment terms for suppliers. *Financial Times*, 24 October.

Robbins, S., Bergman, R., Stagg, I. and Coulter, M. (2006) *Management*, 4th edn. Pearson Prentice Hall, Upper Saddle River, New Jersey.

Rosenau, W., Twede, D., Mazzeo, M. and Singh, S. (1996) Returnable/reusable logistical packaging: a capital budgeting investment decision framework. *Journal of Business Logistics* 17:139.

Rumsey, J. (2008) Brazil steelmaker rolls out fresh strategy. *Financial Times*, 23 July.

Scherr, F.C. (1996) Optimal trade credit limits. *Financial Management* **25**(1):71.

Song, J.-A. (2009) Investing in South Korea: ambitious companies with war-chests look for value. *Financial Times*, 20 May.

Sornette, D. (2003) *Why Stock Markets Crash*. Princeton University Press, Princeton.

Stafford, P. (2009) Special dividend at Hargreaves. *Financial Times*, 2 September.

Starovic, D. and Marr, B. (2003) *Understanding corporate value: managing and reporting intellectual capital*. CIMA, www.valuebasedmanagement.net/articles_cima_understanding.pdf.

Taleb, N. (2007) *Fooled by Randomness*, 2nd edn. Penguin, London.

UK Payments Administration (2009) *Facts and Figures. Cheques and Cheque Clearing: An Historical Perspective*. http://www.ukpayments.org.uk/resources_publications/key_facts_and_figures/cheques_and_bankers'_drafts_facts_and_figures/.

Urry, M. (2008) William Hill confident despite lower profits. *Financial Times*, 27 February.

Weston, J.F., Mitchell, M.L. and Mulherin, J.H. (2004) *Takeovers, Restructuring and Corporate Governance*, 4th edn. Pearson Hall, Upper Saddle River, New Jersey.

Whipp, L. and Garnham, P. (2009) Yen soars despite Japan's troubles. *Financial Times*, 24 January.

Winpenny, J. (2008) Where was the risk in converting my humble fee? Letter to the editor. *Financial Times*, 26 June.

Witzel, M. (2006) Book review: your finance officer's inner warrior. *Financial Times*, 2 April. (Review of *How Financial Managers Can Transform Their Roles and Add Greater Value*, by Jeremy Hope, Harvard Business School Press.)

Wong, S.M.L. (2006) China's stock market: a marriage of capitalism and socialism. *Cato Journal* **26**(3), http://www.cato.org/pubs/journal/cj26n3/cj26n3-1.pdf.

Zhu, A. (2010) *The only responsibility of managers is to maximize shareholder wealth*. http://bizcovering.com/investing/the-only-responsibility-of-managers-is-to-maximize-shareholder-wealth/#ixzz0vgo1glrg, accessed 13 June.

# Internet references

## Academic articles

scholar.google.com.

## Academic articles (more than 5 years old).

www.jstor.com

www.travismorien.com

www.altruistfa.com/readingroom.htm

## Adam Smith

http://www.online-literature.com/view.php/wealth_nations/2

## Behavioural finance

http://www.behaviouralfinance.net/

Links to numerous papers in the area of behavioural finance.

## Beta

www2.ntu.ac.uk/llr/library/betavalues.htm

Source for beta estimates.

## Capital budgeting

ftp://ftp.cba.uri.edu/classes/dash/isida/capitalbudgtingevaluation.pdf

An excellent case study analysis of the role of formal evaluation techniques in the decision making process.

http://www.investopedia.com/terms/c/capitalbudgeting.asp

A basic entry on capital budgeting.

## Capital structure

http://online.wsj.com/article/sb124027187331937083.html

An article detailing some of the history of the effects of capital structure and its contribution to recent recessions.

## 'Common-sense' FT approach to business

www.ft.com

http://creativecapitalism.typepad.com

http://www.samuelbrittan.co.uk/

## Dividends

http://www.direct.gov.uk/en/moneytaxandbenefits/taxes/taxonsavingsandinvestments/dg_4016453

Contains information on the tax rate of dividends in the UK.

http://www.investopedia.com/articles/03/011703.asp

An article on why and how companies pay dividends.

http://www.dividend.com/historical/

A tool to look up the historical dividends of US companies.

http://www.fionaallan.plus.com/results%2020081115.xls

A spreadsheet containing FTSE share information, including dividend yields.

http://bespokeinvest.typepad.com/bespoke/2007/09/historical-di-1.html

A graphical representation of dividend yields on the S&P 500 from 1925–2007.

## Emerging markets and sustainability

http://www.ethicalcorp.com/

## Financial data

finance.yahoo.com.

## International Corporate Governance Network

www.icgn.org

## London Stock Exchange

http://www.londonstockexchange.com/en-gb/

## International finance

There are some very good 'meta' sites in this area, i.e. international business or international finance sites that point to other sites. Two of these are:

http://globaledge.msu.edu/resourceDesk/

http://www.internationaleconomics.net/bizfinance.html#finance

We culled the following very interesting sites from the former:

### Barclays International: Business Banking

Barclays, an offshore banking firm, provides a number of reports for its customers. Economic reports include the European Economics Quarterly Forecast, UK Economic Quarterly Insights and Prospects, Euro Weekly, and Foreign Exchange Weekly. It also provides industry reports for the construction, manufacturing and services sectors.

### Bloomberg Online: Foreign Exchange

The Bloomberg website offers a wide range of tools and information about financial markets. Real-time rates, financial news and currency converters are available for more than 200 currencies.

### International Finance Theory & Policy Analysis

The International Economics Study Center is provided by an academic from George Washington University and includes a textbook online format, so the site contains a vast amount of information for those interested in international finance and cross-country transactions. Also includes a good deal of international

trade information and news available on the main page.

### International Swap and Derivatives Association (ISDA)

This website is the home to a global financial trade association whose members trade negotiated derivatives, covering trades and options in fields such as interest rates, currency, commodities, energy and credit.

### Valore International Finance

Valore International Finance features articles on issues shaping the world of the international executive with a focus in finance. Some of the featured financial articles on the site are a few years old, but the user can find current value in the World at a Glance, Landmarks and Connections pages.

## Internal rate of return

http://apotso.wordpress.com/2006/09/30/evaluation-of-the-merits-and-drawbacks-of-the-use-of-the-internal-rate-of-return-as-an-investment-criterion%e2%80%a6/

## Mergers and acquisitions

http://www.statistics.gov.uk/statbase/product.asp?vlnk=72

The UK National Statistics page on M&A decisions.

http://www.ft.com/indepth/m&a

http://www.guardian.co.uk/business/mergers-and-acquisitions

News sources on recent M&A announcements and developments.

http://investopedia.com/university/mergers/

A basic introduction to M&A for students unfamiliar with the subject.

http://www.econlib.org/library/enc1/takeoversandleveragedbuyouts.html

A history of the development of the M&A corporate culture.

http://www.rba.co.uk/sources/manda.htm

A selection of links to news feeds services and data-bases concerning M&A.

## Microfinance

http://www.grameen-info.org

Grameen Bank.

www.swwb.org

Women's World Banking Network.

www.oecd.org

Organisation for Economic Cooperation and Development (Corporate Governance Code).

## Purchasing power in the UK

http://www.measuringworth.com/ppoweruk/

## Public sector project appraisal

http://www.hm-treasury.gov.uk/data_greenbook_index.htm

'The Green Book', the British government guide to project appraisal for public and voluntary sector projects. Chapters 2 and 5 may be of some interest for private sector practitioners.

## Real options

http://www.real-options.com/overview_intro.htm
http://www.realoptions.org/abstracts.html

Contains information on real options.

## Stakeholder approach to business

www.associatedcontent.com

## Sunk costs

http://sunk-cost.behaviouralfinance.net/

Contains links to several informative resources on sunk costs.

## Treasury and working capital management

www.cfo.com

Chief Financial Officer (CFO) Magazine.

www.treasury-management.com

Treasury Management International Magazine.

http://www.iappnet.org/

International Accounts Payables Professionals website.

http://www.planware.org/workingcapital.htm#2

Planware.com.

http://www.bdc.ca/en/business_tools/calculators/overview.htm?cookie%5ftest=1

Canadian Business Ratio Calculators.

http://www.icai.org/post.html?post_id=2935

Cash Management – Institute of Chartered Accountants of India.

## Valuation and accounting standards

http://www.accountingweb.co.uk/
http://www.accountingweb.co.uk/cgi-bin/item.cgi?id=157890&d=1032&h=1024&f=1026

## Valuation and intangible assets

http://www.intangiblebusiness.com/brand-services/financial-services/press-coverage/why-it-is-hard-to-value-a-mystery~969.html

## Valuation and small business

http://www.smallbusiness.co.uk/channels/small-business-finance/guides-and-tips/24323/valuing-your-business-for-sale.thtml

## WACC

http://thatswacc.com/

# Endnotes

## Chapter 1

[1] A ponzi scheme is a fraudulent investment scheme in which the perpetrator attracts investment funds or deposits by promising high returns or high interest. When the time comes to pay investors, the perpetrator attracts new investors by promising even higher returns, in order to payout to the original investors. Madoff pled guilty on 29 June 2009.

[2] See *Financial Times* 19 September 2005.

[3] See *Financial Times* 13 July 2007.

[4] 'Effective corporate governance requires robust accountability.' Letter from Dr Roger Barker, 12 March 2009 at: http://www.ft.com/cms/s/0/c92f25a0-77e6-11dc-8e4-0000779fd2ac.html

[5] See 'Executive remuneration: Quality over quantity' *Financial Times* 12 October 2007.

[6] For example, see 'Investors up in arms over poor governance' *Financial Times* 12 October 2007.

[7] There are many editions of Wealth of Nations. We have taken the quote from teh online version at: http://www.online-literature.com/view.php/wealth_nations/2.

[8] There are many editions of *Wealth of Nations*. We have taken the quote from the online version at: http://www.online-literature.com/view.php/wealth_nations/2.

[9] Available online at: http://www.mad.co.uk/Main/News/Disciplines/Marketing/IndustryIssues/Articles/e06705f2a3d346d885e00f81b8e7cb2c/Paved-with-good-intentions.html.

[10] See the internet references at the end of the chapter.

## Chapter 3

[1] This was unfortunate for Northern Rock to say the least. As an institution with business primarily in mortgage lending, it had adopted a radical business model in the 1990s, in order to expand rapidly. Rather than financing the majority of mortgages from customer deposits, it was financing them from the rollover of very short-term debt on the wholesale markets. When liquidity dried up in the interbank market at the start of what was to become known as the credit crunch, Northern Rock could no longer borrow money to fund its mortgages and was therefore insolvent.

[2] At the time of going to press there is a great deal of worry in the UK not just about BP's oil spill off the coast of Louisiana in the US, which in itself is a human tragedy and catastrophic environmental disaster, but also about the impact on BP's future and on the value of pension funds, which are heavily exposed to one of the UK's biggest companies. See, for example, the *Daily Telegraph* article by Paul Farrow (5 June 2010).

## Chapter 4

[1] If you use all the decimal places available on your spreadsheet, you will come up with a slightly different answer for value of dividends with supernormal growth, specifically, '£4.91' and '£4.90'.

[2] All extracts from *A Random Walk Down Wall Street* are reproduced by kind permission of the author Burton Malkiel and his publisher W.W. Norton.

[3] In the UK, book value is known as 'net asset value' in contrast to the US where net asset value refers specifically to the net value of mutual funds.

## Chapter 5

1 If you wish to replicate what we did, two additional technical points should be noted. First, dividend data have to be loaded separately and included in the calculation of returns. Second, the stock prices have to be adjusted for stock splits.

2 See, for example, Mira Bar-Hillel, *London Evening Standard,* 14 April 2008.

3 We are grateful to Ibbotson for their kind permission to reproduce this diagram.

## Chapter 6

1 Commodities futures contracts are still market traded at the Chicago commodities futures market, and it is certainly a colourful spectacle. Trading now takes place at the Chicago Mercantile Exchange which still maintains a certain amount of open outcry by traders in trading pits, at a time when many markets have moved to purely electronic trading systems. The traders in the pit announce the number of contracts they want to buy or sell and the price they want to pay or receive. They use their fingers to denote the quantity of contracts. When the trader's palm faces out, he is trying to sell contracts. When the trader's palm faces in, he is buying. You would not want to wave to a friend in case you inadvertently sold 5 million of yen futures!

2 The gearing ratio is the ratio of debt to equity in the firm's capital structure.

## Chapter 7

1 From: news.bbc.co.uk/1/hi/world/south_asia/5164926.stm, 10 July 2006.

2 Reproduced by kind permission of azom.com. The story was published on 7 October 2009 and can be found at: http//www.azom.com/news.asp?NewsID=19202.

## Chapter 8

1 See Column, L. (2008) UK dividends. *Financial Times*, 27 November 2008.

2 We should make the following point. In the *financial management* literature, gearing is the same as leverage, but in the *accounting* literature, gearing may not be the same as leverage. In the UK accounting literature, 'leverage' includes short-term debt as well as long-term debt, but 'gearing' does not. Some UK *accounting* texts have different ratios for gearing and leverage. This is important since many students study accounting as well as finance. We are indebted to an anonymous reviewer for this comment.

## Chapter 9

1 For example, see 'Investors are left to chase increasingly rare dividends', *Financial Times*, 29 November 2008.

2 For example, see 'Royal Bank of Scotland prepares for rights issue', *Financial Times*, 18 April 2008.

3 At the time of writing, Ryanair had actually just paid their first dividend. See *Financial Times*, 1 June 2010.

## Chapter 10

1 The working capital policy of the University of Hawaii can be found at http://www.hawaii.edu/apis/ep/e8/e8201.pdf. We gratefully acknowledge their kind permission to reproduce the excerpt from this document.

2 This article originally appeared in *Treasury Management International* (TMI) magazine [www.treasury-management.com]. It can be found at: http://www.treasury-management.com/showarticle.php?article=1279&pubid=1&issueid=145.

## Chapter 11

[1] See, for example, the Royal British Pharmaceutical Society Information Centre pamphlet on mergers and acquisitions at http://www.rpsgb.org.uk/pdfs/mergers.pdf.

[2] *Financial Times*, 9 March 2009 and 26 January 2009, respectively.

[3] See, for example, the extensive survey of the empirical evidence in Weston *et al.* (2004).

[4] See, for example, 'Japan's other carmaker' at BBC news, http://news.bbc.co.uk/1/hi/business/880093.stm.

# Index